Lecture Notes in Computer Science 15992

Founding Editors

Gerhard Goos
Juris Hartmanis

The series Lecture Notes in Computer Science (LNCS), including its subseries Lecture Notes in Artificial Intelligence (LNAI) and Lecture Notes in Bioinformatics (LNBI), has established itself as a medium for the publication of new developments in computer science and information technology research, teaching, and education.

LNCS enjoys close cooperation with the computer science R & D community, the series counts many renowned academics among its volume editors and paper authors, and collaborates with prestigious societies. Its mission is to serve this international community by providing an invaluable service, mainly focused on the publication of conference and workshop proceedings and postproceedings. LNCS commenced publication in 1973.

Mila Dalla Preda · Sebastian Schrittwieser ·
Vincent Naessens · Bjorn De Sutter

Editors

Availability, Reliability and Security

20th International Conference, ARES 2025
Ghent, Belgium, August 11–14, 2025
Proceedings, Part I

 Springer

Editors
Mila Dalla Preda ⓘ
University of Verona
Verona, Italy

Sebastian Schrittwieser ⓘ
University of Vienna
Vienna, Austria

Vincent Naessens ⓘ
KU Leuven
Ghent, Belgium

Bjorn De Sutter ⓘ
Ghent University
Ghent, Belgium

ISSN 0302-9743 ISSN 1611-3349 (electronic)
Lecture Notes in Computer Science
ISBN 978-3-032-00623-3 ISBN 978-3-032-00624-0 (eBook)
https://doi.org/10.1007/978-3-032-00624-0

Preface

The Twentieth International Conference on Availability, Reliability, and Security (ARES 2025) brings together researchers and practitioners to advance the fields of availability, reliability, and computer security. Following the tradition of previous editions, the conference fosters collaboration and the exchange of ideas across these critical areas of research.

This year, the conference was hosted in Ghent, a vibrant and historic city whose rich cultural heritage, distinguished academic tradition, and welcoming atmosphere offer an ideal setting for scholarly exchange and research collaboration.

This year, the main conference was organized in eleven technical sessions, including a session dedicated to the candidates for the Best Paper Award. We were also honored to host two brilliant keynote speakers: Christian Collberg, Professor at the University of Arizona, renowned for his work in the fields of software protection, intellectual property protection, and reverse engineering resistance, and Bart Preneel, Professor at the Katholieke Universiteit Leuven in Belgium, renowned for his work in the fields of cryptography, information security, and privacy.

ARES 2025 received 162 full papers, 11 SoK papers, and 20 short papers. After desk rejecting 12 papers, we accepted 33 full papers, 1 SoK paper, and 8 short papers that were originally submitted as full papers. For full and SoK papers, this yields an acceptance rate of 19.7%. Each paper, including those submitted by Program Committee members, received a minimum of three reviews. The three best papers were selected by the PC chairs and organizing team for inclusion in the Best Paper Sessions, based on the highest review scores. The Best Paper award was then chosen by the PC chairs and organizing team during the conference, following the Best Paper Sessions, in order to also consider the quality of the presentations.

We thank all the authors for submitting a high volume of quality papers to ARES this year. We are also particularly grateful for the hard work, insights, and support displayed by each of the Program Committee members. Thanks to them, we were able to offer a technically solid program to the attendees. We further thank all workshop chairs for their efforts in organizing engaging workshop sessions.

After years of being organized by a dedicated team from SBA Research, the ARES conference was now for the first time organized by a team from the local host. We specifically want to thank Bettina Jaber from SBA research for the manner in which she prepared the handover, providing tons of documentation and guidance. From the local team, we deeply thank Vicky Wandels, Inge Lason, and Eneko Illarramendi for successfully managing the registrations, the finances, the website, the conference rooms, the social events, the catering, etc.

The General Chair and the Proceedings Chair are included as editors of this volume to reflect their contributions in the preparation of the proceedings.

August 2025   Bjorn De Sutter
                                                             Mila Dalla Preda
                                                            Vincent Naessens
                                                       Sebastian Schrittwieser

Organization

General Chair

Bjorn De Sutter   Ghent University, Belgium

Program Committee Chairs

Mila Dalla Preda   University of Verona, Italy
Sebastian Schrittwieser   SBA Research and University of Vienna, Austria

Steering Committee

Abdelmalek Benzekri   University of Toulouse, France
Francesco Buccafurri   University of Reggio Calabria, Italy
Dominik Engel   Salzburg University of Applied Sciences, Austria
Mathias Fischer   University of Hamburg, Germany
Steven Furnell   University of Nottingham, UK
Stefanie Rinderle-Ma   University of Vienna, Austria
Shujun Li   University of Kent, UK
Christian Doerr   Delft University of Technology, Germany
Pierangela Samarati   Università degli Studi di Milano, Italy
Melanie Volkamer   Karlsruher Institute for Technology (KIT), Germany

Steering Committee Chairs

Edgar Weippl   SBA Research, Austria
A Min Tjoa   TU Vienna, Austria

Workshop Chairs

Bart Coppens   Ghent University, Belgium
Bruno Volckaert   Ghent University, Belgium

Workshop Chair EU Projects Symposium

Florian Skopik   AIT Austrian Institute of Technology, Austria

Proceedings Chairs

Vincent Naessens   KU Leuven, Belgium
Michiel Willocx   KU Leuven, Belgium

Organization Chairs

Vicky Wandels   Ghent University, Belgium
Inge Lason   Ghent University, Belgium

Conference Management

Vicky Wandels   Ghent University, Belgium
Eneko Illarramendi   Ghent University, Belgium

Program Committee

Bert Abrath   Ghent University, Belgium
Isaac Agudo   University of Malaga, Spain
Esma Aïmeur   University of Montreal, Canada
Magnus Almgren   Chalmers University of Technology, Sweden
Saed Alrabaee   United Arab Emirates University, UAE
Todd Andel   University of South Alabama, USA
Mikael Asplund   Linköping University, Sweden
Ali Ismail Awad   United Arab Emirates University, UAE
Sebastien Bardin   CEA LIST, France
Cataldo Basile   Politecnico di Torino, Italy
Ingmar Baumgart   Karlsruhe Institute of Technology, Germany
Bernhard J. Berger   University of Rostock, Germany
Monowar Bhuyan   Umeå University, Sweden
Pascal Birnstill   Fraunhofer, Germany
Gregory Blanc   Institut Mines-Télécom, Télécom SudParis,
                                          Institut Polytechnique de Paris, France
Olivier Blazy   Ecole Polytechnique, France

Aymen Boudguiga	IRT SystemX, France
Nora Boulahia-Cuppens	Polytechnique Montréal, Canada
Alessandro Brighente	University of Padova, Italy
Francesco Buccafurri	Università Mediterranea di Reggio Calabria, Italy
Krzysztof Cabaj	Warsaw University of Technology, Poland
Jordi Castellà-Roca	Universitat Rovira i Virgili, Spain
Marta Catillo	Università del Sannio, Italy
Luca Caviglione	CNR - IMATI, Italy
Mariano Ceccato	University of Verona, Italy
Bo Chen	Michigan Technological University, USA
Sherman S. M. Chow	The Chinese University of Hong Kong, China
Nathan Clarke	University of Plymouth, UK
Marijke Coetzee	North-West University, South Africa
Emilio Coppa	LUISS University, Italy
Tiago Cruz	University of Coimbra, Portugal
Michel Cukier	University of Maryland, USA
Frederic Cuppens	Polytechnique Montreal, Canada
José Maria de Fuentes	Universidad Carlos III de Madrid, Spain
Laurens D'Hooge	Ghent University, Belgium
Nicolás E. Díaz Ferreyra	Hamburg University of Technology, Germany
Tassos Dimitriou	Computer Technology Institute, Greece and Kuwait University, Kuwait
Niels Dossche	Ghent University, Belgium
Pavlos Efraimidis	Democritus University of Thrace, Greece
Günther Eibl	Salzburg University of Applied Sciences, Josef Ressel Center for User-Centric Smart Grid Privacy, Security and Control, Austria
Andreas Ekelhart	SBA Research, Austria
Christian Engelmann	ORNL (Oak Ridge National Laboratory), USA
Santiago Escobar	Universitat Politècnica de València, Spain
Hannes Federrath	University of Hamburg, Germany
Anna Lisa Ferrara	Università degli Studi del Molise, Italy
Umberto Ferraro	Università di Roma, La Sapienza, Italy
Mathias Fischer	University of Hamburg, Germany
Panagiotis Fouliras	University of Macedonia, Greece
Virginia Franqueira	University of Kent, UK
Steven Furnell	University of Nottingham, UK
Sarah Gaballah	Ruhr-Universität Bochum, Germany
Dimitrios Georgoulias	Aalborg University, Denmark
Giorgio Giacinto	Università degli Studi di Cagliari, Italy
Karl M. Goeschka	Vienna University of Technology, Austria
Lorena González Manzano	Universidad Carlos III de Madrid, Spain

Thomas Gross	Newcastle University, UK
Bogdan Groza	Politehnica University of Timisoara, Romania
Sascha Hauke	TU Darmstadt, Germany
Péter Hegedűs	University of Szeged, Hungary
Anne Hennig	University of Bamberg, Germany
Dorjan Hitaj	Sapienza University of Rome, Italy
Stefan Hofbauer	Itenic GmbH, Munich, Germany
Zhen Huang	DePaul University, USA
Michele Ianni	University of Calabria, Italy
Pedro Inácio	Universidade da Beira Interior, Portugal
Martin Gilje Jaatun	SINTEF Digital and University of Stavanger, Norway
Martin Johns	TU Braunschweig, Germany
Nesrine Kaaniche	Telecom SudParis, France
Stylianos Karagiannis	Ionian University, Greece
Kallol Krishna Karmakar	Deakin University, Australia
Sokratis Katsikas	Norwegian University of Science and Technology, Norway
Stefan Katzenbeisser	University of Passau, Germany
Peter Kieseberg	St. Pölten UAS, Austria
Hyoungshick Kim	Sungkyunkwan University, South Korea
Marina Krotofil	Maersk, Denmark
Oksana Kulyk	IT University of Copenhagen, Denmark
Romain Laborde	Université de Toulouse, France
Costas Lambrinoudakis	University of Piraeus, Greece
Jorn Lapon	KU Leuven, Belgium
Sonia Laudanna	Unisannio, Italy
Maryline Laurent	Télécom SudParis, Institut Polytechnique de Paris, France
Olivier Levillain	Samovar, Télécom SudParis, Institut Polytechnique de Paris, France
Shujun Li	University of Kent, UK
Jens Lindemann	Universität Hamburg, Germany
Giovanni Livraga	University of Milan, Italy
Robert Luh	St. Pölten UAS, Austria
Leandros Maglaras	Edinburgh Napier University, UK
Lukas Malina	Brno University of Technology, Czech Republic
Niccolò Marastoni	University of Verona, Italy
Keith Martin	Royal Holloway, University of London, UK
Barbara Masucci	University of Salerno, Italy
Raimundas Matulevicius	University of Tartu, Estonia
Ioannis Mavridis	University of Macedonia, Greece

Rudolf Mayer	Vienna University of Technology, Austria
Wojciech Mazurczyk	Warsaw University of Technology, Poland
Michael Meier	University of Bonn, Germany
Per Håkon Meland	SINTEF Digital, Norway
Weizhi Meng	Lancaster University, UK
Francesco Mercaldo	University of Molise, Italy
Massimo Merro	University of Verona, Italy
Joachim Meyer	Tel Aviv University, Israel
Rodrigo Miani	Federal University of Uberlândia (UFU), Brazil
Aleksandra Mileva	Goce Delcev University, North Macedonia
Lorenzo Musarella	Università Mediterranea di Reggio Calabria, Italy
Stephan Neumann	SaarLB, Germany
Zhenyu Ning	Hunan University, China
Maximilian Noppel	Karlsruhe Institute of Technology, Germany
Christoforos Ntantogian	Ionian University, Greece
Marc Ohm	University of Bonn & Fraunhofer FKIE, Germany
Rolf Oppliger	eSECURITY Technologies, Switzerland
Vinod P.	Cochin University of Science and Technology, Kochi, Kerala, India
Federica Paci	University of Verona, Italy
Miguel Pardal	Universidade de Lisboa, Portugal
Sergio Pastrana	Universidad Carlos III de Madrid, Spain
Sikhar Patranabis	IBM Research India
Sven Peldszus	Ruhr University Bochum, Germany
Günther Pernul	Universität Regensburg, Germany
Pablo Picazo-Sanchez	Halmstad University, Sweden
Alexander Ponticello	CISPA Helmholtz Center for Information Security, Germany
Marie-Laure Potet	University Grenoble Alps, France
Masoom Rabbani	Chalmers University of Technology, Sweden
Pawel Rajba	University of Wroclaw, Poland
Silvio Ranise	University of Trento and FBK, Italy
Pascal Reisert	University of Stuttgart, Germany
Karen Renaud	University of Strathclyde, UK
Christian Reuter	Technical University of Darmstadt, PEASEC, Germany
Junghwan Rhee	University of Central Oklahoma, USA
Golden G. Richard III	Louisiana State University, USA
Giulio Rigoni	Sapienza, University of Rome, Italy
Thomas Rosenstatter	Salzburg University of Applied Sciences, Austria
Michael Rossberg	Technische Universitaet Ilmenau, Germany
Christoph Saatjohann	FH Muenster, Germany

Morteza Safaei Pour	San Diego State University, USA
Pierangela Samarati	Università degli Studi di Milano, Italy
Luis Enrique Sanchez Crespo	University of Castilla-la Mancha, Spain
Riccardo Scandariato	Hamburg University of Technology, Germany
Joern-Marc Schmidt	IU International Hochschule GmbH, Germany
Guido Schmitz	Lancaster University Leipzig, Germany
Jan Seedorf	HFT Stuttgart, Germany
Arnaldo Sgueglia	University of Sannio, Italy
Siamak Shahandashti	University of York, UK
Hervais Simo	Fraunhofer SIT, Germany
Paulo Simões	University of Coimbra, Portugal
Dario Stabili	University of Bologna, Italy
Nazatul Haque Sultan	University of Newcastle, UK
Shamik Sural	Indian Institute of Technology Kharagpur, India
Anum Talpur	University of Hamburg, Germany
Oliver Theel	Carl von Ossietzky University of Oldenburg, Germany
Simon Tjoa	St. Pölten UAS, Austria
Jacob Torrey	Thinkst Applied Research, USA
Katja Tuma	Eindhoven University of Technology, Netherlands
Johanna Ullrich	SBA Research, Austria
Andreas Unterweger	Salzburg University of Applied Sciences, Austria
Emmanouil Vasilomanolakis	Technical University of Denmark, Denmark
Umberto Villano	University of Sannio, Italy
Corrado Aaron Visaggio	University of Sannio, Italy
Stijn Volckaert	KU Leuven, Belgium
Ahmad Samer Wazan	Zayed University, United Arab Emirates
Christos Xenakis	University of Piraeus, Greece
Koen Yskout	KU Leuven, Belgium
Nicola Zannone	Eindhoven University of Technology, Netherlands
Ephraim Zimmer	Technical University of Darmstadt, Germany

Additional Reviewers

Diego Soi	Franziska Schneider
Nikolaos Tsinganos	Dejan Radovanovic
Andreas Menegatos	Tiago Roxo
Soumyadyuti Ghosh	Riccardo Ceccaroni
Reeshav Chowdhury	Daniele Canavese
Jack P. K. Ma	Laurent Mounier
Yagmur Yigit	Pierangelo Loi

Philipp Kühn
Ijeoma Faustina Ekeh
James Ghawaly
Silvia Lucia Sanna
Thrasyvoulos Giannakopoulos
Clemente Galdi
Timo Pohl
Riccardo Ziglio
Anindya Sundar Das
Jef Jacobs
Harry W. H. Wong
August See
Giulia Grani
Georgios Gkoktsis
Konstantinos Giapantzis
Marvin Banse
Riccardo Longo
Aristeidis Farao
Andes Y. L. Kei

Bernardo Sequeiros
Caroline König
Jeetesh Gupta
Ricardo Yaben
Joana C. Costa
Karina Elzer
Max Schirl
Martin Dukek
Chiara Spadafora
Alexander Wallis
Eleni Briola
Nikolaos Pavlidis
Stelvio Cimato
Matthias Börsig
Frank Nelles
Obaidullah Zaland
Josh Dafoe
Simon Althaus
Kilian Demuth

ARES 2025 Keynotes

Crypto Wars: The First 50 Years

Bart Preneel ⓘ

COSIC, KU Leuven, Belgium
bart.preneel@kuleuven.be

Abstract. The ongoing *Crypto Wars* encapsulate the persistent tension between government interests in accessing encrypted data for national security and law enforcement purposes and the imperative to safeguard individual and collective privacy. This keynote provides a brief historical perspective on these conflicts, covering attempts to restrict cryptographic research, government access to secure communications (e.g., the Clipper Chip), stored data disputes (such as Apple vs. the FBI), and the proliferation of surveillance spyware (e.g., NSO Group).

In recent years, the focus has shifted toward end-to-end encrypted communications, with proposals for client-side scanning—a method that scans content on user devices before encryption or after decryption. While officially framed as a tool to detect Child Sexual Abuse Material (CSAM), the technology is also positioned for counterterrorism and combating organized crime. However, such scanning undermines the core principles of encryption, is easily circumvented, and—like all third-party access mechanisms—is susceptible to misuse. Additionally, its reliability is highly questionable. Our recent research has revealed critical flaws in perceptual hash functions used to identify known CSAM, showing that widely adopted schemes suffer from high false positive and false negative rates. Draft regulations have proposed AI-based detection methods for new CSAM and in particular for AI-generated CSAM – this raises additional concerns with respect to feasibility and accuracy.

Meanwhile, law enforcement agencies have significantly expanded their capabilities, leveraging metadata, biometric data, video footage and electronic surveillance, coupled with advanced analytical tools It is highly plausible that these developments offset the challenges for law enforcement investigations presented by the growing use of encryption. The focus should therefore shift toward reinforcing cybersecurity and privacy protections while ensuring transparency in surveillance practices. A broader societal dialogue is crucial to ensure the protection of both society and of fundamental rights.

Issues in Evaluation of Reverse Engineering and Software Protection

Christian Collberg 🆔

Department of Computer Science, University of Arizona, USA
collberg@cs.arizona.edu

Abstract. The area of Man-At-The-End (MATE) software protection and reverse engineering is suffering from an evaluation crisis. The lack of solid and universally accepted evaluation methodologies and benchmark suites has hampered development, made it difficult to fairly compare new algorithms to existing ones, and impossible to answer fundamental questions such as "How long will a particular combination of protection techniques stand up to a particular attack strategy?" or "What attacks are most effective against a particular protection technique?".

This keynote discusses what needs to change in order for the MATE area to gain a solid scientific footing. In particular, we discuss the availability of freely accessible protection tools, the generation of benchmark suites, the design of evaluation methodologies, and the need for a strict policy of artifact availability in scientific publications.

Contents – Part I

Contents – Part II

Privacy-Enhancing Technologies
and Legal Compliance

A Framework for Supporting PET Selection Based on GDPR Principles

Sebastian Pape[1,2]([✉])[ID], Anis Bkakria[3][ID], Badreddine Chah[4][ID],
Maurice Heymann[1][ID], and Sarah Syed-Winkler[1][ID]

[1] Continental Automotive Technologies Gmbh, Frankfurt, Germany
{sebastian.pape,maurice.heymann,sarah.syed-winkler}@continental.com
[2] Goethe University Frankfurt, Frankfurt, Germany
[3] IRT SystemX, Palaiseau, France
[4] CIAD UMR 7533, Univ. Bourgogne-Franche-Comté, UTBM, 90010 Belfort, France

Abstract. The General Data Protection Regulation (GDPR) lists seven privacy principles relating to the processing of personal data and requires the processor to implement appropriate technical and organizational measures (TOMs). In practice, TOMs are often addressed by organizational measures, but technical measures, i.e. Privacy-Enhancing Technologies (PETs), are rarely used to address them. One reason for that might be the challenge to find an appropriate PET. The contribution of our paper is a framework to support the selection of PETs based on GDPR principles. For that purpose, we provide mappings between the trust model and GDPR principles, and between PET types and GDPR principles. Furthermore, we provide an assessment of the different maturity levels of PETs. We evaluated our framework by applying it to three different use cases in the automotive domain and it proved to be highly effective in guiding the identification and selection of candidate PETs.

Keywords: Privacy Enhancing Technology Selection · GDPR Principles · Trust Model

1 Introduction

With the introduction of the General Data Protection Regulation (GDPR) [27] in 2018, the European Union marked a major step forward in data privacy legislation, enforcing comprehensive requirements on how organizations must handle personal data. By establishing this regulation, individuals are empowered to have more control over their personal data, while organizations are held accountable for processing, storing, and collecting their information. The GDPR lists 6 principles in Art. 5 relating to processing of personal data and additionally requires the controller to be able to demonstrate compliance with them (cf. Sect. 2.1). Art. 32 further requires the processor to "implement appropriate technical and organizational measures (TOMs) to ensure a level of security appropriate to the risk". In practice, TOMs are often addressed by organizational measures,

M. Dalla Preda et al. (Eds.): ARES 2025, LNCS 15992, pp. 3–23, 2025.
https://doi.org/10.1007/978-3-032-00624-0_1

that is, integrating legal agreements such as user consent or commissioned data processing into existing processes. Technical measures, i. e. Privacy-Enhancing Technologies (PETs), are rarely used to address the privacy principles [19]. One of the reasons might be that it is still difficult to select, implement, configure, and run most PETs. In this paper, we propose a framework to support the selection of PETs based on the mentioned GDPR principles.

The proposed framework aims to assist in designing service architectures by identifying suitable PETs that are in line with GDPR principles. Architects must define their trust model and the data-related functions of their service. The framework supports identifying the relevant GDPR principles that can be enforced with PETs based on the trust model. Therefore, we map PET types to GDPR principles to support the selection process. Furthermore, a qualitative comparison of PETs is provided to evaluate their trade-offs in terms of utility, practicability, and robustness. We evaluated our framework by applying it to three different use cases in the automotive domain.

The contribution of our paper is a framework for PET selection based on GDPR principles. It is based on mappings between trust model and GDPR principles, and between PET types and GDPR principles; and on an assessment of the PETs' maturity level.

The remainder of this paper is structured as follows: Sect. 2 provides background and reviews related work. Section 3 introduces the methodology of our research. Section 4 describes our framework along with its evaluation in Sect. 5 and the discussion in Sect. 6. Section 7 concludes the work.

2 Background and Related Work

In this section, we recap the GDPR privacy principles and trust models, before briefly discussing related work.

2.1 Background

Privacy Principles According to the GDPR [27, Art. 5 1.], six principles apply when processing personal data:

Lawfulness, Fairness, and Transparency - data is processed lawfully, fairly, and in a transparent manner.
Purpose Limitation - data collection is limited to previously specified, explicit, and legitimate purposes.
Data Minimization - data is adequate, relevant, and limited to what is necessary in relation to the purposes of the data collection.
Accuracy - data is accurate and kept up to date where necessary.
Storage Limitation - data is kept in a form which permits identification of data subjects for no longer than necessary in order to fulfill the purposes.
Integrity and Confidentiality - the data controller should apply appropriate technical or organizational measures to ensure appropriate security of the personal data, including protection against unlawful processing and accidental loss, destruction, or damage.

In addition, the data controller is responsible for complying with previous principles and should be able to demonstrate compliance (**Accountability**).

Trust Models. When dealing with privacy and data protection concerns, trust relations between the data owner and the entity processing and using the data must be considered. Focusing on the previous relation, three main adversary models are considered in the literature [28,32]: In the *untrusted model*, the data owner does not trust any of the entities responsible for processing or using the data to be outsourced. The former is then responsible for correctly enforcing his privacy requirement on the data. In the *semi-trusted model*, the data owner considers the third-party entity going to process or use his or her data as an honest-but-curious entity. It is honest as it is supposed to not deviate from the defined protocol but may attempt to learn as much information as possible about the data owner out of the outsourced data. In the *trusted model*, the data owner trusts a third-party entity, which is in charge of enabling the processing of their data while protecting the private and sensitive parts.

2.2   Related Work

There are proposals for the selection and integration of PETs based on privacy patterns [48,68], privacy strategies [44], or threats [18,20] along some general considerations of privacy requirements in the system engineering process or building systems based on privacy by design [19,35,36]. Drozd [23] maps privacy patterns to privacy principles from the ISO/IEC 29100. Thus, to the best of our knowledge, there is no prior work supporting the selection of PETs based on GDPR principles. This is supported by Kostova et al. [51] who found that only roughly half of the investigated academic papers are providing mappings to PETs at all and further research identifying gaps in the privacy engineering process in practise [65]. Closest to our work is the work by Koolen et al. [50]. They offer guidance on how to assess the concept of 'appropriate TOMs' by considering cybersecurity maturity models. However, we focus on the selection of technical measures, PETs, specifically.

Since our use cases stem from the automotive domain, we also investigated papers discussing the selection of PETs in the automotive domain: Al-Momani et al. [2] explored the usefulness of privacy patterns in improving privacy in future automotive systems. Chah et al. [17,18] use the LINDDUN methodology to identify and analyze privacy threats. Bella et al. [9] investigate privacy policies for cars similar to the recent Mozilla study [15] as well as user concerns and find that privacy for cars is insufficiently understood, mostly due to a lack of awareness. Syed-Winkler et al. [83] propose a system model for enforcing purpose limitation, and Pape et al. [69] propose a system model to identify suitable locations in the vehicle to integrate PETs. Löbner et al. [57,70] evaluate different de-identification techniques based on two automotive use cases.

3   Methodology

This section provides an overview of the underlying methods we used to create the framework. For the assessments and evaluations we did, we followed a rigorous approach of the four-eyes principle: One author proposed a first assessment which together with the corresponding reasoning was discussed with a second author. In case of disagreements, those have been discussed and, if necessary, the corresponding assessment and/or reasoning adjusted.

Application of Trust Models to GDPR Principles. To the best of our knowledge, the relevance of the different GDPR principles and the data processing entity's need to demonstrate its fulfillment to the data owner, have not been covered in related literature. Therefore, we carried out the assessment ourselves: Table 1 shows the result and is presented along with the reasoning in Sect. 4.1.

Framework for Aligning PET Types with GDPR Principles. To map PETs to GDPR principles, we first categorized specific PETs into PET types and classifications. We then mapped these PET types and classifications to four distinct layers, including processing, storage, communication, and physical layer. Subsequently, we analyzed the role of each PET to determine its contribution to GDPR compliance. This involved mapping each PET to the relevant GDPR principles, with a clear justification provided for each connection. The mappings were executed on the basis of existing literature and by discussions between the authors. To offer a concise overview of the relationships between GDPR principles and the corresponding PETs, we present a tabular representation (cf. Table 2 in Sect. 4.2).

Assessment of PET Maturity. For most of the qualitative assessment, we relied on literature benchmarking, drawing from established studies, technical analyses, and empirical results available in research papers and industry reports. For each PET, we referenced the specific literature from which the assessment metrics were derived, ensuring traceability and transparency of the assessment. Additionally, we provided detailed reasoning and supporting evidence to substantiate the assigned evaluations, taking into account factors such as the scope of the benchmarking, the nature of the use case, and the relevance of performance metrics (cf. Table 3 and Table 4 in Sect. 4.3). In cases where insufficient material or no comprehensive benchmarking data was available, we refrained from finalizing an evaluation. Instead, these PETs were noted as requiring further research or more robust empirical validation. This cautious approach ensures that assessments are not based on speculation or incomplete evidence, maintaining the reliability and credibility of the overall evaluation framework.

Evaluation. We used three different use cases from the automotive domain for evaluation: *Platooning* – where a group of vehicles drive together with many privacy challenges especially when trying to find suitable tracks of platoon leaders, *Location-Based Service (LBS)* – trying not to reveal more location information as necessary and still being able to get navigation support to specific points of interests, and *Usage-Based Insurance (UBI)* – when insurance premiums are charged based on the customers' usage and driving habits:

Platooning [7] is a technique closely related to fully automated driving. In this method, a designated platoon leader drives a route and allows other vehicles to join the platoon, following autonomously. This approach enhances both convenience and efficiency. The use case requires vehicles to have a basic set of sensors to sense the environment, cruise control and lane-keep assistance, and positioning including a high-definition map. Leaders announce their routes and followers privately compute their own, verifying leader trustworthiness before joining. While a server can facilitate this, platooning is possible without one. During operation, V2X messages manage smooth merging, departures, and route deviations. The main privacy challenge is to form a platoon without revealing sensitive information about participating vehicles.

Location-Based Services provide personalized, location-aware services such as route optimization, nearby recommendations, and contextual information to enhance the user experience. LBS rely on real-time GPS and user preferences to offer timely, relevant data. To deliver accurate services, the LBS provider (LBSP) collects and processes specific data from users, including current position (GPS data), direction of movement (for anticipating needs), and user queries (preferences for points of interest like restaurants or parks). The reliance of LBS on continuous real-time location data collection brings inherent privacy challenges for users. The sensitive nature of location information can expose users to risks if mismanaged, including potential tracking of movement patterns and revealing personal routines.

Usage-Based Insurance identifies risky driving behaviors to reduce road accidents. This use case focuses on Pay-As-You-Drive Insurance[1] where premiums depend on driving behavior. We explore how Advanced Driver Assistance Systems (ADAS) detect hazardous driving and use vehicle connectivity to update driver profiles dynamically. However, balancing safety incentives with privacy concerns remains a challenge, as does ensuring accurate driver profiling for fair premium calculation.

To evaluate the usefulness and correctness of our framework, we investigated PET candidates based on our framework for each of the three scenarios. We then checked if they can be applied to fulfill one or more of the GDPR principles.

4   Framework for Selection of PETs

One of the primary goals of our framework is to provide the ability to select candidate PETs tailored to specific use cases based on GDPR principles. The use case establishes a detailed framework by defining the entities involved, the data

---

[1] UBI Source: https://www.mobilize-fs.com/fr/actualites/pay-you-drive-et-pay-how-you-drive-nos-premieres-offres-dassurance-connectee.

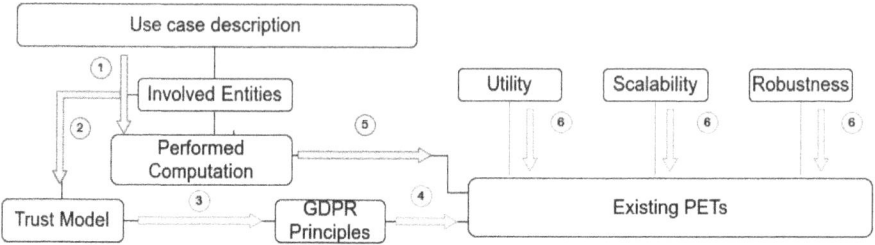

Fig. 1. Proposed Approach: Blue/Green steps are outside/inside the scope (Color figure online)

required, and the computations necessary to achieve their intended functionalities, alongside their corresponding trust levels. Figure 1 provides an overview of the necessary steps. As preparation (blue steps, outside of the scope of our framework), the use case needs to be described, involved entities need to be identified along with the established trust model. The next steps (in green) are in the focus of our framework: Based on the trust model, relevant GDPR principles are identified (step 3, cf. Sect. 4.1). The GDPR principles are then mapped to PET types (step 4, cf. Sect. 4.2 to identify candidate PETs that can be applied to enforce these principles. PETs provide privacy-preserving data processing with varying guarantees (see Tables 3 and 4), such as deterministic encryption, order-preserving encryption, and k-anonymity, each supporting different computational needs. Step 5 of the methodology involves mapping these processing needs to the set of PETs they provide, which allows us to select a set of candidate PETs suitable for a given scenario. We consider steps 1, 2, and 5 (in blue) as part of the use case description as they depend on the exact functions to be evaluated and the involved parties. Thus, our framework only covers the more generic part when the trust model and the mapping of the performed computations to PETs are specified.

Furthermore, we provide an assessment of the maturity of PETs in terms of utility, scalability, and robustness to support the PET selection process (step 6, cf. Sect. 4.3). Finally, trade-offs between utility, privacy, and efficiency must be made specifically for the use case, which is beyond the scope of our framework.

4.1 Application of Trust Model to GDPR Principles

Table 1 shows the application of the trust model towards GDPR principles. We consider two dimensions: *i) Relevance* of the principle, which does not imply that there are irrelevant principles; however, within each trust model, certain principles may have greater relevance than others. *ii) Demonstrability* which refers to the entity's capability not only to follow the principle, but also to provide accountability, which is the last principles of the relevance dimension. For the other principles, in theory the more important property is compliance with the principle (relevance), in practice –especially for semi-trusted and untrusted parties– demonstrability gains on importance.

Lawfulness, Fairness, and Transparency is relevant for untrusted and semi-trusted data processors and owners, but most relevant for those who are untrusted, as this increases the impact should they be caught and their data usage model not comply with the GDPR. For trusted data processors, it is assumed that they will respect the law and may even exceed compliance requirements.

Purpose Limitation is mostly relevant for untrusted and semi-trusted data processors. As these entities are not expected to respect this principle, technical enforcement is crucial. Trusted data processors are expected to adhere to the agreed purpose limitation, regardless of technical enforcement.

Data Minimization is relevant for all data processors, as it limits the risk of unintended data leakage. However, given that semi-trusted and untrusted data processors may be curious, it is even more important to prevent them from accessing unnecessary data.

Accuracy Ensuring the erasure of outdated and inaccurate data is relevant for all data processors. However, it might require the support of third parties, which makes it difficult to enforce in practice. Therefore, the relation to the trust model is moderate and trusted data processors are expected to comply.

Storage Limitation Follows the same argumentation as accuracy.

Integrity and Confidentiality This principle is important for all data processors, as security vulnerabilities may lead to data leakage. However, demonstrating and proving the implementation of security measures is challenging. We consider the importance lower for the trusted data processor, where it is assumed that all necessary measures are in place compared to semi-trusted or untrusted processors.

Accountability is addressed within the discussion of the various principles. Not surprisingly, the desired level of demonstrability increases as trust in the data-owning entity decreases. However, we have not discussed why a user should trust the data owner or processor. One way to gain trust is to demonstrate responsible and lawful data processing to users.

4.2 Mapping GDPR Principles to PET Types

Each of the four distinct layers (Processing, Storage, Communication, and Physical) involve specific PET types to handle sensitive data. Table 2 presents the list of PETs for each layer. These PETs support compliance with one or more GDPR principles, and in the following section, we will clarify the connection between each PET and the corresponding GDPR requirement:

Processing Layer. In this layer, the selected PETs align with one or more of the following GDPR principles: lawfulness, fairness, transparency; purpose limitation; data minimization; integrity and confidentiality; and accountability. First, *Secure and Outsourced Computation* ensures purpose limitation by processing data for specific purposes without exposing raw data and guarantees integrity and confidentiality by encrypting data during processing to prevent

Table 1. Relevance and Demonstrability of GDPR Principles in Relation to the Trust Model

Trust Model / GDPR Principles	Relevance			Demonstrability		
	Untrusted	Semi-trusted	Trusted	Untrusted	Semi-trusted	Trusted
Lawfulness, Fairness, and Transparency	●	◐	○	●	●	○
Purpose Limitation	●	●	◐	●	●	○
Data Minimization	●	●	●	●	●	◐
Accuracy	●	●	◐	●	◐	○
Storage Limitations	●	●	◐	●	◐	○
Integrity and Confidentiality	●	●	●	●	◐	◐
Accountability	●	●/◐	◐	N/A	N/A	N/A

● = high; ◐ = mid; ○ = low

unauthorized access and manipulation. Second, *Anonymization* ensures data minimization so that only the necessary data are processed while removing or concealing identifiers that are not required for the intended purpose. Third, *traceability* techniques, such as data tagging and digital watermarking, comply with data minimization because they allow organizations to track and monitor data use without requiring storage or sharing of excessive personal information. They also partially comply with lawfulness, fairness, and transparency by tracking data use, purpose limitation by enforcing proper usage, and accountability by creating clear audit trails to demonstrate GDPR compliance.

Storage Layer. We identify two types of PETs, including, first, data at rest encryption such as conventional encryption to ensure the integrity and confidentiality of the data. Then, Attribute-Based Encryption (ABE) [11] in the storage layer ensures purpose limitation by restricting access based on specific policies, data minimization by granting access only to necessary data, and integrity and confidentiality by encrypting data and limiting decryption to authorized users. In addition, TEEs [6] ensure compliance with purpose limitation, storage limitation, and the principles of integrity and confidentiality by guaranteeing data integrity, data confidentiality, and code integrity. The storage system partially enforces storage limitation policies by supporting timeline-based deletion, depending on the specific implementation case. Second, immutability, such as in blockchain-based solutions [86], ensures lawfulness, fairness, and transparency by providing a tamper-proof, transparent record of data transactions. It supports integrity and confidentiality by safeguarding data against unauthorized changes while maintaining secure access controls. Additionally, it enhances accountability by creating an auditable and verifiable trail of all actions, ensuring traceability and responsibility.

Communication Layer. This layer incorporates three PET types, which we map to the relevant GDPR principles. First, encryption techniques clearly

Table 2. Mapping PETs to GDPR Principles

Layer	PET & Classification	GDPR Principles	LFT	PL	DM	ACU	SL	IC	ACT
Processing	Secure and outsourced computation	Trusted execution environments [24,52]	✓					✓	
		Private Information Retrieval [34,43,71]	(✓)	✓	✓			✓	
		Homomorphic Encryption [47,89]			✓			✓	
		Secure Multiparty Computation [4]			✓			✓	
		Zero-knowledge proofs [63]			✓			✓	
	Anonymization	Semantic [5,12]			✓				
		Syntactic [62,73]			✓				
		Perturbation [22]			✓				
	Traceability	Data tainting [66]	(✓)	(✓)	✓				(✓)
		Digital Watermarking [66]	(✓)	(✓)	✓				(✓)
Storage	Data at-rest encryption	Conventional encryption						✓	
		Attribute-based encryption [10]		✓	✓			✓	
		Trusted execution environments [6]	✓				(✓)	✓	
	Immutability	Blockchain-based solutions [86]	✓					✓	✓
Communication	Encryption	Symmetric and Asymmetric						✓	
	Anonymity	Mixnet Protocol [72]			✓				
		Tor-related Protocols [60]			✓				
		Random Walk/DHT Protocols [75]			✓				
		DCnet Protocols [75]			✓				
	Authentication	Digital Signature						✓	✓
		Certificateless signature [45]						✓	✓
		Quantum-safe Signatures [79]						✓	✓
		Homomorphic Signature [84]						✓	✓
Physical	Encryption	Transciphering [59]	✓					✓	
		Attribute-based encryption [11]	✓		✓			✓	
	Anonymization	Local Differential Privacy [29]			✓				
		Peudonymization [26]			✓				

LFT: Lawfulness, fairness and transparency; PL: Purpose limitation;
DM: Data minimisation; ACU: Accuracy; SL: Storage limitation;
IC: Integrity and Confidentiality; ACT: Accountability

ensure integrity and confidentiality within the communication layer. Second, anonymity techniques like Mixnet Protocol [72], Tor-related Protocols [60], and Random Walk/DHT [75] Protocols comply with data minimization in the communication layer by obfuscating user identities and reducing the amount of identifiable information transmitted, ensuring only necessary data is exposed. Third, Authentication techniques such as Digital Signatures, Certificateless Signatures [45], Quantum-safe Signatures [79], and Homomorphic Signatures [84] ensure integrity and confidentiality by verifying data authenticity and protecting it from unauthorized access. In addition, it guarantees accountability by creating verifiable records of data interactions and user actions.

Physical Layer. Encryption techniques such as ABE and transciphering [59] can be applied to meet some GDPR principles. For the same reasons explained in the storage layer, the GDPR principles respected are purpose limitation, data minimization, and integrity and confidentiality.

4.3   Assessment of PET Maturity

The maturity assessment of a PET is performed across three key dimensions:

Utility. This dimension assesses whether the application of the PET preserves sufficient data usability for the intended operations. It evaluates if the desired data processing or analysis remains feasible after the PET is enforced.

Practicality and Scalability This dimension focuses on the practical implementation of the PET, particularly its ability to handle large volumes of data efficiently. It considers computational complexity, resource requirements, and scalability in real-world scenarios. The classification in this dimension is based on experimental results provided in the most recent published approaches. Nevertheless, some classifications may be missing due to the absence of recent experimental evaluations for certain proposed PETs.

Robustness of Privacy Guarantees. This dimension evaluates the strength of the privacy protection provided by the PET, categorized into three levels: *i) Low Robustness:* PETs that provide weak privacy guarantees and are vulnerable to well-known attacks (e.g., k-anonymity, which is susceptible to side-knowledge attacks).
ii) Medium Robustness: PETs that offer formal guarantees against specific privacy risks but do not ensure full confidentiality of data. For example, differential privacy provides formal membership privacy guarantees but does not protect the confidentiality of individual data items.
iii) High Robustness: PETs that ensure full confidentiality of data items. These include encryption schemes with strong security properties, such as IND-CPA (indistinguishability under chosen plaintext attack) [31].

These dimensions collectively provide a comprehensive framework for assessing a PET's maturity, helping to determine its suitability for specific privacy requirements and operational contexts. The qualitative evaluation of PET maturity across the different layers – Processing, Storage, Communication, and Physical – is summarized in Tables 3 and 4. For each evaluation, we provide references to the specific paper(s) that informed our assessment, ensuring transparency and traceability. The notation N/A is used to indicate that the evaluated dimension is not applicable or relevant for a particular PET, while ? is used to signify cases where the existing literature does not provide sufficient information to conduct an objective evaluation. This approach ensures clarity in presenting the evaluations while highlighting areas where further research is needed.

5   Evaluation

When we applied our framework to the different use cases, we had the following findings: For the *Platooning* use case [16], the main concern is about secure and

Table 3. Maturity of PETs for Processing Layer

Layer	PET & Classification		Efficiency	Utility	Practicality	Robustness
Secure and outsourced computation	Trusted execution environ.	SGX		● [24,52]	◑ [24,52]	◑ [46,90]①
		Keystone		● [24,52]	◑ [54]	◑ [54]①
		TrustZ.		● [24,52]	◑	?
	Private Information Retrieval	PIR	Computational PIR	● [43,61]	◐ [43,61]	◑ [43,61]
			Information-theoretic PIR	● [34,77]	◑ [34]	● [8]
		Obliv RAM		◑ [71,80]	◑ [71,80]	● [71,80]
	Homomorphic Encryption Based Computation [1]	Partially Homomorphic Encryption	Paillier	◐②	●	◑
			TKKS	◑ [47,89]③	◑ [47,89]	● [47,89]
			BFV	◑ [47,89]③	◑ [47,89]	●
			Hash-ElGamal	◑ [47,89]②	◑ [47,89]	●
			Boneh-Goh-Nissim	◑ [47,89]③	◑ [47,89]	●
		Fully Homomorphic Encryption	Ideal-lattice based	● [47,89]	◐ [47,89]	●
			Over Integers	● [47,89]	◐ [47,89]	●
			LWE based	● [47,89]	◐ [47,89]	●
			NTRU-like	● [47,89]	◐ [47,89]	●
		Functional Encryption	Multi-Client	● [58]	◑ [58]	●
			Single-Client	● [58]	◑ [58]	●
	Secure Multiparty Comp.	Secret Sharing	Additive	● [4]	◐ [4]	●
			Shamir (ECIES)	● [4]	◐ [4]	●
		Garbled Circuits		● [4]	◐ [4]	●
Processing [36]	Anonymization	Zero-knowledge proofs	Non-interactive	N/A	● [63]	●
			Interactive	N/A	● [63]	●
		Semantic Based	Generic	Global Differential Privacy	◑	●	◑①
				Differential Indentifiability	◑ [12]	● [12]	◑①
			Location	Geo-Indistinquishability	◑ [5,64]	● [5,64]	◐①
				δ-privacy	◑ [88]	● [88]	◑⑤
		Syntactic	General	k-anonymity	◑	◑ [73]	◐ [82]
				l-diversity	◐ [62]	◑ [62]	◑ [62]
			-based	t-Closeness	◐ [33]	◑ [33]	◑ [33]
				β-likeness	◑	◑	◑
			Suppression-Based		◐ [78]	◑ [78]	◐ [78]
			Categorization	Perturbation B-likeness	◑	●	◐
		Perturbation Based	Numerical	Noise Addition	◑ [22]	● [22]	◑ [22]
				Geometric perturbation	◑ [21]	● [21]	◑ [21]
	Traceab.	Data tainting		●	◐	◑
		Digital Water.		● [66]	◐ [66]	◑ [66]

① Several implementation attacks are being published each year. The considered adversary model is not always relevant (depending on the use case)

② Pailler cryptosystem provides low utility over the data to be encrypted as it allows only to perform addition on encrypted data

③ CKK and BFV allow to perform computations that can be expressed as additions and a relatively small number of multiplications. In addition, most implementation of the BFV and CKK do not allow bootstrapping.

④ In summary, while differential privacy-based techniques are effective in protecting the presence or absence of specific entities in a database, the responsibility for safeguarding the confidentiality of the data itself lies in implementing comprehensive security measures that encompass encryption, access controls, and secure data handling practices.

⑤ Delta privacy builds upon the principles of geo-indistinguishability and takes into account the temporal correlation of location data. By introducing additional noise and perturbations, it enhances privacy protection by mitigating the risks associated with the analysis of consecutive data points and the potential inference of sensitive information.

Table 4. Maturity of PETs for Storage, Communication and Physical Layer

Layer	PET & Classification		Efficiency	Utility	Practicality	Robustness
Storage	Data at-rest encryption	Conventional encryption	●		◐ ⓖ	●
		Attribute-based encryption	● [10]		● [10]	● [10]
	Immutability	Blockchain-based solutions	●		◐	●
Communication	Encryption	Symmetric and Asymmetric	●		●	●
	Anonymity [75]	Mixnet Protocol	●		◐ [72]	●
		Tor-related Protocols	●		◐ [81]	◐
		Random Walk/DHT Protocols	●		◐ [75]	◐ [75]
		DCnet Protocols	●		◐ [75]	◐ [75]
	Authentication	Digital Signature	●		●	●
		Certificateless signature [45]	● [45]		◐ [45]	◐ [45]
		Quantum-safe Signatures [79]	● [3]		◐ [3]	● [3]
		Homomorphic Signature [84]	● [25]		◐ [25]	● [25]
Physical	Encryption	Transciphering	●		◐ [59]	● [59]
		Attribute-based encryption	●		◐ [11]	● [11]
	Anonymization	Local Differential Privacy	◐		● [29]	◐ [29]
		Peudonymization [26]	●		●	◐

ⓖ Traditional encryption methods are not well-suited for scenarios where data needs to be shared among multiple entities.

outsourced computation as the crucial computations are about the locations and tracks of the platoon leaders and the vehicle trying to join a suitable platoon. Therefore, we considered homomorphic encryption as the candidate. We eventually went with partial homomorphic encryption and found that we could apply CKKS scheme (cf. Chah et al. [16]).

For the *Location and Navigation* use case, we also identified secure and outsourced computation as a significant concern. In this case, two possible approaches were identified: semantic anonymization and the use of a trusted execution environment (TEE). While a trusted execution environment is quite useful for single-user scenarios, it is not scalable for broader applications. Therefore, we focused on semantic anonymization to define a framework for quantifying the privacy loss when interacting with location-based services [13].

For the *Pay as you Drive (PAYD)* use case, the emphasis is again on secure and outsourced computation. The insurance company needs to measure various metrics related to usage and driving behavior, but ideally, not more than necessary. Consequently, our findings indicate that fully homomorphic encryption schemes would be beneficial in this context. The code is available on GitHub[2]. For most use cases, performance is not the main issue as there is

---

[2] PAYD Code: https://github.com/badr007-01/Usage_Based_insurance_DP_HE_from_SUMODataset.git

no need to compute in real time. Furthermore, secret sharing as part of secure multiparty computation comes in handy as it could allow the comparison of different values without revealing more information than necessary.

For all use cases, communication anonymity could also be considered, such as using e. g. Mixnet protocols to conceal users' IP addresses. However, this consideration applies to nearly all scenarios involving online communication. Therefore, the primary concern is whether the associated delay is acceptable, rather than its specificity to our use cases. The structured process provided by our framework, while not directly addressing the selection of PETs in its entirety, proved highly effective in guiding the identification and selection of candidate PETs for the three use cases examined.

6   Discussion

In this section, we first highlight some findings during the creation of the framework, before we discuss limitations and future work.

Coverage of GDPR Principles with PETs. As visible in Table 2, the accuracy cannot be ensured by using PETs. While data governance and management solutions may use dedicated meta data to classify the required freshness of the data, other requirements such as the rectification of false data is more related to dedicated processes than privacy by technology. One reason for this may be that accuracy is considered a soft privacy requirement [20], where it is assumed that the data subject no longer has control over their personal data, and the remaining measures rely on policies, access control, and audits. However, most Privacy-Enhancing Technologies (PETs) aim to minimize data, addressing hard privacy requirements, and therefore, they do not encompass accuracy.

Note, that we specifically started from GDPR principles and not from threats. In industry, often the challenge is to select PETs to implement or support privacy principles rather than addressing specific threats identified by a threat analysis with specific tools such as LINDDUN [87] or PANOPTIC [49].

Differences Between the Layers. Not all GDPR principles are relevant for all layers as the communication layer does not request or store any information; a similar case holds for the physical layer. For the other layers, we see that multiple PETs need to be combined in order to cover most GDPR principles as none can cover all (except accuracy as discussed before).

Anonymity Versus Data Quality. We also came across the well-known issue that the goal of PETs can be in contrast to data quality [85], in particular if we consider PETs such as perturbation which introduce noise to the data. These PETs trade privacy for data quality. On a higher level, this might even be a conflict with the accuracy privacy principle as data with perturbation may not be considered "accurate". The issue can also be observed in a more lightweight manner with data minimization as many machine learning approaches gain a better accuracy if they can be trained with larger amounts of data.

From Selection to Implementation. Additionally, it needs to be mentioned that the correct implementation and usage are crucial. This is a part that is not covered in detail within this work but reflected in the practicability. For example, many semantic anonymizations have the major disadvantage that they are very vulnerable against background knowledge attacks. On the other hand, anonymization except for ZKPs is rather easy to implement. Overall, we observed that Secure MPC and Fully Homomorphic Encryption pose a rather huge computational overhead which reduces the number of potential use cases. Although PHE is orders of magnitude faster than FHE [76], its main issue is its very limited application area due to being reduced to only a single mathematical gate (e.g., secure voting using additive homomorphism). However, FHE, even though libraries such as Microsoft SEAL make continuous progress [74], is hardly used in real-world applications. Similarly, Private Information Retrieval (PIR) in the single-server setting was rather inefficient for a long time. By leveraging a pre-processing phase, SimplePIR could reduce the computational overhead significantly (shifting it to an offline phase still having $O(N)$ with a database size of N) so that the actual computation of the query's answer was at very low cost. But still the communication cost of $O(\sqrt{N})$ is rather high [43]. For the multi-server setting, multiple non-colluding servers are required which is impractical in many real-world applications. On the other hand, there are quite efficient schemes available achieving $N^{o(1)}$ after a near-linear pre-processing phase with an sub-linear communication complexity [53]. Similarly, Günther et al. have demonstrated the potential impact of using GPUs for the pre-processing phase achieving $2.1\times$ speedup compared to the CPU version [34].

6.1   Limitations

While our framework provides valuable insights into the evaluation of PETs, there are several limitations that must be acknowledged.

General Limitations. First, our approach uses the privacy principles of the GDPR as a starting point, which may not encompass all relevant privacy regulations. Second, while we provide a general evaluation of PET efficiency, this cannot replace a dedicated assessment of whether the PET meets specific project requirements, such as response time, storage space, or communication overhead. Such detailed evaluations would need to be tailored to the unique constraints of each application scenario. Furthermore, one needs to evaluate a PET based on their planned trust model, for example ABE requires a semi-trusted third party which does not suit every use case.

Applicability to Other Domains. Although the evaluation was conducted on three scenarios from the automotive domain, we did not rely on properties unique to this domain. Therefore, we are confident that our framework can be adapted for use in other domains; however, additional validation in diverse application areas would further substantiate this claim.

Combination of PETs. Currently, the framework does not support the combination of PETs. It neither accommodates the scenario where different privacy principles necessitate different PETs, potentially increasing the complexity of implementation and configuration—thus making alternative PET choices more attractive—nor does it address the scenario where a single privacy principle may be best implemented by applying multiple PETs.

6.2   Future Work

Cover remaining steps from framework. Our framework did not cover certain preparation steps, such as describing the use case, involved entities, and determining the underlying trust model. Furthermore, the step of aligning the processing needs of the use case with capability of the PETs is only partially supported. While our maturity assessment of the PETs provides some input, the selection process itself is not supported. Future work could address these remaining steps of the framework or at least provide basic support, as they may vary significantly depending on the use case.

Further dimensions for maturity of PETs. The evaluation of PETs also in terms of performance overheads in realistic settings could be expanded. In particular, the availability of easily (re-)usable artifacts (e. g. library, package, component) with the aim to include the dimension of developer-friendliness and necessary implementation efforts in the framework. Those have already been identified by Pallas et al. [65] as important for PET adoption.

Coverage of further privacy principles. Our work is limited to the privacy principles listed in the GDPR in Article 5.1. Not only could the work be expanded to other privacy principles within the GDPR, but also to other privacy-related regulations, such as California Privacy Rights Act of 2020 (CPRA), California Consumer Privacy Act (CCPA) [14], the Brazilian General Data Protection Law (LGPD), or the Act on the Protection of Personal Information (APPI) in Japan. Furthermore, there is no need to restrict the idea to regulatory frameworks. Thus, privacy principles from non-regulatory frameworks, such as the Fair Information Practice Principles (FIPPs) or the OECD Privacy Principles, clearly call for further principles to be properly reflected in the design and implementation of real-world systems as well.

Considering user acceptance criteria for PET selection. Furthermore, it would be interesting to consider any user acceptance effects and criteria for PETs [67] in our framework, e. g. for machine learning [55,56]. User perceptions of PETs considering technology use behavior [42], willingness to pay [37], privacy concerns [39], risk beliefs [40], privacy literacy [41], and perceived anonymity and trust [38] have been investigated in the past by Harborth et al. and shown to have a huge influence on the acceptance of PETs by end users. Therefore, it would be another challenge to include these into the selection process, perhaps along with other economic criteria such as licenses of the PETs, fees and operating costs, and availability of knowledgeable experts.

7   Conclusion

We proposed a framework to support the selection of PETs based on GDPR privacy principles. For that purpose, we provided mappings between a trust model and the GDPR principles and between different PET types and GDPR principles. Furthermore, we assessed different PETs with regards to utility, scalability, and robustness. We evaluated our framework by applying it to three different use cases from the automotive domain and it proved highly effective in guiding the identification and selection of candidate PETs.

While our work helps on the selection of PETs, there is still a gap when it comes to the implementation, configuration and combination of PETs. Furthermore, the challenge of integrating PETs into (existing) architectures of a system may not be trivial as well.

Acknowledgements. This work was suported by the Federal Ministry of Education and Research, Germany (BMBF) under grant number 16KIS1382 and by the Agence Nationale de la Recherche, France (ANR) under grant number ANR-20-CYAL-0008.

References

1. Acar, A., Aksu, H., Uluagac, A.S., Conti, M.: A survey on homomorphic encryption schemes: theory and implementation. ACM Csur. **51**(4), 1–35 (2018)
2. Al-Momani, A., Balenson, D., Mann, Z.Á., Pape, S., Petit, J., Bösch, C.: Navigating privacy patterns in the era of Robotaxis. In: IEEE EuroS&PW, IWPE 2024, pp. 32–39 (2024). https://doi.org/10.1109/EuroSPW61312.2024.00011
3. Alkhulaifi, A., El-Alfy, E.S.M.: Exploring lattice-based post-quantum signature for JWT authentication: review and case study. In: 2020 IEEE 91st Vehicular Technology Conference (VTC2020-Spring), pp. 1–5, IEEE (2020)
4. Aly, A., Nawaz, K., Salazar, E., Sucasas, V.: Through the looking-glass: benchmarking secure multi-party computation comparisons for Relu's. In: International Conference on Cryptology and Network Security, pp. 44–67, Springer (2022)
5. Andrés, M.E., Bordenabe, N.E., Chatzikokolakis, K., Palamidessi, C.: Geo-indistinguishability: differential privacy for location-based systems. In: Proceedings of the 2013 ACM SIGSAC conference on Computer & communications security, pp. 901–914 (2013)
6. Arfaoui, G., Gharout, S., Traoré, J.: Trusted execution environments: a look under the hood. In: 2014 2nd IEEE International Conference on Mobile Cloud Computing, Services, and Engineering, pp. 259–266, IEEE (2014)
7. Balador, A., Bazzi, A., Hernandez-Jayo, U., de la Iglesia, I., Ahmadvand, H.: A survey on vehicular communication for cooperative truck platooning application. Veh. Commun. **35** (2022)
8. Beimel, A., Stahl, Y.: Robust information-theoretic private information retrieval. In: Proceedings of the 3rd International Conference on Security in Communication Networks, pp. 326–341, SCN'02, Springer-Verlag, Berlin, Heidelberg (2002). ISBN 3540004203

9. Bella, G., Biondi, P., Vincenzi, M.D., Tudisco, G.: Privacy and modern cars through a dual lens. In: 2021 IEEE European Symposium on Security and Privacy Workshops (EuroS&PW), pp. 136–143 (2021). https://doi.org/10.1109/EuroSPW54576.2021.00022
10. Bkakria, A.: Robust and provably secure attribute-based encryption supporting access revocation and outsourced decryption. In: IFIP Annual Conference on Data and Applications Security and Privacy, pp. 197–214, Springer (2022)
11. Bkakria, A.: Robust, revocable, forward and backward adaptively secure attribute-based encryption with outsourced decryption. J. Comput. Secur. **31**(6), 727–760 (2023)
12. Bkakria, A., Cuppens-Boulahia, N., Cuppens, F.: Linking differential identifiability with differential privacy. In: International Conference on Information and Communications Security, pp. 232–247, Springer (2018)
13. Bkakria, A., Yaich, R.: A framework for managing multifaceted privacy leakage while optimizing utility in continuous LBS interactions (2024). RL https://arxiv.org/abs/2404.13407
14. California Legislature: California consumer privacy act of 2018 (CCPA) (2018). https://leginfo.legislature.ca.gov/faces/billTextClient.xhtml?bill_id=201720180AB375
15. Caltrider, J., Rykov, M., MacDonald, Z.: It's official: Cars are the worst product category we have ever reviewed for privacy (2023). URL https://foundation.mozilla.org/en/privacynotincluded/articles/its-official-cars-are-the-worst-product-category-we-have-ever-reviewed-for-privacy/
16. Chah, B., Lombard, A., Bkakria, A., Abbas-Turki, A., Yaich, R.: H3PC: enhanced security and privacy-preserving platoon construction based on fully homomorphic encryption. In: 2023 IEEE 26th International Conference on Intelligent Transportation Systems (ITSC), pp. 4086–4093, IEEE (2023)
17. Chah, B., Lombard, A., Bkakria, A., Yaich, R., Abbas-Turki, A.: Exploring privacy threats in connected and autonomous vehicles: an analysis. J. Ubiquit. Syst. Pervas. Netw. **19**(1), 25–32 (2023)
18. Chah, B., Lombard, A., Bkakria, A., Yaich, R., Abbas-Turki, A., Galland, S.: Privacy threat analysis for connected and autonomous vehicles. Proc. Comput. Sci. **210**, 36–44 (2022)
19. Danezis, G., et al.: Privacy and data protection by design-from policy to engineering. arXiv preprint arXiv:1501.03726 (2015)
20. Deng, M., Wuyts, K., Scandariato, R., Preneel, B., Joosen, W.: A privacy threat analysis framework: supporting the elicitation and fulfillment of privacy requirements. Requirements Eng. **16**(1), 3–32 (2011)
21. Domingo-Ferrer, J., Muralidhar, K.: New directions in anonymization: permutation paradigm, verifiability by subjects and intruders, transparency to users. Inf. Sci. **337**, 11–24 (2016)
22. Domingo-Ferrer, J., Trujillo-Rasua, R.: Microaggregation-and permutation-based anonymization of movement data. Inf. Sci. **208**, 55–80 (2012)
23. Drozd, O.: Privacy pattern catalogue: a tool for integrating privacy principles of ISO/IEC 29100 into the software development process. In: Privacy and Identity Management, pp. 129–140 (2016)
24. El-Hindi, M., Ziegler, T., Heinrich, M., Lutsch, A., Zhao, Z., Binnig, C.: Benchmarking the second generation of intel SGX hardware. In: Data Management on New Hardware, pp. 1–8 (2022)
25. Emmanuel, N., Khan, A., Alam, M., Khan, T., Khan, M.K.: Structures and data preserving homomorphic signatures. J. Netw. Comput. Appl. **102**, 58–70 (2018)

26. Englert, R., et al.: ALIIAS: anonymization/pseudonymization with limesurvey integration and ii-factor authentication for scientific research. SoftwareX **24**, 101522 (2023)
27. European Union: Regulation (EU) 2016/679 of the european parliament and of the council of 27 April 2016 on the protection of natural persons with regard to the processing of personal data and on the free movement of such data (2016). URL https://eur-lex.europa.eu/eli/reg/2016/679/oj
28. Franklin, M., Reiter, M.K., Schneier, B.: The secure sockets layer and the future of web security. IEEE Internet Comput. (1999). https://doi.org/10.1109/4236.792812
29. Gallindo, L., Leal, B.F., Cerqueira, L.M., Morais, A., Kim, S.: Performance benchmarking of local differential privacy for mobile devices. In: IEEE International Conference on PerCom Workshops (2022). https://doi.org/10.1109/PerComWorkshops53856.2022.9767402
30. Garrido, G.M., Sedlmeir, J., Uludağ, Ö., Alaoui, I.S., Luckow, A., Matthes, F.: Revealing the landscape of privacy-enhancing technologies in the context of data markets for the IoT: a systematic literature review. J. Netw. Comput. Appl. **207**, 103465 (2022)
31. Goldwasser, S., Micali, S.: Probabilistic encryption. J. Comput. Syst. Sci. **28**(2), 270–299 (1984)
32. Goldwasser, S., Micali, S., Rackoff, C.: The knowledge complexity of interactive proof systems. SIAM J. Comput. **18**(1), 186–208 (1989)
33. Gowda, V.T., Bagai, R., Spilinek, G., Vitalapura, S.: Efficient near-optimal t-closeness with low information loss. In: 2021 11th IEEE International Conference on Intelligent Data Acquisition and Advanced Computing Systems: Technology and Applications (IDAACS), vol. 1, pp. 494–498, IEEE (2021)
34. Günther, D., Heymann, M., Pinkas, B., Schneider, T.: GPU-accelerated PIR with Client-Independent preprocessing for Large-Scale applications. In: 31st USENIX Security Symposium (USENIX Security 22), pp. 1759–1776, USENIX Association, Boston, MA (2022). ISBN 978-1-939133-31-1, URL https://www.usenix.org/conference/usenixsecurity22/presentation/gunther
35. Gürses, S., Troncoso, C., Diaz, C.: Engineering privacy by design. Comput. Privacy Data Prot. **14**(3), 25 (2011)
36. Gürses, S., Troncoso, C., Diaz, C.: Engineering privacy by design reloaded. In: Amsterdam Privacy Conference, vol. 21 (2015)
37. Harborth, D., Cai, X., Pape, S.: Why do people pay for privacy-enhancing technologies? The case of Tor and JonDonym?. In: IFIP SEC (2019). https://doi.org/10.1007/978-3-030-22312-0_18
38. Harborth, D., Pape, S.: Examining technology use factors of privacy-enhancing technologies: the role of perceived anonymity and trust. In: 24th AMCIS 2018, Association for Information Systems (2018)
39. Harborth, D., Pape, S.: Jondonym users' information privacy concerns. In: IFIP SEC (2018). https://doi.org/10.1007/978-3-319-99828-2_13
40. Harborth, D., Pape, S.: How privacy concerns and trust and risk beliefs influence users' intentions to use privacy-enhancing technologies – the case of tor. In: 52nd HICSS (2019). https://doi.org/10125/59923
41. Harborth, D., Pape, S.: How privacy concerns, trust and risk beliefs and privacy literacy influence users' intentions to use privacy-enhancing technologies - the case of tor. ACM SIGMIS Database (2020). https://doi.org/10.1145/3380799.3380805
42. Harborth, D., Pape, S., Rannenberg, K.: Explaining the technology use behavior of privacy-enhancing technologies: the case of tor and Jondonym. Proc. PoPETs (2020). https://doi.org/10.2478/popets-2020-0020

43. Henzinger, A., Hong, M.M., Corrigan-Gibbs, H., Meiklejohn, S., Vaikuntanathan, V.: One server for the price of two: simple and fast single-server private information retrieval. In: 32nd USENIX Security Symposium (USENIX Security 23), pp. 3889–3905, USENIX Association, Anaheim, CA (2023). ISBN 978-1-939133-37-3, URL https://www.usenix.org/conference/usenixsecurity23/presentation/henzinger

44. Hoepman, J.H.: Privacy design strategies. In: IFIP International Information Security Conference, pp. 446–459, Springer (2014)

45. Hussain, S.S., Ullah, S., Ali, I., Xie, J., Inukollu, V.N.: Certificateless signature schemes in industrial internet of things: a comparative survey. Comput. Commun. **181**, 116–131 (2022)

46. Jiang, J., Soriente, C., Karame, G.: On the challenges of detecting side-channel attacks in SGX. In: RAID, pp. 86–98 (2022)

47. Jiang, L., Ju, L.: FHEBench: benchmarking fully homomorphic encryption schemes. arXiv preprint arXiv:2203.00728 (2022)

48. Kalloniatis, C., Kavakli, E., Gritzalis, S.: Addressing privacy requirements in system design: the PRIS method. Req. Eng. **13**, 241–255 (2008)

49. Katcher, S., et al.: The Mitre panoptic™ privacy threat model tutorial. In: 2nd Workshop on Privacy Threat Modeling (WPTM) (2023)

50. Koolen, C., Wuyts, K., Joosen, W., Valcke, P.: From insight to compliance: appropriate technical and organisational security measures through the lens of cybersecurity maturity models. Comput. Law Secur. Rev. **52**, 105914 (2024)

51. Kostova, B., Gürses, S., Troncoso, C.: Privacy engineering meets software engineering. on the challenges of engineering privacy bydesign. arXiv preprint arXiv:2007.08613 (2020)

52. Kumar, S., Panda, A., Sarangi, S.R.: A comprehensive benchmark suite for intel SGX. arXiv preprint arXiv:2205.06415 (2022)

53. Lazzaretti, A., Liu, Z., Fisch, B., Papamanthou, C.: Multi-server doubly efficient PIR. Cryptology ePrint Archive, Paper 2024/829 (2024). URL https://eprint.iacr.org/2024/829

54. Lee, D., Kohlbrenner, D., Shinde, S., Asanović, K., Song, D.: Keystone: an open framework for architecting trusted execution environments. In: Proceedings of the Fifteenth European Conference on Computer Systems, pp. 1–16 (2020)

55. Löbner, S., Pape, S., Bracamonte, V.: User acceptance criteria for privacy preserving machine learning techniques. In: Proceedings of the 18th International Conference on ARES 2023, Benevento, Italy, ACM (2023). https://doi.org/10.1145/3600160.3605004

56. Löbner, S., Pape, S., Bracamonte, V., Phalakarn, K.: Which PPML would a user choose? A structured decision support framework for developers to rank PPML techniques based on user acceptance criteria (2024). https://doi.org/10.48550/arXiv.2411.06995

57. Löbner, S., Tronnier, F., Pape, S., Rannenberg, K.: Comparison of de-identification techniques for privacy preserving data analysis in vehicular data sharing. In: CSCS, pp. 7:1–7:11, ACM (2021). https://doi.org/10.1145/3488904.3493380

58. Marc, T., Stopar, M., Hartman, J., Bizjak, M., Modic, J.: Privacy-enhanced machine learning with functional encryption. In: Sako, K., Schneider, S., Ryan, P. (eds.) ESORICS 2019. LNCS, vol. 11735, pp. 3–21. Springer, Cham (2019). https://doi.org/10.1007/978-3-030-29959-0_1

59. Méaux, P., Park, J., Pereira, H.V.: Towards practical Transciphering for Fhe with setup independent of the plaintext space. Cryptology ePrint Archive (2023)

60. Melloni, A., Stam, M., Ytrehus, Ø.: On evaluating anonymity of onion routing. In: International Conference on Selected Areas in Cryptography, pp. 3–24, Springer (2021)
61. Menon, S.J., Wu, D.J.: Spiral: fast, high-rate single-server PIR via FHE composition. In: 2022 IEEE Symposium on Security and Privacy (SP), pp. 930–947 (2022). https://doi.org/10.1109/SP46214.2022.9833700
62. Nininahazwe, F.S.: Studying L-diversity and K-anonymity over datasets with sensitive fields. In: Sun, X., Pan, Z., Bertino, E. (eds.) ICAIS 2019. LNCS, vol. 11632, pp. 63–73. Springer, Cham (2019). https://doi.org/10.1007/978-3-030-24274-9_6
63. Ornelas, J.M.: On benchmarking zero knowledge proof systems. https://hackmd.io/@heliax/SJU01u5fs (2023)
64. Oya, S., Troncoso, C., Pérez-González, F.: Is geo-indistinguishability what you are looking for?. In: Proceedings of the 2017 on Workshop on Privacy in the Electronic Society, pp. 137–140 (2017)
65. Pallas, F., et al.: Privacy engineering from principles to practice: a roadmap. IEEE Secur. Priv. **22** (2024)
66. Panah, A.S., Van Schyndel, R., Sellis, T., Bertino, E.: On the properties of non-media digital watermarking: a review of state of the art techniques. IEEE Access **4**, 2670–2704 (2016)
67. Pape, S., Harborth, D.: Acceptance factors of privacy-enhancing technologies on the basis of tor and Jondonym. In: Gerber, N., Stöver, A., Marky, K. (eds.) Human Factors in Privacy Research, pp. 299–320, Springer International Publishing (2023). ISBN 978-3-031-28643-8, https://doi.org/10.1007/978-3-031-28643-8_15, URL https://link.springer.com/chapter/10.1007/978-3-031-28643-8_15
68. Pape, S., Rannenberg, K.: Applying privacy patterns to the internet of things' (IoT) architecture. Mobile Netw. Appl. **24**(3), 925–933 (2018). https://doi.org/10.1007/s11036-018-1148-2
69. Pape, S., et al.: A systematic approach for automotive privacy management. In: CSCS, ACM (2023). https://doi.org/10.1145/3631204.3631863
70. Rannenberg, K., Pape, S., Tronnier, F., Löbner, S.: Study on the technical evaluation of de-identification procedures for personal data in the automotive sector. Tech. rep., Goethe University Frankfurt (2021). https://doi.org/10.21248/gups.63413, URL http://publikationen.ub.uni-frankfurt.de/frontdoor/index/index/docId/63413
71. Raskin, M., Simkin, M.: Perfectly secure oblivious ram with sublinear bandwidth overhead. In: Advances in Cryptology – ASIACRYPT 2019: 25th International Conference on the Theory and Application of Cryptology and Information Security, Kobe, Japan, December 8–12, 2019, Proceedings, Part II, pp. 537–563, Springer-Verlag, Berlin, Heidelberg (2019). ISBN 978-3-030-34620-1, https://doi.org/10.1007/978-3-030-34621-8_19, URL https://doi.org/10.1007/978-3-030-34621-8_19
72. Ribarski, P., Antovski, L.: Mixnets: implementation and performance evaluation of decryption and re-encryption types. J. Comput. Inf. Technol. **20**(3), 225–231 (2012)
73. Šarčević, T., Molnar, D., Mayer, R.: An analysis of different notions of effectiveness in k-anonymity. In: International Conference on Privacy in Statistical Databases, pp. 121–135, Springer (2020)
74. SEAL: Microsoft SEAL (release 4.1). https://github.com/Microsoft/SEAL (2023). microsoft Research, Redmond, WA
75. Shirazi, F., Simeonovski, M., Asghar, M.R., Backes, M., Diaz, C.: A survey on routing in anonymous communication protocols. CSUR **51**(3), 1–39 (2018)

76. Sidorov, V., Wei, E.Y.F., Ng, W.K.: Comprehensive performance analysis of homomorphic cryptosystems for practical data processing. arXiv preprint arXiv:2202.02960 (2022)
77. Singh, J., Wei, Y., Zikas, V.: Information-theoretic multi-server private information retrieval with client preprocessing. In: Theory of Cryptography: 22nd International Conference, TCC 2024, Milan, Italy, December 2–6, 2024, Proceedings, Part IV, pp. 423–450, Springer-Verlag, Berlin, Heidelberg (2024). ISBN 978-3-031-78022-6, https://doi.org/10.1007/978-3-031-78023-3_14, URL https://doi.org/10.1007/978-3-031-78023-3_14
78. Slijepčević, D., Henzl, M., Klausner, L.D., Dam, T., Kieseberg, P., Zeppelzauer, M.: k-anonymity in practice: how generalisation and suppression affect machine learning classifiers. Comput. Secur. **111**, 102488 (2021)
79. Sridhar, S.: A Survey of Quantum-safe Digital Signatures and their building blocks. Master's Thesis, NTNU (2021)
80. Stefanov, E., et al.: Path ORAM: an extremely simple oblivious ram protocol. J. ACM **65**(4) (2018). ISSN 0004-5411, https://doi.org/10.1145/3177872, URL https://doi.org/10.1145/3177872
81. Stokkink, Q., Treep, H., Pouwelse, J.: Performance analysis of a tor-like onion routing implementation. arXiv preprint arXiv:1507.00245 (2015)
82. Sun, Y., Yin, L., Liu, L., Xin, S.: Toward inference attacks for k-anonymity. Pers. Ubiquit. Comput. **18**, 1871–1880 (2014)
83. Syed-Winkler, S., Pape, S., Sabouri, A.: A data protection-oriented system model enforcing purpose limitation for connected mobility. In: CSCS, ACM (2022). https://doi.org/10.1145/3568160.3570231
84. Traverso, G., Demirel, D., Buchmann, J.: Homomorphic Signature Schemes: a survey, vol. 1. Springer (2016)
85. Tronnier, F., Pape, S., Löbner, S., Rannenberg, K.: A discussion on ethical cybersecurity issues in digital service chains. In: Cybersecurity of Digital Service Chains - Challenges, Methodologies, and Tools, LNCS, vol. 13300, pp. 222–256 (2022). https://doi.org/10.1007/978-3-031-04036-8_10
86. Wan, Z., Guan, Z., Cheng, X.: Pride: A private and decentralized usage-based insurance using blockchain. In: 2018 IEEE iThings and IEEE GreenCom and IEEE CPSCom and IEEE SmartData, IEEE (2018)
87. Wuyts, K., Joosen, W.: Linddun privacy threat modeling: a tutorial. CW Reports (2015)
88. Xiao, Y., Xiong, L.: Protecting locations with differential privacy under temporal correlations. In: Proceedings of the 22nd ACM SIGSAC Conference on Computer and Communications Security, pp. 1298–1309 (2015)
89. Yang, H., Shen, S., Dai, W., Zhou, L., Liu, Z., Zhao, Y.: Implementing and benchmarking word-wise homomorphic encryption schemes on GPU. Cryptology ePrint Archive (2023)
90. Yoon, H., Lee, M.: SGXDump: a repeatable code-reuse attack for extracting SGX enclave memory. Appl. Sci. **12**(15), 7655 (2022)

Prink: k_s-Anonymization for Streaming Data in Apache Flink

Philip Groneberg[1], Saskia Nuñez von Voigt[1(✉)] [ID], Thomas Janke[1] [ID],
Louis Loechel[1] [ID], Karl Wolf[1] [ID], Elias Grünewald[2] [ID], and Frank Pallas[3] [ID]

[1] Technische Universität Berlin, Berlin, Germany
{saskia.nunezvonvoigt,janke,loechel,k.wolf}@tu-berlin.de
[2] Charité – Universitätsmedizin Berlin, Berlin, Germany
elias.gruenewald@charite.de
[3] Paris Lodron Universität Salzburg, Salzburg, Austria
frank.pallas@plus.ac.at

Abstract. In this paper, we present Prink, a novel and practically applicable concept and fully implemented prototype for k_s-anonymizing data streams in real-world application architectures. Building upon the pre-existing, yet rudimentary CASTLE scheme, Prink for the first time introduces semantics-aware k_s-anonymization of non-numerical (such as categorical or hierarchically generalizable) streaming data in a information loss-optimized manner. In addition, it provides native integration into Apache Flink, one of the prevailing frameworks for enterprise-grade stream data processing in numerous application domains.

Our contributions excel the previously established state of the art for the privacy guarantee-providing anonymization of streaming data in that they 1) allow to include non-numerical data in the anonymization process, 2) provide discrete datapoints instead of aggregates, thereby facilitating flexible data use, 3) are applicable in real-world system contexts with minimal integration efforts, and 4) are experimentally proven to raise acceptable performance overheads and information loss in realistic settings. With these characteristics, Prink provides an anonymization approach which is practically feasible for a broad variety of real-world, enterprise-grade stream processing applications and environments.

Keywords: data stream anonymization · Flink · k-anonymity · privacy engineering

1 Introduction

Stream processing is a core paradigm underlying many modern, enterprise-grade application architectures. From smart energy infrastructures over nearly real-time traffic monitoring and optimization to assistive environments, data are increasingly processed and used on the fly and in real-time while flowing through stream processing pipelines without ever being permanently persisted at all. At

M. Dalla Preda et al. (Eds.): ARES 2025, LNCS 15992, pp. 24–45, 2025.
https://doi.org/10.1007/978-3-032-00624-0_2

the same time, respective applications often collect and process personal and sometimes highly sensitive data, calling for appropriate anonymization.

A widely used approach for privacy protection is k-anonymity [41], which ensures that each entry within a group of k entries is indistinguishable from the others. Extensions such as ℓ-diversity [26] and t-closeness [25] further mitigate risks related to attribute disclosure. These approaches are particularly prominent in scenarios where detailed individual-level data are not needed, but group-level patterns must be preserved. Energy district management serves as a prime example where such privacy guarantees are essential. Here, the focus is not on individual household consumption, but on understanding broader usage patterns across neighborhoods or similar households.

An alternative fundamental concept, differential privacy [13], provides strong mathematical semantic privacy guarantees by adding calibrated noise to the data. While differential privacy provides privacy guarantees beyond the ones of k-anonymity, it introduces noise into data, i.e., specific energy consumption values are inherently uncertain, making stable trend analysis more difficult. For instance, when forecasting energy demand, fluctuations caused by differential privacy could obscure real consumption patterns, leading to suboptimal infrastructure planning. In contrast, k-anonymity preserves data consistency, ensuring that neighborhood-level energy statistics remain reliable over time, which is crucial for energy management.

Despite its advantages, traditional k-anonymity methods were not designed for streaming environments, where data must be anonymized in nearly real time. Stream-specific adaptations of k-anonymity, such as k_s-anonymity [9,36], present a promising prospect by achieving privacy guarantees comparable to their non-streaming counterparts but often focus on numerical values, limiting their applicability to data sets that also contain categorical or hierarchical attributes. Additionally, enterprise-grade systems require efficient, low-latency processing to handle large data volumes without significant performance overhead. These factors are critical for driving the practical adoption of advanced privacy-preserving schemes and for shaping potential regulatory requirements for their implementation in real-world systems [33].

To overcome these limitations and advance the practical applicability of guarantee-providing anonymization schemes in stream-based application architectures, we make the following contributions:

- We present Prink, a privacy-preserving stream anonymization framework that extends the pre-existing CASTLE algorithm and implementation for k_s-anonymization with l-diversity to support categorical and hierarchical generalization, along with the ability to handle multiple sensitive attributes in l-diversity.
- We propose a novel scheme for semantics-aware information loss scheme in the anonymization of non-numerical streaming data, incorporating the support for dynamic generalization trees.

- We introduce a concept for distributing CASTLE's clustering approach across multiple nodes while preserving $k-$ and l-guarantees to achieve the scalability required in real-world streaming applications.
- We provide an open-source implementation designed to seamlessly integrate these functionalities into real-world use cases, employing the established and highly scalable stream-processing framework Apache Flink[1].
- We conduct an experimental evaluation to assess the performance overheads, focusing on latency in realistic settings, demonstrating the practical viability of our approach.

The structure of this paper is as follows. In Sect. 2, we introduce relevant background and related work. Our general approach and the details of our stream-specific anonymization scheme for non-numerical data are provided in Sect. 3. Our evaluation and results are presented in Sect. 4 and further discussed in Sect. 5, before we conclude our paper in Sect. 6.

2 Background and Related Work

In the following, we provide relevant preliminaries for advanced anonymization in streaming architectures.

2.1 Anonymization Techniques and Anonymity Guarantees

To assure the privacy of individuals in the processing of data referring to them, different anonymization techniques are used. These techniques mostly include perturbation, generalization or basic data reduction [5, 19, 27, 28], and provide some level of anonymization. To make these levels measurable and more usable, and to avoid unexpected privacy violations resulting from outlier datapoints, anonymity guarantees such as k-anonymity [41], ℓ-diversity [26] or t-closeness [25] have been established, particularly for publicly releasing static data sets for onward use. These provide very specific and exact levels of anonymity, guaranteeing, for instance, that at least k individuals are indistinguishable from each other in the anonymized data set or that each generalized cluster contains at least ℓ different values for the sensitive attribute.

Since all anonymization techniques reduce or alter the original data, some information is necessarily lost during the anonymization process. To not only provide anonymity guarantees, but also maintain the value of shared, anonymized data (e.g., for subsequent analytics), advanced techniques such as range aggregation for numerical data (assigning distinct values to value ranges) and hierarchical generalization [29, 30, 37, 38] for non-numerical data are used instead of, for instance, removing attributes completely. These techniques provide not just the requirements for the mentioned privacy guarantees, but also try to keep the resulting information loss as low as possible.

---

[1] https://flink.apache.org/.

Having been established in the 2000 s, most respective techniques only work on static data sets such as census data [26, 41]. Further related work applied such techniques to big data architectures [39, 40] including domain hierarchy approaches [7]. For settings with dynamic data, such as frequently updated databases or even continuous data streams, however, they cannot be applied without breaking the to-be provided guarantees. Given that such data-intensive settings particularly shape the collection, processing and use of personal data today, alternative approaches are needed.

2.2   Anonymity Guarantees for Dynamic and Streaming Data

To provide anonymity guarantees and techniques that minimize information loss for dynamic and streaming data, new solutions needed to be created. Respective approaches can be categorized into those following the notion of differential privacy and those adapting pre-existing concepts from k-anonymity (and extensions) to stream-specific givens.

With differential privacy [13, 14], dynamic and streaming data are typically handled through aggregation and noising, ensuring that the impact of individual data points on results remains within specified boundaries.[2] In global differential privacy, a trusted centralized entity holds all raw data and processes queries by providing noisy results, such as sums, counts, or averages. The added noise is calibrated based on the sensitivity of a query and the differential privacy parameter ε that defines the privacy guarantee. Use cases for global differential privacy span a wide range of application, including statistical databases (e.g., for census data [1]), privacy-preserving social network analysis [21], or large-scale trip data analysis [6], often extending to advanced types of aggregations like graph metrics [23] or geospatial analyses [6].

In local differential privacy [14, 22], data are not transmitted in their raw form to a trusted curator but are instead locally anonymized by adding noise before being released. This local noise addition ensures that individual data entries remain private. Data structures such as Bloom filters [16] and FM sketches [31] enable differentially private aggregations, including popularity statistics [10] and cardinality estimations [31]. Local differential privacy is particularly useful for scenarios where many users must report their data to an untrusted party while preserving privacy, such as in location-based services [3, 24], smart metering [15], and large-scale telemetry data collection [11].

Although differential privacy provides strong privacy guarantees, it inherently limits the use of the resulting data—especially in the case of local differential privacy. This limitation arises because the data can only be processed in ways that were anticipated and planned for before implementing a specific, carefully chosen differential privacy mechanism. Additionally, achieving reasonable data utility with differential privacy often requires large volumes of data,

---

[2] Specifically, differential privacy guarantees that the probabilities of outcomes, such as aggregation results, remain nearly identical for two neighboring data sets that differ by only one data point.

further restricting its practical applicability. Moreover, advanced differential privacy mechanisms that extend beyond numerical data are frequently less reusable and necessitate extensive customization for each use case, sometimes introducing unforeseen and non-obvious re-identification risks [20].

Proposals for adapting established approaches of k-anonymity (and extensions) to the specifics of data streams, in turn, initially were of theoretical nature and came without [2,9] or with only rudimentary prototype implementations [36]. Only recently, research on integrating them into real-world streaming systems has gained momentum [34]. Respective endeavors have, however, so far focused on smaller and non-distributed systems, leaving important streaming frameworks such as Kafka or Apache Flink unsupported.

Existing concepts and implementations merely focus on generalizing numerical and occasionally categorical data for anonymization purposes [4]. In reality, however, the data to be anonymized also comprises non-numerical attributes. Different from established $k/\ell/t$-schemes for static data, these are so far not properly covered by existing stream-focused anonymization schemes, especially with regard to the reduction of information loss.

Within these limitations, however, the CASTLE algorithm [9] has established as the prevailing approach for k-anonymizing data streams over alternative ones such as KIDS [43] or K-VARP [32]. CASTLE adapts "traditional" concepts of k-anonymity and l-diversity to the paradigm of stream processing, enriches them with the possibility to additionally noise the data [36], and provides flexible adaptations to use case-specific givens (e.g., timeout constraints). Besides, it has been proven to be on par with state-of-the art non-streaming algorithms for k-anonymization in matters of privacy metrics [8]. CASTLE has thus been chosen as the starting point for our endeavor. Its underlying clustering approach will be introduced in some more detail in Sect. 2.4.

2.3   Apache Flink

Apache Flink is a powerful streaming framework designed for distributed and stateful data processing over continuous streams. Its versatile *Source, Process*, and *Sink* architecture supports a wide range of streaming use cases.

The *Source* component defines the input of the data stream, which can originate from systems like Apache Kafka, Cassandra, external APIs, or even static data collections. Once ingested, the data flows into the *Process* phase, where various processing, analytics, and manipulations are performed using defined process functions. These functions operate in a specified sequence to transform the data. After processing, the data exits the framework through the *Sink*, which could involve logging, further streaming via Kafka, storage in Cassandra, or integration with other systems to handle the output data.

Flink is designed for performance and scalability, operating at in-memory speeds and compatible with containerized environments like Docker, making it suitable for diverse production scenarios. Major companies, including Amazon (Kinesis Data Analytics), Comcast (real-time event stream processing), and

Uber (AthenaX), rely on Flink. Its robust and efficient design solidifies its position as a leading streaming framework, demanding regulatory requirements like data minimization.

2.4 Data Cluster Anonymization CASTLE

CASTLE [9] anonymizes streaming data in a guarantee-providing manner by clustering incoming data tuples based on their quasi-identifiers until a threshold δ is reached, and then anonymizes these clusters through generalization [9,35]. The parameter δ sets the maximum delay a data tuple can experience before it must be released. If a tuple reaches a delay of $\delta - 1$, it is published with its corresponding cluster to ensure timely processing.

To achieve k_s-anonymity, CASTLE ensures that each cluster contains at least k individuals before generalization. The same applies to ℓ-diversity, where the diversity of each sensitive attribute in a cluster is checked before generalization. It is possible that a data tuple belongs to a cluster that has not yet reached the required size of k different individuals when it is about to expire. In such cases, CASTLE merges this cluster with another to ensure the anonymity constraint while minimizing overall information loss. Conversely, if a cluster is too large (exceeding $2k$ individuals), it is split into two smaller clusters to reduce information loss while maintaining privacy guarantees.

To preserve as much information as possible–or, vice versa, to minimize the information loss introduced–in this clustering process, a concept called *enlargement value* is used: Each possible generalization will result in a specific amount of information loss. When a new data tuple needs to be assigned to a cluster, the additional information loss a tuple would introduce to a given cluster is quantified. This amount of increased information loss is called enlargement value and is used to determine the optimal cluster for a new data tuple. The newly arriving tuple is then assigned to the cluster with the smallest enlargement value, balancing privacy and data utility. Noteworthily, tuples remain in their original form until a cluster is to be released as k_s-anonymized output. Only then is the actual generalization applied and the whole cluster is released.

While these mechanisms are suitable for numerical data, CASTLE currently lacks proper loss calculations for non-numerical attributes. Categorical data, such as 'Country' or 'Workplace' can only be fully retained (loss $= 0$) or completely redacted (loss $= 1$), preventing more flexible generalization. Introducing proper loss metrics (and respective generalization capabilities) for such non-numerical attributes to the pre-existing CASTLE algorithm is therefore one of the core contributions herein.

3 Proposal: Prink

For our practical implementation called Prink (<u>Pri</u>vacy Preserving Fli<u>nk</u>), we chose the streaming framework Apache Flink. It offers scalability, fail-safety,

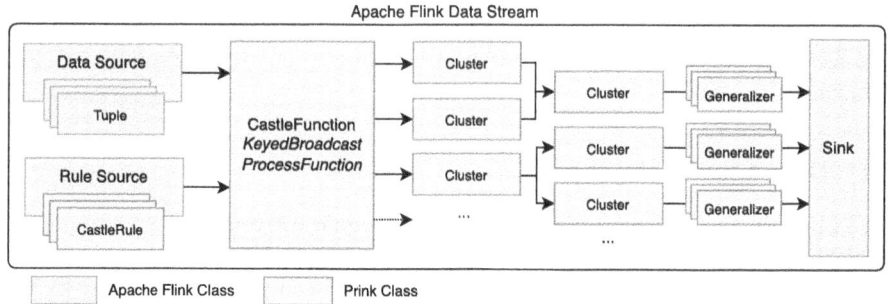

Fig. 1. Prink Architecture in the context of Apache flink data streaming infrastructure.

and robust stream processing capabilities, making it an ideal choice for integrating anonymization techniques. Prink was implemented almost entirely within a single Flink *ProcessFunction*, which simplifies integration into existing or new projects. This approach allows users to easily incorporate Prink at any desired point in their data stream processing pipeline.

Prink's architecture consists of the following core components, depicted in Fig. 1:

– *Rule Broadcasting*: Dynamically updates rules for data processing during runtime.
– *CastleFunction*: The main processing unit responsible for anonymization and interaction with the Flink data stream.
– *Cluster Logic*: Manages groups of data tuples and applies generalization.

3.1 Rule Broadcasting and CastleFunction

Prink uses Flink's native *Tuple* implementation as input and output formats. Tuples support flexible structures with up to 25 attributes of varying data types, making them ideal for dynamic and diverse data streams. This allows Prink to adapt to missing rules or varying input sizes without requiring significant preprocessing.

Prink achieves dynamic flexibility in data stream anonymization through its integration of *CastleRule* objects and Domain Generalization Hierarchies (DGH). The combination of these components ensures that Prink can dynamically adapt to changes in data structures, privacy requirements, and evolving data streams, maintaining both scalability and minimal information loss.

Dynamic adjustments to generalization rules are facilitated by *CastleRule* objects, which are transmitted via a broadcast stream. Each *CastleRule* specifies how an attribute should be generalized, including configurations for loss metrics and sensitive attribute flags. This mechanism allows Prink to accommodate runtime changes in data structures and privacy needs, ensuring operational flexibility and adaptability. To implement these updates efficiently, Prink leverages

Apache Flink's *KeyedBroadcastProcessFunction* rather than a standard *Process-Function*. This specialized function supports two parallel input streams: one for the main data tuples and another for rule updates. By design, it ensures efficient propagation of runtime rule changes across the system while maintaining the essential keying of data tuples to their respective data subjects. This keying mechanism is critical for preserving k_s-anonymity and l-diversity guarantees. Additionally, the architecture supports parallel execution, allowing Prink to scale efficiently for larger data sets and modern containerized environments.

Unlike static data sets, streaming data often introduces new values or requires updates to the attributes being generalized. Prink addresses these challenges through a twofold approach. First, DGHs are instantiated at the cluster level rather than being static global structures. Each CASTLE cluster generates its own DGH instance at creation, ensuring relevance to the current data context. Outdated hierarchies are replaced as clusters are released, enabling efficient adaptation without the need to re-evaluate existing clusters.

Second, Prink extends DGHs dynamically in real-time. Incoming data tuples can carry hierarchical information within their attributes, such as a value "Paris" and its corresponding hierarchy (["Paris", "France", "EU"]). When new relationships are identified, missing nodes and branches are seamlessly added to the DGH of the active cluster. This allows the hierarchy to evolve alongside the data stream, supporting the dynamic nature of streaming scenarios. By integrating these capabilities, Prink maintains consistent and contextually relevant hierarchies, even in rapidly changing data environments.

To ensure efficient generalization and minimal information loss, each dynamically created DGH node tracks the number of data tuples it covers. A node is considered to cover a tuple if its value matches the node or any of its descendants in the hierarchy. This mechanism enables Prink to calculate optimal generalizations for each cluster, maintaining consistent results while minimizing information loss. By combining the flexibility of dynamic rule updates through *CastleRule* with the adaptability of DGHs, Prink provides a robust and scalable anonymization solution tailored to the complexities of real-time data streams.

3.2 Cluster Logic

Within the *CastleFunction*, data tuples are grouped into *Cluster* objects based on generalization rules. For that, the *bestSelection* function finds the best cluster for the new data tuple by leveraging the forementioned concept of enlargement value. Each cluster contains generalizers tailored for different data types, implemented via a *BaseGeneralizer* interface. This modular design simplifies the addition of new generalization strategies, ensuring extensibility for future requirements. Finally, after δ tuples were gathered, in the *delayConstraint* function, the first data tuple's cluster gets generalized and published.

Semantic Generalization Metrics. CASTLE's [9] existing loss metrics for numerical values are insufficient for capturing the complexities of non-numerical, hierarchically generalizable data. Unlike numerical values, non-numerical attributes cannot be easily ordered or bounded, making traditional numerical approaches inapplicable. Instead, the calculation of information loss for non-numerical data must be grounded in the structure provided by DGHs, which leverage the inherent categorical and hierarchical relationships between values.

To address this, we adopt a semantic approach to generalization that minimizes information loss while preserving the relationships between non-numerical data points. Simple numerical mappings often fail in this regard, as they disregard the semantic connections between values. For example, a naive mapping of country/state attributes to numerical values based on their order of appearance loses the semantic relationships, such as the grouping of France and Spain under "EU" or Florida and Virginia under "US". By using DGHs, we address this issue by grouping non-numerical values into higher-order categories, preserving their semantic structure. To ensure the quality of generalization, we apply information loss metrics tailored to these hierarchies, minimizing disruption to data semantics while maintaining robust anonymization.

The Generalized Loss Metric (GLM), one of the wider used information loss metrics, calculates the information loss by assessing the generalization level of a value within the DGH. Formally, the GLM for non-numerical, i.e., categorical attributes, is defined as:

$$GLM(u) = \frac{M_p - 1}{M - 1}, \tag{1}$$

where M_p represents the number of leaf nodes covered by the current generalization node u, and M is the total number of leafs in the hierarchy. In contrast, for a continuous attribute a, the information loss resulting from generalizing its value using an interval $I = [l, u]$ within its domain $[L, U]$ is calculated as $(u-l)/(U-L)$, reflecting the proportion of the domain covered by the generalized interval.

Another metric employed is the Normalized Certainty Penalty (NCP), which evaluates information loss by considering the proportion of values generalized within the hierarchy. For non-numerical data, NCP is calculated as

$$NCP_{Cat}(G) = \begin{cases} 0, & card(u) = 1 \\ card(u)/|A_{Cat}|, & otherwise \end{cases} \tag{2}$$

where $card(u)$ is the number of leaf nodes that are present in the sub-tree of node u, and $|A_{Cat}|$ represents the total number of unique categorical values in the data set. If $card(u) = 1$, the information loss is zero, as no generalization is required. By normalizing the information loss relative to the total attribute diversity, NCP provides a nuanced assessment of the impact of generalization.

Additionally, Prink introduces a dynamic loss metric, the Per Record Request Metric (PRL) [12,17], which adapts to real-time data distributions by factoring in the frequency with which values appear in the stream. The calculation is based on the Requested Number Count (RNC), which tracks the number of times a value from the DGH has been requested. For each generalized node, the total RNC is computed by summing the counts of all its leaf nodes. This total is then divided by the overall number of requests to the DGH, yielding an information loss value that reflects the relative weight of each leaf node. More formally:

$$PRL(G) = \begin{cases} 0, & card(u) = 1 \\ RNC(u)/RNC(root(u)), & otherwise \end{cases}, \qquad (3)$$

where u is the current generalization node. This metric ensures that frequent values are generalized less, preserving their semantic weight. The PRL dynamically aligns information loss calculations with the data distribution, making it effective in k_s settings. To stay adaptable, RNC values are periodically cleared, reflecting evolving weights of attributes. This is especially valuable in dynamic data flows, where value frequencies fluctuate over time. By preserving more information for frequent values, the PRL minimizes information loss while maintaining privacy guarantees.

By introducing these three loss metrics to the CASTLE-based anonymization of data streams, Prink achieves a robust, context-aware approach to generalizing also non-numerical data, enabling Prink to maintain strong privacy guarantees while minimizing information loss.

Attribute Weights in Information Loss Calculation. In Prink, assigning a data tuple to a cluster involves evaluating the information loss for each potential cluster and selecting the one with the lowest average information loss. To provide greater flexibility and align the anonymization process with application-specific priorities, Prink allows the use of attribute weights, implemented as information loss multipliers ranging between 0 and 1.

By default, all attributes have equal weight, meaning their contributions to the total information loss are uniform. In scenarios where certain attributes are more critical for preserving data utility, weights can be adjusted to amplify or reduce their influence. This adjustment of weights, however, is not required for the functionality of Prink; the system operates effectively even without changing the default weights.

When weights are specified, the information loss for each attribute is scaled by its multiplier. Attributes with larger weights (closer to 1) have a higher impact on the total information loss, reducing their likelihood of being generalized. Conversely, attributes with smaller weights (closer to 0) contribute less to the total information loss, making their generalization more likely.

For instance, in cases where attributes are crucial for downstream analysis, assigning higher weights ensures their preservation with minimal generalization. Even if these attributes typically show low information loss under uniform weighting, the applied multipliers prioritize them during the clustering process.

This mechanism ensures that the anonymization process can be tailored to the specific requirements of different use cases. Attribute weights enable the prioritization of certain data characteristics, balancing the trade-off between privacy and utility. Since adjusting the weights is optional, Prink still provides a fine-grained and flexible approach for a wide range of scenarios, even without modifications to the default weights.

Design Choices and Extensibility. To maintain simplicity, all configuration parameters for Prink can be set either through the constructor of the *Keyed-BroadcastProcessFunction* or via rule broadcasting during runtime, ensuring minimal user interaction and reducing the risk of misconfiguration.

Prink's architecture is designed for extensibility. By leveraging the *BaseGeneralizer* interface, developers can add new generalization methods without modifying existing code. This flexibility is especially valuable for advanced privacy guarantees like l-diversity across multiple attributes [18]. By ensuring that each sensitive attribute satisfies the l-diversity requirement independently, Prink can provide robust privacy protection for data sets containing multiple sensitive dimensions. Additionally, Flink's fail-safety mechanisms ensure no data loss during system failures, enhancing the reliability of Prink in production environments.

4   Evaluation

In the following we describe our experimental setup including the details of the data sets and the system environment configurations. We investigate the impact of our proposal Prink on latency and information loss.

4.1   Influencing Factors

Before detailing the experimental setup and results, we discuss the factors that influence Prink's performance and information loss to provide a comprehensive understanding. These factors range from the type of streamed data and rule sets used to specific parameter configurations within Prink.

Parameters. Prink provides parameters to adjust its functionality to suit specific application needs. Below is an overview of key parameters and their impact:

Parameter k: Defines the minimum number of distinct individuals required to ensure k-anonymity, rather than the number of data tuples. This core parameter directly impacts information loss: as k increases, more tuples need to be generalized, which can lead to higher information loss. Additionally, k interacts with other parameters like δ and β, influencing their effects on performance and information loss.

Parameter ℓ: Specifies the minimum number of distinct sensitive attribute values required to satisfy ℓ-diversity. Although less influential than k, ℓ still plays a significant role in determining both performance and information loss.

Number of sensitive Attributes: Prink supports multiple sensitive attributes for ℓ-diversity. An increased number of sensitive attributes requires additional checks, affecting performance. It may also lead to larger generalizations if additional tuples are needed to meet diversity requirements, though this is often dictated by the attribute with the fewest diverse values.

Parameter δ: Determines how many tuples are retained within Prink before generalization. This parameter significantly affects the number of clusters created and the system's overall performance. A low data flow rate can increase the retention time of tuples, impacting throughput. Since δ must always be at least as large as k, its configuration is critical for maintaining both performance and anonymization guarantees.

Parameter β: Limits the number of clusters that can exist simultaneously. While it has minimal impact on information loss, it influences performance by reducing the overhead caused by managing an excessive number of clusters. Balancing this parameter ensures efficient cluster management.

Generalization Rules. The choice of generalization rules primarily depends on the data types of quasi-identifiers, such as integers, floats, or categorical values. However, several aspects can be adjusted to influence the results. A key factor is the type of generalizer used, as quasi-identifiers can often be generalized in multiple ways—for example, converting a postal code (integer) to a broader district or suppressing its last digits. The choice of generalizer directly impacts information loss and data clustering, as highlighted earlier. Properly matching generalizers to specific quasi-identifiers is thus crucial for effective anonymization.

Another key consideration is the approach used for calculating information loss, which directly impacts generalization and cluster enlargement. Generalization rules specify this method, and their configuration can greatly influence the final outcome. The Generalized Loss Metric (GLM) is a common default choice and often provides a solid baseline. However, when applied correctly, the Normalized Certainty Penalty (NCP) can produce more optimal results, offering improved information preservation while still meeting anonymization requirements. For the purpose of this evaluation, we have left the default values unchanged to avoid introducing any fine-tuning that could affect the consistency of the results.

4.2   Data Set

To evaluate Prink, we use the publicly available *ASHRAE - Great Energy Predictor III* data set from the Kaggle challenge.[3] This data set contains meter readings from over one thousand buildings across various sites worldwide. We chose this dataset specifically because it aligns well with our running example of energy district management, where the goal is to anonymize data at the group level (e.g., neighborhood-level energy usage patterns) while preserving relevant aggregate information.

For our analysis, we merge the training data, building metadata, and weather information into a single data set, focusing exclusively on electricity meter readings and buildings with a given year and floor count. This preprocessing results in a data set consisting of $321,728$ data tuples representing hourly electricity

---

[3] https://www.kaggle.com/competitions/ashrae-energy-prediction.

Table 1. ASHRAE electricity meter readings data set.

Attribute	Type	Range	Unique values
building_id	int	[565, 655]	89
timestamp	str	[2016-01-01 01:00, 2016-12-31 23:00]	8736
meter_reading	float	[0.0, 2293.88]	124957
primary_use	str	Categorical (DGH)	7
square_feet	int	[387, 420885]	89
year_built	float	[1903.0, 2016.0]	58
floor_count	float	[1.0, 14.0]	13
air_temperature	float	[1.1, 35.0]	59
cloud_coverage	float	[0.0, 9.0]	4
dew_temperature	float	[−9.4, 17.8]	49
precip_depth_1_hr	float	[−1.0, 8.0]	4
sea_level_pressure	float	[1007.8, 1031.7]	228
wind_direction	float	[0.0, 360.0]	37
wind_speed	float	[0.0, 12.9]	24

smart meter readings from 89 unique buildings, spanning the period from January 1, 2016, to December 31, 2016. We detail our selected quasi-identifier in Table 1. Specifically, the building_id is used as the unique identifier providing k_s-anonymity, while meter_reading serves as the sensitive variable. Although we evaluate only one data set, the use of different quasi-identifiers allows us to cover a variety of data distributions and to access Prink's capability to generalize different attribute types. Several factors related to the data structure influence the performance and the resulting information loss.

One critical factor is the number of quasi-identifiers in the data set. Each additional quasi-identifier increases the complexity of achieving generalization, as all data tuples within a cluster must share the same generalized values for these attributes. This often leads to greater information loss, despite Prink's mitigation efforts through its enlargement value concept. Another important aspect is the uniformity of data tuples. More uniform tuples require less generalization to meet k_s-anonymity, reducing information loss. While this characteristic cannot be controlled in real-world data sets like our evaluation data set, it remains an important consideration in evaluating Prink's performance. Lastly, the ratio of individuals to total number of data tuples significantly impacts both information loss and scalability. Within a cluster, only one tuple per individual contributes to meeting k_s-anonymity, so additional tuples from the same individual may require more generalization, increasing information loss. Furthermore, in parallel execution, Apache Flink ensures that all tuples from a single data subject are processed by the same node, which can limit scalability if the number of data subjects is small.

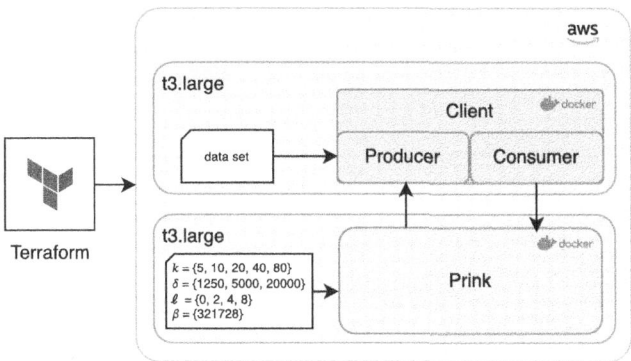

Fig. 2. Benchmarking experiment architecture diagram

4.3 Experimental Setup

We now proceed to outline the design considerations, configurations, and automation processes for the benchmarking experiment. An abstract overview is provided in Fig. 2, which will be further detailed in the following section.

The primary objective of the experiment design is to minimize complexity and eliminate uncontrolled interferences wherever possible. Prink, the system under test (SUT), is deployed on a dedicated virtual machine. A benchmarking client is used to generate load for the SUT, functioning both as a producer and a consumer. This setup not only simplifies deployment but also closely mirrors real-world architectures, where containerization—most commonly through Docker—is a standard practice.

The benchmarking client, implemented in Go, serves as the load generator for Prink. It operates using a configuration YAML file and an example data set. The YAML file specifies key attributes such as networking ports, addresses, and input/output file paths. Upon initialization, the benchmarking client loads configuration variables from the config.yaml file along with the evaluation data set. It begins by launching a single goroutine to sequentially publish each data tuple to Prink. Each published message includes the exact data tuple values, a unique message ID, and an outgoing timestamp (t_s). Messages are retained in Prink until the specified anonymity guarantees are met, as determined by its configuration and incoming message flow. Once these conditions are satisfied, the processed messages are returned to the client. A second goroutine then logs the incoming timestamp (t_e) and appends the processed messages to the result log for further analysis.

To evaluate Prink, the SUT, we conducted benchmarking experiments using 60 distinct parameter configurations, varying key parameters (k, δ, ℓ and β as described in Sect. 4.1 and summarized in Fig. 2). Each configuration was deployed on two AWS t3.large virtual machines (VMs) using an automated Terraform script. This script handled resource provisioning, Prink configuration, Docker container deployment, and retrieval of results. To ensure robust evaluation, each

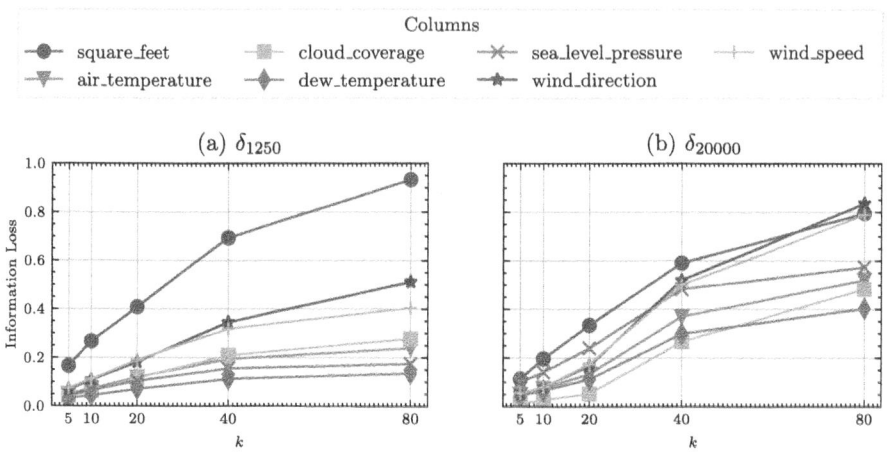

Fig. 3. Evaluation of accuracy through the information loss of attributes.

configuration was tested three times, totaling 180 distinct benchmarking runs. All code and deployment scripts for this evaluation are available in a dedicated GitHub repository[4].

4.4 Evaluation Metrics

Information Loss. Information loss reduction is one of the core requirements of Prink. For the metric itself, the evaluation will use the information loss metrics explained in Sect. 3.2. For our evaluation, we use the Generalized Loss Metric for the calculation of the overall information loss. We calculate the average information loss across all clusters per attribute.

Performance. To ensure Prink's practical viability as an anonymization solution, its performance must be evaluated in terms of latency and its impact on overall application speed. This evaluation focuses on two key aspects of latency.

First, we evaluate the end-to-end latency, which we define as the total time a data tuple spends within Prink before being released back into the main data stream. This latency is determined by calculating as the difference between the timestamp when a tuple enters Prink via the socket and the timestamp when the tuple is returned from Prink through the same socket: $t_e - t_s$. Notably, since this measurement is performed on the client side, the recorded latency includes network transmission time.

Second, we perform a more detailed analysis of Prink's internal processing times, focusing on key operations. This includes measuring time spent in critical functions such as the *bestSelection* process, where a tuple is assigned to the most suitable cluster based on minimal information loss, and the *delayConstraint*

---

[4] https://github.com/PrivacyEngineering/prink-benchmark.

function, activated when δ is exceeded, ensuring timely publication of the cluster containing the oldest data tuple. Furthermore, we measure the *waitTime* between these operations, during which a tuple remains idle, awaiting publication.

Unlike the end-to-end latency measurement, this in-depth analysis is conducted entirely within Prink itself. Consequently, the results are unaffected by network transmission times, offering a clearer and more precise assessment of Prink's internal processing performance. By differentiating between external and internal contributors to latency, this approach provides a holistic evaluation of the system's overall efficiency.

4.5 Results

Information Loss. In Fig. 3, we present the average information loss for each attribute across different k values, with $l = 1$ held constant, and note that no attribute weights were specified, meaning all attributes have equal weight. While it is possible to assign weights to individual attributes, our experiment treats all attributes equally, resulting in generalization being applied uniformly based on the information loss they contribute.

The left-hand Fig. 3 (a) illustrates results for $\delta = 1250$, while the right-hand Fig. 3 (b) corresponds to $\delta = 20,000$. An information loss of 0.0 indicates that no generalization was necessary, and thus no information loss occurred. Conversely, an information loss of 1.0 signifies maximum loss, where the attribute was fully generalized.

Regardless of the attribute, the information loss increases as k grows. This trend is expected, as a higher k requires more distinct individuals—in this case, building IDs with varying attribute values within a cluster–to be generalized. This pattern is consistent for both $\delta = 1250$ and $\delta = 20,000$, although the overall information loss is lower for $\delta = 20,000$.

The attribute with the highest information loss is `square_feet`, explained by its exceptionally large range ($[387, 420885]$) and relatively few unique values (89). These characteristics often cause extensive generalization into large intervals. Notably, the ranking of attributes by information loss varies between the two δ values. For example, `sea_level_pressure` shows minimal information loss at $\delta = 1250$, yet significantly higher loss at $\delta = 20,000$. This variation underscores how higher δ values influence generalization strategies differently. When assigning a data tuple to a cluster, the total information loss across all attributes is calculated, which can lead to discrepancies in attribute-specific generalization. If a particular attribute is more critical for subsequent analysis and requires less generalization, this can be effectively managed by assigning it a higher weight.

Performance. In Fig. 4, we present the average end-to-end latency, the total time a data tuple spends in Prink before being returned to the main data stream. As expected, a higher δ leads to increased latency, with a δ of 1250 resulting in the lowest latency and a δ of 20,000 producing the highest. This occurs because δ directly affects the release timing: with $\delta = 1250$, the cluster containing

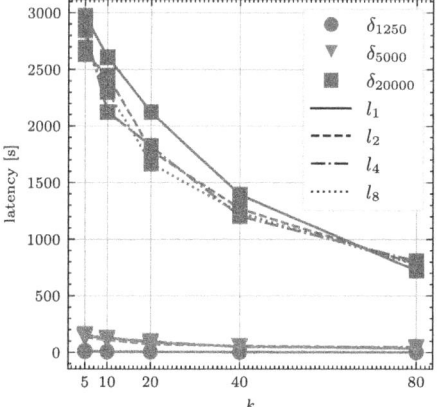

Fig. 4. Evaluation of end-to-end latency (total time a data tuple spends within Prink).

the oldest tuple is released after processing 1250 data tuples, whereas higher δ values increase the waiting time before a tuple is published. Interestingly, latency decreases with higher values of k and l, a trend observed across all parameter settings. Higher k values result in fewer but larger clusters, which reduces the number of information loss calculations for each arriving tuple. Additionally, when a cluster is released, more tuples are released simultaneously compared to configurations with smaller clusters. Together, these effects significantly reduce the overall processing time per tuple.

Prink's internal processing times are depicted in Fig. 5, highlighting the time spent in the *bestSelection* and *delayConstraint* functions, along with the *waitTime* between these two operations. The x-axis represents various parameter configurations, including three different values for δ, k, and l. The y-axis shows the aggregated execution time in milliseconds on a logarithmic scale. Among the three components, the *bestSelection* consistently exhibits the lowest execution time, while the *waitTime* is the longest, highlighting the impact of δ. As δ increases, the execution time across all functions rises, a trend that reflects the extended waiting period imposed by higher δ values. The *bestSelection* function shows the shortest execution times, decreasing further with larger k. This aligns with the observations in Fig. 4, as higher k reduces the number of clusters, thereby minimizing the frequency of information loss calculations. Conversely, the *delayConstraint* function demonstrates longer execution times as k increases. This is due to the formation of fewer but larger clusters at higher k values, requiring more time for generalization because of the greater number of tuples within each cluster. The execution time is measured as the interval between the initiation of *delayConstraint* and the publication of the final tuple in the cluster. Consequently, the extended processing of these larger clusters leads to a higher average execution time.

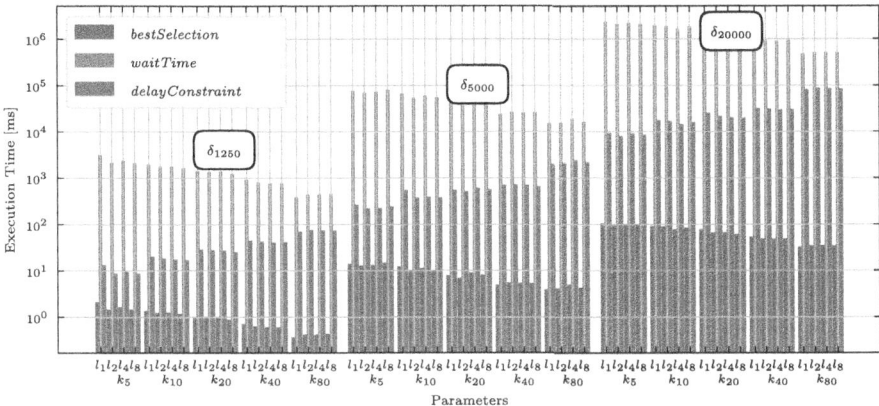

Fig. 5. Evaluation of internal processing times, focusing on key functions: *bestSelection*, *delayConstraint*, and *waitTime* (the interval between these operations).

5   Discussion and Future Work

In this section, we discuss the results in terms of the interaction between performance, utility, and privacy, accessing their impact on the approach's applicability and efficiency. We also address privacy considerations and limitations.

Trade-Off Between Anonymity, Utility and Performance. The results highlight the inherent trade-offs between achieving high levels of anonymity, ensuring low latency, and preserving data utility. In particular, while increasing k provides stronger anonymity guarantees, it also results in higher information loss, as larger clusters require more generalization to ensure indistinguishability among individuals. This interdependency between k and information loss aligns with intuitive expectations and underscores the challenge of maintaining utility as privacy constraints become more stringent.

Our experimental results also reveal an additional dynamic introduced by k_s-anonymization: for the same k, different δ values lead to varying levels of information loss and latency. In fact, a higher δ allows for better generalizations, resulting in lower information loss as clusters can accumulate more tuples over time. However, this comes at the cost of increased latency, as tuples spend more time "waiting" before being published. Conversely, smaller δ values prioritize lower latency but may result in higher information loss due to smaller clusters and less effective generalization. This interplay introduces δ as a new "tuning parameter", offering flexibility to balance the competing demands of privacy, utility, and performance in stream-based applications.

Practical Feasibility. The integration of k_s-anonymity into a Flink-based stream processing architecture has proven feasible by our implementation, with the system demonstrating the ability to balance these competing goals to some extent. However, achieving optimal performance across all three dimensions—anonymity, latency, and utility—remains a complex challenge, as improving one often comes at the cost of the others. These findings highlight the importance of context-specific configurations and the careful adjustment of parameters such as k and δ to meet the needs of different use cases.

Future improvements to Prink could enhance both its accessibility and efficiency. To improve accessibility, Prink could be offered as a packaged Java library via a dependency system, eliminating the need for manual integration. Performance gains could be achieved by caching information loss calculations, reducing redundant computations for unchanged clusters. Another key challenge is dynamic rule updates, as clusters depend on their initialized rule sets to maintain privacy guarantees, complicating seamless rule changes.

Similar to Gal et al. [18], incorporating weighted sensitive attributes could further minimize information loss while preserving required privacy levels. In addition, optimal information loss and utility should be investigated across various business domains. Addressing the anonymization of data sets with numerous sensitive features (e.g., in the medical context), and semi- or non-structured data present another challenge. Extending Prink to support additional privacy-preserving techniques and metrics [42] further strengthen its effectiveness, particularly in scenarios where adversarial risks are high.

Privacy Considerations and Limitations of Prink. Although k_s-anonymity ensures that every released cluster contains at least k distinct individuals, the general limitations of k-anonymity still apply. One key issue is that its provided privacy guarantees are not independent of an attacker's background knowledge. If an adversary has external knowledge about the data set, a re-identification of individuals might be possible despite the anonymization.

Another challenge arises from how generalization is applied dynamically. Since CASTLE adapts its generalization strategies based on the current data structure, the same individual may be generalized differently across time windows. If an attribute remains unchanged but its generalization fluctuates due to temporary data gaps, it could introduce inconsistencies that might be exploited.

6   Conclusion

In summary, this paper presents an effective solution for privacy-preserving data anonymization in stream-based applications. We propose adaptations of k_s-anonymity tailored for non-numerical streaming data, addressing challenges related to dynamic generalization and privacy guarantees. Our approach introduces a novel, semantics-aware information loss scheme and supports scalable, distributed anonymization. We also provide a practical implementation, Prink, based on the Apache Flink framework, and demonstrate its performance through a thorough evaluation. By overcoming key limitations of current anonymization techniques, our work enhances the applicability of privacy-preserving methods to real-world scenarios while maintaining strong privacy protections.

Acknowledgments. This work was supported by the German Federal Ministry of Education and Research as part of the GANGES project under reference number 16KISA033K as well as by the EXDIGIT project, funded by Land Salzburg under grant number 20204-WISS/263/6-6022.

References

1. Abowd, J.M.: The us census bureau adopts differential privacy. In: SIGKDD '18: Proceedings of the 24th ACM International Conference on Knowledge Discovery and Data Mining, pp. 2867–2867 (2018)
2. Al-Zobbi, M., Shahrestani, S., Ruan, C.: Experimenting sensitivity-based anonymization framework in apache spark. J. Big Data **5**(1), 1–26 (2018). https://doi.org/10.1186/s40537-018-0149-0
3. Andrés, M.E., Bordenabe, N.E., Chatzikokolakis, K., Palamidessi, C.: Geo-indistinguishability: differential privacy for location-based systems. In: CCS '13: Proceedings of the 2013 ACM SIGSAC Conference on Computer & Communications Security, pp. 901–914 (2013)
4. Apuan, D.A.: Landscape data transformation: categorical descriptions to numerical descriptors. Int. J. Agric. Biosystems Eng. **5**(9), 512–515 (2011)
5. Ashkouti, F., Sheikhahmadi, A., et al.: DI-Mondrian: distributed improved Mondrian for satisfaction of the L-diversity privacy model using apache spark. Inf. Sci. **546**, 1–24 (2021)
6. Bassolas, A., et al.: Hierarchical organization of urban mobility and its connection with city livability. Nat. Commun. **10**(1), 4817 (2019)
7. Bazai, S.U., Jang-Jaccard, J., Alavizadeh, H.: Scalable, high-performance, and generalized subtree data anonymization approach for apache spark. Electronics **10**(5), 589 (2021)
8. Brunn, C., Nuñez von Voigt, S., Tschorsch, F.: Analyzing continuous k_s-anonymization for smart meter data. In: DPM '23: Proceedings of 18th International Workshop on Data Privacy Management, vol. 14398, pp. 272–282. Springer, Cham (2023). https://doi.org/10.1007/978-3-031-54204-6_16
9. Cao, J., Carminati, B., Ferrari, E., Tan, K.L.: CASTLE: continuously anonymizing data streams. IEEE Trans. Dependable Secure Comput. **8**(3), 337–352 (2010)
10. Cormode, G., Jha, S., Kulkarni, T., Li, N., Srivastava, D., Wang, T.: Privacy at scale: local differential privacy in practice. In: SIGMOD '18: Proceedings of the 2018 International Conference on Management of Data, pp. 1655–1658 (2018)
11. Ding, B., Kulkarni, J., Yekhanin, S.: Collecting telemetry data privately. In: Advances in Neural Information Processing Systems, vol. 30 (2017)
12. Domingo-Ferrer, J., Mateo-Sanz, J.M.: Resampling for statistical confidentiality in contingency tables. Comput. Math. Appl. **38**(11–12), 13–32 (1999)
13. Dwork, C.: Differential privacy. In: ICALP'06: Proceedings of the 33rd International Colloquium on Automata, Languages and Programming, pp. 1–12. Springer, Berlin, Heidelberg (2006). https://doi.org/10.1007/11787006_1
14. Dwork, C., Roth, A., et al.: The algorithmic foundations of differential privacy. Found. Trends® Theor. Comput. Sci. **9**(3–4), 211–407 (2014)

15. Eibl, G., Engel, D.: Differential privacy for real smart metering data. Comput. Sci.-Res. Dev. **32**, 173–182 (2017)
16. Erlingsson, Ú., Pihur, V., Korolova, A.: RAPPOR: randomized aggregatable privacy-preserving ordinal response. In: CCS '14: Proceedings of the 21st ACM SIGSAC Conference on Computer and Communications Security, pp. 1054–1067. ACM (2014). https://doi.org/10.1145/2660267.2660348
17. Gadad, V., Sowmyarani, C.: A novel utility metric to measure information loss for generalization and suppression techniques in privacy preserving data publishing. In: CSITSS '19: Proceedings of the 4th International Conference on Computational Systems and Information Technology for Sustainable Solution, pp. 1–5. IEEE (2019)
18. Gal, T.S., Chen, Z., Gangopadhyay, A.: A privacy protection model for patient data with multiple sensitive attributes. Int. J. Inf. Secur. Priv. **2**(3), 28–44 (2008). https://doi.org/10.4018/JISP.2008070103
19. Gruschka, N., Mavroeidis, V., Vishi, K., Jensen, M.: Privacy issues and data protection in big data: a case study analysis under GDPR. In: Big Data '18: Proceedings of the 2018 IEEE International Conference on Big Data, pp. 5027–5033. IEEE (2018)
20. Houssiau, F., Rocher, L., de Montjoye, Y.A.: On the difficulty of achieving differential privacy in practice: user-level guarantees in aggregate location data. Nat. Commun. **13**(1), 29 (2022)
21. Jiang, H., Pei, J., Yu, D., Yu, J., Gong, B., Cheng, X.: Applications of differential privacy in social network analysis: a survey. IEEE Trans. Knowl. Data Eng. **35**(1), 108–127 (2021)
22. Kasiviswanathan, S.P., Lee, H.K., Nissim, K., Raskhodnikova, S., Smith, A.: What can we learn privately? SIAM J. Comput. **40**(3), 793–826 (2011)
23. Kasiviswanathan, S.P., Nissim, K., Raskhodnikova, S., Smith, A.: Analyzing graphs with node differential privacy. In: TCC '13: Proceedings of the 10th Theory of Cryptography Conference, pp. 457–476. Springer, Berlin, Heidelberg (2013). https://doi.org/10.1007/978-3-642-36594-2_26
24. Kim, J.W., Edemacu, K., Kim, J.S., Chung, Y.D., Jang, B.: A survey of differential privacy-based techniques and their applicability to location-based services. Comput. Secur. **111**, 102464 (2021)
25. Li, N., Li, T., Venkatasubramanian, S.: t-Closeness: privacy beyond k-Anonymity and l-Diversity. In: ICDE '07: Proceedings of the 23rd International Conference on Data Engineering, pp. 106–115. IEEE Computer Society (2007). https://doi.org/10.1109/ICDE.2007.367856
26. Machanavajjhala, A., Gehrke, J., Kifer, D., Venkitasubramaniam, M.: l-Diversity: privacy beyond k-Anonymity. In: ICDE '06: Proceedings of the 22nd International Conference on Data Engineering, pp. 24–24 (2006). https://doi.org/10.1109/ICDE.2006.1
27. Majeed, A., Lee, S.: Anonymization techniques for privacy preserving data publishing: a comprehensive survey. IEEE Access **9**, 8512–8545 (2020)
28. Marques, J.F., Bernardino, J.: Analysis of data anonymization techniques. In: IC3K '20: Proceedings of the 12th International Joint Conference on Knowledge Discovery, Knowledge Engineering and Knowledge Management, pp. 235–241. SCITEPRESS (2020). https://doi.org/10.5220/0010142302350241
29. Martínez, S., Sánchez, D., Valls, A.: Towards k-anonymous non-numerical data via semantic resampling. In: IPMU '12: Proceedings of the 14th International Conference on Information Processing and Management of Uncertainty in Knowledge-Based Systems. Communications in Computer and Information Science, vol. 300,

pp. 519–528. Springer, Berlin, Heidelberg (2012). https://doi.org/10.1007/978-3-642-31724-8_54

30. Martínez, S., Sánchez, D., Valls, A.: A semantic framework to protect the privacy of electronic health records with non-numerical attributes. J. Biomed. Inform. **46**(2), 294–303 (2013). https://doi.org/10.1016/j.jbi.2012.11.005

31. Nuñez von Voigt, S., Tschorsch, F.: RRTxFM: probabilistic counting for differentially private statistics. In: TPSIE '19: Proceedings of the 1st Workshop on Trust and Privacy Aspects of Smart Information Environments, vol. 573, pp. 86–98. Springer, Cham (2019). https://doi.org/10.1007/978-3-030-39634-3_9

32. Otgonbayar, A., Pervez, Z., Dahal, K., Eager, S.: K-VARP: K-anonymity for varied data streams via partitioning. Inf. Sci. **467**, 238–255 (2018)

33. Pallas, F., et al.: Privacy engineering from principles to practice: a roadmap. IEEE Secur. Priv. **22**(2), 86–92 (2024). https://doi.org/10.1109/MSEC.2024.3363829

34. Pallas, F., Legler, J., Amslgruber, N., Grünewald, E.: RedCASTLE: practically applicable k_s-anonymity for IoT streaming data at the edge in node-red. In: M4IoT@Middleware 2021: Proceedings of the 8th International Workshop on Middleware and Applications for the Internet of Things, pp. 8–13. ACM (2021). https://doi.org/10.1145/3493369.3493601

35. Qing-jiang, K., Xiao-hao, W., Jun, Z.: The (p, α, k) anonymity model for privacy protection of personal information in the social networks. In: ITAIC '11: Proceedings of the 6th IEEE Joint International Information Technology and Artificial Intelligence Conference, vol. 2, pp. 420–423 (2011). https://doi.org/10.1109/ITAIC.2011.6030363

36. Robinson, A., Brown, F., Hall, N., Jackson, A., Kemp, G., Leeke, M.: CASTLEGUARD: anonymised data streams with guaranteed differential privacy. In: 2020 IEEE International Conference on Dependable, Autonomic and Secure Computing, International Conference on Pervasive Intelligence and Computing, International Conference on Cloud and Big Data Computing, International Conference on Cyber Science and Technology Congress (DASC/PiCom/CBDCom/CyberSciTech). pp. 577–584 (2020). https://doi.org/10.1109/DASC-PICom-CBDCom-CyberSciTech49142.2020.00102

37. Samarati, P., Sweeney, L.: Protecting privacy when disclosing information: k-anonymity and its enforcement through generalization and suppression (1998)

38. Simi, M., Nayaki, K., Elayidom, M.: An extensive study on data anonymization algorithms based on k-anonymity. IOP Conf. Ser. Mater. Sci. Eng. **225**, 012279 (2017). https://doi.org/10.1088/1757-899X/225/1/012279

39. Sopaoglu, U., Abul, O.: A top-down k-anonymization implementation for apache spark. In: Big Data '17: Proceedings of the 2017 IEEE International Conference on Big Data, pp. 4513–4521. IEEE (2017)

40. Suneetha, V., Suresh, S., Jhananie, V.: A novel framework using apache spark for privacy preservation of healthcare big data. In: ICIMIA '20: Proceedings of the 2nd International Conference on Innovative Mechanisms for Industry Applications, pp. 743–749. IEEE (2020)

41. Sweeney, L.: k-anonymity: a model for protecting privacy. Internat. J. Uncertain. Fuzziness Knowl.-Based Syst. **10**(05), 557–570 (2002)

42. Wagner, I., Eckhoff, D.: Technical privacy metrics: a systematic survey. ACM Comput. Surv. (Csur) **51**(3), 1–38 (2018)

43. Zhang, J., Yang, J., Zhang, J., Yuan, Y.: KIDS: K-anonymization data stream base on sliding window. In: ICFFC '10: Proceedings of the 2nd International Conference on Future Computer and Communication, vol. 2, pp. V2–311. IEEE (2010)

Stop Watching Me! Moving from Data Protection to Privacy Preservation in Crowd Monitoring

Fatemeh Marzani$^{(\boxtimes)}$, Thijs van Ede, Geert Heijenk, and Maarten van Steen

University of Twente, Enschede, The Netherlands
{f.marzani, t.s.vanede, geert.heijenk, m.r.vansteen}@utwente.nl

Abstract. The monitoring of large crowds is essential to optimize traffic flows, ensure safety at large-scale events, and plan effective evacuation routes during emergencies. However, such monitoring rightfully leads to privacy concerns, especially when tracking individuals rather than groups. Existing approaches attempt to address these concerns by pseudonymizing personally identifiable information and restricting the analysis to statistical counts. However, these methods fail to preserve privacy, particularly when small groups can be correlated with external data. To combat this issue, we leverage the idea that crowd monitoring applications are interested in only large crowds (e.g., >100 people) and can deal with low noise levels (e.g., it does not matter whether we count 95 or 105 people). We propose and evaluate two methods that not only protect individual data, but also enhance privacy by introducing varying levels of controlled noise: higher for smaller groups and lower for larger crowd movements. These methods include probabilistically: (1) sampling hash functions and (2) sampling detected identifiers. We show that our methods significantly reduce the risk of re-identification in small crowds while maintaining high precision in large crowd estimations, making them highly effective for privacy-preserving crowd monitoring.

Keywords: Crowd monitoring · pedestrian dynamics · privacy preservation · Bloom filters · homomorphic encryption · privacy-by-design

1 Introduction

Comprehending the crowd dynamics has been a long-standing focus in scientific research. Data collected from crowd behavior can be applied in various fields such as urban planning [1], tourism [2], and enhancing safety and security [3]. Automatic measurement of crowd dynamics enables the gathering of more precise data and is more convenient compared to manual methods. To automate the process, scanners can be installed in public spaces to collect unique identifiers, such as MAC addresses of mobile devices or public transport card identifiers, for each individual. By gathering these identifiers (which can be subject to erroneous

M. Dalla Preda et al. (Eds.): ARES 2025, LNCS 15992, pp. 46–67, 2025.
https://doi.org/10.1007/978-3-032-00624-0_3

detections), interested parties can estimate the crowd size near those scanners, as well as the size of the flows between them. Handling data related to crowds has always been a sensitive and complex challenge. In this work, we distinguish two situations. The first is to count individuals at a specific location and time. The second and most challenging situation involves counting people over time (and perhaps across multiple locations).[1]

In the first case, we can resort to counting detections of unique identifiers during a very short measurement interval (say, a few seconds to at most a few minutes), after which identifiers can be discarded. This limits storing identifiers to a location and time in which they were collected and leaves only the count for further processing.

However, in the second case, we need to store identifiers for future re-identification. Even if an identifier itself cannot be used for the identification of a natural person, as is the case with pseudonyms, storing an identifier for re-identification can easily lead to recognition of patterns that *do* lead to such identification. For example, Montjoye et al. [4] discuss that just four spatio-temporal data points are sufficient to uniquely identify 95% of individuals.

In the context of crowd monitoring systems, there are two fundamental issues that must be considered to prevent individuals from being tracked. First, data protection, which refers to ensuring that identifiers and even pseudonyms are not disclosed to unauthorized parties. Second, ensuring data privacy, which refers to preventing (at all times) the identification of natural persons to unauthorized parties when given the information provided by that system. Although there is existing literature on data protection, ensuring data privacy is much harder, as we cannot foresee which additional information may be available to a party using the system or how the provided information will be used. We observed that existing methods, at best, provide data-protection techniques to count individuals at a specific time. Some approaches also provide data protection over time using anonymous identifiers or encrypted data [5], yet fail to protect privacy. Our novel contribution is to introduce a method that ensures both privacy and data protection.

In our approach, we trust the detecting devices but do not extend this trust to any other party, including the server responsible for performing further processing. For data protection, we store the pseudonyms in Bloom filters (BFs), i.e. probabilistic data structures supporting approximate set operations. After encryption and shuffling, these Bloom filters can be used only for intersection operations and cardinality estimations (and not for membership testing). Encryption ensures that even if the server is compromised, it cannot extract individual identifiers from the data. Shuffling further enhances protection by randomizing the order of bits in the BF, preventing an attacker from inferring membership from the bit positions. Given our data protection measures, breaching privacy is still possible when only a few people are counted: if we count only 1 person at location A, then having additional information about occupancy

---

[1] In this paper, we use pedestrian monitoring as an example, but we can also count more diverse groups of people.

at A, re-identification can be relatively easy. To prevent such re-identification attacks, we intentionally introduce uncertainty *especially* when counting a small number of individuals, yet retain high precision for large groups. The intuition behind our approach is that, in small groups, sampling may not provide a precise representation of the population, which can help protect privacy. However, in larger groups, the sample size also increases, resulting in more precise and reliable estimations. We use this property to deliberately reduce the precision of small crowd estimates in favor of privacy protection. We discuss two different sampling methods:

1. Sampling hash functions
2. Sampling identifiers

The source code for evaluating our methods is publicly available.[2]

2   Related Work

For years, monitoring crowd behavior has been a focus of research, taking advantage of technologies such as Wi-Fi signals and unique device identifiers (e.g., MAC addresses) to estimate crowd densities, flows, and mobility patterns [6–8]. These systems typically rely on the detection of signals emitted by devices carried by individuals, such as smartphones or other Wi-Fi-enabled devices. By capturing and analyzing these signals, researchers can derive valuable insights about crowd behavior. However, these methods often compromise privacy by allowing the tracking and profiling of individuals without their consent [9].

To address these concerns, randomization of MAC addresses was introduced as a countermeasure. This approach ensures that devices periodically generate and use fake MAC addresses instead of their real ones. Although this method mitigates tracking to some extent, studies have shown that inconsistent implementations between different manufacturers still allow reidentification [10]. This limitation exposes individuals to potential privacy breaches. Moreover, for our use case, this limitation significantly impacts the accuracy of crowd flow estimation, undermining the reliability of the data collected for monitoring purposes.

Alternative approaches, such as pseudonymization using hash functions or encryption, have also been explored to mask identifiers [11,12]. In pseudonymization, original identifiers are transformed into pseudonyms through methods such as one-way hash functions or deterministic encryption schemes. However, due to the limited identifier space (e.g., MAC addresses are effectively limited to 2^{24} bits), pseudonyms remain vulnerable to brute-force attacks [13,14]. These weaknesses highlight the need for stronger privacy-preserving mechanisms.

Some methods focus on aggregating data to enhance privacy. Linear counting sketches [15] and k-anonymity-based approaches [11] enable crowd size estimations by grouping data together, making individual identifiers less distinguishable. Similarly, encrypting identifiers in Bloom filters ensures that statistical

---

[2] https://anonymous.4open.science/r/private-bloom-filter/.

counts can be obtained without exposing individual identities [5]. However, these methods are not foolproof, as linkage with external data sources can lead to rei-dentification, especially in sparsely populated areas.

Other privacy-preserving systems, such as DEVCNT [16], avoid completely collecting unique identifiers. Instead, DEVCNT estimates the number of devices in a crowd by detecting and counting active scan events. Although this avoids direct data protection issues, it limits the system to simple counting operations and lacks support for more complex queries, such as intersections or crowd-flow size estimation across locations. These methods collectively underscore the persistent challenge of balancing utility with robust privacy. Although existing techniques offer partial solutions, they often fail to provide the comprehensive privacy guarantees required for practical crowd monitoring systems.

RAPPOR [17] employs a different strategy using differential privacy. It encodes data into Bloom filters and introduces random noise to obscure indi-vidual contributions. RAPPOR is specifically designed for web tracking appli-cations, such as extracting the most frequently visited websites, and does not address Bloom filter intersection challenges for computing the size of crowd flows. Ke et al. [18] introduced DPBloomfilter, which integrates the Random-ized Response mechanism into the Bloom filter to achieve differential privacy for membership queries. Their approach addresses the risks of individual data leakage in standard Bloom filters. Their work primarily focuses on static mem-bership queries, not addressing dynamic crowd flow estimation across locations or epochs, a key feature of our system. Rusca et al. [19] proposed a WiFi-based crowd monitoring system using Bloom filters with fixed initial noise to ensure deniability. However, this added noise cancels out during Bloom filter intersec-tions, making their approach unsuitable for our goal, preserving uncertainty in small group counts during crowd flow analysis.

Recent research has also focused on developing location privacy-preserving techniques for location-based services (LBSs), primarily to prevent adversaries from tracking users, inferring movement patterns, and profiling them. As sur-veyed by Jiang et al. [20], common approaches include spatial cloaking, dummy locations, differential privacy, and cryptographic techniques such as homomor-phic encryption and secure multiparty computation. These methods typically obfuscate location data to protect individual privacy. However, our focus dif-fers from these approaches as we aim to develop a crowd-counting mechanism that preserves privacy. Our method ensures that when the number of people in a location is small, the exact count remains uncertain by design to prevent re-identification. Since LBS privacy techniques focus primarily on anonymizing movement data, they are not directly applicable to our problem.

3 System and Threat Model

Figure 1 shows the setup of our crowd monitoring scenario. We consider a set of trusted scanners $S = (s_1, ..., s_n)$ that are deployed in various locations to detect unique identifiers of people. These scanners record all detected identifiers in a

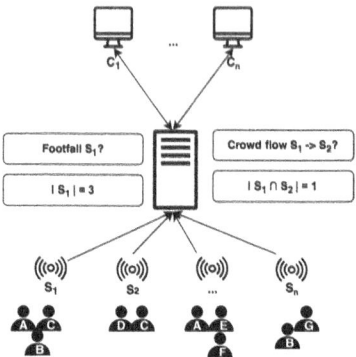

Fig. 1. Overview of the crowd monitoring system setup. Sensors $S = (s_1, ..., s_n)$ collect identifiers, process these and send them to a central processing server. Clients subsequently issue footfall or crowd flow queries to estimate the number of people at given locations.

predetermined time, which we call an epoch e_i. At the end of an epoch, the scanners send their detections to a central processing server p that stores these detections, to continue recording during the next epoch. Authenticated clients $C = (c_1, ..., c_m)$ can subsequently query this server for the size of a crowd in a certain location. We distinguish two types of query:

- *Footfall*: the number of people in a single location during a single epoch.
- *Crowd flow*: the number of people traveling between different locations during a series of (not necessarily consecutive) epochs.

Formally, we define these queries as:

Definition 1. *Footfall:* *Let $D_{s,e}$ be the set of detections made by a scanner s during epoch e. The footfall provided by this scanner is the total count of unique detections $|D_{s,e}|$.*

Definition 2. *Crowd flow:* *Consider a set of scanners $S^* \subseteq S$, a series of (not necessarily consecutive) epochs $E^* = [e_1^*, e_2^*, \ldots, e_k^*]$, along with a series of scanner-epoch pairs $SE = [(s_1^*, e_1^*), \ldots, (s_k^*, e_k^*)]$, with $s_i^* \in S^*$ and $e_i^* \in E^*$. Let $D_{s_i^*, e_i^*}$ be the set of detections by s_i^* during epoch e_i^*. For a given set of scanner-epoch pairs SE, the size of the crowd flow is defined as the size of the intersection of these detection pairs: $|\bigcap_{(s_i^*, e_i^*) \in SE} D_{s_i^*, e_i^*}|$.*

Threat Model

The goal of this work is to provide both data protection and privacy preservation. In this model, we assume that all scanners are trusted, meaning that they can collect and process all identifiers. This is a realistic assumption as adversaries could circumvent the entire system by placing their own scanners to identify individuals. However, the other parties, i.e. the processing server and clients performing queries *cannot* learn the original identifiers (data protection), and should *not* be able to trace an individual with complete certainty (privacy preservation). We assume an honest but curious setting, where all parties follow the given protocol but will try to infer as much information as possible from the system. In this work, we focus mainly on the preservation of privacy, as we build upon other works that provide solutions only for data protection (see Sect. 4). Hence, for simplicity and better understanding, we describe our protocol in a plaintext variant and in Sect. 7, we describe how the protocol can be extended with homomorphic encryption to provide the additional data protection guarantees that other works have already introduced.

4 Background

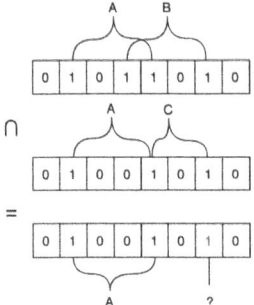

Fig. 2. Behavior of Bloom filter intersection. Intersecting two Bloom filters with ($m = 8$, $k = 2$) by bitwise multiplication, the result is not the same as the Bloom filter of their intersection.

In this paper, we propose methods to enhance privacy in crowd monitoring systems, based on the model introduced by [5], which guarantees data protection. Their system and threat models are similar to ours, except that we focus on privacy preservation on top of data protection. We aim to develop a crowd-monitoring system that preserves privacy and is capable of answering two key types of queries, footfall and crowd flow. Footfall is measured by the cardinality of a single detection set at a specific scanner and epoch, whereas crowd flow is determined by the cardinality of the intersection of detection sets collected from multiple scanners across different time epochs. Stanciu et al. [5] let each scanner store its detections during an epoch in a local Bloom filter. After the epoch, the Bloom filter is encrypted (homomorphically) and sent to a central server for further processing. The scanner subsequently discards all detections and creates a new, empty Bloom filter for the next epoch.

A Bloom filter [21] is a probabilistic data structure used to store whether elements are part of a set, consisting of an array of m bits, initially each set to

0, along with k different hash functions. When adding an element a, the k hash functions are computed on a. Each result points to one of the m array positions, which is then set to 1. To check whether an element is a member of a set, one needs to verify whether all the positions indicated by the k hash functions are set to 1. If we have two sets, A and B, represented as Bloom filters $BF(A)$ and $BF(B)$, respectively, the intersection $A \cap B$ is constructed by computing the bitwise AND operation on $BF(A)$ and $BF(B)$ (see Fig. 2), where we assume that both Bloom filters have the same length m and use the same k hash functions. Due to the probabilistic nature of Bloom filters, the result approximates the intersection of A and B, yet is not guaranteed to be the same as $BF(A \cap B)$. Bloom filters may reveal false positive membership tests (false negatives cannot occur). This is because positions associated with an element can also be marked as 1 by the hashes of other elements. However, the parameters of the Bloom filter can be adjusted to achieve a desired probability of false positives (p) when the maximum number of elements in the set (n) is known.

We use Bloom filters to compute footfall and crowd-flow queries, considering the cardinality of the sets involved. The cardinality of a Bloom filter c can be estimated using the following formula, where t is the number of bits set to 1:

$$c = -\frac{m}{k} \ln \left(1 - \frac{t}{m} \right) \tag{1}$$

To perform a query, the system follows this procedure. Scanners encode their detections into Bloom filters and transmit them to the server at the end of each epoch. To ensure data protection, each Bloom filter is encrypted using a homomorphic encryption scheme before transmission. This allows the server to process the data—such as computing intersections for crowd flow queries—without learning the underlying identifiers. Upon receiving a query from a client, the server begins crafting a response by gathering the necessary data generated by scanners. For crowd flow queries, it generates a new Bloom filter through a bitwise AND of the corresponding Bloom filters. Then, it shuffles the positions to obscure any discernible patterns, transforming the Bloom filter into a randomized array of 0s and 1s (but without affecting the number of bits set to 1), before delivering the result to the client. The server is trusted to conduct the shuffling, as it is considered an integral part of the protocol, with the assumption that it will execute it accurately. After decrypting the shuffled Bloom filter, the client computes the desired statistical count using Eq. 1, as the count of 1s remains unaffected by the shuffling.

Stanciu et al. [21] proposed that the exclusive provision of statistical counts for crowd monitoring data could protect privacy, rather than using techniques such as anonymization, which removes personal identifiers. However, statistical outputs still present risks of individual identification. Using publicly available statistics, adversaries can conduct reconstruction attacks with the objective of identifying probable instances of individuals. These statistical reports can be linked to additional data using linkage techniques (see Vatsalan et al. [22]). Providing additional data about the monitored group becomes simpler when the group size is smaller, thus making the attack easier.

5   Methods

Regardless of the estimator we use for counting footfall or crowd flow, our goal is to have relatively high precision for high counts and low precision for low counts to protect privacy. Estimators operating on Bloom filters rely on the count of bits set to 1. Our key insight is to introduce controlled imprecision by giving a consumer access to a sample t^* of the actual number of bits t from which they can estimate the original count. The smaller the subset, the less precise the estimation, which helps obscure individual contributions to small counts. Specifically, we examine two methods to sample the number of bits that contribute to the estimate $t^* < t$: (1) sampling Bloom filter hash functions and (2) sampling detected identifiers. Bloom filters inherently introduce some inaccuracy due to false positives, and our methods leverage this property to further enhance privacy while maintaining utility for large-scale crowd monitoring.

5.1   Sampling Hash Functions

In this method, we use a standard Bloom filter of size m, using k hash functions. Each hash function h_i has a probability of q being used (and thus $1 - q$ of being skipped), deterministically determined by the element being inserted.[3] This determinism ensures consistency when sampling hash functions are applied to every identifier. This is crucial to maintain reliability when intersecting Bloom filters at different locations containing the same element. This method ensures that not all bits are used for inserting an item into the Bloom filter. By selectively including hash functions, we effectively reduce the number of set bits. However, given the reduced number of bits (which we call t^*), we cannot use Eq. 1 as this formula assumes knowledge of the total number of bits that *would* be set without using our selection method. Therefore, we estimate the value of t from the subsample t^* using the following formula:

$$t = m \left(1 - \left(1 - \frac{t^*}{m} \right)^{\frac{1}{q}} \right) \tag{2}$$

When substituting t in Eq. 1 with the Eq. 2, we can simplify the computation for estimating the count of inserted items to:

$$c = -\frac{m}{k \times q} \ln \left(1 - \frac{t^*}{m} \right) \tag{3}$$

We have proved the derivations in Appendix A.

5.2   Sampling Identifiers

Consider a standard Bloom filter with a length of m and k hash functions. To reduce the number of bits to be used to estimate the size of the original set, each

---

[3] Using a seeded random function where the inserted element determines the seed.

identifier is inserted into the Bloom filter with probability q. It is crucial for this process to yield consistent decisions for each identifier to ensure the reliability of Bloom filter intersections when computing crowd flow. In other words, the decision to insert the detection of identifier ID is always the same, independent of when and where ID is detected. The total number of items inserted into the Bloom filter is estimated by modifying the original formula to account for the sampling identifier with probability q, as shown in Eq. 3.

6   Evaluation

In this section, we evaluate how effectively our solutions estimate statistical counts for both footfall and crowd flow while enhancing privacy through controlled uncertainty, particularly in low-density crowd areas. While simple footfall counts can be directly obtained from Bloom filters without additional processing, crowd flows involve analyzing movement patterns across different locations or times, which requires processing intersected Bloom filters. We use generated detections[4] instead of real-world detections because they allow us to precisely control and measure privacy across a wide range of crowd flow scenarios, enabling us to comprehensively evaluate the precision of the system. Specifically, we compare the system's estimated statistical output with actual values obtained from controlled simulations. We performed $1,000$ repeated experiments using both the standard Bloom filter used in [5] and our sampling techniques, thoroughly evaluating their uncertainty levels across varying footfall and crowd flow sizes. To do so, we explore different combinations of parameters for Bloom filters and sampling methods. For the hash functions of the Bloom filters, we use MurmurHash3[5] for its efficiency and use of seed, providing an arbitrary number of hash functions.

The estimated number of identifiers in a Bloom filter may differ from the actual count for two reasons. First, the estimation is based on the probability of certain bits being set, which can vary as hash functions in Bloom filters have a probability of mapping different elements to the same position. Second, hash collisions during the intersection of multiple Bloom filters can cause bits to be marked incorrectly (see Fig. 2), leading to discrepancies in the count for crowd flow queries. When we use sampling methods instead of inserting all crowd detections into Bloom filters, we expect significant differences between the actual count and the estimated count, especially with low actual counts and sampling does not provide a reliable representation.

We used the Root Mean Square Error (RMSE) to evaluate how closely the estimated count of inserted identifiers in the Bloom filter matches the actual count. It serves as a statistical measurement of the average deviation of predicted

---

[4] To have precise control over the size of detection sets and the count of shared identifiers between them, we generate sets of random unique identifiers to directly represent detections, mimicking pre-collected data.

[5] A. Appleby, *MurmurHash3*, 2016. Available at: https://github.com/aappleby/smhasher/wiki/MurmurHash3.

values from actual values. In this research, RMSE quantifies the precision of the estimated count by measuring how closely it aligns with the actual count over $1,000$ repeated experiments.

$$RMSE = \sqrt{\frac{1}{x}\sum_{i=1}^{x}(c_{t_i} - c_i)^2} \tag{4}$$

Here, x represents the total number of experiments ($x = 1,000$), c_{t_i} represents the actual count of inserted identifiers, and c_i represents the estimated count. A lower RMSE value indicates better agreement between the estimated and actual counts, reflecting higher precision in the estimation process.

By employing RMSE, we can calculate the relative error using the formula:

$$\text{relative error} = \max\left(0, \frac{c_t \pm \text{RMSE}}{c_t}\right) \tag{5}$$

Here, c_t represents the actual count of inserted identifiers. Relative error represents the range within which the estimated value lies relative to the actual value, expressed as a ratio of the actual value. For a specific estimated value, if relative error $= 1$, then the estimated value is equal to the true value, which indicates that there is no deviation. If relative error > 1, then the estimated value is greater than the true value, suggesting an overestimation. If relative error < 1, then the estimated value is lower than the true value, indicating an underestimation. We select the maximum value between 0 and the computed error. Since we cannot predict a negative number of observations for footfall or crowd flow, estimating a negative value lacks a meaningful interpretation.

6.1   Footfall Queries

To evaluate the impact of the proposed methods on the uncertainty of footfall query estimation, we use a standard Bloom filter configured for $1,000$ insertions ($n = 1,000$) and a false positive rate set at 0.01 ($p = 0.01$). Using the formulas $m = \frac{n \ln p}{(\ln 2)^2}$ and $k = \log_2 p$ we determine the length of the Bloom filter ($m = 9586$) and the optimal number of hash functions ($k = 7$) based on the given parameters n and p. Subsequently, we ran experiments by inserting detection sets ranging in size from 1 to $1,000$ into the Bloom filter. Each experiment is repeated $1,000$ times with distinct sets of identifiers to ensure the robustness of our evaluation. Finally, we compute the Root Mean Square Error (RMSE) for footfall queries. In this section, we outline the configurations employed for each method and subsequently present the results obtained.

Sampling Hash Functions. We conducted experiments using different probability values, $q \in \{0.01, 0.02, 0.04, 0.0833, 0.1667, 0.3333, 1\}$.[6] In Fig. 3a, the

---

[6] Reflecting sampling rates of one out of $100, 50, 25, 12, 6, 3$, and 1, respectively.

observed trends and values align closely with our expectations, reducing the value of q results in a higher relative error. This effect becomes especially notable when handling a small number of observations, while its impact diminishes for larger footfall sizes. For privacy-sensitive footfall sizes, particularly when the footfall size is 1, the system provides an intentionally uncertain output to enhance privacy. In this case, there is only a single detection, making direct estimation highly sensitive. When using a standard Bloom filter ($q = 1$), the relative error remains between 0.99 and 1.00. However, setting q to 0.3333 significantly increases the relative error, expanding its range to 0.20–1.79. When q is reduced to 0.01, the error range broadens drastically to 0–4.41, introducing uncertainty that effectively protects individual privacy. A relative error close to 1 suggests that the estimated count is highly precise. However, larger relative errors (e.g., 0–4.41 for $q = 0.01$ and footfall size 1) indicate greater uncertainty in the estimated count, making it difficult to determine the exact number of detections. This design choice prioritizes privacy for small footfall sizes. For larger footfall sizes, the relative error stabilizes. When the footfall size is $1,000$, a standard Bloom filter ($q = 1$) yields a relative error range of 0.99–1.00. With $q = 0.3333$, this range slightly shifts to 0.98–1.01, while reducing q to 0.01 results in an error range of 0.88–1.11. Since the relative error stays close to 1, the estimations remain reliable and useful for planning.

Sampling Identifiers. In methods Sect. 5.1 and 5.2 described, the parameter q determines whether to include an item (regardless of whether we are dealing with a hash function or an identifier) in the Bloom filter. However, its effect on the Bloom filter may vary due to the context in which it is used. In method Sect. 5.1, q determines the probability of executing each hash function during the insertion of an item into the Bloom filter. This means that for each hash function, there is a chance of q that it will be applied. In method Sect. 5.2, q represents the probability of including an identifier in the Bloom filter. This probability directly influences the level of privacy and the number of identifiers stored in the Bloom filter. A lower q means that fewer identifiers are stored, improving privacy by reducing the likelihood of individual identification. In contrast, a higher q results in more identifiers being included, potentially compromising privacy by making individual representations more precise.

To assess the impact of detecting an identifier and to ensure a fair comparison with sampling hash functions, we use the same set of q values for our experiments. The results are shown in Fig. 3b. As expected, decreasing the value of q correlates with an increase in relative error. This increase becomes particularly noticeable when dealing with a limited number of detections, whereas its impact diminishes for larger footfall sizes. For example, when q is set to 1 (i.e., using a standard Bloom filter) with a footfall size of 1, the relative error ranges between 0.96 and 1.03. However, with q set to 0.3333, the relative error increases substantially, ranging from 0 to 2.40. Setting q to 0.01 further increases the error range between 0 and 11.40. The broader range of error observed with smaller footfall sizes offers advantages in terms of privacy concerns. In contrast, with a footfall size of $1,000$, the use of a standard Bloom filter produces a relative error range of 0.99 to 1.00. When q is adjusted to 0.3333, this range changes to 0.95 and 1.04, while setting it to 0.01 causes the range to expand merely to 0.69 and 1.30.

When comparing the results of sampling hash functions (method Sect. 5.1) and sampling identifiers (method 5.2), we observe similar overall trends. In both approaches, reducing q significantly increases the relative error for smaller footfall sizes, providing greater privacy compared to the standard Bloom filter ($q = 1$) used in [5]. For $q = 0.01$ both methods introduce a substantial increase in relative error for small footfall sizes, reflecting their shared goal of obscuring individual detections. However, sampling identifiers (method Sect. 5.2) generally result in a wider error range compared to sampling hash functions (method Sect. 5.1), particularly when the footfall size is as low as 1. For larger footfall sizes, the difference between the two methods becomes less significant. Both converge to a relative error close to 1.

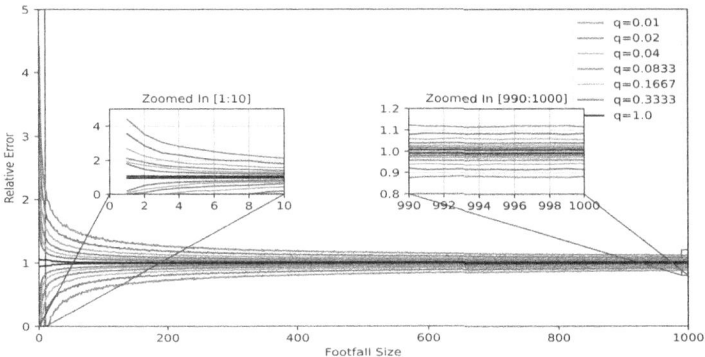

(a) Sampling hash functions to include.

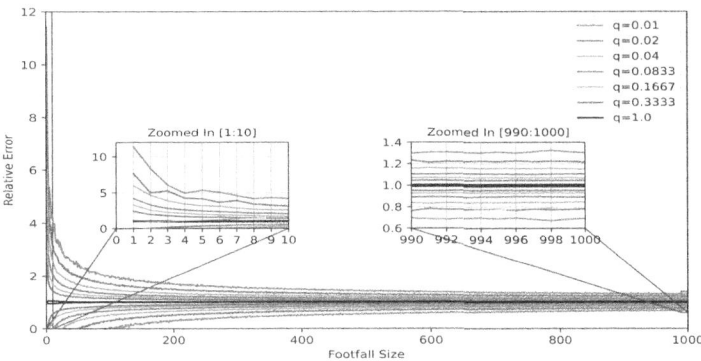

(b) Sampling identifiers to include.

Fig. 3. Relative error of footfall queries. Footfall size ranging from 1 to 1,000. Bloom filter parameters: $n = 1,000$ and $p = 0.01$ using our proposed method.

6.2 Crowd-Flow Queries

Crowd flow is determined by the size of the intersection of multiple detection sets at different locations. In the system, these detection sets are represented by Bloom filters. To compute the size of the intersection of these Bloom filters, we use bitwise multiplication, which provides an estimate of the intersection of the underlying sets within the Bloom filters. It is important to note that the Bloom filter resulting from the bitwise multiplication operation on Bloom filters representing sets of detections is different from the Bloom filter representing the intersection of those sets of detections. Specifically, the same bits may be set in two Bloom filters, BF1 and BF2, due to different elements: one belonging only to BF1 and the other only to BF2. These bits will be incorrectly set to 1 in the bitwise multiplied Bloom filter (see Fig. 2). Consequently, the resulting number of set bits in the bitwise multiplied Bloom filter may not accurately represent the cardinality of the intersection of the two sets.

The number of bits set after performing a bitwise multiplication on BF1 and BF2, denoted as $t_\wedge$, is the sum of two terms:

- The number of bits set due to the actual intersection of elements in both sets $(t_\cap)$.
- The number of bits set caused by the hash collisions described above $(rbits)$.

Consequently, the resulting Bloom filter from the bitwise multiplication of Bloom filters representing detection sets may differ from the Bloom filter representing their actual intersection. Thus, the formula used to estimate the number of common detections in sets tends to overestimate the actual counts. Papapetrou et al. [23] proposed an enhancement in estimating the number of common detections by incorporating not just the 1's in the resulting Bloom filter, but also those in the Bloom filters employed for bitwise multiplication. For t_1, t_2, and $t_\wedge$, representing the counts of bits set to 1 in two Bloom filters to be multiplied and in the resulting Bloom filter, respectively, the estimation formula is as follows:

$$c_\wedge = \frac{\ln(m - \frac{t_\wedge \times m - t_1 \times t_2}{m - t_1 - t_2 + t_\wedge}) - \ln(m)}{k \times \ln(1 - \frac{1}{m})} \tag{6}$$

To optimize two Bloom filters and assess the impact of our methods on crowd flow, we use the following setting. To reduce the impact of $rbits$ on the intersection and optimize the Bloom filters, we create a larger but sparser Bloom filter as suggested by Mitzenmacher [24]. Sparse Bloom filters have low entropy, which decreases the possibility of hash collisions. We design the Bloom filters for 10,000 items and a false positive rate of 0.01. Then, we insert two randomly generated sets, each containing 1,000 detections. We varied the number of common detections from 1% to 100% of the respective total detections of 1,000 individuals.

To apply Eq. (6), a consumer would require knowledge of the responses to associated footfall queries alongside the crowd-flow query, allowing for the determination of parameters t_1 and t_2. This approach aligns with our system model, as consumers are allowed to initiate such queries and does not entail any additional computationally intensive operations. To prevent leaking information from other queries, one potential approach is to use fully homomorphic encryption (FHE) which would allow *the server* to perform calculations for crowd flow using parameters such as t_1, t_2, and $t_\wedge$ on encrypted data. The final output (crowd flow) remains encrypted, and only the consumer can decrypt it. This ensures that all intermediate data and computations remain secure, preventing accidental data exposure. We discuss this idea in more detail in Sect. 7.1. We employ Eq. 6 throughout the evaluation to estimate statistical counts on crowd flows, where we are especially interested in the error of our count compared to the actual size of the crowd flow. Adjustments to the formula are necessary for each method based on the sampling parameters.

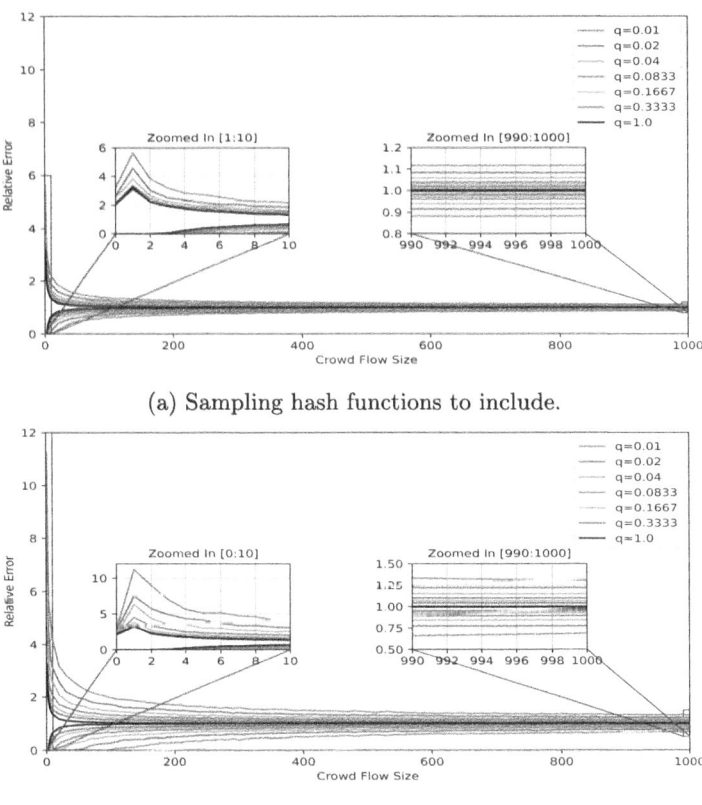

(a) Sampling hash functions to include.

(b) Sampling identifiers to include.

Fig. 4. Relative error of crowd flow queries with a crowd size of 1,000 in both locations, and a crowd flow size ranging from 0 to 1,000. Bloom filter parameters: $n = 10,000$ and $p = 0.01$ using our proposed method.

Sampling Hash Functions. We conducted experiments with different probability values $q \in \{0.01, 0.02, 0.04, 0.0833, 0.1667, 0.3333, 1\}$. Analogous to Eq. 3, we adjusted the crowd-flow estimation formula (6) to:

$$c_\wedge = \frac{\ln\left(\frac{(m-t_1^*) \times (m-t_2^*)}{m \times (m-t_1^*-t_2^*+t_\wedge^*)}\right)}{k \times q \times \ln\left(\frac{m-1}{m}\right)} \tag{7}$$

The results are shown in Fig. 4a. The results indicate that smaller values of q introduce greater uncertainty in crowd-flow estimation compared to using the standard Bloom filter with $q = 1$. Specifically, for small groups (e.g., crowd-flow size $= 1$), the relative error range is wider for smaller values of q. For example, when $q = 0.01$, the error can reach 5.64 for a crowd-flow size of 1, compared to an error of 3.23 when $q = 1$. By increasing the error in estimations, it becomes more difficult for an observer to determine the exact number of individuals in the crowd flow, thereby protecting individual privacy.

In larger crowds (e.g., crowd-flow size $= 1,000$), the relative errors decrease, but remain slightly higher for decreased values of q. For example, at $q = 1$, the narrow error range is between 0.998 and 1.002, while at $q = 0.01$, the relative error range is between 0.88 and 1.12. This shows that the system maintains accuracy and precision in estimating larger crowd sizes, ensuring that it is useful for planning and management.

Optimizing the value of q depends on the specific requirements of the application for privacy and utility. Smaller q values are beneficial for improving privacy in smaller groups, while maintaining higher q values ensures accurate estimation of crowd-flow sizes.

Sampling Identifiers. For a fair comparison of the methods, we repeated the experiment using the same set of probability values q. Since we are sampling identifiers with a probability of q, we adjust the crowd-flow estimation formula (6) by dividing it by q. This adjustment makes the formula equivalent to (7).

The results (in Fig. 4b) show that we achieved our goal of introducing a higher relative error in small groups for privacy preservation by decreasing the sampling probability q. Specifically, for small groups (e.g., crowd-flow size $= 1$), the relative error is significantly higher for lower values of q, with an error of 11.26 for crowd flows of size 1 when q is 0.01 and 3.26 when q is 1. This higher error occurs because smaller groups have fewer identifiers, and sampling at lower probabilities reduces this even more. This makes the estimation less accurate and more random, which helps to protect individual privacy in less crowded areas. In contrast, for larger crowds (e.g., crowd-flow size $= 1,000$), the relative error remains relatively small across all values of q. Even at the lowest sampling probability of $q = 0.01$, the error is only 1.31, and decreases further as q increases, reaching 1.00 at $q = 1$. This indicates that the system remains reliable and precise for crowd flow size estimation in crowded areas, making it effective for planning and management purposes.

Overall, both sampling hashes and detected identifiers effectively balance privacy preservation in small groups with precise crowd flow size estimation in larger groups. In Sect. 7.4 we compare the two methods in terms of potential privacy breaches.

7 Discussion

7.1 Privacy Enhancement Using Fully Homomorphic Encryption

Fully homomorphic encryption (FHE) [25] enables both addition and multiplication operations on encrypted data, allowing confidential computations required for privacy enhancement. By applying FHE, statistical computations, such as counting set bits in an Encrypted Bloom Filter (EBF), can occur without decryption. Unlike the current approach requiring server shuffling of EBFs, FHE eliminates the client's access to raw data. The result—a simple, encrypted count— is returned to the client, ensuring that the Bloom filters remain confidential, regardless of server behavior. While FHE provides significant privacy advantages, Bloom filters' size intensifies computational overhead. Segmenting Bloom filters into smaller blocks is a potential optimization for future research.

7.2 Identifiers for Detection of Individuals

Crowd-monitoring systems study pedestrian activity in public areas using sensors to gather identifiable data. Although our approach is independent of the chosen identifiers, some identifiers may be more suitable than others. In [5], the authors suggest using the MAC addresses of devices carried by individuals as identifiers. Recently, many Wi-Fi enabled devices have started using MAC address randomization. This means that devices replace their original MAC addresses with random ones during probe requests, according to the manufacturers' rules. The system can accurately estimate the number of devices, and thus the number of individuals, as long as each identifier belongs to a single device. However, some randomization techniques assign multiple identifiers to a single device, which can cause potential problems. For example, if a device uses several random MAC addresses within the same epoch, it can result in overestimating footfall. Additionally, if devices change their MAC addresses between epochs, it can easily cause underestimation of crowd flows, as the same device might be seen as different ones. To address these challenges, future work should focus on finding more reliable identifiers to accurately count footfall and crowd flow sizes. Although identifiers such as MAC addresses are generally subject to consent requirements, our system avoids this by ensuring privacy by design. Identifiers are processed only within trusted scanners, immediately encoded into encrypted Bloom filters, and then discarded. No raw or linkable data is stored or transmitted, and outputs are noisy and aggregated, preventing identification and need for consent.

7.3 Trade-Off Between Privacy and Utility

We recommend optimizing hyperparameter q based on the specific application and sensitivity to privacy. This trade-off between privacy and utility can be adjusted to suit different scenarios. For scenarios prioritizing precise crowd monitoring with less emphasis on privacy, such as managing foot traffic during a large public event (e.g., a music festival), higher values of q provide sufficient data for accurate analysis of crowded areas. Conversely, in privacy-sensitive applications (e.g., monitoring pedestrian traffic in a quiet residential neighborhood), lower q values enhance privacy. This reduces the data granularity, ensuring residents' privacy while still providing approximate metrics for urban planning. By adjusting q, we can find the right balance between privacy and utility to suit the specific needs of the application.

7.4 Comparison of Privacy-Enhancing Methods

We propose two methods to intentionally reduce the precision of estimates in sparse areas, each offering privacy and utility trade-offs. Method 5.2 applies the sampling probability q directly to the identifiers, meaning fewer identifiers are represented in the Bloom filter. While this approach increases privacy by reducing the contribution of individual identifiers, it also leads to higher errors as fewer bits are set in the filter, lowering its precision. Moreover, this method may not guarantee equal privacy for all identifiers. For instance, if certain identifiers are consistently included and the query result is zero, an adversary could infer that the individual associated with the included identifier is absent, thus compromising their privacy. On the other hand, Method Sect. 5.1 uses q to probabilistically include specific hash functions, effectively controlling the number of set bits in the Bloom filter. This approach achieves results comparable to Method Sect. 5.2 but avoids the issues associated with inconsistent identifier representation. By balancing precision and privacy, Method Sect. 5.1 ensures that errors remain manageable while minimizing the risk of privacy violations. Therefore, we recommend Method Sect. 5.1 as the preferred approach for improving privacy in crowd-monitoring systems.

8 Conclusion

We address the challenge of protecting privacy in crowd monitoring systems by limiting the amount of information that can be inferred about individuals. We achieve this by carefully limiting the granularity of data, ensuring that data about small groups is imprecise to prevent reidentification. In sparsely populated areas, this approach reduces privacy risks, while in densely populated regions, where accurate data is essential, our methods remain reliable and effective.

Our evaluation using simulated data confirms the effectiveness of our approach. By adjusting hyperparameters, we can balance privacy and utility, making the system adaptable to a wide range of real-world scenarios, from large public events to more privacy-sensitive environments. Future work should focus on refining these techniques, particularly exploring fully homomorphic encryption to enhance privacy while limiting computational overhead. In addition, the identification of more reliable and consistent identifiers will be crucial to improve the accuracy of crowd flow and footfall estimations. Our study contributes to the development of privacy-preserving crowd monitoring systems that protect individual privacy while delivering valuable insights for planning.

Acknowledgements. This research is funded by the Dutch Research Council (NWO) through the PERSPECTIEF Program P21-08 'XCARCITY'. We gratefully acknowledge their financial support.

A Appendix

A.1 Footfall

Sampling Hash Functions. Starting equation:

$$t = m \left(1 - \left(1 - \frac{1}{m} \right)^k \right)$$

Substitute for t^*:

$$t^* = m \left(1 - \left(1 - \frac{1}{m} \right)^{kq} \right)$$

If we let:

$$\left(1 - \frac{1}{m} \right) = a, \quad \text{then:}$$

$$\frac{t}{m} = 1 - a^k \quad \Longrightarrow \quad a^k = 1 - \frac{t}{m} \quad \text{(Equation I)}$$

$$\frac{t^*}{m} = 1 - a^{kq} \quad \Longrightarrow \quad a^{kq} = 1 - \frac{t^*}{m} \quad \text{(Equation II)}$$

Apply Equation (I) into Equation (II), then:

$$1 - \frac{t^*}{m} = \left(1 - \frac{t}{m} \right)^q$$

Taking the q-th root of both sides:

$$\left(1 - \frac{t^*}{m} \right)^{\frac{1}{q}} = 1 - \frac{t}{m}$$

Rearranging:

$$\frac{t}{m} = 1 - \left(1 - \frac{t^*}{m} \right)^{\frac{1}{q}}$$

Finally:

$$t = m \left(1 - \left(1 - \frac{t^*}{m} \right)^{\frac{1}{q}} \right)$$

Starting equation:

$$c = -\frac{m}{k} \ln\left(1 - \frac{t}{m}\right)$$

Substitute:

$$t = m\left(1 - \left(1 - \frac{t^*}{m}\right)^{\frac{1}{q}}\right)$$

This leads to:

$$c = -\frac{m}{k} \ln\left(1 - \frac{1}{m}\left[m\left(1 - \left(1 - \frac{t^*}{m}\right)^{\frac{1}{q}}\right)\right]\right)$$

Simplifying:

$$c = -\frac{m}{k} \ln\left[\left(1 - \frac{t^*}{m}\right)^{\frac{1}{q}}\right]$$

Finally:

$$c = -\frac{m}{k} \cdot \frac{1}{q} \ln\left(1 - \frac{t^*}{m}\right)$$

Sampling Identifiers. When sampling the identifier to insert them into the Bloom filter with a probability q, the standard BF estimator can be corrected by dividing estimated value by q:

$$c = \frac{c}{q}$$

A.2   Crowd Flow

Sampling Hash Functions. Let BF_1 and BF_2 be the Bloom filters of sets S_1 and S_2, respectively. The Bloom filters have length m and share the same k hash functions. $BF_\wedge$ is the Bloom filter created by a bitwise AND of BF_1 and BF_2. c denotes the cardinality of $S_1 \cap S_2$, and t_x denotes the count of the true bits set in the Bloom filter BF_x. In the paper by Papapetrou et al. [23], it is proved that:

$$t_\wedge = t_\cap + r_{\text{bits}} \tag{8}$$

$$t_\wedge = t_\cap + \frac{(t_1 - t_\cap) \times (t_2 - t_\cap)}{m - t_\cap} \tag{9}$$

In the standard Bloom filter, the expected number of bits set to 1 after inserting c elements using k hash functions in a Bloom filter of size m is given by:

$$t_\cap = m\left(1 - \left(1 - \frac{1}{m}\right)^{c \times k}\right)$$

Substituting this into the formula 9, we get:

$$t_\wedge = \frac{t_1 \times t_2 + m\left(1 - \left(1 - \frac{1}{m}\right)^{k \times c}\right) \times (m - t_1 - t_2)}{m\left(1 - \frac{1}{m}\right)^{k \times c}} \tag{10}$$

Thus, in the standard Bloom filter, the expected number of common items in both sets (c) will be:

$$c = \frac{\ln\left(m - \frac{t_\wedge m - t_1 t_2}{m - t_1 - t_2 + t_\wedge}\right) - \ln(m)}{k \ln\left(1 - \frac{1}{m}\right)}$$

When running each hash function with a probability of q, the expected number of bits set to 1 after inserting c elements is given by:

$$t_\cap = m\left(1 - \left(1 - \frac{1}{m}\right)^{k \times q \times c}\right)$$

Substituting this into the formula 9, we get:

$$t_\wedge = \frac{t_1 \times t_2 + m\left(1 - \left(1 - \frac{1}{m}\right)^{k \times q \times c}\right) \times (m - t_1 - t_2)}{m\left(1 - \frac{1}{m}\right)^{k \times q \times c}} \tag{11}$$

Thus, the expected number of common items in both sets (c) is:

$$c = \frac{\ln\left(\frac{(m - t_1) \times (m - t_2)}{m(m - t_1 - t_2 + t_\wedge)}\right)}{kq \ln\left(\frac{m-1}{m}\right)}$$

Sampling Identifiers. When sampling the identifier to insert them into the Bloom filter with a probability q, the standard BF estimator can be corrected by dividing estimated value by q:

$$c = \frac{c}{q}$$

References

1. Southworth, M.: Designing the walkable city. J. Urban Planning Dev. **131**(4), 246–257 (2005). https://doi.org/10.1061/(ASCE)0733-9488(2005)131:4(246)
2. Lai, Y., Kontokosta, C.E.: Quantifying place: Analyzing the drivers of pedestrian activity in dense urban environments. Landscape Urban Planning **180**, 166–178 (2018). https://doi.org/10.1016/j.landurbplan.2018.08.018
3. Martella, C., Li, J., Conrado, C., Vermeeren, A.: On current crowd management practices and the need for increased situation awareness, prediction, and intervention. Saf. Sci. **91**, 381–393 (2017). https://doi.org/10.1016/j.ssci.2016.09.006

4. de Montjoye, Y.A., Hidalgo, C.A., Verleysen, M., Blondel, V.D.: Unique in the crowd: the privacy bounds of human mobility. Sci. Rep. **3**(1), 1376 (2013). https://doi.org/10.1038/srep01376

5. Stanciu, V.D., Steen, M.v., Dobre, C., Peter, A.: Privacy-preserving crowd-monitoring using bloom filters and homomorphic encryption. In: Proceedings of the 4th International Workshop on Edge Systems, Analytics and Networking, EdgeSys '21, pp. 37–42. Association for Computing Machinery, New York (2021). https://doi.org/10.1145/3434770.3459735

6. Musa, A.B.M., Eriksson, J.: Tracking unmodified smartphones using wi-fi monitors. In: Proceedings of the 10th ACM Conference on Embedded Network Sensor Systems, pp. 281–294. SenSys '12. Association for Computing Machinery, New York (2012). https://doi.org/10.1145/2426656.2426685

7. Schauer, L., Werner, M., Marcus, P.: Estimating crowd densities and pedestrian flows using wi-fi and bluetooth. In: Proceedings of the 11th International Conference on Mobile and Ubiquitous Systems: Computing, Networking and Services, pp. 171–177. MOBIQUITOUS '14, ICST (Institute for Computer Sciences, Social-Informatics and Telecommunications Engineering), Brussels, BEL (2014). https://doi.org/10.4108/icst.mobiquitous.2014.257870

8. Bonné, B., Barzan, A., Quax, P., Lamotte, W.: Wifipi: involuntary tracking of visitors at mass events. In: 2013 IEEE 14th International Symposium on "A World of Wireless, Mobile and Multimedia Networks" (WoWMoM), pp. 1–6 (2013). https://doi.org/10.1109/WoWMoM.2013.6583443

9. Cunche, M., Kaafar, M.A., Boreli, R.: Linking wireless devices using information contained in wi-fi probe requests. Pervasive Mob. Comput. **11**, 56–69 (2014), https://doi.org/10.1016/j.pmcj.2013.04.001

10. Vanhoef, M., Matte, C., Cunche, M., Cardoso, L.S., Piessens, F.: Why mac address randomization is not enough: An analysis of wi-fi network discovery mechanisms. In: Proceedings of the 11th ACM on Asia Conference on Computer and Communications Security, ASIA CCS 2016, pp. 413–424. Association for Computing Machinery, New York (2016). https://doi.org/10.1145/2897845.2897883

11. Stanciu, V.D., van Steen, M., Dobre, C., Peter, A.: k-anonymous crowd flow analytics. In: MobiQuitous 2020 - 17th EAI International Conference on Mobile and Ubiquitous Systems: Computing, Networking and Services, MobiQuitous 2020, pp. 376–385. Association for Computing Machinery, New York (2021). https://doi.org/10.1145/3448891.3448903

12. Ferguson, N., Schneier, B., Kohno, T.: Cryptography Engineering: Design Principles and Practical Applications. Wiley (2010). https://doi.org/10.1002/9781118722367

13. Demir, L., Cunche, M., Lauradoux, C.: Analysing the privacy policies of wi-fi trackers. In: Proceedings of the 2014 Workshop on Physical Analytics, WPA 2014, pp. 39–44. Association for Computing Machinery, New York (2014). https://doi.org/10.1145/2611264.2611266

14. Marx, M., Zimmer, E., Mueller, T., Blochberger, M., Federrath, H.: Hashing of personally identifiable information is not sufficient. In: SICHERHEIT 2018, pp. 55–68. Gesellschaft für Informatik e.V., Bonn (2018). https://doi.org/10.18420/sicherheit2018_04

15. Kamp, M., Kopp, C., Mock, M., Boley, M., May, M.: Privacy-preserving mobility monitoring using sketches of stationary sensor readings. In: Blockeel, H., Kersting, K., Nijssen, S., Železný, F. (eds.) Machine Learning and Knowledge Discovery in Databases, pp. 370–386. Springer, Heidelberg (2013). https://doi.org/10.1007/978-3-642-40994-3_24

16. Lim, R., Zimmerling, M., Thiele, L.: Passive, privacy-preserving real-time counting of unmodified smartphones via zigbee interference. In: 2015 International Conference on Distributed Computing in Sensor Systems, pp. 115–126 (2015). https://doi.org/10.1109/DCOSS.2015.13

17. Erlingsson, U., Pihur, V., Korolova, A.: Rappor: Randomized aggregatable privacy-preserving ordinal response. In: Proceedings of the 2014 ACM SIGSAC Conference on Computer and Communications Security, pp. 1054–1067. CCS '14. Association for Computing Machinery, New York, NY, USA (2014). https://doi.org/10.1145/2660267.2660348

18. Ke, Y., Liang, Y., Sha, Z., Shi, Z., Song, Z.: Dpbloomfilter: securing bloom filters with differential privacy. arXiv preprint arXiv:2502.00693 (2025)

19. Rusca, R., Carluccio, A., Casetti, C., Giaccone, P.: Privacy-preserving wifi-based crowd monitoring. Trans. Emerging Telecommun. Technol. **35**(3), e4956 (2024), https://doi.org/10.1002/ett.4956

20. Jiang, H., Li, J., Zhao, P., Zeng, F., Xiao, Z., Iyengar, A.: Location privacy-preserving mechanisms in location-based services: a comprehensive survey. ACM Comput. Surv. **54**(1) (2021). https://doi.org/10.1145/3423165

21. Bloom, B.H.: Space/time trade-offs in hash coding with allowable errors. Commun. ACM **13**(7), 422–426 (1970). https://doi.org/10.1145/362686.362692

22. Vatsalan, D., Christen, P., Verykios, V.S.: A taxonomy of privacy-preserving record linkage techniques. Inf. Syst. **38**(6), 946–969 (2013). https://doi.org/10.1016/j.is.2012.11.005

23. Papapetrou, O., Siberski, W., Nejdl, W.: Cardinality estimation and dynamic length adaptation for bloom filters. Distributed Parallel Databases **28**(2), 119–156 (2010). https://doi.org/10.1007/s10619-010-7067-2

24. Mitzenmacher, M.: Compressed bloom filters. In: Proceedings of the Twentieth Annual ACM Symposium on Principles of Distributed Computing, pp. 144–150. PODC '01. Association for Computing Machinery, New York (2001). https://doi.org/10.1145/383962.384004

25. Rivest, R.L., Adleman, L., Dertouzos, M.L., et al.: On data banks and privacy homomorphisms. Found. Secure Comput. **4**(11), 169–180 (1978). https://api.semanticscholar.org/CorpusID:6905087

Cross-Jurisdictional Compliance with Privacy Laws: How Websites Adapt Consent Notices to Regional Regulations

Xander Smeets[1] ⓘ, Michele Campobasso[2] ⓘ, and Nicola Zannone[1(✉)] ⓘ

[1] Eindhoven University of Technology, Eindhoven, The Netherlands
x.l.j.a.smeets@student.tue.nl, n.zannone@tue.nl
[2] Forescout Technologies, Eindhoven, The Netherlands
michele.campobasso@forescout.com

Abstract. Tracking cookies have been widely used for targeted advertising, raising privacy concerns due to their invasive nature. In response, jurisdictions such as the EU, UK, California, and Canada have enacted privacy laws to regulate online tracking. This study examines the compliance of 535 websites with these laws. To do so, we define a set of legal requirements and assess website compliance through region-specific simulated visits. Consistent with prior research, we find widespread privacy violations. Additionally, websites that adapt their privacy interfaces based on visitor location tend to violate EU and UK regulations more frequently while showing higher compliance with Californian requirements. No significant compliance trend was observed for Canadian regulations.

Keywords: Cookie · Consent · Cookie Banner · Legal Compliance

1 Introduction

In recent years, organizations have extensively collected user behavior data to create profiles for targeted advertising [66, 70]. However, large-scale data collection raises significant privacy concerns. To address these concerns, several jurisdictions have enacted privacy laws. For instance, California introduced the California Consumer Privacy Act (CCPA) [64], while the EU implemented the ePrivacy Directive [19] and the General Data Protection Regulation (GDPR) [20]. The ePrivacy Directive mandates user consent before placing cookies, and the GDPR establishes legal criteria for valid consent.

In response to privacy laws, many websites display *consent notices* (also known as cookie banners) asking users to accept cookies. However, research shows that these notices often fail to meet legal requirements [47, 56]. This is unsurprising, as targeted advertising—heavily reliant on cookies—remains a key revenue source for many websites [3, 40], creating incentives for manipulative consent mechanisms [61]. Most studies on privacy legislation and consent notices focus on a single jurisdiction, such as the EU [46, 55, 56] or California [68]. Moreover, little research has examined whether websites adapt privacy interfaces based on user location. Understanding whether and how websites adjust to different legal frameworks is crucial for assessing the effectiveness of privacy laws, identifying variations in compliance, and evaluating geographic

M. Dalla Preda et al. (Eds.): ARES 2025, LNCS 15992, pp. 68–91, 2025.
https://doi.org/10.1007/978-3-032-00624-0_4

disparities in user privacy protections. Investigating cross-jurisdictional compliance can offer insights into whether companies prioritize certain regulations over others and help policymakers refine enforcement strategies.

This study aims to assess website compliance with privacy laws across four jurisdictions—the EU, the UK, California, and Canada—focusing on legal requirements for consent and privacy options. To this end, we analyze 535 websites from the EU, the UK, the US, and Canada across three categories: news, e-commerce, and government. We examine the privacy laws of these four jurisdictions to identify legal requirements on consent and privacy settings. Compliance is evaluated by simulating visits from different regions to determine adherence to these requirements. Additionally, we investigate whether websites modify their privacy interfaces based on visitor location and analyze how this behavior influences compliance.

Our main contributions are as follows:

- Our analysis of privacy regulations provides a consolidated and updated overview of the legal requirements applicable to consent notices across multiple jurisdictions.
- Our study shows that websites comply more with local regulations than with extraterritorial ones, even when laws such as the GDPR and CCPA extend beyond their borders. This highlights the challenges of enforcing extraterritorial privacy laws and their impact on compliance.
- Our results also show that websites adapt privacy options to visitor location rather than applying the strictest regulation. This suggests that privacy is primarily perceived as a compliance obligation, highlighting the need to explore incentives for stronger privacy protections.
- Our findings indicate that privacy laws defining precise interface requirements, such as the CCPA, promote more standardized privacy controls, while technology-agnostic regulations such as the GDPR result in significant variation.

The remainder of the paper is organized as follows. Section 2 discusses the legal background for privacy interfaces and prior work on privacy choices on the Internet. Section 3 introduces our research questions and describes the methodology for answering them. Section 4 provides an overview of our results and answers to the research questions. Section 5 discusses the implications of our work. Finally, Sect. 6 concludes the paper.

2   Background and Related Work

2.1   Legal Frameworks

This section reviews the most relevant legislation in the EU, UK, US, and Canada.

European Union: The European Union has enacted several directives and regulations related to privacy. The most relevant to our work are the ePrivacy directive and the GDPR.

ePrivacy Directive: The ePrivacy directive [19] defines obligations for telecommunications service providers. In particular, article 5(3) requires the explicit and informed consent of the users before cookies (or any other form of data) can be stored or read from their devices [16,37,38]. The only exception to this rule applies to cookies which

Table 1. GDPR consent aspects.

GDPR consent aspect	Description
Freely given	User should be provided with a *genuine choice* between giving and refusing consent [20, rec. (42)]
Specific	Consent should be given for *specific purposes* [20, art. 6(1)(a)]. This is usually interpreted as requiring separate consent for each of the purposes for which processing of data is desired [25]
Informed	Users should be *made aware* of the *identity of the data controller* (i.e., the organization determining how and for what purposes data is processed [20, art. 4(7)]), as well as the *purposes of the data processing* [20, rec. (42)]. In addition, the information provided to the user must be *clear and comprehensive* [25]
Unambiguous	Consent needs to be expressed through a *clear and affirmative action of the user* [25]

are strictly necessary[1] to transmit data over the network [1] or to provide services that have been explicitly requested by the user.

GDPR: The GDPR [20] grants users several privacy rights and imposes obligations on organizations processing data of individuals in the European Economic Area (EEA). One key obligation is to establish a legal basis for data processing [20, art. 6(1)], which must be one of the following: (1) consent (2) performance of a contract (3) compliance with a legal obligation (4) vital interests (5) public interest (6) legitimate interests. As noted before, the ePrivacy Directive mandates consent as the legal basis when storing non-essential data (e.g., cookies) on a user's device. For consent to be valid, it must be *freely given, specific, informed,* and *unambiguous* [20, art.4(11)], hereafter referred to as *GDPR consent aspects* (Table 1). Additionally, consent requests must be clearly distinguishable from other matters [20, art.7(2)], and users must be informed of their right to withdraw consent, which must be as easy as granting it [20, art. 7(3)].

United Kingdom: Despite Brexit, the privacy-related EU regulations still largely apply in the UK. For instance, Article 5 of the ePrivacy directive and article 6 of the Privacy and Electronic Communications (EC Directive) Regulations [59] have been incorporated in UK law. In addition, the UK has chosen to retain the GDPR as part of its domestic law as part of the *European Union (Withdrawal) Act* [52]. The UK has, however, made some modifications to the GDPR as it applies in the UK [58]. The resulting version of the GDPR is known as the UK GDPR [21]. For our study, the UK GDPR can be considered equivalent to the EU's GDPR.

California: The California Consumer Privacy Act (CCPA) [64], later amended by the California Privacy Rights Act (CPRA) [65], establishes privacy rights for California residents, even when temporarily outside the state [64, § 1798.140(i)]. It grants individuals control over their personal data and imposes obligations on businesses handling such information. In particular, the CCPA grants rights to delete [64, §1798.105], correct [64, §1798.106], and access [64, §1798.110] personal data. Additionally, businesses must provide a 'notice at collection' [63, § 7012(a)], informing users about data collection, its intended use, and whether the data is sold or shared. However, unlike the GDPR, which regulates data collection, the CCPA primarily governs data use after collection. This distinction is highlighted in the California Code of Regulations, which states that cookie banners alone do not satisfy opt-out requirements for data sale or sharing [63, § 7026(a)(4)]. Businesses that sell or share personal data must provide an opt-out option and inform users via a '*Do Not Sell or Share My Personal Information*'

---

[1] The necessity should be from the user's perspective, not the website's [1].

(DNSMPI) [68]) link on their homepage. Those processing *sensitive* personal information must also offer a '*Limit the Use of My Sensitive Personal Information*' link [63, §7014], though both may be combined into a single '*Your Privacy Choices*' or '*Your California Privacy Choices*' link with a designated opt-out icon [63, § 7015].

It is worth noting that CCPA obligations apply only to businesses meeting at least one of the following criteria [64, §1798.140(d)(1)]: (1) annual gross revenue exceeding $25 million, (2) buying, selling, or sharing the personal information of at least 100,000 consumers, or (3) deriving at least 50% of revenue from selling or sharing personal information. Nonprofits and government agencies are exempt [44].

Canada: Canada has two privacy laws similar to those in the EU: the Personal Information Protection and Electronic Documents Act (PIPEDA) [49] and Canada's Anti-Spam Legislation (CASL) [50]. PIPEDA mandates businesses to follow privacy principles when handling personal data, while CASL regulates the installation of '*computer programs*', including cookies. In case of conflict, CASL takes precedence [50, §2].

PIPEDA: PIPEDA applies the National Standard of Canada's personal information protection principles [49, Sched. 1] to organizations. These principles include: (1) accountability, (2) identifying purposes, (3) consent, (4) limiting collection, (5) limiting use, disclosure, and retention, (6) accuracy, (7) safeguards, (8) openness, (9) individual access, and (10) challenging compliance. The second and third principles are the most relevant for our work. The second principle requires organizations to identify and disclose the purposes for collecting and using personal information, generally before collection. Previously collected data can only be repurposed after obtaining user consent. The third principle mandates knowledgeable consent before collecting, using, or sharing personal data, similar to GDPR's informed consent. Users must be able to withdraw consent at any time, and consent cannot be a condition for accessing goods or services, aligning with EU regulations. However, unlike EU law, PIPEDA allows implied consent; for example, not checking a box can be considered valid consent [49, Sched.1, §4.3.7(b)], whereas the EU requires explicit user action (i.e., no pre-ticked boxes).

Although PIPEDA applies broadly to "organizations" [49, §4(1)], some are exempted, similar to California's CCPA. Notably, government institutions (as defined in Canada's Privacy Act [51]) are excluded. Additionally, PIPEDA does not apply to intra-provincial data activities when a province has privacy laws deemed "substantially similar" [49, §26(2)(b)]. Currently, this exemption applies in several provinces [48].

Canada's Anti-Spam Legislation: CASL prohibits the installation of computer programs without the express consent of the owner or authorized user of a computer located in Canada [50, §8(2)]. The law defines "computer programs" broadly, covering cookies, HTML, JavaScript, and any executable code that runs via another program previously installed with consent [50, §10(8)(a)]. When expressing consent is required, users must be informed of both the purpose of the consent request [50, §10(1)(a)] and the function of the program being installed [50, § 10(3)]. Although this rule resembles the EU ePrivacy Directive, CASL presumes user consent for certain programs, including cookies, unless users explicitly indicate otherwise [50, §10(8)(b)]. In practice, this means a user is considered to have consented unless they disable cookies in their browser [10].

Cookies and advertising choices

If you agree, we may use your personal information from any of these Amazon services to personalize the ads we show you on other services. For example, we may use your Prime Video Watch history to personalize the ads we show you on our Stores or on Fire TV. We may also use personal information we receive from third parties (like demographic information). If you decline, your choices will apply by 6 March 2024. Learn more.

In addition, if you agree, we'll also use cookies to complement your shopping experience across the Amazon stores as described in our Cookie notice. Your choice applies to using first-party and third-party advertising cookies on this service. Cookies store or access standard device information such as a unique identifier. The 103 third parties who use cookies on this service do so for their purposes of displaying and measuring personalised ads, generating audience insights, and developing and improving products.

In any case, we use cookies and similar tools that are necessary to enable you to make purchases, to enhance your shopping experiences and to provide our services, as detailed in our Cookie notice. We also use these cookies to understand how customers use our services (for example, by measuring site visits) so we can make improvements. Click "Decline" to reject, or "Customise" to make more detailed advertising choices, or learn more. You can change your choices at any time by visiting Cookies and advertising choices. To learn more about how and for what purposes Amazon uses personal information (such as Store order history or Prime Video Watch history) and cookies, please visit our Privacy notice and our Cookie notice.

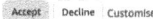

Fig. 1. Amazon consent notice

2.2 Consent Gathering and Enforcement

Websites use various methods to collect user consent, and these methods vary depending on regulatory frameworks in place. Common methods, especially in the EU and UK, include consent notices (e.g., Fig. 1) that inform users about the use of cookies and third-party data sharing while providing options to accept or reject cookies with different levels of granularity. Some jurisdictions rely on implied consent, treating continued site usage as agreement, while others (e.g., California) mandate opt-out mechanisms.

The design of consent notices strongly influence user decisions, often raising concerns about legal compliance. Despite existing regulations, many websites employ deceptive or non-compliant mechanisms, driven by the profitability of targeted advertising. Research on this issue primarily examines two interconnected aspects: the use of *dark patterns* in consent interfaces and their *compliance with legal requirements*. While dark patterns are used to manipulate users into consenting, studies focusing on legal compliance assess whether organizations meet the requirements outlined in privacy laws.

Dark patterns are deceptive design techniques that nudge users toward choices favoring the organization rather than their own privacy interests. First introduced by Brignull [8,9], these techniques have been systematically categorized in various taxonomies [24]. For instance, the consent notice in Fig. 1 exemplifies the 'interface interference' dark pattern by visually prioritizing the 'Accept' button to encourage user consent. The widespread use of dark patterns raises concerns about compliance with privacy regulations. Recognizing their manipulative nature, the European Data Protection Board (EDPB) advises against their use [17], while regulations such as the Digital Services Act [22], Digital Markets Act [23], and California's CCPA [64] explicitly prohibit them. Several studies have examined the prevalence of dark patterns on websites and their impact on user interactions with consent notices [4,5,28,67]. Soe et al. [61] manually analyzed 300 news websites and found that 297 employed some form of dark pattern in their consent mechanisms. Gunawan et al. [26] compared websites and mobile apps offering the same services, revealing that every service used at least one dark pattern, with notable variations between platforms. Similarly, Habib et al. [28] found that 88% of 603 UK websites utilized at least one dark pattern. Kirkman et al. [36] developed an automated system to detect dark patterns, identifying 3,744 instances across 2,417 consent notices.

Most studies on legal compliance have primarily examined the GDPR, leaving other regulations comparatively underexplored. Santos et al. [56] define six legal requirements for cookie banner text in the EU, emphasizing clarity, specificity, and informed consent. Paci et al. [46] assessed the compliance of Android apps, categorizing consent requirements into six key aspects, including prior consent, specificity, and ease of revocation. Similarly, Santos et al. [55] identify 22 legal requirements based on the ePrivacy directive and GDPR, highlighting additional concerns such as readability and accessibility. Van Nortwick and Wilson [68] investigate compliance with the CCPA, particularly the requirement for a 'Do Not Sell My Personal Information' link on websites. Their study also considers whether or not DNSMPI links are hidden for users outside California, as well as exemptions to the CCPA.

While many studies have examined the compliance of privacy interfaces across a diverse set of popular websites, often selected using the Tranco list or market research reports [6,27,28,35,39,47,54,56,68], only a few have investigated how these interfaces vary based on user location. Dabrowski et al. [12] found that websites commonly request cookie consent only when accessed from the EU, while US visitors receive no such prompts. Rasaii et al. [54] observed a higher prevalence of consent notices for EU users compared to those outside the EU. Van Eijk et al. [18] further examined the role of top-level domains (TLDs) and found that TLDs strongly predict consent notice prevalence, whereas user location had a limited effect, except for .com domains where location did influence notice display. Given the discrepancies in findings, further research is needed.

Beyond improperly obtaining consent, another major privacy violation occurs when websites disregard users' choices. Several studies have examined the enforcement of user decisions, revealing that consent refusals are often mishandled [39,47]. For example, research has shown that some websites record users as having given consent even when they have not [39]. Moreover, tracking is not limited to cookies—fingerprinting and other tracking techniques are often used even when users explicitly reject cookie-based tracking [47]. In some cases, rejecting consent has paradoxically increased the number of third parties receiving user data [47]. To counteract such practices, Bollinger et al. [6] developed CookieBlock, a browser extension that uses machine learning to categorize cookies and enforce user preferences. Privacy violations are not limited to websites—similar issues have been found in mobile applications. Several studies have shown that many Android apps share user data with third parties without first requesting consent [38,42,43]. Nguyen et al. [42] analyzed these violations by examining the third-party domains contacted by mobile apps, highlighting the extent of unauthorized data sharing.

2.3 Gaps in Prior Work

Most prior studies have primarily focused on the requirements imposed by the EU's ePrivacy Directive and GDPR. While some works have examined privacy regulations outside the EU, they typically analyze non-EU legislation in isolation rather than in conjunction with EU laws. As a result, little is known about how websites adapt their privacy interfaces when serving users in different regulatory environments. Investigating these differences is important for assessing whether websites tailor their privacy

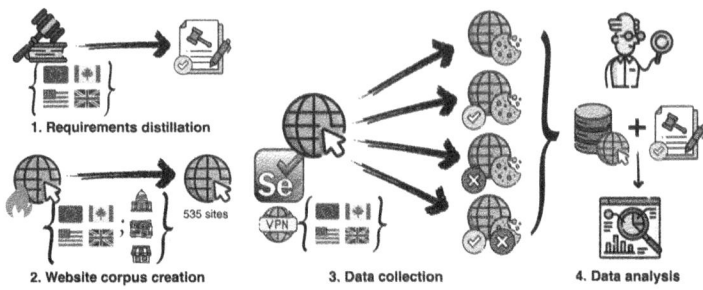

Fig. 2. A schematic overview of the methodology.

practices to the legal obligations of the user's jurisdiction, or maintain a uniform app-roach irrespective of user location. To the best of our knowledge, only a few studies have explored the impact of user location on privacy interfaces. Notably, Van Eijk et al. [18] examined regional differences in consent notices but focused primarily on visual char-acteristics, such as notice presence, height, word count, and button/link counts, leaving a more detailed analysis for future work. Similarly, Rasaii et al. [54] investigated how user location affects consent notices and the availability of CCPA-mandated DNSMPI links but did not comprehensively assess compliance with broader CCPA requirements.

By systematically analyzing privacy interfaces and compliance across multiple jurisdictions, our study offers insights into how regulatory frameworks influence web-site behavior. If privacy interfaces and compliance levels vary significantly across coun-tries, this suggests that regulatory requirements play a dominant role in driving privacy practices rather than a website's internal privacy policies or user-centric commitments. Understanding such patterns is valuable for regulators evaluating the impact of different legal frameworks, and for users and consumer associations assessing how companies handle privacy across jurisdictions.

3   Methodology

The gap identified in the previous section leads us to the following research questions:

RQ1 *To what extent do the origin and category of websites determine whether they present different privacy-related interfaces to visitors from different regions?*
RQ2 *To what extent do the origin and category of websites determine whether they comply with the requirements posed by the privacy legislation that applies by virtue of the location of their visitors?*
RQ3 *If websites present different privacy-related interfaces to visitors from different regions, are they more likely to comply with privacy regulations?*

These questions aim to provide an understanding of how user location influences the privacy mechanisms displayed by websites.

Figure 2 shows an overview of the methodology used to answer the research ques-tions. First, we distilled a set of requirements to be met by websites from privacy reg-ulations and prior work (Sect. 3.1). Then, we created a corpus of websites (Sect. 3.2).

Next, we collected data on the websites in our corpus from the perspective of each region (Sect. 3.3). Finally, we analyzed each website's compliance with the identified requirements and used regression models to answer our research questions (Sect. 3.4).

3.1   Requirements Distillation

From the legal frameworks discussed in Sect. 2.1, we obtained the requirements from the associated privacy laws and prior work. The requirements were initially defined by one of the authors and iteratively refined with the other authors until a consensus was reached. These requirements, outlined in Tables 2, 3, and 4, served as the foundation for systematically evaluating websites' compliance with privacy obligations.

3.2   Website Corpus Creation

For our study, we built a corpus of websites based on two properties: geographic *origin* and *category*. We selected sites from the countries covered in the legal requirements analysis (Sect. 2.1) to examine compliance with different regulations. The included websites span over three categories—*news*, *government*, and *e-commerce*—to explore

Table 2. Requirements applying to sites under EU privacy laws.

ID	Requirement	GDPR consent aspect	Sources
EU01	A consent notice should contain a visibly highlighted link to the privacy/cookie policy.	Informed	[2, 17]
EU02	The consent notice text should be readable.	Informed	[17, 55]
EU03	The purposes for which cookies are being stored should be explicitly mentioned in the consent notice/privacy policy.	Informed	[2, 13, 17]
EU04	Expiration date of cookies should be disclosed to users when obtaining consent.	Informed	[17, 71]
EU05	Third party sharing should be disclosed to users when obtaining consent.	Informed	[17, 71]
EU06	Links to privacy policy of third party should be provided.	Informed	[17, 71]
EU07	Controller's identity is present in privacy policy.	Informed	[14, 55]
EU08	What cookies are being stored is present in the cookie policy.	Informed	[14]
EU09	The existence of the right to withdraw consent should be present in the notice.	Informed	[14]
EU010	Emotional language should not be used.	Informed	[17]
EU011	The legal basis for processing must be mentioned.	Specific	[13]
EU012	Consent must be given separately for each purpose.	Specific	[15, 17, 55]
EU013	The accept and reject mechanisms should be displayed using the same type of form element, and at the same level of the consent notice.	Freely given	[17]
EU014	If a form element is highlighted, it must be the most restrictive one (i.e. the most privacy-friendly one).	Freely given	[15]
EU015	Rejection of consent should be as easy as giving consent.	Freely given	[15, 17]
EU016	There should be no pre-selected boxes in any level of the consent notice.	Freely given	[17, 55, 71]
EU017	Legitimate interest should not be used as a legal basis for storing non-necessary cookies.	Freely given	[16, 37, 38, 42, 43]
EU018	The font size in a consent notice should be readable.	Unambiguous	[17]
EU019	Conditional tense should not be used in a consent notice.	Unambiguous	[17]
EU020	After withdrawing consent, non-necessary cookies should not be present.	Unambiguous	[14]
EU021	A consent notice should produce a visual effect when interacted with.	Unambiguous	[17]
EU022	If consent is declined, no non-necessary cookies should be placed.	Freely given	[17]
EU023	No non-necessary cookies should be placed without user interaction.	Freely given	[6, 17, 55]
EU024	Consent must be withdrawable via the same electronic interface.	Freely given	[14, 55]
EU025	A site's content must be accessible without providing consent. (e.g. no cookie walls)	Freely given	[17, 55]

how the type of organization affects compliance. These categories were selected based on their distinct business model: news websites often rely on advertising revenue, e-commerce platforms use tracking to personalize product recommendations, and government websites are typically non-profit. Government websites serve as a baseline in our study, as they are expected to adhere more closely to their country's legal privacy frameworks.

Table 3. Requirements applying to sites under Californian privacy laws.

ID	Requirement	Sources
US01	If information is shared with third parties, the website should show a 'Do Not Sell or Share My Personal Information' link in the header or footer of the homepage.	[64, § 1798.135(a)(1)] [63, § 7015(a)] [63, § 7013(c)]
US02	Before or at the moment of collecting users' personal information, (a link to) a notice at collection should be provided to them.	[63, § 7012(c)]
US03	If the notice at collection is provided using a link to a privacy policy, then the link should bring the user to the part of the privacy policy containing the required information.	[63, § 7012(f)]
US04	The notice at collection should include a list of the categories of personal information which is gathered.	[63, § 7012(e)(1)]
US05	The notice at collection should include the purposes for which (categories of) personal information are collected and used.	[63, § 7012(e)(2)]
US06	The notice at collection should describe whether each category of information is sold or shared.	[63, § 7012(e)(3)]
US07	The notice at collection should include the retention period for each category of personal information (or the criteria used to determine that period).	[63, § 7012(e)(4)]
US08	If the business sells or shares personal information, the notice at collection should include a link to a notice of right to opt-out of sale/sharing.	[63, § 7012(e)(5)]
US09	The notice at collection should include a link to the business's privacy policy.	[63, § 7012(e)(6)]
US010	If the business uses and/or discloses sensitive personal information, the website should show a 'Limit the Use of My Sensitive Personal Information' link in the header or footer of the homepage.	[64, § 1798.135(a)(1)] [63, § 7014(c)]
US011	A business should provide an email address for submitting requests to delete, correct, and know if it operates exclusively online. Otherwise, it should provide both a toll-free telephone number and a website-based method for submitting such requests.	[64, § 1798.130(a)(1)(A, B)] [63, § 7020(a, b)]
US012	The user should not be required to create an account to exercise the right to opt-out of sale/sharing.	[64, § 1798.135(c)(1)] [63, § 7026(c)]
US013	The user should not be required to create an account to exercise the right to limit the use and disclosure of sensitive personal information.	[64, § 1798.135(c)(1)] [63, § 7027(d)]
US014	The business should not discriminate against the user for exercising their rights.	[64, § 1798.125(a)(1)]

We built our corpus using country- and category-specific lists of popular websites provided by PressGazette and market research firms Semrush and SimilarWeb.[2] These sources yielded 1025 unique websites across all countries and categories. To assess the reliability of this list, we used Cloudflare Gateway to check whether each website exists and whether its origin and category match the original classification. Due to limited access to Cloudflare's API, we developed a configurable DNS resolver that selectively queried websites in specific Cloudflare categories, enabling us to retrieve data for all candidate sites. We excluded websites that were inaccessible or whose origin or category did not align with the initial classification (e.g., a US website popular in Canada). This resulted in a final set of 535 unique websites, distributed by origin and category as shown in Table 5.

---

[2] We excluded sources, like the Tranco list, that lack information on website origin or category.

Table 4. Requirements applying to sites under Canadian privacy laws.

ID	Requirement	Sources
CA01	The purposes for which personal information is collected shall be made available to users at/before the time of collection of personal information.	[49, Sched. 1, § 4.2.3]
CA02	Consent must be obtained for the collection, use and disclosure of personal information.	[49, Sched. 1, § 4.3.1]
CA03	Consent must not be required as a condition of the supply of a product or service (beyond what is required to fulfil the explicitly specified, and legitimate purposes).	[49, Sched. 1, § 4.3.3]
CA04	Consent must be withdrawable at any time (subject to legal or contractual restrictions and reasonable notice).	[49, Sched. 1, § 4.3.8]
CA05	Cookies which are legally placed by a third party should not technically present themselves as first-party cookies.	[45]

3.3   Data Collection

We assume that websites must comply with the privacy laws of the country where the user is physically located at the time of access, which is typically determined using their IP address. Accordingly, we assess the compliance of a website with a given law if the user's IP address originates from the country where the law applies. To this end, we accessed the websites in our corpus using an IP address from each country through a VPN. For every location, we collected the source code of the webpage and video recordings demonstrating and navigating the consent notices and privacy policy on every website. Additionally, we stored the cookies present on the website, categorized by type, such as necessary, analytics, or advertising. For the EU and UK, we recorded the cookies at multiple stages: *(i)* before any user interaction, *(ii)* after giving consent, *(iii)* after rejecting consent, and *(iv)* after giving consent, withdrawing it, and refreshing the page. For California, we captured cookies after giving consent and observed the website's response to the Global Privacy Control signal [53]. For Canada, we collected cookies after giving consent and after opting out of cookies. This comprehensive data collection provided the foundation for evaluating how websites from different countries comply with privacy regulations.

We recall that the CCPA does not apply to non-profit organizations, government agencies, or websites that fail to meet any of the criteria specified in Sect. 2.1. Websites that do not meet these criteria were removed from the data collection process when websites were visited using an IP address from California. To determine whether a website was owned by a non-profit or government organization, we manually reviewed the website content. We also evaluated whether the website had at least 100,000 visitors from

Table 5. An overview of the number of sites from each origin and category.

Origin	Category			Total
	News	E-commerce	Government	
EU	90	67	58	215
UK	30	30	34	94
US	30	34	58	122
Canada	30	38	36	104
Total	180	169	186	535

California using Semrush data [68] and whether its owning organization had annual revenues exceeding $25 million by gathering from freely available corporate records and online resources, including market research firms and Wikipedia. This approach ensured that our analysis focused solely on websites subject to the CCPA's jurisdiction.

We accessed all websites using Google Chrome, with the collection process partially automated using Python and Selenium [62]. Automation handled tasks such as navigation, cookie management, and data recording, while manual supervision ensured completeness and data quality, for example, verifying that all relevant elements were captured. Cookie data was primarily collected using the CookieBlock browser extension [6], which categorizes cookies by type (e.g., necessary, analytics, advertising). For technical reasons, some data was manually gathered using the 'Get cookies.txt' browser extension [34].

3.4   Data Analysis

This section details how we measured our constructs (*differences in privacy interfaces* and *compliance with requirements*) and the regression models used in the analysis.

Differences in Privacy Interfaces: To assess whether privacy-related interfaces differ based on a visitor's country, we examine three criteria. First, we check if the website is accessible in some countries but not others. Second, we evaluate whether a consent notice is displayed to visitors from certain countries but not to others. Third, we analyze whether a "Do Not Sell or Share My Personal Information" link is visible to visitors from specific countries. The accessibility of the website, as well as the presence of a consent notice or "Do Not Sell" link, is determined through visual inspection. The difference in the privacy interface is expressed as a binary variable: 1 if a country-level difference is identified in at least one of the three criteria, and 0 otherwise.

Compliance with Requirements: To evaluate the compliance of websites with legal and normative privacy expectations, we operationalized the requirements in Sect. 3.1 by defining concrete assessment criteria grounded in prior work. Each requirement was assessed through visual inspection, HTML source analysis, or automated tool support, depending on its nature. Visual inspection was used to evaluate interface elements such as the presence of a cookie wall (EU25), required information (e.g., EU03, EU04, EU07, EU09), and the visual display and placement of buttons (e.g., EU13, EU14). HTML source analysis helped identify structural elements like the presence of specific links (e.g., EU01, EU06) or font size (EU18). Automated tools supported criteria involving text analysis. For example, the readability of consent notices (EU02) was assessed using the textstat Python library and the Flesch-Kincaid Grade Level, with scores of 8.5 or lower considered acceptable [41,69]. Sentiment neutrality (EU10) was evaluated using the NLTK library, with an absolute compound score below 0.65 indicating neutral phrasing [32]. A full overview of the criteria and their assessment methods is provided in [60]. Each requirement was labeled as *satisfied*, *not satisfied*, or *not applicable*. Requirements were considered not applicable when the website's context rendered them irrelevant. For example, requirements concerning consent notice presentation (e.g., font size) do not apply to websites that do not display such notices. To address ambiguous or borderline cases, we adopted an iterative refinement process in which the authors discussed any unclear interpretations of the requirements. These discussions led to refinements of the criteria and ensured they were applied consistently across all websites. To quantify compliance, we computed a *compliance ratio* for each website, defined as the number of satisfied requirements divided by the total number of applicable requirements (i.e., excluding those marked as not applicable). All applicable requirements contributed equally to the ratio.

Regression Analysis: To address the research questions outlined in Sect. 3, we defined three regression models, summarized in Table 6. Model 1 investigates RQ1 by examining how the origin and category of a website influence the presence of differences in the consent notice shown when the website is accessed from different locations. Model 2 focuses on RQ2 by exploring the relationship between the compliance ratio and the origin and category of websites. Model 3 addresses RQ3, analyzing whether the presence of differences is a predictor of a website's compliance ratio, while also using the origin and category of websites as control variables to ensure the reliability of the results.

Table 6. Equations for the regression models used to describe the results.

Model	Equation
Model 1	$difference = \beta_0 + \beta_1 \cdot category + \beta_2 \cdot origin$
Model 2	$compliance = \beta_0 + \beta_1 \cdot category + \beta_2 \cdot origin$
Model 3	$compliance = \beta_0 + \beta_1 \cdot category + \beta_2 \cdot origin + \beta_3 \cdot difference$

For RQ2 and RQ3, we further analyze compliance with respect to specific GDPR consent aspects (cf. Table 1). In these cases, the compliance ratio is recalculated based on the requirements associated with each aspect, as detailed in Table 2. This analysis evaluates whether the influence of website origin, category, or the presence of differences is consistent across all consent aspects or varies by aspect.

Logistic regression was performed for Model 1, while quasi-binomial logistic regression was used for Models 2 and 3. Factors with regression coefficients showing a p-value below 0.05 were considered statistically significant. We tested the models for RQ2 and RQ3 using two datasets: one comprising all websites in the corpus and another restricted to websites for which all requirements are applicable. This allows us

Table 7. Summary of analyzed websites per country, including the presence of privacy interfaces and the number of sites violating at least one requirement.

		# sites analyzed				Differ	Privacy interface present				At least one violation			
		EU	UK	CA	Cali		EU	UK	Canada	California	EU	UK	Canada	California
Tot		535	535	535	315	138 (25.8%)	361 (67.5%)	368 (68.8%)	302 (56.5%)	87 (27.6%)	523 (97.8%)	525 (98.1%)	473 (88.4%)	312 (99.1%)
Origin	EU	215	215	215	127	23 (10.7%)	189 (87.9%)	188 (87.4%)	184 (85.6%)	2 (1.6%)	215 (100%)	213 (99.1%)	180 (83.7%)	127 (100%)
	UK	94	94	94	58	31 (33.0%)	89 (94.7%)	92 (97.9%)	69 (73.4%)	25 (43.1%)	94 (100%)	94 (100%)	79 (84.0%)	58 (100%)
	US	122	122	122	67	55 (45.1%)	46 (37.7%)	47 (38.5%)	21 (17.2%)	56 (83.6%)	115 (94.3%)	116 (95.1%)	117 (95.9%)	64 (95.5%)
	CA	104	104	104	63	29 (27.9%)	37 (35.6%)	41 (39.4%)	28 (26.9%)	4 (6.4%)	99 (95.2%)	102 (98.1%)	97 (93.3%)	63 (100%)
Category	News	180	180	180	152	78 (43.3%)	163 (90.6%)	165 (91.7%)	109 (60.6%)	50 (32.9%)	180 (100%)	180 (100%)	177 (98.3%)	150 (98.7%)
	E-comm	169	169	169	156	46 (27.2%)	123 (72.8%)	128 (75.7%)	120 (71.0%)	36 (23.1%)	161 (95.3%)	164 (97.0%)	155 (91.7%)	155 (99.4%)
	Govt	186	186	186	7	14 (7.5%)	75 (40.3%)	75 (40.3%)	73 (39.3%)	1 (14.3%)	182 (97.9%)	181 (97.3%)	141 (75.8%)	7 (100%)

to examine whether websites bound by the complete set of requirements exhibit distinct compliance patterns compared to the entire dataset.

4   Results

Table 7 summarizes the presence of relevant privacy interfaces across countries, showing how many websites display these interfaces based on user location. It also reports the number of sites analyzed for compliance in each country and those violating at least one requirement in that country. Note that the number of websites assessed for California is lower due to the applicability of the CCPA (see Sect. 3.3).

We can observe that approximately 70% of websites display a consent notice in the EU, 71% in the UK, and 61% in Canada. In California, 28% of websites provide a "Do Not Sell" link, which may also include a "Limit the Use of My Sensitive Personal Information" or "Your Privacy Choices" link. Around 26% of websites exhibit differences in privacy interfaces based on user location. Notably, almost all websites analyzed violate at least one legal requirement, revealing substantial compliance gaps. In the EU, UK, and California, over 90% of websites fail to meet at least one applicable requirement. In Canada, approximately 88% of the websites exhibit at least one violation; this trend is consistent across all website categories and countries of origin, with at least 75% of websites in every category failing to comply with at least one requirement.

Table 8 analyzes compliance with GDPR consent requirements when websites are accessed from the EU and UK. The results show that full compliance with consent aspects is notably rare. For most consent aspects, at least 69% of websites fail to meet at least one requirement. An exception is the 'specific' consent aspect, where compliance may be higher due to the limited number of applicable requirements (only two). These findings highlight widespread violations of GDPR requirements.

4.1   RQ1: Differences in Privacy Interfaces

Presence of Privacy Interfaces: Figure 3 presents the results of the regression analysis examining the presence of privacy interfaces based on website origin and category; coefficients are reported in [60]. The McFadden pseudo R-squared values, ranging from 0.33 to 0.55, indicate that the models account for approximately 33–55% of the variance

Table 8. Number of sites violating at least one requirement per consent aspect, reported separately for access from the EU and the UK.

		Freely given		Informed		Specific		Unambiguous	
		EU	UK	EU	UK	EU	UK	EU	UK
Tot		485 (90.7%)	489 (91.4%)	490 (91.6%)	502 (93.8%)	276 (51.6%)	269 (50.3%)	434 (81.1%)	478 (89.4%)
Origin	EU	196 (91.2%)	196 (91.2%)	202 (94.0%)	203 (94.4%)	84 (39.1%)	81 (37.7%)	166 (77.2%)	188 (87.4%)
	UK	81 (86.2%)	80 (85.1%)	90 (95.7%)	92 (97.9%)	27 (28.7%)	14 (14.9%)	73 (77.7%)	84 (89.4%)
	US	113 (92.6%)	114 (93.4%)	103 (84.4%)	109 (89.3%)	88 (72.1%)	93 (76.2%)	104 (85.3%)	110 (90.2%)
	CA	95 (91.4%)	99 (95.2%)	95 (91.4%)	98 (94.2%)	77 (74.0%)	81 (77.9%)	91 (87.5%)	96 (92.3%)
Category	News	178 (98.9%)	177 (98.3%)	177 (98.3%)	179 (99.4%)	51 (28.3%)	61 (33.9%)	168 (93.3%)	177 (98.3%)
	E-comm	160 (94.7%)	163 (96.5%)	156 (92.3%)	158 (93.5%)	80 (47.3%)	67 (39.6%)	137 (81.1%)	157 (92.9%)
	Govt	147 (79.0%)	149 (80.1%)	157 (84.4%)	165 (88.7%)	145 (78.0%)	141 (75.8%)	129 (69.6%)	144 (77.4%)

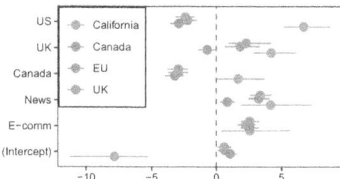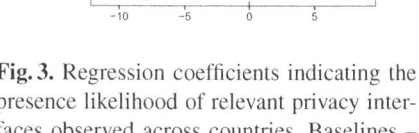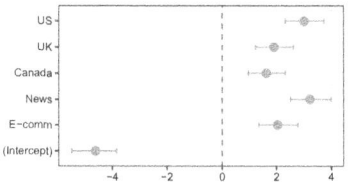

Fig. 3. Regression coefficients indicating the presence likelihood of relevant privacy interfaces observed across countries. Baselines – origin: EU; category – government.

Fig. 4. Regression coefficients indicating the presence of a difference in privacy interfaces among countries. Baselines – origin: EU; category – government.

in the data. The analysis reveals that EU and UK websites are more likely to display consent notices compared to US and Canadian websites. "Do Not Sell" links are most frequently observed on US websites and least likely on EU websites. These results are consistent with companies prioritizing compliance with local laws. Privacy interfaces, regardless of type, are more common on e-commerce and news websites. Government websites, being non-commercial and less reliant on tracking technologies that require consent, are the least likely to display privacy interfaces, including consent notices.

Differences Between Regions: Figure 4 illustrates the relationship between differences in privacy interfaces across regions and a website's origin or category; the coefficients are reported in [60]. The McFadden pseudo R-squared value of 0.30 indicates a moderate model fit, accounting for roughly 30% of the variance in the data. The results show that non-EU websites are more likely to exhibit differences in privacy interfaces compared to EU government websites. Similarly, e-commerce and news websites are more likely to have such differences than EU websites. One explanation is that non-EU websites, often written in English, are more likely to target an international audience. In contrast, EU websites, typically written in local languages, tend to focus on domestic users. Internationally oriented websites are incentivized to adjust privacy interfaces based on visitor location to align with regional laws, enabling them to maximize revenue by limiting privacy options in areas with less stringent regulations. The higher prevalence of differences on e-commerce and news websites compared to government websites likely reflects their commercial nature. Government websites, being non-commercial, have less incentive to tailor privacy options based on location, as their primary focus is providing public services to their local audience rather than generating revenue. In contrast, e-commerce and news websites may strategically adapt privacy interfaces to meet minimum legal requirements by region.

ANSWER TO RQ1. The origin and category of a website significantly influence whether privacy-related interfaces vary based on visitor location. Non-EU websites and commercial sites, such as e-commerce and news, are more likely to adjust their privacy interfaces across regions, whereas EU and government websites tend to present consistent interfaces focused on domestic users. These findings suggest that the adoption of tailored privacy interfaces is often driven by commercial incentives.

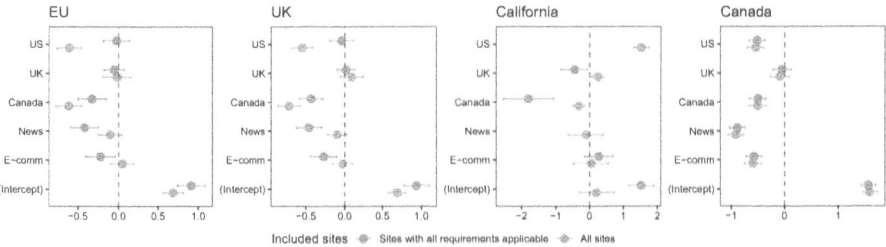

Fig. 5. Regression coefficients of the observed variables w.r.t. the compliance ratio (Model 2). Plot titles indicate the region of visit.

4.2   RQ2: Compliance with Requirements

Figure 5 presents the results of the regression analysis examining the relationship between a website's origin and category and its compliance with requirements from each region. The regression coefficients are reported in [60].[3] For each region, the plot shows the results for all websites and for the ones for which all requirements from that region apply.

The analysis reveals that North American websites are less compliant with EU and UK laws than European websites, which aligns with our expectations. When considering only websites where all requirements apply, we can observe significant shifts in coefficients. News and e-commerce websites appear less compliant, whereas US and Canadian websites show greater compliance. This shift is likely due to the exclusion of US and Canadian government websites, which generally do not display consent notices. As a result, the model increasingly relies on website category rather than origin to explain compliance patterns. Figure 5 also shows that US websites are more likely to comply with Californian requirements than EU websites. Similarly, UK websites are more likely than EU websites to comply with these requirements, but only when all UK websites are considered. When restricting the analysis to websites for which all Californian requirements apply, UK websites show lower compliance. This discrepancy may stem from differences in geolocation-based requirements, such as US10 and US13, where websites requesting geolocation data may fail to display "Do Not Sell" links or other CCPA-mandated information. Canadian websites consistently exhibit lower compliance with Californian requirements than EU websites.

Compliance with Canadian requirements depends more on website category than origin, with government websites being significantly more compliant than news and e-commerce sites. CA01, CA03, and CA04 show near-universal compliance (see [60]), while CA02 and CA05 show most variations. CA02 assesses whether advertising or social media cookies persist after opting out. Government websites, which rarely use ads, have fewer violations, whereas news and e-commerce sites often rely on third-party

---

[3] The pseudo R-squared values vary across models. For models assessing compliance with EU, UK, and Canadian requirements, values range from 0.12 to 0.23, indicating a moderate explanatory capacity. In contrast, models evaluating compliance with Californian requirements have pseudo R-squared values between 0.50 and 0.55, reflecting a stronger fit.

opt-out mechanisms, which set opt-out cookies that CookieBlock classifies as advertising cookies, leading to violations. CA05 identifies third-party cookies disguised as first-party cookies, often for analytics. Government websites use fewer analytics cookies, leading to higher compliance, while news and e-commerce sites frequently deploy such trackers, making category a strong predictor of CA05 compliance.

To better understand compliance with EU and UK requirements, we analyzed individual GDPR consent aspects. The results are shown in Fig. 6 for the EU; the ones for the UK are similar. Regression coefficients for this analysis are provided in [60].[4] The results highlight differences in compliance with specific consent aspects based on website origin and category. News websites are more likely to violate requirements for freely given consent but perform better in informing users. These patterns remain consistent across datasets, except in models addressing unambiguous consent. This could be explained by the fact that websites cannot request consent ambiguously if they do not request consent at all.

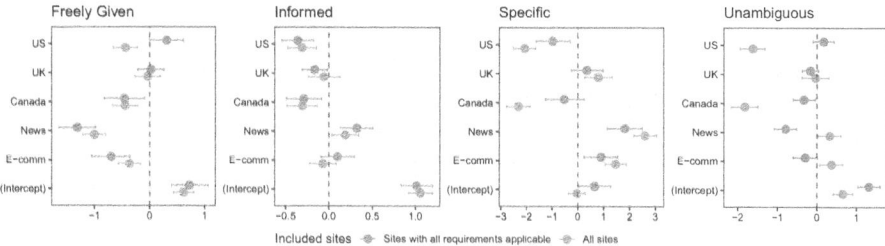

Fig. 6. Regression coefficients of the observed variables w.r.t. the compliance ratio with EU requirements for GDPR consent aspects.

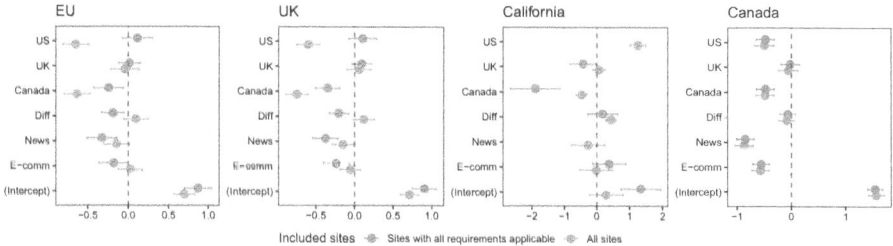

Fig. 7. Regression coefficients of the observed variables w.r.t. the compliance ratio (Model 3). Plot titles indicate the region of visit.

---

[4] The pseudo R-squared values for these models vary considerably. Models including all websites range from 0.04 to 0.47. When considering only websites for which all requirements apply, values range from 0.12 to 0.23. The lower fit in informed consent models for all websites is likely due to the inclusion of websites without consent notices, which inherently fail to inform users.

ANSWER TO RQ2. The compliance of websites with privacy laws varies by origin and category, with North American websites less compliant with EU and UK regulations but more aligned with Californian laws. Commercial websites, especially news and e-commerce, show lower compliance, as their reliance on tracking and third-party services often leads to violations. These findings suggest that compliance is driven by legal risks and business practices rather than uniform standards, highlighting the need for stronger enforcement measures where compliance is low.

4.3   RQ 3: Relation Between Differences in Privacy Interfaces and Compliance

Figure 7 presents the results of the regression analysis examining the relationship between the use of different privacy interfaces when accessing the website from different locations and compliance with requirements; coefficients are reported in [60].[5] For each region, the plot shows the results when considering all websites and when considering only the websites for which all requirements from that region apply.

For EU and UK requirements, we find that websites exhibiting a different consent notice are less likely to comply when analyzing only those where all requirements are applicable. This relationship, however, becomes insignificant when considering all websites, possibly because the broader set includes, for instance, websites inaccessible from certain regions, thus inevitably exhibiting a different behavior when accessed from different regions. To further analyze this correlation, we investigated compliance with EU and UK requirements at the level of individual GDPR consent aspects. Figure 8 shows the results for the EU; we refer to [60] for the results for the UK and coefficients.[6] The use of different privacy interfaces positively correlates with consent being freely given and specific, but no significant relationship is found for informed consent. Across all websites, we observe a positive relationship. However, when focusing only on sites where all requirements apply, we find that consent requests tend to be more ambiguous. This may be because sites that do not request consent at all cannot do so ambiguously.

For Californian requirements, significant correlations are only observed when considering all websites. This may be because requirements US10 and US13 are inapplicable if geolocation information is not requested. Nonetheless, the positive relationship between differences and compliance when considering all websites suggests that differences may directly influence compliance with Californian law. Higher compliance among websites showing different privacy interfaces may reflect characteristics of websites subject to the CCPA. Websites operated by larger organizations, which have stronger incentives to comply with privacy laws, may tailor privacy options based on visitor locations, displaying only region-specific choices.

For Canadian requirements, the presence of a difference in the displayed privacy interface does not significantly impact compliance rates. This aligns with earlier findings: news and e-commerce websites are more likely to have differences (Sect. 4.1),

---

[5] The pseudo R^2 values range from 0.15 to 0.23 for EU, UK, and Canadian requirements and from 0.54 to 0.56 for Californian requirements, indicating a stronger relationship for California.

[6] The pseudo R-squared values range from 0.04 to 0.13 for informed consent and from 0.16 to 0.52 for the other consent aspects, suggesting reasonable fits except for informed consent.

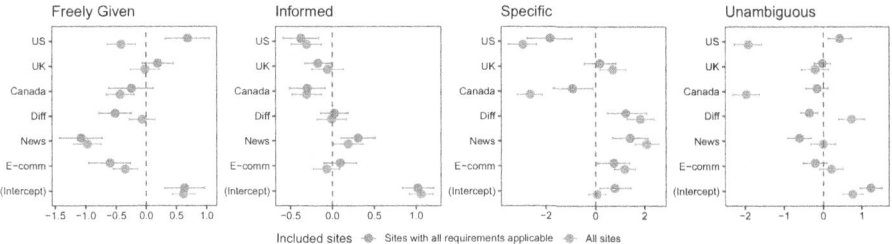

Fig. 8. Regression coefficients of the observed variables w.r.t. the compliance ratio with EU requirements for GDPR consent aspects.

while government websites are more likely to comply with Canadian requirements (Sect. 4.2). This suggests that differences may act as a confounding variable for website categories rather than directly determining compliance. Additionally, the limited number of Canadian requirements could contribute to the weak relationship, as discussed in Sect. 4.2.

ANSWER TO RQ3. Websites presenting different privacy interfaces to visitors from different regions are not necessarily more likely to comply with privacy regulations. While differences are linked to higher compliance with Californian requirements, they are associated with lower compliance in the EU and UK and show no significant impact in Canada. These findings suggest that organizations should focus on meeting legal requirements directly rather than relying on region-specific consent interfaces, as their adoption alone does not necessarily imply compliance.

5 Discussion

Extraterritoriality of Privacy Laws: Regulations such as the GDPR and CCPA apply extraterritorially, based on the data subject's location rather than that of the data controller or processor. However, websites generally comply more with regulations from their country of origin (cf. Sect. 4.2). One reason could be that organizations prioritize laws that can be enforced against them. If a company has no offices, employees, or assets in a jurisdiction, enforcement may be difficult, reducing the incentive to comply. Another factor is uncertainty about extraterritorial laws, as organizations may wrongly assume these do not apply to them. Clearer regulatory guidance is needed to address these challenges, particularly for businesses operating across jurisdictions. Regulators could provide more accessible interpretations of privacy laws, while researchers could identify ambiguities in their application. At the same time, regulators need automated detection to help streamline compliance monitoring, allowing them to identify violations more efficiently and expand monitoring efforts beyond manual investigations.

Websites' Perception of Privacy: Although EU privacy regulations are often 'exported' to other countries [57], a phenomenon known as the Brussels effect [7], our findings show that organizations tailor privacy options to visitors' locations instead of applying the strictest standards globally. This suggests the Brussels effect may be weaker than previously thought and that many organizations treat privacy primarily as a compliance requirement rather than a user right. This lack of incentive is further supported by [30], which found that most websites notified about potential GDPR non-compliance in their cookie banners neither responded nor updated their interfaces, reflecting limited willingness to improve their privacy practices. Future work could explore this further to identify incentives that encourage organizations to offer stronger privacy protections.

Standardization of Privacy Information & Options: Our investigation suggests that privacy laws with detailed requirements such as the CCPA promote the consistent adoption of a standardized interface, whereas general regulations such as the GDPR lead to significant variation in interfaces, potentially hindering users' decision-making and complicating compliance. European regulators should consider stricter guidelines on presenting privacy information and options. Standardized icons (as explored by e.g. [29,31], or as currently mandated by CCPA [63, § 7015(b)]) or machine-readable privacy information could improve user understanding and better align privacy practices with GDPR's intent.

Compliance Frameworks: During data collection, we observed that many websites create their privacy interfaces using consent management platforms (CMPs) from a small group of vendors (Table 9). The choice of CMP often dictates aspects of the privacy interface, including button placement, text, and font size. Since these elements affect compliance, CMPs can significantly influence a website's compliance ratio. Future work could examine how CMP vendors affect compliance rates; additionally, analyzing the effect on compliance of CMP configuration options could help vendors refine their tools and guide organizations in configuring CMPs to better align with privacy requirements. This discussion is particularly relevant in the context of the IAB Europe Transparency & Consent Framework (TCF) industry standard. While the TCF specifies required privacy information [33], it allows flexibility in presentation. Greater standardization by industry organizations could enhance the accessibility and usability of privacy interfaces.

Table 9. Results of a preliminary analysis of the CMP vendors used on websites. The analysis does not account for websites that use multiple CMPs simultaneously.

CMP vendor	Number of websites
Didomi	31
Google Funding Choices	21
InMobi	27
OneTrust	72
Sourcepoint	32

5.1 Threats to Validity

Construct Validity. Our interpretation of laws such as the GDPR and CCPA may introduce biases in defining compliance requirements. For example, while the CCPA mandates disclosure using predefined categories, we accepted similar descriptions, which may have been too lenient. Conversely, our strict interpretation of GDPR rules on legitimate interests for commercial purposes may be overly rigid in light of recent court rulings [11]. While these factors could affect specific assessments, most requirements were derived from literature, ensuring overall robustness. Another limitation is the use of a compliance ratio that weighs all requirements equally, regardless of their significance or frequency of violation. Future research should explore more nuanced compliance metrics to enhance result reliability.

Internal Validity. A threat to internal validity concerns the collection and classification of cookies. Distinguishing third-party cookies from those originating through external mechanisms (e.g., opt-out tools) is challenging. Additionally, reliance on CookieBlock for categorization introduces a risk of misclassification, potentially leading to incorrect compliance assessments. Another threat arises from using VPN services to simulate visitor locations. Websites may misidentify user locations, though we observed only one such case, suggesting minimal impact. Determining CCPA applicability posed challenges due to inconsistent corporate records and revenue estimates. When official figures were unavailable, we relied on secondary sources, which may be inaccurate. Additionally, using parent company revenues may have led to overestimation, as CCPA aggregation rules apply only to commonly branded entities [64, § 1798.140(d)(2)]. Finally, despite our verification efforts (cf. Sects. 3.2 and 3.3), a few misclassifications may have persisted; for instance, some political news websites were misclassified as government websites, affecting compliance assessments, particularly under the CCPA.

External Validity. Our dataset of 535 websites may be too small to generalize our findings. Additionally, since we focus on popular websites, our results may not fully represent the broader Internet. Expanding our dataset, potentially through automation, could improve representativeness. Furthermore, some organizations, such as the Canadian federal government and British news publisher Reach plc, have multiple websites in our corpus. Since these sites often share privacy policies, their overrepresentation may skew observed trends, reflecting institutional practices rather than broader industry patterns.

6 Conclusion

This study investigated the differences in privacy interfaces when websites are accessed from different regions and their impact on compliance with privacy laws. To this end, we identified a set of requirements for assessing websites' compliance with privacy laws from the EU, the UK, California, and Canada. We conducted a study evaluating the compliance of 535 websites with these requirements, simulating visits from the countries where the laws were enacted. Our findings revealed that approximately 25% of websites displayed regional differences, which were more common among non-EU websites compared to EU websites. Moreover, nearly all websites violated at least one requirement. Websites with region-specific privacy interfaces were less likely to meet EU and UK requirements but were more likely to comply with Californian regulations, while no significant relationship was observed for Canadian requirements. Additionally, North American websites showed lower compliance with EU and UK requirements but higher compliance with the CCPA compared to EU websites. Future work should focus on expanding the dataset to include more websites, enhancing the scalability and reliability of compliance assessments. Further research could also explore the motivations and incentives that drive privacy compliance, offering insights on how to improve regulatory practices.

References

1. Art. 29 Data Protection Working Party. Op. 04/2012 on Cookie Consent Exemption (2012)
2. Art. 29 Data Protection Working Party. Guidelines on transparency for Reg. 2016/679 (2018)
3. Bekh, A.: Advertising-based revenue model in digital media market. Econviews: Review of Contemporary Entrepreneurship, Business, and Economic Issues, 33(2), 547–559 (2020)
4. Berens, B.M., Dietmann, H., Krisam, C., Kulyk, O., Volkamer, M.: Cookie Disclaimers: Impact of Design and Users' Attitude. In: ARES. ACM (2022)
5. Bermejo Fernandez, C., Chatzopoulos, D., Papadopoulos, D., Hui, P.: This Website Uses Nudging: MTurk Workers' Behaviour on Cookie Consent Notices. In: HCI. ACM (2021)
6. Bollinger, D., Kubicek, K., Cotrini, C., Basin, D.: Automating Cookie Consent and GDPR Violation Detection. In: USENIX Security Symposium, pp. 2893–2910 (2022)
7. Bradford, A.: The Brussels Effect. Northwest. Univ. Law Rev. **107**(1), 1–67 (2012)
8. Brignull, H.: Dark Patterns: User Interfaces Designed to Trick People (2010)
9. Brignull, H.: Dark Patterns: Deception vs. Honesty in UI Design (2011)
10. Canadian Radio-television and Telecommunications Commission. Canada's Anti-Spam Legislation Requirements for Installing Computer Programs (2020)
11. Court of Justice of the European Union. Koninklijke Nederlandse Lawn Tennisbond v Autoriteit Persoonsgegevens. ECLI:EU:C:2024:857 (2024)
12. Dabrowski, A., Merzdovnik, G., Ullrich, J., Sendera, G., Weippl, E.: Measuring Cookies and Web Privacy in a Post-GDPR World. In: PAM, pp. 258–270. Springer (2019)
13. EDPB. Guidelines 2/2019 on the processing of personal data under Article 6(1)(b) GDPR in the context of the provision of online services to data subjects (2019)
14. EDPB. Guidelines 05/2020 on consent under Regulation 2016/679 (2020)
15. EDPB. Guidelines 4/2019 on Article 25 Data Protection by Design and by Default (2020)
16. EDPB. Report of the work undertaken by the Cookie Banner Taskforce (2023)
17. EDPB (European Data Protection Board). Deceptive design patterns in social media platform interfaces: how to recognise and avoid them (2023)
18. v. Eijk, R., Asghari, H., Winter, P., Narayanan, A.: The Impact of User Location on Cookie Notices (Inside and Outside of the European Union). In: ConPro (2019)
19. European Parliament and Council of the European Union. Directive 2002/58/EC concerning the processing of personal data and the protection of privacy in the electronic communications sector (Directive on privacy and electronic communications) (2002)
20. European Parliament and Council of the European Union. Regulation (EU) 2016/679 on the protection of natural persons with regard to the processing of personal data and on the free movement of such data, and repealing Directive 95/46/EC (GDPR) (2016)
21. European Parliament and Council of the European Union. Regulation (EU) 2016/679 on the protection of natural persons with regard to the processing of personal data and on the free movement of such data (UK GDPR) (2016)

22. European Parliament and Council of the European Union. Reg. (EU) 2022/2065 on a Single Market For Digital Services and amending Directive 2000/31/EC (Digital Services Act) (2022)
23. European Parliament and Council of the European Union. Regulation (EU) 2022/1925 on contestable and fair markets in the digital sector and amending Directives (EU) 2019/1937 and (EU) 2020/1828 (Digital Markets Act) (2022)
24. Gray, C.M., Kou, Y., Battles, B., Hoggatt, J., Toombs, A.L.: The Dark (Patterns) Side of UX Design. In: Conference on Human Factors in Computing Systems, pp. 1–14. ACM (2018)
25. Gray, C.M., Santos, C., Bielova, N., Toth, M., Clifford, D.: Dark patterns and the legal requirements of consent banners: an interaction criticism perspective. In: Conference on Human Factors in Computing Systems. ACM (2021)
26. Gunawan, J., Pradeep, A., Choffnes, D., Hartzog, W., Wilson, C.: A comparative study of dark patterns across web and mobile modalities. ACM Hum.-Comput. Interact., 5 (2021)
27. Gundelach, R., Herrmann, D.: Cookiescanner: an automated tool for detecting and evaluating GDPR consent notices on websites. In: ARES. ACM (2023)
28. Habib, H., Li, M., Young, E., Cranor, L.: "Okay, whatever": an evaluation of cookie consent interfaces. In: Conference on Human Factors in Computing Systems. ACM (2022)
29. Habib, H., et al.: Toggles, Dollar Signs, and Triangles: How to (In)Effectively Convey Privacy Choices with Icons and Link Texts. In: Conference on Human Factors in Computing Systems. ACM (2021)
30. Hennig, A., Dietmann, H., Lehr, F., Mutter, M., Volkamer, M., Mayer, P.: Your Cookie Disclaimer is Not in Line with the Ideas of the GDPR. Why? In: Human Aspects of Information Security and Assurance, pp. 218–227. Springer (2022)
31. Holtz, L.-E., Zwingelberg, H., Hansen, M.: Privacy policy icons. In: Privacy and Identity Management for Life, pp. 279–285. Springer (2011)
32. Hutto, C., Gilbert, E.: VADER: a parsimonious rule-based model for sentiment analysis of social media text. Internat. AAAI Conf. on Web and Social Media, vol. 8(1), 216–225 (2014)
33. IAB Europe. TCF Standardisation Principles
34. kairi003. Get cookies.txt LOCALLY (2024)
35. Khandelwal, R., Nayak, A., Harkous, H., Fawaz, K.: Automated cookie notice analysis and enforcement. In: USENIX Security Symposium, USENIX Association (2023)
36. Kirkman, D., Vaniea, K., Woods, D.W.: DarkDialogs: automated detection of 10 dark patterns on cookie dialogs. In: EuroS&P, pp. 847–867. IEEE (2023)
37. K. Kollnig, R. Binns, M. Van Kleek, U. Lyngs, J. Zhao, C. Tinsman, and N. Shadbolt. Before and After GDPR: Tracking in Mobile Apps. *Internet Policy Review*, 10(4), 2021
38. Kollnig, K., et al.: A fait accompli? an empirical study into the absence of consent to third-party tracking in android apps. In: SOUP, pp. 181–196. USENIX Association (2021)
39. Matte, C., Bielova, N., Santos, C.: Do cookie banners respect my choice? measuring legal compliance of banners from IAB Europe's transparency and consent framework. In: IEEE Symposium on Security and Privacy, pp. 791–809 (2020)
40. Müller, S., Goswami, S., Krcmar, H.: Monetizing Blogs: Revenue Streams of Individual Blogs. In: European Conf. on Information Systems (2011)
41. National Cancer Institute. Simplification of Informed Consent Documents - Recomms (2006)
42. Nguyen, T.T., Backes, M., Marnau, N., Stock, B.: Share First, Ask Later (or Never?) Studying Violations of GDPR's Explicit Consent in Android Apps. In: USENIX Security Symposium, pp. 3667–3684. USENIX Association (2021)
43. Nguyen, T.T., Backes, M., Stock, B.: Freely given consent? studying consent notice of third-party tracking and its violations of GDPR in android apps. In: SIGSAC Conference on Computer and Communications Security, pp. 2369–2383. ACM (2022)
44. Office of the Attorney General of the State of California. California Consumer Privacy Act (CCPA) (2023)

45. Office of the Privacy Commissioner of Canada. Policy position on online behavioural advertising (2021)
46. Paci, F., Pizzoli, J., Zannone, N.: A comprehensive study on third-party user tracking in mobile applications. ACM, In ARES (2023)
47. Papadogiannakis, E., Papadopoulos, P., Kourtellis, N., Markatos, E.P.: User Tracking in the Post-cookie Era: How Websites Bypass GDPR Consent to Track Users. In: The Web Conference, pp. 2130–2141. ACM (2021)
48. Parliament of Canada. Personal Information Protection and Electronic Documents Act – Exemptions for Organizations in Alberta, British Columbia, and Quebec and for Personal Health Information Custodians in New Brunswick, Newfoundland, Labrador, and Nova Scotia. https://laws-lois.justice.gc.ca/eng/acts/P-8.6/ (2000)
49. Parliament of Canada. Personal Information Protection and Electronic Documents Act (2019)
50. Parliament of Canada. An Act to promote the efficiency and adaptability of the Canadian economy by regulating certain activities that discourage reliance on electronic means of carrying out commercial activities, and to amend the Canadian Radio-television and Telecommunications Commission Act, the Competition Act, the Personal Information Protection and Electronic Documents Act and the Telecommunications Act (2023)
51. Parliament of Canada. Privacy Act (2023)
52. Parliament of the United Kingdom of Great Britain and Northern Ireland. European Union (Withdrawal) Act 2018 (2018)
53. Privacy Community Group. Global Privacy Control - Take Control Of Your Privacy
54. Rasaii, A., Singh, S., Gosain, D., Gasser, O.: Exploring the Cookieverse: A Multi-Perspective Analysis of Web Cookies. In: PAM, pp. 623–651. Springer (2023)
55. Santos, C., Bielova, N., Matte, C.: Are cookie banners indeed compliant with the law? Deciphering EU legal requirements on consent and technical means to verify compliance of cookie banners. Technology and Regulation, pp. 91–135 (2020)
56. Santos, C., Rossi, A., Sanchez Chamorro, L., Bongard-Blanchy, K., Abu-Salma, R.: Cookie Banners, What's the Purpose? Analyzing Cookie Banner Text Through a Legal Lens. In *Workshop on Privacy in the Electronic Society*, WPES '21, pp. 187–194. ACM (2021)
57. Scott, M., Cerulus, L.: Europe's new data protection rules export privacy standards worldwide (2018)
58. Secretary of State of the United Kingdom of Great Britain and Northern Ireland. The Data Protection, Privacy and Electronic Communications (Amendments, EU Exit) Reg. 2019 (2020)
59. Secretary of State of the United Kingdom of Great Britain and Northern Ireland. The Privacy and Electronic Communications (EC Directive) Regulations 2003 (2020)
60. Smeets, X.: Do websites truly value your privacy? An analysis of privacy requirement compliance among websites differing between jurisdictions. Master's thesis, Eindhoven University of Technology (2024)
61. Soe, T.H., Nordberg, O.E., Guribye, F., Slavkovik, M.: Circumvention by design - dark patterns in cookie consent for online news outlets. ACM, In NordiCHI (2020)
62. Software Freedom Conservancy. Selenium (2024)
63. State of California. California Code of Regulations - Title 11, Division 6, Chapter 1 - California Consumer Privacy Act Regulations
64. State of California. California Consumer Privacy Act of 2018 (2018)
65. State of California. California Privacy Rights Act of 2020 (2020)
66. Ur, B., Leon, P.G., Cranor, L.F., Shay, R., Wang, Y.: Smart, useful, scary, creepy: perceptions of online behavioral advertising. ACM, In Symposium on Usable Privacy and Security (2012)

67. Utz, C., Degeling, M., Fahl, S., Schaub, F., Holz, T.: (Un)informed Consent: Studying GDPR Consent Notices in the Field. In: CCS, pp. 973–990. ACM (2019)
68. van Nortwick, M., Wilson, C.: Setting the bar low: are websites complying with the minimum requirements of the CCPA? In: PoPETs Proceedings, pp. 608–628 (2022)
69. Walters, K.A., Hamrell, M.R.: Consent Forms, Lower Reading Levels, and Using Flesch-Kincaid Readability Software. Drug information journal: DIJ / Drug Information Association **42**(4), 385–394 (2008). https://doi.org/10.1177/009286150804200411
70. Yayla, A., Dincelli, E., Parameswaran, S.: A Mining Town in a Digital Land: Browser-Based Cryptocurrency Mining as an Alternative to Online Advertising. Information Systems Frontiers (2023)
71. Zanfir-Fortuna, G.: Planet49 CJEU Judgment brings some 'Cookie Consent' Certainty to Planet Online Tracking (2019)

Network and Communication Security

On the Feasibility of Fingerprinting Collaborative Robot Network Traffic

Cheng Tang$^{(\boxtimes)}$, Diogo Barradas, Urs Hengartner, and Yue Hu

University of Waterloo, Waterloo, Canada
{c225tang,dbarrada,urs.hengartner,yue.hu}@uwaterloo.ca

Abstract. This study examines privacy risks in collaborative robotics, focusing on the potential for traffic analysis in encrypted robot communications. While previous research has explored low-level command recovery in teleoperation setups, our work investigates high-level motion recovery from script-based control interfaces. We evaluate the efficacy of prominent website fingerprinting techniques (e.g., Tik-Tok, RF) and their limitations in accurately identifying robotic actions due to their inability to capture detailed temporal relationships. To address this, we introduce a traffic classification approach using signal processing techniques, demonstrating high accuracy in action identification and highlighting the vulnerability of encrypted communications to privacy breaches. Additionally, we explore defenses such as packet padding and timing manipulation, revealing the challenges in balancing traffic analysis resistance with network efficiency. Our findings emphasize the need for continued development of practical defenses in robotic privacy and security.

Keywords: Encrypted traffic analysis · Privacy · Robot teleoperation

1 Introduction

In recent years, robotics has rapidly evolved to become an integral part of many industries and domains, including manufacturing, healthcare, transportation, and even personal use, in a fully autonomous fashion or shared-control fashion such as teleoperation [21]. Among the recent trends in robotic applications, the healthcare and service sectors have seen increased options, thanks to the advent of collaborative robots, i.e., robots intended for close contact with humans [26]. In this context, examples of robotic applications such as surgical assistants [15] bring benefits such as increased dexterity and precision [16], and applications in home assistance [41] guarantee independent living and healthy aging.

However, the integration of robotics in direct interaction with humans also introduces significant privacy concerns [34]. The continuous communication between robots and control interfaces, often encrypted yet susceptible to traffic analysis (i.e., the examination of communication metadata like the volume of communication or the frequency of packet exchanges), can enable malicious actors to infer critical information about end users (e.g. a patient's health status, medical procedures being performed, or daily routines in care settings). Such breaches not only pose risks to individual privacy but can also compromise trust in adopting robotic systems. The privacy threat is not just a matter of unauthorized data access; it extends to the potential misuse of sensitive information, which can have far-reaching implications for end-users and service providers [11].

Previous work [34] has begun exploring the potential leakage of robotic operations through the analysis of encrypted traffic, focusing on the recovery of low-level commands sent to a robot via the analysis of features such as packet lengths and inter-arrival times. While prior research is tailored to robots controlled by teleoperation interfaces and to the classification of low-level motions via deep learning, we employ signal processing to extract command messages in script-based robot control interfaces. By classifying actions based on temporal dependencies via classical machine learning, our model requires few data samples and could potentially be more easily extended across various robotic systems.

We study potential threats arising from traffic analysis in robotic operations, focusing our analysis on the traffic generated by collaborative robots. We start by leveraging established traffic analysis techniques used in the related domain of website fingerprinting, such as k-FP [19] or Tik-Tok [31], to extract features from our network traces and classify robot actions. However, we find that these methods are unable to account for detailed temporal relationships between sequences of command messages, critical for identifying robotic actions (Sect. 5).

To address these shortcomings, we introduce a novel traffic classification approach based on signal processing techniques (Sect. 6). Our core insight is that distinct robot operation commands generate specific traffic sub-patterns, which can be accurately identified through the application of signal correlation and convolution techniques. Further, we develop and evaluate custom traffic analysis defenses for robot operations. Inspired by existing techniques, we implement two metadata obfuscation mechanisms: padding and packet timing manipulation. We analyze the performance overhead of different defense configurations and assess their effectiveness in mitigating traffic analysis.

In our evaluation, we conduct experiments over a network traffic dataset comprising four robotic actions that were manually generated. The results of our experiments show that our signal processing-based classification technique is able to identify these actions with an accuracy of 97%, thus revealing that adversaries might be able to infer sensitive robotic actions from encrypted network traffic alone. In turn, our experiments with traffic analysis defenses suggest that balancing traffic analysis resistance with network efficiency is challenging in practical settings, casting the need for additional work towards the development of practical defenses that can be widely applied to the robot operation scenario.

2   Background

2.1   Control Interfaces in Robotics

Robotic control interfaces primarily fall into two categories: script-based control and teleoperation, each generating distinct traffic patterns with privacy implications, particularly in encrypted communication settings. Our focus is on script-based control, which is particularly relevant to collaborative robotics.

Script-Based Control. In this model, robots execute predefined scripts that automate tasks with minimal human intervention. The controller sends structured command messages, and the robot executes them accordingly. For example, a domestic robot may be programmed to open curtains at a set time or sort recyclables from trash. These scripts, written in programming languages or proprietary software, define task logic that has evolved from simple sequences to complex behaviors influenced by perception, probabilistic decision-making, and machine learning. Commands are transmitted from the controller to the robot's onboard computer, which executes actions and generates feedback. This feedback–such as vision, location, or object classification–is sent back to the controller and influences subsequent commands. For instance, in a pick-and-place task, the feedback helps determine grasp adjustments or movement corrections.

Teleoperation. This interface allows human control of robots through real-time mimicry or high-level command execution, but relies on human input for online adjustments. It uses devices like joysticks or VR interfaces to translate human actions into robotic movements, with feedback (e.g., sensory data, video) aiding the operator's situational awareness. Unlike script-based control, where feedback informs automated planning, teleoperation relies on human interpretation.

Privacy Implications. Both control modalities produce structured network traffic that can be analyzed to infer robotic tasks or operator intent. In script-based control, adversaries may identify routine procedures by analyzing patterns in command sequences, while in teleoperation, they may infer operator actions based on message timing and frequency. In sensitive applications like healthcare, recurring message patterns could indicate medical routines, while specific sensory data exchanges might reveal patient information or caregiving activities. In our work, we focus on fingerprinting the network traffic generated by a specific collaborative robot (the Kinova Gen3 arm, described below), which can autonomously execute a series of high-level commands via script-based control.

2.2   The Kinova Robotic Arm and APIs

Figure 2 illustrates the Kinova Gen 3 robotic arm, a commercially available robotic arm, accessible to industry, research institutions, and also individual consumers. It is utilized in healthcare and research contexts [10,17,30], providing a rich API with protocols, functions, and libraries for high-level and low-level control. Communication with the Kinova Gen 3 robotic arm is secured using encrypted channels (e.g., TLS) to ensure data integrity and confidentiality.

High-level API Controls. The high-level API abstracts robotic movements, allowing developers to issue complex commands with ease. For example, in a "pick and place" task, the robot's controller sends a structured sequence of movement commands to navigate to an object, followed by gripper commands to grasp, transport, and release it. These high-level commands generate uniform and consistent network traffic patterns (see Sect. 4), as each command maps to a predictable sequence of movements and corresponding data packets.

Low-level API Controls. Low-level controls provide granular access to individual joints, real-time sensor feedback, and custom control algorithms. In tasks like picking and placing, this allows precise wrist and finger adjustments for accurate object handling. Since these controls rely on frequent adjustments and feedback loops, they introduce greater variability in network traffic, as each sensor reading and movement adjustment contributes to a more dynamic packet flow.

Privacy Implications. The interaction between the controller and the Kinova arm generates network traffic patterns that can inadvertently reveal operational details. High-level API controls share similarities with script-based control methods (see Sect. 2.1), as both rely on predefined command sequences that shape network traffic patterns. While high-level APIs abstract robot interactions, the potential for traffic analysis and privacy risks remain comparable to those observed in script-based control. Throughout our study, we focus on fingerprinting the network traffic generated by the Kinova Gen3 arm when controlling it via scripts that rely on the arm's high-level API controls, as these facilitate the analysis of command sequences for abstract and complex tasks.

2.3   Encrypted Traffic Fingerprinting

Encrypted traffic fingerprinting denotes a traffic analysis technique based on the examination of the metadata of encrypted traffic [1,14]. By inspecting traffic characteristics like overall communication volume, packet sizes, or inter-packet timing, an eavesdropper can build a profile of the network behavior of some Internet-based application under a given workload (i.e., a traffic *fingerprint*), and then re-identify the occurrence of the same workload by matching its fingerprint.

While we now address earlier efforts aimed at fingerprinting robot traffic, we refer to Sect. 9 for a broader perspective about other traffic fingerprinting contexts (e.g., website [37], video [33], and IoT [9] fingerprinting).

Reconstruction of Robot Operations from Encrypted Traffic. Shah et al. [34] discuss reconstructing robot high-level movements from lower-level movements in teleoperation scenarios, where an operator directly controls the robot using a movement controller. This approach contrasts with our focus, which lies on script-based applications and reconstructing traffic patterns by analyzing sequences of command messages. Shah et al.'s methodology, which employs a simple neural network with a single hidden layer to analyze encrypted traffic data for identifying robot movements and reconstructing workflows, is tailored to teleoperated systems with a dynamic operator control. This differs from our context of scripted robotic actions, making their approach not directly applicable to our experiments due to the distinct setups involved.

3   Methodology

This section describes our evaluation methodology. First, we describe our threat model and our experimental testbed. Then, we detail the metrics used to evaluate the success of attacks and defenses applied to robot control traffic.

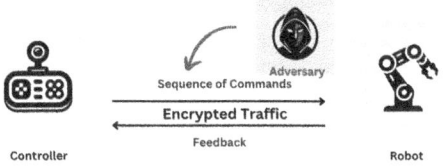

Fig. 1. Depiction of our threat model.

3.1   Threat Model

Our threat model is illustrated in Fig. 1, where an adversary is assumed to passively listen to the communication between a robot and its controller. As an example, considering a healthcare scenario, the robot could be located in a user's home while being remotely controlled by an operator within a hospital facility. **Fingerprinting Setting.** The adversary's goal is to identify the robot's actions by analyzing traffic patterns generated during control operations, including the exchange of commands and feedback. Beyond recognizing actions, the adversary may also seek to infer fine-grained details, such as the exact commands enabling a given action. These insights could allow near real-time activity prediction.

In general, traffic fingerprinting attacks assume either a *closed-* or *open-world* setting [37], depending on the adversary's knowledge. In the *closed-world* setting, which we assume, the adversary knows that the robot is only able to perform a restricted set of actions (monitored set), and aims to identify which of these actions has been performed. In sensitive healthcare environments, repeated command patterns linked to a concrete set of medical procedures could inadvertently reveal patient-specific information. For instance, a sequence of actions unique to a particular therapy may expose a patient's treatment regimen.

Adversary's Capabilities. We assume that the adversary has the following main capabilities: First, the adversary has their own robot and controller, whose model/version is identical to the one used by the target user. This allows the adversary to use its own robot (and unrestricted API access) to study traffic patterns. This level of access provides them with a comprehensive understanding of potential traffic patterns, thus offering them a strategic advantage in predicting and interpreting traffic flows. Second, the adversary has the capability to eavesdrop the traffic exchanged between the robot and its controller, e.g., by wiretapping the Internet connections of a given household [13]. Third, the adversary can use multiple techniques to analyze traffic flows towards generating features that can help characterize traffic traces (e.g., deriving summary statistics or well-defined patterns through signal processing operations). Finally, the adversary can use machine learning techniques for helping it interpret the command sequences issued to the robot and identify actions issued via the controller.

We also assume that the adversary is limited in its operation. Specifically, the adversary is unable to break the cryptographic primitives used for securing the control channel, and the adversary has no control over the endpoints engaged in communication–thus, both the controller and the robotic arm are trusted.

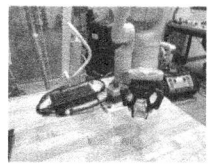 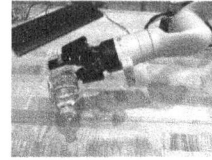 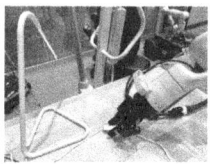 

(a) Pick and place.   (b) Pour water.   (c) Turn on switch.   (d) Press key.

Fig. 2. The Kinova robotic arm executing four actions.

3.2 Experimental Setup

Hardware and Software Configuration. Our experiments leverage a Kinova Robotic Arm Gen3 [22], which remotely receives commands and returns feedback to a workstation acting as a controller. This workstation runs Ubuntu 20.04 LTS and is configured with a 2.40 GHz Intel Core i7-8700T CPU and 32 GB RAM. The workstation and the robotic arm are interconnected using Ethernet cabling to ensure a reliable communication. We use the Kinova API v2.3.0 for controlling the robotic arm and generating command patterns, configuring it to enable TLS-based encrypted communication between the robot and the controller. To capture the encrypted traffic exchanges between the robot and the controller for our analysis, we use `tcpdump` on the controller workstation.

Robot Actions Dataset. We obtain our dataset by collecting the network traces exchanged between the robot and its controller when instructing the robot to execute four distinct actions: a) picking up and placing an object, b) pouring water, c) turning on a switch, and d) pressing a key. Figure 2 provides a depiction of the robotic arm while performing each of these actions. The actions share a certain degree of similarity; for instance, both pouring water and turning on a switch involve fluid motions and subtle changes in the robot's articulation, which could be reflected in the traffic patterns as similar command message sequences, making it challenging to distinguish between them accurately. The duration of each trace also varies significantly across actions to capture cases where users might take different times to complete the same action. However, all our samples are bounded to a minimum and maximum completion time of 5 and 30 s.

We collect a total of 200 samples: 50 for each action. The robot executes actions according to a set of predefined rules that an operator (ourselves) writes in scripts. However, data collection depends on the robot's physical operation, which cannot be easily parallelized without additional robots (unavailable to us). The catalog of commands we execute includes different combinations of Cartesian motions (i.e., instructions to move the robot arm in a straight line along the X, Y, and Z axes), the opening/closing of a gripper claw, and adjustments of the gripper's speed. This flexibility allows us to capture a multitude of real-world *trajectories*, where different operators may script the completion of an identical task with a different number of high-level commands or change their order. Each action sample follows a unique trajectory, composed of sub-tasks (e.g., movement, object manipulation) executed at varying points in time. Sub-tasks differ in speed, waypoints, object locations, and task-specific parameters (e.g., pouring angles), enhancing trajectory diversity. We leave the exploration of automatic traffic sequence generation other approaches to generate command traffic sequences automatically (e.g., via GANs [42]) to future work.

Considered Traffic Analysis Attacks. For showcasing the potential threats of traffic analysis attacks on robot traffic, we leverage the open-source implementations of attacks used in the context of website fingerprinting (Sect. 5), including CUMUL [29], k-FP [19], Tik-Tok [31], and Robust Fingerprinting (RF) [35]. These attacks rely either on manually-engineered traffic features (CUMUL, k-FP), or latent features extracted via deep learning (Tik-Tok, RF).

Considered Traffic Analysis Defenses. We consider two defenses inspired by constant-rate padding approaches [5] (Sect. 7). The first involves padding individual packets to enforce uniform packet lengths. The second transmits fixed-size packets at a constant rate, potentially including dummy packets, while ensuring compliance with the scheduling constraints required for robot communication.

ML Models' Evaluation. The models employed in our study are trained and tested using stratified 10-fold cross-validation to mitigate the impacts of bias in the dataset. We refrain from using an additional validation set since we use all machine learning models with their default hyperparameter configurations.

3.3   Metrics

Attack Evaluation Metrics. We leverage accuracy as our main metric to assess attack performance. Accuracy is defined as the ratio of the number of correctly classified observations to the total number of observations. We also make use of confusion matrices to visualize attack performance across the multiple action classes by inspecting the distribution of correct and incorrect predictions.

Defense Evaluation Metrics. We primarily focus on two aspects: the reduction of an attack's *accuracy* (effectiveness), and the impact of the defense on the robot's performance (efficiency). We measure the efficiency of the defense through the *bandwidth utilization* and *latency increase* experienced by the robot's activities. To compute bandwidth utilization overheads, we compare the amount of additional data exchanged due to the defense. To compute latency impacts, we compute the delays introduced in the communication between the robot and the controller, and assess the potential impacts of such delays on the correct operation of the robot and its ability to complete a designated task.

4   Characterization of Robot Actions

In this section, we characterize the actions composing our dataset, showcasing both the inter-class and intra-class variability of the generated traffic traces.

Individual Commands have Stable Traffic Signatures. Figure 3 shows two different network traces for a Cartesian command and a gripper movement command, respectively. We can see that different executions of the same command result in similar traffic patterns, but that these patterns also differ amongst each

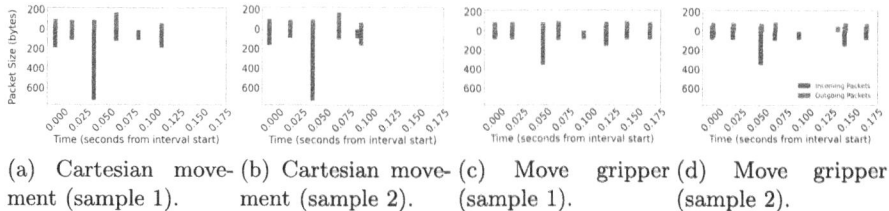

(a) Cartesian move-
ment (sample 1).
(b) Cartesian move-
ment (sample 2).
(c) Move gripper
(sample 1).
(d) Move gripper
(sample 2).

Fig. 3. Network traces for two kinds of commands.

different kind of command. Cartesian commands move the robot arm in 3D space
and typically span a shorter period of time compared to gripper position commands. These Cartesian movements usually elicit a longer feedback packet from
the robot arm, indicative of the arm's positional adjustments in a 3D space. In
contrast, gripper position command messages control the opening and closing of
the robot's gripper, and consist of packets just over 100 bytes in either direction.
Different Actions Result in Different Traffic Patterns. Figure 4 shows
example traffic patterns for the four classes of actions included in our dataset,
showcasing both incoming and outgoing traffic from the point of view of the
controller workstation. At a high level, we can see that each different action
generates a disparate traffic pattern. For instance, the pick and place action
(Fig. 2a) generally involves at least two distinct gripper command messages,
before and after the act of picking and placing an object. This is reflected in
the traffic as two dense clusters of gripper position or speed command messages,
indicating the gripper's motion to open and close. Despite the two actions being
markedly dissimilar, the traces generated by the pour water action (Fig. 2b)
exhibit some similarities tied to specific commands that instruct the closing of
the gripper to grab the bottle and opening it after pouring.

In turn, actions such as turning on a switch (Fig. 2c) or pressing a key
(Fig. 2d) involve a tapping motion, which requires the robot to close the gripper beforehand. These actions do not necessitate additional gripper motions but
it may open if required by subsequent tasks. The timing between Cartesian
command messages also provide information; tapping motions are usually swift,
leading to shorter intervals between command messages. Other details include
the observation of interleaved occurrence of different commands. For instance,

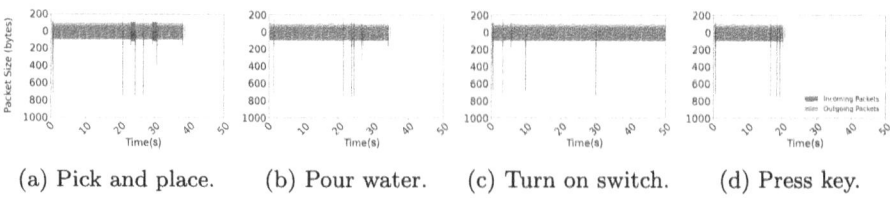

(a) Pick and place.   (b) Pour water.   (c) Turn on switch.   (d) Press key.

Fig. 4. Examples of robot actions' packet lengths over time.

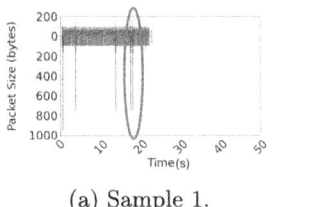 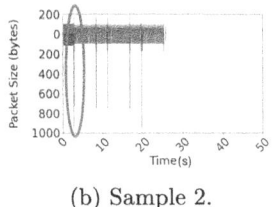

(a) Sample 1.   (b) Sample 2.

Fig. 5. Examples of two "turn on switch" network traffic traces.

in the pick and place action, we can observe the presence of Cartesian command message between two gripper command messages, as seen in Fig. 4c around the 25 s mark. These temporal dependencies that are characteristic to each action may provide actionable information for building an effective classifier.

Traffic Patterns for a Given Action are Highly Variable. Figure 5 presents two variations of the turn on switch action, showcasing that the traffic patterns for a given action can also be distinct and challenging to recognize by simple observation. The composition of individual commands sent to the robot can help us identify an action, such as the short period of time between two Cartesian commands, as circled green in Fig. 5a, and a gripper command (closing the gripper) at the start of the action to prepare for the tapping motion, immediately followed by a Cartesian command message, as circled in green in Fig. 5b.

The results of our characterization suggest that there are multiple sources of information in robot traces that may be leveraged for enabling their accurate classification. Next, we experiment with different traffic classification approaches and assess whether these enable the successful identification of robot actions.

5   Exploiting Known Attacks for Action Identification

Multiple classifiers have been proposed for traffic fingerprinting, with website fingerprinting being one of the most well-studied contexts. In this section, we outline how popular classifiers operate, explain their feature selection rationale, and evaluate their performance when fingerprinting robot operation traffic.

5.1   ML-Based Website Fingerprinting Attacks

We now describe four traffic analysis attacks used for website fingerprinting. **CUMUL** [29]. The features used in this attack include the number of incoming and outgoing packets, total bandwidth used in each direction. Additional features are drawn from the cumulative sum of packets' sizes at different instants of a trace. The attack uses a Support Vector Machine with an RBF kernel.

k-FP [19]. This attack combines features used in previous attacks with novel traffic characteristics, leading to a systematic analysis of 150 traffic features. The attack works by building a fingerprint for each web page using a modification of the Random Forest algorithm, and classifies them using k-Nearest Neighbors.

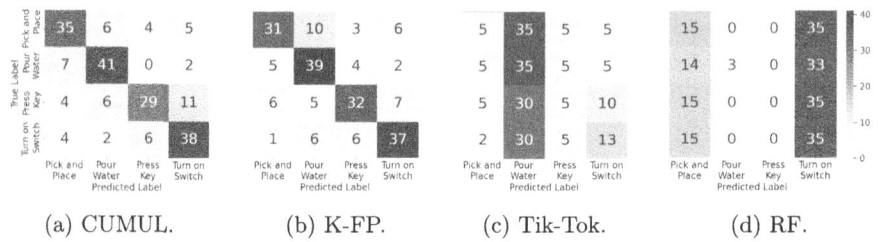

(a) CUMUL.   (b) K-FP.   (c) Tik-Tok.   (d) RF.

Fig. 6. Confusion matrices for website fingerprinting attacks on robot traffic.

Tik-Tok [31]. This attack builds-up on Deep Fingerprinting (DF) [37] and is based on a deep convolutional neural network (CNN) that extracts latent features from network traces to classify websites. Its input is based on a directional-timing representation of traffic, obtained by multiplying a packet's direction (incoming/outgoing represented as -1/+1) with its inter-packet arrival time.

Robust Fingerprinting (RF) [35]. This attack introduces a Traffic Aggregation Matrix (TAM), which divides network traffic into fixed-size time windows. It identifies website-specific traffic signatures by leveraging TAM's spatial structure to extract hierarchical patterns using a CNN-based classifier.

5.2   Attacking Robot Operation Traffic

We now present our main findings after applying the classifiers introduced above for attempting the identification of robot actions issued via the controller.

Existing Website Fingerprinting Attacks Fail to Identify Robot Actions. The attacks introduced in the previous section obtain a poor accuracy in identifying the robotic actions in our dataset. k-FP and CUMUL achieve accuracies of 69.5% and 71.5%, respectively, while models relying on deep learning, such as RF, struggle with limited data, performing only marginally better than random guessing. In particular, the Tik-Tok attack reaches just 29.0% accuracy, while RF attains 26.5%. Figure 6 illustrates the confusion matrices for each classifier.

Why Do These Attacks Fail? The relatively low performance of these attacks in identifying robot actions can be attributed to a set of fundamental differences in the nature of robotics traffic compared to web traffic. As we observed in Sect. 4, the robotic actions considered in our work generate highly variable traffic patterns with intricate temporal dependencies that may not be typically present in web traffic. Among these, we highlight nuanced variations in gripper speed and position commands, as well as specific timing intervals between Cartesian command messages. Our results suggest that these dynamic characteristics are not effectively captured by traditional website fingerprinting classifiers, failing to adequately capture local information in a trace, for example, the exact timing at which specific robot operation commands are placed.

What Can We Do About It? We argue that the presence of command-specific patterns in robotics traffic, such as visible instances of gripper command

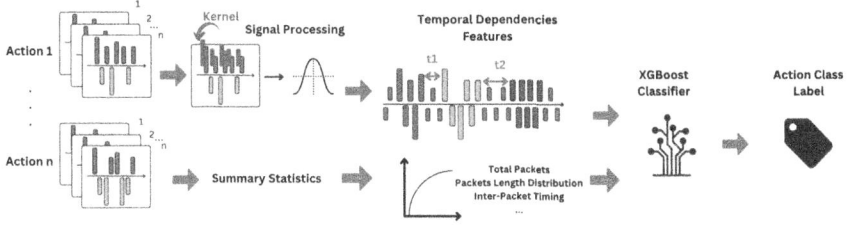

Fig. 7. Overview of our signal processing-based traffic analysis pipeline.

messages or distinct intervals between Cartesian commands, demands a more specialized approach for accurate classification. These patterns exhibit structured temporal dependencies that standard classifiers designed for web traffic struggle to capture effectively. Next, we depart from the use of established classifiers used for fingerprinting network traffic, and introduce a new fingerprinting approach based on signal processing techniques, which allow us to better analyze temporal structures, extracting features inherent to the different commands composing robotic actions without high data requirements and computational cost.

6 Signal Processing-Based Robot Action Identification

In this section, we introduce a new signal processing-based method to detect network events, and explore whether an adversary could use these methods to enhance robotic action identification capabilities.

Traffic Analysis Pipeline Overview. Figure 7 depicts a bird's-eye view of our analysis pipeline. Network traces representing different actions start by undergoing a set of signal processing operations (correlation and convolution, see Sect. 6.1) whose results we rely on to build a set of temporal dependency features. These features are then combined with a set of more generic summary statistics obtained from the network traces (inspired in those used by the ML classifiers analyzed in Sect. 5). Finally, we use these features to train (and later test the success of) an XGBoost [7] classifier geared at identifying the actions performed by the robot. We employ XGBoost given that it is known to outperform other classical machine learning models in both computational speed and model performance, and has been successfully used for traffic analysis [4].

Next, we describe our signal processing approach, detail how it is able to recognize temporal dependencies and statistical features of robot control traffic, and show how our method achieves a high accuracy in robot action identification.

6.1 Pattern Matching Operations

Our traffic analysis methodology places a large emphasis on the recognition of traffic patterns by leveraging two basic mathematical operations: *convolution* and *correlation*. Next, we provide the necessary background on these operations and then address how their results can be composed into a set of temporal dependencies and statistical features that help us build an accurate classifier.

Convolution. Convolution is a mathematical operation that combines two signals to produce a third, which reflects how the shape of a signal is modified by the other. For two discrete signals $x[n]$ and $h[n]$, their convolution is given by:

$$(x * h)[n] = \sum_{m=-\infty}^{\infty} x[m] \cdot h[n-m]$$

Here, $h[n]$ can be thought of as a "kernel" or "filter" that is slid across $x[n]$. In the realm of traffic pattern recognition, if $x[n]$ is the observed traffic and $h[n]$ is a known pattern, then a significant spike in $(x * h)[n]$ at a particular n indicates the presence of the known pattern in the observed traffic at that point.

Correlation coefficient. The correlation coefficient, often denoted r, quantifies the linear relationship between two signals. For two discrete signals $x[n]$ and $y[n]$, their correlation at lag m is:

$$r[m] = \sum_{n=-\infty}^{\infty} x[n] \cdot y[n+m]$$

The value of $r[m]$ peaks when $x[n]$ and $y[n+m]$ align most closely. In the context of traffic analysis, $x[n]$ could be a known command pattern and $y[n]$ the observed traffic pattern. A peak in $r[m]$ indicates the presence of the command pattern within the observed traffic at lag m. Correlation coefficients have been used in other traffic analysis tasks, e.g., anomaly detection and correlation [6,28].

We find that both correlation and convolution play an important role in detecting repetitive patterns within encrypted traffic. While the operations are closely related, they offer different interpretations and can be combined.

6.2   Signal Processing-Based Traffic Features

In our analysis, we utilize both convolution and correlation-based techniques to extract information on different types of command messages. Some command messages are one-time-only patterns, where convolution is particularly effective. This method allows us to highlight these singular patterns within the broader traffic data. In contrast, other commands are repetitive and may have varying duration; these are better captured using the correlation coefficient to reduce noise and false positives. For instance, we use the correlation coefficient for detecting command messages like gripper speed, where patterns are recurring. Our work primarily focuses on three types of command messages: Cartesian movements, gripper movements, and gripper speed adjustments. Each type presents unique pattern characteristics in network traffic. When introducing a new command message type for detection, we explicitly assess the nature of the command's traffic pattern. This assessment guides our decision on whether to

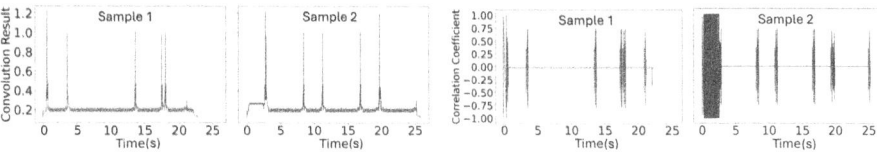

(a) Convolution for "turn on switch".   (b) Correlation for "turn on switch".

Fig. 8. Convolution and correlation results for two "turn on switch" samples.

apply convolution–best for one-time, distinct patterns–or the correlation coefficient, which excels in identifying and analyzing recurring patterns within the traffic.

Next, we present two sets of traffic statistics extracted via convolution and correlation, and show how we combine them into features for our classifier.

Convolution-Based Statistics. Consider the results of the convolution operation (Fig. 8a) applied to the two original "turn on switch" action traces depicted in Fig. 5. We can see that the convolution result is close to or above 1, meaning that the convolution operation is able to identify significant matches between the observed traffic pattern and the known command pattern. This indicates that the specific features or sequences in the traffic that correspond to the "turn on switch" action are effectively highlighted by the convolution process.

We used a kernel designed to match the expected traffic pattern of the "turn on switch" action. The kernel was crafted based on the sequence of packet sizes and intervals that we observed in our preliminary analysis for this action. Later in Sect. 6.3, we expand on the implications of selecting an adequate convolution kernel and of finding an adequate threshold for extracting command message information. By convolving this kernel with the observed traffic data, we sought to amplify parts of the signal that match the expected pattern. We determined a threshold to pinpoint instances where the convolution identifies segments in the traffic that correspond to the "turn on switch" action, based on our kernel.

After obtaining the convolution results, we extract a set of statistics from the resulting signal to build a set of convolution-based features. Table 1 presents a summary of the features derived from our analysis. The example in Table 1 shows the features from the second "turn on switch" sample. We observe that there are six Cartesian command messages issued during the sample duration, as reflected in the total of six clusters detected. For example, on average, there is a gap of approximately 4 s between each cluster. Additionally, higher-level information such as the total time span and average time gap provides insights into the general dynamics of the action: how frequently the Cartesian command messages are issued and whether they are closely spaced. The maximum convolution value can offer an idea about the number of parameters specified in the Cartesian command message, as this typically results in larger feedback packets.

Correlation-Based Statistics. Figure 8b depicts the results of the correlation coefficient operation for two original "turn on switch" action traces, previously shown in Fig. 5. We can observe a distinct difference in the traffic pattern of

Table 1. Convolution features for "turn on switch" (sample 2).

Metric	Value
Mean	0.2454
Standard Deviation	0.096
Median	0.2172
25th Percentile	0.2163
75th Percentile	0.2616
Maximum	1.2160
Minimum	0.1181
Skewness	6.0470
Kurtosis	48.9907
Total Clusters	6
Total Time Span	16.9991
Average Time Gap	3.3998

Table 2. Correlation features for "turn on switch" (sample 2).

Metric	Value
Mean	-0.0019
Standard Deviation	0.5653
Median	0.0
25th Percentile	0.0
75th Percentile	$5.3926e-17$
Maximum	1
Minimum	-1
Skewness	0.0039
Kurtosis	-0.1747
Number of Clusters	1
Total Length of Clusters	2.0910
Average Length of Clusters	2.0910
Total Time Span of Analysis	2.0910
Average Time Gap between Clusters	0

the two samples. The first sample does not exhibit any clusters, suggesting the absence of gripper speed commands, despite a high initial value. Conversely, the second sample displays a prominent cluster at the start, lasting $\sim$2 s.

To enhance the accuracy of our detection, we establish a criterion where a cluster must consecutively last over 1 s to be considered a positive match. This threshold aligns with the inherent activity of gripper speed commands, which typically persist for a certain duration to maintain a consistent speed or force applied by the gripper, thereby ensuring that we accurately identify when and for how long these commands are present in the action traffic.

Table 2 provides a summary of the correlation coefficient statistics, offering details similar to those discussed in the convolution analysis. In this context, the cumulative and average lengths of clusters offer additional insights into the duration of commands. We employ the correlation coefficient to identify command messages that exhibit varying recurring patterns (e.g., the gripper speed command) as a means to reduce noise and false positives. By analyzing these statistics, we can, for instance, ascertain the duration of gripper movements.

Our Classifier's Feature Set. The aforementioned convolution and correlation-based statistics comprise the main fuel for our traffic classifier. Specifically, the detection of each new command message allows us to refine the set of the above statistics with fine-grained information about commands' temporal dependencies. We obtain features for our model by processing these statistics into a summarized representation of messages' temporal dependencies.

Concretely, our features include the *average time between clusters*, shedding light on the intervals between command groups; *total number of clusters*, quantifying the diversity of patterns; *total length of all clusters*, giving an aggregate duration of detected patterns; and *average length of clusters*, indicating the typical duration of individual patterns. The *time gaps between consecutive clusters* highlight intervals between patterns, while *skewness and kurtosis* offer insights into their distribution. The *total time span of clusters* provides data about the start of the first to the end of the last cluster, and the *average time gap between clusters* showcases the average intervals between these occurrences. Collectively, these features paint a detailed picture of the robot's operational patterns, capturing not only the frequency and duration of command messages but also transitions and relationships within them. In addition, we also include in our final feature set a collection of common summary statistics extracted from network traffic (akin to k-FP [19]) and that relate to the timing and volume of communication (e.g., number of packets exchanged, or average inter-packet timing).

6.3 Convolution Parameters

The results of our convolution operation are mostly guided by the choice of two parameters: the convolution kernel, and a threshold for determining the occurrence of a command message. Below, we detail our choice for both parameters.

Convolution Kernel. We find that the choice of the convolution kernel–a pattern used to detect similar patterns in the observed data–does not significantly impact accuracy. Essentially, a kernel represents the overall shape or signature of a particular type of traffic pattern, such as a Cartesian or gripper position command message. For example, a kernel might be derived from a typical pattern of packet sizes and intervals observed for a specific robot command. We test this by using 10 different kernels for each type of command message, each extracted from 10 distinct samples of that command. Despite these variations, the accuracy of our traffic pattern detection remains consistent. This suggests that our method is robust to variations in the kernel, capable of accurately identifying traffic patterns regardless of slight differences in the kernel's shape.

Convolution Threshold. Figure 9a shows the variation in our classifier's accuracy across different convolution threshold (t) values. The threshold is based on the range of convolution results obtained when the normalized signal is convolved with the normalized kernel, using the normalization factor derived from the kernel itself. A threshold value of 0 means that every positive convolution result, no matter how small, is classified as a Cartesian command message. This can lead to a high rate of false positives, as even minimal similarities between the observed traffic and the kernel are flagged as matches. Conversely, a threshold of 1.3 sets a very high bar for detection, meaning that only very strong matches–those with convolution results exceeding this value–are considered true positives. This strict criterion can increase the likelihood of false negatives, as it may overlook less pronounced but still relevant patterns. In our analysis, we find that a threshold value of approximately 0.9 strikes an optimal balance.

6.4 Evaluation of Our Approach

Our traffic analysis pipeline achieves an accuracy of 97% in the robot actions dataset, thus showcasing the potential for network adversaries to compromise the

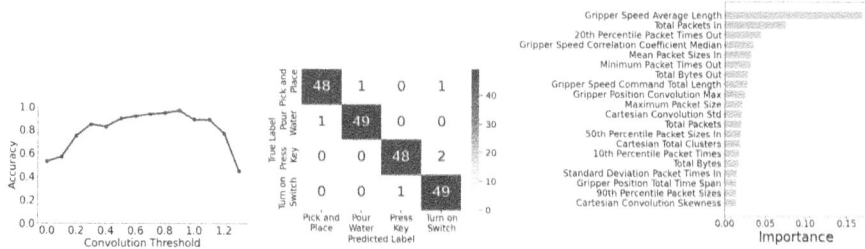

(a) Acc. for threshold t. (b) Conf. mat. $(t = 0.9)$.   (c) Top 20 features $(t = 0.9)$.

Fig. 9. Classification results.

privacy of users through the accurate recognition of robot activities. Figure 9b depicts the confusion matrix of our classifier on the robot's actions dataset, allowing for two interesting observations. First, we can see that the classifier occasionally mispredicts the "pick and place" and "pour water" with one another. This misclassification likely stems from the similar sequence of movements shared by these actions, which involve the gripper's opening and closing motions used for grabbing and placing an object. Second, actions that involve tapping motions, such as pressing a key and toggling a switch, are also occasionally misclassified as each other. Indeed, both classes exhibit quick and sharp motion patterns, which are typical of tapping actions, and thus distinct from the more fluid and prolonged actions of picking, placing, and pouring. Our classifier uses these patterns to accurately distinguish between these two sets of actions.

Feature Importance. The top 20 most important features for our classifier's performance (depicted in Fig. 9c) comprise a mix of signal processing and summary statistics elements. Feature importance is determined based on the average *gain*, which measures the improvement in the loss function when a feature is used for splitting in the XGBoost model. From the signal processing category, the gripper speed average length emerges as the most significant feature, followed by the gripper speed command correlation coefficient median, ranking as the fourth most important, highlighting the role of gripper movement clusters in the classification. On the other hand, from the summary statistics category, the total number of incoming packets and the 20th percentile of outgoing packet inter-arrival times stand out as the second and third most important features, respectively. This highlights that different classes exhibit variations not only in the total number of packets sent but also in the timing between these packets.

7   Towards Efficient Defenses

Here, we explore different defense mechanisms and determine their effectiveness in protecting robotic operations from traffic analysis attacks. We evaluate two defenses: one based on the simple *padding of packet sizes*, and a more complex one developed by ourselves, which we named *latency-aware traffic modulation*.

At the core of the defense mechanisms we consider lies a concern over how these defenses may impact the correct and timely operation of the robot. As it stands, the robot can only proceed with another action after it has received an entire command message and feedback messages about that same command (both possibly segmented over multiple packets). Delaying this cycle would lead to delays in action execution. To ensure that action correctness and operational efficiency are maintained, the content within the command and feedback messages must be sequentially delivered before any robotic action can be executed. Moreover, the messages exchanged between the robot and the controller while a command's execution is ongoing should also not be delayed.

7.1 Considered Defenses

Padding Packet Sizes. This defense obfuscates the size of packets, making it more challenging for an adversary to discern patterns based on packet size. This method does not introduce additional latency, as it does not affect the transmission time of the packets. However, it does result in additional bandwidth overhead due to the transmission of larger-sized packets. The defense mechanism rounds up each packet size to the nearest multiple of $x * 100$ bytes. We assume x to be an integer ranging from 1 to 10 since the maximum packet size observed in our traces was under 1000 bytes. We also assume padding to occur only up to the maximum MTU size of 1500 bytes. For example, a packet of size 360 bytes would be padded to 400 bytes if $x = 2$ (nearest multiple of 200) and to 500 bytes if $x = 5$, while a packet of size 960 bytes would be padded to 1500 bytes if $x = 8$.

Latency-Aware Traffic Modulation. This defense strategy is inspired by constant-rate traffic analysis defenses (in the likes of Tamaraw [5]), which involve the use of a fixed packet size for all messages. Generically, applying such a defense to our setting would cause the segmentation of any robot command or feedback message larger than this fixed size into several packets of equal size, or, alternatively, the padding of the contents of small messages to meet this fixed packet size. Then, all packets would be sent at a specific and fixed time interval.

However, the above method can introduce delays, particularly if the frequency of packet transmission does not align with the speed at which the robot's controller operates. Concretely, the Kinova Gen3 robotic arm features a closed-loop control system operating at a frequency of 1 kHz. Our analysis of the robot operation traffic revealed that the command message type with the *shortest inter-packet intervals* is the speed command, which averages about 80 packets per second. Any latency in a single command/feedback message that results in the message arriving noticeably late to the controller is unacceptable.

To address this, we developed a *latency-aware traffic modulation* scheme that helps maintain latency within an acceptable range while adequately obfuscating traffic patterns. Like constant-rate defenses, our technique still relies on sending dummy packets to fulfill fixed packet sending rates and padding short packets to meet the pre-configured fixed packet size. However, we leave packets longer than this fixed size (and which cannot be broken down without exceeding the acceptable latency range) at their original size. In turn, packets that can be segmented into multiple smaller packets without resulting in unacceptable delays are appropriately split. This approach still introduces some latency, but can keep it within an acceptable range for the robotic arm's operation [22].

As a concrete formulation, let s_o be the original packet size, and let s_p be the predefined padded packet size. Let L be the permissible latency 0.001 s in the case of running the Kinova controller and t_i be the chosen time interval for transmitting each packet. The calculated packet size s_c and the number of segments n into which the original packet is divided can be defined as follows:

$$s_c = \begin{cases} s_p & \text{if } s_o \leq s_p, \\ \frac{s_o}{\left\lceil \frac{L}{t_i} \right\rceil} & \text{if } \left\lceil \frac{s_o}{s_p} \right\rceil \cdot t_i > L, \quad (1) \\ s_p & \text{otherwise.} \end{cases} \qquad n = \begin{cases} 1 & \text{if } s_o \leq s_p, \\ \left\lfloor \frac{L}{t_i} \right\rfloor & \text{if } \left\lceil \frac{s_o}{s_p} \right\rceil \cdot t_i > L, \quad (2) \\ \left\lceil \frac{s_o}{s_p} \right\rceil & \text{otherwise.} \end{cases}$$

7.2   Evaluation of Defenses

Padding-Only Defense. Figure 10a illustrates the relationship between the accuracy of our classifier and the size of padded packets when the simpler padding-only defense is employed. The classifier retains a relatively high accuracy (above 80%) for packets padded to the nearest multiple of 700 bytes ($x = 7$), decreasing its accuracy to ~40% when packets are padded to the nearest multiple of 1000 bytes ($x = 10$). Figure 10b depicts the average bandwidth overhead percentage of the defense when considering our robot actions dataset. As observed, the overhead percentage increases linearly with the padding size, reaching approximately 700% overhead when the padding size is set to the nearest multiple of 800 bytes ($x = 8$). At this padding size, the accuracy of our classifier is still relatively high (~70%). Thus, we conclude that this defense is largely ineffective for low padding sizes, achieving only a moderate protection for a large bandwidth overhead.

Latency-Aware Traffic Modulation Defense. For evaluating this defense, we perform a set of experiments with different permissible latency: 0.01s, matching the fastest average command speed, specifically for speed commands; 0.001s, aligning with the controller's operational frequency, and; 0.0001s, the frequency allowing the transmission of the shortest command/feedback message. While the

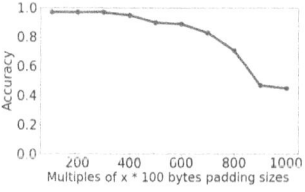

(a) Classifier's accuracy.

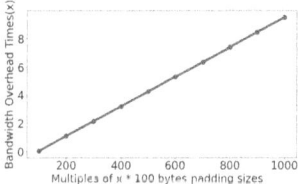

(b) Bandwidth overhead.

Fig. 10. Results for the padding-only defense.

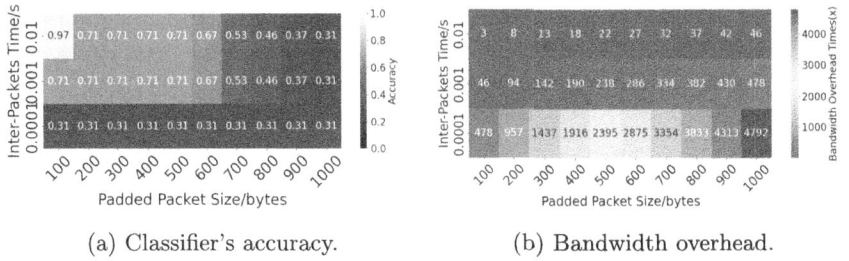

(a) Classifier's accuracy.   (b) Bandwidth overhead.

Fig. 11. Results for the latency-aware defense.

speed command typically exhibits the fastest average frequency, some command messages contain packets with significantly smaller single inter-packet intervals.

Figure 11a illustrates the relationship between the effectiveness of our defense mechanism and the degree of packet padding and segmentation applied to robot traffic. We can see that, for fixed packet sending rates of 0.01s and 0.001s, the defense is only reasonably effective once packets are also padded to a large size (900 bytes for degrading classification accuracy below 40%). However, we can also see that, for all the padding sizes under test, sending packets at a fixed frequency of 0.0001s is sufficient for reducing the accuracy of the classifier to approximately 30%. Figure 11a also suggests that an adversary may still be able to infer information about the actions being performed (accuracy of ∼30%) due to the total time duration of each action (which we do not obfuscate).

Figure 11b shows the bandwidth overhead incurred by the latency-aware traffic modulation defense. Bandwidth overheads increase both with the packet sizes and with the packet sending frequency used in the defense. The figure suggests that the latter cause more pronounced bandwidth overhead, given the additional packets exchanged per time unit. When sending packets at a 0.01s rate, the defense reduces our attack's accuracy to 31% but incurs a staggering 478 times bandwidth overhead. This trade-off is not practical in realistic settings, indicating a pressing need for the development of low-delay defense strategies.

8   Limitations and Future Work

Extension to the Open-World. Our evaluation matches that of a closed-world attack [35] where we attempt to distinguish between a restricted set of four different actions performed by the robot. In the future, we aim to analyze the effectiveness of our approach in the open-world setting [40], where the robot is allowed to perform a range of tasks beyond those the adversary seeks to identify. **Traffic Analysis Under Varying Network Conditions.** We assumed a stable and high-performance network connection that was free from interference (e.g., packet drops, jitter, etc.). Future work could consider the analysis of robot traffic under varying network conditions. Different network environments may introduce unique challenges and opportunities for attack and defense strategies [3].

Measuring Robot Traffic Information Leakage. We aim to explore more systematic methods for evaluating information leakage in robot traffic [8,24, 39]. Automating a security evaluation pipeline for robotics applications could enhance the overall effectiveness of security assessments applied to these systems.

9   Related Work

The fingerprinting scenarios we enumerate below target the re-identification of traffic that follows relatively stable patterns. We argue that fingerprinting robot actions presents unique challenges – complex robot activities might involve a variable number of smaller operations which can be performed in different orders and last for different amounts of time. In our work, we rely on a new set of manually-engineered features based on signal processing operations, combining these with traffic statistics that have been used before for fingerprinting purposes.
Website Fingerprinting. Despite the use of encrypted tunnels, web traffic retains traffic patterns that allow eavesdroppers to map those patterns to specific websites [19]. Website fingerprinting mappings were traditionally built using manual features and classical ML [19,29], but recent work leverages deep learning for higher accuracy [31,35,37]. There also exists prolific literature on defenses [25], ranging from rather secure but inefficient constant-rate padding defenses [5], to more efficient defenses like FRONT [18] or RegulaTor [20].
Video Fingerprinting. Video streaming protocols that adjust their bit rates in response to network conditions manifest traffic patterns that fluctuate based on the video content and its resolution, enabling the development of fingerprinting techniques which can identify a given video being streamed, even if it is encrypted [32,33]. Proposed defenses include the generation of synthetic video flows that shield the videos being watched by users [38], or noise addition [23].
IoT Device Fingerprinting. IoT devices exhibit predictable traffic patterns which are only partially shrouded by encryption, enabling eavesdroppers to infer which specific devices operate within a household [2]. Different approaches for IoT device fingerprinting have focused both on the collection of summary statistics from IoT device traffic [9,27], or on the analysis of network traces with deep neural networks [12]. Existing defenses include improved padding schemes [13] and the perturbation of traffic flows through deep learning methods [36].

10   Conclusion

In this paper, we investigated encrypted traffic analysis in robotics, emphasizing its implications for sensitive applications (e.g., domestic, healthcare). Leveraging machine learning classifiers fueled with signal-based processing features, we were able to discern robotic actions from encrypted traffic patterns, shedding light on significant privacy concerns. Our findings highlight potential vulnerabilities within robotic communication channels, calling for the development of enhanced security measures as the deployment of collaborative robots becomes widespread.

Acknowledgments. This work was supported in part by a seed grant jointly awarded by the University of Waterloo's Cybersecurity and Privacy Institute and RoboHub. We thank RoboHub for providing us with access to the Kinova Gen 3 robotic arm.

Disclosure of Interests. The authors have no competing interests to declare that are relevant to the content of this article.

References

1. Al-Naami, K., et al.: Adaptive encrypted traffic fingerprinting with bi-directional dependence. In: Proceedings of ACSAC (2016)
2. Apthorpe, N., Reisman, D., Feamster, N.: A smart home is no castle: privacy vulnerabilities of encrypted IoT traffic. In: Proceedings of the DAT Workshop (2016)
3. Bahramali, A., Bozorgi, A., Houmansadr, A.: Realistic website fingerprinting by augmenting network traces. In: Proceedings of ACM CCS (2023)
4. Barradas, D., Santos, N., Rodrigues, L.: Effective detection of multimedia protocol tunneling using machine learning. In: Proceedings of USENIX Security (2018)
5. Cai, X., Nithyanand, R., Wang, T., Johnson, R., Goldberg, I.: A systematic approach to developing and evaluating website fingerprinting defenses. In: Proceedings of ACM CCS (2014)
6. Chen, N., Chen, X.S., Xiong, B., Lu, H.W.: An anomaly detection and analysis method for network traffic based on correlation coefficient matrix. In: Proceedings of SCALCOM-EMBEDDEDCOM (2009)
7. Chen, T., Guestrin, C.: XGBoost: a scalable tree boosting system. In: Proceedings of ACM KDD (2016)
8. Cherubin, G.: Bayes, not naïve: security bounds on website fingerprinting defenses. PoPETs **4** (2017)
9. Chowdhury, R.R., Aneja, S., Aneja, N., Abas, E.: Network traffic analysis based iot device identification. In: Proceedings of ACM BDIOT (2020)
10. Colucci, G., Tagliavini, L., Carbonari, L., Cavallone, P., Botta, A., Quaglia, G.: Paquitop. arm, a mobile manipulator for assessing emerging challenges in the covid-19 pandemic scenario. Robotics **10**(3) (2021)
11. Denning, T., Matuszek, C., Koscher, K., Smith, J.R., Kohno, T.: A spotlight on security and privacy risks with future household robots. attacks and lessons. In: Proceedings of ACM UbiComp (2009)
12. Dong, S., Li, Z., Tang, D., Chen, J., Sun, M., Zhang, K.: Your smart home can't keep a secret: towards automated fingerprinting of IoT traffic. In: Proceedings of ACM AsiaCCS (2020)
13. Engelberg, A., Wool, A.: Classification of encrypted IoT traffic despite padding and shaping. In: Proceedings of WPES (2022)
14. European Union Agency for Cybersecurity: Encrypted traffic analysis (2019). https://www.enisa.europa.eu/publications/encrypted-traffic-analysis
15. Fiorini, P., Goldberg, K.Y., Liu, Y., Taylor, R.H.: Concepts and trends in autonomy for robot-assisted surgery. Proc. of the IEEE **110**(7) (2022)
16. França, R.P., Monteiro, A., Arthu, R., Iano, Y.: The evolution of robotic systems: overview and its application in modern times. Safety , Security, and Reliability of Robotic Systems (2020)

17. Gillini, G., et al.: A dual-arm mobile robot system performing assistive tasks operated via p300-based brain computer interface. Ind. Robot **49**(1) (2022)
18. Gong, J., Wang, T.: Zero-delay lightweight defenses against website fingerprinting. In: Proceedings of USENIX Security (2020)
19. Hayes, J., Danezis, G.: k-fingerprinting: a robust scalable website fingerprinting technique. In: Proceedings of USENIX Security (2016)
20. Holland, J.K., Hopper, N.: Regulator: a straightforward website fingerprinting defense. PoPETs **2022**(2) (2022)
21. Kebria, P.M., Abdi, H., Dalvand, M.M., Khosravi, A., Nahavandi, S.: Control methods for internet-based teleoperation systems: a review. IEEE Trans. Hum.-Mach. Syst. **49**(1) (2018)
22. Kinova Robotics: Kinova gen3 robotic arm (2023). https://www.kinovarobotics.com/product/gen3-robots
23. Li, H., Niu, B., Wang, B.: Smartswitch: efficient traffic obfuscation against stream fingerprinting. In: Proceedings of SecureComm (2020)
24. Li, S., Guo, H., Hopper, N.: Measuring information leakage in website fingerprinting attacks and defenses. In: Proceedings of ACM CCS (2018)
25. Mathews, N., Holland, J.K., Oh, S.E., Rahman, M.S., Hopper, N., Wright, M.: SOK: a critical evaluation of efficient website fingerprinting defenses. In: Proceedings of IEEE S&P (2023)
26. Mihelj, M., et al.: Collaborative robots. Robotics (2019)
27. Msadek, N., Soua, R., Engel, T.: IoT device fingerprinting: Machine learning based encrypted traffic analysis. In: Proceedings of the IEEE WCNC (2019)
28. Nasr, M., Houmansadr, A., Mazumdar, A.: Compressive traffic analysis: a new paradigm for scalable traffic analysis. In: Proceedings of ACM CCS (2017)
29. Panchenko, A., Lanze, F.: Website fingerprinting at Internet scale. In: Proceedings of NDSS (2016)
30. Pulikottil, T.B., Caimmi, M., D'Angelo, M.G., Biffi, E., Pellegrinelli, S., Tosatti, L.M.: A voice control system for assistive robotic arms: preliminary usability tests on patients. In: Proceedings of IEEE BioRob (2018)
31. Rahman, M.S., Sirinam, P., Mathews, N., Gangadhara, K.G., Wright, M.: Tik-tok: the utility of packet timing in website fingerprinting attacks. In: PoPETs (2020)
32. Reed, A., Kranch, M.: Identifying HTTPS-protected Netflix videos in real-time. In: Proceedings of ACM CODASPY (2017)
33. Schuster, R., Shmatikov, V., Tromer, E.: Beauty and the burst: Remote identification of encrypted video streams. In: Proceedings of USENIX Security (2017)
34. Shah, R., Ahmed, C.M., Nagaraja, S.: Can you still see me?: identifying robot operations over end-to-end encrypted channels. In: Proceedings of ACM WiSec (2022)
35. Shen, M., Ji, K., Gao, Z., Li, Q., Zhu, L., Xu, K.: Subverting website fingerprinting defenses with robust traffic representation. In: Proceedings of USENIX Security (2023)
36. Shenoi, A., Karthik, P., Sabharwal, K., Jialin, L., Divakaran, D.M.: ipet: privacy enhancing traffic perturbations for IoT communications. PoPETs **2** (2023)
37. Sirinam, P., Imani, M., Juarez, M., Wright, M.: Deep fingerprinting: Undermining website fingerprinting defenses with deep learning. In: Proceedings of ACM CCS (2018)
38. Vaskevich, A., Dahanayaka, T., Jourjon, G., Seneviratne, S.: Smaug: streaming media augmentation using CGANs as a defence against video fingerprinting. In: Proceedings of IEEE NCA (2021)

39. Veicht, A., Renggli, C., Barradas, D.: Deepse-WF: unified security estimation for website fingerprinting defenses. PoPETs **2** (2023)
40. Wang, T.: High precision open-world website fingerprinting. In: Proceedings of IEEE S&P (2020)
41. Wilson, G., et al.: Robot-enabled support of daily activities in smart home environments. Cogn. Syst. Res. **54** (2019)
42. Yin, Y., Lin, Z., Jin, M., Fanti, G., Sekar, V.: Practical GAN-based synthetic IP header trace generation using netshare. In: Proceedings of ACM SIGCOMM (2022)

Domainator: Detecting and Identifying DNS-Tunneling Malware Using Metadata Sequences

Denis Petrov[1]([✉]) [iD], Pascal Ruffing[1] [iD], Sebastian Zillien[2] [iD], and Steffen Wendzel[2] [iD]

[1] Worms University of Applied Sciences, Worms, Germany
{petrov,ruffing}@hs-worms.de
[2] Ulm University, Ulm, Germany
{sebastian.zillien,steffen.wendzel}@uni-ulm.de

Abstract. For a few years, malware with tunneling (or: covert channel) capabilities has been on the rise. While malware research led to several methods and innovations, the detection and *differentiation* of malware solely based on its DNS tunneling features is still in its infancy. Moreover, no work so far has used the DNS tunneling traffic to gain knowledge over the current *actions* taken by the malware.

In this paper, we present Domainator, an approach to detect and differentiate state-of-the-art malware and DNS tunneling tools without relying on trivial (but quickly altered) features such as "magic bytes" that are embedded into subdomains. Instead, we apply an analysis of sequential patterns to identify specific types of malware. We evaluate our approach with 7 real-world malware samples and tunneling tools and can identify the particular malware based on its DNS traffic. We further infer the rough *behavior* of the particular malware through its DNS tunneling artifacts. Finally, we compare our Domainator with related methods.

Keywords: Covert Channels · DNS · Malware · Tunneling

1 Introduction

Tunneling data through a protocol that is not meant for such activities provides malware authors with the capabilities of transporting stolen data and subsequent command and control messages to and from a C2 server in a hidden manner. Their focus on evading traditional detection methods allows the malware and its communication channel(s) to remain undiscovered. As such tunnels break the security policy of their environments in a stealthy manner, literature refers to these as *covert channels* [28]. More than 100 recent cases of malware employing covert channels have been summarized by Strachanski *et al.* [26] (2024), Knöchel and Karius [15] (2024) as well as Caviglione and Mazurczyk [5] (2022).

Network tunneling exploits features of common Internet protocols [5], with DNS being the most frequently used protocol for this purpose [26]. While the

© The Author(s) 2025
M. Dalla Preda et al. (Eds.): ARES 2025, LNCS 15992, pp. 118–140, 2025.
https://doi.org/10.1007/978-3-032-00624-0_6

detection of network-specific covert channels was studied for years, there is still a lack regarding the *differentiation* – or: *identification* – of malware. Moreover, studies on detecting or identifying network covert channels usually target *purely academic* implementations.

This paper aims to address this gap by showing that we can not only *detect* but *identify* (i.e., separate) *real-world* DNS-based malware, and also understand its *behavior*. In particular, our contributions are the following:

1. We introduce a methodology for the identification of *real-world* malware samples on the network-level;
2. Targeting DNS-based tunneling, we are able to differentiate multiple malware samples solely based on statistical features of their subdomain utilization that we feed into a Random Forest classifier;
3. We show that our classification approach can be used to detect malware *behavior*, i.e., we can tell which action a malware performs;
4. We further show that we can identify malware samples even when their communication pattern is slightly modified;
5. We provide our dataset to the scientific community.

The remainder of the paper is structured as follows. We cover fundamentals and related work in Sect. 2 and present our methodology in Sect. 3. We evaluate our approach in Sect. 4, which also introduces the analyzed malware samples. Section 5 discusses our methodology while Sect. 6 concludes.

2   Related Work and Fundamentals

2.1   Related Work

Establishment of DNS Tunnels. A plethora of methods exist to *embed* covert messages into network traffic, see, e.g., the following survey publications [20,27, 28]. Recent findings unveiled that the predominant protocol utilized by malware is DNS [26]. Summarized, to hide secret information in DNS traffic, attackers exploit the header fields of the DNS protocol and the values of the DNS entries that are attached to the header (these are called *resource records*).

Detection of DNS Tunnels. Several papers study the *detection* of network covert channels, including DNS-based ones, see, e.g., [19,27] for comprehensive overviews. The related work on detecting DNS-based covert channels and tunneling barely addresses real-world malware traffic and almost exclusively focuses on academic tools and methods. Moreover, it targets the detection (and not the identification) of these tools. Known approaches for detecting DNS-based covert channels and tunneling are the following: Gao *et al.* [10] aims to detect DNS-based tunnels using a framework called GraphTunnel, which leverages graph neural networks to model DNS recursive resolution processes as graphs. By aggregating node and edge features with the GraphSage framework, GraphTunnel achieves 100% accuracy in detecting both known and unknown DNS tunnels, even in challenging environments with wildcard DNS where it maintains an F1-score of 99.78%. In addition to detecting tunnels, GraphTunnel accurately identifies DNS tunneling tools with a success rate of more than 98.57%. In contrast, Born and Gustafson focus on character frequency analysis to detect DNS tunnels [3]. Their approach uses unigram, bigram, and trigram models to detect anomalies in the frequency patterns, based on the observation that domain names typically follow Zipf's law. This method effectively identifies DNS tunnels by highlighting deviations from expected character frequency distributions. With a focus on machine learning, Buczak *et al.* [4] develop a method for detecting DNS tunnels by applying Random Forest classifiers to analyze features extracted from PCAP data. The authors curated a dataset by extracting relevant features from DNS traffic, such as domain name length, query types, and packet length, enabling them to effectively distinguish between normal DNS activity and tunneling activity. Their approach achieved a detection accuracy of over 95%, demonstrating the effectiveness of Random Forest models in identifying DNS tunnels. Similarly, in the work of Alkasassbeh and Almseidin [1], the detection of DNS tunneling using machine learning techniques is explored, with a particular focus on evaluating the effectiveness of different classifiers. In their experiments, Random Forest classifiers again produced the best results, achieving a precision of 98% in detecting DNS tunneling traffic. Žiža *et al.* [30] have also shown an approach based on Random Forests that has an accuracy of 99.7%. Machmeier *et al.* [17] utilize dynamic time warping as a distance metric to achieve an F1-Score above 99.99%, proving the potential of similarity-based approaches for the detection of DNS tunneling. The FANCI [25] system focuses on the domain portion, targeting infections making use of domain generation algorithms. The approach considers multiple categories of features (linguistic, statistical and structural ones), calculated on the given domain name. Another recent study has outlined detection approaches for both network-based malware communication and other forms of media, summarizing them in a comprehensive overview [2]. While these works target the bare detection of DNS tunnels, our work additionally aims to identify the particular malware that generated the observed DNS traffic. Moreover, we attempt to determine the behavior of the malware solely by analyzing its network communication, regarding which we found no related works.

Malware Identification. In addition to the detection, research also covers malware *identification*. A few recent works address this problem: Dittmann *et al.* analyze identification and attribution of steganographic algorithms for MP3 audio [7], and a forensic trace map for malware that employs steganographic artifacts in digital images was introduced by Kiltz *et al.* [14]. The only work dealing with *network*-based malware identification was provided by Zillien *et al.* [29] but was focusing on a testbed and not on any (DNS-related) experiments.

Anomaly Detection Using Sequences. Chandola *et al.* provide a comprehensive survey on anomaly detection in discrete sequences [6]. The authors categorize existing research into three main approaches: sequence-based anomaly detection, which focuses on identifying entire sequences that deviate from the norm;

subsequence-based anomaly detection, which involves detecting anomalous subsequences within longer sequences; and pattern frequency-based anomaly detection, which identifies anomalies based on unusual frequency patterns of specific sequences. The survey provides a detailed review of techniques for each of these formulations, offering insights into how different approaches can be applied across various domains. In [16], Loganathan *et al.* introduce a sequence-to-sequence (Seq2Seq) pattern learning algorithm for real-time anomaly detection in network traffic. The authors propose a multi-attribute model that predicts sequences of TCP packets based on prior sequences using a Seq2Seq encoder-decoder architecture. The model effectively learns the expected order of packets, allowing it to identify deviations that signal potential anomalies or intrusions, achieving an accuracy of 97% for detecting anomalous TCP packets.

2.2   Fundamentals on DNS-Utilization by Malware

Due to the crucial nature of DNS for a successful communication on the Internet, it is also an attractive target for threat groups and their malware, with the aim of keeping their communication inconspicuous.

As DNS does not support arbitrary payload transfer natively, malicious actors utilize its request and response structure by having a malware issue DNS queries for a domain registered and controlled by them. The data transferred by the client-side of the communication channel is inserted as a subdomain string, which can then be read and interpreted by a remote C2 server. Such communication is indirect, with a DNS resolver standing between the client and the server, with the communication loop being visualized in Fig. 1. When the length of the data, which the malware attempts to exfiltrate, exceeds either a pre-defined value or the maximum allowed size for a DNS packet, it is split into multiple smaller chunks that are sent individually, usually coupled with an offset value to indicate which part of the message is transferred. In order to keep the domains valid and the requests less suspicious, the plain-text data often has undergone some form of encoding or encryption. Depending on the malware implementation, the record types chosen for the DNS queries may vary. On the C2 server, the request is processed, a fitting response is created and again encoded into a meaningful string for the resource record type used. This may be an IP address in the case of record types *A* and *AAAA*, or another subdomain for *CNAME*.

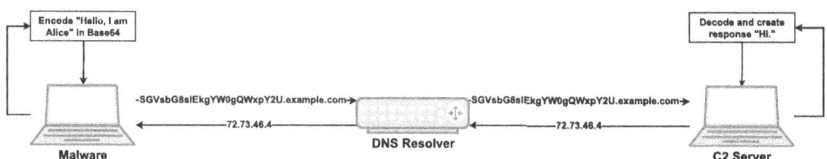

Fig. 1. A visualization of the malware instance communicating with its C2 server

3   Framework and Dataset

3.1   The Domainator DNS Covert Channel Detection Framework

To gather the data necessary for our evaluation, we have constructed an isolated physical testbed environment on which we can observe the analyzed malware samples. The testbed consists of a Windows- and Linux-based computer where the malware is executed, a Linux-based computer that acts as a DNS resolver, as well as the host for the respective C2 server in a separate module, and a router connecting the computers into a local network.

For the execution of each malware sample, the client-side device was reset to the initial state it had before any malware infection took place. In addition to that, no debugging or malware analysis tools were present on the system at the same time as the malware to prevent any external influences. Since our goal is to analyze the original network traffic generated by the malware, we made sure that it was not recognized or influenced by any local antivirus and malware detection tools. To this end, we deactivated the in-built antivirus software (e.g., Windows Defender), since some of the used samples were easily detected. This enables an unobstructed communication that we can build our DNS-based malware identification upon.

On the server-side, an instance of the open-source tool DNSChef [13] was utilized as a DNS resolver. Based on the domain name in the DNS query, DNSChef has been configured to either respond with a dummy IP address or to forward the packet to an address the C2 server can listen on. When a packet is captured by the server, it interprets the request and returns an appropriate answer, which is also handled by the resolver. The list of domains to be forwarded is compiled from domains we have observed during the operation of the malware samples in Sect. 3.2. This allows the simulation of an authentic network communication for both malicious and non-malicious requests.

A limiting factor for the reproduction of the malicious communication is the lack of knowledge regarding the hardware or software, as well as their exact implementation, that the threat group used originally with the associated sample. In order to replicate this command and control setup, we have either recreated the C2 server by examining the malware and its traffic, and determining the expected responses, or have used already available implementations, e.g., the publicly available C2 server for Saitama [9]. Every C2 server listens for traffic coming from the DNS resolver with a destination port *53* and parses for the domains utilized by the respective malware instance. The network packets are then processed by filtering the subdomains, based on the record type and the current malware requirements. Due to the distinctive nature of each malware, the procedures of the server in this step are highly individual. Following, a fitting reply is constructed and sent to the client as a DNS response.

3.2   Selection and Description of DNS Malware and Tunneling Tools

To cover various DNS data exfiltration methods and their use in malicious scenarios, we have chosen a list of seven tools: five cases of DNS-utilizing malware, including two different implementations of the same malware, as well as two open-source tools, at least one of which has been utilized in malicious campaigns:

RogueRobin is a malware created by the Iranian-linked DarkHydrus threat group [21], targeting government figures within the Middle East. There are two known versions of the malware, the main differences between being the delivered payload: either a PowerShell-based script or a C# executable [23]. They also differ in the approach used for encoding the data that is sent through the DNS communication channel. We have analyzed both versions of the malware and created a C2 server for each so that we can explore their capabilities.

Initially, the *PowerShell version* runs various checks to test whether it is being run within a virtual environment or a debugger [23]. If those tests are passed, it begins rotating between the DNS record types stored in a hard-coded list and sends a DNS query for each one, in an attempt to find out which records can be used successfully for communication. The very first request is also utilized by the malware as a way to register itself with the C2 server. It inserts the process ID as a *base64* encoded string into the subdomain of the query, and expects to get an integer value back, that is used as a unique ID [23]. If the response to any of the requests was not successful or valid, the malware would repeat the query, before moving to the next record. After each resource type has been tested, an evaluation string is sent back to the server [11], indicating which records were successful. The complete transfer of this string is considered by the malware as a job and is designated with an ID, that is sent alongside the encoded data. Longer data strings are split into chunks that are sent separately, in which case the job ID aids to rebuild the original full message. A sample DNS request, which transfers data, has the following structure: *uniqueID|-|jobID|-|dataOffset|isMoreFlag|-|encodedData.example.com*. The malware also gathers and transfers information about the victim system and the user, before querying the C2 server for any available jobs.

The *.NET version* executes a similar initial sequence utilizing a round-robin resource record rotation, with the list of record types having a different order [11]. The data in this version uses a hexadecimal encoding, which is then fully converted into letters through a simple, hard-coded substitution alphabet. The malware also includes a character at the beginning of each covert message, indicating the current mode, i.e., data transfer. When sending data back to the server, .NET RogueRobin separates the hidden data into two parts, one containing meta information about the data and the other being the data itself. To distinguish between each part, a single character from a pre-defined list is inserted. An example packet that sends data from the victim would have the form of *mode|uniqueID|jobID|dataOffset|isMoreFlag|sepChar|encodedData.example.com*. For non-data transferring queries, the covert message would also include a single hard-coded character either at the end or behind the *jobID* position.

Saitama is a malware that was targeted towards Jordanian government officials. It was first analyzed by Malwarebytes [18], which is the main source for our initial analysis. On the command and control side, we have employed a publicly available C2 server implementation [9]. In comparison to *RogueRobin*, *Saitama* establishes longer pauses between each sent packet and utilizes a form of base36 encoding with a mixed character positions to introduce randomness in the resulting string. An additional preventative measure to reduce the similarity of each malware run is the internal counter that chooses a random number upon execution, and is then utilized in the data encoding. The initial request *Saitama* makes is a registration query that requests an ID it can be identified by later. The ID itself is sent back as the last octet of an IPv4 address, while other responses use each octet to encode the covert response. Subsequently, the malware retrieves a job from the C2 server, which can either be from a list of pre-defined commands or a custom one that will take more DNS queries to be acquired. Once the job is complete, the sample sends the result back to the server in chunks. In the case of no available jobs, it initiates a form of a keep-alive connection which sends a burst of packets in an interval of six to eight hours.

Symbiote is a type of malware that specifically targets Linux-based systems and was first analyzed by Intezer, which our description is mainly based on [12]. Its main target has been the infiltration of banks in Latin America. Unlike other typical malware, *Symbiote* is not a standalone executable, instead, being a shared object file that inserts itself into running processes. To achieve this, it uses the *LD_PRELOAD* environment variable to ensure that it is loaded first in every new process [22]. There are five known versions of *Symbiote*, with only two implementing their own DNS covert communication protocol. A later version of the malware uses a modified version of the DNS tunneling tool DNSCat2, which we will discuss later. The primary objective of *Symbiote* is providing remote access to the compromised system and stealing credentials by capturing them from SSH or SCP processes. It uses two different communication approaches. For exfiltration, the data is encrypted, encoded into hexadecimal format and embedded into DNS *A*-record queries using the following format: *packetNumber|.|machineID|.|hexEncPayload.example.com*. The packet number begins at 11111 and is incremented for each sent chunk. The machine ID, made up of data from the *uname* syscall, helps to differentiate between infected systems.

The second communication method is used to download scripts from its C2 server for further attacks. To accomplish this, it uses a similar approach, with the utilized resource record being changed to *TXT*. It uses the following query format: *packetNumber|.|machineID.example.com*. For this mode, the packet number starts at 0, which indicates that the malware requests the ED25519 signature of the script. This is later used to verify the downloaded data and prevent the malware from executing scripts from other sources. The packet number is then incremented, signaling the actual start of the download. As the size of DNS packets is limited, the script must be split into chunks and transmitted individually. The server can determine the respective chunk through the packet number in the requests. The selected chunk is encrypted and sent in the DNS response.

DNSCat2 is an open-source remote control tool, which utilizes DNS tunneling [24]. It strongly focuses on command and control functionality like file upload or download and tunneling shell sessions. DNSCat2 offers two operation modes, a "typical" connection through a local DNS Server and a direct connection. The direct connection uses UDP on port 53 and mimics DNS traffic to some extent but will not hold up against a proper inspection. The "typical" mode uses actual DNS requests that are sent through a local DNS server. Similar to other tools, DNSCat2 offers various configuration options to tailor the behavior to different networking environments. By default, it uses encrypted connections between client and server, and a single server can interface with multiple client simultaneously. The complexity of DNSCat2 is also observed in the communication protocol itself, which possesses TCP-like components, e.g., sequence numbers and acknowledgments. Internal commands of DNSCat2 follow another protocol that works on top of the low-level protocol. The binary data is transported through the DNS requests/responses as a hex-encoded string.

Symbiote DNSCat2 [12] is a modified DNSCat2 version of Symbiote, presumably customized by the same attack group. The changes mainly concern how the tool can be started. The reverse-engineered binary revealed that the attackers removed the argument parameters of the main function and created a custom *argv* variable with the following fixed parameters: `--no-encryption --dns domain=git.bancodobrasil.dev,type=TXT`. These are used to initialize the tool and set up a connection to the C2 server through *TXT* record messages. The transferred data is not being encrypted, instead applying a base64 encoding.

Iodine [8] is a general-purpose tunneling tool that can transport IPv4 traffic through the DNS protocol, offering a vast and versatile set of parameters and settings. The main use case is to gain Internet access in a network where general Internet access is blocked, but DNS traffic is still allowed through the firewall. This could be used to circumvent captive portals in public Wi-Fi networks or to exfiltrate information from corporate networks. As it is a tunneling software, it focuses on bidirectional communication, session stability and throughput. The general concept of the tunneling is similar to the samples mentioned above.

3.3   Generation of Data for the Evaluation

In a real attack scenario, the DNS communication would be hidden within a multitude of non-malicious traffic. When evaluating our malware identification framework, we must take that into consideration. However, due to the testbed having no Internet access, it is not possible to have ordinary, user-generated traffic directly mixed with the malware traffic. We resolve this by expanding the dataset with legitimate traffic, as described in Sect. 3.4.

We have chosen a total of seven "scenarios" where the malware samples are executed and the traffic produced by them is recorded. The scenarios are meant to cover different aspects of the communication and to gain an ample overview of the malware behavior. Every possible combination of a malware and scenario has been created (as long as the feature covered by the scenario is part of the capabilities of the malware). To have a consistent and comparable dataset across all of our malware samples, some of the recordings were conducted with a set time limit that is based on the recorded scenario. The scenarios are:

1. Handshake (HS) - observes the start-up sequences initiated by the malware. In this mode the custom-made C2 server is available and ready to respond

to any requests, thus the malware can register and display its behavior in a realistic infection scenario. Due to each malware having a unique initial chain of requests, we have designated all traffic produced up to the first Idle/Keep Alive request, as the Handshake of the malware. For that reason, the recordings have contrasting lengths and sizes, as well as no fixed duration.

2. Handshake with Fake Internet (HS Fakenet) - inspects the traffic generated by the malware when the C2 server is unavailable or unreachable. The mode intends to mimic a realistic infection scenario, and therefore a fake Internet connection was established between the victim and our uplink server. While the malware will be unable to register with a legitimate C2 server, we are interested in the behavior and frequency of the requests sent by the infected device. The recordings are limited to 30 min.

3. Handshake Offline (HS Offline) - a scenario similar to the Handshake with Fake Internet, where no network connection is simulated, therefore none of the requests sent by the victim device are answered. While there is no change in the C2 server accessibility from the previous mode, this scenario allows us to observe whether the behavior of the malware undergoes any changes when a system is completely offline. Equivalent to the Handshake with Fake Internet, the recordings were done over a 30 min time period.

4. Idle/Keep Alive - a mode that enables the C2 server and observes the communication after the initial Handshake. This means a connection with the malware has been established but no jobs will be sent to the sample once the handshake is complete. Due to some malware samples implementing pause intervals to make their traffic less recognizable, we have decided each recording of this mode to have a $12\,h$ length.

5. Steal SSH key through upload (UL SSH) - a plausible infection scenario for a job which utilizes the malware to upload the contents of a file from the victim machine to the C2 server. To have a more representative set of data, we have decided to record this scenario with both a 4096 bit RSA and an ED25519 private key. For consistency, we have used the exact same keys for each malware sample. There is no set time limit for the recordings, instead storing all of the packets from the job acquisition until the last packet.

6. Steal Large File (UL File) - a scenario that utilizes the same malware capabilities as the Steal SSH scenario. The goal is to see how each sample handles a larger file, i.e., a MS Office Word document. To do that, we first encode the document into base64, and then proceed with the upload. We used the same file for each sample, and the recording length varies between them.

7. Download of a File (DL File) - the last scenario transfers a file from the C2 server to the infected device. Contrasting the previous upload modes, the malware sends requests which may contain metadata, rather than stolen information, so that the commanding server can interpret it and respond with segments of the file. In real infection circumstances, this file could be additional instructions, another stage of the malware, or a new malware altogether. We have chosen to use a network scanner tool, as it fits the use-case while being relatively light in size. Nevertheless, due to the limited space and

frequencies of the requests, sending the full file may take extremely long time, so we limited the recordings to a maximum of 12 h.

Table 1 shows all the combinations of malware and scenarios that we recorded. As the SSH scenario uploads two separate files, each has been stored in its own recording, making a total of 8 possible recordings for each tool or malware.

Table 1. Malware and open-source tools with their scenario combinations.

Malware and Tools	Handshake	HS Fakenet	HS Offline	Keep Alive	UL SSH	UL File	DL File
RogueRobin PS	✓	✓	✓	✓	✓	✓	✓
RogueRobin .NET	✓	✓	✓	✓	✓	✓	✓
Saitama	✓	✓	✓	✓	✓	✓	✓
Symbiote	-	-	-	-	✓	✓	✓
Symbiote DNSCat2	✓	✓	✓	✓	✓	✓	✓
DNSCat2*	✓	✓	✓	✓	✓	✓	✓
Iodine	✓	✓	✓	✓	✓	✓	✓

*Dnscat2 has been used in a malware campaign

3.4 Expanding the Collected Dataset

While the recorded network traffic covers a broad range of the potential tunneling usage, taking each recording as a single sample is not sufficient for a meaningful analysis. This is due to the low total number of samples available to training and testing our methodology, as we would be grouping all requests from the same domain. In addition, it is not an efficient approach that can be applied to a live-environment as the full recording may take a long period of time to be captured. For this reason, we have taken an approach that combines all of the recordings into a single set of data and then processes n packets under the same domain in a sliding window. The packets in this combined dataset follow a consistent scenario sequence and have the same order as they have been sent in. Likewise, the packet order in each window follows the original order of the traffic recording. This also leads to some windows containing traffic from two scenarios, which would mirror an authentic classification attempt in the wild.

We have analyzed various window size configurations and did not notice a major difference in the results. For this reason, we have chosen a size of 10 packets per window, as this allows Domainator to not only be used *post factum*, but also in a live setting with a manageable number of requests that are necessary to do the identification. As there may not always be a full window of 10 requests, especially in the case of legitimate domains, we have set a minimum of 3 requests per window that are necessary for the calculation of the statistical features.

Although the order of the scenarios does not influence our results, we have built a plausible attack configuration which takes the following arrangement:

Handshake Offline → Handshake Fakenet → Handshake →
Download → Idle → Steal RSA → Steal ED25519 → Steal File

The recordings done with the live malware contain all the additional legitimate packets that were sent by other services during the execution. However, the malware produces a much higher amount of traffic in comparison to the rest of the applications, thus building an imbalanced ratio of malicious and non-malicious traffic.

To have more equal proportions between these, we have added legitimate, non-malicious DNS requests from a dataset recorded in the span of a day on a DNS resolver managed by an Internet service provider [30]. The authors have anonymized the timestamps and the true user IP addresses, but have kept the adjustments consistent to the real traffic, i.e., all requests from a single user are mapped to the same new address. Additionally, two exfiltration tools were executed during the recorded period – *Iodine* and *DNSExfiltrator*. The dataset also recognizes the presence of benign data exfiltration performed by two distinct antivirus tools, namely *Eset* and *McAfee*. All exfiltration requests have been marked as such, so that they can be separated from the rest of the data, and were used by us as part of the validation in Sect. 4.4.

In addition to that, we have created a validation set consisting of recordings of our malware samples that were not utilized in the training. These recordings follow a similar malware-scenario pairing, but for each one of them a different parameter was changed or the code itself was modified to simulate possible adjustments an adversary could undertake to evade a detection algorithm. These changes include new files being uploaded or downloaded, the removal of used domain names, changes in the used resource records, changes in the encoding algorithm and alphabet, and reduction or increase of the communication capacity per DNS request. The goal of this set is to validate the identification process and its robustness to distortions in the traffic.

3.5   Feature Selection

When analyzing any of the given malware samples, a fairly simple approach would be to search for re-occurring fixed strings which uniquely identify the sample (e.g., subdomains which always begin with a certain substring). We call such values *magic bytes* and consider their utilization an insufficient solution because they could be changed by the malware authors by adjusting a single variable. Doing detection over specific anomalies can also lead to the incorrect classification of anomalous-looking traffic originating from legitimate sources, e.g., antivirus software. Moreover, it is not possible to reliably identify such magic bytes in most cases.

We decided to work independent of such magic bytes and have concentrated our efforts on creating a set of statistical values which capture the overall characteristics of the traffic generated by the malware, instead of the individual requests. When detecting tunneling presence in network flows, the metrics used by the papers described in Sect. 2 have already shown to be effective, as they search for anomalies not usually present in legitimate traffic. However, when attempting to do identification, there is an overlap of the anomalous characteristics, as each sample is malicious. Using our windowing approach, we analyze a snippet of the traffic and build all pair combinations within an individual window. Following, various string metrics are calculated for every combination, resulting in a subdomain similarity score for each metric. We take the scores on a per metric basis, and determine the mean value, thus assigning similarity scores to the window itself, which act as the input features to our detection and identification classifiers. The string metric features are listed on the right side of Fig. 2. Our approach has also been visualized in Fig. 2, with the possible combinations of DNS requests being shown on the left side of the graphic, and the calculated mean scores resulting in the features on the right side.

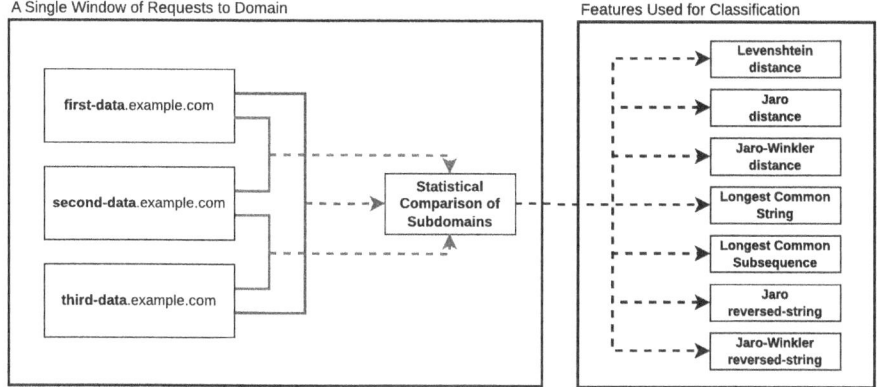

Fig. 2. A single window of three requests and their combination into the statistical metrics. Each metric consists of the mean value for the window.

The Levenshtein distance, as well as the Jaro and Jaro-Winkler similarities, provide data on the number of edits it takes to get from one string to the other. As each malware has a different implementation of its communication protocol, there is a contrast between the order of occurring changes and their execution in consecutive requests sent to the C2 server. It is also not unusual for the communication protocol to include a form of a victim ID, a job ID or a counter, which add some repetitiveness to the requests. The Jaro-Winkler similarity considers such reoccurring elements at the beginning of the strings by having a scaling component that results in a higher similarity score. To cover a broader comparison, we also calculate the Jaro and Jaro-Winkler scores for the reversed strings, so that subdomains ending in the same suffix can also be weighted correspondingly. Furthermore, it is possible that static patterns within the strings are separated by a chunk of dynamic data. The longest common subsequence covers such cases by matching two strings and finding equivalent segments, even with gaps of variable length. In contrast, the longest common substring searches for an uninterrupted pattern of matching characters, and in the case of multiple separated sequences, it considers only the longest one. The combination of these features results in traffic windows exhibiting similar subdomain patterns to be grouped together. These clusters are distinguishable from one another, which allows a classifier to correctly identify a future window without relaying on specific spatial and temporal variables, e.g., the timestamp or the timings between the packets.

Using the combination of the scenario recordings and the legitimate traffic, we built a dataset containing 43, 212 windows, with the total number of windows for each malware being presented in Table 2. The data was split into a train part and a test part, with a proportion of 80% to 20%, which were subsequently passed to a simple classifier. Although we have analyzed various classification and regression methods, our approach showed the greatest potential with a Random Forest classification, due to its overall score and efficiency. In our final approach, we have trained multiple such classifiers, with all of them utilizing the same input features. The evaluation is split into several stages, which can either work separately or be put together into a pipeline. For all results, we have listed the scores of the Random Forest classifiers.

Table 2. Number of windows in the full dataset, together with their distribution per action

Type of Traffic	Total	Handshake	Keep Alive	Upload	Download
Legitimate	15,914	–	–	–	–
RogueRobin PS	3,005	24	1,106	114	1,761
RogueRobin .NET	3,043	23	930	524	1,566
Saitama	242	8	6	158	70
Symbiote	697	–	–	23	674
Symbiote DNSCat2	7,331	7	4,319	21	2,984
DNSCat2	8,054	8	4,269	23	3,754
Iodine	4,926	9	4,297	14	606

4 Results and Evaluation

4.1 Malware Detection

Our initial step was to conduct a binary classification, where all non-legitimate traffic was labeled as malicious. The goal of this was to examine whether we can create a detection algorithm that can differentiate between the malicious and non-malicious windows using the described features. The classifier had an overall accuracy (F1-Score) of 0.966, with a macro average precision of 0.958 and recall of 0.970. The false-positive rate lies at 1.2%. The distribution of the predicted labels and the associated ROC curve are shown in Fig. 3.

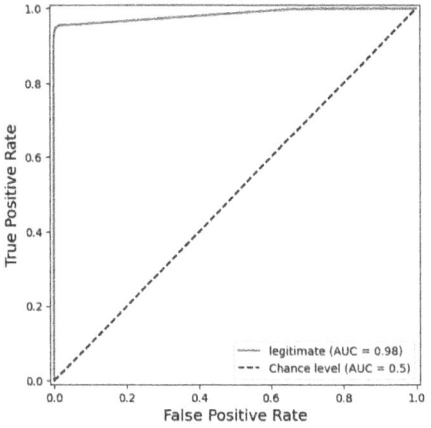

Fig. 3. ROC curve: malware detection

Table 3. Classification results for the malware detection

	Predicted		
Actual	Malic.	Legitim.	**F1-Score**
Malicious	5,201	259	**0.955**
Legitimate	38	3,145	**0.972**
hline			**0.966**

4.2 Malware Identification

The next step was to increase the granularity of the classification by having each malicious window be labeled as the malware that it originates from. This creates the broader task of not only detecting the presence of malicious DNS requests, but also separating and identifying each sample. The classifier achieved an F1-score of 0.964, similar to the accuracy of the previous binary approach, with the more precise scores being shown in Fig. 4a. The macro precision of the classifier is 0.982, while its recall is 0.911. Figure 4b presents the ROC curves.

In both of these cases, there appears to be an outlier scenario that the classifier is not able to correctly detect and identify. The *Idle* traffic produced by PowerShell RogueRobin continuously sends the same packet requesting a new job ID from the server. This leads to a statistical uniformity that is consistent with the behavior observed by a big portion of the non-malicious traffic. For the detection of the 259 windows falsely identified as legitimate in Tab. 3, 221 (85%) can be attributed to this scenario. Although not impactful to our classifiers, due to the smaller number of windows, the *Idle* windows of Saitama have the same communication pattern and are incorrectly identified as legitimate traffic.

4.3 Scenario Identification

Subsequently, we implement identification of the behavior and actions the tools have undertaken. An action is defined as the function currently executed by the tool and correlates to the scenarios in Sect. 3.3. The traffic within our dataset can be categorized into four such actions: performing the initial handshake, being idle, downloading a file, and uploading a file. Although some of our designed scenarios cover the same action (e.g., multiple *Uploads*), these can be joined into a singular group and therefore pose no obstruction to the classification. Non-malicious traffic performs none of these actions. The distribution of windows for each action has been described in Tab. 2.

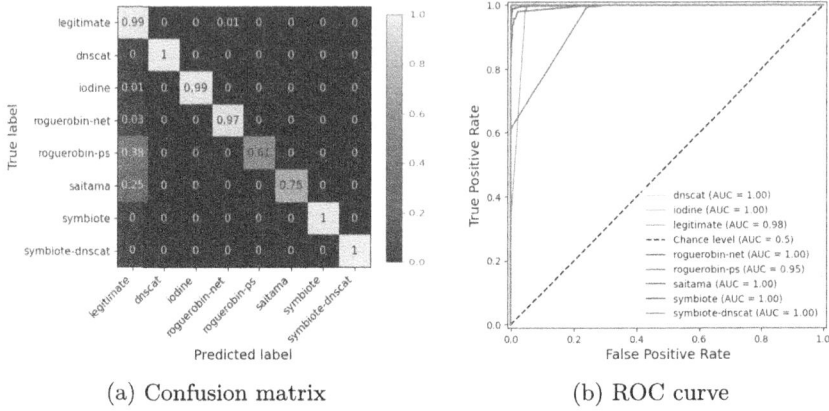

(a) Confusion matrix   (b) ROC curve

Fig. 4. Malware identification results

An imbalance between the number of DNS requests for the actions can be observed, as it is ordinary that the malware sends more packets during the more data transfer intensive actions. While it can skew the score of the classifier, it is more authentic to a real infection scenario. However, a limitation resulting directly from this design choice is the very small number of DNS requests within the handshake action, due to the tools requiring to do it only once at the beginning of their interaction with the C2 server. As a result of this, we have decided to exclude this action from the scenario identification.

There are two approaches that can be used for the training of the classifier. The first one attempts to identify the window directly, without any previous steps being taken, while the second one assumes that the window has already been identified as malicious and removes the legitimate traffic from the dataset. While both approaches led to a similar accuracy of 0.857 and 0.876, the inclusion of the legitimate traffic in the first approach skews the results as the precision and recall of the respective classifier are 0.832 and 0.804, in comparison to 0.892 and 0.881 for the second one. The main difference between the two is caused by PowerShell RogueRobin and Saitama traffic being identified as non-malicious, similarly to the malware identification.

The results of the identification done by the approach without legitimate traffic, as visualized in Fig. 5, show that the classifier is struggling with two of the actions recorded with DNSCat2. The cause for this is the usage of the same patterns during the download of a file and idle operation which our statistical features cannot differentiate. Although the approach with no legitimate traffic correctly classifies the idle traffic of RogueRobin, a different malware sample (e.g., Saitama) producing the same unchanged DNS requests would lead to identical inaccuracies. A further refinement of the method could have the identification task be performed in two separate stages – the first identifies the specific malware, and the second classifies the action.

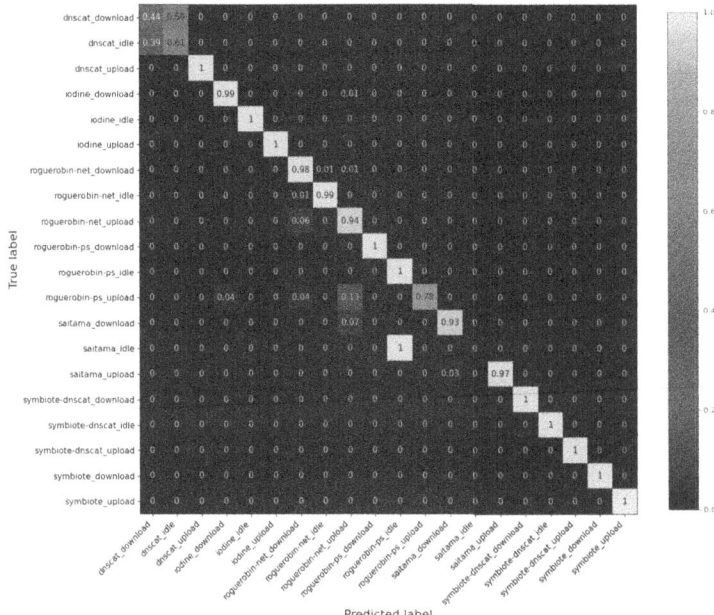

Fig. 5. Confusion matrix with the scores of the scenario identification classifier

We have also evaluated a more generalized scenario classification in which the malware is not taken into account but the classifier has to identify what action is being performed. As the training dataset mixes windows from different tools for the same actions, which means the used patterns are not complimentary to one another, it is performing worse than the more precise approaches. However, the goal of this form of classification would be to attempt identifying malicious actions taken by malware which is not in the dataset, but has a similar communication protocol. The results of this method are visualized in Fig. 6, and the overall accuracy is 0.878, with macro precision of 0.889 and recall of 0.878.

4.4 Validation

In addition to the classification of the initial dataset, we wanted to analyze how well the classifiers can manage traffic produced by the same malware and tools, but with adapted settings. These adapted settings are: different files being uploaded, altered domains and resource records, a modified set of used encoding characters, and a modified size of the data that is sent with each request. Although we have not crossed each tool with each setting variation, we have built an ample validation dataset which we passed to our trained classifiers.

The evaluation of this dataset was done by taking each PCAP file and computing the statistical windows, then letting the classifier make its prediction. Subsequently, an average score is calculated for the whole file. Table 4 shows most of the entries of this dataset, together with the averaged F1-scores for the

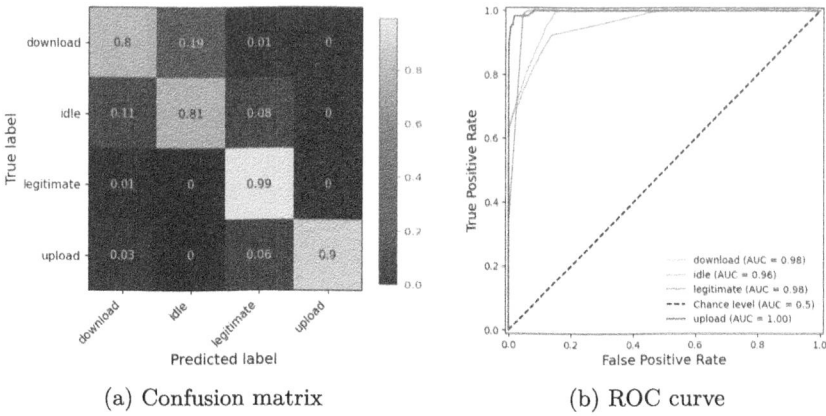

(a) Confusion matrix   (b) ROC curve

Fig. 6. Generalized scenario identification results

malware and scenario classifiers. As the validation dataset contains overlaps of malware-scenario pairings with similar changes (e.g., Iodine Upload with multiple different files being uploaded), the repetitions have been omitted from the table, unless there is a stark discrepancy in the prediction accuracy. Although not written explicitly under the changes, for every download and upload scenario, the file sent through the channel was different from the ones utilized in the training set. We observe the lowest results in cases where the encoding was fully changed, or the length of the tunneled subdomains has been starkly increased or decreased. We also recognize that the versatility of the open-source tools leads to lower results, due to the vast number of adjustable parameters, which can produce widely different traffic.

We have also validated the process on the exfiltration requests present in the [30] dataset with real traffic. These can be put into two categories based on their intentions, with the antivirus data being considered non-malicious, and the requests initialized by the authors to transfer files as malicious. Although the whitelisting of non-malicious domains that utilize DNS tunneling is possible and would prevent them from being detected as malicious, our goal is to test whether the granularity of our features can lead to them not being detected as malicious in the first place. In addition to that, the inclusion of a tunneling tool outside the ones in our training dataset allows us to examine how the classifiers handle the detection and identification of an unknown malware.

The results for both classifications are presented in Tab. 5. For the identification portion of the table, only labels that were predicted more than 10 times are listed, in order to keep the visualization compact. In the case of non-malicious tunneling, we observe high accuracy in the detection classifier, with an F1-score of 0.951. A similar F1-score is shown by the identification predictions, with most of the misidentifications being attributed to the two open-source tools in our training dataset. For the McAfee tunneling channel, there were also 4 incorrect identifications as the Symbiote Dnscat2 implementation and a single

Table 4. Classification results of the validation dataset

Malware	Scenario	Changes	F1-Score Malware	F1-Score Scenario
Symbiote	Upload		1.0	1.0
Symbiote	Download		0.99	0.99
Saitama	Upload		0.6	0.8
RR-PS	Upload	Data transfer length	0.17	0.46
RR-PS	Idle		0.0	0.0
RR-PS	Download		0.88	0.88
RR-PS	Download	Removed used RRs	0.88	1.0
RR-NET	Upload		0.94	0.90
RR-NET	Upload	Data transfer length	0.74	0.72
RR-NET	Upload	Removed used domains	0.94	0.83
RR-NET	Upload	Encoding character set	0.90	0.84
RR-NET	Idle	Encoding character set	0.95	0.93
RR-NET	Download		0.91	0.84
Iodine	Upload	Length to 200 chars	0.90	0.95
Iodine	Upload	Length to 100 chars	0.04	0.0
Iodine	Idle	Used encoding chars	0.98	0.98
Iodine	Idle	Utilised resource record to TXT	0.94	0.94
Iodine	Idle	Utilised resource record to A	0.99	0.99
Iodine	Download	Transfer length to 200 chars	0.75	0.75
Iodine	Download	Transfer length to 150 chars	0.54	0.50
DNSCat2	Upload		0.94	0.91
DNSCat2	Upload	Data encoding method	0.03	0.02
DNSCat2	Idle	Utilised resource record to CNAME	1.0	0.65
DNSCat2	Idle	Encoding method and resource record	0.0	0.0
DNSCat2	Download		1.0	0.4
DNSCat2	Download	Data encoding method	0.0	0.0

misclassification as RogueRobin-Net. Additionally, the Eset exfiltration showed 1 identification as Symbiote Dnscat2.

Although the classifiers have no concept of how to categorize the DNSExfiltrator traffic, it is correctly detected as malicious in just over 75% of the cases. However, the identification shows a much higher rate of uncertainty, with a mostly even split between the window being designated as legitimate traffic, or as being produced by Saitama, Dnscat2 or Iodine. The variance in which malware or tool the DNSExfiltrator is associated with, can be explained by the usage of different parameters (i.e., maximum domain name length and encoding) by the authors. As the true label of these requests is not within the classes of the classifier, all of these predictions considered "incorrect", and thus significantly reduce the overall F1-score of the identification validation.

The Iodine traffic generated by the authors is in much smaller quantities compared to the other tools. A more in-depth analysis of the requests also showed that most of these are part of the handshake routine, separated by sporadic idle traffic. This mixture and alternation of non-exfiltration activities causes the detection classifier to have a very low success rate at predicting whether the traffic is malicious. The proportions of irregular traffic have an even starker effect on the tool identification, with none of the elements being correctly classified. Beside the identification as legitimate traffic, there are also 3 classifications as RogueRobin-Net and 1 as RogueRobin-PS.

Table 5. Classification results for the validation of third-party traffic

Tool		Predicted Detection		Predicted Identification				
	Actual	Malic.	Non-malic.	Saitama	Dnscat2	Iodine	Legitim.	Others
Eset	Non-malic.	149	11,627	0	52	73	11,650	1
McAfee	Non-malic.	48	880	0	2	14	907	5
Iodine	Malic.	4	25	0	0	0	25	4
DNSExfilt.	Malic.	3,661	1,065	997	1,101	1,554	1,074	0

While there is no full overlap of the investigated tools, we have also evaluated our approach on the dataset provided by the authors of the GraphTunnel [10] framework. The dataset contains multiple recordings of both *Iodine* and *dnscat2* traffic, with the *Iodine* file names suggesting alternation between the used resource records. However, no specifications are given for any of the other parameters. The captured *dnscat2* traffic was detected and identified correctly by our classifiers with an accuracy of 0.9. Although the performed actions are not given, our behavior classifier overwhelmingly suggests the presence of a file upload, together with idle traffic. The *Iodine* traffic identification was less successful, as the classifier recognized the tool about half the time in the files designated as *NULL* and *TXT* resource records, as well as the recording named *private*. The rest of the recordings, indicated as *A*, *MX*, *CNAME* and *SRV* had a prediction rate of less than 0.05. According to our behavior classifier, the tool provides download functionality. Manual inspection of the recordings shows the main difference between them appears to be in what actions were performed, with the *NULL*, *TXT* and *private* recordings exhibiting traffic very similar to our *Iodine-Download* scenario, and the remainder being of unclear behavior. The provided normal traffic was correctly detected as non-malicious with a rate of 0.96, ascertaining a low false-positive rate on previously unseen traffic.

4.5   Result Comparison

Although in Sect. 2 we have listed multiple other tools that cover tunneling detection as their main goal, none of them have made their models and feature extraction partially or fully available. For this reason, we cannot fairly evaluate their approaches on our dataset containing real malware samples, and therefore have chosen to compare the results to the ones that have been provided in each work, as shown in Tab. 6.

While our detection approach achieves a slightly lower detection score, none of the other tools have attempted to detect *real* malware, i.e., they solely covered

Table 6. Result comparison with other similar tools

Tool	Malware Count	Open-Source Count	Tunnel Detection	Tunnel Identification	Behavior Identification
Domainator (our approach)	5	2	0.966	0.964	0.857
GraphTunnel (2024) [10]	0	7	1.000	0.986	n/a
Žiža et al. (2023) [30]	0	2	0.998	n/a	n/a
Alkasassbeh et al. (2023) [1]	0	1	0.97	n/a	n/a
Buczak et al. (2016) [4]	0	4	0.95	n/a	n/a

open-source DNS tunneling tools. Further, our approach is the first to perform an identification of real-world malware traffic (GraphTunnel also identified tools but did not cover real-world malware). Given this more challenging task, our detection score of 0.964 can be considered promising. Furthermore, `Domainator` is the first attempt to identify specific *actions* taken by the malware based on its DNS tunneling activities, and thus no comparison can be drawn to other tools. The achieved score of 0.857 is acceptable for this specific task.

5 Discussion

`Domainator` differentiates between certain malware samples and their actions, based on DNS tunneling behavior. Our method solely relies on the metadata analysis of subdomain strings, i.e., it works independently of other DNS characteristics that are utilized by malware, such as the transferring of commands and payloads in `TXT` answer records, which provides a high embedding capacity.

`Domainator` is tailored to aid the classification and attribution of upcoming malware families. Therefore, DNS traffic of new malware must be recorded, e.g., in our testbed. If the traffic matches certain sequential patterns identified by our research, it might be linked to the specific type of malware that we associate with the particular pattern. As discussed in Sect. 4.3, we are unable to successfully identify some idle scenarios, which is caused by the idle behavior of the malware continuously sending identical requests and thus closely resembling legitimate traffic. During our evaluations, we observed only PowerShell RogueRobin and Saitama being incorrectly classified for those reasons, but future malware with such idle behavior could result in similar misclassifications. Although the per window false-positive rate of the non-malicious traffic is already low, adding a per domain threshold based on malicious window count can further lower the per domain false-positive-rate.

Limitations We investigated 7 malware samples and tools that exploit subdomain strings in the DNS protocol. Other or future malware samples could apply covert channel techniques for DNS in alternative ways, e.g., based on different hiding patterns [27]. Such malware would most likely require us to adjust the set of selected DNS features for appropriate detection. Moreover, future versions of the analyzed malware might change their behavior or encoding strategy for subdomains. This could influence detectability and would also require adjustments of our features. The identification of future malware outside of our current set would not be possible without retraining the classifier with the traffic from the new malware, as the classifier would have no knowledge of it. Versatile tools like *Iodine* would also benefit from multiple parameter setups being added to the dataset, due to the vastly different tunneling traffic it can produce based on those settings, as seen in our validation results. Finally, we experimented solely with a limited set of simple classifiers and evaluating alternative, more complex machine learning methods might improve our results.

Provision of Data Our traffic dataset is available on GitHub: https://github.com/dreamingdust/domainator-dataset.

6   Conclusion

We introduced a sequence-based detection and differentiation approach for malware using DNS-based covert channel techniques. We utilize only the subdomain portions of the domains sent in the DNS requests as a vector to calculate statistical metrics. These features were used to train a generic Random Forest classifier, which can be used for both the *detection of DNS tunneling traffic* and the *identification of the malware*. Our approach is even able to *identify the action undertaken by the malware* (e.g., file upload or download), utilizing the same statistical features. In future work, we plan to extend our research to additional protocols of the TCP/IP protocol suite, especially to HTTP(S).

Acknowledgments. Parts of the research work have been funded by the ATTRIBUT project, *Agentur für Innovation in der Cybersicherheit*, Germany, program "Existenzbedrohenden Risiken aus dem Cyber- und Informationsraum Hochsicherheit in sicherheitskritischen und verteidigungsrelevanten Szenarien" (HSK), *https://www.cyberagen- tur.de/tag/hsk/*. Project website: *https://attribut.cs.uni-magdeburg.de*. This publication was financially supported by the Worms University of Applied Sciences, Germany.

Disclosure of Interests. The authors have no competing interests to declare that are relevant to the content of this article.

References

1. Alkasassbeh, M., Almseidin, M.: Machine learning techniques for accurately detecting the DNS tunneling. In: Intelligent Comput. Springer (2023)
2. Badar, L.T., Carminati, B., Ferrari, E.: A comprehensive survey on stegomalware detection in digital media, research challenges and future directions. Signal Process. **231**, 109888 (2025)
3. Born, K., Gustafson, D.: Detecting DNS tunnels using character frequency analysis. arXiv, cs.CR(1004.4358) (2010)
4. Buczak, A.L., Hanke, P.A., Cancro, G.J., Toma, M.K., Watkins, L.A., Chavis, J.S.: Detection of tunnels in PCAP data by random forests. In: Proceedings of the Annual Cyber and Information Security Research Conference (CISRC '16'). ACM (2016)

5. Caviglione, L., Mazurczyk, W.: Never mind the malware, here's the stegomalware. IEEE Secur. Priv. **20**(5), 101–106 (2022)
6. Chandola, V., Banerjee, A., Kumar, V.: Anomaly detection for discrete sequences: a survey. IEEE Trans. Knowl. Data Engin. **24**(5), 823–839 (2012)
7. Dittmann, J., Kraetzer, C., Alemann, J., Birnbaum, B.: Forensic trace analysis for MP3 based stego-malware: exemplary study for stego-algorithm and capacity attribution to derive YARA rules for malware identification. In: Proceedings of the IHMMSec, pp. 101–112. ACM (2024)
8. E. Ekman & Iodine Contrib. iodine (2024). https://github.com/yarrick/iodine
9. Fox-IT. Saitama C2 Server (2024). https://github.com/fox-it/saitama-server
10. Gao, G., et al.: GraphTunnel: robust DNS tunnel detection based on DNS recursive resolution graph. IEEE Trans. Inf. Forens. Secur. (2024)
11. Ironnet. The siren song of RogueRobin (2020). https://www.ironnet.com/blog/dns-tunneling-series-part-3-the-siren-song-of-roguerobin
12. Kennedy, J., The BlackBerry Threat Research & Intelligence Team: Symbiote Deep-Dive: Analysis of a New, Nearly-Impossible-to-Detect Linux Threat (2022). https://intezer.com/blog/research/new-linux-threat-symbiote/
13. Kacherginsky, P.: DNSChef (2023). https://github.com/iphelix/dnschef
14. Kiltz, S., Dittmann, J., Loewe, F., et al.: Forensic image trace map for image-stego-malware analysis: Validation of the effectiveness with structured image sets. In: Proceedings of the IHMMSec, pp. 125–130. ACM (2024)
15. Knöchel, M., Karius, S.: Text steganography methods and their influence in malware: a comprehensive overview and evaluation. In: Proceedings of IHMMSec, pp. 113–124. ACM (2024)
16. Loganathan, G., Samarabandu, J., Wang, X.: Sequence to sequence pattern learning algorithm for real-time anomaly detection in network traffic. In: Canadian Conference on Electrice & Computing Engineering (CCECE), pp. 1–4 (2018)
17. Machmeier, S., Heuveline, V.: Detecting DNS tunnelling and data exfiltration using dynamic time warping. In: Cyber Security in Network Conference, pp. 83–91 (2024)
18. Malwarebytes. Saitama (2022). https://www.threatdown.com/blog/apt34-targets-jordan-government-using-new-saitama-backdoor/
19. Mazurczyk, W., Wendzel, S., Zander, S., Houmansadr, A., Szczypiorski, K.: Information Hiding in Communication Networks. Wiley (2016)
20. Mileva, A., Panajotov, B.: Covert channels in TCP/IP protocol stack-extended version. Open Comput. Sci. **4**(2), 45–66 (2014)
21. MITRE ATT&CK. DarkHydrus (2023). https://attack.mitre.org/groups/G0079/
22. MITRE ATT&CK. Hijack Execution Flow: Dynamic Linker Hijacking (2023). https://attack.mitre.org/techniques/T1574/006/
23. Palo Alto Networks. RogueRobin (2018). https://unit42.paloaltonetworks.com/unit42-new-threat-actor-group-darkhydrus-targets-middle-east-government/
24. R. Bowes & Contrib. DNSCat2 (2024). https://github.com/iagox86/dnscat2
25. Schüppen, S., Teubert, D., Herrmann, P., Meyer, U.: FANCI: feature-based automated NXDomain classification and intelligence. In: Proceedings of the USENIX Security '18, pp. 1165–1181. USENIX Assoc. (2018)
26. Strachanski, F., Petrov, D., Schmidbauer, T., Wendzel, S.: A comprehensive pattern-based overview of stegomalware. In: Proceedings of the ARES '24. ACM (2024)
27. Wendzel, S., Zander, S., Fechner, B., Herdin, C.: Pattern-based survey and categorization of network covert channel techniques. ACM Comput. Surv. **47**(3) (2015)

28. Zander, S., Armitage, G., Branch, P.: A survey of covert channels and counter-measures in computer network protocols. IEEE Commun. Surv. Tutor. **9**(3), 44–57 (2007)
29. Zillien, S., Petrov, D., Ruffing, P., Gross, F.: A development framework for TCP/IP network steganography malware detection. In: Proceedings of the IHMMSec, pp. 95–100. ACM (2024)
30. Žiža, K., Tadić, P., Vuletić, P.: DNS exfiltration detection in the presence of adversarial attacks and modified exfiltrator behaviour. Int. J. Inf. Secur. **22**(6), 1865–1880 (2023)

Mitigation of PFCP Attacks in 5G Networks: Dynamic Defense Through Moving Target Defense and Honeynets

Aitor Landa-Arrue[1]([✉]) [iD], Jasone Astorga[2] [iD], Iñaki Garitano[3] [iD],
and Aitor Urbieta[1] [iD]

[1] Ikerlan Technology Research Centre, Basque Research and Technology Alliance (BRTA), P.J.M. Arizmendiarrieta, 2, 20500 Arrasate/Mondragón, Spain
{alanda,aurbieta}@ikerlan.es
[2] Department of Communications Engineering, Faculty of Engineering, University of the Basque Country UPV/EHU, Alameda Urquijo s/n, 48013 Bilbao, Spain
jasone.astorga@ehu.eus
[3] Department of Electronics and Computing, Mondragón Unibertsitatea, Goiru, 2, 20500 Arrasate/Mondragón, Spain
igaritano@mondragon.edu

Abstract. The growing demand for enhanced network capabilities, driven by the exponential increase in connected devices, has led to the widespread adoption of Fifth-Generation (5G) networks. While these networks significantly improve speed, latency, and scalability, they remain susceptible to evolving cyber threats. Despite security advancements introduced by 5G, such as robust authentication methods like 5G-AKA and improved user identity protection through Subscription Permanent Identifiers and Subscription Concealed Identifiers, critical vulnerabilities persist. Particularly, attacks targeting the User Plane Function via the Packet Forwarding Control Protocol can modify packet forwarding rules, manipulate or disrupt user sessions, and degrade network services, posing substantial risks to operators and end-users. To address this challenge while enabling the analysis of adversarial behavior, this work proposes a mechanism based on a Moving Target Defense (MTD) strategy. The proposed approach isolates malicious actors within a honeynet environment, thereby enhancing threat detection and mitigation. By leveraging MTD principles, the proposed framework enhances network resilience, reduces the impact of the attacks, and strengthens overall 5G security. Additionally, it ensures adaptive protection against evolving threats, supporting the reliable and robust delivery of next-generation network services. The effectiveness of the proposed framework is evaluated through a testbed simulating a 5G environment, demonstrating that the additional latency introduced by the security mechanisms is limited and does not compromise overall network performance. Thus, the proposed solution provides effective and adaptive protection against evolving threats, supporting reliable and robust delivery of next-generation network services.

Keywords: 5G · PFCP · Mitigation · MTD · Cyber deception · Honeynets

M. Dalla Preda et al. (Eds.): ARES 2025, LNCS 15992, pp. 141–162, 2025.
https://doi.org/10.1007/978-3-032-00624-0_7

1   Introduction

In the context of a connected society, the adoption of Fifth-Generation (5G) networks, as a response to the requirements of increasingly connected devices, brings several advantages to connection performance. However, 5G networks also bring new security challenges, not only for ensuring the security of end-users but also for guaranteeing the security of underlying services [20].

The evolution of mobile networks has brought significant advancements in security mechanisms, particularly with the transition to 5G. Compared to previous generations, 5G introduces a more robust authentication framework, 5G-Authentication and Key Agreement (5G-AKA), which enhances mutual authentication between the User Equipment (UE) and the network while mitigating identity exposure risks [29]. Unlike its predecessors, 5G-AKA incorporates stronger cryptographic techniques to protect against replay attacks, man-in-the-middle attacks, and user traceability threats. A key improvement is the introduction of Subscription Permanent Identifier (SUPI) and Subscription Concealed Identifier (SUCI), which replace the clear-text transmission of user identities, a critical vulnerability in previous generations such as Forth Generation (4G) Long-Term Evolution (LTE) [11].

SUPI serves as a unique and permanent identifier for each subscriber but is never transmitted in plaintext over the air. Instead, the SUCI, an encrypted version of the SUPI, is generated using a public key encryption mechanism before being sent over the network, significantly reducing the risk of identity exposure and location tracking [11].

The present work focuses on securing core network services. To this end, it assumes a scenario where the Session Management Function (SMF) and Network Exposure Function (NEF) services were previously compromised. In this context, this paper proposes a mechanism to respond to the identified attack through the implementation of cyber deception techniques.

The term cyber deception describes techniques that attempt to mislead the attackers of a system by altering the attack surface without the knowledge of the attacker [22]. This prevents the attacker from recognizing or compromising the system [22], including techniques such as Moving Target Defense (MTD) and honeynets. Honeynets are networks specifically designed to lure and analyze attackers by simulating real environments while monitoring their actions. They are composed of multiple honeypots, which are decoy systems or services that mimic legitimate ones to attract and study malicious activity [17]. In our case, the honeynet corresponds to the 5G core network, where the honeypots consist of 5G services deployed in a separate network.

Our contribution is summarized as a mitigation solution that preserves end-user security by dynamically redirecting malicious traffic from the compromised SMF to a high-interaction honeynet, effectively isolating the attacker from legitimate critical network services. The redirection is done by two proxies that translate Internet Protocol (IP) addresses, leading the attacker to believe the connection is established with legitimate services. This mechanism prevents unauthorized modifications of user sessions and enables the monitoring of attacker behavior for timely defensive actions.

The structure of the paper is as follows: the background Sect. (2) delineates the primary technologies involved in this study; the threat modeling Sect. (3) identifies the main attack vectors within the network; the related work Sect. (4) presents the most relevant research efforts related to this study; the conducted proposed approach Sect. (5) describes the design and the main concepts of the implemented mitigation framework; the testbed Sect. (6) details the experimental environment used to evaluate the effectiveness of the proposed solution and discusses experimental results obtained; the subsequent Sect. (7) outlines future research directions; and finally, the conclusions (8) summarize the key findings of this study.

2   Background

This section explains the technologies employed in the work, which are indispensable for a comprehensive understanding of the subject.

2.1   5G Networks

The 5G networks are distinguished by their enhanced features in comparison to their predecessors. These features include reduced latency, increased bandwidth, and the capacity for supporting massive communications between devices [7].

The architecture of 5G networks is regarded as distributed by default. Two primary planes are specified in the architecture definition: the control plane and the user plane. These planes can be both logically and physically distributed, enabling services to be deployed throughout the cloud-continuum.

Moreover, modifications have been made to the network architecture, with the implementation of the Service-Based Architecture (SBA) [14] for the development of services that manage network users. The adoption of a microservice-based architecture in 5G networks promotes service encapsulation and results in a more loosely coupled and scalable design. Nevertheless, this architectural choice also expands the attack surface by generating additional microservices, potentially vulnerable to external or internal threats.

The ETSI standard TS 123.501 [13] defines 18 Network Functions (NFs) and the interfaces between them to connect each other. Nevertheless, not all NFs are implemented in existing solutions as illustrated in Fig. 1.

2.2   Moving Target Defense

MTD techniques, categorized as cyber deception techniques, involve altering the attack surface of a solution to confuse the attackers and impede their ability to compromise it. These techniques can be classified based on the mechanism that triggers them or the attribute that is modified by using MTD techniques [32]. Two categories of triggers are identified:

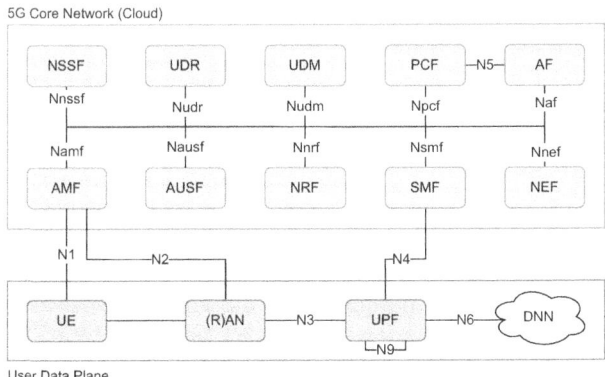

Fig. 1. ETSI [13] defined non-roaming 5G network architecture.

1. **Event-based triggers.** They initiate MTD techniques in response to specific events.
2. **Time-based triggers.** They initiate MTD techniques after a designated time interval has elapsed.

Depending on the attribute to be modified, MTD techniques can be further categorized into three types: shuffling, diversity, and redundancy.

1. **Shuffling.** Shuffling techniques focus on modifying the parameters of the solution, such as changing IP addresses, routing tables, or network protocols.
2. **Diversity.** Diversity techniques modify the platform on which the solution is running, such as changing the operating system of the service, the virtualization system, or the programming language of the service.
3. **Redundancy.** Redundancy techniques replicate services so that if the operation of the main service is altered, a replica can be used to replace the affected service.

It is important to note that these techniques are not mutually exclusive, and their combination can yield more complex solutions. However, some studies [3] have also highlighted that the combination of these techniques can result in an overload for the system in charge of their management due to the high cost in terms of resources.

2.3   Honeynets

Honeynets are groupings of several honeypots or trap nodes in a network dedicated to capturing attackers. Honeypots can be classified by purpose or by level of interaction [17]. Honeypots are cybersecurity decoys that attract attackers by imitating real systems, offering false data and services while discreetly monitoring their actions to dissuade threats and drain resources. Honeypots can be either research or production, depending on their purpose. In the field of research, honeypot devices are designed to collect data and information regarding cyberattacks within the honeypot. The researcher or administrator can then process this data to draw conclusions about the attacks and create a mitigation plan for those attacks. In contrast, production honeypots prioritize network protection and the reduction of potential threats in a real network environment. Their primary objective is to capture the attacker, thereby preventing them from reaching the real network. Instead, they focus their efforts on attacking the trap network.

In terms of interaction level, they can be categorized as high interaction, medium interaction, or low interaction [17].

- Honeynets with a **high interaction** level are the closest to the original application and allow the attacker to use the different network services as if they were using the legitimate network.
- **Medium interaction honeynets**, while demonstrating reliability in relation to the original network, are subject to limitations that hinder the full utilization of network services by attackers.
- **Low interaction honeynets**, on the other hand, simulate specific functions of the network and do not allow use beyond these functions.

3   Threat Modeling in the User Plane

In 5G networks, the user plane is particularly susceptible to external adversarial actions and connectivity impairments. Among its constituent elements, the gNodeB (gNB) and the User Plane Function (UPF) are considered the most critical, owing to exploitable vulnerabilities in the GPRS Tunneling Protocol (GTP) (N3 interface) and Packet Forwarding Control Protocol (PFCP) (N4 interfaces) protocols that may compromise confidentiality, integrity, or availability.

3.1   Overview of Threat Vectors

Three principal categories of attacks targeting the user plane have been delineated:

- **False Base Station attack.** These man-in-the-middle exploits involve the deployment of an illegitimate gNB by an adversary, thereby enabling interception or alteration of UE and other services communications [15,19,25]. Moreover, this attack can serve as a foundation for more sophisticated attacks [18,28].
- **GTP tunneling protocol-based attacks.** GTP tunneling protocol-based attacks are Distributed Denial-of-Service (DDoS) attacks where an attacker overloads the UPF by establishing numerous connections, leading to service degradation [6]. A more advanced variant, PFCP-in-GTP, encapsulates PFCP requests within GTP packets to evade firewalls and disrupt user sessions [23, 24], as detailed in Sect. 3.2.

– **PFCP protocol-based attacks.** These attacks allow adversaries to manipulate traffic control, modify active sessions, redirect data, or disrupt network services. By injecting or altering PFCP messages, attackers can evade security mechanisms, degrade network availability, and compromise the integrity and confidentiality of user connections.

Thus, the common element among the mentioned attacks is the UPF service, which becomes a critical component of the user plane from a security perspective due to its role as a gateway for user traffic when accessing the Internet or other applications. Furthermore, it stores user sessions in its memory, facilitating the management of each traffic of the client. Therefore, it assumes a pivotal role in the operation of the network and the facilitation of client-application connectivity. Hence, this study focuses on the analysis of the third type of attack: PFCP-based attacks.

3.2   PFCP Attacks for Session Manipulation

The UPF is responsible for routing user traffic according to the policies established in the user sessions. Therefore, modification of these sessions could result in access to unauthorized information or denial of service if the session policies indicate that packets from a user should be dropped. This attack is possible through the PFCP protocol, which is used to manage the sessions between the SMF and the UPF.

According to Radoglou-Grammatikis et al. [27] and Amponis et al. [4,5], the classification of PFCP attacks is divided into four groups, with the classification based on the PFCP request.

1. **PFCP session establishment request.** It is a Denial-of-Service (DoS) attack that involves sending a high volume of legitimate session establishment requests, thereby overloading the capacity of the UPF to handle all requests.
2. **PFCP session modification request (by DROP tag).** The objective is to modify the policies implicit in user sessions. This results in Forwarding Action Rule (FAR) rules being modified with the DROP action to discard packets with which the rule is associated. This may result in the UE losing the connection to the Data Network (DN). Nevertheless, it should be mentioned that even though the UE is disconnected from the DN, it is still connected to the 5G core through the Radio Access Network (RAN).
3. **PFCP session modification request (by DUPL tag).** This attack seeks to flood the UPF with the duplication of the same rule of a session, which generates that for the same type of traffic, the UPF has more than one possible path to forward that traffic. This can generate unexpected behavior due to duplication of traffic in the DN. In addition, this attack can lead to a DDoS attack if the flooding attack is scaled to multiple users.
4. **PFCP session deletion request.** This attack attempts to disconnect the UE through the submission of a high volume of session deletion requests. Consequently, the only way to reconnect would be by creating a new session or moving to another gNB.

4   Related Work

This part describes the existing landscape of attack and mitigation strategies within 5G and Beyond-5G (B5G) networks, with the primary goal of safeguarding them against cyber threats. For that, attack management emphasizes cyber deception techniques. The section is structured into three subsections: firstly the current works about PFCP attacks management are analysed, then, how MTD can be used for attack mitigation is explained, finally, the works about honeynets in 5G networks are reviewed.

4.1   PFCP Attacks Handling

PFCP attacks are designed to manipulate user sessions; however, they have received considerably less research attention than other types of cyberattacks. The majority of the existing literature focuses on detecting these attacks rather than addressing their mitigation. As PFCP is a protocol specific to 5G networks, the following works primarily concentrate on 5G network environments.

Radoglou-Grammatikis et al. [27] propose an Intrusion Detection System (IDS) for the detection of these attacks. This IDS is divided into seven modules, ranging from traffic capture to attack detection with explainability and a notification module. The detection is performed by two modules: one dedicated to the detection of PFCP traffic and the other to analyze TCP/IP traffic. The PFCP module (PFCP Artificial Intelligence (AI) Detection Engine) uses a decision tree algorithm, specifically Classification And Regression Tree (CART). The authors also mention the use of a specific PFCP dataset for model training. Still, the paper does not discuss any mitigation once the attack is detected.

In their research, Pell et al. [24] assume a compromised SMF service is the starting point for an attack on user sessions. In this case, an anomaly detection process is implemented using deep learning, specifically utilizing Long-Short Term Memory (LSTM) networks. Regarding the handling of detected malicious requests, they propose either discarding them or removing them.

As discussed in the work of Pell et al. [24], PFCP-in-GTP attacks are also considered, as they can evade detection by firewalls due to their encapsulation within the PFCP protocol. In this particular instance, Pell et al. [24] identify the origin of these packets within the SMF service. However, the study by Park et al. [23] identifies the source of the packets within the UE, thereby classifying this as a more critical attack. This distinction results in the potential for modification of the session of the user by an end user.

The authors Sheiki et al. [30] further propose the detection of attacks in distributed environments using federated learning in conjunction with LSTM. However, the mitigation of attacks is not a consideration in the paper.

Amponis et al. [4] discuss the challenges in detecting these attacks from the perspective of an end user, noting that end-users may not be aware of changes due to the absence of logs reflecting session state changes. They propose a future direction for creating a mechanism to synchronize logs between services, enabling them to detect and respond to session changes.

Additionally, Park et al. [23] introduce the concept of PFCP-in-GTP attacks, which aims to compromise the UPF by encapsulating the malicious PFCP packets in GTP packets. By using these techniques, they are able to avoid packet inspection. A straightforward approach is to inspect the packets looking for PFCP header in order to intercept those packets. However, in this case, the header of the packet is a GTP header. Thus, the packets are not identified as suspicious by the inspector. If the attack results are successful, the attacker can introduce arbitrary commands in the 5G core network and provoke unexpected behaviors. The table below (Table 1) shows the highlight of each work.

Table 1. PFCP attack management state-of-the-art.

Ref.	Attack Detection	Detection Methodology	Attack Mitigation
[27]	●	CART	○
[24]	●	LSTM	○
[23]	●	Custom detection algorithms	○
[30]	●	FL+LSTM	○
[4]	○	-	◐

● Addressed topic.   ○ Not addressed topic.   ◐ Partially addressed topic.

Table 1 illustrates that research on the protocol primarily focuses on detecting attacks using AI. However, only one study [4] addresses mitigation, and even then, only at a theoretical level. While it proposes mitigating the attack through log synchronization, this approach has not been implemented in practice.

4.2 MTD as Attack Mitigation

After detecting attacks, it is necessary to mitigate the impact of the attack on the system so that the damage caused is the least possible and causes the least possible disruption to the services offered to the end user.

Using MTD techniques, a combination of diversity and shuffling techniques is proposed by Alavizadeh et al. [3]. Specifically, Virtual Machine (VM) Live Migration shuffling is proposed to change the location of VMs and Operative System (OS) diversification. However, the paper mentions that combining both MTD techniques substantially increase the use of extra resources.

There has been limited research on integrating MTD in 5G/B5G networks. Soussi et al. propose MERLINS [31], an MTD framework that employs Deep Reinforcement Learning (DRL) algorithms to mitigate Advanced Persistent Threats (APT). Their solution can also be operated under SLAs. Abdelhay et al. [1] suggest a solution for privacy and security that uses MTD to shuffle IPs and mitigate DDoS attacks in the 5G core network. The privacy topic is covered by using the Software-Defined Perimeter (SDP) zero-trust technique.

Dantas Silva et al. [9] propose MADS, an MTD approach that mitigates scanning attacks without impacting Quality-of-Service (QoS). It monitors the byte counter of the Software-Defined Networks (SDN) controller and introduces delays when a threshold is exceeded. The switch then infers the source interface of the attacker, though MADS remains vulnerable to advanced attacks such as slow-rate attacks [9].

Table 2. MTD as attack mitigation state-of-the-art.

Ref.	Decision process	Cost-effective	MTD technique	MTD trigger	Mitigated attack	5G/B5G application
[3]	HARM	●	S, D	*Undefined*	*Undefined*	○
[31]	DRL	●	S	Hybrid	APT	●
[1]	*Undefined*	○	S	Time	DDoS	●
[9]	Custom	●	S	Event	Scanning attacks	●

● Addressed topic.   ○ Not addressed topic.   ◖ Partially addressed topic.
S: Shuffling.   D: Diversity.   R: Redundancy.   APT: Advance Persistent Threats.   HARM: Hierarchical Attack Representation Model.

From Table 2, it can be concluded that the most commonly used MTD technique is shuffling system attributes. The table includes a study not specifically focused on 5G; this is because the study performed by Alavidazeh et al. [3] combines multiple MTD techniques, which is uncommon and challenging from the resource management perspective. Regarding the efficiency of the solutions, most of them employ cost-effective approaches. Meanwhile, the triggers for MTD techniques vary across studies, utilizing event-based, time-based, or hybrid mechanisms depending on the approach.

Current literature shows that MTD techniques, primarily involving shuffling of IP addresses or VM migration, have been successfully employed against general threats like DDoS or APT attacks in various network contexts. However, their integration into 5G networks remains limited, and existing solutions often focus on isolated MTD techniques rather than comprehensive approaches. Hence, this work proposes a MTD-based approach to mitigate PFCP-specific attacks in 5G core networks.

4.3   Honeynets in 5G Networks

The utilization of honeynets in conjunction with MTD techniques has gained significant traction. Qin et al. [26] have conducted a comprehensive survey, which draws parallels between numerous papers employing both technologies. However, Qin et al. [26] identify several areas where honeynets show potential for enhancement:

- The absence of datasets.
- The lack of mechanisms for deployment cost optimization.
- The need for consensus on the utilization of quantitative metrics for evaluating solutions.

– The limitation of testbeds and applications.

Furthermore, most of the papers presented in [26] related to MTD and honeypots do not have 5G core network as a use case.

Alani et al. [2] propose a honeytwin approach for Sixth Generation (6G) networks based on SDN networks. In this case, the replicated services by the honeypots are Internet of Things (IoT) devices that use the network to communicate with other services. The distinction between honeytwin and honeynet is outlined by contrasting their function. Honeytwin is characterized as a service that replicates an IoT device, while a honeypot is designed to emulate a client computer or server in a generic manner [2]. They propose an efficient Machine Learning (ML)-based attack detection system that, after detecting malicious traffic, is able to redirect the traffic to a honeytwin using a SDN router. Nevertheless, the honeytwin and the redirection process is applied to an end-application (IoT device). Thus, 5G/6G core network service security is not addressed.

Escolar et al. [12] developed a mitigation mechanism based on network flow redirection, Network Slicer. In this case, the mechanism is an evolved version of a flow redirector that launches the honeynets in different network slices so that the malicious flow is isolated in a different slice from the legitimate one. Once the network slices have been configured, the slices designated for the attacker are provisioned with a reduced allocation of resources, with the aim of constraining both bandwidth and priority. In these network slices where the honeynet is hosted, information about the behavior of the attacker is collected.

Beltran et al. [21] propose on-demand honeypot deployment with attacker redirection. The proposed system is a cyber deception system that stealthily redirects suspicious TCP connections to honeypots, which are created instantaneously and mimic real systems. This redirecting of connections is intended to fool attackers, protect legitimate assets, and learn from the actions of attackers. The system utilizes an SDN/Network Function Virtualization (NFV)-based architecture, which ensures that it is both fast and unobtrusive. This architecture guarantees that attackers will not notice the redirection, even in scenarios with high traffic loads. The results of the study demonstrate the effectiveness and realism of the system, as well as its low impact on communications latency.

Table 3 shows that while honeynets are widely used in ICS environments, their adoption in 5G core network, remains limited. This highlights an opportunity to implement honeynets in the 5G core network and address the previously mentioned limitations in the work of Qin et al. [26].

5   Proposed Approach for PFCP Attack Mitigation

The proposed solution aims to mitigate PFCP session modification and deletion attacks launched by a single attacker. It involves the creation of a high-interaction honeynet that simulates the 5G core realistically at the time the core is compromised. This approach consists of redirecting the attacker to the honeynet, isolating them to analyze their intentions, observing their interactions

Table 3. Summary of Works on Honeynets and MTD

Ref.	Approach	Limitations	5G application
[26]	Honeynets + MTD review. Identifies key gaps.	No datasets, cost optimization metrics, or testbeds	○
[2]	Honeytwin for 6G (SDN, IoT). ML-based redirection.	Only for IoT, does not protect core 5G/6G	●
[12]	Traffic redirection via network slicing. Attack isolation.	Requires network slicing, does not cover internal attacks	●
[21]	On-demand honeypots Stealthy attack redirection.	TCP only, limited evaluation	○

with different network services, and gaining insight into their behavior. The proposed architecture (see Fig. 2) manages the traffic from SMF and gNB services to the UPF service by proxies that execute redirection tasks in the event of an attack, thereby redirecting the attacker to the honeynet.

The objective of the attacker is to compromise the sessions of the UEs by modifying them using the PFCP protocol. The threat model under considera-

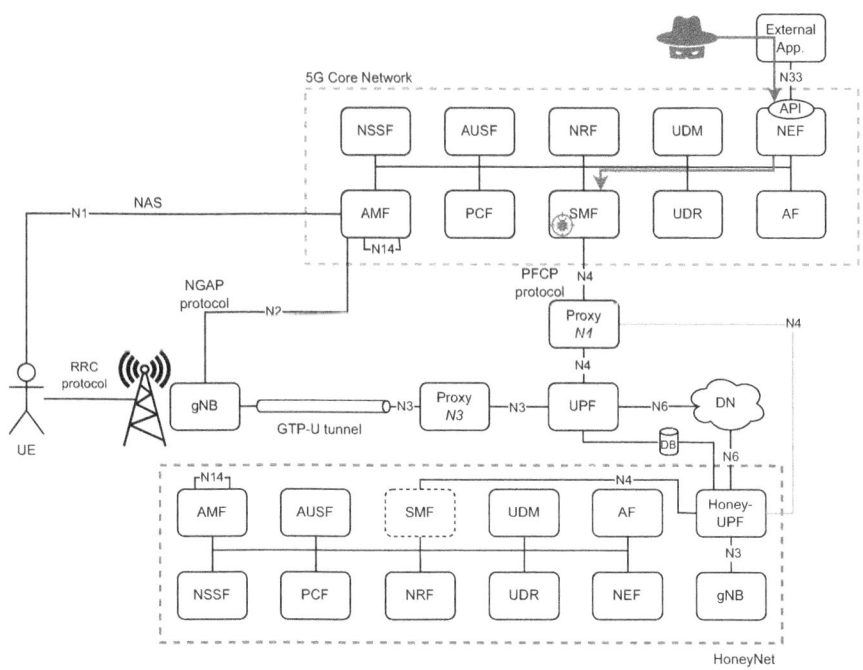

Fig. 2. Solution overall architecture.

tion assumes that the security of the core network has been previously compromised, thereby enabling a single attacker to gain access to the SMF service. This access is gained externally and through a network connection. This access can be obtained from the NEF NF, which is directly exposed to the network as part of the Northbound Application Programming Interface (API) of the 5G core [16]. Consequently, NEF exposes the core functionalities to the outside of the network for consumption by third-party applications, such as management and orchestration applications. Therefore, several authors [8,10] consider the NF and the possibility that it can be compromised as critical. Hence, the misconfiguration of NEF can result in unauthorized access to the various 5G core resources, as well as the violation of the confidentiality and integrity of the NF.

It is crucial to consider those conditions when mitigating the attack, as the objective is to ensure that the attacker remains unaware of the redirection to the honeynet. This means that the loss of the network connection to the SMF service during mitigation or the cessation of the attack must be prevented. Thus, it avoids the modification of the behavior of the attacker.

In the proposed scenario, session-related PFCP messages are identified as the primary messages capable of modifying a UE session. Within these messages, a distinction is made between requests and responses. Requests are those formulated from the SMF, making them more susceptible to spoofing. Within the requests, those specified in Sect. 3.2 are of particular concern.

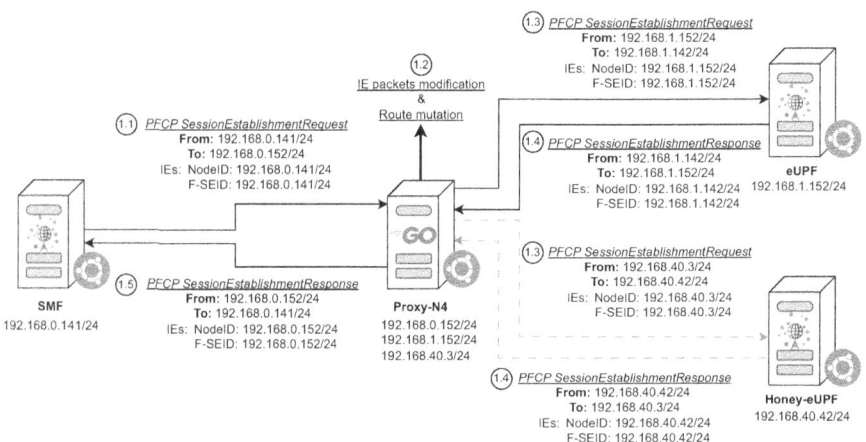

Fig. 3. IP translation representation.

Figure 3 shows how the PFCP session establishment requests are handled in the system. First, the SMF sends the PFCP SessionEstablishmentRequest (1.1), and then the proxy performs the route mutation by translating the IPs and modifying the Information Elements (IEs) of the packet (1.2). Depending on the route chosen by PROXY-N4, the packet will be forwarded to legitimate eUPF or to honey-eUPF (1.3). When the packet reaches eUPF, it is processed, and the response is generated and sent back to the proxy (1.4). Finally, the proxy translates the IP and IEs (1.2) and redirects the response back to the SMF (1.5).

The primary functions of the proxies include IP translation and the modification of PFCP packets, including Session Establishment Request/Response and Association Setup Request/Response. These four types of packets, handled by the UPF service, contain IEs in which session information is stored. Among them, the IP of the legitimate UPF is stored as identifiers in NodeID and Fully Qualified Session Endpoint Identifier (F-SEID). In the case that the UPF is not reachable when the packets reach the SMF, the SMF fails and terminates its process, or the packets are routed incorrectly. Consequently, it is imperative to substitute the IPs with those of the IEs, thereby ensuring that, from the perspective of the SMF, the proxies are recognized as the UPF. For the same reason, a proxy is required to manage traffic on the N3 interface. This is due to the fact that the parameters that have been previously modified are transmitted from the SMF to the Access and mobility Management Function (AMF) and from the AMF to the gNB. Consequently, for the establishment of the GTP tunnel, the gNB will seek the IP of the proxy without receiving an answer if those packets are not redirected to the UPF.

The use of proxies that dynamically modify IP addresses and routing configurations constitutes a form of MTD, specifically categorized as IP and route shuffling techniques, aimed at enhancing network resilience against attacks.

In order to integrate and mitigate the compromised SMF in the honeynet, the use of snapshots of the virtual machines used to virtualize the 5G core is proposed, preserving the state of the processes in the honeynet (stateful snapshot), assuming that the data contained in the core up to the time of the attack is compromised. The designated snapshot manager would function as an external monitoring service (orchestrator), with the permissions to access the hypervisor that oversees the virtualization of services.

In the case that the orchestrator is alerted of a potential attack, it will initiate the process of creating snapshots of the virtual machines and subsequently deploying them. Following the deployment of the core snapshot as a honeynet, SMF traffic is directed to this honeynet.

In the deployment of the snapshot as a honeynet, the legitimate core continues to serve the users, which may result in the creation of new sessions during the deployment. This potential inconsistency in session synchronization with the UPF of the honeynet can be mitigated by maintaining UPF sessions in a database for subsequent synchronization.

5.1   UPF Synchronization

The communication between the legitimate UPF and the honeynet UPF presents a synchronization challenge. This synchronization ensures that the honeynet has access to the sessions recorded in the legitimate core up until the creation of the honeynet.

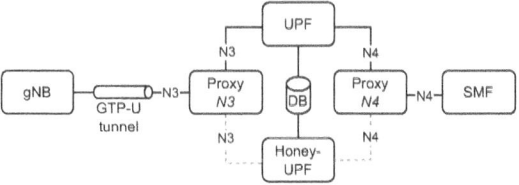

Fig. 4. Synchronization approaches for multiple UPFs by shared database.

Although various methods exist for synchronizing multiple UPFs, the proposed approach employs a shared database as the synchronization mechanism (see Fig. 4). In this approach, upon processing the packets transmitted by the SMF, each UPF stores the messages corresponding to sessions and nodes in a database designed to be compatible with UPFs. Besides, the integration of the shared database required modifications to the original UPF service. When an update occurs, the database notifies all listening UPFs of the changes, ensuring continuous and consistent synchronization.

This approach ensured the continuity of sessions established during the deployment interval, facilitating access to the most up-to-date information for the honeynet UPF upon connection. Subsequent to the deployment of the UPF of the honeynet, the database becomes the proprietary domain of the honeynet, thereby ensuring that legitimate sessions added to the database are not reflected in the honeynet.

6   Functional Validation

The implementation of the proposed approach (depicted in Fig. 5) involved the utilization of a virtual server equipped with 28 CPU cores and 32GB of RAM, on which Oracle VirtualBox hypervisor has been used to deploy 10 Oracle VirtualBox virtual machines. These virtual machines were configured to distribute the 5G core services, two proxies (one on the N4 interface and the other on the N3 interface), and databases.

The elements constituting this deployment can be categorized into five groups. The first group consists of RAN simulation of the 5G core, for which UERANSIM has been used. The second group consists of the 5G core, which is implemented by Free5Gc. The third group consists of a database compatible with UPFs, for which MongoDB is used, but alternative database systems may be considered. It is important to evaluate the advantages and disadvantages of different database systems, for example, latency, scalability, ease of integration, and data consistency, in order to determine which one best meets the objective of the solution. The fourth group consists of two proxies for traffic redirection, which are implemented as Go applications using PFCP and network-related libraries. The fifth group consists of a honeynet to isolate the attacker inside. The honeynet is a stateful snapshot of the 5G core VMs.

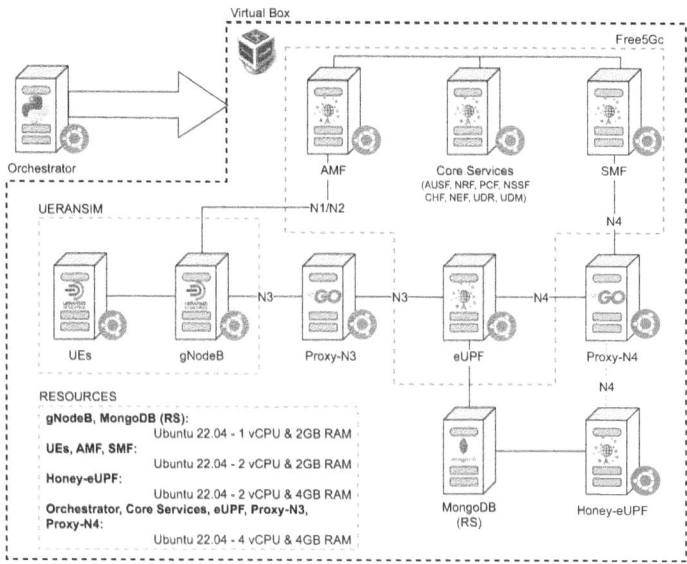

Fig. 5. Deployed testbed architecture.

It is noteworthy that the UPFs have been modified compared to the original version of Free5Gc, and thus, they are now designated as evolved-UPFs (eUPFs). The functionality to communicate with the database has been incorporated, with a dedicated thread being allocated to monitor database changes and execute the necessary actions. The new functionalities are based on the session and node management functions provided by Free5Gc and focus on reflecting their actions in the database. Additionally, although it is not a function officially supported by the Free5Gc UPF, it is also capable of deleting nodes from the database.

In the context of database management, MongoDB has been selected for implementation due to its ChangeStream system, which facilitates the triggering of notifications upon execution of database operations. This functionality is particularly advantageous in scenarios where a UPF modifies or inserts a document into the database, as it enables the notification of all eUPFs that are configured for monitoring.

To support synchronization and ensure fault tolerance, a MongoDB replica set configuration was utilized. This setup comprises a primary node, secondary nodes, and an arbitrator, with a lightweight Python application managing configuration adjustments during snapshot deployments. During these deployments, one of the secondary nodes is temporarily detached, reconfigured for the decoy environment, and replaced by a new secondary node to maintain consistency. This mechanism contributes to isolating the decoy environment from the legitimate network, thereby safeguarding session integrity (see Fig. 6).

The proxies are configured to monitor network interfaces for messages corresponding to the specified target service. In the case of PROXY N4, it listens

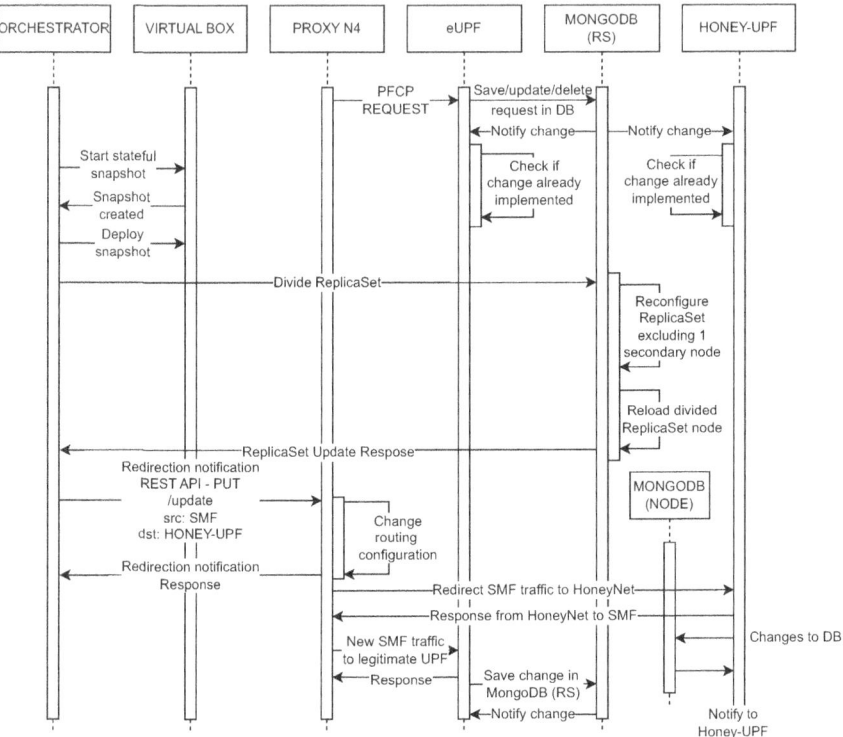

Fig. 6. Interactions between database and different services.

on interfaces where the SMF, the eUPF, and the eUPF of the honeynet are configured. When traffic is directed to any of these services, the proxy redirects it through the corresponding interface. The N3 proxy functions similarly, but in this case, it facilitates communication between the gNB and the legitimate eUPF and honey-eUPF. As previously mentioned, the proxies also modify the NodeID and F-SEID parameters of the packets to ensure the SMF operates correctly. This is due to the eUPF and SMF populating these fields with their actual IP addresses; however, neither of these services is aware of the IP addresses of the other, as they are on different networks. Consequently, the proxies perform IP translation to maintain connectivity and consistency. Additionally, both proxies provide a Representational State Transfer (REST) API interface, allowing the orchestrator to instruct them via Hypertext Transfer Protocol (HTTP) requests when to initiate traffic redirection towards the honeynet. These orchestrator-triggered HTTP requests can be observed in the Wireshark workflow shown in Fig. 7, which illustrates the complete process of IP translation, proxy communication, and redirection management between SMF and UPF services.

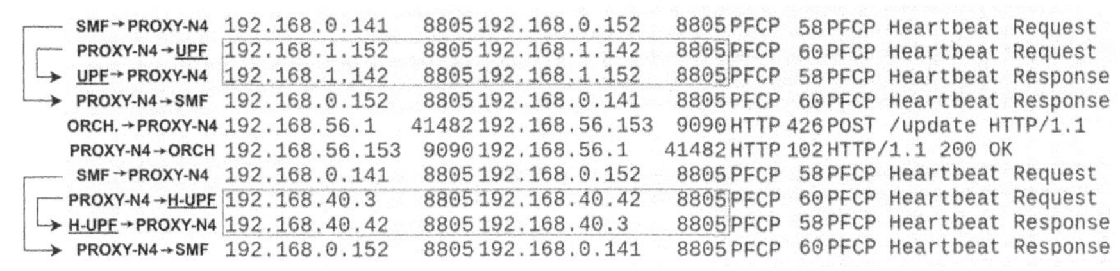

```
      SMF→PROXY-N4  192.168.0.141    8805 192.168.0.152    8805 PFCP  58 PFCP Heartbeat Request
      PROXY-N4→UPF  192.168.1.152    8805 192.168.1.142    8805 PFCP  60 PFCP Heartbeat Request
      UPF→PROXY-N4  192.168.1.142    8805 192.168.1.152    8805 PFCP  58 PFCP Heartbeat Response
      PROXY-N4→SMF  192.168.0.152    8805 192.168.0.141    8805 PFCP  60 PFCP Heartbeat Response
     ORCH.→PROXY-N4 192.168.56.1    41482 192.168.56.153   9090 HTTP 426 POST /update HTTP/1.1
     PROXY-N4→ORCH  192.168.56.153   9090 192.168.56.1    41482 HTTP 102 HTTP/1.1 200 OK
      SMF→PROXY-N4  192.168.0.141    8805 192.168.0.152    8805 PFCP  58 PFCP Heartbeat Request
      PROXY-N4→H-UPF 192.168.40.3    8805 192.168.40.42    8805 PFCP  60 PFCP Heartbeat Request
      H-UPF→PROXY-N4 192.168.40.42   8805 192.168.40.3     8805 PFCP  58 PFCP Heartbeat Response
      PROXY-N4→SMF  192.168.0.152    8805 192.168.0.141    8805 PFCP  60 PFCP Heartbeat Response
```

Fig. 7. Wireshark capture where the IP translation and redirection are shown.

6.1 Results

Considering the testbed described in Sect. 6 and later illustrated in Fig. 5, the performance of the proposed solution has been measured. For this purpose, traces of the delay introduced by the proxy implementation and the eUPF have been collected. The introduction of these new services inevitably impacts performance compared to the default 5G core solution, where network traffic is not forwarded, nor are user session data stored in a shared database. Consequently, the additional delay introduced by these components can be observed in contrast to the default delay in direct communication between the UPF and SMF.

The new functionalities introduced in the core enable interaction with a database, which translates into operations and requests that introduce a delay between queries and responses. Similarly, the proxy facilitates IP translation and the deserialization and serialization of the PFCP protocol to modify IEs in the requests. These modifications also impact the performance of communications between services, although in exchange for enhanced security features that contribute to a more secure application.

In Fig. 8, the median delay of various PFCP requests is displayed, ranging from the moment a single user is connected to the 5G core until there are 50 users in the network. The solid lines along with the "x" and "o" markers indicate the median delay for each event, whether it is a user connecting to the network, modifying their connection, or disconnecting. This median is calculated over 30 rounds for each type of request. Additionally, the dashed line represents the overall median delay computed across all users.

In Fig. 8a, the difference in delay when the user establishes a session with the 5G core can be observed. The graphs show that the median delay in direct service-to-service communication is nearly 18 ms, whereas in our solution, it approaches 96 ms.

Meanwhile, in Fig. 8b, the difference in delay is shown once the session has been established and a modification request is made. As shown, the delay in our solution reaches 85 ms, whereas in the default solution, it reaches 13 ms.

Regarding session deletion, the obtained delay is shown in Fig. 8c, where it can be observed that the delay gap is similar to the previous operations. More specifically, the difference between the proposed approach and the default deployment is due to the operations in the database. It is important to highlight that

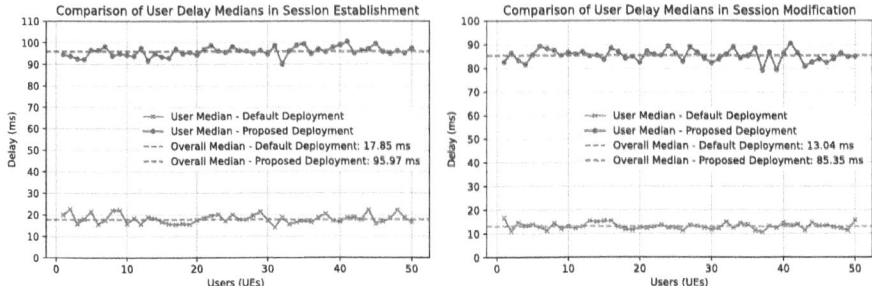

(a) Session establishment delay compari- (b) Session modification delay comparison
son between the proposed approach and between the proposed approach and the de-
the default Free5Gc deployment.   fault Free5Gc deployment.

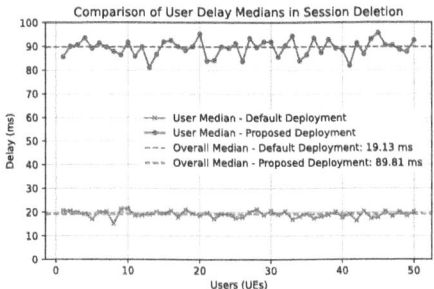

(c) Session deletion delay comparison between the proposed approach and the default Free5Gc deployment.

Fig. 8. Comparison of user delay at the proposed approach.

these operations, while essential for ensuring synchronization and consistency of
the environment, are relatively costly in terms of latency.

The difference in delay is mainly due to database write operations. After collecting traces at various points within the UPF to measure the delay introduced
by each function involved in session establishment and modification, it has been
observed that these operations introduce an approximate delay of 50 ms. Additionally, the proxy, due to address resolution requests and message forwarding,
contributes an additional delay of approximately 30 ms.

In this regard, it is important to note that the proposed solution is currently
in a Proof-of-Concept (PoC) phase, where resource optimization has not been a
primary focus. At this stage, the primary focus has been to design and develop
the architecture to handle the PFCP attacks. In fact, the development of proxies
and eUPF has been the main task.

7   Future Lines

Although the proposed solution has proven effective in mitigating PFCP-based attacks through MTD and honeynets, future research should focus on three strategic dimensions to enhance system maturity and operational viability:

- **Performance and Scalability Optimization.** Mitigating latency and ensuring efficient resource utilization remain critical to sustaining the responsiveness of the system. The current architecture introduces overhead through proxies and database interactions, which could be reduced by leveraging advanced parallelization techniques and adopting real-time data storage solutions such as in-memory or stream-based systems. Furthermore, scenarios involving multiple concurrent attackers must be addressed, with emphasis on optimizing snapshot orchestration to avoid redundant deployments and ensure scalability under stress.
- **Resilient and Autonomous Defense Mechanisms.** To reduce reliance on manual oversight, future work should incorporate autonomous anomaly detection mechanisms capable of triggering mitigation workflows with minimal false positives. Behavioral analysis using machine learning models could enable early identification of malicious PFCP messages, limiting unnecessary snapshot deployments. In addition, improving session-level traceability and state supervision can support early detection of lateral movement and session hijacking attempts, reinforcing the overall resilience of the system.
- **Integration with Emerging 5G Technologies.** Given the increasing adoption of SDN and NFV in 5G infrastructures, future research should explore how MTD and honeynet strategies can dynamically integrate with these paradigms to enable policy-driven security controls. Similarly, overcoming current synchronization limitations among UPF nodes benefits from distributed clustering and load-balancing across the N3 and N4 interfaces, improving service continuity. Finally, exploring adaptive and context-aware MTD strategies provides a more balanced trade-off between security posture and network performance, particularly in dynamic traffic environments.

Addressing these three pillars will help consolidate the mitigation strategy into a robust, intelligent, and flexible solution tailored for the security demands of modern 5G core networks.

8   Conclusions

As stated in Sect. 3.2, most of the existing research on attacks targeting the PFCP protocol primarily focuses on attack detection, while mitigation strategies remain largely underexplored. This gap highlights a critical vulnerability within the 5G core network, where the lack of effective countermeasures leaves key infrastructure components exposed to persistent and evolving threats. Given that the 5G core network is responsible for handling user sessions, mobility management, and resource allocation, any unauthorized manipulation of session parameters could lead to severe security risks, such as session hijacking, service disruption, or unauthorized access to network resources.

In response to this issue, the framework proposed in Sect. 5 provides an effective mitigation strategy by redirecting suspicious traffic to a honeynet, isolating the attacker while preserving the integrity of legitimate network operations. A key strength of this approach is its ability to keep the session of the attacker active without noticeable disruptions, allowing security mechanisms to gather intelligence on the attack patterns without triggering evasive actions from adversaries. However, despite the effectiveness of this solution, a crucial challenge remains: ensuring continuous monitoring of user sessions to detect and respond to unauthorized modifications in real-time.

Ultimately, addressing the lack of mitigation strategies in the 5G core is crucial for securing next-generation networks. By bridging this gap, we can significantly improve the robustness of network infrastructures, safeguarding both service providers and end-users from sophisticated cyber threats.

Acknowledgments. This work was supported in part by the Spanish Ministry of Science and Innovation in the project EnablIng Native-AI Secure deterministic 6G networks for hyPer-connected envIRonmEnts (6G-INSPIRE) (PID2022-137329OB-C44). It was partially supported by CRITIC Project Grant PLEC2024-011222 funded by AEI/10.13039/501100011033, FEDER, and EU.

Disclosure of Interests. The authors have no competing interests to declare that are relevant to the content of this article.

References

1. Abdelhay, Z., Bello, Y., Refaey, A.: Toward zero-trust 6gc: a software defined perimeter approach with dynamic moving target defense mechanism. IEEE Wireless Commun. **31**, 74–80 (2024). https://doi.org/10.1109/MWC.001.2300358
2. Alani, M.M.: HoneyTwin: securing smart cities with machine learning-enabled SDN edge and cloud-based honeypots. J. Parallel Distributed Comput. **188**, 104866 (2024). https://doi.org/10.1016/J.JPDC.2024.104866
3. Alavizadeh, H., Kim, D.S., Jang-Jaccard, J.: Model-based evaluation of combinations of Shuffle and Diversity MTD techniques on the cloud. Future Generation Comput. Syst. **111**, 507–522 (2020). https://doi.org/10.1016/J.FUTURE.2019.10.009
4. Amponis, G., et al.: Threatening the 5G core via PFCP DoS attacks: the case of blocking UAV communications. Eurasip J. Wireless Commun. Netw. **2022**(1), 1–27 (2022). https://doi.org/10.1186/S13638-022-02204-5/FIGURES/6
5. Amponis, G., et al.: 5G Core PFCP intrusion detection dataset. In: International Conference on Modern Circuits and Systems Technologies, MOCAST 2023 - Proceedings (2023). https://doi.org/10.1109/MOCAST57943.2023.10176693
6. Andrade, D.P., Akkaya, K., Perez-Pons, A., Uluagac, S., Sahin, A.: Ddos attack detection and mitigation in 5g networks using p4 and sdn. In: IEEE Conference on Local Computer Networks (LCN) pp. 1–9 (Sep 2024). https://doi.org/10.1109/LCN60385.2024.10639648

7. Barakabitze, A.A., Ahmad, A., Mijumbi, R., Hines, A.: 5G network slicing using SDN and NFV: a survey of taxonomy, architectures and future challenges. Comput. Netw. **167** (2 2020). https://doi.org/10.1016/j.comnet.2019.106984

8. Batalla, J.M., et al.: Security Risk Assessment for 5G Networks: National Perspective. IEEE Wireless Commun. **27**(4), 16–22 (2020). https://doi.org/10.1109/MWC.001.1900524

9. Dantas Silva, F.S., Neto, E.P., Nunes, R.S., Souza, C.H., Neto, A.J., Pascoal, T.: Securing software-defined networks through adaptive moving target defense capabilities. J. Netw. Syst. Manag. **31**(3), 1–28 (2023). https://doi.org/10.1007/S10922-023-09746-Z/TABLES/2

10. Dolente, F., Garroppo, R.G., Pagano, M.: A vulnerability assessment of open-source implementations of fifth-generation core network functions. Future Internet 2024, vol. 16(1), p. 1 (Dec 2023). https://doi.org/10.3390/FI16010001

11. Eleftherakis, S., Otim, T., Santaromita, G., Zayas, A.D., Giustiniano, D., Kourtellis, N.: Demystifying privacy in 5g stand alone networks. In: ACM MobiCom 2024 - Proceedings of the 30th International Conference on Mobile Computing and Networking, pp. 1330–1345 (5 2024). https://doi.org/10.1145/3636534.3690696, /doi/pdf/10.1145/3636534.3690696?download=true

12. Escolar, A.M., Wang, Q., Calero, J.M.A.: Enhancing honeynet-based protection with network slicing for massive Pre-6G IoT smart cities deployments. J. Netw. Comput. Appli. **229**, 103918 (2024). https://doi.org/10.1016/J.JNCA.2024.103918

13. ETSI: TS 123 501 - V15.3.0 - 5G; System Architecture for the 5G System (3GPP TS 23.501 version 15.3.0 Release 15). Tech. rep., ETSI (2018). https://portal.etsi.org/TB/ETSIDeliverableStatus.aspx

14. ETSI: TS 123 502 - V17.12.0 - 5G; Procedures for the 5G System (5GS) (3GPP TS 23.502 version 17.12.0 Release 17). Tech. rep., ETSI (2024). https://portal.etsi.org/TB/ETSIDeliverableStatus.aspx

15. Ferrag, M.A., Maglaras, L., Argyriou, A., Kosmanos, D., Janicke, H.: Security for 4G and 5G cellular networks: a survey of existing authentication and privacy-preserving schemes. J. Netw. Comput. Appli. **101**, 55–82 (2018). https://doi.org/10.1016/J.JNCA.2017.10.017

16. Gao, S., Lin, R., Fu, Y., Li, H., Cao, J.: Security threats, requirements and recommendations on creating 5G network slicing system: a survey. Electronics**13**(10), 1860 (2024). https://doi.org/10.3390/ELECTRONICS13101860

17. Javadpour, A., Ja'fari, F., Taleb, T., Shojafar, M., Benzaïd, C.: A comprehensive survey on cyber deception techniques to improve honeypot performance. Comput. Sec. **140**, 103792 (2024). https://doi.org/10.1016/J.COSE.2024.103792

18. Karakoc, B., Fürste, N., Rupprecht, D., Kohls, K.: Never let me down again: bidding-down attacks and mitigations in 5G and 4G. In: WiSec - Proceedings of ACM Conference on Security and Privacy in Wireless and Mobile Networks, pp. 97–108 (May 2023). https://doi.org/10.1145/3558482.3581774

19. Kim, H.: 5g core network security issues and attack classification from network protocol perspective. J. Internet Serv. Inform. Sec. **10**, 1–15 (2020). https://doi.org/10.22667/JISIS.2020.05.31.001

20. Liyanage, M., et al.: A survey on zero touch network and service management (ZSM) for 5G and beyond networks. J. Netw. Comput. Appli. **203**, 103362 (2022). https://doi.org/10.1016/J.JNCA.2022.103362

21. Lopez, P.B., Nespoli, P., Perez, M.G.: Cyber deception reactive: Tcp stealth redirection to on-demand honeypots (2024). https://arxiv.org/abs/2402.09191

22. López, P.B., Pérez, M.G., Nespoli, P.: Cyber deception: state of the art, trends and open challenges (2024). https://arxiv.org/abs/2409.07194

23. Park, S., Kwon, S., Park, Y., Kim, D., You, I.: Session management for security systems in 5G standalone network. IEEE Access **10**, 73421–73436 (2022). https://doi.org/10.1109/ACCESS.2022.3187053

24. Pell, R., Moschoyainnis, S., Shojafar, M.: LSTM based anomaly detection of PFCP signaling attacks in 5G networks. IEEE Consumer Electr. Mag. (2024). https://doi.org/10.1109/MCE.2024.3353177

25. Pell, R., Moschoyiannis, S., Panaousis, E., Heartfield, R.: Towards dynamic threat modelling in 5g core networks based on mitre att&ck (2021). https://arxiv.org/abs/2108.11206

26. Qin, X., Jiang, F., Cen, M., Doss, R.: Hybrid cyber defense strategies using Honey-X: a survey. Comput. Netw. **230**, 109776 (2023). https://doi.org/10.1016/J.COMNET.2023.109776

27. Radoglou-Grammatikis, P., et al.: 5GCIDS: An Intrusion Detection System for 5G Core with AI and Explainability Mechanisms. In: 2023 IEEE Globecom Workshops, GC Wkshps 2023 pp. 353–358 (2023). https://doi.org/10.1109/GCWKSHPS58843.2023.10464667

28. Ramezanpour, K., Jagannath, J., Jagannath, A.: Security and privacy vulnerabilities of 5G/6G and WiFi 6: survey and research directions from a coexistence perspective. Comput. Netw. **221**, 109515 (2023). https://doi.org/10.1016/J.COMNET.2022.109515

29. Scalise, P., Boeding, M., Hempel, M., Sharif, H., Delloiacovo, J., Reed, J.: A systematic survey on 5g and 6g security considerations, challenges, trends, and research areas. Future Internet **16**, 67 (2024). https://doi.org/10.3390/FI16030067

30. Sheikhi, S., Kostakos, P.: Advancing Security in 5G Core Networks Through Unsupervised Federated Time Series Modeling. 7a6cf2d6-c1ed-404a-8f83-806e8c2abcd8 pp. 492–497 (Sep 2024). https://doi.org/10.1109/CSR61664.2024.10679491

31. Soussi, W., Christopoulou, M., Gur, G., Stiller, B.: MERLINS - moving target defense enhanced with Deep-RL for NFV in-depth security. In: 2023 IEEE Conference on Network Function Virtualization and Software Defined Networks, NFV-SDN 2023 - Proceedings, pp. 65–71 (2023). https://doi.org/10.1109/NFV-SDN59219.2023.10329594

32. Tan, J., et al.: A survey: when moving target defense meets game theory. Comput. Sci. Rev. **48**, 100544 (2023). https://doi.org/10.1016/j.cosrev.2023.100544

Striking Back at Cobalt: Using Network Traffic Metadata to Detect Cobalt Strike Masquerading Command and Control Channels

Clément Parssegny[1,2]($\boxtimes$) (ID), Johan Mazel[1] (ID), Olivier Levillain[2] (ID), and Pierre Chifflier[1]

[1] ANSSI, Paris, France
[2] SAMOVAR, Télécom SudParis, Institut Polytechnique de Paris, 91120 Palaiseau, France
clement.parssegny@ssi.gouv.fr

Abstract. Off-the-shelf software for *Command and Control* is often used by attackers and legitimate pentesters looking for discretion. Among other functionalities, these tools facilitate the customization of their network traffic so it can mimic popular websites, thereby increasing their secrecy. Cobalt Strike is one of the most famous solutions in this category, used by known advanced attacker groups such as "Mustang Panda" or "Nobelium".

In response to these threats, Security Operation Centers and other defense actors struggle to detect *Command and Control* traffic, which often use encryption protocols such as TLS. Network traffic metadata-based machine learning approaches have been proposed to detect encrypted malware communications or fingerprint websites over Tor network.

This paper presents a machine learning-based method to detect Cobalt Strike *Command and Control* activity based only on widely used network traffic metadata. The proposed method is, to the best of our knowledge, the first of its kind that is able to adapt the model it uses to the observed traffic to optimize its performance. This specificity permits our method to performs equally or better than the state of the art while using standard features thus easier to use in a production environment and more explainable.

Keywords: Cobalt Strike · Command and Control · Detection · Machine Learning · Network Metadata

1 Introduction

Command and Control (C2) is used by attackers to control several compromised hosts, forming networks called *botnets*. A usual architecture for these botnets is the client/server botnet. In order to operate, this model of botnet uses communication channels where the server sends commands to infected hosts that will execute them and then transmit the results back. These channels have evolved over the years. First, they used IRC as their transport protocol. Then, HTTP,

© The Author(s), under exclusive license to Springer Nature Switzerland AG 2025
M. Dalla Preda et al. (Eds.): ARES 2025, LNCS 15992, pp. 163–185, 2025.
https://doi.org/10.1007/978-3-032-00624-0_8

HTTPS and DNS became commonly employed. Recently, off-the-shelf commercial [48] or open source [25–27] software that were originally designed for Red team audits, have been used by malicious actors [17,28,63,65].

Cobalt Strike [12] is the most popular example of these frameworks [55], used by both legitimate pentesters and real threat actors [16,37]. It can set up a full kill chain targeting Windows systems with several attackers collaborating simultaneously [39]. This situation drives organizations to do everything they can to neutralize identified Cobalt Strike-linked malicious infrastructure [67].

In Cobalt Strike, *Command and Control* communication channels can be customized to mimic benign services, based on different configuration profiles. Moreover, this off-the-shelf software supports TLS to encrypt its communications. Both masquerade and encryption strengthen Cobalt Strike's protection against detection. However, the metadata related to the size, the direction or the timings of the communication can still be leveraged for detection.

Botnet detection has been the goal of previous work through different ways. Many used an approach based on machine learning [4,18,24,32,36,49,52,69]. However, as these Botnet *Command and Control* channels rely on various protocols such as IRC [23,36], HTTP [32] or DNS [4,18], approaches used for the detection vary. While some research monitored a precise network's activity, measuring anomalies as deviations from a computed profile [24,30,61], others preferred to inspect packet contents to search for specific characteristics of compromise [49]. As encryption use increased [22], network traffic metadata began to be used to identify C2 traffic from benign traffic [52]. However, up to our knowledge, malware targeted in existing works did not have a masquerade capability similar to Cobalt Strike. A Cobalt Strike detection method [53] has been proposed. It is however limited regarding Cobalt Strike configurations and the training data is biased. More recently, a deep learning approach has been presented [70]. However, it does not take the masquerading capability of Cobalt Strike into account while using dubious feature construction steps. In this paper, we focus on the capability for Cobalt Strike to obfuscate and hide C2 traffic inside messages imitating benign services. We address the existing work shortcomings and provide a detailed performance evaluation based on configurations used in the wild.

Thus, our goal is to design a method to detect Cobalt Strike C2 traffic despite its masquerade and encryption capabilities. This method works with different configuration profiles and network protocols. Since configurations are easily modified and deployed in Cobalt Strike, it is also central for our detection method to be easily extensible to seamlessly include new configurations. Our main contribution is a machine learning-based method to detect Cobalt Strike C2 traffic using only network traffic's metadata. One advantage of this approach is that it is not based on Deep Packet Inspection (DPI) at all but can still produce good performance, even with unsophisticated and standard features. Indeed, we observe mean F_1 scores between 0.78 and 1 with a 95% threshold confidence interval, equaling or slightly improving previous approaches. These features also show good performance on clear and encrypted Cobalt Strike traffic from real-world attacks.

Our paper is structured as follows. Section 2 describes existing work on C2 channel detection. Section 3 portrays the working principle of Cobalt Strike's *Command and Control* feature. Section 4 presents the threat model we consider. Section 5 depicts our method. Section 6 details our results. Finally, Sect. 7 and Sect. 8 discuss of our work and of our future work.

2   Related Work

C2 channel detection is inherently linked to botnet detection as it is the communication method for such networks. Decades ago, these botnets were based on IRC channels [1,29,30] on which attackers would send commands for victims to execute. Then, HTTP [40] and DNS [41] became widely used protocols for C2.

Several papers searched for botnet by profiling the normal activity of the studied network before measuring the distance of a sample in comparison with the benign one [24,30,61]. Another method used is DPI [7,68]. The principle is to inspect payloads to detect botnet messages [29,49] or to identify protocols [30] for correlation detection. However, this method is only possible when the studied traffic is not encrypted [1,23,32,36,49] which is hardly the case now as the use of TLS increases continuously for both benign [22] and C2 traffic. Although methods like entropy computing [18,74] were used to improve detection methods.

To accommodate the increasing use of encryption [22], papers that try to identify malicious traffic within encrypted communications have been published. They focus on machine learning techniques applied to TLS handshake such as `ClientHello`, `ServerHello` or `Certificate` records [4,5,52,69]. However, TLS 1.3, released in 2018,encrypts most of the handshake records [19]. An overview of how machine learning has been applied for C2 detection is presented in Table 1. It is noticeable that a majority of the research formalized this problem as a binary classification problem but then differ in the protocols studied. Moreover, while other articles generally study one specific protocol in a known configuration to evaluate and compare different machine learning methods, our work concentrates on a unique method based on traffic metadata applied to a larger panel of configurations and protocols used in the wild. We thus argue that the masquerading capability of Cobalt Strike C2 traffic constitutes a unique challenge and we carefully design our proposed approach to address this challenge. Furthermore, few works detail the number of malicious configurations they are studying, which has a detrimental influence on reproducibility and the generalization capability of their method.

It is also important to note that traffic metadata have also been used in active methods to detect and fingerprint C2 servers and infected hosts. More specifically, TLS metadata present in the handshake messages were studied by academics [59,60] and industrial actors whose tools [2,3,56] have been integrated to scanning platforms [8] and are routinely used in CTI reports [33]. Finally, industrial research focused on detecting Cobalt Strike and understanding its components to better fight against one of their client's main threat [31,50,64].

Our method has common ground with the work of Anderson et al. [4] but we apply it to the Cobalt Strike framework. Van der Eijk et al. [20] designed

Table 1. Comparison of machine learning-based methods for C2 channels detection. Clas.: Classification type (B: Binary, M: Multiclass); Mw.: Malware; CS: Cobalt Strike; Feat. type: Feature Type (M: Metadata, D: Deep Packet Inspection); Reprod.: Reproducibility; Feat. imp. analysis: Feature Importance Analysis. Variability is the number of malicious classes used in the datasets e.g. the number of botnets or the number of malleable profiles.

Authors	Ref.	Yr.	Clas.	IRC	HTTP	DNS	TLS	Feat. type	Type	Variability	Open code	Open data	Feat. imp. analysis
Nivargi et al.	[49]	'06	B	√	-	-	-	M/D	Mw.	?	-	-	-
Livadas et al.	[36]	'06	B/M	√	-	-	-	M	Mw.	1	-	-	-
Kondo et al.	[32]	'07	B	√	√	-	-	M	Mw.	5	-	-	-
Dietrich et al.	[18]	'11	B	-	-	√	-	M	Mw.	11	-	-	-
Warmer	[69]	'11	B	-	-	-	√	M	Mw.	4	-	-	-
Garcia et al.	[24]	'14	B	√	√	-	-	M	Mw.	10	-	√	-
Anderson et al.	[4]	'16	B	-	√	√	√	M/D	Mw.	?	-	-	√
Anderson et al.	[5]	'20	M	-	-	-	√	M	Mw.	?	√	√	√
Pai et al.	[52]	'20	B	-	-	-	√	M	Mw.	?	-	-	-
Van der Eijk et al.	[20]	'20	B	-	√	-	√	M	CS	1	-	-	√
Ramos et al.	[53]	'22	B	-	√	-	√	M	CS	?	-	-	-
Ramos et al.	[54]	'23	B	-	-	-	√	M	CS	29	-	-	-
Yang et al.	[70]	'24	B	-	-	-	√	M/D	CS	?	√	√	-
Our work		**'25**	**B**	-	√	√	√	**M**	**CS**	4	√	√	√

a threshold-based method to detect Cobalt Strike using network traffic metadata. However, there are limitations to their work. First, they only detect one profile mimicking Amazon. We address this issue by experimenting on four different profiles that mimic four distinct websites. Then, they use empirically and manually chosen values as thresholds for their detection algorithm. Finally, they only use the accuracy as performance metric. As their data contains much more benign instances than malicious ones, their results are biased. We address this potential bias due to the dataset imbalance by using a carefully designed training procedure and appropriate metrics. More recently, Ramos et al. [54] used multi-flow features to detect Cobalt Strike HTTPS sessions. This approach has an objective close to ours, but their method focuses on a different scale of the communication. Before this, Ramos et al. [53] used supervised machine learning to detect Cobalt Strike C2 traffic, but their work suffers from several limitations. First, they do not specify the number nor the details of the publicly available and randomly generated malleable profiles used to train their different models. Hence, there is no assurance that their work is based on a realistic deployment situation. This also restricts the reproducibility of their results. We address this issue by using profiles known to be deployed in the real world for our experiments and by documenting them. Then, their dataset construction process suffers from some limitations. They use both HTTP and HTTPS traffic for their malicious traffic while only HTTPS traffic is used for the benign part. This biases packet size-related network features. We avoid this bias by using both HTTP and HTTPS for benign traffic. We also take the DNS C2 use case into account while they do not. Also, they transform categorical features into integers that encode the rank in terms of decreasing appearance frequency in the dataset. Thus the most frequent value is encoded as "1", the second most frequent value as "2", etc. This brings an order relation between initially unordered values and thus a bias for many methods such as tree-based Random Forest, which is put forward in the paper, or linear models such as Logistic Regression. Thus, we argue that their model is too limited in terms of malleable profiles and biased to be successful in a production environment. Finally, they do not analyze the feature importance of their model, as shown in Table 1. This prevents from understanding why the model is efficient to detect Cobalt Strike C2 traffic. We address this issue by computing the Mean Decrease in Impurity (MDI) of the different features used in our experiments. More recently, Yang et al. [70] used a deep learning approach to detect HTTPS traffic from Cobalt Strike. Their approach suffers from several issues that we address in this work. First, they are only taking HTTPS traffic into account. By using one protocol, they omit several uses of Cobalt Strike C2 traffic. We address this issue by proposing a method taking all the protocols usable to connect with a C2 server in Cobalt Strike. Then, they do not consider the different malleable profiles they gathered in their datasets. Moreover, by using only the default configuration in their C2 traffic generation lab, they ignore the main difficulty regarding Cobalt Strike C2 traffic detection which is its masquerading capability and the associated configuration diversity [31], as pictured in Subsect. 5.2. We address this issue by studying several configurations. Furthermore, their approach based on deep learning may not be suitable in production environment as the detection is harder to explain. Finally, some features, such as tokenized encrypted *Application Data* payload exhibits dubious usefulness. We address this issue by using common metadata features and explainable algorithms.

The detection of Cobalt Strike's C2 traffic can also fall within the more general subject of detecting covert channels. Our use case can be formalized as the detection of a Covert Storage Channel (CSC) with a passive warden as presented in "The prisoner problem" [58]. This problem has been studied in several papers gathered in surveys [38,71]. However, these detection techniques can not apply to covert channels with a high degree of customization and an encryption of the application layer which contains the payload, as in Cobalt Strike. Machine learning approaches have also been explored [21] but mainly for the DNS protocol [6] or timing based covert channels [9]. However, these detection techniques are making the hypothesis that a single method and protocol are used by the covert channel and that this information is known by the defender. As Cobalt Strike is capable of using several protocols and methods to masquerade its malicious traffic, we need a generic method able to adapt to different configurations.

3   Cobalt Strike

Cobalt Strike is an off-the-shelf penetration testing framework written in Java and targeting Windows operating systems. This section details the working principles of *Command and Control* communications in Cobalt Strike. Subsection 3.1 deals with the general architecture. Then, Subsect. 3.2 describes the different possibilities brought by malleable profiles and how C2 protocols work.

3.1   Architecture

Command and Control in Cobalt Strike is based on three elements: a server controlled by the attacker, a Beacon on each compromised system and a client used by the attacker to control the server. Figure 1 illustrates how these components interact with each other. The server is at the center of communications between attackers and compromised systems. It forwards commands from the attackers and perform on-demand initial exploitation executable generation. In particular it creates Listeners and Beacons, the two agents of the C2 communication, based on the configured malleable profile. Beacons are executed on a compromised system in order to execute C2 commands selected by the attacker and sent by a Listener that is running on the server side. Finally, the client is a graphical interface used by the attacker to interact with the server.

3.2   Malleable Profiles

Command and Control configuration in Cobalt Strike is based on malleable profiles. These profiles are files that define the behavior used during the communication between the attacker server and the Beacons installed on the target [13]. A malleable profile contains all the parameters structuring the generated traffic, in particular the metadata used to impersonate benign traffic such as the values of the HTTP headers parameters, the encoding method used to obfuscate the payload or the "sleeptime" between two C2 communications. The malleable profile may also define a TLS certificate as Cobalt Strike can use an existing or self-signed certificates to create HTTPS C2 channels. As multiple servers can use the same profile (see Subsect. 5.2), detecting a profile may allow one to identify several servers that use similar malleable profiles.

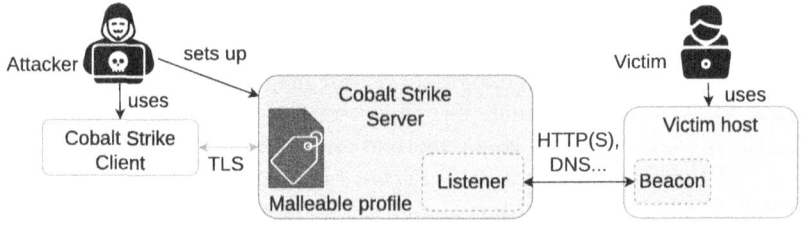

Fig. 1. Cobalt Strike architecture.

Communication behaviors can be defined for different protocols within a single profile as Cobalt Strike supports HTTP, HTTPS, DNS, SMB and TCP. In the following, we focus only on HTTP(S) and DNS protocols because SMB and TCP are only used in a peer-to-peer connection between two Beacons and not between a Beacon and a server. This Beacon-only communication is designed to limit the number of hosts calling out to the server during lateral movements [15].

The C2 communication can be described in four steps. First, at configurable time intervals (with or without jitter), the Beacon contacts the Listener on the server with identification metadata to check if there are commands to execute. This is called a "check-in". Then, the Listener responds with the attacker's commands or, if there is none, with the default answer defined in the profile. Once the output of the commands is known, the Beacon sends it to the server with a different request. This request also contains authentication metadata, so the server can sort the requests when several Beacons are used. Finally, the Listener can send a final answer which is optional. For HTTPS, a TLS handshake is executed to fetch the orders and post the outputs. The version of TLS used depends on the OpenJDK version used by Cobalt Strike. The DNS communication is slightly more complex than the HTTP(S) one but follows the same logic. An illustration of these protocols is presented in Fig. 2.

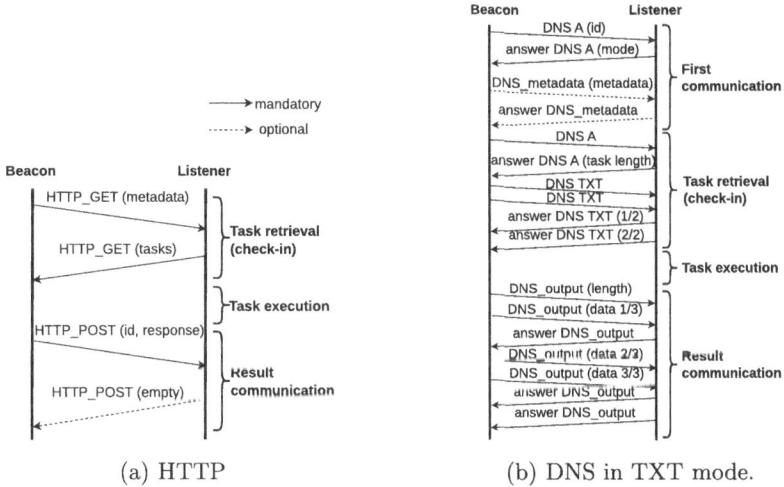

(a) HTTP   (b) DNS in TXT mode.

Fig. 2. Examples of C2 communications based on HTTP and DNS.

4   Threat Model

We consider the following threat model. The attacker controls an external C2 server and at least one compromised machine inside the supervised network, running a Cobalt Strike Beacon. Thus, these two hosts establish C2 channels using either HTTP, HTTPS or DNS. We, as defenders, can passively monitor incoming and outgoing network traffic, but we cannot analyze the application layers. To put it in a covert channel detection context, as described by Simmons [58], we are a passive warden trying to detect a Covert Storage Channel between the Cobalt Strike server and the infected host which are the two prisoners.

Our goal is then to distinguish C2 communications from benign traffic.

5   Method

We detail the proposed method in the following parts. Subsection 5.1 outlines its general principle. Subsection 5.2 presents our data generation processes while Subsect. 5.3 depicts the feature extraction of the metadata for the datasets' construction. Subsection 5.4 describes our machine learning method.

5.1   Principle

Our objective is to detect Cobalt Strike C2 communications, using only network traffic metadata. This method should work with different malleable profiles and should be extensible to easily take into account new malleable profiles.

The use of malleable profiles makes it complex to detect Cobalt Strike C2 channels using patterns in headers or payload. The encryption of the application layers introduced by recent changes in security protocols, such as TLS 1.3, DNS over HTTPS or encrypted `Client Hello` (formerly limited to an encrypted `Server Name Indication`) also adds to the detection obstacles regarding packet content inspection. Supervised machine learning models based on metadata are thus an answer to masquerade and encryption.

We use a supervised machine learning model for each "group" of malleable profiles we consider, each profile in a "group" mimicking the same benign traffic. This facilitates the extension of the proposed method to new profiles. Our method aims to select the most relevant model regarding the context to obtain the best performance. Thus, with our method, a single model may help detect slightly different malleable profiles, for example derived from the public repository [14]. The proposed method is depicted in Fig. 3. First, we make the hypothesis that we know the protocol used by the traffic to be classified (e.g. based on the UDP/TCP ports). Because the purpose of Cobalt Strike is to be stealthy and overcome firewalls, we suppose attackers use the same ports as benign traffic. Then, we check if a domain name is available in the traffic metadata. This information may be present in various locations such as the *Host* header for HTTP or the *Server Name Indication* for TLS. If we cannot extract a domain name, we check if the remote IP address belongs to a subnet part of a domain present in a known malleable profile (such as `3.0.0.0/15` which belongs to Amazon). If the observed traffic is linked to a known domain, we apply a machine learning model trained with malicious and benign traffic specific to this domain. Otherwise, we use several models, each trained with domain-specific malicious traffic and generic benign traffic.

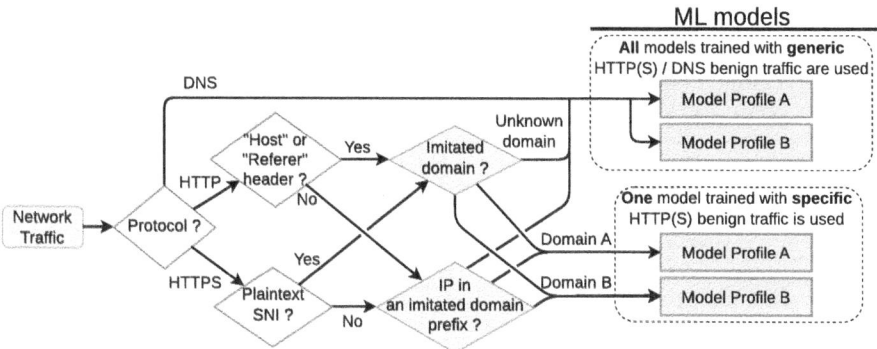

Fig. 3. Proposed method to detect Cobalt Strike C2 traffic. We use machine learning models trained on traffic which uses the same protocol (HTTP, HTTPS or DNS) as the observed traffic. Each model is trained using benign traffic as indicated on the figure and malicious traffic generated using the related profile.

5.2   Data Collection

We set up two platforms to generate network traffic. The first one is based on a virtualized architecture to run *Command and Control* scenarios and capture the malicious traffic generated by the attack. The second one uses an automation framework to mimic user activity and create benign traffic as close as possible to real traffic. We also use external benign traffic datasets to minimize bias. The details of the data used in our experiments are listed in Table 2.

Malicious Traffic. Because Cobalt Strike is a tool designed for Windows attacks, we use a Windows Server 2022 virtual machine (VM) as the victim. The remaining part of the Vagrant-based architecture is composed of two Debian 11 VMs. One is the Cobalt Strike server, and the other is a `bind9` server used in DNS-based C2 channels experiments.

Our detection approach targets network traffic observed between hosts (i.e. not on the host themselves). TCP offloading mechanisms are thus deactivated with the `ethtool` package to respect the default Ethernet *Maximum Transmission Unit* (MTU) value of 1 500 bytes. C2 commands, listed in Table 3, are chosen to be diverse regarding the amount of generated traffic and provided functionality. We also gather malicious Cobalt Strike C2 traces from Malware Traffic Analysis (MTA) [47] to test our method and features on real-world attacks.

Benign Traffic. The benign traffic generation process is based on the Python bindings to the Selenium framework. This tool is used to simulate web browsing-related user inputs. Therefore, we write a script adapted to each service spoofed by Cobalt Strike that we study. For example, the script for Amazon search and select items based on predefined search terms as the corresponding studied

Table 2. Number of instances (TCP or UDP flow) used in our experiments.

Traffic Type / Malleable Profile	Protocol	(B)enign / (M)alicious	Instance Count
Generic traffic (UPC+UPNA+CTU)	HTTP	B	73 873
	HTTPS	B	74 019
	DNS	B	279 455
Default profile	HTTPS	M	247
	DNS	M	7 618
Amazon	HTTP	M	172
	HTTPS	M	160
		B	615
	DNS	M	23 507
Smashburger	HTTPS	M	129
		B	230
jQuery	HTTP	M	2 225
		B	99
MTA Jan. 31st [42]	HTTPS	M	158
MTA May 23th [43]	HTTPS	M	121
MTA Jul. 12th [44]	HTTPS	M	803
MTA Oct. 3rd [45]	HTTPS	M	203
MTA Nov. 6th [46]	HTTP	M	2 208

Cobalt Strike profile uses "item search" like requests. Meanwhile, we capture the generated network traffic. We also use generic traffic from external datasets from the Universitat Politècnica de Catalunya (UPC) [7,66], the Universidad Pública de Navarra (UPNA) [34,35] and the Stratosphere IPS project of the Czech Technical University (CTU) [62] to minimize the bias of the benign traffic dataset. To use this traffic with our malicious data and minimize bias again, only flows that respect our condition on MTU are kept as stated in Sect. 5.2. It is then split by protocol we want to study: HTTP, HTTPS or DNS.

Choice of Targeted Malleable Profiles. Cobalt Strike provides its own malleable profile set [14] with an official repository containing 32 malleable profiles based on popular services and known attackers. Because this dataset does not provide any information about its use in attacks, our choice of malleable profiles is based on the Beacon dataset published by NCC [31]. It contains more than 120 000 Cobalt Strike Beacons fetched in the wild between 2018 and 2022.

We extract every profile in the dataset based on the IP/port pair and the month of its collection to avoid duplicates. After determining the domain

Table 3. C2 commands used for malicious traffic generation.

Command	Action
bhashdump	Dump local passwords hashes
blogonpassword	Dump passwords with Mimikatz
bls	List current directory
bmimikatz	Use a Mimikatz command
bnet	Run a network module command
bportscan	Scan the network using *Beacon*'s port scanner
bps	List processes
bpwd	Print current directory path
brun	Run a console command
bpowershell	Run a console command (**brun** variant)
bscreenshot	Take and send a screenshot

mimicked for each of them by looking at the headers parameters, we apply a fuzzy hashing algorithm, TLSH, to get a ranking of the most used profiles [51]. We also use DBSCAN to cluster profiles with small differences, even if the mimicked domain value is different. DBSCAN parameters are $\epsilon = 30$ and $minPts = 2$. Here, the ϵ parameter is the maximal distance between two TLSH digests as defined in [51] within a cluster. Based on this information, we select three domains: amazon.com, code.jquery.com which are the two most mimicked domains and smashburger.com which has a significant low number of unique profiles for a great number of instances. The 10 most mimicked domains are listed on Table 4. Finally, for each of these three chosen websites, we select the most common profile that we adapt so the C2 server answers with realistic answers. For example the jQuery profile returns the legitimate code after receiving a command result. The hash of the profiles used are listed in Table 5.

As many web services now enforce the use of HTTPS, the jQuery profile is chosen for the HTTP experiments. Indeed, this service is still accepting HTTP requests while others enforce HTTPS connections. For the HTTPS experiments, we use self-signed certificates generated by Cobalt Strike with mimicked parameters such as the Common Name for more stealthiness. Additionally, we use the default profile for testing HTTPS and DNS detection. This profile is found in several hundreds instances in the NCC dataset but with much variations, making it difficult to establish the correct count.

5.3 Dataset Construction

Once the network traffic is captured, we extract the metadata to build the dataset. This is done by using the Zeek analysis framework [73]. Our Zeek scripts fetch the metadata for each flow, i.e. each TCP or UDP connection, from an input

Table 4. Top 10 most common domains mimicked in the Cobalt Strike's Beacons dataset published by NCC group [31]. Each Beacon is counted once per month per (IP, port) couple. Nb: Number.

Spoofed domain	Nb of TLSH-based grouped profiles	Nb of instances	Nb of unique profiles
code.jquery.com	30	4 949	601
www.amazon.com	36	3 662	243
download.windowsupdate.com	42	993	145
locations.smashburger.com	2	827	3
www.google.com	40	722	195
www.bing.com	29	548	92
ocsp.verisign.com	24	520	54
www.microsoft.com	33	360	67
onedrive.live.com	15	316	63
audio-sv5-t1-3.pandora.com	7	281	38

Table 5. Hashes of the different malleable profiles used.

Malleable Profile	SHA-1 hash
Default	cb8632399e2c07b7b69e2403f3d543ac870176a4
Amazon	e3ee5e42845ef28a19fd6dd39b418acab279582d
jQuery (with realistic answers)	9b6551fb41c96b47f3e4153a0603458166fe44c6
Smashburger	1561b087573c535fc953336b509df88de82b75ba

network capture. We also make sure to remove flows without any exchanged data, e.g. from a port scanning, as it would bring bias in the learning process.

Netflow is a protocol developed by Cisco to collect information and statistics on an IP network traffic based on *flows*. A *flow* is described using different values that differ between the versions of the protocol. We choose Netflow v5 [10] and Netflow v9 [11] features for our experiments. We limit our work on this metadata as they are standard and easy to collect in a production environment. We also extend these 2 sets with features computed on Netflow information to improve the classification process. Finally, we compute two ratios. One is the ratio of the total size of packets received to the total size of packets sent while the other is the same logic applied to the number of packets. Ramos et al. [53] uses three other features from a standard Zeek log [72]. The first is the ordered history of the TCP flags received in a flow. The second is the transport protocol used (TCP or UDP) while *service* is an inference on the application protocol based on the destination port e.g. 53 for DNS. These feature groups are presented in Table 6.

Table 6. Used network traffic features. ext.: extended; $\mathcal{B}$: bi-direction (Beacon to Listener and Listener to Beacon jointly) ; $\mathcal{U}$: uni-directional (Beacon to Listener and Listener to Beacon separately) ; $\mathcal{A}$: all directions (bi-direction and two uni-directions) ; R: $\frac{received}{sent}$ ratios ; S: sent packets only (Beacon to Listener); L3/4: Layer 3/4. Byte counts are based on the layer payload.

Feature group name	Nb packets	Packet size	OSI layer used for size	Duration	TCP flags	TCP history	Protocol	Service
Netflow v5	$\mathcal{B}$	total ($\mathcal{B}$)	L3	√	√	-	-	-
Netflow v5 ext.	$\mathcal{B}$	total & mean ($\mathcal{B}$)	L3	√	√	-	-	-
Netflow v9	$\mathcal{U}$	total ($\mathcal{U}$); minimum & maximum (S)	L3	√	√	-	-	-
Netflow v9 ext.	$\mathcal{A}$; R	total & mean ($\mathcal{A}$); minimum & maximum (S); R	L3	√	√	-	-	-
Ramos et al. [53]	$\mathcal{B}$	total ($\mathcal{B}$)	L4	-	-	√	√	√

5.4 Machine Learning: Pre-processing, Algorithm and Metrics

After constructing the datasets, we apply supervised machine learning classification techniques. First, we scale the features using standardization. Then, we run a Random Forest algorithm, which is known to give good results and understandable explanation compared to other methods such as deep learning-based ones. We use a stratified k-fold cross-validation with a common value of $k = 10$ for the learning process to limit the bias from the imbalance between the proportion of benign and malicious traffic in the dataset. Finally, we use a grid search for hyperparameter tuning and optimize our performance. It tunes the number of trees (10, 100 or 500), the quality of a split criterion (gini or entropy), the depth achievable by a tree (2, 5, 10, 15 or 20) and the minimum of sample for a split to occur (2, 5, 10 or 50).

Because we are in a security use case where alerts are processed by human beings, it is important to limit the number of false positives. Thus, we choose the F_1 score as a metric. We also use precision and recall metrics to better analyze the performances of the models. To measure the importance of each feature in the decision of the model, we use the Mean Decrease in Impurity (MDI).

Table 7. Mimicked activities and network traffic used in experiments. The labels of the experiments associated are listed in the last column. Smashb.: Smashburger.

Mimicked activity	Targeted malleable profile traffic (protocol)	Benign traffic (protocol)	Experiment label
Website browsing	Amazon (HTTP)	Amazon (HTTPS)	Az/Az (HTTP)
		Generic (HTTP)	Az/Gen (HTTP)
	Amazon (HTTPS)	Amazon (HTTPS)	Az/Az (HTTPS)
		Generic (HTTPS)	Az/Gen (HTTPS)
	Smashb. (HTTPS)	Smashb. (HTTPS)	Sb/Sb (HTTPS)
		Generic (HTTPS)	Sb/Gen (HTTPS)
	Default (HTTPS)	Generic (HTTPS)	D/Gen (HTTPS)
JS library download	jQuery 3.6 (HTTP)	jQuery (HTTP)	jQ/jQ (HTTP)
		Generic (HTTP)	jQ/Gen (HTTP)
DNS	Default (DNS)	Generic (DNS)	D/Gen (DNS)
	Amazon (DNS)		Az/Gen (DNS)

6 Results

The goal of these experiments is to evaluate the performance of the models used in our method which are depicted in purple boxes in Fig. 3. We compare them to the Random Forest approach of Ramos et al. [53] which is put forward in their article as it has a good F_1 score and the smallest false positive rate. Yang et al. [70] is not considered as deep learning is not easily explainable.

The different sets of features and malleable profiles used are depicted in Table 6 and Table 7. Netflow uses the layer 3 payload size, designated in the following as "size". To visualize the results, we generate box plots of the F1 scores of the different models in Fig. 4. Each box plot is based on the 10 values from the 10 cross-validation folds.

Our preliminary experiments show that the duration feature has a strong impact on the model's performance. This may be explained by the fact that our malicious server and victim are located in a virtualized environment where there is less RTT and jitter whereas the benign traffic is generated using servers in the wild. We also observe a strong impact of CWR and ECE TCP flags, explained by the fact that benign traffic datasets are generated using Linux operating systems which disable these flags by default, whereas the malicious traffic is necessarily produced by Windows hosts where these flags are enabled by default. To limit this bias, we perform experiments without the duration or these two flags.

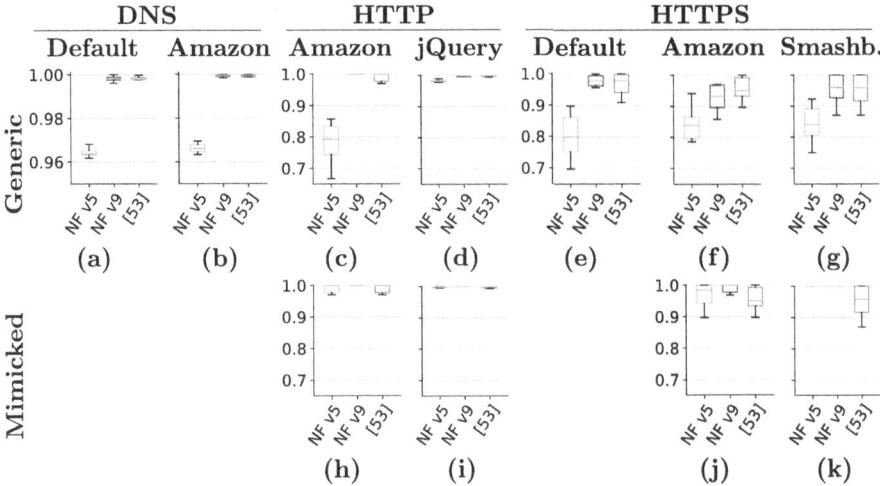

Fig. 4. F_1 score of the different models. Ramos et al. [53] uses generic DNS or HTTP and HTTPS combined benign traffic. Smashb.: Smashburger, NF: NetFlow

We present our results in the following parts. First, Subsect. 6.1 deals with the case of DNS C2 traffic. Then, Subsect. 6.2 compares the performances of the two methods when no known profile can be linked to the observed traffic. Subsection 6.3 analyzes the results when a known domain can be linked to the traffic observed. Finally, in Subsect. 6.4, we apply our method and compare the performances of Netflow features to those Ramos et al. [53] propose using publicly shared malicious traces [42–46]. As we observe that the extended feature sets only slightly improve the performance, we focus on the basic sets which are easier to collect in a production environment. Thus we compare three methods: our method with Netflow v5 features, our method with Netflow v9 features (both without the features discarded in the previous paragraph), and Ramos et al. [53] method.

6.1   Detection of DNS C2 Traffic

We first evaluate the DNS protocol use case. The experiments pictured in Fig. 4 (a) and (b), are approaching the maximum F1 score of 1. A straightforward observation is the score improvement when Netflow v9 features are used compared to Netflow v5. The Mean Decrease in Impurity (MDI) used to measure the importance for each feature in Fig. 5 (a) shows that the total size of data exchanged is the most important feature whereas the number of packets is not important at all. We manually checked that Cobalt Strike is using standard DNS streams composed mostly of 2 packets which is similar to benign traffic.

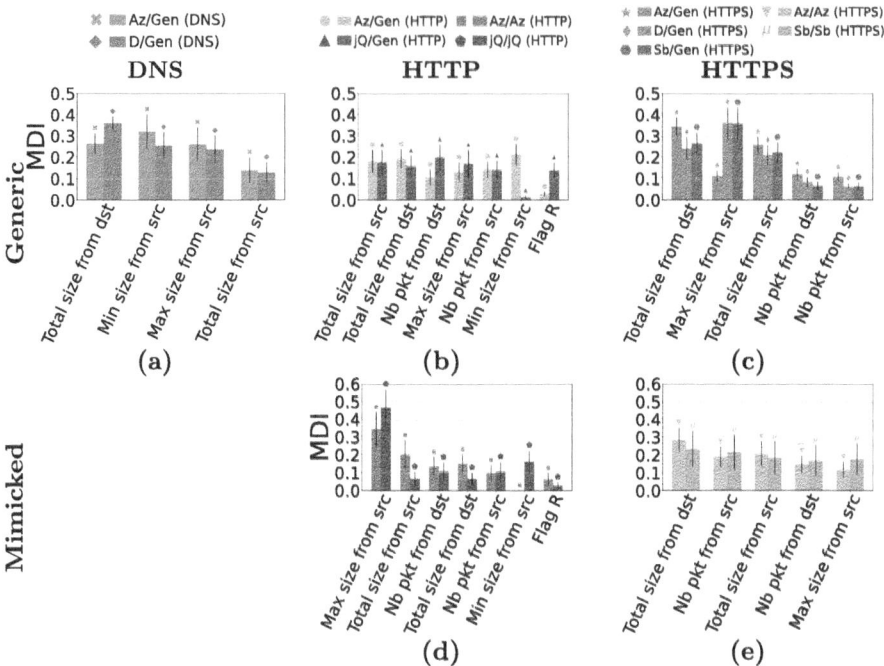

Fig. 5. Feature importance based on MDI with a confidence interval at a 99% threshold for Netflow v9. Only features with a mean value greater than 0.04 are kept. Az: Amazon, D: Default, Gen: Generic, jQ: jQuery, Sb: Smashburger, pkt: packet, src: source (client), dst: destination (server), R: Reset.

> **Takeaway**
>
> To summarize our results on DNS C2, the performance of the three methods are close as they all include the payload size as a feature, which is visibly the biggest difference between malicious and benign DNS traffic. However, our features are easier to collect and more adapted to production environments.

6.2 Detection of HTTP(S) C2 Traffic Linked to an Unknown Domain

We then compare both methods when the traffic can not be associated to a known imitated domain. Again, we observe a great improvement in the detection capability of our model using Netflow v9 features compared to Netflow v5. The detection performance is lower for HTTPS Web browsing-masquerading C2 among generic traffic than DNS traffic, as pictured in Fig. 4 (e) to (g). This is caused by the diversity of traffic in the generic dataset, having thus more samples similar to the malicious ones. This lowers the recall and thus the F_1 score.

The MDI for each feature in experiments with Netflow v5 shows that the total size of data exchanged has the most impact. We also observe in Fig. 5 (b) and

(c) that, in general with Netflow v9 features, the payload size's extremums from the source have a bigger impact on the decision than the number of packets. This is because the size of the payload for a profile has predefined values during check-ins. For instance, Amazon profile based Beacon sends data up to 1480 bytes while the minimum is 20 bytes. Check-ins without commands exhibit this minimum size, and are thus easy to identify. Moreover, the data exfiltration by the Beacon implies that a lot of data is sent by the source, which contrasts with a benign activity where the client receives more data than it sends. Hence, features built on traffic from the source are more crucial for the final decision.

> **Takeaway**
>
> To summarize, the performance of our method with Netflow v9 is similar to the method proposed by Ramos et al. [53]. However, the features we use are easier to collect. Netflow v5 can also be used with lower performance scores.

6.3 Detection of HTTP(S) C2 Traffic Linked to a Mimicked Domain

Then we study the case when masquerading traffic can be linked to a known imitated domain. Unlike the approach described in Ramos et al. [53], the method we propose select a specialized model to perform the detection. The improvement of performance by using Netflow v9 compared to Netflow v5 is still observed but, more important, the F1 score is greater than with Ramos et al. [53] in all experiments as the median has an equal or higher value and the box plot is tighter, as seen in Fig. 4 (h) to (k).

For Netflow v5 features, we note that the feature importance difference between the total size and the number of packets is less significant when the benign traffic is specific to the domain mimicked by Cobalt Strike. We suppose that specific benign traffic has a smaller variation in numbers of packets than generic benign traffic, justifying closer feature importance values. Moreover, Fig. 5 (d) shows the impact of the maximum size sent by the client for HTTP experiments. Again, check-ins without commands stand out when compared to specific benign traffic.

> **Takeaway**
>
> To summarize our results on generated C2 traffic, we obtain good performances with the Netflow v9 based feature sets. Furthermore, the use of specific traffic significantly improves the different scores compared to generic traffic. Thus, a method that selects a specific model matching the observed traffic provides the best performances and outperforms the approach proposed by Ramos et al. [53].

6.4 Detection of Documented Real-World Cobalt Strike Traffic

Finally, we apply our method to Cobalt Strike C2 traffic collected in 2023 [42–46]. To minimize bias, we study traces with at least a hundred Cobalt Strike TCP flows. This malicious traffic has been collected during real-world attacks

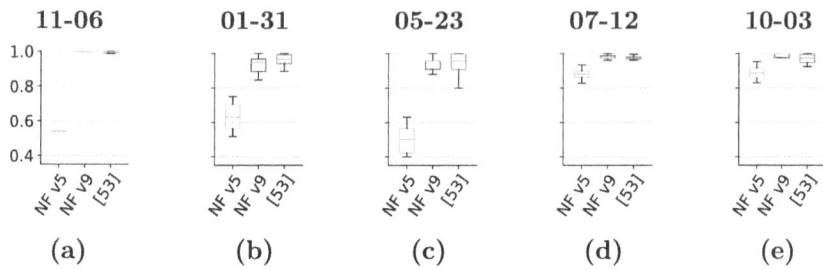

Fig. 6. F_1 score with a confidence interval at a 95% threshold for detecting masqueraded Cobalt Strike C2 observed in the wild. Ramos et al. [53] uses generic HTTP and HTTPS combined benign traffic. NF: NetFlow.

by Malware Traffic Analysis [47], as presented in Sect. 5.2. The four traces with HTTPS traffic, detailed in Table 2, contain unencrypted SNIs. However, as they do not correspond to any targeted profile, our method uses several models trained with generic HTTPS benign traffic, as depicted on the bottom of Fig. 3.

We observe that our method obtains downgraded performances. This may be occurring because the correct profile is not present inside training data. On the contrary, for a trace containing HTTP traffic with a known referer header corresponding to jQuery [46], our method uses one model trained with jQuery HTTP benign traffic. We then obtain a F_1 score of 0.99, as pictured in Fig. 6 (a). We manually extract and check afterwards that the malleable profile used in this trace is, in fact, a jQuery mimicking profile.

To evaluate the capability of Netflow features-based models to detect real-world HTTPS Cobalt Strike traffic, we train four models on the HTTPS selected traces. We then compare our results to those obtained with the method proposed by Ramos et al. [53], as pictured in Fig. 6 (b) to (e). Metrics values are presented in Table 8, including precision and recall. We observe that in most cases, models based on Netflow v9 features equals or outdo the performances reached by Ramos et al. [53]. Thus, Netflow v9 based models are proficient to detect external HTTPS C2 but Netflow v5 can also be used to create simpler yet effective models.

> **Takeaway**
>
> To summarize, our method applied to real-world traces performs well when the profile can be identified (see results for the jQuery profile [46]). Then, we show that Netflow features-based models' performance roughly equals Ramos et al. [53] and surpass it in some cases. Thus our method's performance is optimal when diverse profiles are used for training, as this increases the probability to use a specific model matching the traffic studied. These experiments show similar results as those in virtualized environment.

Table 8. Metrics rounded down to one hundredth with a 95% threshold confidence interval of the experiments in comparison with Ramos et al. [53]. Exp: Experiment, P: precision, R: recall, H: HTTP, HS: HTTPS, D: DNS.

Exp.	Netflow v5			Netflow v9			Ramos et al. [53]		
	F_1	P	R	F_1	P	R	F_1	P	R
Az/Az (H)	.98±.02	1±0	.96±.04	.99±0	1±0	.99±.01	.98±.01	.99±.01	.98±.02
Az/Gen (H)	.78±.04	.85±.05	.72±.06	.99±.01	.99±.01	.99±.01			
jQ/jQ (H)	.99±0	.99±0	.99±0	1±0	1±0	1±0	.99±0	.99±0	.99±0
jQ/Gen (H)	.98±0	.98±0	.97±0	.99±0	1±0	.99±0			
Az/Az (HS)	.96±.02	1±0	.94±.04	.99±.01	.99±.01	.98±.01	.95±.02	1±0	.91±.04
Az/Gen (HS)	.84±.05	.88±.05	.81±.06	.92±.02	.99±.01	.87±.05			
Sb/Sb (HS)	.99±.01	.98±.02	1±0	1±0	1±0	1±0	.95±.03	1±0	.91±.06
Sb/Gen (HS)	.84±.04	.88±.05	.81±.07	.95±.03	1±0	.91±.06			
D/Gen (HS)	.80±.05	.87±.05	.75±.07	.97±.01	1±0	.95±.02	.96±.02	1±0	.94±.04
D/Gen (D)	.96±0	.95±0	.97±0	.99±0	.99±0	.99±0	.99±0	.99±0	.99±0
Az/Gen (D)	.96±0	.96±0	.97±0	.99±0	.99±0	.99±0	.99±0	.99±0	.99±0
01-31 (HS)	.60±.10	.68±.11	.63±.09	.92±.05	1±0	.88±.06	.94±.05	1±0	.89±.05
05-23 (HS)	.49±.05	.54±.08	.48±.09	.93±.04	.99±.01	.87±.07	.94±.04	1±0	.89±.05
07-12 (HS)	.88±.02	.87±.03	.88±.02	.98±0	1±0	.96±.01	.97±0	1±0	.95±.02
10-03 (HS)	.88±.02	.91±.03	.87±.04	.98±0	1±0	.97±.02	.96±.02	1±0	.93±.04
11-06 (H)	.56±.04	.99±0	.40±.06	.99±0	1±0	.99±0	.99±0	1±0	.99±0

Exp.	Netflow v5 extended			Netflow v9 extended			Ramos et al. [53]		
	F_1	P	R	F_1	P	R	F_1	P	R
Az/Az (H)	.98±.01	1±0	.97±.03	1±0	1±0	1±0	.98±.01	.99±.01	.98±.02
Az/Gen (H)	.82±.03	.88±.06	.78±.05	.98±.01	.98±.01	.97±.02			
jQ/jQ (H)	.99±0	.99±0	.99±0	.99±0	1±0	.99±0	.99±0	.99±0	.99±0
jQ/Gen (H)	.98±0	.98±0	.97±0	.99±0	.99±0	.99±0			
Az/Az (HS)	.97±.01	.97±.03	.97±.02	.99±0	.99±.01	1±0	.95±.02	1±0	.91±.04
Az/Gen (HS)	.86±.03	.91±.02	.81±.07	.91±.03	.98±.01	.85±.06			
Sb/Sb (HS)	.99±.01	.98±.02	1±0	1±0	1±0	1±0	.95±.03	1±0	.91±.06
Sb/Gen (HS)	.86±.05	.92±.05	.82±.08	.94±.02	1±0	.89±.05			
D/Gen (HS)	.80±.05	.88±.05	.74±.07	.96±.01	1±0	.93±.02	.96±.02	1±0	.94±.04
D/Gen (D)	.96±0	.95±0	.97±0	.99±0	.99±0	.99±0	.99±0	.99±0	.99±0
Az/Gen (D)	.96±0	.96±0	.97±0	.99±0	.99±0	.99±0	.99±0	.99±0	.99±0

7 Ethics, Discussion and Future Work

We acknowledge that inspecting packets has an ethical impact on privacy. However, we argue that we minimize this impact by searching only for the domain name and that our method still provides good results when no domain is linked to the observed traffic. Moreover, the traffic generated in our work is not captured from real users' activity. We identify three main limitations to our work. First, the number of malicious samples in our experiments is low as we have a limited number of attack scenario to run on our platform. This prevents us from obtaining optimal results but collecting more information about real use of Cobalt Strike can help to improve our datasets. Second, the number of malleable profiles studied is still limited while being higher than in most related works.

This is because we limit our experiments to three popular profiles detected in the wild. This may explain the downgraded performances observed during the evaluation of our method on external HTTPS traces. Finally, the generic traffic datasets used are a few years old. More recent datasets would result to models closer to the current state of network traffic. These limitations will be addressed in future work.

We plan to extend this work along three axes. The first axis is to continue our experiments on other kinds of profiles. In a C2 communication, the victim sends more data than it receives. However, the tested profiles mimic activities where the victim receives more data than they send, making the detection easier. By studying the capability to detect data-sending oriented profiles such as cloud storage uploads or videoconferencing, we suppose it would help to better estimate the efficiency of other models and improve the coverage offered by our method. The second axis is the evaluation of a general performance of our method. We are also interested in the domain generalization of our method inside malleable profile groups (see Sect. 5.2), i.e. how well a model trained on data from a single profile performs on samples from close-related malleable profiles. This work will be based on the TLSH-based groups presented in Table 4. Finally, the third axis is to extend this work towards other frameworks [27] and Cobalt Strike extensions that are used in the wild [57]. We hypothesize that the performance may be preserved as the proposed method is not based on Cobalt Strike's specific parameters.

8   Conclusion

In this paper, we propose a new network traffic metadata-based machine learning method to detect Cobalt Strike masquerading C2 traffic. This passive detection method, in opposition with previous work, is based on unsophisticated but widely used features so it can be easily deployed in production environments. It can also adapt the model used to the observed traffic to optimize its performance. We evaluate the performance of this method on data generated using several widely used Cobalt Strike configurations deployed in a realistic virtualized architecture. We are the first paper providing such detailed, documented and reproductible evaluation. We show that a Random Forest model can detect Cobalt Strike masquerading *Command and Control* with or without encryption. We also show that this method performs better than the state of art when mimicked websites or services can be identified, and provides similar results to previously proposed approaches when it is not the case. Finally, we show that our method performance is similar to a previously proposed method on real-world attacks while using more standard features. The artifacts to reproduce the results of this paper are released at https://github.com/cp-tsp/ares2025-artifacts.

References

1. Abu Rajab, M., Zarfoss, J., Monrose, F., Terzis, A.: A multifaceted approach to understanding the botnet phenomenon. In: ACM SIGCOMM IMC (2006)

2. Althouse, J.: Tls fingerprinting with ja3 and ja3s (2019). https://engineering.salesforce.com/tls-fingerprinting-with-ja3-and-ja3s/

3. Althouse, J.: Ja4+ network fingerprinting (2023). https://blog.foxio.io/ja4%2B-network-fingerprinting

4. Anderson, B., McGrew, D.: Identifying encrypted malware traffic with contextual flow data. In: AISec (2016)

5. Anderson, B., McGrew, D.: Accurate tls fingerprinting using destination context and knowledge bases (2020)

6. Buczak, A.L., Hanke, P.A., Cancro, G.J., Toma, M.K., Watkins, L.A., Chavis, J.S.: Detection of tunnels in pcap data by random forests. In: CISRC 2016 (2016)

7. Bujlow, T., Carela-Español, V., Barlet-Ros, P.: Independent comparison of popular dpi tools for traffic classification. Comput, Nets (2015)

8. Censys: Jarm in censys search. https://docs.censys.com/docs/ls-jarm

9. Chen, S., Lang, B., Liu, H., Li, D., Gao, C.: Dns covert channel detection method using the lstm model (2021)

10. Cisco: NetFlow v1, v5, v7 and v8 (2007). https://www.cisco.com/c/en/us/td/docs/net_mgmt/netflow_collection_engine/3-6/user/guide/format.html

11. Cisco: NetFlow v9 (2011). https://www.cisco.com/en/US/technologies/tk648/tk362/technologies_white_paper09186a00800a3db9.html

12. CobaltStrike: https://www.cobaltstrike.com

13. CobaltStrike: https://www.cobaltstrike.com/help-malleable-c2

14. CobaltStrike: Official malleable profiles repository (2014). https://github.com/Cobalt-Strike/Malleable-C2-Profiles

15. CobaltStrike: (2022). https://hstechdocs.helpsystems.com/manuals/cobaltstrike/current/userguide/content/topics/listener-infrastructure_peer-2-peer.htm

16. CrowdStrike: (2018). https://www.crowdstrike.com/blog/meet-crowdstrikes-adversary-of-the-month-for-june-mustang-panda/

17. Cybereason. https://www.cybereason.com/blog/sliver-c2-leveraged-by-many-threat-actors

18. Dietrich, C., Rossow, C., Freiling, F., Bos, H., van Steen, M., Pohlmann, N.: On botnets that use dns for command and control. In: EC2ND (2011)

19. Rescorla, E.: Mozilla: RFC on TLS 1.3. https://www.rfc-editor.org/rfc/rfc8446

20. Vincent van der Eijk, C.S.: Detecting Cobalt Strike beacons in NetFlow data (2020)

21. Elsadig, M.A., Gafar, A.: Covert channel detection: machine learning approaches. IEEE Access, 38391–38405 (2022)

22. Felt, A.P., Barnes, R., King, A., Palmer, C., Bentzel, C., Tabriz, P.: Measuring https adoption on the web. In: USENIX Security (2017)

23. Freiling, F., Holz, T., Wicherski, G.: Botnet tracking: exploring a root-cause methodology to prevent distributed denial-of-service attacks. In: ESORICS (2005)

24. García, S., Grill, M., Stiborek, J., Zunino, A.: An empirical comparison of botnet detection methods. Elsevier Advanced Technology Publications (2014)

25. Github: https://github.com/looCiprian/GC2-sheet

26. Github: https://github.com/YDHCUI/manjusaka

27. Github: https://github.com/BishopFox/sliver

28. Google Cybersecurity Action Team (2023). https://services.google.com/fh/files/blogs/gcat_threathorizons_full_apr2023.pdf

29. Gu, G., Porras, P., Yegneswaran, V., Fong, M.: Bothunter: detecting malware infection through ids-driven dialog correlation. In: USENIX Security (2007)

30. Gu, G., Zhang, J., Lee, W.: Botsniffer: detecting botnet command and control channels in network traffic. In: NDSS Symposium (2008)

31. Hu, Y.Z.: Mining data from cobalt strike beacons (2022). https://www.nccgroup.com/us/research-blog/mining-data-from-cobalt-strike-beacons
32. Kondo, S., Sato, N.: Botnet traffic detection techniques by c&c session classification using svm. Adv. Inform. Comput. Secur. (2007)
33. Kravensecurity: C2 hunting: How to find c2 servers with shodan (2024). https://kravensecurity.com/c2-hunting-using-shodan/
34. Labayen, V., Magaña, E., Morató, D., Izal, M.: Network traffic and code for machine learning classification. Mach. Learn. Netw. (2020)
35. Labayen, V., Magaña, E., Morató, D., Izal, M.: Online classification of user activities using machine learning on network traffic. Comput, Nets (2020)
36. Livadas, C., Walsh, R., Lapsley, D., Strayer, W.T.: Using machine learning techniques to identify botnet traffic. In: LCN (2006)
37. Microsoft (2021). https://www.microsoft.com/en-us/security/blog/2021/05/27/new-sophisticated-email-based-attack-from-nobelium/
38. Mileva, A., Panajotov, B.: Covert channels in tcp/ip protocol stack - extended version-. Open Comput. Sci. (2014)
39. MitreAtt&ck: https://attack.mitre.org/software/S0154/
40. MitreAtt&ck: https://attack.mitre.org/techniques/T1071/001/
41. MitreAtt&ck: https://attack.mitre.org/techniques/T1071/004/
42. MTA: https://www.malware-traffic-analysis.net/2023/01/31/
43. MTA: https://www.malware-traffic-analysis.net/2023/05/23/
44. MTA: https://www.malware-traffic-analysis.net/2023/07/12/
45. MTA: https://www.malware-traffic-analysis.net/2023/10/03/
46. MTA: https://www.malware-traffic-analysis.net/2023/11/06/
47. MTA: https://www.malware-traffic-analysis.net/2023/
48. Nayak, C.: https://bruteratel.com/
49. Nivargi, V., Bhaowa, M., Lee, T.: Machine Learning Based Botnet Detection (2006)
50. Mavis, N.: The art and science of detecting Cobalt Strike (2020)
51. Oliver, J., Hagen, J.: Designing the elements of a fuzzy hashing scheme. In: EUC (2021)
52. Pai, K., Shubhodeep, M., Madhusoodhana, S.: Novel tls signature extraction for malware detection (2020)
53. Ramos, F.M., Wang, X.: A machine learning based approach to detect stealthy cobalt strike c&c activities from encrypted network traffic. Mach. Learn. Netw. (2022)
54. Ramos, F.M., Wang, X.: Detecting stealthy cobalt strike c&c activities via multi-flow based machine learning. In: ICMLA (2023)
55. Red Canary: Threat detection report (2022). https://resource.redcanary.com/rs/003-YRU-314/images/2022_ThreatDetectionReport_RedCanary.pdf
56. Salesforce: Easily identify malicious servers on the internet with jarm (2020). https://engineering.salesforce.com/easily-identify-malicious-servers-on-the-internet-with-jarm/
57. SentinelOne (2023). https://www.sentinelone.com/blog/geacon-brings-cobalt-strike-capabilities-to-macos-threat-actors/
58. Simmons, G.J.: The prisoners' problem and the subliminal channel. In: Advances in Cryptology, pp. 51–67 (1984)
59. Sosnowski, M., Zirngibl, J., Sattler, P., Carle, G.: DissecTLS: a scalable active scanner for TLS server configurations, capabilities, and TLS fingerprinting. In: PAM 2023 (2023)
60. Sosnowski, M., et al.: Active TLS stack fingerprinting: characterizing TLS server deployments at scale. In: TMA 2022 (2022)

61. Staniford-chen, S., et al.: Grids : A graph based intrusion detection system for large networks (1998)
62. Stratosphere: Stratosphere laboratory datasets (2015). https://www.stratosphereips.org/datasets-overview
63. Talos: https://blog.talosintelligence.com/manjusaka-offensive-framework
64. O'Leary, T.J., Bonner, T., Janus, M., Given, D., Wickens, E.. Simpson, J.: Finding Beacons In The Dark (2021)
65. Unit42 (2022). https://unit42.paloaltonetworks.com/brute-ratel-c4-tool/
66. UPC (2015). https://historic.cba.upc.edu/monitoring/traffic-classification.html
67. US district court for the eastern district of New York (2023). https://noticeofpleadings.com/crackedcobaltstrike/
68. Wang, K., Stolfo, S.: Anomalous payload-based network intrusion detection. In: RAID (2004)
69. Warmer, M.: Detection of web based C2 channels. Ph.D. thesis (2011)
70. Yang, X., Ruan, S., Yue, Y., Sun, B.: Petnet: plaintext-aware encrypted traffic detection network for identifying cobalt strike https traffics. Comput, Nets (2024)
71. Zander, S., Armitage, G., Branch, P.: A survey of covert channels and countermeasures in computer network protocols (2007)
72. Zeek: conn.log. https://docs.zeek.org/en/master/logs/conn.html
73. Zeek: Zeek framework official website. https://zeek.org/
74. Zhang, H., Papadopoulos, C., Massey, D.: Detecting encrypted botnet traffic (2013)

Towards Deterministic DDS Communication for Secure Service-Oriented Software-Defined Vehicles

Florian Frank[1]([⊠])[iD], Dominik Püllen[1][iD], Alexandru Kampmann[2][iD], and Stefan Katzenbeisser[1][iD]

[1] University of Passau, Passau, Germany
{florian.frank,dominik.puellen,stefan.katzenbeisser}@uni-passau.de
[2] RWTH Aachen University, Aachen, Germany
kampmann@embedded.rwth-aachen.de

Abstract. Software-defined vehicles, which rely on zonal architectures, run multiple applications on a small number of control units. This requires deploying several applications on a single platform, which introduces significant challenges in ensuring strict time boundaries for safety-critical operations due to shared physical resources and full-stack operating systems. To address these challenges, this paper proposes a time-aware scheduler implemented on an FPGA within an MPSoC for the widely adopted DDS standard, allowing time-critical data to bypass the slow and unpredictable OS-level networking layers. The scheduler enables prioritized processing of time-critical data within fixed and predictable time slots while preventing starvation of low-priority data. Moreover, we introduce a method to define QoS profiles, which allow forwarding time-critical traffic in guaranteed time slices to automotive applications running on the MPSoC's CPUs. That way, we guarantee strict real-time requirements with minimal latency and an overall jitter below $2\,\mu s$. Finally, we outsource DDS security operations to a hardware-implemented cryptographic algorithm and demonstrate a PUF-based key extraction method with 99.33% reliability. The approach enables highly deterministic processing of DDS traffic with integrated security by design.

Keywords: Software-Defined Vehicles · DDS · FPGA · Physical Unclonable Functions

1 Introduction

The Transformation of automobiles into automated Software-Defined Vehicles (SDVs) requires new hardware and software architectures to address numerous challenges, particularly handling large data volumes in real-time, seamless software updates, and cost-effective maintenance.

Traditionally, vehicles used highly optimized embedded control units to perform specific tasks. These control units communicated through tailored automotive protocols such as CAN or FlexRay.

M. Dalla Preda et al. (Eds.): ARES 2025, LNCS 15992, pp. 186–208, 2025.
https://doi.org/10.1007/978-3-032-00624-0_9

The increasing number of functions in SDVs (e.g., automated driving, V2X communication) necessitates improvements in scalability, modularity, resource utilization efficiency and a reduction in wiring complexity. These demands led to fewer but more powerful controllers referred to as High-Performance Computing (HPC) platforms. They are interconnected in Ethernet networks and run full-stack operating systems, allowing the parallel execution of multiple applications.

In the software layer, SDVs tend to incorporate Service Oriented Architectures (SOAs) because they increase modularity, enable dynamic software management, and improve maintainability. Prominent communication middlewares for SOAs are SOME/IP [24] and Data Distribution Service (DDS)[5], often combined with Time Sensitive Networking (TSN) [11] to ensure predictable latencies. Another key feature is that SDVs communicate through external interfaces with other traffic participants, the infrastructure, and data centers. Exchanging information such as current position, speed, route plans, and intended maneuvers with remote participants enhances driving safety. However, it also increases the risk of cyber threats.

To effectively mitigate such risks, security measures must become an integral component of SDVs [19]. For instance, DDS provides the DDS security specification [18], while the Automotive Service-Oriented software Architecture (ASOA) has a dedicated security extension [20].

Although security measures are essential, they come at the cost of higher latencies and potentially violate real-time constraints as they impose additional and possibly unpredictable computational overhead. This can be particularly critical when multiple services are deployed on a single HPC platform and share hardware resources. For example, interference between time-critical packets may occur within a shared communication stack if various services run on a single control unit.

This work addresses these challenges by proposing an architectural design for HPC platforms that guarantees deterministic, low-latency, and secure communication. More precisely, we make the following contributions:

- An Architecture for Multi-Processor System On Chip (MPSoC) with a pipelined, Field Programmable Gate Array (FPGA)-based solution ensuring low latency and deterministic processing of DDS traffic on HPC platforms. In this work, deterministic behavior refers to the ability to ensure predictable timing within fixed boundaries, independent of the system load.
- Demonstration of dynamic prioritization and time-aware scheduling in hardware, forwarding data within precise timing constraints while supporting the dynamic behavior of service-oriented architectures.
- A hardware-based security solution integrating cryptographic algorithms with minimal delay, using a low-cost Physical Unclonable Function (PUF)-based key generation system with 99.33% robustness to eliminate external cryptographic operations and minimize the Trusted Computing Base (TCB).
- Comprehensive evaluation of the architecture's timing behavior and security.

2   Related Work

This section provides an overview of various works focusing on minimizing latency and jitter in service-oriented architectures using reconfigurable hardware.

Scordino *et al.* [22] introduced the Elastic Gateway (eGW), a hardware architecture for accelerating DDS in automotive networks. It processes frames in three stages: ingress (normalization), processing (dynamic prioritization), and egress (transmission) while supporting TSN-based Quality of Service (QoS). In contrast to their approach of adding a normalization step, our solution directly processes Real-Time Transport Protocol (RTPS) frames for lower latency. Furthermore, this work does not address the challenge of integrating security measures into time-critical systems, as discussed in this work.

Lienen *et al.*[16] published a paper describing an intra-FPGA data distribution service for ReconROS, optimizing Robot Operating System 2 (ROS2) communication by FPGA-based hardware acceleration. It reduces memory access, improves performance, and ensures predictable real-time behavior. Unlike our approach, which enables frame prioritization and various OS platforms, this solution runs exclusively on ReconOS and lacks packet prioritization capabilities.

Sugata *et al.* [23] proposed a method to accelerate ROS publish-subscribe messaging by offloading ROS nodes to an FPGA with a simplified hardware-implemented network stack. The implementation is divided into two phases: registering publishers and subscribers at a master node, which is implemented in software, while the subsequent data transmission is accelerated in hardware. However, their approach is limited by the network stack, which supports only one port and one session for data communication. In contrast, our solution enables multiple services to communicate over different ports while supporting packet prioritization in hardware, offering enhanced flexibility and performance.

Rosa *et al.* [21] introduced DerechoDDS, a DDS middleware using Remote Direct memory Access (RDMA) for low-latency communication. It supports four QoS policies for data durability, impacting bandwidth and consistency. However, the authors only evaluate bandwidth and latency savings while not analyzing deterministic timing, which is this work's primary focus.

As we present a key generation method based on ring oscillator PUFs, an overview of some FPGA-based PUF solutions relevant to this work are given:

Budnik *et al.* [6] implemented a ring oscillator PUF for Zynq® UltraScale+™ FPGAs using five-stage oscillators placed on four different physical locations on the FPGA. The oscillators occupy 512 LookUp Tables (LUTs), generating 130 bit responses. In contrast, we use a Linear-Feedback Shift Register (LFSR)-based oscillator pair selection to generate 256 bit from 2×16 oscillators, reducing the area consumption. We achieve a uniqueness of 43.87%, comparable to the 43.64% reported in their paper, while our reliability reaches 99.33%, marginally higher than the 98.91% reported in their work.

Kareem *et al.* [15] implemented ring oscillators on Xilinx FPGAs, focusing on placement strategies for Arty A7 FPGAs. Our work, targeting Zynq®

UltraScale+^{TM}, also addresses consistency and robustness of repeated PUF measurements, which is not discussed in their work.

Further works on PUFs targeting Xilinx FPGAs are presented in [9,25].

Compared to existing solutions, our approach uniquely combines deterministic timing in automotive SOAs with integrated hardware security features.

3   Service-Oriented Architectures for SDVs

SOAs are design paradigms for distributed systems, where functionalities are encapsulated as modular services that interact through a publish-subscribe pattern. In general, publishers distribute data, and subscribers receive it. Instead of directly addressing subscribers, data is sent to designated topics, allowing registered subscribers to receive the published information. Subscribers can dynamically subscribe to topics, enhancing system flexibility and modularity, features particularly beneficial in domains such as vehicular networks. In SDVs, this communication paradigm serves as the foundation for any kind of interactions between Electronic Control Units (ECUs), cameras, or sensors.

This modularity enables starting, rescheduling, and updating services, replacing the rigid and static software architectures of the past.

These advantages have made DDS a standard for SOAs and part of the AUTomotive Open Systems ARchitecture (AUTOSAR) Adaptive and Classic platforms since 2018 [5]. Furthermore, it has also been an integral component of the ROS 2 framework [17]. As a prominent SOA middleware, DDS is widely adopted across automotive, aviation, military, and robotics domains. Unlike other SOA standards, it employs a decentralized discovery mechanism, enabling the seamless runtime addition of new services without requiring a central broker.

In DDS, topics define specific data types and are augmented with QoS parameters to enforce policies such as real-time constraints, redundancy, bandwidth optimization, and caching. This work presents a hardware-based network stack parser that efficiently processes Ethernet frames up to the RTPS protocol, which is the wire protocol of DDS. It supports advanced features like filtering, prioritization, and scheduling defined by QoS parameters.

4   Architecture and Design

In this section, we will first provide a high-level overview of the hardware-accelerated package filtering, scheduling, and security architecture. We begin with an explanation of the core functionalities of each component at a coarse level, followed by a more detailed explanation of all components that make up the entire architecture in the following sections. The proposed architecture is designed for MPSoCs including one or multiple CPUs, referred to as the Processing System (PS), and an FPGA, referred to as the Programming Logic (PL). On the PS, multiple DDS-based services can be deployed to operate various tasks within an automotive ecosystem, while exchanging DDS traffic with the PL. This paper primarily focuses on the design placed on the PL, which enables

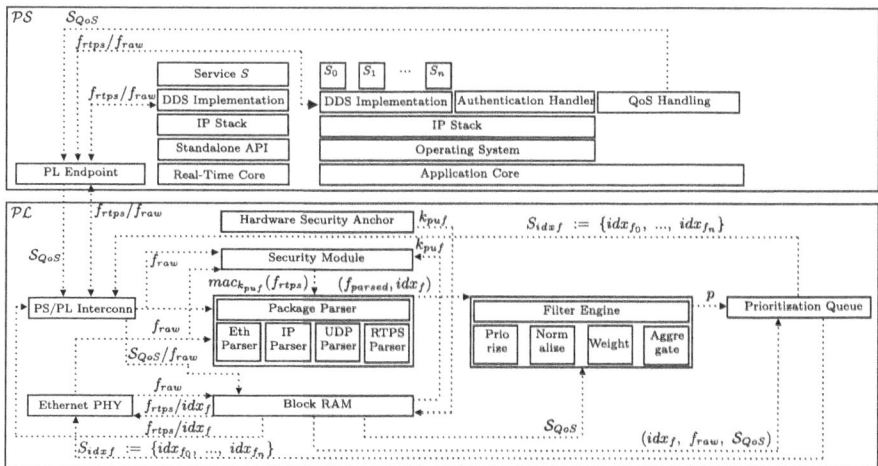

Fig. 1. Overview of the entire architecture targeting MPSoCs.

customized hardware designs with highly predictable timing. An overview of the full architecture is given in Fig. 1.

In general, the PL architecture is designed as a pipeline where messages corresponding to services are received, parsed, prioritized, and scheduled. Simultaneously, their integrity and authenticity are assessed before being forwarded to the service, running on the PS. When sending data frames, services on the PS transmit them to the PL, passing through the same pipeline before being forwarded to the Ethernet PHY.

The architecture follows a modular approach on the PS and PL, featuring interchangeable software components on the PS and replaceable modules m on the PL. A module is defined as an encapsulated unit of a hardware design with well-established interfaces that enable seamless interaction with other modules. The implementation of individual modules is detailed in Sect. 5.

The pipeline is initiated at the *Ethernet PHY* when data is received, or at the *PS/PL Interconnection* when outgoing data is transmitted from a service running on the PS. At this stage, raw RTPS frames f_{raw}, potentially assigned to different services running on one of the cores on the PS are decomposed into fragments that match the pipeline's data bus size, shared across all modules.

In the next pipeline stage, the fragments are forwarded in parallel to the *Packet Parser, Block RAM* module, and *Security Module*. The *Packet Parser* extracts and interprets all header fields, allowing the frame's protocol stack to transform the fragments of f_{raw} into a structured set of parsed fields, f_{parsed}.

Simultaneously, the *Security Module* ensures the authenticity and integrity of the frame while significantly reducing latency by leveraging highly efficient hardware-accelerated cryptographic algorithms. The third parallel pipeline operation involves storing the raw frame f_{raw} in the *Block RAM* module. Storing the frame in block RAM allows the frame to be loaded and forwarded in prioritized order to the PS or Ethernet PHY after prioritization and scheduling.

The next module in the pipeline is the *Filter Engine*, which receives the parsed fields f_{parsed} returned by the *Packet Parser* and computes a priority p to determine the order of processing of RTPS frames. This priority can be calculated dynamically through various evaluation methods, including simple comparisons (e.g., comparing GUID prefixes in DDS traffic), ordering operations (e.g., based on timestamps), or by more complex functions, calculated on the previously parsed fields. The resulting priorities are normalized and weighted, resulting in a single priority p for each individual RTPS frame. The set of evaluation methods and weights is dynamically configurable on the PS and transmitted over the *PS/PL Interconnection* module to the PL. This information, along with dynamically adjustable parameters required for the scheduler, is denoted as S_{QoS} and stored in block RAM, accessible to the *Filter Engine,* as well as the next component in the pipeline, the *Prioritization Queue*.

This module implements a time-aware scheduler, which arranges indices to RTPS frames idx_f, previously stored in *Block RAM* based on their priority p and forwards them in dedicated time slices defined in S_{QoS}, either to the PS for data reception or to the Ethernet PHY for data transmission. Those modules fetch the frames from block RAM, identified by idx_f, and delivers the RTPS frames f_{rtps} to the appropriate destination.

This implementation can be considered a dynamic framework for prioritizing and scheduling of DDS traffic. It offers a fine-grained, dynamically adjustable prioritization mechanism that can be refined during runtime, making it particularly suitable for highly dynamic SOAs, as those in SDVs, where static prioritization methods may become insufficient. Furthermore, this approach guarantees compliance with hard real-time constraints by leveraging the highly predictable timing of the PL, where the core components of our architecture are implemented. By utilizing predefined time slices within the *Priority Queue*, real-time communication is ensured without starvation of lower priority traffic.

Finally, to complement the deterministic and performance-centric architecture and to provide a small TCB, a cryptographic key k_{puf} is directly retrieved from the FPGA, stored in Block RAM, and forwarded to the *Security Module*. The key is generated by the *Hardware Security Anchor*, which encapsulates a PUF to derive cryptographic keys directly from the PL, avoiding the need to store keys or transmit them from the PS during runtime.

4.1 Prioritization of RTPS Frames

On HPC platforms, particularly when multiple services share a single network interface, it is crucial to determine the order in which data frames are forwarded to the DDS service running on the PS, or when RTPS frames are transmitted from services to the network bus. Instead of using a static prioritization function, a dynamic framework is provided that not only calculates priorities but also allows adjustable weighting, enabling more fine-grained control on the prioritization. For example, by assigning higher weight to soon-to-expire deadlines, while additionally increasing the priority of specific subscribers and publishers. This step is followed by the aggregation and normalization of priorities into a single priority, denoted as p. For this purpose, the prioritization algorithm extracts specific values of interest from the RTPS frames, denoted as $S_{par} := \{par_0, \ldots, par_n\}$. Parameters $par_i \in S_{par}$ may correspond to deadlines or identifiers of specific readers or writers. Second, the module uses the extracted parameters to invoke a set of $\mathbb{N}$-valued evaluation functions $S_{\mathcal{F}_{eval}} := \{\mathcal{F}_{eval_0}, \ldots, \mathcal{F}_{eval_n}\}$. These evaluation functions accept a parameter par_i and a constant value $const_i$. For example, $const_i$ could be a constant subscriber identifier, and par_i pointing to the identifier of the currently processed frame. The evaluation function $\mathcal{F}_{eval_i}(par_i, const_i)$ compares them, returning a priority $\tilde{p} \in \mathbb{N}$. In general, $\mathcal{F}_{eval_i}$ can range from simple comparisons to complex operations, each returning a priority $\tilde{p}$. Third, this module normalizes the priorities $\tilde{p}$ to the predefined priority range $p_i' \in [p_{min}, p_{max}]$ utilizing a normalization function $\mathcal{F}_{norm}$ (e.g., min-max normalization), resulting in the normalized priority p_i'. Once normalized, the resulting priorities are weighted by multiplying the corresponding weight w_i to each priority value $\tilde{p}_i$. Finally, the normalized and weighted priorities are aggregated to produce a single priority $p \in \mathbb{N}_0$, which forms the basis for arranging the frame in the Prioritization Queue. The weighting and subsequent aggregation, resulting in a single priority p are computed as follows:

$$p = \frac{1}{|S_p|} \sum_{i=1}^{|S_p|} p_i' \cdot w_i; p \in [p_{min}, p_{max}] \wedge p \in \mathbb{N}_0 \qquad (1)$$

The parameter sets $S_{\mathcal{F}_{eval}}$, $S_{const} := \{const_0, \ldots, const_n\}$, and S_w can be dynamically optimized based on the scheduled services and are defined within the QoS parameter set S_{QoS}.

4.2   Prioritization Queue

The Prioritization Queue is required to guarantee deterministic timing and uses a variant of time-aware scheduling, as specified in IEEE 802.1 TSN [12]. Time-aware scheduling defines distinct time slices to meet hard real-time deadlines while reserving additional time slices for best-effort communication, preventing the starvation of lower-priority traffic.

Such a scheduler consists of several components, including multiple priority queues that store frames of a particular priority p. The priority of all n queues represents the normalized priority range $[p_{min}, p_{max}]$, with each queue assigned a particular priority p. Each of these has a gate, controlled by a binary value, that determines when a packet can be pushed to the output queue. If the gate is open (1), the packet is dequeued; otherwise, it is not. The data in the output queue is then forwarded to the PS/PL Interconnection module or Ethernet PHY, which transmits the assigned frames $S_{f_{rtps}}$ to the services running on the PS or to the network bus. An example of a time-aware scheduler with four queues is shown in Fig. 2.

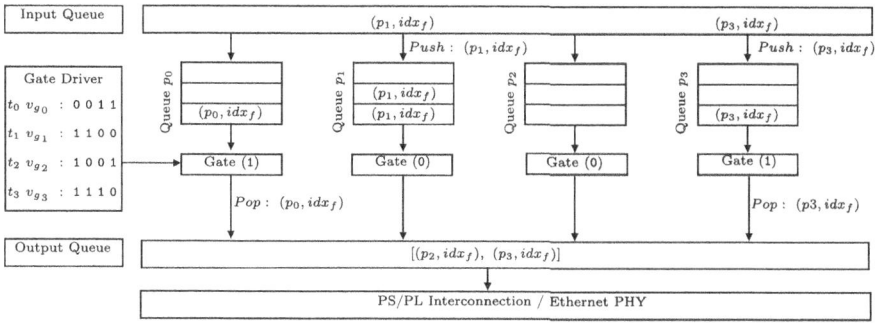

Fig. 2. Example of a time-aware scheduler with four priority queues.

The Gate Driver manages the gates of each priority queue using distinct gate vectors v_g, periodically set at specific times t_i. Thereby, a list of time slices $S_t = \{t_0, \ldots, t_n\}$ defines the turnaround time of this component, with each time point configuring the gate vectors v_g. Each gate at t_i is assigned a value, ensuring $|v_g| = |[p_{min}, p_{max}]|$. Thereby, when multiple priority queues dequeue data at t_n, the indices of the dequeued frames, $S_{idx_f} := \{idx_{f_0}, \ldots, idx_{f_n}\}$ are forwarded to the PS or Ethernet PHY in descending priority.

Similar to the parameters used in the priority calculation, the time slices S_t and the corresponding set of gate vectors $S_{v_g} := \{v_{g_0}, \ldots, v_{g_n}\}$, where $|S_t| = |S_{v_g}|$, are adjustable and stored as elements of S_{QoS} in block RAM.

4.3   Security Module

Ensuring authenticity, integrity, and confidentiality of messages without compromising performance is critical in automotive ecosystems. Therefore, we focus on securing intra-vehicle networks within automotive SOAs, which face security risks, especially from external connectivity like V2X communication.

As the existing DDS security standard imposes a high performance overhead, primarily due to computationally heavy cryptographic operations such as the Advanced Encryption Standard (AES) it may violate real-time performance.

Therefore, we adopt a lightweight security implementation described in [20]. In contrast to the DDS security standard, this approach provides a solution divided into two phases: an authentication phase that involves a non-real-time critical authentication and key exchange with a central security server at vehicle startup, distributing session keys derived from a root key. The second phase (runtime protection) focuses on data protection of RTPS frames. Building on this solution, we specifically focus on runtime protection, as this phase is critical for ensuring deterministic and low-latency communication. However, the authentication phase is not real-time critical and can be implemented in software.

Within the runtime protection phase, authentication and integrity protection are achieved by computing a Message Authentication Code (MAC) on an RTPS frame, denoted as $mac_{k_{puf}}(f_{rtps})$. The resulting checksum and a nonce are appended to the RTPS frame f_{rtps}. Furthermore, the MAC of received RTPS frames can be verified. This method can be easily implemented on FPGAs.

Moreover, since MACs are only as secure as the cryptographic keys used, addressing the problem of key management is essential. To solve this problem, we avoid storing cryptographic keys in non-volatile memory and minimize interaction with the PS, especially after initialization. Instead, we derive these keys directly from the PL using strong hardware fingerprints based on PUFs. As the compatibility of PUFs with the measures presented in [20] was already described, we improve this approach using a more efficient PUF implementation based on ring oscillators, seamlessly integrated within the overall architecture. PUFs exploit minor manufacturing variations to produce a key, k_{raw}. As k_{raw} may suffer small instabilities, it is subjected to error correction to derive a stable key, k_{puf}, which is stored in volatile block RAM only during runtime and is subsequently used by the MAC. This approach offers benefits in performance and security by providing a great source of entropy, allowing the generation of multiple keys as detailed further in Sect. 5.6.

5   Implementation

This section covers key implementation aspects derived from the design as outlined in Sect. 4. The implementation is tailored for an Zynq® UltraScale+™ ZCU102 evaluation board, hosting multiple CPUs, programmable logic, and various I/O ports. However, the design can be adjusted for other MPSoCs. Similar to the design, the implementation is divided into two parts: the PS, hosting two CPUs, and the PL. On the PL, all modules derived from the design (m) are implemented as dedicated SystemVerilog/Verilog modules or encapsulated within one or multiple custom IP-cores. This implementation achieves high throughput by enabling pipelining in almost all modules, supporting a 128 bit databus size.

To further reduce latency, data transmission to block RAM and the evaluation of the Security Module and Filter Engine are implemented in three parallel pipelines. These pipelines converge before entering the Prioritization Queue, which synchronizes with completing the longest pipeline. DDS services are executed on the CPUs of the PS, with the ability to exchange data across the PL.

5.1   PS Implementation

On the PS, we adopted an implementation of the DDS standard building on the lightweight DDS implementation embeddedRTPS [14]. The PS of the Zynq® UltraScale+™ ZCU102 includes a Real-time Processing Unit (RPU), Application Processing Unit (APU), and a graphical processor, allowing us to run this implementation either on the APU, supported by a PetaLinux operating system, or as bare-metal application on the RPU. This work focuses primarily on the RPU implementation, enabling precise measurements of the timing, unaffected by interference from the non-deterministic Linux kernel. embeddedRTPS features a layer that abstracts the implementation from the underlying operating system and architecture. Within this work, this layer is tailored to support the execution as a standalone program on the RPU. The entire implementation is controlled by an event-driven single loop scheduler to ensure deterministic timing. This scheduler manages tasks such as transmitting periodic service discovery messages and processing incoming and outgoing data frames triggered by events originating from precise hardware timers, or interrupts fired when RTPS data is available. The previously mentioned abstraction layer enables the reception and transmission of packets, such as discovery messages, which are not prioritized by our implementation. For this purpose, we use the LwIP stack, which provides low-level functionalities not implemented in hardware, such as the Address Resolution Protocol (ARP) protocol. This stack is integrated through its callback functionality, which is triggered when incoming data is available. These callbacks initiate events that are subsequently processed by the scheduler.

The callback behavior is adopted for receiving prioritized data from our PS/PL Interconnection, triggered by the Prioritization Queue, which initiates data transmission at dedicated time slices. By using an interrupt line on the PS, the system invokes a callback and processes it as an event (similar to handling incoming data from the LwIP stack) to retrieve the data from a shared memory segment efficiently. We utilize the Advanced eXtensible Interface Bus (AXI)-Full protocol for receiving prioritized frames from the PL to enable high throughput.

As a proof-of-concept, we support Ethernet communication on the PL using the AXI Ethernet Subsystem IP-core [1]. Incoming data frames are transferred into a shared memory segment of the RPU's Network Interface (NETIF) memory segment and directly forwarded to the PL. However, future work would require a hardware IP stack to eliminate delays caused by transmitting data to the RPU's memory segment.

5.2   PS/PL Interconnection Module

To implement the interconnection between the PS and PL, we utilize the well-established AXI protocol. As this section focuses on high throughput and the transmission of single RTPS frames, the AXI-Full variant is employed, which supports burst transmissions, unlike the AXI-Lite protocol. This approach enables the transmission of data bursts with up to one beat per clock cycle. Our design features a beat size of 128 bit and a maximum burst size of 95, allowing the transmission of 1520 B of data in a single sequence to achieve high throughput. This configuration was chosen to enable the transmission of the maximum Ethernet frame length of 1518 B in one sequence. The remaining two bytes are used as opcode to distinguish whether QoS parameters (S_{QoS}) are being updated or whether an RTPS message encapsulated within an Ethernet frame is being transmitted to the PS.

5.3   Package Parser and Prioritization Algorithm

Like most modules of our implementation, the Package Parser functions as a pipeline supporting a 128 bit data bus, processing all static header fields of each protocol layer and continuously forwarding the parsed frames. After parsing the static header fields, each RTPS submessage is parsed in a single clock cycle if its size is less than or equal to the data bus size; otherwise, it requires several cycles equal to the submessage size divided by the 128 bit bus width.

The parsed fields are sent directly to the Filter Engine, which is configured by the previously transmitted set of QoS parameters. The properties within parsed frames, used to prioritize $\mathcal{S}_{par}$ and the corresponding evaluation methods $\mathcal{S}_{\mathcal{F}_{eval}}$, are extracted based on predefined opcodes and processed in dedicated Verilog tasks. Calculating single priorities $\tilde{p}$ is performed within a single clock cycle per 128 bit frame, taking advantage of the parallelism of optimized hardware designs. Our prototype implementation was tested with a maximum of five parallel priority calculation methods but can be easily scaled at the cost of higher area utilization. Upon receiving a 128 bit portion of a single frame, normalization, weighting, and aggregation are executed within three clock cycles.

5.4   Block RAM Module

To efficiently handle large amounts of data and avoid storing full RTPS frames within the Prioritization Queue, we use the Block RAM generator IP-core [2], configured with dual ports (one port is used for reading and the other for writing). This IP-core is configured with a data width of 128 bit and a read/write depth of 8192 entries, ensuring compatibility with the globally defined bus width. This module is connected to a custom-developed module that manages data storage and retrieval from block RAM using a ring buffer mechanism.

5.5   Prioritization Queue

For a compact hardware design, the Prioritization Queue operates exclusively on addresses idx_f to frames in the Block RAM module, instead of processing the frames directly. For this reason, it receives tuples of addresses and priorities from the Packet Parser. The Prioritization Queue aligns with our pipeline approach by storing a frame index idx_f in a priority queue within a single clock cycle, eliminating the need for additional buffering. This approach is supported by the implementation of a scheduler driven by three `always` blocks relying on a shared clock source. The first `always` block stores the incoming frame index pairs in respective priority queues. The second block controls the gate driver, updating its gate vector within each time slice. Finally, the third block retrieves the frame index, concatenates the addresses, and transmits the data to the PS/PL Interconnection or Ethernet PHY, where it is loaded from block RAM and forwarded to the PS or network.

The gate vectors and corresponding time units are retrieved from $\mathcal{S}_{QoS}$. The prototype implementation was tested with eight priority queues, following the IEEE 802.1 TSN standard [12].

5.6   Security Implementation

Our proposed security implementation consists of two components. The first component is the Security Module, which implements an integrity protection and validation mechanism based on the SipHash MAC algorithm [4]. This algorithm uses a cryptographic key provided by the Hardware Security Anchor, which features a ring oscillator-based PUF.

Security Module: The core component of this module is a SipHash implementation, which offers a balanced trade-off between security and performance while enabling efficient hardware acceleration. The algorithm is structured in three phases: initialization, compression, and finalization. In the initialization phase, it XORs four internal 64 bit states with a 128 bit key, while the compression phase processes one or multiple 64 bit input blocks. During the third phase, the finalization phase, multiple SipRounds are performed to produce a 64 bit hash value. The number of SipRounds in both phases is configurable. We selected two rounds in the initialization and four for finalization to balance throughput and security, as recommended by the authors of this algorithm [4]. To integrate SipHash into our pipelining approach with a 128 bit data bus, we implemented a variant of Hirose's Double Block Length Compression Function [10] by integrating the Verilog SipHash implementation by Joachim Strömbergson [13]. This method doubles the input size of the MAC algorithm by employing two parallel SipHash instances, offering a 128 bit input and enabling a pipelined operation. Only a tiny buffer is required to handle the additional clock cycles needed for initialization and compression.

Hardware Security Anchor: Within this module, we adopt a ring oscillator-based PUF, based on the implementation from Jimenez *et al.* [8]. As this PUF was developed for Xilinx Artix-7 FPGAs, we extend and adapt this implementation for compatibility with Zynq® UltraScale+™ architectures. The implementation employs two groups of 16 oscillators, with each oscillator consisting of three inverters and a NAND gate to activate self-oscillation. Two 16-to-1 multiplexers select an oscillator from each group. Therefore, $16 \times 16 = 256$ bit responses can be derived from the PUF design. This implementation uses a LFSR with a seed to derive the combinations of ring oscillators selected by the two multiplexers. A control unit manages the PUF execution, utilizing a 10 MHz reference counter to determine when the comparison of the two groups is completed and a new key bit is generated. A shift register appends single response bits to the output response until a 256 bit output is generated. The oscillators are positioned so that the paths within each oscillator have equal line lengths. Otherwise, the comparisons return biased and predictable responses. This arrangement necessitates manual floorplanning. To prevent interference with other components in the implementation, we allocate exclusive space within a dedicated clock management region and ensure that no other hardware is placed in this area.

All ring oscillators are placed on equal SLICEL (Logic) units, with the inverters and NAND gates implemented within these rows as LUTs of type LUT6.

Above these oscillators, we have placed symmetric counters for each ring oscillator group, along with a comparator between the two rows of counters. Since the
arrangement of slices and other components, like block RAM or arithmetic units,
differs significantly from the structure of the Artix-7, it is challenging to identify
symmetric paths. Subsequently, we manually placed all components iteratively
to optimize the PUF parameters of robustness and uniformity. To evaluate the
uniqueness of the PUF, we have implemented a script to automate the placement
of oscillators within each clock management region on the FPGA, which shares
a similar structure. To analyze the PUF responses, we use a serial interface to
send the seed for the LFSR and receive the response. This interface is removed
before integrating the PUF into the architecture.

Keys must be fully reproducible to allow the generation and verification
of MACs. However, since PUFs inherently exhibit instability, slight deviations
also occur in the PUF presented in this work, making error-correction mechanisms necessary. Therefore, we employ the commonly used Bose-Chaudhuri-
Hocquenghem (BCH) error correction code; specifically, we use an implementation by Dill *et al.* [7]. This implementation turns a raw and slightly unstable
PUF response k_{raw} into a stable one. To obfuscate physical characteristics and
to distill the entropy of the response, we hash the corrected PUF response,
resulting in a 128 bit cryptographically usable key k_{puf}, reusing the two parallel
SipHash implementations. This key is temporarily stored in block RAM to avoid
compromising the pipeline's performance by the PUF readout.

6   Evaluation

This section evaluates the key performance indicators of our solution, focusing on
latency and its ability to meet hard real-time guarantees. Precisely, we assess the
overall latency and, more importantly, the Worst-Case Execution Time (WCET)
that the system can reliably guarantee. The second part of this section focuses
on assessing the security implementation, including the hardware-accelerated
cryptographic implementations and the analysis of the ring oscillator-based PUF
assessing its key properties: robustness, uniqueness, and uniformity.

Evaluation Platform and System Configuration: We evaluate our approach on the Xilinx UltraScale+^{TM} platform, which resembles the hardware
architectures commonly used in automotive HPCs. This platform offers a
powerful Arm® Cortex®-A53 quad-core APU, as well as an Arm® Cortex®-
R5 dual-core RPU and programmable logic. Specifically, we chose a Zynq®
UltraScale+^{TM} ZCU102 board, which offers various interfaces, including an
onboard Gigabit Ethernet interface and four additional Enhanced Small Form-
factor Pluggable (SFP+) ports, to which we connect a Gigabit extension network
card to evaluate the throughput and performance of our MPSoC-based design.
The performance evaluation in this section is conducted by a standalone application running on a single core of an Arm® Cortex®-R5 processor.

Our FPGA design is configured as a pipeline with a data bus width $m_d =$ 128 bit to ensure high throughput. Furthermore, we configured the AXI-Full interface to allow transfers consisting of up to 95 bursts, enabling the transmission of 12160 bit in 95 clock cycles. This setup allows the processing of Ethernet frames with a Maximum Transmission Unit (MTU) of 1500 B to be sent as a single burst. The hardware design on the PL is driven by the PL fabric clock provided by the Zynq® UltraScale+™ MPSoC Processing System IP configured with 150 MHz. All components in the design are driven by this clock, except for the PUF implementation, which uses a 10 MHz clock derived from the fabric clock, as well as the AXI 1G/2.5G Ethernet Subsystem IP Core, which requires a 156.25 MHz hardwired clock source. The frequency of the fabric clock is chosen based on the evaluated Worst Negative Slack (WNS), as discussed in Sect. 6.1, to optimize throughput, reduce latency, and ensure reliable operation.

6.1   Performance Evaluation

To evaluate the deterministic behavior and latency of the proposed architecture, we assess each module in our design separately, particularly under worst-case conditions. This approach enables us to provide a precise estimation of the minimum latency we can reliably guarantee for RTPS frames to be processed and to determine whether strict real-time requirements can be met. In this work, we adopt a top-down evaluation approach by first analyzing the latency on the RPU, followed by an analysis of the interconnection interface between the PS and PL. Finally, we evaluate the timing guarantees achievable by each module deployed on the PL.

Time Savings Through Bypassing the LwIP Stack: First, to evaluate the impact of our solution on the RPU's timing, we analyze the time savings achieved by bypassing the LwIP stack. Precisely, we measure the time elapsed from the availability of data at the NETIF layer to the reception of frames by the callback function on the RPU, which triggers a scheduler event within the standalone embeddedRTPS implementation. To perform this experiment, we transmit RTPS frames with embedded payloads of 8 B, 16 B, 64 B, 512 B, and 1024 B through a local network, where they are received by a Gigabit SFP+ interface on the Zynq® UltraScale+™ ZCU102.

As shown in Fig. 3, the LwIP stack introduces a maximum overhead of 3.8 μs for payload sizes of 8 B, increasing to as much as 12.12 μs for payloads of 1024 B.

After bypassing the frames, the time required to process RTPS messages becomes identical to the time needed to receive frames from the network interface. This duration primarily depends on the timing characteristics of the single-loop scheduler of the DDS implementation.

The aforementioned latencies can be entirely avoided by bypassing the LwIP stack and directly forwarding the RTPS frames to the DDS service. As shown in the subsequent sections, this measure significantly improves performance, as functionality outsourced to the FPGA is processed within just a few nanosec-

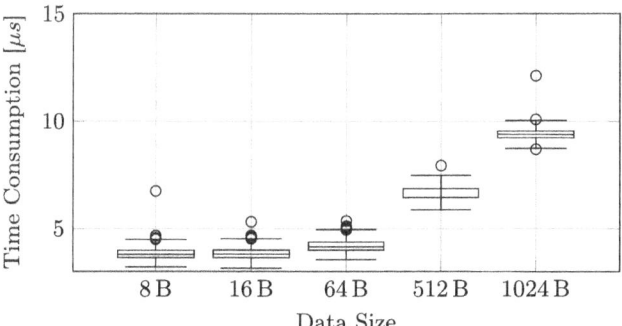

Fig. 3. Time consumption for processing RTPS frames by the LwIP stack with different payload sizes.

onds. Meanwhile, the Ethernet implementation underlying the LWIP stack, similar to our PS/PL Interconnection module, utilizes an AXI interface.

PS/PL Interconnection Module: Next, we evaluated the impact of the PS/PL Interconnection module on the timing characteristics of the architecture. To measure latency in isolation, we implemented a loopback mechanism that enables transmitting data samples of varying lengths from the RPU to the PL across the AXI interface. Those samples are routed back to the RPU to measure the round-trip time. More specifically, the time elapsed between sending data to the PL and its availability in shared memory is captured. This availability is indicated by a rising edge from the PL sent to the Zynq processing system, which triggers a callback function on the RPU. The callback function is registered with the highest interrupt priority (0) on the RPU to measure the time consumption in isolation. More importantly, it allows us to determine the maximum jitter, which is critical for calculating the WCET. Furthermore, the shared memory segments for sending and receiving are subdivided into two distinct areas, to prevent read-write conflicts and to prove reliable transmission across the interface in both directions. These measurements were performed by a bare-metal program executed on a single-core Arm® Cortex™-R5F processor. The boxplot in Fig. 4 shows the absolute latency and jitter when performing round-trip time experiments with different burst sizes collected from 50,000 measurements.

A dataset of this size is essential for making reliable conclusions about timing guarantees. As described in the subsequent section, we run the design on the PL driven by a 150 MHz clock and a bus size of 128 B, while the PS operates at a clock frequency of 500 MHz. Furthermore, Fig. 4 illustrates that the majority of all measurements have a maximum latency variation of about 1 μs. Only when 16384 bit in a single burst are transmitted, the variation is well under 2.5 μs, while the total maximum latency is only 77.97 μs. A single 128 bit message can be transmitted and read back within a maximum time of less than 1.2 μs.

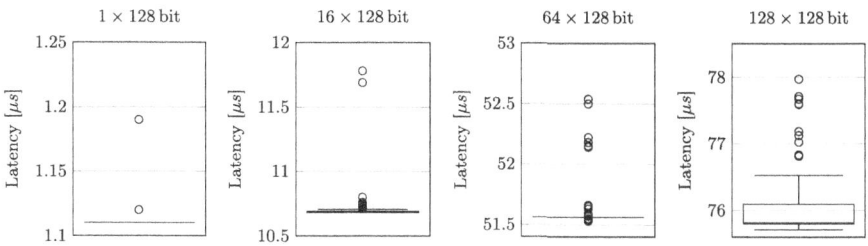

Fig. 4. Round-trip time at different burst sizes on an Arm® Cortex™-R5F.

PL Latency Evaluation: To assess the latency of PL architecture, the fully integrated design must first be synthesized, placed, and routed. Afterward, the post-implementation timing analysis provided by Vivado 2022.1 is used to determine the WNS of our design. The WNS occurs within the Ethernet MAC IP-core requiring 6.025 ns. As $f_{max} = \frac{1}{WNS}$ a theoretical maximum clock frequency $f_{max} = 165.975$ MHz would be possible. The module operates with a fixed clock frequency of 156.25 MHz. To prevent any instabilities and to later support direct communication with the Ethernet PHY on the PL our design is driven by a 150 MHz clock. Based on this frequency combined with the number of clock cycles used by each module in our architecture, we can estimate the timing of the entire PL implementation. This implementation consists of three parallel pipelines: one stores data in the Block RAM module, another processes data within the Security Module, and the third executes the Packet Parser. Therefore, we evaluate the number of clock cycles each pipeline requires to complete its task on the current frame before forwarding the frame to the Filter Engine and Prioritization Queue. This evaluation can be seen in Table 1 showing the number of clock cycles and the timing consumption by the PS/PL Interconnection module, followed by the three pipelines. The timing is assessed for various payload sizes embedded into DATA submessages transmitted at a frequency of 150 MHz. Only RTPS messages with a total size of up to 1472 B are considered, as more significant message sizes would be fragmented, exceeding the MTU, when accounting for the 20 B IPv4 header and a 8 B UDP header, as our prototype implementation currently does not support fragmentation.

The *PS/PL Interconnection* module receives full Ethernet frames, dividing them into 128 bit blocks to forward them to the modules on the PL. To evaluate the time consumption, we leverage the System Integrated Logic Analyzer (ILA) IP-core [3]. With burst support, each additional 128 bit transmission on the PL requires one extra clock cycle, equivalent to 6.67 ns at a clock frequency of 150 MHz. Moreover, every burst incurs a constant overhead of 6 clock cycles, starting with the write address setup on the AW Channel and continuing until both the WVALID and WREADY signals are asserted, enabling a burst data transmission in subsequent cycles. An additional clock cycle is necessary to send an acknowledgment on the B Channel, indicating that the data was transmitted. Since the received data from this module is directly forwarded to other modules

Table 1. Analysis of clock cycles per module and corresponding time consumption based on a clock frequency of 150 MHz.

RTPSPayload Size	PS/PL Interface		Parsing		BlockRAM		Security	
	Cycles	Time	Cycles	Time	Cycles	Time	Cycles	Time
	[CC]	[ns]	[CC]	[ns]	[CC]	[ns]	[CC]	[ns]
8 B	16	146.52 ns	11	73.26 ns	10	66.67 ns	17	113.22 ns
16 B	17	153.18 ns	11	73.26 ns	11	73.26 ns	17	113.22 ns
64 B	20	173.16 ns	14	93.24 ns	14	93.24 ns	20	133.2 ns
512 B	48	359.64 ns	42	279.72 ns	42	279.72 ns	48	319.68 ns
1024 B	80	572.76 ns	74	492.84 ns	74	492.84 ns	80	532.8 ns

on the PL prior sending an acknowledgment through the B Channel, it is not considered part of the pipeline and not contributing to the critical path. The time required to send data to the PS is assumed to be similar to that of a read operation.

The *Packet Parser* generates a constant overhead of 4 clock cycles per RTPS frame. This overhead arises from the following parsing tasks: the 112 bit Ethernet header is parsed in a single clock cycle, while 16 bit of the IP frame are parsed in the same clock phase. Additionally, the remaining 144 bit of a 20 B IP frame are parsed in two additional clock cycles, while the constant 8 B UDP header is processed alongside the final segment of the IP frame. The remaining bits of the same frame are used to decode portions of the 20 B RTPS header, which is fully parsed within the fourth clock cycle. Next, we analyze the number of clock cycles necessary to parse the different RTPS submessages, which is defined as follows: Let cc_{sub} represent the number of clock cycles required to parse an RTPS submessage, $|f_{sub}|$ the size of the RTPS submessage, and $m_d = 128$ bit the size of the data bus. The number of clock cycles, denoted as cc_{sub}, required to parse a submessage can be expressed as:

$$cc_{sub} = \begin{cases} 1 & \text{if } |f_{sub}| \leq m_d \\ \left\lceil \frac{|f_{sub}|}{m_d} \right\rceil & \text{if } |f_{sub}| > m_d \end{cases}$$

Overall, the delay caused by the *Packet Parser* is defined by $cc_{prs} := 4 + cc_{sub}$. This implementation was evaluated with different types of RTPS frames. In our example, a typical data frame consists of the following submessages: a 128 bit INFO_DEST submessage (parsed in 1 clock cycle), a 96 bit INFO_TS submessage (parsed in 1 clock cycle). The subsequent DATA submessage includes 28 bit of metadata, such as identifiers of publishers and subscribers and serialization information. For instance, a payload of 16 B results in a 44 B DATA submessage, which is parsed in 3 clock cycles. Additionally, an attached 256 bit HEARTBEAT submessage requires two clock cycles to finish parsing. Finally, resulting in 7 clock cycles for parsing the submessages and 11 clock cycles or 77.26 ns in total.

The *Filter Engine* is synchronized with the parsing pipeline and starts calculating priorities based on the portions of the Ethernet frame that have already been parsed. Once all required data fields are received, normalization, weighting, and aggregation are performed, which requires two additional clock cycles.

To store data using the *Block RAM module*, the required clock cycles are given by $cc_{bram} := \left\lceil \frac{|f_{raw}|}{m_d} \right\rceil$, with $m_d = 128\,\mathrm{bit}$. To store a frame with a 16 B payload resulting in a total of 166 B that must be saved by the Block RAM module, including the Ethernet, IP, UDP, and RTPS headers and RTPS metadata. This operation requires 11 clock cycles, assuming a data width of 128 bit.

Furthermore, the third parallel pipeline processes data within the *Security Module*, including the SipHash implementation by Joachim Strömbergson [13]. This implementation is able to perform a SipRound in a single clock cycle. Since the SipHash-2-4 variant is used in this work, six SipRounds need to be calculated. One cycle is required for initialization to set the key and the first 64 bit block. The compression phase requires two cycles for the SipRounds and two additional cycles for control operations. As we operate with two SipHash instances in parallel, every additional 128 bit input block requires an additional cycle during the compression phase. After all input blocks have been processed, the finalization phase requires five clock cycles: four for the SipRounds and one for control operations. The MAC is calculated on the full RTPS frame, which contains 108 B of metadata. Therefore, computing the MAC for a 16 B payload requires compressing 124 B of input data, which is afterward forwarded to the two SipHash cores. This process requires a total of 17 clock cycles, or 113.22 ns, considering a 150 MHz clock.

Since the pipeline processing the cryptographic operations requires the longest time to complete, the Prioritization Queue waits for the pipeline to finish before proceeding. Upon successful validation, the block RAM address of a RTPS frame together with its aggregated priority is assigned to a priority queue, a process completed in a single clock cycle. In parallel, the gate driver sets the appropriate gates, handled in a dedicated `always` block, while an additional `always` block forwards the block RAM addresses for transmission to the PS/PL interconnection module. Through this design of three parallel `always` blocks, the module enables precise gate timing control with a granularity of three clock cycles.

Finally, we evaluated the time consumption for the PUF readout within the Hardware Security Anchor, which requires a large number of 65,997 clock cycles to generate a 256 bit PUF response. This duration is primarily due to the sequential selection of ring oscillator pairs and comparing their counter values after a reference counter reaches 256. This is necessary because smaller counter values lead to unstable behavior. Specifically, counting the reference counter to 256 for each of the 256 comparisons results in 65,536 cycles. The remaining 461 cycles are necessary for control operations, such as managing the control state machine, while the BCH-based error correction consumes 54 cycles, and 11 cycles are needed for the hash operation using the SipHash algorithm. Since this part of the design operates at a clock frequency of 10 MHz, approximately 6.61 ms are required to read out the PUF. Due to this relatively high latency, the readout is performed only during system startup, and the response is stored in volatile block RAM for subsequent use.

6.2   Security Evaluation

To evaluate the proposed security concept, we specifically focus on analyzing the cryptographic key forming the foundation for the security implementation built on top. This analysis examines the key properties of robustness, uniqueness, and uniformity on the raw PUF responses, using the most commonly used PUF metrics. The software-based security implementation, partially offloaded to hardware in this work, is evaluated in [20].

Robustness: Cryptographic algorithms, such as those used in this work, rely on the avalanche effect, where even minor changes in the key result in significantly different outcomes. Thus, providing a fully stable cryptographic key k_{puf} to the Security Module is crucial, requiring a nearly stable raw PUF response. At the same time, minor instabilities can be corrected using error correction codes, specifically BCH codes, as discussed in this paper. To evaluate the robustness of the ring oscillator PUF, the fractional intra-device Hamming distance ($\mathcal{HD}_{intra}$) is calculated, which measures the variation between pairs of responses generated by the same PUF. A $\mathcal{HD}_{intra} = 0\%$ indicates that a pair of responses of the same PUF placed within a dedicated clock region produce identical responses. Figure 5 illustrates the robustness of ring oscillator PUFs instantiated in each available clock region of the evaluation board, identified by their X and Y positions on the board's physical layout.

Each PUF within a clock region is repeatedly measured 1,000 times at room temperature. Afterward, each of the 1,000 iterations is compared with each other using $\mathcal{HD}_{intra}$. Our design demonstrates excellent robustness values, achieving an average $\mathcal{HD}_{intra}$ of 0.67%, thus providing 99.33% stable PUF bits. A single outlier is located at clock region X3 Y5, where the $\mathcal{HD}_{intra}$ is 5.08%. To achieve these values, we iteratively optimized all ring oscillators' placement to enhance the performance of the PUF. Modifying the position of a single LUT may result in unstable or biased behavior.

Uniqueness: This property indicates that when two different ring oscillator PUFs are initialized with the same challenge, they produce completely different responses, thereby enabling the derivation of distinct keys. In our case, $\mathcal{C}$ corresponds to the seed of the LFSR. To verify this property, the fractional inter-Hamming distance ($\mathcal{HD}_{inter}$) between the two responses is calculated. An $\mathcal{HD}_{inter}$ of 50% is preferred, indicating that the responses differ by fifty percent of their bits, achieving the maximum uniqueness. Due to the structure of FPGAs, we are able to evaluate uniqueness on a single device by placing ring oscillators in different clock regions and computing their uniqueness. For each of those, we select the PUF response that appears the most frequently among the

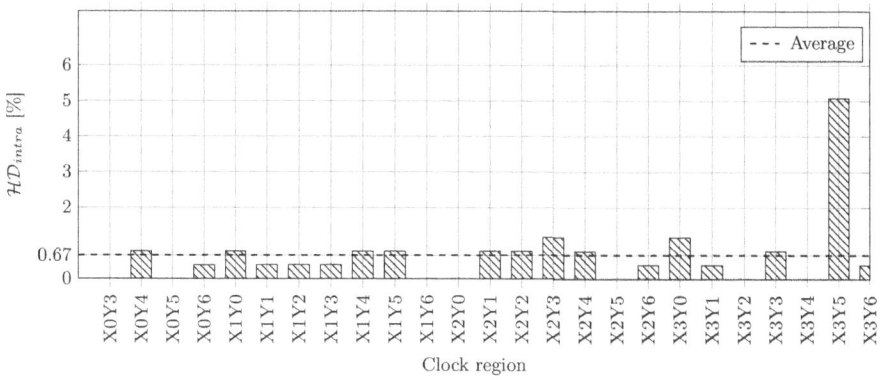

Fig. 5. Bar chart showing robustness values across all clock regions.

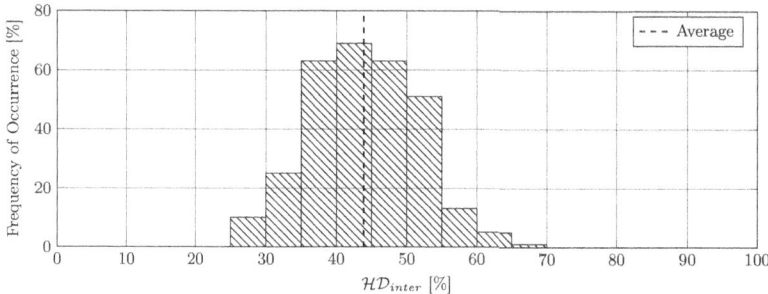

Fig. 6. Histogram of inter-device Hamming distances evaluated from PUF responses across all clock management regions.

1000 collected responses. A histogram showing the distribution of the $\mathcal{HD}_{inter}$ when comparing each PUF response with each other is illustrated in Fig. 6.

The average Hamming distance is 43.87%, which is acceptable, while below the ideal value of 50%, particularly when entropy is further improved through post-processing. In this work, entropy is enhanced by using SipHash as cryptographic hash function to distill the entropy into 128 bit keys derived from the 256 bit PUF responses.

Uniformity: The last property we evaluate is uniformity, which refers to the ratio of logical zeros and ones in each PUF response. This ratio should be equally distributed, assessed by calculating the Hamming weight for the most frequent PUF response collected from each PUF placed in an individual clock region of the Xilinx UltraScale+^{TM} board. A total of 25 different PUFs are evaluated, with no configurable logic possible in the regions X0Y0, X0Y1, and X0Y2. The evaluation results show some variability in certain regions, while many PUFs return values close to 50%, which are preferred among those with biased uniformity.

A value close to 50% indicates a uniform distribution of logical 0s and 1s, a key property for guaranteeing the unpredictability of the derived cryptographic key (Table 2).

Table 2. Average Uniformity values of ring oscillators placed in each clock region.

		Column			
		0	1	2	3
Row	0	/	58.2	61.72	52.73
	1	/	60.55	65.23	75.0
	2	/	47.27	73.44	50.78
	3	41.02	62.11	82.81	56.25
	4	57.81	76.56	61.72	35.94
	5	47.27	56.25	74.61	69.14
	6	34.77	45.31	75.78	55.47

7   Conclusion and Discussion

In this work, we present a novel architecture that guarantees deterministic timing in DDS-based service-oriented architectures targeting SDVs by utilizing MPSoC architectures. This approach directly processes RTPS messages on an FPGA, where message parsing, prioritization, and scheduling are performed. To align with the principles of service-oriented architectures, a method is introduced to dynamically adjust QoS parameters that allow for a flexible adoption of the prioritization algorithm based on the services scheduled on the PS. Furthermore, since security operations can be time-critical and may compromise real-time constraints, we use a hardware implementation of SipHash to perform integrity checks. The key stems from a ring oscillator PUF, implemented on the PL, eliminating the need for additional communication between the PS and PL, while allowing to derive a fully stable key. Additionally, we analyzed the deterministic behavior of each component within the prototype, beginning with the modules on the PL, where we identified a maximum latency of less than 300 ns for processing an RTPS frame with 64 bit payload. On the PS, we could show that we can save more than $4\,\mu s$ by bypassing the LwIP stack, more than ten times higher than the latency caused by the FPGA acceleration. Within this work, we can guarantee deterministic timing with granularity below $2\,\mu s$, the maximum observed jitter. However, to further reduce latency and enhance deterministic timing guarantees, all RTPS frames should be received and processed directly on the PL instead of filtering them on the NETIF layer of the PS. Finally, hardware-based synchronization of multiple HPCs is beyond the scope of this work and therefore left for future research.

Acknowledgments. This work has been accomplished within the projects "autotech.agil" (FKZ01IS22088X). We acknowledge the financial support for the projects by the Federal Ministry of Education and Research of Germany (BMBF).

References

1. Advanced Micro Devices, Inc.: LogiCORE IP AXI Ethernet (2012). https://docs. amd.com/v/u/en-US/ds759_axi_ethernet. [Version v3.01a; Online; Accessed 29 May 2025]
2. Advanced Micro Devices, Inc.: LogiCORE IP Block Memory Generator (2012). https://www.xilinx.com/products/intellectual-property/block_memory_generator.html#documentation. [Version v7.1; Online; Accessed 29 May 2025]
3. Advanced Micro Devices, Inc.: System Integrated Logic Analyzer v1.1] (2023). https://docs.xilinx.com/v/u/en-US/pg261-system-ila. [Online; Accessed 29 May 2025]
4. Aumasson, J.-P., Bernstein, D.J.: SipHash: a fast short-input PRF. In: Galbraith, S., Nandi, M. (eds.) INDOCRYPT 2012. LNCS, vol. 7668, pp. 489–508. Springer, Heidelberg (2012). https://doi.org/10.1007/978-3-642-34931-7_28
5. AUTOSAR: Specification of Data Distribution Service in Classic Platform (2022). https://www.autosar.org/fileadmin/standards/R22-11/CP/AUTOSAR_SWS_ClassicPlatformDataDistributionService.pdf. [Online; Accessed 29 May 2025]
6. Budnik, M.: Design and evaluation of a Ring Oscillator based Physically Unclonable Function (2023). http://essay.utwente.nl/95895/
7. Dill, R., Shrivastava, A., Oh, H.: Optimization of multi-channel BCH error decoding for common cases. In: 2015 International Conference on Compilers, Architecture and Synthesis for Embedded Systems (CASES), pp. 59–68 (2015)
8. Gabriel Jimenez: RO_PUF (2022). https://github.com/Gabalo/RO_PUF. [Online; Accessed 29 May 2025]
9. GU, C., Chang, C.H., Liu, W., Hanley, N., Miskelly, J., O'Neill, M.: A large scale comprehensive evaluation of single-slice ring oscillator and PicoPUF bit cells on 28nm Xilinx FPGAs. In: Proceedings of the 3rd ACM Workshop on Attacks and Solutions in Hardware Security Workshop. ASHES'19, pp. 101–106. Association for Computing Machinery, New York, NY, USA (2019)
10. Hirose, S.: Some plausible constructions of double-block-length hash functions. In: Robshaw, M. (ed.) Fast Software Encryption, pp. 210–225. Springer, Heidelberg (2006)
11. IEEE Standards Association: TSN Profile for Automotive In-Vehicle Ethernet Communications. https://standards.ieee.org/ieee/802.1DG/7480/. [Online; Accessed 29 May 2025]
12. IEEE Standards Association: IEEE Standard for Local and Metropolitan Area Networks–Media Access Control (MAC) Service Definition - Corrigendum 1: Logical Link Control (LLC) Encapsulation EtherType. IEEE Std 802.1AC-2016/Cor 1-2018 (Corrigenda to IEEE Std 802.1AC-2016), pp. 1–13 (2018)
13. Joachim Strömbergson: SipHash (2022). https://github.com/secworks/siphash/. [Online; Accessed 29 May 2025]
14. Kampmann, A., Wüstenberg, A., Alrifaee, B., Kowalewski, S.: A portable implementation of the real-time publish-subscribe protocol for microcontrollers in distributed robotic applications. In: 2019 IEEE Intelligent Transportation Systems Conference (ITSC), pp. 443–448 (2019)

15. Kareem, H., Dunaev, D.: Towards performance optimization of ring oscillator PUF using Xilinx FPGA. In: 2022 17th Iberian Conference on Information Systems and Technologies (CISTI), pp. 1–6 (2022)

16. Lienen, C., Middeke, S.H., Platzner, M.: FPGADDS: an intra-FPGA data distribution service for ROS 2 robotics applications. In: 2023 IEEE/RSJ International Conference on Intelligent Robots and Systems (IROS), pp. 6261–6266 (2023)

17. Macenski, S., Foote, T., Gerkey, B., Lalancette, C., Woodall, W.: Robot operating system 2: design, architecture, and uses in the wild. Sci. Robot. **7**(66), eabm6074 (2022)

18. Object Management Group: DDS Security (2024). https://www.omg.org/spec/DDS-SECURITY/1.2/PDF. [Version 1.2; Online; Accessed 29 May 2025]

19. Petit, J., Shladover, S.E.: Potential cyberattacks on automated vehicles. IEEE Trans. Intell. Transp. Syst. **16**(2), 546–556 (2015)

20. Püllen, D., Frank, F., Christl, M., Liu, W., Katzenbeisser, S.: A security process for the automotive service-oriented software architecture. IEEE Trans. Veh. Technol. **73**(4), 5036–5053 (2024)

21. Rosa, L., Song, W., Foschini, L., Corradi, A., Birman, K.: DerechoDDS: strongly consistent data distribution for mission-critical applications. In: MILCOM 2021 - 2021 IEEE Military Communications Conference (MILCOM), pp. 684–689 (2021)

22. Scordino, C., Mariño, A.G., Fons, F.: Hardware acceleration of data distribution service (DDS) for automotive communication and computing. IEEE Access **10**, 109626–109651 (2022)

23. Sugata, Y., Ohkawa, T., Ootsu, K., Yokota, T.: Acceleration of publish/subscribe messaging in ROS-compliant FPGA component. In: Proceedings of the 8th International Symposium on Highly Efficient Accelerators and Reconfigurable Technologies. HEART '17. Association for Computing Machinery, New York, NY, USA (2017)

24. Völker, L.: Scalable service-Oriented MiddlewarE over IP (SOME/IP) (31524). https://some-ip.com/standards.shtml. Accessed 29 May 2025

25. Xin, X., Kaps, J.P., Gaj, K.: A configurable ring-oscillator-based PUF for Xilinx FPGAs. In: 2011 14th Euromicro Conference on Digital System Design, pp. 651–657 (2011)

TSA-WF: Exploring the Effectiveness of Time Series Analysis for Website Fingerprinting

Michael Wrana[✉], Uzma Maroof, and Diogo Barradas

University of Waterloo, Ontario, Canada
{mmwrana,uzma.maroof,diogo.barradas}@uwaterloo.ca

Abstract. Website fingerprinting (WF) is a technique that allows an eavesdropper to determine the website a target user is accessing by inspecting the metadata associated with the packets she exchanges via some encrypted tunnel, e.g., Tor. In this paper, we explore whether classical time series analysis techniques can be effective in the WF setting. Specifically, we introduce TSA-WF, a pipeline designed to closely preserve network traces' timing and direction characteristics, which enables the exploration of algorithms designed to measure time series similarity in the WF context. Our evaluation with Tor traces reveals that TSA-WF achieves a comparable accuracy to existing WF attacks in the *single-tab* setting. TSA-WF did not outperform existing attacks in the *multi-tab* setting, but was uniquely able to pinpoint the approximate instant at which a given website of interest was visited within a multi-tab trace.

Keywords: Time series · Tor · Traffic analysis · Website fingerprinting

1 Introduction

Privacy-conscious internet users often seek to hide their web activities from network surveillance apparatuses. Technologies such as Tor and VPNs respond to users' privacy needs by providing anonymous and encrypted access to websites. Instead of directly accessing a website, Tor and VPNs rely on intermediate nodes that bridge the communication between clients and their intended destinations.

Unfortunately, the above privacy-enhancing technologies do not sufficiently hide the network metadata (e.g., packet sizes and timing, or the overall volume of communication) associated with a user's connection [20]. For this reason, existing research has shown that an eavesdropping adversary is capable of determining the websites that a target user is visiting by comparing her traffic patterns with the patterns generated when accessing a pool of websites of interest. This technique, website fingerprinting (WF), poses significant privacy risks [16].

WF techniques have existed for nearly two decades but struggled to achieve satisfactory performance for real world usage [9]. Recent advances in machine learning (ML) and deep learning (DL) enabled eavesdropping adversaries to

M. Dalla Preda et al. (Eds.): ARES 2025, LNCS 15992, pp. 209–220, 2025.
https://doi.org/10.1007/978-3-032-00624-0_10

create sophisticated models that can accurately identify websites while requiring less training data, or in the early stages of page loading. As of today, WF attacks can achieve high success rates against Tor [18] or VPNs, and can even detect accesses to multiple websites in sequence or simultaneously [3,8].

Our work departs from the observation that, despite the existence of numerous refined techniques for the analysis of time series data, the usefulness of such techniques has only been briefly touched upon within the WF context [17]. We comprehensively explore the potential of classical time series analysis techniques to act as the main driver for matching website traces in the context of WF attacks. To this end, we devise TSA-WF, a time series analysis pipeline tailored to WF comprised of three components: a) a distance calculator that combines different time series analysis techniques to quantitatively determine the similarity between website traces; b) a classifier which uses distance scores to execute a WF attack, and; c) a tool that provides additional context to WF attacks' results by pinpointing the approximate instant at which a monitored website is accessed within a multi-tab trace, thus compensating for the information loss incurred by current attacks during their feature extraction phase.

The evaluation we conducted using recent Tor traces indicates that TSA-WF, when used as an independent attack, is on par with state-of-the-art WF classifiers in the single-tab setting, achieving a classification accuracy of 92.2% for undefended traces. While TSA-WF is subpar compared to existing DL methods when applied to merged sequences of traces (i.e., the multi-tab setting), TSA-WF can be combined with existing attacks to provide valuable insights on why websites are (mis-)classified in this setting. In particular, in the 3-Tab setting, TSA-WF can pinpoint the approximate location of a monitored website within the multi-tab traces to within 8k packets 82.2% of the time.

Contributions. We summarize our main contributions as:

- We design TSA-WF [21], a time series analysis pipeline geared towards WF which is compatible with multiple time series matching algorithms.
- We evaluate TSA-WF resorting to multiple time series similarity measures, and compare its accuracy with that of existing WF attacks in the single-tab and multi-tab settings using merged, overlapped, and defended Tor traces.
- We show how TSA-WF augments the capabilities of WF attacks by pinpointing the approximate location of specific website traces in multi-tab settings.

2   Background and Related Works

2.1   Website Fingerprinting

Threat Model. The typical threat model for a WF attack involves a user, Alice, attempting to privately browse the internet over Tor while an adversary aims to determine the sequence of websites she is visiting without cryptographically breaking her communication. To prepare a WF attack, the adversary first builds a database of *fingerprints* for the websites (e.g., Alexa top-100) it wishes to monitor before Alice visits them. Then, the adversary launches the attack by comparing its database of monitored website traces with the traces observed in the network once Alice has visited a given website. WF attacks are typically launched in two different scenarios and settings, which we discuss below.

In a *closed-world* scenario, the assumption is that Alice visits a website which is amongst a limited set of websites monitored by the adversary, and for which the adversary collects sample traces as part of its database [20]. In an *open-world* scenario, Alice is allowed to access both monitored and unmonitored websites (i.e., the web at large). In the *single-tab* setting, the adversary knows when Alice starts and stops loading each website. In the *multi-tab* setting the adversary can only see a merged trace, potentially containing packets from multiple websites accessed in sequence or simultaneously overlapping [22].

WF Attacks. Early WF attacks, such as k-Fingerprinting [5], use manually crafted features combined with ML classifiers in the single-tab setting [9]. Deep Fingerprinting (DF) [18] introduced a CNN-based architecture that uses a *directional* representation, where traces are sequences of positive (+1) and negative (-1) ones, depending on whether a packet is incoming or outgoing. Tik-Tok [15] uses DF's architecture but includes packet timing information (by multiplying a packet's direction with its inter-arrival time). WF research has also focused on DL-based classifiers and feature extraction methods to expand attacks' scope towards a multi-tab setting. ARES [3] uses an ensemble DNN to classify multi-tab traces with high accuracy. Jin *et al.* [8] use a transformer model which can identify a potentially arbitrary number of websites within a multi-tab trace.

WF Defenses. Constant rate padding defenses, such as Tamaraw [1], uniformize traffic by forcing packet transmission with a fixed size at a fixed rate. More efficient padding-based defenses include adaptive padding (e.g., WTF-PAD [9]) and randomized padding (e.g., FRONT [4]) approaches, which strategically transmit dummy packets to conceal the real network patterns generated by a given website access. A more recent defense that also aims to uniformize traffic, RegulaTor [7], focuses on shaping the packet burst patterns that frequently occur in download traffic. In our work, we concentrate on padding-centric defenses, but refer the reader to an extensive analysis of the broader space of WF defenses [13].

2.2   Time Series Analysis

Dynamic time warping (DTW) is the primary classical time series analysis measure that has seen consistent use for matching website traces in the context of WF [17]. In this work, we explore the use of three additional time series matching techniques that are deemed effective for a wide range of applications which depend on the computation of time series' similarity. *Euclidean* distance has been used as a time series comparison metric to detect attacks in network traffic [23]. *STUMPY* [12] improves the efficiency of computing the normalized euclidean distance metric using a matrix profile along with other optimizations. STUMPY has been previously used for time series anomaly detection [6]. Finally, *compression-based-distance* (CBD) [11] is an indirect measure for comparing the

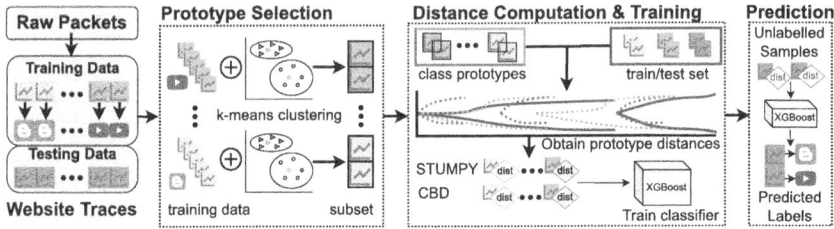

Fig. 1. Depiction of TSA-WF's pipeline for performing a WF attack.

distance between two time series. In CBD, time series are converted into symbols that can be stored as a text file. Then, these files are compressed (e.g., .zip, .rar) and the difference in their sizes are compared. Compression-based measures have been used for anomalous web traffic analysis [19].

3 The Architecture of TSA-WF

We design and implement a WF pipeline named TSA-WF (*Time-Series Analysis for Website Fingerprinting*). We implemented TSA-WF in ~5 000 lines of Python code to enable further experimentation by the WF research community [21].

3.1 Prototype Selection

The first phase of the TSA-WF pipeline determines which samples to use as the best representatives of a website, denoted as a class' *prototype* (PT). Below, we describe three different approaches to finding a class prototype. In Sect. 4 we show that *clustering trace features* is the most effective approach.

Random Selection. Prototypes could be chosen by randomly selecting a few traces per website from the training set. However, this may lead to choosing prototypes based on traces that a) might be outliers for a particular class, or that; b) are not sufficiently representative of diverse intra-class patterns.

Clustering Raw Traces. In this approach, we organized each trace into a number of features equal to the number of packets. The value of each feature is equal to the packet's y-value in the time series (i.e., time and direction). To select prototypes, we applied k-means clustering to the feature set, and the centroid of each cluster is ultimately selected as a class prototype. We observed that packet traces obtained by visiting the same website tend to form clearly defined clusters. While we hypothesize that these clusters may result from varying network conditions while traces are collected from the live Tor network [14], the above suggests that class prototypes can indeed be chosen using clustering.

Clustering of Trace Features. Despite producing visually separable clusters, the previous approach treats the integer representation of each packet as a separate feature for clustering. In this setting, k-means has to operate over potentially

Algorithm 1. Compute best match between a prototype and a trace

```
1: s ← [...]                                          ▷ The prototype we are using to represent a website
2: t ← [...]                                          ▷ The trace containing an unknown website
3: n ← [STUMPY(), EUC(), WED(), CBD(), DTW()]    ▷ List of measures for comparing traces
4: procedure COMPUTEDIST(s, t)
5:     d ← [len(t) − len(s), n]                       ▷ A list of all the computed distances
6:     for j = 0 → len(n), compute_dist = n[j] do     ▷ For each distance function in n
7:         for i = 0 → len(t), i += len(s) do    ▷ Traverse a sliding window of t with size len(s)
8:             d[i, j] = compute_dist(s, t[i : i + s])  ▷ Compute similarity between s and the window
9:     return min(d[:,j])                             ▷ Return the minimum of each distance measure
```

thousands of dimensions, leading to "curse of dimensionality" issues that statistical models suffer from when reasoning about samples in highly-dimensional spaces. As an alternative, we extracted the set of ≈150 summary statistics used by Hayes *et al.* [5] from each website trace and used those features for clustering.

3.2   Distance Computation and Training

The second phase of TSA-WF computes the distance between the (few) selected prototypes from each website (i.e., class) and all other trace samples in the training data. These distances will be later used to train a classifier assuming that the distances from a class' prototypes to samples of its own class should be smaller that the distances obtained when comparing the prototype to samples which belong to other classes. TSA-WF combines the distances computed with euclidean (with and without weights), STUMPY, CBD, and DTW by representing trace similarity as a vector n with five cells (one for each distance measure we consider).

Calculating Distances. Algorithm 1 details the computation of the distance between a class prototype and a training sample. Function `ComputeDist` (line 4) finds the minimum distance between a prototype s and sample t (both stored as lists containing the trace representation). In the (unlikely) scenario that the prototype length exceeds the trace length, we reverse t and s.

Training a Classifier. After the distances between all class prototypes and samples comprising the training set have been computed, TSA-WF trains a classifier using the resulting $[n]$-shaped distance vectors. A simple approach for using distance vectors to issue predictions is to determine a threshold for each class, such that every sample either belongs to a particular class or not depending on whether its distance is below a set threshold for that class. The thresholds for each class can be determined by recording the distance scores obtained by comparing a prototype with training samples from the same class. In our experiments, we report the best matching label for both single- and multi-tab traces.

A threshold classifier assigns labels based on the distance between the sample and other prototypes from the *same* class. However, it does not evaluate the distance between the sample and the prototypes of all possible classes. By using an ML-based classifier, TSA-WF makes labeling decisions based on the similarity between the prototype and examples of every *other* class as well. Our results (Sect. 4.1) suggest that gradient-boosted decision trees (as implemented by XGBoost) [2] make for an effective model for TSA-WF's final classification step.

3.3 Prediction

The final phase of TSA-WF predicts labels for a set of samples where the label associated with the monitored website contained therein is unknown. Recall that we assume unlabeled single-tab samples to either contain monitored or unmonitored websites, while multi-tab traces contain a single monitored website amongst an arbitrary number of unmonitored websites. First, the distance between each unlabeled sample and the class prototypes used for training are calculated. Then, the classifier included in TSA-WF's pipeline (Sect. 3.2) assigns a label based on the training class that the sample is most similar to.

3.4 Untangling Multi-tab Traces

An adversary interested in launching a multi-tab WF attack must decide: a) which monitored website(s) are contained within a traffic sample, and; b) at which instant is the monitored website located in that sample. All WF attacks must achieve the former by definition but, to the best of our knowledge, existing attacks do not attempt the latter. TSA-WF is capable of jointly performing a) and b), or use the results of another attack for a) and compute b) independently.

We determine the location of the monitored website within an unlabeled trace sample is as follows. First, we train a classifier that determines the class of the monitored trace within an unlabeled sample. This can either be TSA-WF's own classifier (described previously) or sourced from elsewhere (e.g., a pre-existing WF attack). Next, we record the labels assigned by the classifier for each unlabeled sample. Finally, we select one prototype from the class assigned by the chosen WF attack and compute the distance between it and the trace sample. The packet index where the smallest distance was computed is TSA-WF's guess for the location of the monitored website within a multi-tab sample.

4 Evaluation

Before presenting our main experimental results, we first provide context for the dataset and the existing work that TSA-WF is compared with.

Dataset. We evaluate TSA-WF with the Tor traffic dataset used in the state-of-the-art multi-tab DL-based attack of Jin *et al.* [8]. It contains 100 traces per each of 50 different monitored websites ($100 * 50 = 5\,000$) and 5 000 traces from unmonitored websites, totaling 10 000 single-tab traces. We generate 1 000 multi-tab traces for each monitored website ($1\,000*50 = 50\,000$), and divide them into a 90/10 training/testing split. To create a multi-tab trace with x tabs, we take one random monitored website and merge/overlap it with $x - 1$ random unmonitored website traces. Thus, each multi-tab trace contains precisely one monitored website and, in each experiment, a WF attack must identify which of the 50 monitored websites was included in the trace. This is consistent with prominent multi-tab WF attacks (e.g., [3]) that also finely control the composition of multi-tab traces. We also include settings where we assume that each trace comprising a merged trace may overlap adjacent traces by up to 40%.

Trace Distance Measures. To compute the distance between websites' prototypes and other traces contained in TSA-WF's training/testing data, we use existing code for STUMPY, the numpy implementation of euclidean distance, the tslearn implementation for DTW, and our own implementation of CBD.

WF Attacks. We compare TSA-WF on single-tab against k-Fingerprinting [5] (k-FP), Deep Fingerprinting [18] (DF), and Tik-Tok [15]. We compare the effectiveness of TSA-WF in the multi-tab setting with ARES [3].

WF Defenses. We evaluate the considered WF attacks against traces shielded using three well-known WF defenses. WTF-PAD [10] (W-P), FRONT [4], and RegulaTor [7] (RT). We used two configurations of FRONT (F-T1 and F-T2) [20].

4.1   Parameter Tuning

As an initial round of experiments, we limited data availability to samples pertaining to the simpler closed-world scenario and single-tab setting. Our task was to determine reasonable settings for three main parameters of TSA-WF. The results from this round of experiments indicated that clustering using k-means (Table 1) with two prototypes (Table 2) and classifying with XGBoost (Table 3) achieved the best performance. In the following sections, we use these optimal combination of hyperparmeters to score TSA-WF. We also determined that the best weighting approach for weighted euclidean distance was inverse logarithmic.

4.2   TSA-WF's Effectiveness on Single-Tab Traces

In Table 4, we evaluate the efficacy of TSA-WF in the open-world scenario and single-tab setting and compare it to WF attacks that operate in the same regime.

Classification by Individual Distance Measures. Initially, we evaluate our time-series method by employing each distance measure independently. STUMPY exhibits the highest classification accuracy (87.9%) when compared to all other approaches. That is, Euclidean (EUC), Weighted Euclidean (WED), Compression-Based Distance (CBD), and Dynamic Time Warping (DTW).

Classification by Combining Distance Measures. Each time series similarity measure captures different aspects of website trace matching and confers benefits in certain respects while lacking in others. As anticipated, TSA-WF's accuracy increased when the pipeline's prediction model is supplied with the feature vectors obtained from combining multiple measures, resulting in an accuracy of 92.2% – 4.3% higher compared to STUMPY alone

Table 1. Accuracy of the clustering methods.

Method	Accuracy
k-means	0.888
AP	0.885
DBSCAN	0.872
OPTICS	0.873

Table 2. Accuracy of PT clustering features.

PTs.	Rand.	Clust.	k-FP
1	0.864	0.870	0.870
2	0.871	0.880	**0.888**
3	0.878	0.889	0.895
4	0.883	0.893	0.900
5	0.884	0.895	**0.904**

Table 3. Accuracy of the ML&DL classifiers.

Classifier	Accuracy
Decision Tree	0.860
Random Forest	0.888
XGBoost	**0.890**
CNN	0.790
MalConv	0.830

Table 4. Accuracy of different WF attacks in the single- and multi-tab (merged traces only) open-world scenario. Each column shows the scores using traces with 1 to 7 tabs.

Attack Method	# of Tabs			
	1-Tab	3-Tab	5-Tab	7-Tab
STUMPY	0.879	0.505	0.397	0.340
Euclidean	0.816	0.440	0.340	0.298
WED	0.875	0.480	0.369	0.380
CBD	0.758	0.384	0.260	0.204
DTW	0.857	-	-	-
STUMPY+CBD	0.886	0.502	0.400	0.339
STUMPY+EUC	0.897	0.517	0.400	0.346
STUMPY+WED	0.909	0.517	0.408	0.344
STUMPY+CBD+EUC	0.893	0.520	0.406	0.345
STUMPY+WED+EUC	0.912	0.520	0.410	0.348
STUMPY+WED+DTW	0.904	-	-	-
STUMPY+EUC+DTW	0.913	-	-	-
STUMPY+WED+EUC+CBD	0.913	**0.522**	**0.412**	**0.351**
STUMPY+WED+EUC+DTW	0.915	-	-	-
All	**0.922**	-	-	-
ARES [3]	-	0.875	0.710	-
DF [18]	0.758	-	-	-
Tik-Tok [15]	0.796	-	-	-
k-FP [5]	0.898	-	-	-

Benchmarking WF Attacks on Undefended Traces. We also benchmarked a set of prominent WF attacks on the same dataset used to evaluate TSA-WF above. As shown in Table 4, TSA-WF's classification pipeline (fueled by all distance measures) outperformed Tik-Tok, DF, and k-FP, distancing itself from the accuracy achieved by k-FP by 2.4%.

Benchmarking WF Attacks on Defended Traces. In Table 5, we compare TSA-WF's performance (using STUMPY) with other attacks in the open-world setting, when WF defenses were applied to traces. TSA-WF achieves similar performance to existing WF attacks, outperforming Tik-Tok by 1.5% vs. FRONT-T1 and 4.0% vs. FRONT-T2, as well as outperforming k-FP by 2.7% vs. RegulaTor. However, Tik-Tok outperforms TSA-WF by 0.8% vs. WTF-PAD.

4.3   TSA-WF's Effectiveness on Multi-Tab Traces

Merged Traces. In this experiment, we compare the performance of TSA-WF with existing work designed for the multi-tab setting in the open-world scenario. First, similarly to our observations in the single-tab setting, we can see in Table 4 that the standalone use of STUMPY in TSA-WF's pipeline still

Table 5. Acc. of WF on defended 1-Tab open-world traces.

Attacks	Defenses	
	W-P	RT
TSA-WF	0.735	**0.633**
DF	0.727	0.490
Tik-Tok	**0.743**	0.508
k-FP	0.692	0.606
	F-T1	**F-T2**
TSA-WF	**0.722**	**0.756**
DF	0.664	0.677
Tik-Tok	0.707	0.716
k-FP	0.656	0.709

Table 6. Acc. of WF on multi-tab open-world traces using WF defenses.

Attack	Def.	# of Tabs		
		3-Tab	5-Tab	7-Tab
TSA-WF	W-P	0.278	0.185	0.146
	RT	**0.280**	**0.208**	0.171
	F-T1	0.295	0.213	0.165
	F-T2	0.313	0.220	0.176
ARES	W-P	**0.584**	**0.416**	-
	RT	0.071	0.097	-
	F-T1	**0.469**	**0.324**	-
	F-T2	**0.581**	**0.391**	-

Table 7. Acc. of WF on multi-tab open-world traces, with overlaps between 0% and 40%.

Attack	Ovl.	# of Tabs		
		3-Tab	5-Tab	7-Tab
TSA-WF	10%	0.450	0.344	0.295
	20%	0.423	0.314	0.254
	40%	0.386	0.273	0.210
ARES	10%	0.806	0.619	-
	20%	0.771	0.590	-
	40%	0.761	0.586	-

reaps most of the benefits when compared to the combined usage of distance measures. Specifically, we can observe that TSA-WF (STUMPY) achieves an accuracy of 50.5% for the 3-Tab scenario, while the combination of STUMPY, WED, euclidean, and CBD distances achieves an accuracy of 52.2%, only 1.7% better. However, we also see that, in the multi-tab setting, CBD helped improve TSA-WF's accuracy, as opposed to the single-tab setting where its use provided no advantage.

Second, we see that TSA-WF was not able to outperform state-of-the-art deep learning-based attacks designed for the multi-tab setting. The table shows that TSA-WF (equipped with STUMPY only) achieved an accuracy of 50.5% in the 3-Tab setting and 39.7% in the 5-Tab setting, revealing a gap of 37% and 31.3% in accuracy, respectively, when compared with ARES.

Note that we did not evaluate ARES in the 7-Tab setting as it truncates traces after 10k packets (similarly to DF's and Tik-Tok's behavior), thus losing important contextual information. While it would be possible to admit larger inputs by adding hidden layers to ARES, this would require non-trivial transformations to ARES's DNN. We did not evaluate DTW on multi-tab traces since distance calculations take much longer, making it intractable.

Defended Merged Traces. Table 6 describes the accuracy of TSA-WF (w/ STUMPY) on defended traces created from 3/5/7 tabs. Recall TSA-WF's undefended accuracies of 50.5% and 39.7% in the 3-Tab and 5-Tab settings. The results of Table 6 show a decrease in accuracy between 19.2% (vs. FRONT-T2) and 22.7% (vs. WTF-PAD) for 3-Tab and between 17.7% (vs. FRONT-T2) and 21.2% (vs. WTF-PAD) for 5-Tab. Recall ARES' undefended accuracy of 87.5% and 71.0% in the 3-Tab and 5-Tab settings. Table 6 shows ARES experienced an accuracy reduction between 29.1% (vs. WTF-PAD) and 80.4% (vs. RegulaTor) for 3-Tab and between 29.4% (vs. WTF-PAD) and 65.6% (vs. RegulaTor) for 5-Tab. While RegulaTor was the most effective defense against TSA-WF for 1-Tab (see Table 5), WTF-PAD was the best defense against it for 3 and 5 tabs.

Overall, TSA-WF had a smaller relative decrease in accuracy compared with ARES, but still failed to outperform ARES against most defenses.

We note that ARES is highly ineffective against traces defended using RegulaTor and posit two reasons for this result. Firstly, the deep learning architecture of ARES is closely related to that of DF – indeed, ARES' local profiling component uses the same 32-layer CNN architecture as DF. For this reason, we expect ARES' performance to be similarly impacted by the same perturbations introduced by the RegulaTor defense. Secondly, RegulaTor traces are significantly longer compared to the other defenses. On average, when considering the 3-Tab setting, ARES truncates RegulaTor-generated traces at 46% of their length, vs. only ≈30% for FRONT-T1, FRONT-T2, and WTF-PAD. Trace truncation is likely to have a negative impact on the performance of ARES, although we saw similarly low scores in both the 3-Tab and 5-Tab settings. We note that ARES has not previously been evaluated against WF defenses, and we expect our results may stir follow-up research into its robustness against such safeguards (e.g., by triggering potential extensions to its model architecture).

Overlapped Traces. Lastly, in Table 7, we compare the accuracy obtained by TSA-WF (w/ STUMPY) and ARES when identifying a monitored website amongst 3, 5, and 7 tab traces that have been overlapped to different degrees. For a (maximum) 10% overlap, the accuracy of TSA-WF decreased (from 50.5% and 41.2%) by 5.0% in the 3-Tab setting and by 6.8% in the 5-Tab setting. In ARES, we observed a slightly larger decrease of 6.9% in the 3-Tab setting and 9.1% in the 5-Tab setting. As expected, we can see a trend that larger overlaps between traces lead to an overall decrease in classification accuracy.

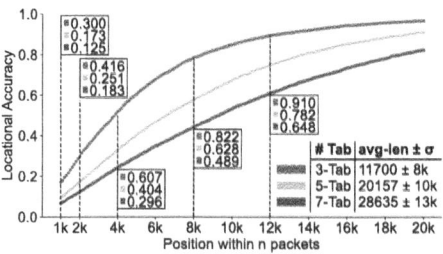

Fig. 2. TSA-WF's ability to locate the monitored website to within n packets.

4.4   Untangling Multi-tab Traces

In Fig. 2, we depict the accuracy of TSA-WF when pinpointing the approximate location of a monitored website within an open-world multi-tab trace. For each unlabeled sample, we begin by taking the prototype associated with the monitored class label predicted by TSA-WF. Then, we infer that monitored website's location in the multi-tab trace by finding the packet index where the minimum distance occurs (i.e., best match) between itself and the multi-tab trace being labeled. The reported accuracy value represents the percentage of monitored websites which were correctly located to within n packets of the true location. Overall, TSA-WF was able to correctly identify the location of the monitored website with an accuracy between 30.0% and 91.0% for 3-Tab traces, 17.3% and 78.2% for 5-Tab traces, and 12.5% and 64.8% for 7-Tab traces. In the 3-Tab setting, TSA-WF correctly located the monitored website to within 4 000 packets with an accuracy of 60.7%, which is similar to its overall accuracy on undefended 3-Tab traces (52.2%) with a difference of +8.5%. In the 5-Tab and 7-Tab settings, TSA-WF located the monitored website to within 4 000 packets with an accuracy of 40.4% (−0.8% vs. undefended) and 29.6% (−5.5% vs. undefended). We posit that as the number of tabs increases, the ability for TSA-WF to locate the website of interest to within one trace's length decreases faster than its classification accuracy, likely due to the increased chance for mismatches as a larger number of unmonitored websites are added to the merged trace.

5 Conclusions

In this paper, we reframed WF attacks as a time series matching problem. Our evaluation showed that a time series analysis pipeline designed for website fingerprinting (TSA-WF) achieves similar performance to state-of-the-art attacks in the open-world single-tab setting, both for undefended and defended website traces. Furthermore, we described how TSA-WF can augment the capabilities of existing multi-tab WF attacks by pinpointing the approximate instant at which a monitored website is accessed within a multi-tab trace.

Disclosure of Interests. The authors have no competing interests to declare that are relevant to the content of this article.

References

1. Cai, X., Nithyanand, R., Wang, T., Johnson, R., Goldberg, I.. A systematic approach to developing and evaluating WF defenses. In: Proceedings of ACM CCS (2014)
2. Chen, T., Guestrin, C.: XGBoost: a scalable tree boosting system. In: Proceedings of ACM KDD (2016)
3. Deng, X., et al.: Robust multi-tab website fingerprinting attacks in the wild. In: Proceedings of IEEE S&P (2023)
4. Gong, J., Wang, T.: Zero-delay lightweight defenses against website fingerprinting. In: Proceedings of USENIX Security (2020)
5. Hayes, J., Danezis, G.: k-fingerprinting: a robust scalable website fingerprinting technique. In: Proceedings of USENIX Security (2016)
6. He, X., Li, Y., Tan, J., Wu, B., Li, F.: One-shot seasonal-trend decomposition for online time series anomaly detection. Proc. VLDB Endow. (2023)
7. Holland, J.K., Hopper, N.: Regulator: a straightforward website fingerprinting defense. In: PoPETs (2022)

8. Jin, Z., Lu, T., Luo, S., Shang, J.: Transformer-based model for multi-tab website fingerprinting attack. In: Proceedings of ACM CCS (2023)
9. Juarez, M., Afroz, S., Acar, G., Díaz, C., Greenstadt, R.: A critical evaluation of website fingerprinting attacks. In: Proceedings of ACM CCS (2014)
10. Juarez, M., Imani, M., Perry, M., Díaz, C., Wright, M.: WTF-PAD: toward an efficient website fingerprinting defense for tor. CoRR abs/1512.00524 (2015)
11. Keogh, E.J., Lonardi, S., Ratanamahatana, C.A., Wei, L., Lee, S., Handley, J.C.: Compression-based data mining of sequential data. Data Min. Know. Discov. (2007)
12. Law, S.: STUMPY: a powerful and scalable python library for time series data mining. J. Open Source Softw. (2019)
13. Mathews, N., Holland, J.K., Oh, S.E., Rahman, M.S., Hopper, N., Wright, M.: SoK: a critical evaluation of efficient WF defenses. In: Proceedings of IEEE S&P (2023)
14. Nunes, V., Brás, J., Carvalho, A., Barradas, D., Gallagher, K., Santos, N.: Enhancing the unlinkability of circuit-based anonymous communications with k-funnels. In: PACMNET (2023)
15. Rahman, M.S., Sirinam, P., Mathews, N., Gangadhara, K.G., Wright, M.: Tik-tok: the utility of packet timing in website fingerprinting attacks. In: PoPETs (2020)
16. Rimmer, V., Preuveneers, D., Juarez, M., van Goethem, T., Joosen, W.: Automated feature extraction for WF through DL. In: Proceedings of NDSS (2018)
17. Rupprecht, D., Kohls, K., Holz, T., Pöpper, C.: Breaking LTE on layer two. In: Proceedings of IEEE S&P (2019)
18. Sirinam, P., Imani, M., Juarez, M., Wright, M.: Deep fingerprinting: undermining website fingerprinting defenses with deep learning. In: Proceedings of ACM CCS (2018)
19. de la Torre-Abaitua, G., Lago-Fernández, L.F., Arroyo, D.: On the application of compression-based metrics to identifying anomalous behaviour in web traffic. Log. J, IGPL (2020)
20. Veicht, A., Renggli, C., Barradas, D.: Deepse-WF: unified security estimation for website fingerprinting defenses. In: PoPETs (2023)
21. Wrana, M., Maroof, U., Barradas, D.: TSA-WF. https://doi.org/10.5281/zenodo.14991323
22. Xu, Y., Wang, T., Li, Q., Gong, Q., Chen, Y., Jiang, Y.: A multi-tab website fingerprinting attack. In: Proceedings of ACSAC (2018)
23. Zhou, R., Wang, X., Yang, J., Zhang, W., Zhang, S.: Characterizing network anomaly traffic with euclidean distance-based multiscale fuzzy entropy. Secur. Commun. Netw. (2021)

Generalized Encrypted Traffic Classification Using Inter-flow Signals

Federica Bianchi$^{(\boxtimes)}$ [ID], Edoardo Di Paolo [ID], and Angelo Spognardi [ID]

Computer Science Department, Sapienza University of Rome, Rome, Italy
{bianchi,dipaolo,spognardi}@di.uniroma1.it

Abstract. In this paper, we present a novel encrypted traffic classification model that operates directly on raw PCAP data without requiring prior assumptions about traffic type. Unlike existing methods, it is generalizable across multiple classification tasks and leverages inter-flow signals—an innovative representation that captures temporal correlations and packet volume distributions across flows. Experimental results show that our model outperforms well-established methods in nearly every classification task and across most datasets, achieving up to 99% accuracy in some cases, demonstrating its robustness and adaptability.

Keywords: Encrypted Traffic Analysis · Network Security · Machine Learning

1 Introduction

Network traffic analysis is a fundamental aspect of cybersecurity, network management, and performance optimization. Analyzing network activity provides valuable insights into communication patterns, the services and applications in use, and potential security threats. As a result, traffic analysis plays a key role in a wide range of real-world applications, from securing enterprise networks and detecting malware to enhancing service quality and protecting user privacy. In recent years, the increasing adoption of encryption protocols has rendered plaintext payload analysis ineffective, shifting the focus to methods based on machine learning and deep learning. Encrypted traffic analysis supports multiple critical goals [21], including the *identification of network assets* like IoT systems and mobile devices, enabling better asset management and vulnerability assessment. It also facilitates *network characterization* by evaluating service quality and user experience metrics. Moreover, it plays a key role in *privacy leakage detection*, revealing user activities and accessed apps, services, or websites through encrypted traffic. Finally, it is crucial for identifying malicious behavior and anomalies, a need underscored by the rising prevalence of malware and attacks on enterprise, IoT, and blockchain infrastructures.

This work was supported by project SERICS (PE00000014) under the NRRP MUR program funded by the EU-NGEU.

Despite the broad applicability of encrypted traffic classification, most existing research typically focuses on developing a method tailored to a single task and is rarely evaluated in multiple analysis goals, limiting the generalizability. Moreover, previous work focuses mainly on statistical features extracted from packets or within individual flows (intra-flow level), with only a few exploring relationships among multiple flows over time (inter-flow level) and integrating insights from multiple perspectives [17, 25, 26].

To address these limitations, we present a novel encrypted traffic classification model that is both generalizable across multiple domains and does not require prior assumptions about traffic type. Our approach proves effective across various tasks, including mobile application and website fingerprinting, malware detection, IoT device fingerprinting, and general traffic classification (with and without VPN), making it a highly versatile solution. Although our model has been tested on the aforementioned tasks, it also holds significant potential for application in other encrypted traffic classification tasks due to its generalizability. Another key innovation of our method is the introduction of signals, a novel inter-flow representation that captures temporal correlations among flows and packet volume distributions. Drawing inspiration from telecommunications and signal processing [18], we treat network flows as temporal signals. Unlike statistical features, which summarize flow characteristics in isolation, signals model how multiple flows interact over time, offering a richer context-aware classification of encrypted traffic. To our knowledge, this is the first general-purpose encrypted traffic classifier using inter-flow signal representations.

The main contributions of this paper can be summarized as follows:

- We propose a general-purpose encrypted traffic classification model that successfully generalizes across multiple analysis goals.
- We introduce a novel inter-flow representation, called signals, which captures temporal correlations among flows and packet volume distributions.
- We conduct an extensive evaluation across eight diverse datasets, covering multiple encrypted traffic classification tasks.
- We compare our approach against well-established methods across the same datasets, demonstrating superior performance in all classification tasks.

2   Related Work

One of the main applications of encrypted network traffic analysis has been the identification of mobile applications. FlowPrint [25] analyzed temporal correlations among destination-related features of network traffic at the inter-flow level and created a database of application-specific fingerprints. When classifying new traffic, their method generated a corresponding fingerprint and matched it against the database. *Taylor et al.* in AppScanner [24] adopted machine learning models using statistical features at the intra-flow level and packet sizes to recognize apps. More recent methods leverage deep learning. *Pham et al.* [17] proposed MAppGraph, a method that classifies mobile applications by constructing a communication graph of network destinations for each app. The nodes of the graph for each app are defined by tuples of IP addresses and ports of the services connected by the app, while the edges represent weighted communication correlations among these nodes. They then used deep graph convolutional neural networks (DGCNN) to learn the various communication behaviors of mobile apps. Some works, instead, feed raw packet bytes directly into deep learning models, such as in PEAN [10].

Website fingerprinting aims to identify the specific website visited by a user despite encryption mechanisms. Many methods leverage machine learning to infer web activity [20,22], while others leverage deep learning approaches, such as in [4,27], in which they classify websites visited using CNNs.

Generic traffic classification targets broad service categories (e.g., email, VoIP). *Chen et al.* [3] employed Long Short-Term Memory (LSTM) on message size sequences for early prediction, while *Luo et al.* [13] proposed a self-supervised method for traffic classification to enhance flow representations using trace data.

Encrypted traffic analysis has also been widely used to distinguish malicious activity from benign traffic. The approaches range from traditional machine learning classifiers [6,8] to deep models. *Feng et al.* [5] introduced a two-layer CNN-AutoEncoder to classify malware, while more recently *Liu et al.* [12] modeled temporal patterns in Dalvik opcode sequences with LSTM and temporal convolutional network (TCN). In IoT device fingerprinting, statistical profiling has been effective [23], while recent efforts employ deep learning for IoT malware detection [1].

3 Problem Definition

Encrypted network traffic classification categorizes network traffic according to different analysis goals. Indeed, traffic can be generated from various sources, such as mobile applications, web pages or websites, services, malware, etc.

Unlike approaches that classify individual traffic *flows* or *packets*, our method operates on *traffic chunks*. A traffic chunk is a bounded segment of network traffic that spans a specific time window, which may include multiple concurrent or sequential flows. Formally, let P be the set of all the observed **network packets** in a monitored traffic session. Each packet $p_j \in P$ belongs to a specific **network flow**, which consists of a series of packets sharing the standard 5-tuple:

$$\langle src_{ip}, dst_{ip}, src_{port}, dst_{port}, proto \rangle, \tag{1}$$

where src_{ip} and dst_{ip} are the source and destination IP addresses, src_{port} and dst_{port} are the source and destination ports, and $proto$ is the transport-layer protocol. A **traffic chunk** C_i is defined as a set of packets occurring within a fixed time window W, such that:

$$C_i = \{p_j \in P \mid t_j \in [t_{start}, t_{start} + W]\}. \tag{2}$$

where t_j is the timestamp of packet p_j, t_{start} is the starting time of the chunk and W is the pre-defined window duration.

A traffic chunk may contain different flow communication scenarios:

- **Single Flow Communication**: Occurs when a network interaction involves one isolated flow between a client and server, exhibiting simple request-response behavior, without concurrent or sequential connections.
- **Sequential Flow Communication**: Involves multiple flows initiated sequentially for different stages of the communication. Each flow contributes to a broader activity.
- **Concurrent Flow Communication**: In many real-world scenarios, end-points initiate multiple flows in parallel towards different network destinations to manage different aspects of the communication.

Since we evaluate our model on multiple classification tasks, the ground-truth label varies depending on the task. For mobile applications, it identifies the specific application in use. In website classification, it corresponds to the accessed site, whether through standard or VPN-protected browsing. For malware detection, the label distinguishes between benign and malicious traffic. In service classification, it indicates the type of network service (e.g., chat, email, VoIP, etc.). Finally, for IoT classification, it reflects the type of IoT device involved in the communication.

4   Methodology

We propose a general traffic classification method that operates directly on raw PCAP files, without assumptions about the nature of the traffic. This flexible design supports various analysis goals, including mobile application fingerprinting, website fingerprinting, generic traffic classification, malware detection, and IoT traffic classification. To achieve effective classification, we extract features at multiple representation levels. At the inter-flow level, we introduce **signals**, a key novelty of our work, which capture temporal relationships, volume, and timing across flows within the same time window. We also compute statistical features at the packet and intra-flow levels for detailed insights into flow behavior and packet distributions.

Traffic Pre-processing. Following prior work [16,17,25], we filter out packets based on port numbers, discarding traffic from common background services (e.g., DNS, DHCP). These ports are typically not related to specific apps, services, or websites and do not offer distinguishing characteristics for classification [17,27]. Removing them reduces irrelevant variation and improves the clarity of traffic features for classification. After PCAPs are filtered, we split them into smaller **chunks**, or time windows, of network activity, to improve computational efficiency and analytical precision. Segmenting traffic into manageable portions reduces the complexity and overhead associated with analyzing large captures, essential for real-time or high-volume scenarios. Additionally, breaking down traffic into time windows allows us to focus on discrete periods of network communication, enabling a finer-grained analysis of the traffic temporal dynamics, as network behavior can vary over time. To prevent information loss at the boundaries of these time windows, we introduce an **overlap** parameter, which defines the fraction of two consecutive chunks that overlap. Without overlap, some traffic patterns occurring near chunk edges may be split between consecutive windows, leading to fragmented representations. Choosing the time window duration and overlap involves trade-offs. Short windows capture fine-grained interactions but can be noisy and fragmented, while longer ones smooth out fluctuations and provide a broader perspective, but risk obscuring short-term behaviors and delaying classification. Similarly, large overlaps preserve continuity but add redundancy, whereas small overlaps are more efficient but may disrupt dependencies between related flows. We empirically tune these parameters for optimal balance.

Traffic Representation. To achieve a thorough understanding of traffic patterns, we represent them at multiple levels: packet level, intra-flow level, and inter-flow level. This choice comes from the intuition that traffic may leak different kinds of information based on the viewpoint of the analysis, each providing valuable insights into its behavior and the overall dynamics of the network. At the **inter-flow level**, we aim to leverage the **temporal relationships** between the sending and receiving of packets across multiple flows. The key hypothesis underlying this representation is that network communications generate discernible patterns in flow initiation and sequencing, which can be used for traffic classification. When analyzing the network behavior of communicating endpoints within specific time windows (i.e., chunks), we observe the scenarios outlined in Sect. 3, namely single flow communication, sequential flow communication, and concurrent flow communication. Traditional studies on encrypted traffic classification typically isolate individual flows for analysis. In contrast, our approach wants to capture these sequential and concurrent flow communication scenarios, examining how flows **coexist** and **interact** within the same temporal context. This provides a more holistic representation that integrates both the byte volume and the temporal relationships between flows, such as flows initiation, sequencing, and overlap. To capture these inter-flow dynamics, we represent network traffic as a discrete time series signal. This transformation moves beyond simple flow classification by analyzing traffic as a structured sequence that encapsulates both the exchanged data volume and the key temporal features of flow interactions. The general idea is that each chunk is transformed into a **unified signal** that aggregates all packets exchanged during that time window, regardless of whether they originate from a single flow or multiple concurrent flows. The rationale behind constructing a unified signal is to capture the endpoint global communication pattern, rather than focusing on individual flows.

With this unified signal, we aim to: (i) capture the volume of transmitted data across all flows within the chunk, along with the temporal structure of packet transmissions, revealing distinct traffic patterns; (ii) quantify each flow contribution to the overall network activity, helping to identify dominant interactions in data transfer; and (iii) analyze flow interactions to help distinguish different types of traffic. For example, mobile applications may exhibit consistent flow initiation and overlap patterns—such as connections to authentication servers, content delivery networks, or analytics services. This predictable behavior suggests that the initiation of flows follows a relatively consistent pattern in both timing and volume.

Signal Creation. Each network packet is represented as a tuple containing its **timestamp** and **packet length**:

$$p_j = (t_j, l_j), \tag{3}$$

where t_j represents the time at which the packet was transmitted as recorded in the PCAP file (approximated in seconds for analysis) and l_j denotes its size in bytes. A network flow F_k is then defined as an ordered sequence of packets that share the same five-tuple identifier, as defined in Eq. 1:

$$F_k = \{(t_1^k, l_1^k), (t_2^k, l_2^k), ..., (t_{n_k}^k, l_{n_k}^k)\} \quad \text{where } t_1^k < t_2^k < \cdots < t_{n_k}^k. \tag{4}$$

Each flow consists of packets exchanged between a client and a server, and multiple flows may be present within a given traffic chunk, as described in the previous sections. To construct a single **unified signal** from multiple flows (sequential or concurrent), we aggregate their packet information over a coherent time axis to ensure that all flows are synchronized within the time window of the chunk, aligning their packet data into a cohesive representation.

Let $F = \{F_1, F_2, ..., F_n\}$ represent the set of flows within a chunk. We determine the minimum and maximum timestamps across all flows:

$$t_{\min} = \min_{k=1,\cdots,n} \min_{i=1,\cdots,n_k} t_i^k, \quad t_{\max} = \max_{k=1,\cdots,n} \max_{i=1,\cdots,n_k} t_i^k. \tag{5}$$

Then, we define T as a discretization of the interval $t_{\min}$ to $t_{\max}$ with a step size δ, which can be chosen arbitrarily:

$$T = \{t_{\min}, t_{\min} + \delta, ..., t_{\max}\}. \tag{6}$$

For each flow F_k, we compute its **amplitude**, which represents the total transmitted data volume, computed as follows:

$$A_k = \sum_{j=1}^{n_k} l_j^k. \tag{7}$$

Each packet is then mapped onto the time axis, and the value of the signal at each timestamp is computed by summing the contributions of all active flows:

$$S(T_{min} + \delta t) = \sum_{k=1}^{n} A_k \sum_{j=1}^{n_k} l_j^k \mathbf{1}_{[T_{min}+\delta t, T_{min}+\delta(t+1))}(t_j^k), \quad t = 0, \cdots, \frac{T_{max} - T_{min}}{\delta}. \tag{8}$$

where, given a set B,

$$\mathbf{1}_B(x) = \begin{cases} 1 & \text{if } x \in B, \\ 0 & \text{otherwise.} \end{cases} \tag{9}$$

By scaling the signal values with amplitude, we ensure that each flow influence is proportional to its total traffic volume within the chunk. High-volume flows contribute more significantly, while low-volume flows have a lesser impact.

Table 1. List of features extracted for incoming packets, outgoing packets, and their combined set.

	Features
Packet-Level	Total Number of Packets, Maximum Packet Size, Minimum Packet Size, Mean Packet Size, Variance of Packet Size, Standard Deviation of Packet Size, Mean Absolute Deviation of Packet Size, Skewness of Packet Size, Kurtosis of Packet, Size Percentiles (10th to 90th)
Intra-Flow Level	Mean Flow Duration (Seconds), Mean Flow Size (Bytes), Total Number of Flows, Standard Deviation of Flow Duration, Mean Number of Packets per Flow

Min-Max Normalization is applied to maintain comparability across signals of different chunks. In addition to constructing the signal, we compute and normalize the inter-arrival times of packets across all flows. These inter-arrival times capture patterns such as burstiness, network congestion, or application-specific timing characteristics. By incorporating both the aggregated traffic signal and inter-arrival times, our method effectively captures the overall data volume and flow significance and the timing characteristics of packet exchanges.

To our knowledge, this approach of deriving a single application-level signal from overlapping flows has not been previously explored in the literature.

At the **packet** and **intra-flow levels**, we extract statistical features that describe both individual packets and their corresponding flows. This choice is motivated by their demonstrated effectiveness in the literature [20], where statistical features have consistently yielded strong results in network traffic analysis. In particular, packet level features capture the statistical properties of individual packets within a chunk. These features are extracted separately for incoming packets, outgoing packets, and their combined set. On the other hand, intra-flow features describe the behavior of individual flows, capturing how packets are transmitted over time. All the extracted features are summarized in Table 1.

Traffic Analysis. During Traffic Analysis, the extracted features are processed to derive meaningful insights about the encrypted network traffic. Our approach derives insights from traffic patterns and distributions that describe the behavior of network flows and packets. We employ **Random Forest**, a well-established machine learning technique effective in high-dimensional data, such as that from network traffic.

5   Evaluation

We implemented our model in Python, using Scapy [2] PCAP processing and analysis and the scikit-learn library for the Random Forest classifier. To assess the performance of our proposed method, we conducted an evaluation on eight different datasets (MAppGraph [17], PostQuantumTLS [14], Cross Platform [19], ISCX-VPN and ISCX-nonVPN [7], CICAndMal2017 [9], IoT-Sentinel [15] and CSTNET-TLS 1.3 [11]) and compared our approach with Flowprint [25] and MAppGraph [17]. Flowprint was selected as it is a well-established knowledge-based approach for mobile traffic classification, while MAppGraph is one of the

Table 2. Results and comparison of our method with MAppGraph and Flowprint across different datasets.

Model	Our Method				MAppGraph				Flowprint			
Dataset	Acc.	Prec.	Rec.	F1	Acc.	Prec.	Rec.	F1	Acc.	Prec.	Rec.	F1
MAppGraph	**0.9517**	0.9473	0.9385	0.9418	0.9346	0.9364	0.9346	0.9347	0.8664	0.8718	0.8664	0.8662
PostQuantumTLS	0.5013	0.5624	0.5013	0.4941	0.3684	0.2663	0.2760	0.2612	**0.7077**	0.7177	0.7077	0.6927
Cross Platform	0.3418	0.5088	0.3120	0.2748	0.2686	0.1853	0.2130	0.1862	**0.8692**	0.9070	0.8692	0.8745
ISCX-VPN	**0.9903**	0.9895	0.9882	0.9885	0.8846	0.6988	0.7195	0.7055	0.9484	0.9728	0.9484	0.9557
ISCX-nonVPN	**0.9918**	0.9887	0.9811	0.9845	0.9244	0.9022	0.8875	0.8915	0.7791	0.8770	0.7791	0.8150
CICAndMal2017	0.8308	**0.8315**	0.8285	0.8295	**0.8518**	0.7507	0.6467	0.6755	0.7836	0.7837	0.7836	0.7829
IoT-Sentinel	**0.9280**	0.9198	0.9293	0.8878	0.6553	0.6002	0.5451	0.5481	0.7084	0.7084	0.7084	0.7084
CSTNET-TLS 1.3	**0.7497**	0.7408	0.7079	0.7142	-	-	-	-	0.1953	0.1987	0.1953	0.1834

few methods that classify chunks of traffic, making it a suitable choice for direct comparison with our approach.

We evaluated our model on various datasets in order to address an assorted range of network traffic classification challenges, including mobile application fingerprinting, website fingerprinting, traffic classification (with and without VPN), and IoT device fingerprinting. All experiments use an 80:20 train-test split and standard metrics—accuracy, precision, recall, and F1-score. We tested various window-overlap configurations to optimize performance per dataset. The evaluated time window sizes included *300s*, *200s*, *80s*, *50s*, *30s*, and *10s*, with overlaps of *180s*, *120s*, *30s*, *10s*, *2s*, and *1s*. For each dataset, we selected the window-overlap combination that produced the highest accuracy, and all reported results correspond to this best-performing configuration. For fair comparative evaluation, we used the official implementations of MAppGraph[1] and FlowPrint[2]. The MAppGraph implementation was used without modification, except for an added module to convert PCAP files to CSVs (as the original implementation assumes CSV input). We tested the same range of window sizes and overlaps for parameter tuning. For FlowPrint, we installed the library via `pip`, preprocessed the PCAPs to extract flows, generated fingerprints, and subsequently performed app recognition.

Analysis of Results. Our method demonstrates (Table 2) robust classification performance on almost all tested datasets, achieving high accuracy across all analysis goals. It operates without assumptions about the type of analysis goals considered and achieves consistent performance across a diverse range of datasets. These results suggest that our signal-based inter-flow features, combined with statistical representations, effectively capture characteristics of different types of encrypted traffic. In particular, our method achieves outstanding results in the general traffic classification task, reaching 99.03% accuracy on ISCX-VPN and 99.18% on ISCX-nonVPN. Additionally, it performs very well in IoT device detection (92.80% on IoT-Sentinel) and malware

---

[1] https://github.com/soeai/mappgraph.git.
[2] https://flowprint.readthedocs.io/en/latest/index.html.

classification (83.08% on CICAndMal2017). However, we encountered limitations with datasets like Cross Platform and PostQuantumTLS. These datasets pose a challenge, particularly for methods that classify chunks of traffic, as they contain only one PCAP per app, with a maximum capture duration of five minutes. The short duration of these PCAPs results in very limited network activity, which complicates the extraction of meaningful statistical features. When divided into smaller chunks, these limited captures result in segments that may lack the packet volume and traffic diversity needed to extract meaningful statistical features. Furthermore, signal generation can be affected by these short PCAPs, as the flow duration is limited and the number of concurrent flows captured is minimal.

Comparison with MAppGraph and Flowprint. Table 2 shows that our method outperforms existing approaches in most cases. MAppGraph, like our method, classifies chunks of traffic rather than individual flows. It struggles with smaller datasets, such as CrossPlatform (26.96%) and PostQuantumTLS (36.84%), likely for our same reasons. Despite sharing a chunk-based approach, MAppGraph's performance remains lower than ours across most datasets. Notably, our method outperforms MAppGraph even on its own dataset, and it achieves higher accuracy in the general traffic classification task (ISCX-VPN and ISCX-nonVPN), website fingerprinting (CSTNET-TLS 1.3), and IoT device recognition (IoT-Sentinel), demonstrating its better adaptability across different traffic classification tasks. Although MAppGraph achieves a higher accuracy (85.18%) compared to our method (83.08%) on the CICAndMal2017 dataset, it demonstrates significantly lower precision (75.07% vs. 83.15%) and recall (64.67% vs. 82.85%). This distinction is important in malware detection tasks: lower precision means that MAppGraph is more likely to generate false positives, flagging legitimate traffic as malicious, while lower recall implies that MAppGraph may miss some malicious traffic, leaving malware undetected. FlowPrint, in contrast, uses a knowledge-based approach, generating fingerprints for applications. This methodological difference may explain why FlowPrint performs better on smaller datasets, namely Cross Platform and PostQuantumTLS. However, despite its strong general performance across multiple classification tasks, Flow-Print never surpasses our method except for the previously mentioned datasets. Importantly, both FlowPrint and MAppGraph struggle in the CSTNET-TLS 1.3 dataset. This is likely due to their reliance on network destinations and ports for graph construction. When working with websites, especially those with fewer unique IP-port pairs, these methods face difficulty in creating meaningful graphs and in capturing enough network diversity to make accurate classifications. While these approaches work well for mobile application fingerprinting, for which they were specifically developed—due to the typical presence of many distinct network destinations contacted by apps—they do not perform as well for websites. As a result, on CSTNET-TLS 1.3 dataset, MAppGraph is unable to even create the graphs needed to test the model, while FlowPrint achieves only 19.53% of accuracy. This limitation highlights a failure in generalizability.

6   Conclusions and Future Works

In this paper, we proposed a general-purpose encrypted traffic classification model that operates across multiple analysis goals without prior assumptions about traffic type. A key innovation of our approach is the signal-based inter-flow representation, which captures temporal correlations and packet volume distributions across flows, providing a richer and more context-aware representation of encrypted network traffic. Our evaluation across eight datasets demonstrates the effectiveness and adaptability of our method, consistently outperforming state-of-the-art models in mobile application recognition, website fingerprinting, malware detection, IoT fingerprinting, and general traffic classification. Future work will focus on improving performance with small datasets and short PCAPs, exploring with other machine and deep learning models for enhanced accuracy, and investigating real-time encrypted traffic detection for dynamic environments.

References

1. Ali, S., Abusabha, O., Ali, F., Imran, M., Abuhmed, T.: Effective multitask deep learning for IoT malware detection and identification using behavioral traffic analysis. IEEE TNSM (2023). https://doi.org/10.1109/TNSM.2022.3200741
2. Biondi, P.: Scapy. http://www.secdev.org/projects/scapy
3. Chen, W., Lyu, F., Wu, F., Yang, P., Xue, G., Li, M.: Sequential message characterization for early classification of encrypted internet traffic. IEEE TVT (2021)
4. Cui, W., Chen, T., Chan-Tin, E.: More realistic website fingerprinting using deep learning. In: (ICDCS) (2020). https://doi.org/10.1109/ICDCS47774.2020.00058
5. Feng, J., Shen, L., Chen, Z., Wang, Y., Li, H.: A two-layer deep learning method for android malware detection using network traffic. IEEE Access (2020). https://doi.org/10.1109/ACCESS.2020.3008081
6. Garg, S., Peddoju, S.K., Sarje, A.K.: Network-based detection of android malicious apps (2017). https://doi.org/10.1007/s10207-016-0343-z
7. Habibi Lashkari, A., Draper Gil, G., Mamun, M., Ghorbani, A.: Characterization of encrypted and vpn traffic using time-related features (2016). https://doi.org/10.5220/0005740704070414
8. Lashkari, A.H., A.Kadir, A.F., Gonzalez, H., Mbah, K.F., Ghorbani, A.A.: Towards a network-based framework for android malware detection and characterization. In: PST (2017). https://doi.org/10.1109/PST.2017.00035
9. Lashkari, A.H., Kadir, A.F.A., Taheri, L., Ghorbani, A.A.: Toward developing a systematic approach to generate benchmark android malware datasets and classification. In: ICCST (2018). https://doi.org/10.1109/CCST.2018.8585560
10. Lin, P., Ye, K., Hu, Y., Lin, Y., Xu, C.Z.: A novel multimodal deep learning framework for encrypted traffic classification. IEEE/ACM Trans. Netw. (2023). https://doi.org/10.1109/TNET.2022.3215507
11. Lin, X., Xiong, G., Gou, G., Li, Z., Shi, J., Yu, J.: Et-BERT: a contextualized datagram representation with pre-training transformers for encrypted traffic classification. In: WWW (2022). https://doi.org/10.1145/3485447.3512217, http://dx.doi.org/10.1145/3485447.3512217

12. Liu, H., Gong, L., Mo, X., Dong, G., Yu, J.: Ltachecker: lightweight android malware detection based on Dalvik opcode sequences using attention temporal networks. IEEE Internet Things J. (2024). https://doi.org/10.1109/JIOT.2024. 3394555
13. Luo, Z., Li, Y., Tan, S., He, D.: Enhancing flow embedding through trace: a novel self-supervised approach for encrypted traffic classification (2024). https://doi.org/ 10.1109/IJCNN60899.2024.10651222
14. Mankowski, D., Wiggers, T., Moonsamy, V.: Post Quantum TLS for Android (0.1.0) (2023). https://doi.org/10.5281/zenodo.7950522
15. Miettinen, M., Marchal, S., Hafeez, I., Asokan, N., Sadeghi, A.R., Tarkoma, S.: IoT sentinel: automated device-type identification for security enforcement in IoT. In: IEEE ICDCS (2017). https://doi.org/10.1109/ICDCS.2017.283
16. Oh, S., Lee, M., Lee, H., Bertino, E., Kim, H.: AppSniffer: towards robust mobile app fingerprinting against VPN. In: WWW (2023). https://doi.org/10. 1145/3543507.3583473
17. Pham, T.D., Ho, T.L., Truong-Huu, T., Cao, T.D., Truong, H.L.: MAppGraph: Mobile-App Classification on Encrypted Network Traffic using Deep Graph Convolution Neural Networks. In: ACSAC (2021). https://doi.org/10.1145/3485832. 3485925
18. Picone, J.: Signal modeling techniques in speech recognition. Proc. IEEE (1993). https://doi.org/10.1109/5.237532
19. Ren, J., Dubois, D.J., Choffnes, D.: An international view of privacy risks for mobile apps (2019). Unpublished manuscript
20. Shen, M., Liu, Y., Zhu, L., Xu, K., Du, X., Guizani, N.: Optimizing feature selection for efficient encrypted traffic classification: a systematic approach. IEEE Netw. (2020). https://doi.org/10.1109/MNET.011.1900366
21. Shen, M., et al.: Machine learning-powered encrypted network traffic analysis: a comprehensive survey. IEEE Commun. Surv. Tutor. (2023). https://doi.org/10. 1109/COMST.2022.3208196
22. Shen, M., Zhang, J., Chen, S., Liu, Y., Zhu, L.: Machine learning classification on traffic of secondary encryption. In: IEEE GLOBECOM (2019). https://doi.org/10. 1109/GLOBECOM38437.2019.9013272
23. Sivanathan, A., et al.: Characterizing and classifying IoT traffic in smart cities and campuses. In: IEEE INFOCOM WKSHPS (2017). https://doi.org/10.1109/ INFCOMW.2017.8116438
24. Taylor, V.F., Spolaor, R., Conti, M., Martinovic, I.: Robust smartphone app identification via encrypted network traffic analysis. IEEE TIFS (2018). https://doi. org/10.1109/TIFS.2017.2737970
25. van Ede, T., et al.: FlowPrint: semi-supervised mobile-app fingerprinting on encrypted network traffic. In: NDSS (2020). https://doi.org/10.14722/ndss.2020. 24412
26. Wang, X., et al.: Combine intra- and inter-flow: a multimodal encrypted traffic classification model driven by diverse features. Comput. Netw. (2024). https:// doi.org/10.1016/j.comnet.2024.110403
27. Zhang, Z., Liu, L., Lu, X., Yan, Z., Li, H.: Encrypted network traffic classification: a data driven approach. In: IEEE BdCloud (2020). https://doi.org/10.1109/ISPA-BDCloud-SocialCom-SustainCom51426.2020.00114

IoT & Embedded Systems Security

SHIELD: Scalable and Holistic Evaluation Framework for ML-Based 5G Jamming Detection

Jiali Xu[1(✉)], Aya Moheddine[1], Valéria Loscrì[1], Alessandro Brighente[2], and Mauro Conti[2]

[1] Inria Centre at the University of Lille, 59650 Villeneuve d'Ascq, France
{jiali.xu,aya.moheddine,valeria.loscri}@inria.fr
[2] Department of Mathematics, University of Padova, 35131 Padova, Italy
{alessandro.brighente,mauro.conti}@unipd.it

Abstract. Jamming remains a significant threat to 5G network reliability and security, despite extensive research. This work addresses critical scalability and robustness gaps in previous approaches by introducing SHIELD: a scalable, holistic framework to evaluate jamming interference and support Machine Learning (ML)-based detection techniques without relying on costly external hardware. To validate our approach, we developed a realistic 5G testbed featuring a power-modulated jammer, commercial off-the-shelf Android devices, and a Software-Defined Radio (SDR)-based Radio Access Network (RAN). Our experiments demonstrate this setup generates complex interference patterns challenging prior detection methods. SHIELD's novel methodology involves synchronously collecting native logs from User Equipment (UE) and Next-Generation Node B (gNB), capturing a comprehensive view of network behavior. It overcomes existing methods' shortcomings against subtle, long-term interference by employing a robust preprocessing pipeline with interpolation and sliding-window aggregation for multi-layer feature extraction. We assess several lightweight classifiers (Support Vector Machines (SVM), K-Nearest Neighbors (KNN), Gradient Boosting (GB), Random Forest (RForest)) across diverse real-world scenarios. Our evaluation reveals that while existing methods may exceed 90% accuracy in controlled settings, their performance can drop below 70% under varying conditions. In contrast, SHIELD's log-based framework maintains approximately 94% accuracy on unseen data, offering a scalable, cost-effective, and robust solution for large-scale 5G deployments.

Keywords: 5G Networks · Wireless Security · Jamming Attack · Pattern Analysis · Anomaly Detection

1 Introduction

Cellular networks form the backbone of modern communication systems, connecting millions of users through voice calls, internet browsing, and various data-intensive applications. These networks rely on seamless Radio Frequency (RF)

© The Author(s), under exclusive license to Springer Nature Switzerland AG 2025
M. Dalla Preda et al. (Eds.): ARES 2025, LNCS 15992, pp. 235–256, 2025.
https://doi.org/10.1007/978-3-032-00624-0_12

signal transmission between mobile devices, such as smartphones and base stations. The emergence of advanced technologies like 5G has enabled unprecedented speed, capacity, and reliability. However, the open and shared nature of wireless channels brings inherited vulnerabilities [4, 23], including radio jamming interference—a fundamental threat that extensive research has not fully eliminated.

Jamming, though not a novel concept, remains a critical wireless attack. By injecting disruptive RF signals on the same frequencies that cellular networks use, adversaries can degrade performance, increase latency, and cause dropped calls or total communication failure, effectively leading to denial-of-service scenarios. Such disruptions not only frustrate end users but can have serious implications in sectors dependent on uninterrupted connectivity, such as healthcare, transportation, and critical infrastructure.

Traditionally, detecting and mitigating jamming attacks has required specialized hardware, such as spectrum analyzers and advanced signal processing systems [20, 25], to capture RF fingerprints. These methods can be costly and lack scalability, making them unsuitable for wide deployment in end devices. Furthermore, the proposed methodologies in prior works often focus on a single network entity, relying on measurements either from the RAN or the UE, which limits the holistic analysis of system behavior. Additionally, many existing detection methods [5, 6, 10, 13, 14, 21] primarily address simplistic jamming profiles, such as constant or reactive jammers. These types of interference often produce overt and consistent disruptions, making them more amenable to detection. However, sophisticated adversaries can employ more subtle, power-modulated jamming strategies that generate less predictable interference patterns. Such complex variants pose significant challenges to conventional techniques, particularly those validated predominantly through simulations, which may not fully capture the intricacies of real-world 5G operational dynamics and hardware interactions.

Being aware of these gaps in the current literature, we propose the SHIELD framework. The main contributions of this work are: (1) We construct a power-modulated jammer and integrate into a near-realistic 5G setup using commercial off-the-shelf Android devices and an SDR-driven RAN. We reproduce several detection methods from prior studies in our testbed to demonstrate the challenge of detecting such complex jamming profiles. Additionally, we collect data directly from these devices to validate the effectiveness of our subsequent proposals, highlighting the limitations of existing techniques under more subtle jamming scenarios. (2) We propose an approach that captures features from native UE logs and gNB traces to remove excessive hardware dependencies. This approach includes an efficient preprocessing pipeline that preserves crucial signals and filters out non-jamming fluctuation, providing a scalable and holistic analysis toward accurate and robust jamming detection. (3) We design an evaluation method that balances performance with resilience to varying real-world conditions, a dimension the literature often overlooks. We illustrate this approach with several lightweight yet highly accurate ML models, ensuring a broader applicability of these detection approaches beyond a single, strictly controlled environment.

The remainder of this paper proceeds as follows: In Sect. 2, we review related work on jamming detection and ML-based anomaly detection to highlight existing challenges and gaps. Section 3 describes our proposed SHIELD framework in detail, including the design of a power-modulated jammer, our cross-layer data collection approach, and the preprocessing pipeline used to extract and aggregate features from native logs. Section 4 presents our experimental setup, evaluation results, and comparative analysis of various ML models. In Sect. 5, we discuss the implications of our findings, the limitations of the current approach, and potential directions for future work. Finally, Sect. 6 concludes the paper with a summary of our contributions and insights.

2   Related Work

This section reviews the landscape of jamming approaches in wireless communication networks, focusing on 5G environments. It also examines recent jamming analysis and detection techniques developed specifically for 5G systems.

2.1   Jamming Attacks in 5G Networks

Jamming attacks have been extensively examined in wireless networks because they can disrupt communication by injecting noise into the same frequencies used by legitimate devices. Exploiting the broadcast nature of wireless media, a jammer can overwhelm RF signals and effectively target the availability of network resources, creating serious security challenges. Such attacks pose risks across a variety of wireless applications, from the Internet of Things (IoT) and wireless sensor networks to vehicular communications and 5G infrastructure.

Jamming strategies can be categorized based on how they interfere with network operations, each requiring distinct detection and mitigation methods [23]. (i) Constant jammers emit signals at a single frequency to continuously block legitimate communication. This tactic is straightforward but power-intensive, making it more easily detected by monitoring uncommonly high interference levels. (ii) Deceptive jammers mimic legitimate network signals, causing nodes to process false information or remain silent; their resemblance to valid traffic makes detection challenging. (iii) Random jammers transmit interference at irregular intervals, improving stealthiness while complicating detection. Finally, (iv) reactive jammers [29] transmit only upon sensing network activity, aligning their interference with legitimate transmissions to save energy and avoid easy identification.

Researchers have investigated these attack types to assess their impact on network performance and to develop targeted countermeasures. Savadatti et al. [28] offered a comprehensive taxonomy of jamming attacks in 5G, classifying them by factors such as jammer characteristics, attack methodology, and security implications. Similarly, a thorough survey in [25] analyzed a wide spectrum of jamming threats and countermeasures in modern wireless systems, highlighting the unique vulnerabilities introduced by high-frequency bands, massive MIMO

(Multiple-Input Multiple-Output) antennas, and network slicing in 5G. Other works have focused on specific attack scenarios. Flores et al. [11] demonstrated that targeted uplink jamming can reduce the throughput of a specific UE by 100% if a jammer exploits resource allocation information. Salehi et al. [27] explored how deep reinforcement learning can enable adaptive jammers to disrupt resource blocks assigned to network slices, indicating that adversaries are increasingly sophisticated.

While existing research has extensively examined various jamming profiles, many studies focus on attacks like constant, deceptive, or reactive jamming. These often induce consistent and easily identifiable network impacts, enabling simpler detection via traditional approaches optimized for such straightforward interference patterns. However, reliance on these simpler jamming models, often evaluated within simulated environments, provides limited insight into the efficacy of detection techniques against more sophisticated, real-world threats (we further demonstrate this in Sect. 4.2). In practice, network environments are dynamic, and adversaries are likely to employ jammers that create more subtle and complex interference to evade detection. To address this critical gap, our work introduces and evaluates defenses against a power-modulated jammer. This type of jammer, by design, generates unpredictable interference effects through time-varying amplitude patterns. By incorporating this more realistic threat model within a physical testbed, SHIELD aims to develop and validate detection approaches that are robust against such complex, evasive jamming scenarios, thereby highlighting the necessity for evaluations that move beyond simplistic simulated attacks.

2.2   Anomaly and Attack Detection in 5G Networks

Given the growing scale and complexity of 5G, anomaly detection is integral to maintaining secure and reliable communications. Various ML approaches have been proposed to detect malicious activities in real-time. Lam et al. [19] introduced a Software-Defined Security (SDS) framework employing Convolutional Neural Network (CNN) to identify anomalous network traffic, achieving a high detection rate for both benign and malicious flows. Rahman et al. [26] discussed the use of diverse ML algorithms—including KNN and K-prototype—for anomaly detection in the inherently stochastic 5G environment. Their work showed that integrated or ensemble techniques can outperform single-method approaches.

Other research efforts have explored deep learning in depth. Doan et al. [8] applied deep neural networks to detect anomalies without degrading 5G performance. Issa et al. [15] demonstrated a deep learning solution for anomaly detection and traffic forecasting in 5G core networks. Meanwhile, Arjoune et al. [4] examined 5G NR vulnerabilities to jamming, offering insights into diverse jamming models and the effectiveness of existing defenses. Alenazi et al. [1] used a deep-hybrid learning method to identify wireless cyberattacks in 5G, surpassing traditional ML methods in accuracy.

Recent studies have applied specialized ML models to 5G jamming scenarios. Bousalem et al. [7] explored deep learning to detect jamming in vehicular-to-infrastructure (V2I) and vehicular-to-network (V2N) communications, emphasizing the importance of reliable data exchange. Hachimi et al. [13] presented a multi-stage ML-based intrusion detection system for 5G Cloud-RAN, focusing on jamming attack classification while minimizing false negatives. Jere et al. [16] combined supervised learning with Bayesian inference to detect jamming in 5G Non-Standalone (NSA), achieving high accuracy. Arjoune et al. [3] used Hoeffding Decision Trees for real-time jamming detection, enabling rapid training to mitigate attacks effectively. Asemian et al. [6] proposed a robust deep learning architecture for over-the-air detection of smart and barrage jamming, incorporating Discrete Wavelet Transform (DWT) for high-accuracy classification under various Signal-to-Jamming-and-Noise Ratio (SJNR) conditions.

Beyond algorithmic approaches, researchers have investigated the role of specific features and device-side data. Forssell [12] leveraged UE-measured Signal-to-Interference and Noise Ratio (SINR) for both detection and localization, revealing how signal quality metrics can serve as vital inputs for interference identification. Kryszkiewicz et al. [18] emphasized 5G NR Radio Resource Control (RRC) measurement reports to augment jamming detection, demonstrating the importance of device-native capabilities in crafting robust security solutions.

We conclude the following persisting gaps while ML and deep learning techniques have advanced anomaly and jamming detection in 5G: (1) Many studies [32] still focus on overly simplistic jamming profiles that favor detection. (2) Few efforts collect data simultaneously from both the UE and gNB perspectives, creating an incomplete view of network anomalies. (3) Some complex and high-accuracy solutions [20] rely on external hardware to capture physical-layer signals, restricting scalability to the fast-expanding 5G environment. (4) Many existing solutions rely heavily on simulations, raising concerns about their real-world applicability. These limitations highlight the need for a more scalable, holistic, cross-layer approach that leverages practical, system-wide data from both ends of the 5G communication link.

3   Proposed Framework: SHIELD

We propose SHIELD (Fig. 1) to address challenges that current detection methods fail to overcome: scalability and holisticness. We present this framework as an end-to-end solution, that incorporates wireless jamming modules and ML flows for assessing jamming interference on both the UE and gNB in a 5G environment. It includes (1) a controlled wireless jamming implementation that challenges existing defenses and serves as the target in the evaluation pipeline; (2) a cross-end data collection mechanism that merges UE logs and gNB traces to quantify system behavior under jamming; (3) a robust and efficient preprocessing methodology to extract rich contextual information from raw logs; and (4) a rigorous evaluation methodology that employs a primary dataset for training and initial validation, and a distinct, separately collected dataset—which we term the robustness test set—to measure ML model resilience against new, unseen operating conditions.

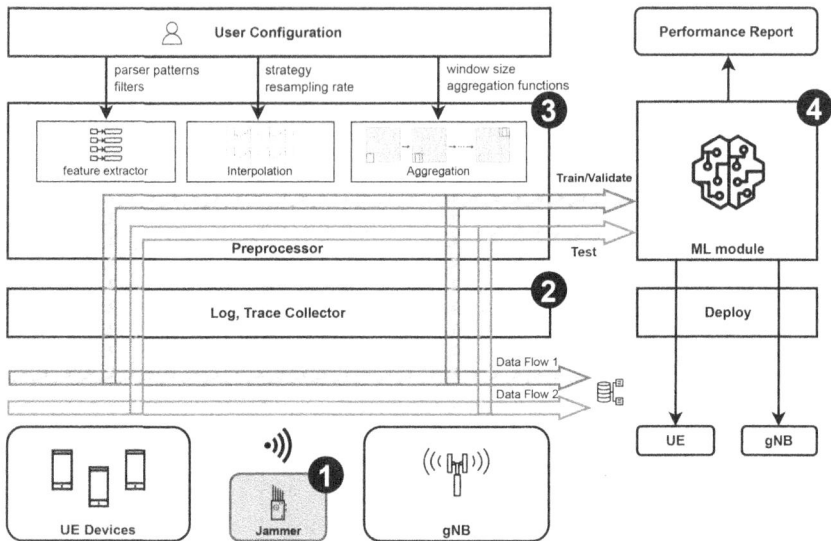

Fig. 1. Architecture of the SHIELD Framework. The diagram illustrates the end-to-end pipeline, including ❶ UE devices, gNB, and the power-modulated jammer testbed setup; ❷ the Log and Trace Collector for synchronized data acquisition from UE and gNB; ❸ the configurable Preprocessor with feature extraction, interpolation, and aggregation modules, which feed into the ML module using distinct data flows for training/validation (from the primary dataset) and robustness testing (from the separate test set); and ❹ the ML module for model deployment and performance reporting.

3.1 Controlled Jamming Interference

We assume an adversary can position a jamming signal emitter between the UE and gNB, use competitive signal power, and interfere with uplink and downlink control channels. Rather than severing connectivity—which would trigger obvious alarms—the adversary aims to degrade performance subtly and prolong interference without immediate detection.

A key element of this framework is a controllable jamming module to impact the system behavior. In this study, we implemented a power-modulated jammer that simulates intentional interference by periodically varying its amplitude. Unlike constant or reactive jammers, a power-modulated jammer leverages sinusoidal amplitude patterns to produce a variable-power noise profile, making its interference less predictable and more reflective of real-world adaptive jamming scenarios. Our experimental results demonstrate that this jamming technique compromises several existing data-driven detection approaches, highlighting the need for more robust detection methods, as discussed in the following Sect. 4.2.

We design the jammer to operate autonomously without external inputs. It generates the interference signal based on the following parameters:

– *Sampling Rate* r_{samp}: Controls the frequency resolution of the signal, enabling more precise manipulations of jamming characteristics as the rate increases.

– *Slot Length* L_{slot}: Defines the interval—expressed in samples—at which the amplitude pattern resets, adding structured periodicity that can mimic pulsed or intermittent jamming scenarios.

– *Amplitude Range* (min_A, max_A): Governs the power of the emitted signal, supporting a wide variety of jamming strengths.

– *Pattern Frequency* f_{pat}: Determines the rate of sinusoidal oscillations in amplitude, allowing the jammer to vary its power in real time and evade straightforward detection.

The jammer produces complex output signals using Algorithm 1. The jamming signal is structured around slots to generate bursts of interference. Within each slot, the amplitude resets based on an adjustable sinusoidal pattern through various pattern frequency f_{pat} and sampling rate r_{samp} values. This pattern design allows the jammer to fluctuate its power dynamically over time and challenge the static noise filter of wireless systems.

Algorithm 1. Power-Modulated Jamming.

Require: Sampling Rate r_{samp}, Slot Length L_{slot}, Amplitude Range (min_A, max_A),
  Pattern Frequency f_{pat}
Ensure: Jamming Signal J_{signal}
1: Initialize time index $n \leftarrow 0$
2: Compute amplitude modulation factor: $\mathcal{A}_m \leftarrow \frac{1}{2}(max_A - min_A)$
3: **while** Jamming is active **do**
4:   Compute amplitude modulation for current time step:

$$\mathcal{A}(n) \leftarrow min_A + \mathcal{A}_m \times \left(1 + \sin \left(\frac{2\pi n f_{pat}}{r_{samp}} \right) \right)$$

5:   Generate jamming signal:

$$J_{signal}(n) \leftarrow \mathcal{A}(n) \times Noise(n)$$

6:   Transmit $J_{signal}(n)$
7:   Increment time index: $n \leftarrow n + 1$
8:   **if** $n \bmod L_{slot} = 0$ **then**
9:     Reset amplitude pattern for the next slot
10:   **end if**
11: **end while**

3.2   Data Source and Context

Recent work [12] suggests that rich metrics and telemetry embedded in system logs, generated by end devices during regular network operations, can reveal signatures of jamming attacks. In our proposed approach, the detection system is deployed directly on the UE or gNB device itself, utilizing native logs and traces to capture how the system behaves under jamming interference. This choice of deployment allows the system to access data directly from the device, which is readily available and avoids the need for additional probing tools or specialized hardware. Specifically, by mining these native logs, we can enable ML-based jamming detection without requiring extra infrastructure.

This deployment strategy offers several advantages: (1) Improved data accessibility: By collecting device-level metrics that are available by default, we eliminate the need for additional probes or external hardware, making the system self-contained and easier to deploy in a large-scale, distributed manner. (2) Multi-layer view of the network: The collected data spans both Media Access Control (MAC)-related metrics (e.g., signal quality, Modulation and Coding Scheme index) and system-level insights (e.g., resource usage reports, scheduling decisions). This cross-layer data provides a comprehensive view of network behavior under jamming interference, strengthening detection accuracy. (3) End-to-end observation: By monitoring both device endpoints (the UE and gNB), we gain a holistic view of how jamming impacts normal network operations. This end-to-end perspective enhances the detection of subtle anomalies in the communication process. (4) Real-time detection capability: Since the detection system relies solely on existing device logs, it can function autonomously, enabling online jamming detection. This makes it feasible to run self-contained algorithms (such as TinyML [9]) on the UE and gNB, which simplifies deployment across multiple devices and facilitates collaborative jamming detection.

We adopt different traffic profiles while capturing this data. First, we use the `iperf3` utility at configurable rates to create controlled, replicable traffic that simulates common use cases (e.g., streaming video). This profile provides stable performance under standard conditions and minimizes non-jamming factors, which helps isolate the jammer's impact. Second, we run actual real-world applications such as online gaming or video streaming on the UE to reflect realistic 5G usage. This additional context broadens our analysis and ensures that the dataset covers diverse traffic patterns beyond the scripted tests.

3.3   Preprocessing Methodology

A robust preprocessing strategy is essential for any ML pipeline. Our contribution includes a methodology specifically tailored for 5G logs and traces that enriches raw information to ensure reliable jamming detection under diverse real-world conditions. It contains steps that extract informative features, bridge gaps in temporal data, and construct representative aggregated samples.

Feature Extraction. We start by parsing text-based log messages, which often arrive in key-value structures with embedded tags. We apply adaptable regular expression patterns to detect explicit measurements (e.g., signal strength and quality) in log messages. We also include contextual system-level signals derived from logging behavior (e.g., the frequency of repeated errors, the time gaps between critical events).

Extracted features must show sufficient variation and relevance. We discard those that stay constant, appear too rarely, or lack meaningful insights for classification. We can further customize parsing rules to match the log formats of each manufacturer. A consistent feature mapping across heterogeneous devices ensures that our pipeline remains portable and scales to multi-vendor deployments.

Interpolation. Two significant challenges arise when converting features into unified time-series data. (1) Different log types have unique logging rates, leading to uneven timestamps or long gaps for certain metrics. As illustrated in Fig. 2, Reference Signal Receiving Power (RSRP) measurements in Android logs appear irregularly, causing missing entries in our consolidated dataset. (2) Some traces include invalid entries due to unpredictable hardware malfunctions that are unrelated to jamming interference.

We address these issues with an interpolation-based data cleaning process. We focus on two approaches: (i) forward filling, which propagates the last valid reading until a new data point is observed, and (ii) polynomial interpolation (in particular, the Lagrange method), which fits an n-th degree polynomial to neighboring samples for a smoother transition. Forward filling works best for categorical features (e.g., network mode or carrier band) that do not vary continuously. Polynomial fitting is more effective for quantitative metrics to produce smoother time-series data (as shown in Fig. 2). By filling these gaps consistently, we ensure resilience of our subsequent ML models to such randomness.

Aggregation. Jamming detection often benefits from capturing temporal patterns, as a single instant of data might not reflect deeper trends. Studies such as [16] found that sequential time-series based Recurrent Neural Network (RNN)-type models (e.g., Long Short-Term Memory (LSTM) or Gated Recurrent Unit (GRU)) outperform purely instantaneous classifiers in jamming detection, but those models come with higher computational costs. To achieve a balance between complexity and accuracy, we use a sliding window aggregation stack. The window buffer size can be tuned to meet different objectives: a larger window captures extended temporal trends but risks slower detection, while a smaller window provides faster reactions and higher sensitivity but less contextual depth.

Within each window, we compute statistical metrics—mean, standard deviation, median, amplitude, skewness, and kurtosis—across the chosen features. These metrics highlight persistant patterns rather than instantaneous values. This design helps filter out noise from environmental factors and focus on identifying meaningful interference patterns.

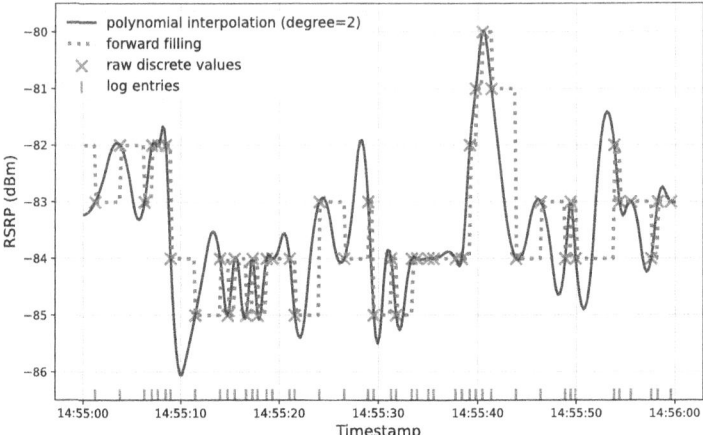

Fig. 2. Comparison of interpolation techniques for handling missing/invalid data in log entries. The plot shows raw discrete RSRP measurements from Android logs alongside the output of forward filling and polynomial interpolation (degree = 2) over a one-minute interval, illustrating how interpolation creates a continuous time-series.

3.4   ML Assessment on Robustness

An often-overlooked aspect in anomaly detection is ensuring resilience when real-world conditions deviate from those in lab experiments. Many studies apply a train-test split to a single, homogeneously collected dataset. This often results in overlapping feature distributions between training and testing subsets, and leads to overly optimistic performance estimates (e.g., test accuracies nearing 99%) that may not hold when models are deployed in production environments. Such approaches often lack a clear justification for the distinction between their training and test sets, potentially risking data leakage and yielding models that are not robust to real-world variability.

To address this gap and ensure a more rigorous assessment of generalization, SHIELD employs a two-data-collection strategy. First, we collected a primary dataset under a consistent set of experimental conditions. This primary dataset is partitioned into a training set and a validation set for hyperparameter tuning. Second, we meticulously collected an entirely separate dataset, termed the robustness test set, under demonstrably different network conditions (e.g., varying UE-gNB distances, presence of obstacles, and operating temperature). As we demonstrate with Kernel Density Estimation (KDE) plots in Sect. 4.1 (Fig. 4), the feature distributions in this robustness test set differ significantly from those in the primary dataset, confirming it represents a genuinely unseen and more challenging evaluation scenario.

4   Experiment and Results

We evaluated our proposed framework in a quasi-realistic 5G testbed, comprising an open-source 5G core (Open5GS [24]) and a software-emulated RAN running on the srsRAN [30] stack, and a bladeRF 2.0 micro SDR. A OnePlus Nord 2T 5G device served as the UE and was situated close to the gNB within a range from 10 to 15 m. Its logs were collected via Android Debug Bridge (ADB). To introduce interference, we employed a power-modulated jammer with 1 m close to the gNB—running on another bladeRF 2.0 micro and transmitting at power levels equivalent to the gNB—that varied its transmit amplitude over time. This setup was hosted in an nonanechoic indoor environment.

To simulate traffic, we ran iperf3 in UDP mode at 10 Mbps to approximate scenarios such as video streaming or other bandwidth-intensive applications. We also collected subsets in which the UE streamed live Youtube content to incorporate a real-world scenario. Figure 3 illustrates key iperf3 performance metrics—bandwidth, jitter, and packet loss—captured over time. Around the midpoint of the measurement period, when the jammer becomes active, the bandwidth begins to decrease, while both jitter and packet loss exhibit noticeable increases. These trends clearly demonstrate the interference introduced by the power-modulated attack.

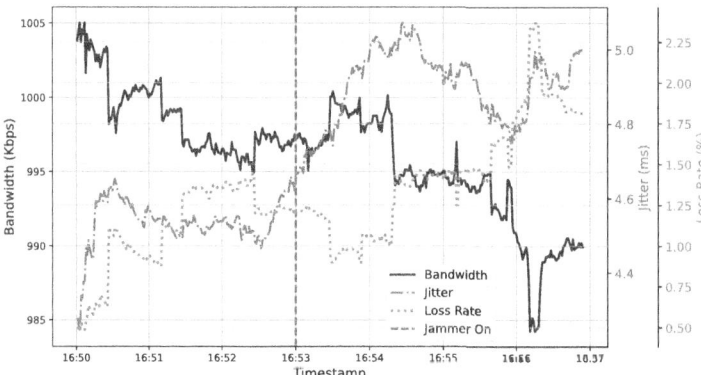

Fig. 3. Impact of Power-Modulated Jamming on Key Performance Indicators (KPIs) from iperf3. The graph shows bandwidth, jitter, and packet loss rate over time, with the vertical dashed line indicating the activation of the power-modulated jammer, demonstrating its negative effect on network performance.

4.1   Data Description

We collected logs and traces from both the UE and gNB while toggling between normal operation and jamming interference. We recorded timestamps at the start and end of jamming interference to facilitate accurate dataset labeling, 0 (normal) or 1 (jammed). For class balancing, we enabled the jammer halfway through each session, allowing the normal and jammed segments to be comparable in duration.

On the UE side, we collected timestamped log entries from the radio buffer. These raw logs contained significant redundancy and irrelevant information related to jamming. To enhance relevance, we applied filters that specifically focused on signal strength reports—RSRP, Reference Signal Received Quality (RSRQ), and SINR—which previous studies [12,18] have demonstrated to be effective for jamming detection. Additionally, we selected AT command records associated with modem operations, including ERFTX for setting transmit power, ECSQ for requesting signal quality, and ETHERMAL for reading thermal reports.

The gNB traces contained rich information including signal power, throughput, and packet transmission metrics (e.g., Physical Uplink Shared Channel (PUSCH), Physical Uplink Control Channel (PUCCH), bit rates, packet success/failure counts). We initially referenced [33], which offers a comprehensive set of features for analyzing network performance in both normal and attack scenarios. However, its complexity and wide range of features introduced excessive noise, obscuring the effects of specific attack patterns. To enhance cross-scenario performance, we refined our dataset by selecting a subset of features most relevant to jamming detection. Specifically, we removed features such as mean values that are susceptible to fluctuations from unexpected network variations while preserving informative indicators that effectively capture jamming-induced anomalies.

As we described in previous Sect. 3.3, two primary data challenges exist: irregular time intervals in the UE logs and a high volume of missing values in the gNB logs. To address these issues, we first pivoted the data and then applied Lagrange polynomial interpolation, resampling each dataset to a uniform 200 ms interval. Next, we used sliding-window aggregation (e.g., mean, standard deviation) to capture contextual trends indicative of jamming events. After discarding uninformative features, we obtained two balanced datasets for binary classification:

–UE Dataset: 6,259 samples (3,202 normal, 3,057 jammed) and 72 features.
–gNB Dataset: 6,958 samples (3,491 normal, 3,467 jammed) and 66 features.

Finally, we analyzed the feature distributions within our primary dataset and our separate test set using KDE. This analysis aimed to assess how individual features and feature pairs differentiate between normal and jammed conditions, and critically, to confirm the distributional differences between the two sets. We selected the top four features from each data source (UE and gNB) based on feature importance rankings from our optimal RForest model. As shown in Fig. 4a and 4c for the training portion of our primary dataset, these selected features or feature pairs display significant shifts under interference, indicating the jammer's distinct impact on system behavior within that initial collection context. More importantly, Fig. 4b and 4d illustrates the KDE plots for these same features from our test set. A comparison reveals notably different underly-

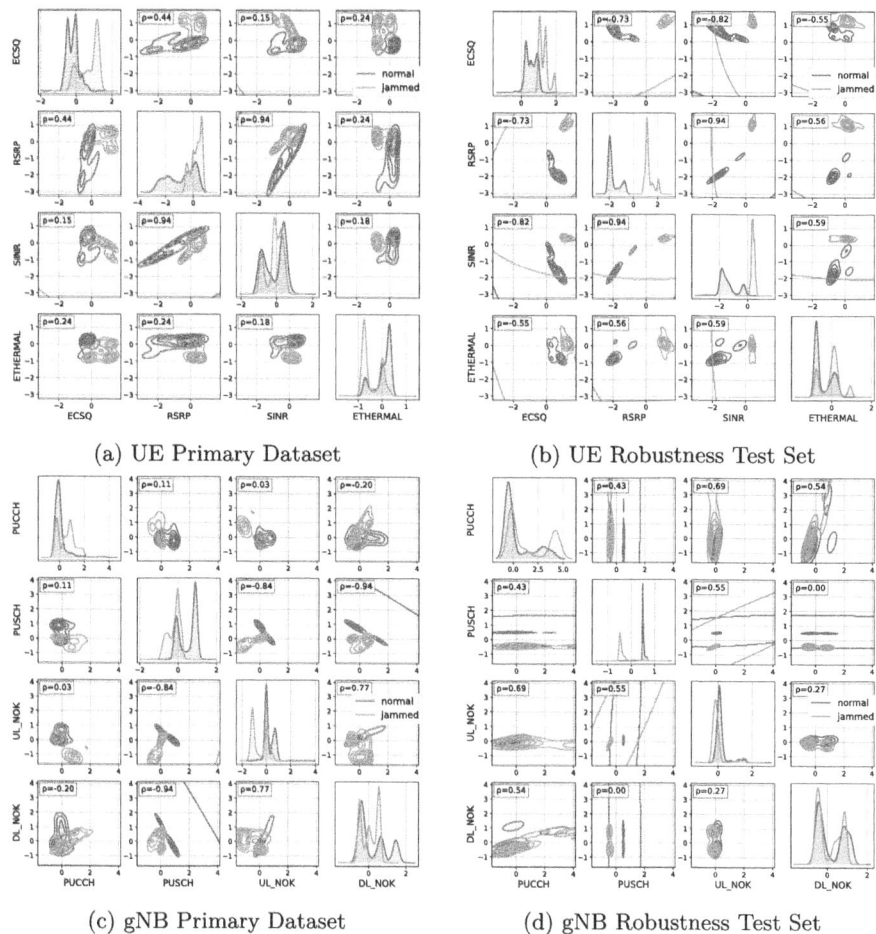

(a) UE Primary Dataset

(b) UE Robustness Test Set

(c) gNB Primary Dataset

(d) gNB Robustness Test Set

Fig. 4. KDE analysis comparing the distributions of top-ranking features. Subfigures (a) and (c) display feature distributions from our primary dataset for UE and gNB respectively. Subfigures (b) and (d) display distributions of the same features from the separate robustness test set for UE and gNB respectively. The distinct distributions in (b) and (d) compared to (a) and (c) highlight the different operating conditions, crucial for evaluating model generalization.

ing distributions for these features. Consequently, evaluating models against this separate dataset provides a more rigorous test of cross-scenario generalization.

4.2   Benchmarking and Limitations of Existing Detection Methods

To benchmark SHIELD and illustrate the challenges posed by our power-modulated jamming scenario, we evaluated several jamming detection methods from existing literature [5,10,14,31,32]. These particular works were selected

for multiple reasons: firstly, they represent common and lightweight ML classifiers frequently adopted for jamming or anomaly detection in wireless networks;
secondly, they utilize input features similar to those considered foundational in
many detection systems, such as packet delivery ratio (PDR), bad packet ratio
(BPR), and basic signal strength metrics (Received Signal Strength Indicator
(RSSI), Signal-to-Noise Ratio (SNR)); and thirdly, assessing their performance
with their originally proposed feature sets and without our proposed preprocessing pipeline allows for a clearer understanding of their baseline resilience. Table 1
summarizes these approaches, their reported accuracies in prior work, and their
performance on our primary dataset's validation split and subsequently on our
separate robustness test set. Our primary goal in this comparative analysis was
to highlight the performance gap that can emerge when methods validated in
controlled or simulated environments confront more complex, real-world interference patterns. Consistent with SHIELD's design philosophy to avoid deployment
overhead, we excluded approaches requiring specialized hardware or external IQ
sampling, such as RF fingerprinting [20].

Table 1. Comparative analysis of state-of-the-art jamming detection methods.
Reported accuracies in the original studies vs. performance on our validation split
and our separate robustness test set.

Method	Input Features	Reported Accuracy	Validation Accuracy	Test Accuracy
SVM	PDR, Packet Counts	95% [32], 98.55% [31]	73.48%	36.49%
RForest	PDR, BPR, RSSI	81% [10], 96.6% [5], 98.61% [31]	66.67%	53.65%
Hybrid-Tree	PDR, BPR, SNR, RSSI	99.5% [14]	76.51%	70.91%

–SVM-based Approach: Abhishek et al. [32] proposed a low-power SVM classifier operating on cumulative PDR and counts of successful or erroneous packets
(Packet Counts) over 20-second intervals. Their ns-3 simulation on urban mobility scenario reported over 95% detection accuracy, even when jamming affected
only 20%–40% of transmission time. When we evaluated this approach on our
dataset, the accuracy dropped to 73.48%, with a notable imbalance between
precision (100%) and recall (48.53%). This indicates a strong bias toward predicting attacks and overlooking normal traffic. When evaluated on our test set,
the accuracy declined drastically to 36%, suggesting the SVM was unable to
generalize beyond the conditions it saw in training.

–RForest Methods: Multiple works in the literature [5,10,31] adopt RForest
classifiers using metrics such as PDR, BPR, RSSI, and SNR. While some papers
briefly mention extended features, they often rely on instantaneous values rather
than time-cumulative or aggregated metrics. Reported accuracies ranged from
81% to nearly 98% in simulations using ns-3 [10] or Matlab [31]. However, our
experiments under realistic conditions resulted in 66.67% validation accuracy,
which dropped to 53.65% on the test scenario. This shortfall highlights the challenge of detecting subtle, power-modulated attacks that differ from the jamming
profiles in simulation.

–Hybrid-Tree Classifier: Hone et al. [14] designed a hybrid tree-based design that combines decision trees with isolation trees to better detect unseen anomalies. This method featured fine-grained isolation trees on decision tree leafs to further classify false-negative entries. They used data from C-band modems and jamming source from an Agilent E4438C signal generator, achieving near-perfect 99.5% detection in controlled tests. They further tested robustness using the open WSN-DS dataset and reached 83.9% accuracy. However, their accuracy dropped to 76.51% on our validation split and 70.91% on the test scenario. Although this approach was more robust than other classifiers, it still fell substantially short of its originally reported performance.

4.3   Evaluation of the Proposed ML Pipeline

The results from previous subsection suggest an insufficient performance of existing jamming detection. To evaluate our proposed preprocessing pipeline, we incorporated four ML classifiers that are common, computationally efficient and scalable even to edge devices—SVM, KNN, GB, and RForest—to demonstrate the viability of data-driven jamming detection.

We trained four classifiers using grid search and 10-fold cross-validation to tune hyperparameters. Table 2 summarizes these optimal configurations and the resulting F1-scores across both the UE and gNB datasets. For each pipeline, we employed different scoring strategies, as illustrated in Fig. 5a and 5c. Overall, all four models converged successfully and reached roughly 90% validation accuracy, though their performance varied between the UE and gNB datasets. The gNB dataset appeared more sensitive to jamming signals, enabling better detection, while the UE dataset introduced slightly more noise. Notably, SVM tended to excel at recall, minimizing false negatives where jammed states are flagged as normal.

To rigorously assess generalization to new conditions, we further tested the models on our separate robustness test set. As demonstrated by the KDE plots in Fig. 4b and 4d, the feature distributions in this set exhibit significant shifts compared to the primary training data. Consequently, when evaluated on this genuinely unseen data, the performance of our trained models typically dropped relative to their scores on the validation split. The results from Fig. 5b and 5d highlights the challenge of maintaining detection accuracy outside the initial operating conditions:

–SVM showed substantial performance declines under unfamiliar conditions but maintained strong recall score, suggesting it was prone to predict anomalies at the risk of false positives. The linear kernel's decision boundaries struggled to capture the intersection of the two classes, limiting its generalization. Nonetheless, this propensity to over-predict anomalies implies that its negative predictions can be quite reliable, making SVM a competitive candidate for normal-case prediction in a model-stacking framework.

–KNN performed reliably in controlled settings and achieved reasonable classification accuracy. However, its performance dropped significantly when faced with varying conditions, reflecting the limitations of a distance-based approach

that may be too simplistic for handling complex, context-dependent jamming patterns. Despite these shortcomings, KNN remains attractive for certain applications because of its low computational cost and ease of retraining.

–*GB and RForest* consistently demonstrated strong performance across both UE and gNB datasets, and sometimes even improved on the test set. GB favored higher precision over recall, occasionally overlooking some jamming events while reducing false positives. In contrast, RForest struck a more even balance among these metrics. Both models appeared less vulnerable to environmental changes and maintained robust performance in sophisticated operational contexts.

In general, the experimental results confirm that all these models achieved reasonable detection performance, revealing specific strengths and shortcomings of each model. Meanwhile, tree-based methods (GB and RForest) delivered outstanding robustness to evolving conditions.

5   Discussion

Our evaluation demonstrates that a carefully designed data pipeline—one that synchronizes UE logs and gNB traces, applies interpolation and aggregation, and utilizes robust ML algorithms—can effectively detect jamming in quasi-realistic

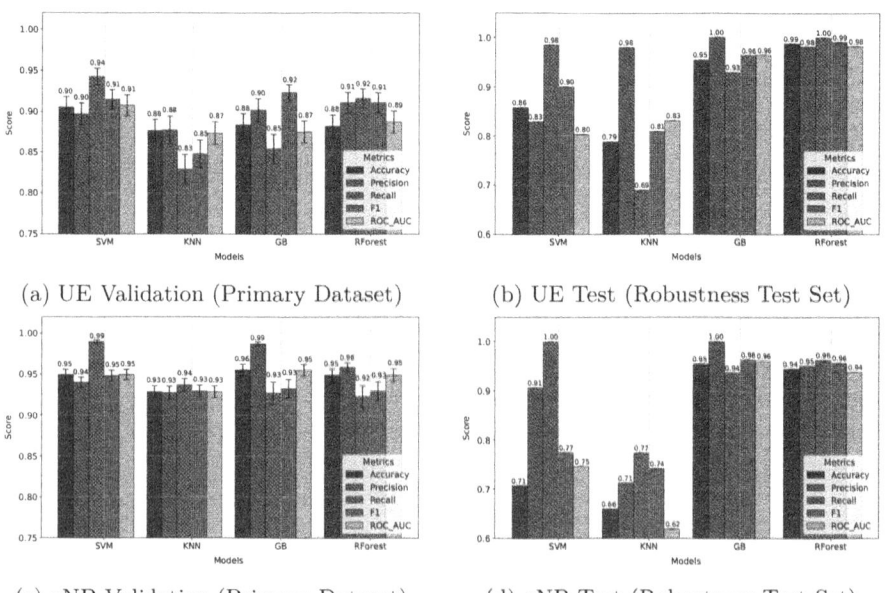

(a) UE Validation (Primary Dataset)   (b) UE Test (Robustness Test Set)

(c) gNB Validation (Primary Dataset)   (d) gNB Test (Robustness Test Set)

Fig. 5. Accuracy, precision, f1, recall and roc-auc scores for each model. Subfigures (a) and (c) show performance on the validation split of the primary UE and gNB datasets, respectively. Subfigures (b) and (d) show performance on the separate robustness test set for UE and gNB data, respectively, to ensure robustness assessment against unseen conditions.

Table 2. Hyperparameter tuning search space and optimal configurations for each ML model. The optimal settings, determined by maximizing the F1-score during 10-fold cross-validation on the training split of the primary UE (*) and gNB (+) datasets, are presented.

Model	Hyperparameter	Values	F1-score (UE)	F1-score (gNB)
SVM	C	**0.01***+, 0.1, 10, 100	0.9147	0.9479
	kernel	**linear***+, rbf, poly, sigmoid		
	gamma	scale, auto, 0.01, 0.1, 0.5, **1***+		
	degree	2, 3, 4, **5***+		
	tol	1e−5, **1e−4***+, 1e−3		
k-NN	n_neighbors	3, **5**+, 7, **9***, 11, 15, 20	0.8475	0.9291
	weights	**uniform***, **distance**+		
	algorithm	**auto**+, **ball_tree***, kd_tree, brute		
	p	**1***+, 1.5, 2		
GB	n_estimators	**50***, 100, 200, **300**+, 500	0.9229	0.9326
	learning_rate	1e−3, 0.01, 0.05, **0.1**+, **0.2***, 0.3		
	min_samples_split	**2***, 5, **10**+		
	min_samples_leaf	1, **2***+, 5, 10		
	max_depth	**3**+, **5***, 10, 20		
	max_features	**sqrt***, **log2**+, None		
	subsample	**0.5***+, 0.7, 1.0		
RForest	n_estimators	50, 100, **200***, 300, **500**+	0.9107	0.9291
	min_samples_split	**2**+, **5***, 10		
	min_samples_leaf	1, **2**+, **5***, 10		
	max_depth	10, **20***, 50, **None**+		
	max_features	**sqrt**+, **log2***, None		
	bootstrap	**True***+, False		

5G deployments. Previous research proposed similar detection approach basing on same algorithms. Our findings show that without a holistic pre-analysis of system metrics, these established models (e.g., SVM, RForest) cannot consistently detect a power-modulated jammer. By contrast, our pipeline, which leverages native logs from both ends of the link and employs tailored preprocessing, bridges this gap and maintains reasonable performance across different environmental scenarios. These results suggest that even basic ML algorithms gain considerable robustness when trained with a well-designed feature set and cleaning process. Moreover, many prior works [9] have discussed the feasibility of deploying such low-cost algorithms on edge devices (e.g., TinyML), enabling real-time, on-device predictions consistent with the broader trend toward online detection.

In addition, our cross-scenario evaluation demonstrates that on-device logs inherently provide rich information for jamming detection at scale. This scalability aspect addresses a known drawback in prior works, where solutions either hinge on external hardware or rely on limited simulation environments. Admittedly, RF-based jamming analysis—such as building RF fingerprinting [20]—can provide more precise interference profiles. However, these approaches require specialized probes and produce vast amounts of raw IQ data, which can be impractical and costly to manage over large or heterogeneous networks. In contrast, our native log-based strategy delivers a more affordable, easily deployable option. While we have not benchmarked our solution directly against hardware-based probes, our results confirm that our proposed pipeline can provide high and robust detection rates. Therefore, we believe the on-device anomaly detection is the future trend of security solutions, especially in expanding 5G and IoT ecosystems where budget constraints and complexity often limit hardware installation.

5.1   Limitations and Future Directions

Limited Scope of Diversity and Single Jamming Modality. While the SHIELD framework itself aims to be general, the current evaluation remains narrow. Although we presented a quasi-realistic 5G environment to validate our framework, the testbed relied heavily on one power-modulated jamming profile, one specific SDR platform, a single phone model, and a single site setup.

We justified by theory and comparative analysis that power-modulated jammers, which subtly degrade performance over time, can be more challenging to detect than simpler constant or reactive jammers. Successfully detecting such a stealthy attack illustrates our framework's potential. Moreover, because our data pipeline does not rely on any unique jammer characteristics, it can adapt to other jamming profiles with minimal effort.

Future work should incorporate more diverse hardware (including different chipset vendors or OS variants, and multiple SDR/RF front ends), various sophisticated deployment scenarios, and more complex jamming strategies-ranging from reactive and random attacks to AI-aided adaptive interference. Broader coverage of devices, network conditions, and interference patterns would validate the framework's generalizability and ensure that it remains robust under heterogeneous 5G deployments.

Fine-Grained Detection and Mitigation. Our present approach primarily identifies whether a jamming attack is active, without distinguishing its intensity or specific interference patterns. More detailed detection strategies could provide insights such as jammer power levels or temporal patterns of interference. This information would be especially valuable for refined countermeasures, such as altering scheduling or power-control parameters on the gNB side. Future work could integrate jamming localization or self-healing network responses to maximize resilience.

Advanced Techniques on Jamming Analysis. In this work, we focused on four relatively simple ML algorithms, mainly to illustrate how systematic feature engineering and aggregation can boost performance. However, jamming analysis extends well beyond these methods. Model stacking, adaptive or online learning, and more extensive feature engineering could further advance detection reliability and resilience against evolving jamming threats.

Large-scale data collection represents a major availability concern for researchers in the wireless security domain. Running real-device experiments, especially in industrial settings, demands substantial resources, and many devices impose strict constraints on data capture rates (e.g., Teltonika RUTX50 5G Router yields stably one log entry every five seconds). This limitation reduces the amount of high-resolution data, complicating efforts to train complex models such as deep neural networks. Efficient data augmentation techniques offer an appealing solution to address data scarcity. Recent studies [2,17] highlight how generative models can extend existing datasets and improve anomaly detection generalizability.

Opportunities also remain for exploring advanced detection (e.g. RNN [16]) and mitigation strategies that incorporate richer contextual information. Rather than deploying separate models on individual network components, future efforts can aggregate predictions from multiple entities to improve detection reliability. Further mitigation options, such as pinpointing the jammer's location, could be integrated into post-detection actions to increase overall network resilience. Reinforcement learning techniques, similar to those proposed by Mowla et al. [22], could dynamically adjust responses based on ongoing detection results, further strengthening the system against evolving jamming threats.

6   Conclusion

This work introduced SHIELD, an end-to-end framework designed to evaluate jamming interference in 5G networks using native logs from both the UE and the gNB. Departing from hardware-heavy solutions that rely on specialized RF probes, SHIELD harnessed existing device-side resources, which offered a scalable, cost-effective, and versatile alternative for real-world deployment. Through synchronized data collection, advanced preprocessing (e.g., interpolation, aggregation), and robust ML assessment pipeline, we demonstrated reliable jamming detection across diverse conditions.

By examining both normal and power-modulated jamming scenarios, we highlighted the importance of holistic, cross-layer data and rigorous validation across varying network environments. Our results showed that different ML models excelled in distinct ways, emphasizing how careful feature engineering and pipeline design could significantly enhance detection accuracy and system resilience. Additionally, we underscored how real-time log-based techniques could reduce overhead and speed up deployment timelines relative to more equipment-intensive detection schemes.

Looking ahead, we plan to extend SHIELD's capabilities through online learning, model stacking, and transfer learning methods. These enhancements can further adapt detection pipelines to shifting traffic profiles and evolving jamming strategies in an ever-changing 5G landscape. Another priority involves integrating SHIELD into existing network management and security systems, aiming for unified, real-time defenses that can proactively respond to suspicious patterns. By uniting lightweight, log-centered data collection with advanced analytics, SHIELD seeks to raise security standards and build greater resilience against jamming threats in 5G and next-generation wireless networks.

Acknowledgments. This research was made possible with support from the Horizon Europe research and innovation program of the European Union, under grant agreement number 101092912 (project MLSysOps).

References

1. Alenazi, B., Idris, H.E.: Wireless intrusion and attack detection for 5G networks using deep learning techniques. Int. J. Adv. Comput. Sci. Appl. **12**(7) (2021)
2. Alhoraibi, L., Alghazzawi, D., Alhebshi, R.: Generative adversarial network-based data augmentation for enhancing wireless physical layer authentication. Sensors **24**(2) (2024). https://doi.org/10.3390/s24020641. https://www.mdpi.com/1424-8220/24/2/641
3. Arjoune, Y., Faruque, S.: Real-time machine learning based on Hoeffding decision trees for jamming detection in 5G new radio. In: 2020 IEEE International Conference on Big Data (Big Data), pp. 4988–4997. IEEE (2020)
4. Arjoune, Y., Faruque, S.: Smart jamming attacks in 5G new radio: a review. In: 2020 10th Annual Computing and Communication Workshop and Conference (CCWC), pp. 1010–1015. IEEE (2020)
5. Arjoune, Y., Salahdine, F., Islam, M.S., Ghribi, E., Kaabouch, N.: A novel jamming attacks detection approach based on machine learning for wireless communication. In: 2020 International Conference on Information Networking (ICOIN), pp. 459–464 (2020). https://doi.org/10.1109/ICOIN48656.2020.9016462
6. Asemian, G., Amini, M., Kantarci, B., Erol-Kantarci, M.: Over-the-air double-threshold deep learner for jamming detection in 5G RF domain. arXiv preprint arXiv:2403.02645 (2024)
7. Bousalem, B., Silva, V.F., Boualouache, A., Langar, R., Cherrier, S.: Deep learning-based smart radio jamming attacks detection on 5G V2I/V2N communications. In: GLOBECOM 2023-2023 IEEE Global Communications Conference, pp. 7139–7144. IEEE (2023)
8. Doan, M., Zhang, Z.: Deep learning in 5G wireless networks-anomaly detections. In: 2020 29th Wireless and Optical Communications Conference (WOCC), pp. 1–6. IEEE (2020)
9. Dutta, D.L., Bharali, S.: TinyML meets IoT: a comprehensive survey. Internet Things **16**, 100461 (2021). https://doi.org/10.1016/j.iot.2021.100461. https://www.sciencedirect.com/science/article/pii/S2542660521001025
10. Feng, Z., Hua, C.: Machine learning-based RF jamming detection in wireless networks. In: 2018 Third International Conference on Security of Smart Cities, Industrial Control System and Communications (SSIC), pp. 1–6 (2018). https://doi.org/10.1109/SSIC.2018.8556709
11. Flores, M.E., Poisson, D.D., Stevens, C.J., Nieves, A.V., Wyglinski, A.M.: Implementation and evaluation of a smart uplink jamming attack in a public 5G network. IEEE Access (2023)

12. Forssell, H., Mungara, R.K., Ferrante, G.C., Tullberg, H.: UE-assisted jamming detection in 5G NR. In: ICC 2023 - IEEE International Conference on Communications, pp. 5216–5220 (2023). https://doi.org/10.1109/ICC45041.2023.10279513

13. Hachimi, M., Kaddoum, G., Gagnon, G., Illy, P.: Multi-stage jamming attacks detection using deep learning combined with kernelized support vector machine in 5G cloud radio access networks. In: 2020 International Symposium on Networks, Computers and Communications (ISNCC), pp. 1–5. IEEE (2020)

14. Hong, S., Kim, K., Lee, S.H.: A hybrid jamming detection algorithm for wireless communications: simultaneous classification of known attacks and detection of unknown attacks. IEEE Commun. Lett. **27**(7), 1769–1773 (2023). https://doi.org/10.1109/LCOMM.2023.3275694

15. Issa, A., Kandil, N., Hakem, N.: Deep learning-based anomaly detection for 5G core mobility management. In: 2023 Fifth International Conference on Advances in Computational Tools for Engineering Applications (ACTEA), pp. 25–29. IEEE (2023)

16. Jere, S., Wang, Y., Aryendu, I., Dayekh, S., Liu, L.: Bayesian inference-assisted machine learning for near real-time jamming detection and classification in 5G new radio (NR). IEEE Trans. Wirel. Commun. (2023)

17. Jiang, X., et al.: NetDiffusion: network data augmentation through protocol-constrained traffic generation. Proc. ACM Meas. Anal. Comput. Syst. **8**(1) (2024). https://doi.org/10.1145/3639037

18. Kryszkiewicz, P., Hoffmann, M.: Open ran for detection of a jamming attack in a 5G network. In: 2023 IEEE 97th Vehicular Technology Conference (VTC2023-Spring), pp. 1–2 (2023). https://doi.org/10.1109/VTC2023-Spring57618.2023.10201067

19. Lam, J., Abbas, R.: Machine learning based anomaly detection for 5G networks. arXiv preprint arXiv:2003.03474 (2020)

20. Li, Y., et al.: Jamming detection and classification in OFDM-based UAVs via feature- and spectrogram-tailored machine learning. IEEE Access **10**, 16859–16870 (2022). https://doi.org/10.1109/ACCESS.2022.3150020

21. Ma, J., Li, Q., Liu, Z., Du, L., Chen, H., Ansari, N.: Jamming modulation: an active anti-jamming scheme. IEEE Trans. Wireless Commun. **22**(4), 2730–2743 (2023). https://doi.org/10.1109/TWC.2022.3213572

22. Mowla, N.I., Tran, N.H., Doh, I., Chae, K.: AFRL: adaptive federated reinforcement learning for intelligent jamming defense in FANET. J. Commun. Netw. **22**(3), 244–258 (2020). https://doi.org/10.1109/JCN.2020.000015

23. Mpitziopoulos, A., Gavalas, D., Konstantopoulos, C., Pantziou, G.: A survey on jamming attacks and countermeasures in WSNs. IEEE Commun. Surv. Tutor. **11**(4), 42–56 (2009)

24. Open5GS: Open5GS. https://open5gs.org/

25. Pirayesh, H., Zeng, H.: Jamming attacks and anti-jamming strategies in wireless networks: a comprehensive survey. IEEE Commun. Surv. Tutor. **24**(2), 767–809 (2022)

26. Rahman, A.U., et al.: Network anomaly detection in 5G networks. Math. Model. Eng. Probl. **9**(2) (2022)

27. Salehi, S., et al.: Smart jamming attack and mitigation on deep transfer reinforcement learning enabled resource allocation for network slicing. IEEE Trans. Mach. Learn. Commun. Netw. (2024)

28. Savadatti, S., Kuldeep Dhariwal, S., Krishnamoorthy, S., Delhibabu, R.: An extensive classification of 5G network jamming attacks. Secur. Commun. Netw. **2024**(1), 2883082 (2024)

29. Schulz, M., Gringoli, F., Steinmetzer, D., Koch, M., Hollick, M.: Massive reactive smartphone-based jamming using arbitrary waveforms and adaptive power control. In: Proceedings of the 10th ACM Conference on Security and Privacy in Wireless and Mobile Networks, WiSec 2017, pp. 111–121. Association for Computing Machinery, New York (2017). https://doi.org/10.1145/3098243.3098253
30. srsRAN: srsRAN. https://github.com/srsran
31. Upadhyaya, B., Sun, S., Sikdar, B.: Machine learning-based jamming detection in wireless IoT networks. In: 2019 IEEE VTS Asia Pacific Wireless Communications Symposium (APWCS), pp. 1–5 (2019). https://doi.org/10.1109/VTS-APWCS.2019.8851633
32. Venkata Abhishek, N., Gurusamy, M.: JaDe: low power jamming detection using machine learning in vehicular networks. IEEE Wirel. Commun. Lett. **10**(10), 2210–2214 (2021). https://doi.org/10.1109/LWC.2021.3097162
33. Xavier, B.M., Dzaferagic, M., Martinello, M., Ruffini, M.: Performance measurement dataset for open ran with user mobility and security threats. Comput. Netw. **253**, 110710 (2024)

AARC-FE: Electrical Assembly Authentication with Random Convolution Kernels and Fuzzy Extractors

Christian Spinnler$^{(\boxtimes)}$ ⓘ, Torsten Reißland ⓘ, and Norman Franchi ⓘ

Institute for Smart Electronics and Systems, Friedrich-Alexander-University Erlangen Nürnberg, Erlangen, Germany
{christian.spinnler,torsten.reissland,norman.franchi}@fau.de

Abstract. Identity management of devices in the Internet of Things (IoT) has become an essential part of a secure IoT infrastructure. Enrollment and authentication is performed based on public key infrastructure (PKI) in state-of-the-art deployments. This ensures device authenticity based on certificates. To mitigate the risk of compromised certificates and to strengthen the security, the certificates can be created on the device during enrollment based on physical properties, such as a physical unclonable function (PUF) of the device or a connected secure element.

Identity management of devices in the Internet of Things (IoT) has become an essential part of a secure IoT infrastructure. Enrollment and authentication is performed based on public key infrastructure (PKI) in state-of-the-art deployments. This ensures device authenticity based on certificates. To mitigate the risk of compromised certificates and to strengthen the security, the certificates can be created on the device during enrollment based on physical properties, such as a physical unclonable function (PUF) of the device or a connected secure element.

To add further physical properties to the device identity, we propose AARC-FE: Electrical **A**ssemblie **A**uthentication with **R**andom **C**onvoultion Kernels and **F**uzzy **E**xtractors. This is a new approach for hardware fingerprint creation of a serial communication interface. The proposed solution uses characteristics of the analog signal introduced by manufacturing variances, which are made detectable by using random convolutional kernels. The features produced by the convolution are transformed in a two-step approach to suit the requirements of a fuzzy extractor that is used to create strong keys for the observed communication interface.

We create a stochastic model for evaluating the analog domain and transfer this model to a SPICE-based simulation of a common communication bus: I^2C . To characterize the approach, metrics for Physical Unclonable Functions (PUFs) and authentication systems are applied.

The evaluation shows, that AARC-FE is a feasible approach for key generation of an electrical assembly. Depending on the chosen parameters, the authentication system achieves an equal error rate (EER) as low as 0.09.

With this approach, it is possible to detect attacks such as device swapping or sniffing attacks on a serial communication bus. The system

M. Dalla Preda et al. (Eds.): ARES 2025, LNCS 15992, pp. 257–277, 2025.
https://doi.org/10.1007/978-3-032-00624-0_13

derives asymmetric keys from the analog values of the communication bus and can thus participate in standard public key authentication schemes.

1 Introduction

The transition to Internet of Things (IoT) has created many new challenges, one of which is the identification and authentication of a large amount of heterogeneous and connected devices that are deployed in a variety of operational areas. This issue creates even more impact as the convergence of information technology (IT) and operation technology (OT) is in full progress through the rise of Industry 4.0. In smart city infrastructures, IoT devices might be exposed outside a secured perimeter, so that malicious actors can easily gain access to the hardware of a device. At the same time, IoT devices are under high cost pressure, which means that protection against hardware manipulation is usually omitted. This opens up new attack vectors and, therefore, requires additional countermeasures to check the authenticity of a device, its peripherals, attached sensors, and actors.

In order to prevent an adversary from tampering the device, different solutions exist [8]: making the components physically inaccessible, e.g., by pouring them in resin, using tamper-resistant envelopes, enclosures, or fingerprinting of electrical characteristics, e.g., using PUFs.

In most cases, it is not economically feasible for IoT device vendors to implement physical tamper protection, as it requires additional steps in a manufacturing process, which is why we do not consider physical tamper protection suitable for a common IoT device. It is also impractical in many cases: special solutions would be required for wired sensors, and a damaged envelope would eventually render a device unusable. Therefore, the challenge is to make fingerprinting technologies available for entire device assemblies.

Device fingerprinting technologies have gained the interest of researchers and industry in recent years to improve the reliability and security of systems. There are a wide variety of fingerprinting solutions. They range from PUF-based hardware fingerprinting, device behavior fingerprinting, to radio frequency (RF) fingerprinting [9,16,18], all of which target different use cases.

In this article, we focus on hardware fingerprinting, which describes a method to prove the authenticity of the hardware of a device. The hardware fingerprint of a device is similar to a biometric fingerprint of humans: tiny variances are used to create a unique and collectible characteristic. These characteristics are implicitly or explicitly added during the manufacturing process [16].

According to Sanchez et al. [18], fingerprinting solutions can be distinguished by three properties: (i) the application scenario they are used for, (ii) how the fingerprint is evaluated and (iii) the data source that is used for fingerprinting. As described in [19], it is important to understand that the data source is also the only component that is actually secured by the fingerprint. Most hardware fingerprinting solutions incorporate only the characteristics of a single component of the device, which is often a property of the device's system-ona-chip (SoC).

However, IoT devices are assembled out of a multitude of components, such as a a central processing unit (CPU), non-volatile memory (NVM), volatile memory, communication interfaces, sensors and actuators, digital signal processors (DSPs) or other SoCs and co-processors. The components of a device, and also the peripherals externally connected to a device, communicate through electrical communication buses such as UART, I^2C or SPI.

Contributions. In this work a new method is proposed to improve the authenticity of an IoT device. Following the taxonomy proposed by Spinnler, Labs, and Franchi [19], the method can secure the electrical communication bus and peripherals of the device. This is achieved by verifying the validity of a cryptographic key, which is derived from the electrical signal of a communication bus that is commonly available on IoT devices. We provide the following contributions:

– A system architecture of a fingerprinting approach for device assemblies which uses modern time series analysis algorithms with a fuzzy extractor using a secure sketch for key extraction
– A stochastic model of the underlying data source to estimate its entropy and the derived key strength
– An implementation and analysis of the approach on simulated data with SPICE

Structure. The remainder of this work is structured as follows: Related work and the state-of-the-art (SOTA) is presented in Sect. 2. In Sect. 3, we present the proposed system architecture, followed by Sect. 4 where we develop the stochastic model of the fingerprinting approach and analyze its feasibility and limitations. In Sect. 5, we implement the proposed fingerprinting architecture with data from a SPICE simulation, followed by a security analysis in Sect. 6. Finally, we will conclude our work.

2   State of the Art

In the following section, we provide information about similar methods for fingerprinting and PUFs.

2.1   Physical Unclonable Functions

PUF based security is an active field of research, finding popularity in many technical areas [16]. PUFs are usually separated into *weak* and *strong* PUFs. Weak PUFs have a limited set of challenge-response-pairs (CRPs) and are therefore often used for key derivation. Instead of storing a private key directly on a NVM, the secret is derived from a weak PUF, thus improving security. For example, the derived key can be used in a public key infrastructure (PKI) to create a device identity certificate.

Strong PUFs are used in a different way: they provide an exceptionally large amount of CRPs and authentication procedures make use of that. During enrollment, a data base is created in a secure environment, storing CRPs of the device. During operation, a verifier will send a challenge and authenticate the device by receiving the expected response. These approaches have the advantage of providing lightweight security as no cryptographic primitive needs to be executed on the device itself. However, strong PUF based approaches are vulnerable for machine learning (ML) modeling attacks as has been shown in several publications [20].

In [8], the authors improve the resistance to tampering of devices by using an envelope that is a capacitive sensor that is used as a PUF. An evaluation unit detects any change in capacitance, which leads to an alarm and the destruction of confidential data such as keys. Furthermore, the key cannot be recovered because the envelope's capacitance has changed by such an amount that a new key generation would result in a different key. The solution proofs secure against tampering of the housing of a device as the attacker has to damage the envelope in order to open the device.

2.2   Device Fingerprinting

Device fingerprinting, often referred to as hardware fingerprinting, behavior fingerprinting or RF fingerprinting incorporates many different approaches to identify a device or to detect anomalies on a device or in a system. Most fingerprinting approaches nowadays use ML to accomplish the task [18,19].

The authors of [6] aim to detect malicious devices on the ARINC 429 Avionic Bus. Therefore, they propose a system that records the communication on the bus with an analog-digital converter (ADC). The differential bus signal is segmented into different signal transition types, i.e., falling, rising, high, and low, making it independent of the actual data that are transmitted. An anomaly detector is used to find suspicious variations in the analog signal of the communication. The anomaly detector is implemented as a local outlier factor algorithm. This approach requires a learning phase of "normal" segments, enabling the identification of an "anomaly".

The authors of [12] propose another approach. In order to authenticate an analog temperature sensor, they excite the sensor by applying a sinusoidal signal. Their approach relies on the assumption that the electrical characteristics of the analog sensor distort the signal in a unique way. A sensor is authenticated if the root-mean-square (RMS) value of the frequency response of a sensor is within a predefined margin of a previously recorded "golden" frequency response.

The concept most similar to this work is designed by Jäger and Lorych [10]. They measure the step response of an RC low-pass filter that is connected to an SPI communication bus. Their goal is to detect sniffing devices on the bus. They achieve this by measuring a "golden" step response and averaging the initial measurements. During operation, later measurements are compared against this golden step-response. They evaluated different spatial metrics as similarity measures. The system decides on a precomputed threshold by maximizing the accuracy score of the system. In a final step, they implement the fingerprint in Device Identifier Composition Engine (DICE) to extend it with the functionality of hardware attestation.

In contrast to PUF-based systems, approaches based on fingerprinting mostly lack a security evaluation with a stochastic model to provide insight of the reliability and min-entropy of the systems. The evaluation is mostly done by providing the confusion matrix of the anomaly detector.

2.3   Time Series Analysis

In the following section, a short introduction to time series analysis (TSA) is provided as our proposed architecture is based on TSA methods. TSA can be understood as the extraction of meaningful characteristics of a time-series signal. Time-series signals are data points that have a chronological order, e.g., voltage measurements. Typical applications of TSA include forecasting and classification of time series data.

Our approach uses the concepts of *random* convolutional kernels introduced by ROCKET [4] and MINIROCKET [5]. The authors of the articles found that most TSA methods with SOTA accuracy have high computational complexity, require long training times, and therefore do not scale well to large data sets. The authors wanted to provide a very efficient method for TSA with SOTA classification accuracy. They achieved this with a method they called ROCKET (Random Convolutional Kernel Transform). Their method does not require training of specific convolution kernels as in conventional convolutional neuronal network (CNN), instead it uses a huge amount of kernels with a wide variety of values. It produces two features: the maximum value and a feature called *proportion of positive values (PPV)*. PPV simply represents the fraction of positive values in a time series: $\text{PPV}(C) = \frac{1}{n} \sum [c > 0]$. MINIROCKET was stripped down to be quasi-deterministic. It uses a reduced number of kernels and removes almost all randomness from the kernel parameters. The kernel values are limited to only two values by default, making it possible to apply optimization for processing time. In addition, it uses PPV as a single feature omitting the maximum value. By applying these and some additional optimizations, MINIROCKET performs even faster than ROCKET while maintaining the same accuracy. A detailed description of MINIROCKET is provided in Sect. 5.1.

The main reasons we decided to use MINIROCKET are the following three:

1. **High classification performance:** The method provides one of the best classification performances on average on the UCR archive [3].
2. **Fast computing time:** Among the common TSA algorithms MINIROCKET is fast, making it a suitable choice for devices with limited resources.
3. **No training required:** This allows us to apply the method to data where we cannot provide a complete training data set. There is no domain knowledge necessary for MINIROCKET.

We want to take advantage of these features to build a time-series-based authentication scheme.

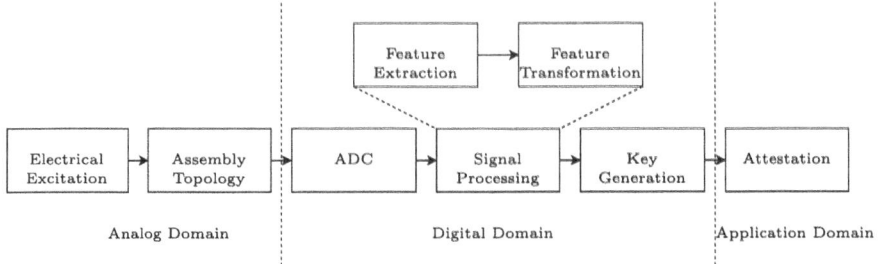

Fig. 1. System Architecture for electrical assembly fingerprinting.

3   System Architecture

In this section, we introduce the architecture of the system and its components of our proposed fingerprinting approach.

3.1   Attacker Model

The AARC-FE shall withstand a certain attacker who performs malicious operations on a device. We will assume an attacker who has physical access to an IoT device. The attacker wants to tamper with peripherals or components, e.g. a I^2C connected sensor, of the device. This can be achieved by exchanging the components with malicious or counterfeit components or examining the communication on the bus. As a result, the system needs to reliably detect exchanged components or probes on the bus.

3.2   Overview

An overview of the proposed fingerprinting approach is shown in Fig. 1. In its essence, the system provides a key which is created from the electrical circuit to which it is connected. If the electrical circuit has been modified, e.g. by removing or exchanging components or by adding a sniffing probe, the key cannot be reproduced any more, resulting in an unauthenticated assembly. A more detailed analysis will be provided in Sect. 5.

We divide the system into three parts: (i) analog domain, (ii) digital domain and the (iii) application domain, which we will describe in the following.

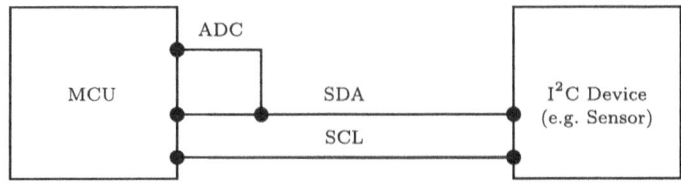

Fig. 2. System Architecture for electrical assembly fingerprinting of the I^2C bus.

Analog Domain. The analog domain represents the PUF-like structure. The assembly topology creates a unique electrical structure that encompasses the characteristics of the electrical conductors and all connected components[1]. A detailed analysis can be found in Sect. 4. The electrical excitation can be seen as a challenge passed to the electrical structure. The excitation can be generated by any component i.e. , we can simply use the signal transmitted by a component on the bus. In the case of a digital communication, this is equal to a step response or an electrical discharge on the bus. In Fig. 2, the simplified measurement setup is depicted: an ADC is connected to a microstrip which is the data lane of the communication bus. In a real implementation, it would be necessary to add a measurement amplifier to accordingly scale the signal.

Digital Domain. The digital domain is the main evaluation unit of the system. It digitizes the analog response of the electrical assembly PUF with an ADC. Only for evaluation purposes, the signal is divided into comparable segments as low-high, high-low, steady-high, and steady-low. This is important as for the evaluation we want to be sure that the fingerprinting performance arises from the variances in the signal, and not from the random *digital word* that is transmitted [6]. In addition to that, the digitized signal is processed in three steps: (i) extracting features with MINIROCKET, (ii) transforming the features by performing quantization and binarization on the feature values and (ii) applying the Fuzzy Extractor (FE) logic. The FE logic derives a key from the representation of the received binary time signal. The key is created once during the enrollment phase. It gets reproduced during operation for each authentication request. The key, generated by FE, is used to derive additional keys for the application domain and should be handled in a Trusted Computing Base (TCB) to not leak private information to any untrusted part of the system.

The process will be discussed in more detail in Sect. 5 with Fig. 5 and Fig. 6.

Application Domain. The application domain is responsible for attesting the authenticity of the electrical assembly. During the enrollment phase, the application domain requests a private/public key-pair creation. The application domain can act as a verifier itself or it can transmit the public key to another party that performs attestation. The authentication scheme requires the application domain to send a random nonce to the evaluation unit. The unit needs to sign the nonce with its reproduced private key. The application domain can verify the correctness of the private key using the previously exchanged public key. The private key gets destroyed after each authentication request. This part of the system will not be the focus for this paper; instead we just want to refer to suitable implementations, e.g. DICE for device authentication [7,13,14].

---

[1] E.g., this could be an I^{2}C bus with several connected sensors.

4 Stochastic Model of the Analog Domain

In the following section, we show the underlying mechanics of the proposed approach and its feasibility. Therefore, we will analyze the stochastic behavior of a simplified system model in the analog domain as depicted in Fig. 1.

4.1 Randomness in Components

The fundamental assumption for the fingerprinting approach is that each component in an electrical circuit deviates from its nominal value. Therefore, we decompose the impedance value Z of each component into four distinct values:

- Z^N: the nominal value of the component, i.e. the value the designer chose for it.
- Z^V: the time invariant variation of the component. This value is added by the manufacturing process and persists throughout the life of the component.
- Z^T: the time variant variation of the component. It incorporates parasitic effects, such as changes in value as a result of temperature and aging over time.
- Z^R: noise of the component, e.g. thermal noise.

Therefore, the overall impedance of a component is the sum of its previously defined impedance values:

$$Z = Z^N + Z^V + Z^T + Z^R \ . \tag{1}$$

For the analysis in this work, a time-invariant setup is assumed, which sets the value for $Z^T = 0$. The nominal value of the component is constant: $Z^N \sim Z_0$. The variation introduced by the manufacturing process is modeled as $Z^V \sim \mathcal{N}(\mu_V = 0, \sigma_V^2)$, where $\mathcal{N}$ denotes the Gaussian distribution. Consequently, the noise value of the components is $Z^R \sim \mathcal{N}(\mu_R = 0, \sigma_R^2)$, where $\sigma_R^2 << \sigma_V^2$. This results in a total impedance $Z \sim \mathcal{N}(Z_0, \sigma_V^2 + \sigma_R^2)$.

On a printed circuit board (PCB) multiple components add up to the overall impedance, e.g. of a transmission line. The single impedances are assumed to be identically distributed (i.i.d.) random variables (RVs). With the assumption that RVs can be measured independently with a resolution of Δ, it is possible to calculate an upper bound of the system's entropy, that is, the sum of the single entropies. According to [2], the entropy of a single, discretized continuous RV can be calculated as

$$H^{\Delta} = \sum_{i=0}^{N-1} \mathrm{ld} \left(\frac{\sigma_{V_i}}{\Delta} \sqrt{2\pi e} \right) \ . \tag{2}$$

However, in a complex system, it is likely infeasible to measure each impedance value independently. Instead, the components and their behavior are described with the help of the transfer function $H(s)$ of the assembly. This

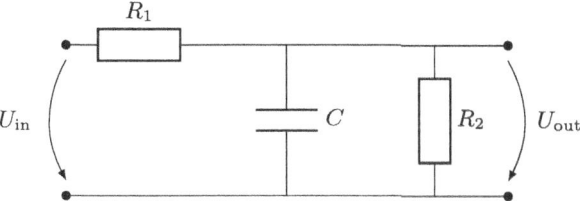

Fig. 3. Simple low-pass filter mimicking the behavior of a bus system with capacitive characteristics as described in [10].

makes it possible to show the correlation between the randomness grade of components, i.e. the variance σ_V^2, and the variance of the gain ($|.|$) of the output signal $\sigma_{|H|}^2 = \text{Var}(|H(s)|)$ for a set of different transfer functions. This is examined by simulating the transfer functions with the component values sampled from their Gaussian distribution with different variances.

4.2   Simulating the Analog Domain

In a previous work Jäger and Lorych [10] used an analog signal, a step response, of an electrical circuit to detect tampering. To evaluate this approach further, the simulation in our work follows the idea of a fingerprint with a step response on a simple RC circuit. The RC circuit represents a transmission line, neglecting a possible inductance L for simplicity. Two aspects are evaluated: (i) the variance of the output gain $\sigma_{|H|}^2$ depending on the components' variance σ_V^2 and (ii) the impact of wide-spread electrical structures, i.e. , the spatial spread of the transmission line, on the variance.

We simulate the transfer function of the circuit depicted in Fig. 3. Compared to Fig. 2, the voltage U_{out} is measured by ADC and U_{in} is the excitation signal, i.e. the data word transmitted on the I²C bus. The transfer function has low-pass characteristics:

$$H(s) = \frac{R_1}{sCR_1R_2 + R_1 + R_2} . \tag{3}$$

The components R_1, R_2 and C are all following a Gaussian distribution of the same variance $\sigma_V^2 = [0.01, 0.1, 0.2]$ and nominal values $R_1^N = 1\Omega$, $R_2^N = 1\text{M}\Omega$ and $C^N = 1\text{pF}$. For simulation, a normalized variance is used, depending on the nominal component value: $\hat{\sigma}_V^2 = Z^N \cdot \sigma_V^2$. For each iteration, the phase and gain are calculated on discrete values of s. To simulate the wide-spread electrical structure, a ten-times concatenated transfer function is simulated by creating the product in the Laplace domain:

$$H_{\text{concat}}(s) = \prod_{n=1}^{10} H(s) . \tag{4}$$

According to the low-pass characteristics of (3), high frequencies result in a low output gain. Therefore, the effects of the randomness of the components are most visible in low frequencies. This effect increases with concatenation of the transfer function.

Figure 4 shows the empirical cumulative distribution function (ECDF) of the gain values of the single transfer function in the left column and the gain of the concatenated transfer function in the right column. The first row represents the results with a variance of $\sigma_V^2 = 0.01$, and the other rows are interpreted accordingly. Investigation of the simulated gain values reveals that these values are close to a Gaussian distribution[2]. The simulation clearly shows a positive correlation between the variance of the components σ_V^2 and the gain[3] values of the transfer function $\sigma_{|H|}^2$. Furthermore, it can be observed that the frequency of the input signal influences the variance of the gain.

In Table 1 we provide the numerical results of the simulation with the output variance and the discrete entropy (2), assuming an ADC with 12 bit resolution and a sampling range of $0-2\,\mathrm{V}$, resulting in an absolute resolution of $\Delta = 488\,\mu\mathrm{V}$. The concatenated topology with the highest input variance results in the highest entropy.

To conclude this analysis, we used a simplified system model to show the positive correlation between component variance and gain variance of a transfer function. This proves the general underlying concept. In the next section, we will use this concept in a more advanced scenario.

Table 1. Variance of transfer function output and discrete entropy with $N_{\mathrm{MC_V}} = 5000$ for 100 Hz

	topology	variance σ_V^2		
		0.01	0.1	0.2
$\sigma_{|H|}^2$	RRC	0.034	0.34	0.69
	RRC Concat.	0.38	3.78	7.59
H^Δ	RRC	8.18bit	11.52bit	12.50bit
	RRC Concat.	11.64bit	14.98bit	15.96bit

5   Fingerprinting a Communication Bus in the Digital Domain

This section describes the processing of the fingerprinting system in the digital domain depicted in Fig. 1. Contrary to the work of Jäger and Lorych [10] the proposed fingerprinting approach in this work uses the communication signal of a bus system to create a unique identifier, which gets affected when the system bus is manipulated. As stated earlier, it is not feasible to sample the RVs directly for the usage in the fingerprinting approach, but instead, the signal traversing the circuit of the communication bus is recorded and used for fingerprinting.

---

[2] Converting the gain to voltage values, does not significantly distort the distribution.
[3] and phase.

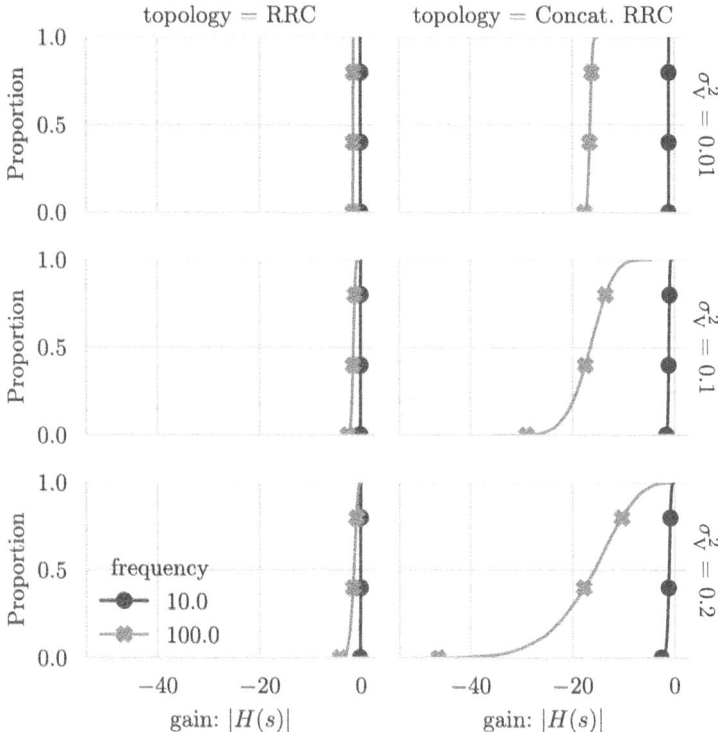

Fig. 4. The ECDF of the gain (magnitude) value of U_{out} with a step-function U_{in} transformed by (3). The left column depicts the step-response of a single transfer function, whereas the right column shows a concatenated transfer function (4). The rows have varying variance σ_V^2. It is clearly visible that an increasing variance of the components lead to a increased variance of the output $\sigma_{|H|}^2$.

5.1 Feature Extraction with Random Convolution Kernels

The randomness of the system arises from the variances introduced in Sect. 4.1. However, in this approach we do not measure the values directly but use the step response of the system, which depends on the absolute values of Z. In a practical implementation, the step response is acquired by an ADC resulting in a vector $\mathbf{x}$ of voltage values x_{n-1}.

To generate meaningful features from the time series data we use MINIROCKET. The authors Dempster, Schmidt, and Webb [5] provide the transform of one input time series $\mathbf{x} = [x_0, x_1, \ldots, x_{n-1}]$ and a kernel $\mathbf{w} = [w_0, w_1, \ldots, w_{m-1}]$ with dilation d as

$$\mathbf{x} * \mathbf{w}_d = \sum_{j=0}^{m-1} x_{i-\left(\left\lfloor \frac{m}{2} \cdot d \right\rfloor + (j \cdot d)\right)} \cdot w_j, \ \forall i \in \{0, 1 \ldots, n-1\}. \tag{5}$$

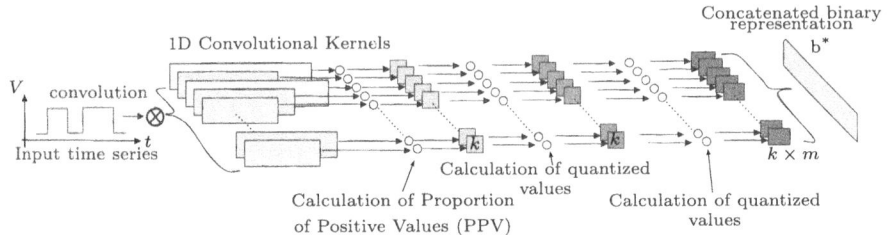

Fig. 5. System Architecture for electrical assembly fingerprinting.

With a kernel length of $m = 9$ there are $2^9 = 512$ possibilities from which MINIROCKET uses a subset of 84 kernels. The authors chose this value empirically. Furthermore, to make use of mathematical optimization, the kernels are constructed from only two values $\alpha = -1$ and $\beta = 2$, with the kernel having three β and the rest α values. In the default configuration with dilation and padding, a multiple of 84 kernels is used, resulting in 9996 features. In the default configuration, the bias values $\mathbf{a}$ are sampled from the quantiles of a single randomly drawn convolution output. For a more detailed investigation of the transform, we highly recommend the primary literature.

Together with the bias values $\mathbf{a}$ of the transform we get the PPV of the input time series vector with $\mathbf{v} = \text{PPV}(\mathbf{x} * \mathbf{w_d} - \mathbf{a})$. This creates a vector of features $\mathbf{v} = [v_0, v_1, \ldots, v_k] \ \{v_k \in \mathbb{R} : [0, 1]\}$, where k is a parameter that defines the number of features generated by MINIROCKET.

In our approach, we only use a total number of $k = 84 \cdot 6 = 504$ kernels, resulting in 504 features. Furthermore, our approach does not sample the bias value randomly from the training data set but instead only from a single time series. This corresponds to the idea that in a real-world implementation no training data would be available to fit the bias value, but instead the algorithm will run on a single device from which the bias value is sampled.

5.2   Encoding and Fuzzy Extraction

In the consecutive steps of data processing, we want to use block codes to correct noisy fingerprint responses. Therefore, the use of real-valued numbers is impractical. Instead, the features are transformed into a binary vector $\mathbf{b} = [b_0, b_1, \ldots, b_k] \ \{b_k \in \{0, 1\}\}$. This is accomplished by first discretizing the vector $\mathbf{v}$ into i intervals resulting in vector $\mathbf{q}$. The amount of intervals is called *support*, i.e., the support describes in how many intervals the values in $\mathbf{v}$ are divided. After quantization, each interval is encoded in a $(2, 4)$-bit Gray code or 4-bit Linearly Separable Subcode (LSSC) [11]. Other codes are possible, but we select Gray codes, as they are very common and maintain uniformity. To compare a different code and as it was tested by Rathgeb *et al.* [17] as well, we also apply LSSC. The number of bits m is shown in the right of Fig. 5 and depends on the decoding scheme. The binary vector $\mathbf{b}$ is concatenated into a single representation $\mathbf{b}^*$ which is of length $k \cdot m$.

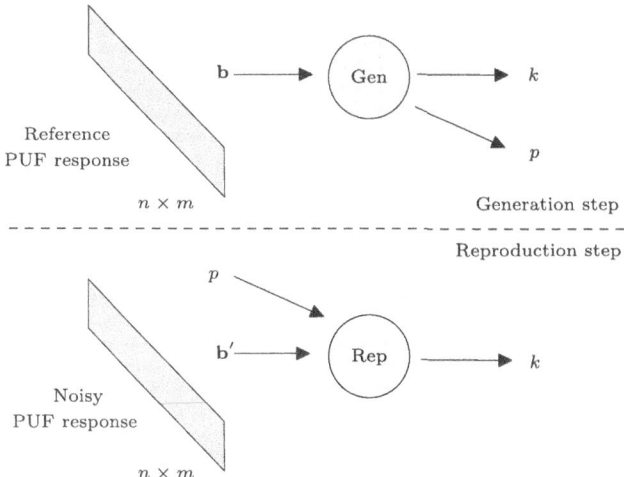

Fig. 6. FE construction with generation *Gen* and reproduction *Rep* step.

The encoded time series **b*** is fed into the Fuzzy Extractor (FE) as a Secure Sketch (SS) construction for key generation *Gen*, as shown in the upper part of Fig. 6. The algorithm is described in Algorithm 1. The generation step produces a key r that can be used for further cryptographic operations and public helper data p, which is used for a later reproduction *Rep* of a noisy encoded time series **b*** as described in Algorithm 2. The symbol $\oplus$ is the exclusive-or (XOR) operator and the *Hash* function is used to generate a uniform distributed hash value of the input value. c_s represents the error correction codes (ECC) for the random string s.

Algorithm 1. Fuzzy Extractor: Generation
_____

Require: b^*

$s \leftarrow Random$

$c_s \leftarrow Encode(s)$

$\hat{s} \leftarrow s \oplus b$

$p \leftarrow \hat{s}, c_s$

$r \leftarrow Hash(b^*)$
_____

The FE scheme uses Reed-Solomon (RS) block codes for error correction. The RS codes are configured as $[n, k]$ codes, with n as the block length of the code and k the message length. In order to have an optimal error correction, the reliability of the construction must be taken into account and is investigated in Sect. 6.1.

Algorithm 2. Fuzzy Extractor: Reproduction

Require: $b^{*\prime}$, p

    $\hat{s}, c_s \leftarrow p$

    $s' \leftarrow \hat{s} \oplus b^{*\prime}$

    $s \leftarrow Decode(s', c_s)$

    $b^* \leftarrow \hat{s} \oplus s$

    $r \leftarrow Hash(b^*)$

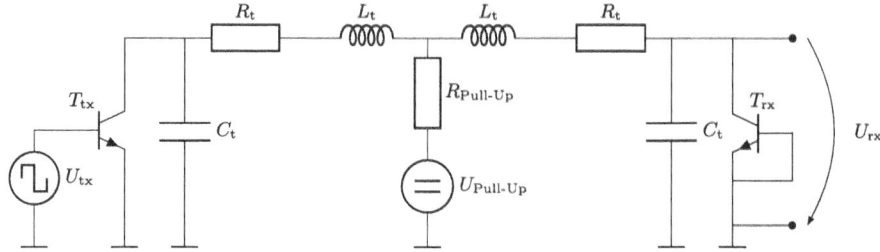

Fig. 7. Simplified equivalent circuit of an I²C bus for MC simulation. U_{tx} is a randomly generated rectangular signal, which simulates the transmission of random bits on the data bus. $U_{\text{Pull-Up}}$ is a constant voltage. The U_{rx} is the received and transformed signal.

5.3 Simulation of a Communication Bus

To analyze this approach, the simulation, which was introduced in Sect. 4.2, is adjusted to correspond to an I²C communication bus. The simulation is based on SPICE. PySpice[4] is used to create the MC simulation with a netlist similar to the schematic in Fig. 7, which corresponds to an I²C circuit. In the MC simulation, the time-invariant variation Z^{V} of the components and the additional noise of the components Z^{R} are sampled from a Gaussian distribution with the corresponding normalized variances $\hat{\sigma}_{Z_V}^2$ and $\hat{\sigma}_{Z_R}^2$. For bipolar transistors, a standard SPICE model of an NPN transistor is used. To simulate a common data transmission over the I²C bus, a random bit pattern is generated and used as the input signal U_{tx}. The transformed signal U_{rx} is stored in a data base for later processing.

The received voltage $U_{\text{rx}}(t)$ for an arbitrary set $S = \{\hat{\sigma}_V^2, \hat{\sigma}_R^2\}$ is depicted in Fig. 8, showing a subset of the MC simulation. The voltage across the transistor T_{rx} is used as an input data source for the proposed fingerprinting approach and is assigned to the time series vector $\mathbf{x}$ in the following. In the MC simulation N_{MC_V} different classes, that is, samples from the RV Z^{V} are simulated. For each class, additional N_{MC_R} noisy readings are simulated, resulting in a total number of $N_{\text{MC}} = N_{\text{MC}_R} \cdot N_{\text{MC}_V}$. The number of samples from both RVs, Z_V and Z_R is $N_{\text{MC}_V} = N_{\text{MC}_R} = 100$, resulting in a total number of iterations of $N_{\text{MC}} = 10000$. The simulation results in a matrix $\mathbf{X}$ with $\mathbf{x}_i \, \forall i \in \{0, 1, \ldots, N_{\text{MC}} - 1\}$ rows.

---

[4] https://pyspice.fabrice-salvaire.fr/.

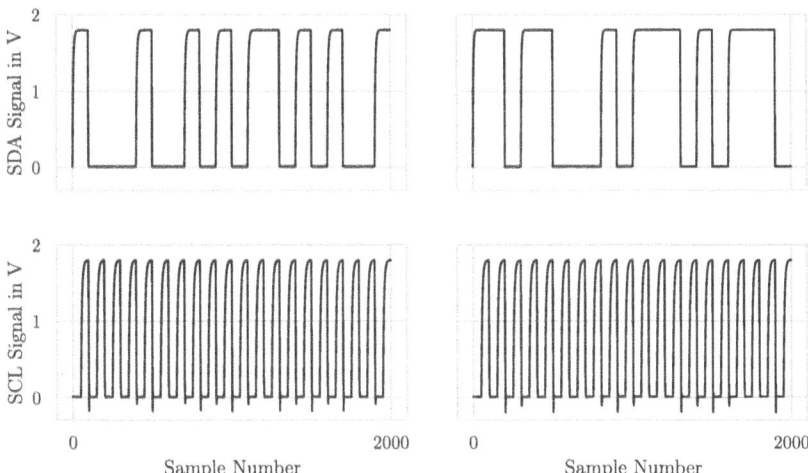

Fig. 8. Subset of MC simulation of I^2C transmission with varying Z^V. The plots depicts the voltage $U_{rx}(t)$.

6   Security of the Proposed Concept

To assess the security of the proposed scheme, metrics for PUFs are applied to evaluate the system in Sect. 6.1. In a second step, the complete authentication system is evaluated by providing the EER of differently parameterized configurations.

For the evaluation to be representative, the data signal depicted in Fig. 8 is segmented into similar segments, such as the edge rising or falling, or the high or low value, as introduced in Sect. 1. For the evaluation in this section, only the rising edges are used.

6.1   Metrics for PUFs and Authentication Systems

In this section, we provide suitable metrics to characterize PUFs and authentication systems. The metrics for PUFs are calculated from the raw data of a PUF, whereas the metrics for the authentication systems are applied to the processed data.

Metrics for PUFs. The binary output of the proposed scheme makes it possible to use metrics for binary PUFs to further evaluate the system. Maiti, Gunreddy, and Schaumont [15] provided a comprehensive list of metrics for PUFs and further classified both Arbiter-PUF (APUF) and Ring-Oscillator-PUF (RO PUF) with their proposed metrics. The metrics they identified as important are: (i) uniformity, (ii) reliability, (iii) steadiness (iv) uniqueness, (v) diffuseness, (vi) bit-aliasing, (vii) probability of misidentification (PMSID). For the proposed PUF construction we analyze the uniformity, reliability, and uniqueness. Steadiness

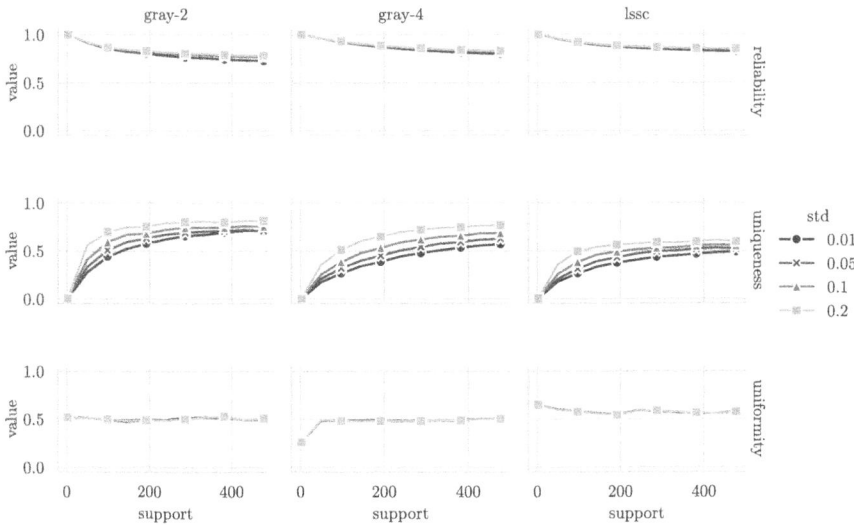

Fig. 9. Different metrics evaluating the performance of different coding schemes for the PUF depending on the variance of the simulated components.

will not be evaluated; however, it is an important metric that indicates reliability under certain operating conditions. Diffuseness is only useful if we have a large set of CRPs, which is not the case in this evaluation. Bit-aliasing seems not useful for analog PUFs as we have a rather vague spatial correlation. The PMSID is highly dependent on the length of the PUF response, and as we can arbitrarily scale the length, this metric is not evaluated.

Uniformity. This metric is similar to the Hamming weight and its desired value is 0.5, since for security purposes a uniformly distributed binary vector is the optimum, indicating that the probability of 0s and 1s is equally distributed and therefore equally likely.

Reliability. This metric characterizes the reliability of bit readouts over time. In its worst case, $reliability = 0$, the bit has a random behavior and is therefore maximally unreliable. In the best case, $reliability = 1$ the bit is always evaluated to the same value. A value of 0.6 therefore characterizes a bit as random in only 40% of the evaluations.

Uniqueness. Uniqueness characterizes bits at a specific position of the bit stream in different instances of PUFs. However, the metric is again related to the Hamming weight, this time across different instances of PUFs instead of the single PUF as in uniformity. A value of 1 is ideal as it describes the percentage of bits that have a Hamming weight of 0.5 and are therefore truly random across different instances of PUFs.

The evaluation of the concatenated binary representation $\mathbf{b}^*$ defined in Sect. 5.2 is depicted in Fig. 9. The figure compares the previously defined metrics for three different codes with a varying variance of the input components. The uniformity (lower row) is good for all setups, with a minor bias for LSSC. The 2-bit Gray code has a more noisy uniformity than the 4-bit Gray code, which could mean that more bits smooth out a bias. Reliability (upper row) also shows minor differences between the three coding schemes. The reliability value of the 2-bit Gray code has the strongest decline. In contrast, of the uniqueness values, the 2-bit gray code has the strongest increase, followed by the 4-bit gray code. Both reach similar values at higher support values. The LSSC, however, is limited in the maximum value of uniqueness compared to the others.

It becomes clear that the fingerprint construction is highly dependent on the number of supports. It is therefore crucial to find a suitable working point by adjusting the authentication system.

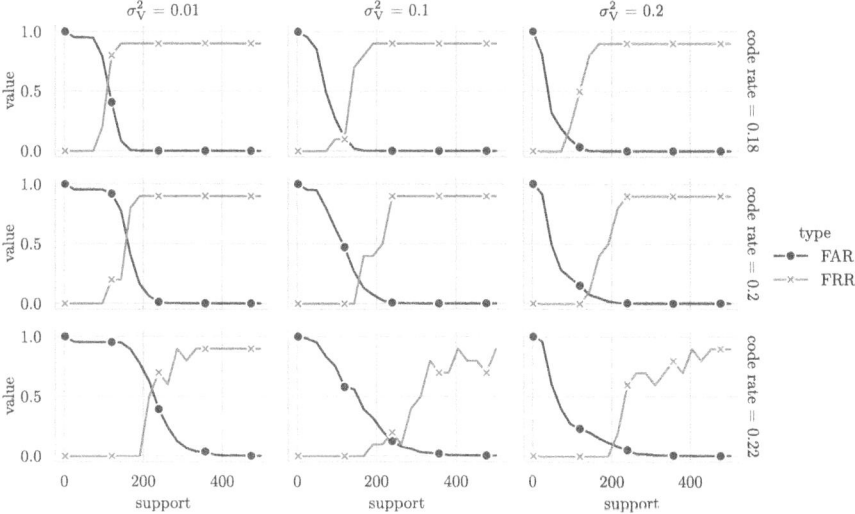

Fig. 10. The FAR and FRR of 4-bit Gray codes with varying ECC lengths with different analog models (different variance of the components). (Color figure online)

Metrics for Authentication Systems. Authentication systems are often characterized by the false acceptance rate (FAR) and false rejection rate (FRR) [1]. The authentication system can be tuned to have a lower FAR or FRR, depending on the application. A common parameter to characterize the performance of the authentication system is the Equal Error Rate (EER), i.e. , when FAR and FRR are equal. A low EER is desirable, as it describes an authentication system with low FRR and FAR. With true positives tp, true negatives tn, false positive fp and false negative fn they are defined as:

$$FRR = \frac{tn}{tp + fn} \tag{6}$$

$$FAR = \frac{fp}{tn + fp} \tag{7}$$

The proposed authentication system of Sect. 5.2 is tested using simulated data from 5.3. To reduce computation time, only 300 samples from Z^V, i.e. the different classes, and 10 samples from Z^N, i.e. repeated and noisy class readings are analyzed.

The resulting metrics are depicted in Fig. 10. Only fingerprints encoded with the 4-bit Gray code are depicted, as there is not much difference compared to the others. What can be seen is the high dependence on the input variance σ_V^2, which is represented by the column of the chart. It is intuitive that the lower the variance of the input variables, the worse the performance of the authentication system, i.e. the higher the EER. In contrast, a higher variance results in better performance, i.e. a lower EER. Furthermore, the Reed-Solomon code is configured for different code rates. The code rate is set around 0.2 as this corresponds quite well to the reliability parameter, taken from Fig. 10. A lower code rate leads to an EER already with a coarser quantization (*support* < 200) interval, and the curves appear relatively sharp. With a higher code rate, the curves have more flat shapes and an EER that is reached with a higher quantization *support* > 200. That means that for a higher code rate, there is a larger area, where there are no false rejections for the authentication system. The numerical results are visible in Table 2. The best values for the EER are 0.09 and 0.10 which are within the error of the evaluation.

Table 2. EER for 4-bit Gray code with different code rates according to different variance of the simulated components.

code rate	variance σ_V^2		
	0.01	0.1	0.2
0.18	0.56	0.11	0.13
0.20	0.55	0.20	**0.09**
0.22	0.56	0.16	0.1

6.2   Discussion of the Results

We first want to discuss the results according to the PUF metrics introduced in Sect. 6.1. The authors of [15] used the metrics to compare a RO PUF and a APUF, therefore, we can directly compare AARC-FE against the two other PUFs. The results are provided in Table 3. The selected AARC-FE configuration has a support value of 140 with the 4-bit Gray code and $\sigma_V^2 = 0.2$, as this falls together with the lowest EER of the setup. It is recognizable, that the RO PUF outperforms both other PUF constructions. However, AARC-FE has slightly better uniformity and uniqueness compared to APUF. AARC-FE has the worst reliability: almost every tenth bit is unreliable, whereas for APUF and RO PUF only every hundredth bit is unreliable. The RO PUF and the APUF are explicit hardware constructions to provide good PUF performance, whereas AARC-FE is built on existing electrical structures. It is therefore not surprising that they can provide a significantly higher reliability.

Table 3. Comparison of different PUFs by a subset of the metrics introduced by Maiti, Gunreddy, and Schaumont [15].

	APUF	RO PUF	AARC-FE	Ideal Value
Uniformity	55.69%	50.56%	47.70%	50%
Reliability	99.76%	99.14%	90.77%	100%
Uniqueness	36.75%	94.07%	59.63%	100%

A similar approach presented by Gilboa-Markevich and Wool [6] reaches an EER of < 0.01 with real data, which is, compared to the presented results, better by about one magnitude. However, their approach requires sufficient data to train the classifier, whereas AARC-FE does not require any prior knowledge about the signal.

The performance of the AARC-FE is mainly dependent on the variance of the components captured by the fingerprint. The results for the normalized variance of 0.01 do not appear to be sufficient for an authentication system, as the EER always has a very high value regardless of the configuration. This aligns with the results of Sect. 4.2, where a lower variance of the input results in a low variance of the output. However, we could show that using larger electrical assembly topologies, the overall variance increases. As it is quite hard to estimate the manufacturing variances, and therefore the input variance, of an electrical assembly, it might be feasible to say that only large electrical assemblies should be used for such an approach for now, as it cannot be guaranteed that the variance of the components alone is sufficient for a good authentication performance.

Therefore, the proposed system in its current state might be used as an additional security measure e.g. in an embedded system to test the authenticity of a device assembly, making it possible to detect changes in the assembly. It is not feasible to use it as a single trust anchor.

7 Conclusion

In this work, we presented a new concept for fingerprinting communication bus systems, from the ground-laying system model to a possible authentication system implementation. We evaluated each processing step with a suitable metric and showed the basic feasibility of this approach, requiring no more than an ADC and a suitable measurement amplifier attached to the communication line that should be fingerprinted.

In concluding this work, some questions remain open for further investigation. For a practical implementation, the time-variant effects (see Z^{T} in Sect. 4) must be analyzed. Furthermore, the authors have already recorded a real-world dataset with a deterministic testbed which needs investigation. In addition, AARC-FE is implemented in an embedded system for real-world analysis, investigating resource usage and reliability.

Due to its generic black-box approach, AARC-FE is feasible for technologies other than communication buses e.g. I^2C , and should be applied and tested on other data sources, such as behavior and RF fingerprinting solutions.

Acknowledgments. This work has been partially funded by the German Federal Ministry of Education and Research in the ZEUS project VE-ASCOT (#16ME0271) and by the Federal Office for Information Security in the project 6G-ReS (01MO23013E).

Disclosure of Interests. The authors have no competing interests to declare that are relevant to the content of this article.

References

1. Aniello, L., Halak, B., Chai, P., Dhall, R., Mihalea, M., Wilczynski, A.: Securing hardware supply chain using PUF. In: Halak, B. (ed.) Authentication of Embedded Devices: Technologies, Protocols and Emerging Applications, pp. 115–144, Cham (2021)
2. Cover, T.M., Thomas, J.A.: Elements of Information Theory, New York (1991)
3. Dau, H.A., et al.: The UCR time series archive. IEEE/CAA J. Automatica Sinica (2019)
4. Dempster, A., Petitjean, F.,Webb, G.I.: ROCKET: exceptionally fast and accurate time series classification using random convolutional kernels. Data Min. Knowl. Disc. (2020)
5. Dempster, A., Schmidt, D.F., Webb, G.I.: MINIROCKET: a very fast (almost) deterministic transform for time series classification. In: Proceedings of the 27th ACM SIGKDD Conference on Knowledge Discovery & Data Mining, pp. 248–257 (2021)
6. Gilboa-Markevich, N., Wool, A.: Hardware fingerprinting for the ARINC 429 avionic bus. In: Chen, L., Li, N., Liang, K., Schneider, S. (eds.) Computer Security – ESORICS 2020, pp. 42–62, Cham (2020)
7. Trusted Computing Group: DICE Attestation Architecture (2020)
8. Immler, V., Obermaier, J., König, M., Hiller, M., Sig, G.: B-TREPID: battery-less tamper-resistant envelope with a PUF and integrity detection. In: 2018 IEEE International Symposium on Hardware Oriented Security and Trust (HOST), pp. 49–56 (2018)
9. Jagannath, A., Jagannath, J., Kumar, P.S.P.V.: A comprehensive survey on radio frequency (RF) fingerprinting: traditional approaches, deep learning, and open challenges. arXiv preprint arXiv:2201.00680 (2022)

10. Jäger, L., Lorych, D.: Remote attestation extended to the analog domain. In: The 16th International Conference on Availability, Reliability and Security, Vienna Austria, pp. 1–10 (2021)

11. Lim, M.-H., Teoh, A.B.J.: Linearly Separable SubCode: a novel output label with high separability for biometric discretization. In: 2010 5th IEEE Conference on Industrial Electronics and Applications, pp. 290–294 (2010)

12. Lorenz, F., et al.: Fingerprinting analog IoT sensors for secret-free authentication. In: 2020 29th International Conference on Computer Communications and Networks (ICCCN), Honolulu, HI, USA, pp. 1–6 (2020)

13. Lorych, D., Jäger, L.: Design space exploration of DICE. In: Proceedings of the 17th International Conference on Availability, Reliability and Security, Vienna Austria, pp. 1–10 (2022)

14. Lorych, D., Jäger, L., Fuchs, A.: Acceleration of DICE key generation using key caching. In: Proceedings of the 19th International Conference on Availability, Reliability and Security, pp. 1–8, New York (2024)

15. Maiti, A., Gunreddy, V., Schaumont, P.: A systematic method to evaluate and compare the performance of physical unclonable functions. In: Athanas, P., Pnevmatikatos, D., Sklavos, N. (eds.) Embedded Systems Design with FPGAs, pp. 245–267, New York (2013)

16. McGrath, T., Bagci, I.E., Wang, Z.M., Roedig, U., Young, R.J.: A PUF taxonomy. Appl. Phys. Rev. (2019)

17. Rathgeb, C., Merkle, J., Scholz, J., Tams, B., Nesterowicz, V.: Deep face fuzzy vault: implementation and performance. Comput. Secur. (2022)

18. Sanchez, P.M.S., Valero, J.M.J., Celdran, A.H., Bovet, G., Perez, M.G., Perez, G.M.: A survey on device behavior fingerprinting: data sources, techniques, application scenarios, and datasets. IEEE Commun. Surv. Tutorials (2021)

19. Spinnler, C., Labs, T., Franchi, N.: SoK: a taxonomy for hardware-based fingerprinting in the internet of things. In: Proceedings of the 19th International Conference on Availability, Reliability and Security, pp. 1–12, New York (2024)

20. Tobisch, J., Aghaie, A., Becker, G.T.: Combining optimization objectives: new modeling attacks on strong PUFs. IACR Trans. Cryptogr. Hardw. Embed. Syst. (2021)

In Specs We Trust? Conformance-Analysis of Implementation to Specifications in Node-RED and Associated Security Risks

Simon Schneider[1]([✉])(iD), Komal Kashish[2], Katja Tuma[3](iD),
and Riccardo Scandariato[1](iD)

[1] Hamburg University of Technology, Hamburg, Germany
`simon.schneider@tuhh.de`
[2] Siemens Mobility, Berlin, Germany
[3] Eindhoven University of Technology, Eindhoven, Netherlands

Abstract. Low-code development frameworks for IoT platforms offer a simple drag-and-drop mechanism to create applications for the billions of existing IoT devices without the need for extensive programming knowledge. The security of such software is crucial given the close integration of IoT devices in many highly sensitive areas such as healthcare or home automation. Node-RED is a framework to build applications from *nodes* that are contributed by open-source developers. Its reliance on unvetted contributions and lack of security checks raises the concern that the applications could be vulnerable to attacks, thereby posing a security risk to end users. The low-code approach could imply that users lack the technical knowledge to mitigate or even realize such security concerns.

This paper focuses on *hidden* information flows in Node-RED nodes, meaning flows that are not captured by the specifications. They could (unknowingly or with malicious intent) cause leaks of sensitive information to unauthorized entities. We report the results of a conformance analysis of all nodes in the Node-RED framework, for which we compared the numbers of specified inputs and outputs of each node against the number of sources and sinks detected with CodeQL. The results show, that 55% of all nodes exhibit more possible flows than are specified. A risk assessment of a subset of the nodes showed, that 28% of them are associated with a high severity and 36% with a medium severity rating.

Keywords: IoT · security · conformance analysis · information flow analysis · Node-RED · low-code

1 Introduction

The number of Internet of Things (IoT) devices has seen a tremendous boom over the last decade and they have seamlessly become a part of the everyday world. From industrial control systems to fitness bands, from smart security systems to

© The Author(s), under exclusive license to Springer Nature Switzerland AG 2025
M. Dalla Preda et al. (Eds.): ARES 2025, LNCS 15992, pp. 278–300, 2025.
https://doi.org/10.1007/978-3-032-00624-0_14

medical instruments, more and more devices enter the cyberspace continuously to increase the efficiency of their industries. Predictions for the number of IoT devices being installed in the coming years reach up to 100 billion [18]. The grave financial and personal costs that can occur from compromised systems via IoT devices in critical and sensitive domains has lead to active research on the challenges faced ([1, 17, 40]), ongoing work ([23, 25]), and possible mitigation approaches ([3, 8, 37, 38]). The physical devices' need for software has been the propelling factor for IoT software development platforms that realize a wide range of functionality by abstracting many complex activities into simple interfaces, for example, the management of sensor data streams from hardware devices or communication with other entities, thus tackling some unique challenges for developers of IoT software [35]. The highest level of abstraction is reached by *low-code* or *no-code* frameworks, which simplify the development process into graphical drag-and-drop interfaces, allowing even users with low or no programming knowledge to create applications for IoT devices [7, 29]. Frameworks that also follow an open-source approach rely on contributions from developers to realize the abstraction of the code-intensive software development into low-code functionalities, promising to increase the amount of available functionalities by leveraging the work of numerous developers.

Problem. However, this also introduces security challenges since the frameworks' code is no longer created by a single authority that can implement secure development practices and open-source contributions are not vetted. With insecure software being a major issue for the security of IoT devices [15], this could result in less secure IoT devices. Low-code development frameworks could potentially provide insufficiently secured software to users that do not have the capabilities to address or even realize this issue, resulting in vulnerable IoT devices that can be compromised by attackers and have serious security implications.

This paper presents the results of an investigation of one possible security issue in such low-code development frameworks, hidden information flows. We have performed a conformance analysis of the nodes in the Node-RED ecosystem to identify hidden information flows. In this context, "hidden" information flows are flows that can occur in the implemented node but are not considered in the node's specification, i.e., not captured by the specified numbers of inputs and outputs. These are relevant for the described scenario, since they and their security implications likely go unnoticed by the end user of the ecosystem. Therefore, we performed a risk assessment of identified information flows. The conducted study investigated the above-described security issue faced by low-code open-source development frameworks for IoT devices by shedding light on the extent of information flows that could expose sensitive information to unauthorized entities and are not marked as such by the code's specifications. Although Node-RED is likely not used in critical domains, it is an important low-code platform. This paper addresses the following research questions:

❓ **RQ1: What is the prevalence of hidden information flows in the Node-RED ecosystem?**

We performed a conformance analysis of all node packages (the components used to create IoT applications) provided by Node-RED. An information flow analysis with CodeQL revealed the implemented sources and sinks, and the node packages' specifications the intended inputs and outputs. Comparing these numbers determined the conformance case (convergence, divergence, or absence).

> ❓ **RQ2: How severe are the risks for users of the Node-RED ecosystem introduced by the hidden information flows?**

All hidden information flows can be seen as a compliance issue from a software development perspective, but not all hidden information flows necessarily pose a security issue. To assess the extent to which the detected non-conformances impose security threats to users of the ecosystem, we manually assessed a subset of the detected information flows concerning their security risk and severity.

Contributions. This paper presents three key contributions. First, we introduce a methodology to analyze hidden information flows in Node-RED packages. The methodology is also supported by an open-source implementation[1], which includes a reusable list of manually identified sources and sinks in node packages. Second, we study all available Node-RED packages and report on the identified hidden information flows. Contextually, we also provide an assessment of the risks for end users. Third, we offer a discussion of potential mitigations that could be implemented in the Node-RED platform.

Paper Structure. The rest of this paper is structured as follows: Sect. 2 describes background information on the technologies used for the conformance analysis; Sect. 3 presents the methodology of the conducted study; Sect. 4 contains the results of the conformance analysis and the risk assessment of information flows; Sect. 5 discusses the presented results; Sect. 6 presents the related work; and Sect. 7 concludes this paper.

2   Background

In this work, we use CodeQL to perform information flow analysis on nodes from the Node-RED framework and conduct a conformance analysis based on the results. The following presents background on the above technologies.

2.1   Node-RED

Node-RED is an open source project originally developed by IBM that allows the creation of flow-based IoT applications. The platform follows the low-code paradigm, i.e., applications can be developed with *nodes*, which are software components that realize specific functionalities and interact with other such nodes via input and output ports. A multitude of nodes are available that can, for example, connect with hardware sensors and actuators, access online services

---

[1] **Implementation**: github.com/tuhh-softsec/node-red-conformance-analysis

such as mail servers or social media platforms, or interact with system resources such as files. Individual nodes can communicate by exchanging messages via the Node-RED runtime API. The job of the application developer is mainly visual. The developer selects nodes and wires them together into an application (called *flow*) that realizes the intended business functionality. When one node's output is connected to another node's input, messages sent by the upstream node are forwarded to the downstream one. Only in exceptional cases does the developer have to resort to writing JavaScript code themselves, for example, by using the "function" node, which follows the function-as-a-service paradigm.

A node consists of JavaScript/TypeScript files, an HTML file, and an additional JSON file for packaging. The node's functionality is implemented in standard JavaScript and can interact with the framework via the Node-RED runtime API. The HTML file contains a number of definitions needed for integration into the Node-RED framework, styling configurations for the visual editor, help texts, and other information. Most importantly for this work, the HTML file also specifies the number of inputs and outputs of the node. In the following, we call the JavaScript files defining the node's behavior its *implementation* and the HTML file providing information about it its *specification*.

Nodes are made available via the Node.js package manager *npm* and are indexed in the *Node-RED library*. The library lists all available *node packages*, which contain at least one node each, but usually multiple ones that belong to the same functionality complex. The library contains some official and many third party nodes that are created by independent developers. The exact ratio of official to open-source nodes can not reliably be determined, but the vast majority of available nodes are developed by open-source contributors. As of April 2020, a request must be submitted to Node-RED to add a node to the official library. It is not clear if and how requests are vetted, but the requirement for a request is for technical reasons and not to enforce any regulations. Given the context of the platform, it is unlikely that extensive checks concerning the security or other properties of the packages are applied, if any.

2.2   CodeQL

Information flow analysis is used to determine how data traverses a program and how it is changed. The typical use case is for the identification of information leaks or other unwanted and unforeseen software behavior. It can detect *sources* and *sinks* of information, i.e., places where information is created or enters the program (e.g., user-provided input) and places where information leaves the system (e.g., when it is sent to a server). The analysis then identifies possible connections between sources and sinks, i.e., program behavior that leads to information from a source propagating and reaching a sink. Following the related literature [20], we refer to sources and sinks collectively as *endpoints*.

CodeQL[2] is an open-source tool distributed by GitHub that enables information flow analysis and is often used to automate security checks. It works by

---

[2] CodeQL: codeql.github.com.

transforming the analyzed code into a relational database capturing an abstract syntax tree, data flow graph, and control flow graph that can be analyzed via a custom query language. Issues that are to be detected are expressed as queries and a query engine detects any occurrences of these patterns in the database. Any possible flow of information through the program is modeled, including flows through transformation operations as known from taint analysis [30].

We use CodeQL to identify information flows in Node-RED nodes, thus revealing all endpoints over which a node can communicate during operation.

2.3   Conformance Analysis

Conformance analysis is the widely used process of checking for deviations between any two system artifacts to detect discrepancies between *what is* and *what should be*. In our work, we check the conformance between the implementation and specifications of nodes in the Node-RED framework. The specified inputs and outputs are extracted from the nodes' HTML specifications, and the implemented endpoints are identified via an information flow analysis with CodeQL.

The outcome of a conformance analysis can be one of three cases, *convergence*, *absence*, or *divergence*. In our analysis, we have two variables (sources/inputs and sinks/outputs) and therefore more nuanced cases. For comparability and simplicity, we aggregate them into the standard three cases. In the context of this work, they are defined as: **convergence** – specifications and implementation coincide, i.e., the number of detected sources is the same as the number of specified inputs and the number of sinks is the same as the number of specified outputs; **divergence** – more sources and/or sinks are detected than are specified, regardless of the second variable; **absence** – fewer sources and/or sinks are detected than specified for both variables or for one and the second variable matches the specifications. The generalization of measurements where, e.g., only the observed inputs divert from the specified ones while the outputs converge leads to a loss of information. However, we did not gain any further analysis insights when considering the more nuanced results.

The case of convergence is the desired one in any conformance analysis. In the context of this work, absences are an issue mainly from a software engineering viewpoint. We focus on divergences in this paper, as they are the most important cases from a security point of view. Additional "hidden" information flows are potentially security- and privacy-relevant.

3   Methodology

Figure 1 shows the methodology of the conducted work, structured into five steps. They are presented in detail below.

3.1 Crawling of the Node-RED Library

As first step in the study (step ① in Fig. 1), the Node-RED library was crawled to retrieve the source code of all node packages currently listed. A custom script was implemented that scrapes all node package identifiers from the library's official website[3]. At the time of the analysis, September 10th 2024, 5051 node packages were listed. The analysis script then retrieved the source code of 5032 of the listed node packages from the npm package manager. The other 19 node packages (0.4% of the library) had broken download links. From the downloaded node packages, 133 (2.6% of the library) were excluded because they did not contain any nodes. Instead, they contain other content related to Node-RED, such as customizations to change the appearance of the development dashboard or tools that support users in the development. A further 101 node packages (2.0% of the library) were removed because they did not contain parsable specifications. After these steps, the source code of 4798 valid node packages remained (95.0% of the library).

The valid node packages contained 17603 individual nodes. Figure 2a shows the distribution of the number of nodes per node package, excluding the 10 most extreme outliers because they skew the graph. Four of these outliers are node packages containing more than 100 individual nodes (507, 195, 137, and 134 nodes), the other six range between 61 and 96 nodes. Most of the valid node packages (2035) contain a single node.

Figure 2b shows the distribution of the size of node packages in lines of code (LOC), considering functional code. The figure does not show the highest per-

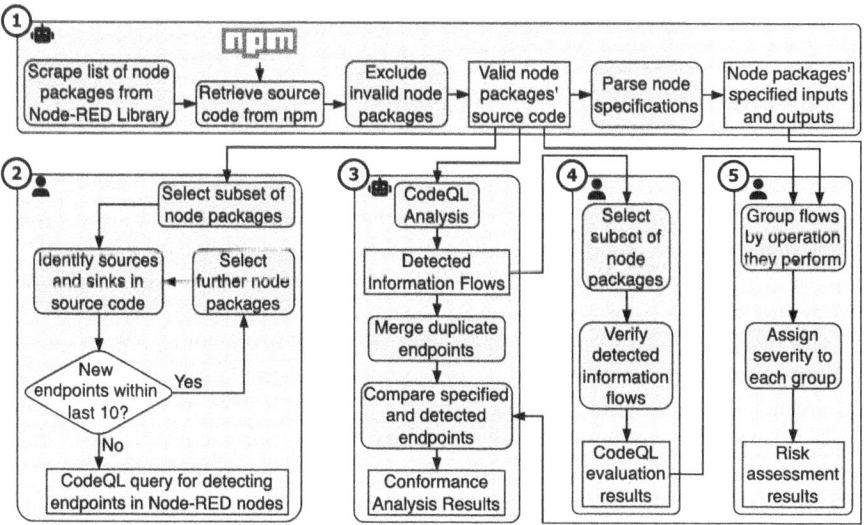

Fig. 1. Methodology of the conducted study. ▲ = manual step, 🤖 = automated step

---

[3] flows.nodered.org/search?type=node.

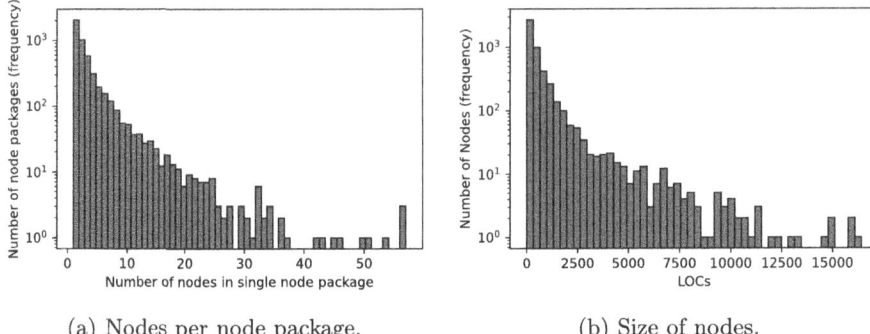

(a) Nodes per node package.   (b) Size of nodes.

Fig. 2. Distribution of (a) the number of nodes per node package (not showing the ten highest outliers) and (b) the size of nodes in LOC (not showing the 100th percentile). Outliers excluded because they skew the graph.

centile of values, since they would skew the graph. The largest node package has a size of 148397 LOC. Another outlier has 114110 LOC, the remaining 49 values in the 100th percentile are below 100000 LOC. As shown in the plot, the majority of node packages contains up to 2500 LOC.

For later use in the conformance analysis, the node packages' specifications were parsed by the analysis script to retrieve the numbers of specified inputs and outputs of each node. For this, the HTML files in each node package were searched for the parameters *inputs* and *outputs*, considering all different formats of how these parameters are defined throughout the library.

3.2   Identification of Nodes' Endpoints

A CodeQL query was required that captures the sources and sinks that CodeQL should consider in its information flow analysis (step ②). The query needed to be created manually, since the endpoints are specific to the Node-RED ecosystem and no such resource could be found anywhere. To this end, we selected a subset of all valid node packages and manually analyzed their source code to identify sources and sinks of information flows. The sample size of nodes was chosen such that the margin of error is below 10% with a confidence level of 95%, resulting in 97 node packages to be analyzed. The margin of error is tolerated due to the high required manual effort, as indicated by the size of node packages shown in Fig. 2b. From our experience of the variability of the source code of nodes in the ecosystem, this number is sufficiently high to create a comprehensive CodeQL query. To mitigate the introduced error nevertheless, we additionally considered saturation by analyzing further node packages after the initial set of 97 until no new endpoints were encountered within the last ten analyzed ones.

The analyzed samples should cover major node packages that are most often used in Node-RED flows and which are often developed and maintained by a team of experienced developers over a long time, as well as less common nodes that are created by independent developers with possibly less rigor. Therefore, half of the samples were selected from the most popular nodes based on the number of downloads within the last week (this metric is used for ranking in the Node-RED library), and the other half randomly from all valid node packages.

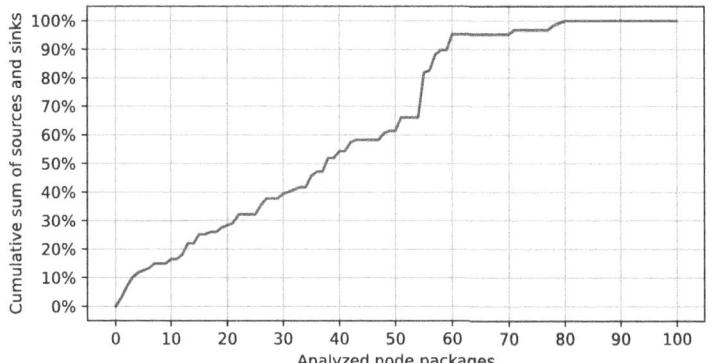

Fig. 3. Saturation of manually detected sources and sinks in the analyzed node packages. $100\% \triangleq 127$ endpoints.

For the analysis, all JavaScript, TypeScript, and HTML files in the node packages were manually examined. We identified all methods, variables, and functions in the code that serve as a source or sink (see Sect. 2.2). Figure 3 visualizes the saturation progression, showing the cumulative number of detected endpoints against the number of analyzed node packages. It shows, that 90% of the overall sources and sinks were identified in the first 60 node packages and that no new sources or sinks were encountered within the last 20 analyzed node packages. Thus, the formulated saturation criterion was met by analyzing the initial 97 node packages and no further samples were analyzed.

The process identified 59 sources and 68 sinks (127 endpoints in total). They were translated into a CodeQL query, following the documentation of the query language QL^4. To verify the correctness, we ran it without information flow analysis, i.e., such that only the location of detected sources and sinks is reported. For each of the 127 endpoints, we selected one of its manually identified occurrences in the source code and verified that CodeQL detected this location.

3.3 Conformance Analysis

The conformance analysis (step ③) was performed on the granularity of node packages instead of individual nodes. Although an analysis of individual nodes would allow for a more detailed assessment, information flows detected by CodeQL cannot be reliably assigned to an individual node if it is contained in a

---

[4] codeql.github.com/docs.

node package with other nodes. In cases where, e.g., nodes within a package share recurring functionality in custom libraries, a detected flow can not always be reliably assigned to an individual node. Since the nodes in a node package are created by the same (group of) developer(s), we can assume that their level of conformance between implementation and specification should be similar.

Each node package was transformed into a CodeQL database and the query created in step ② was applied to each database by custom scripts that execute the commands as indicated in the official CodeQL documentation. An individual CodeQL result file per node package resulted from the analysis that listed all possible information flows within the node package. Then, duplicate endpoints within the results were merged. Since CodeQL considers all possible information flows between endpoints, it can detect multiple flows that have the same source and sink, for instance, if they differ in a hard-coded input parameter. In addition, flows can have different sources but the same sink or vice versa. Since the argumentation in this article is on the level of individual endpoints, such duplicates had to be resolved to identify distinct endpoints. The merging was realized by a custom script that considers the file, line number, and method, function, or variable that form the endpoint to clearly identify distinct endpoints.

Finally, the number of identified sources and sinks per node package was compared against the number of specified inputs and outputs as parsed from the specifications in step ①. Based on this comparison, the conformance case (convergence, absence, or divergence, see Sect. 2.3) of each node package was determined and some statistics such as the exact number of additional or missing endpoints were calculated. The results are presented below in Sect. 4.1

3.4   Evaluation of CodeQL's Correctness

To evaluate the accuracy of the used analysis pipeline, we manually checked the correctness of a subset of the information flows that CodeQL detected (step ④). The information flow analysis with CodeQL is the only step in the methodology that is subject to major threats to its validity, due to its complex nature and the impact of the created query's quality on the results. All other steps are simple and robust, and their correctness was easily verified during their implementation.

For the evaluation, we selected a subset of all valid node packages following the same process as for the creation of the CodeQL query and ensuring that no node package that had been used to create the query was used for this evaluation, since this could thwart the results. All information flows detected by CodeQL in the thus selected 97 node packages were manually checked for their correctness. Specifically, it was checked for each flow reported by CodeQL whether the source and sink were valid and whether a control flow was possible during the node's execution in which information from the source propagates to the sink.

CodeQL detected 964 information flows across the 97 analyzed node packages. The manual checking yielded 951 true positives and 13 false positives, resulting in a precision of 0.99. Considering the chosen margin of error, the precision is seen as sufficiently high to draw conclusions about the Node-RED ecosystem from our conformance analysis. The false positives detected were caused by ambiguous variable names, e.g., a variable called "key" being detected as a source that referred to a key in a dictionary instead of an encryption key.

Note that, while it would be desirable to check for additional information flows not detected by CodeQL, such an analysis is extremely labor intensive and error-prone and out of the scope of this work – compare the sizes of node packages reported in Fig. 2b . We hope for the emergence of a dataset that could serve as the ground truth for such a study, thus allowing for an evaluation of CodeQL's recall. Currently, only its precision can be evaluated by us. Due to this, we cannot make sound statements about absence cases in the conformance analysis and therefore focus on divergence cases in the discussion of the results.

3.5   Risk assessment (Step ⑤)

Since not all detected divergences necessarily pose a security risk, we assessed the impact of the identified divergent information flows on the security of users. To this end, the risk associated with a subset of the information flows detected by CodeQL was evaluated. While the conformance analysis was performed on the level of endpoints, the risk assessment needed to consider complete information flows, to take into account the sensitivity of the transferred data.

The same set of node packages as for the evaluation of CodeQL's correctness (step ④) was used for this assessment because these information flows' correctness had been manually verified. The selection was not restricted to divergent node packages because it is not possible to distinguish between the information flows within a node that had been considered by its specifications and those that are divergent. Therefore, information flows from any node package are suitable for this process. The CodeQL results of each sample were analyzed manually, and all detected information flows were classified by the action they perform and the type of data they send. Here, an action refers to functionalities such as displaying an error message, writing to a file, sending a message to another node, etc. The grouping by type of data sent was based on the data's sensitivity.

The first author performed the classification following an inductive approach, where each assessed information flow was assigned to a group indicating the performed action and the type of transferred data. An information flow was assigned to an existing group if a suitable one existed and a new group for it was created otherwise. Afterwards, groups were revised and merged if they could be generalized without loosing specificity about the induced risk, e.g., if the performed action of two groups were different but comparable from the perspective of a risk assessment.

A severity level was then assigned to each resulting group in a discussion with three authors, indicating the risk introduced by each group of information flows. The assessment of the severity was influenced by (i) the sensitivity of the transferred data, (ii) the context to which data is exposed (local or outside), and (iii) the possible impact of exposed data on the program's control flow. We assumed an attacker model where only the development process with Node-RED is confidential, and all other contexts could potentially be observed by an attacker, since the developed programs are deployed on IoT devices that usually run autonomously without supervision and can also be located such that physical access is not controlled. The assessment followed a worst-case classification in cases of ambiguity where the risk depended on the deployment context.

The classification was performed for all information flows detected by CodeQL before they are merged in the later stages of the conformance analysis. We did so to not lose information due to the merging. If, for example, CodeQL detects two flows for two different information objects from the same input to the same output, these are merged into one in the conformance analysis. However, the two information objects can be of different sensitivity and therefore have different security implications when exposed. Performing the risk assessment before the merging thus provides more accurate results.

3.6   Threats to Validity

The conclusions drawn from the presented results are subject to some threats to validity. We present possible limitations and how we mitigated them.

Internal. Some of the presented results are based on the work of one individual researcher, which introduces the risk of researcher bias and errors during the analysis. We addressed this threat by discussing the critical parts and intermediate results of the analysis process with the other authors. A second limitation is introduced by the exploratory nature of the conducted study, for which no existing ground truth could be used to validate the correctness of the non-conformance analysis. The evaluation of CodeQL's correctness (see Sect. 3.4) is a mitigation for this. The important CodeQL query also had to be created by us and was repeatedly checked for its correct capturing of all manually identified sources and sinks in the analyzed node packages. The results of the CodeQL evaluation and the iterative creation of the query indicate, that the analysis pipeline functions as intended, as far as we could check it in the given context.

External. Since we analyzed the complete population of the investigated domain (the library of Node-RED node packages), the generalization of the presented results is not an issue. However, the results should not be generalized to, e.g., other IoT development frameworks without verifying comparability.

Construct. Conformance analysis is a suitable tool to investigate compliance between different system artifacts and is commonly used for this purpose. Using the specifications as representation of the design level model and the information flow analysis as representation of the implementation is in line with the related literature. Using the nodes' specifications as comparator for the information flows detected by CodeQL might not be suitable for other analyses because they are developer-created and therefore not reliable, however, this is exactly the mismatch we aimed to investigate. Consequently, it is seen as fitting in our case.

The risk assessment was conducted on information flows detected in both divergent and non-divergent node packages. Therefore, the conclusions drawn are

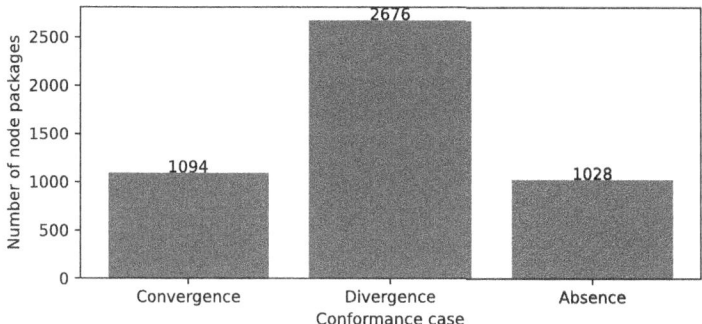

Fig. 4. Results of the non-conformance analysis. n = 4798.

not solely based on the risks introduced by divergent flows. At the construction level, it is not possible to distinguish between flows that were considered by the developer when creating the specifications and those that were not. Thus, selecting only divergent flows for the risk assessment was not possible. Furthermore, the applied methodology was a deliberate design decision to avoid potential bias that could arise if all assessed flows were known to be divergent.

Finally, using static analysis might not be suitable for cases where configurations influence how nodes behave at runtime. Still, it is considered the best tool for the conducted investigation, as such cases should be rare.

4   Results

The conformance analysis of all valid (analyzable) node packages in the Node-RED library and the risk assessment of a subset of the detected flows were performed following the methodology presented in Sect. 3.3 and Sect. 3.5. A replication package for the presented results is made available [6].

4.1   RQ1: Conformance Analysis

The CodeQL information flow analysis of the node packages' source code using the query created in step ② yielded a total of 58807 detected information flows. After merging duplicate endpoints in the flows, 42590 endpoints across all analyzed node packages remained. Comparing each node package's specified inputs and outputs against the number of identified endpoints resulted in the classification of each node package into one of the three conformance cases. Figure 4 shows the results of this classification. Within the 4798 valid node packages at the time of analysis, 1094 (22.8%) were classified as convergence cases, 2676 (55.8%) as divergence cases, and 1028 (21.4%) as absence cases. In terms of individual nodes contained in the node packages, there are 2240 individual nodes assigned to the convergence case, 10903 to the divergence case, and 4807 to the absence case. As a ratio of individual nodes per node package, the convergence case has 2.05

individual nodes per node package, the divergence case 4.06, and the absence case 4.67. Concerning the size of the node packages in lines of code (LOC), the nodes in the convergence case have 270 LOC per node package on average, the nodes in the divergence case 1492 LOC per node package, and the nodes in the absence case 950 LOC per node package. Comparing the two above measures shows that individual nodes in the convergence case have 132 LOC on average, 367 LOC per node in the divergence case, and 204 LOC per node in the absence case.

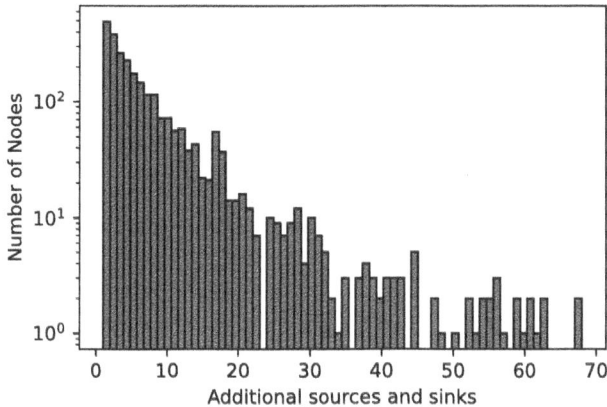

Fig. 5. Distribution of the combined number of additional sources and/or sinks per divergent node package as histogram. Not showing the highest percentile because they skew the graph.

Figure 5 presents a histogram of the number of additional endpoints per node package that is classified as divergent. It does not show the outliers in the highest percentile for readability purposes. The 100th percentile contains 27 values, ten of them are values between 70 and 100, 16 further ones reach up to 194, and the highest value lies at 556 combined additional sources and sinks. On average, there are 2.9 additional sources and 5.3 additional sinks per node package in the divergent node packages, i.e., 8.2 additional endpoints in sum. This is an average of 2 additional endpoints per node.

❶ **RQ1:** Figure 4 shows the distribution of the node packages in the Node-RED library of nodes across the three conformance cases. 55% of the node packages were classified as divergent, i.e., containing hidden information flows. On average, a divergent node had 2 additional endpoints.

4.2   RQ2: Risk Assessment

The risk assessment was performed based on the 951 information flows detected by CodeQL within the selected subset of 97 node packages that were manually verified to be correct in step ④ of the methodology (see Sect. 3.4). For 12 of the 951, the type of transferred data could not be determined with certainty, and they were therefore not considered in the further assessment, yielding 939 remaining information flows. By manually analyzing the source code of the node packages and following the methodology presented in Sect. 3.5, 18 different groups were created to classify the information flows.

Table 1. Results of the risk assessment. Identified groups in the detected information flows, the number and precentage of flows in each group, and the assigned severity of the introduced security risk. Separated by the passed information.

Information	Group description	Flows		Severity
Sensitive information	Display sensitive information in terminal	37	(3.9%)	high
	Display sensitive information in dashboard	46	(4.9%)	medium
	Log sensitive information	31	(3.3%)	high
	Send sensitive information to external server	31	(3.3%)	high
	Write sensitive information to file	3	(0.3%)	high
	Send sensitive information to framework	11	(1.2%)	medium
Error message	Log error message	16	(1.7%)	high
	Display error message in dashboard	110	(11.7%)	medium
	Display error message in terminal	18	(1.9%)	high
Input message	Send input message to other node	323	(34.4%)	low
	Log input message	56	(6.0%)	high
	Send input message to ext. hardware device	2	(0.2%)	high
	Display input message in dashboard	175	(18.6%)	medium
	Write input message to file	6	(0.6%)	high
	Send input message to external server	22	(2.3%)	high
	Display input message in terminal	28	(3.0%)	high
Misc.	Misc. low severity	10	(1.1%)	low
	Misc. high severity	14	(1.5%)	high

Table 1 presents the groups, the number of information flows that were assigned to each, and the severity assessment associated with each group.

When comparing the different groups, it is apparent that the type of transferred information does not affect the severity, only the context to which it is exposed. As we realized late during the analysis, each group's type of transferred data can contain sensitive information. The first block of groups in Table 1 (with *Sensitive information* in the column *Information*) are groups directly related to sensitive information. These are information flows that handle entities such as passwords, encryption keys, usernames, etc. The second block of groups (*Error message* in column *Information*) cover information flows that handle error messages. While standard error messages of existing libraries and frameworks are usually innocuous, they can also contain information that should not be disclosed. Especially when they are customized by developers, they often contain sensitive information. Multiple CWEs refer to this issue (CWE-209 *Generation of Error Message Containing Sensitive Information*[5] as well as other more specific CWEs) and it has been noted in the literature as well [16,31]. Finally, the third block of groups in Table 1 (*Input message* in column *Information*) contains groups that handle the input message a node received from other upstream nodes. These messages also often contain sensitive information required for the node's functionality. After establishing that all information could potentially be sensitive, the context to which it is exposed remains the only factor to determine the risk imposed by an information flow. We retain the created grouping nevertheless to give a more nuanced classification.

Table 2 summarizes the results of the risk assessment by the assigned severity rating. A low severity can be assumed for 35.5% of the information flows, a medium severity for 36.4%, and a high severity for 28.1%.

---

❶ RQ2: Table 2 provides the answer to RQ2, summarizing the results of the risk assessment of a subset of detected information flows into the severity ratings. A high severity is associated with 28% of information flows, a medium severity with 36% of analyzed flows.

---

5   Discussion

5.1   Divergences in the Node-RED Ecosystem

The results presented in Sect. 4.1 paint a concerning picture of the state of conformance between the implementation and specifications of the nodes in the Node-RED ecosystem. More than half of the node packages and an even higher proportion of the individual nodes are detected to be divergent, with an average of 8.2 additional endpoints per node package or 2 additional endpoints per individual node. Many node packages show dozens of additional endpoints in the implementation compared to the specifications. As the histogram in Fig. 5 shows, most node packages have only one or a few additional endpoints. This could suggest that many cases can be explained by minor negligence by the developer instead of a more substantial problem. The consequences, however,

Table 2. Results of the risk assessment summarized per severity rating.

Severity	Flows	Percentage
Low	333	35.5%
Medium	342	36.4%
High	264	28.1%

---

[5] https://cwe.mitre.org/data/definitions/209.html.

can be the same as for a node package with many additional endpoints. Overall, the observed numbers show a disconnection between implementation and specifications that make the specifications useless in their current form.

This disconnection can not be explained by differing definitions of inputs and outputs, since a large portion of node packages were also classified as absence cases. Further, no such definition could be found from Node-RED, therefore, the results at the least show a lack of consensus among the open-source developers.

Since it cannot be determined which endpoints were considered by the developers when creating a node's specifications and therefore, which are the divergent endpoints, discussing the origins of divergences in detail is speculative. However, as an intermediate step of the risk assessment, Table 1 also shows the type of endpoints that are prevalent in the nodes, regardless of the conformance case. As shown there, most of the identified information flows either display information in the terminal or the development dashboard, or they log information. Interestingly, these are likely not required for the corresponding nodes' functionalities in the majority of cases. Instead, they mostly concern the development or maintenance process, both of which are not performed by the typical end-user of the IoT devices but rather the developers of the applications. This also suggests that a possible mitigation for part of the issue at hand might be to simply remove or disable these parts of the code without breaking their functionality.

The average number of individual nodes per node package and the LOC per node package per conformance case suggest that smaller, less complex node packages tend to be divergent. On the other hand, the groups of absence and divergence node packages show a higher average number of nodes per node package. This could indicate that node packages with a high number of nodes have a tendency for non-conformance in general. Intuitively, this observation seems reasonable, given that the increasing complexity and size of the codebase for larger node packages also add mental load for the developer(s) and make it more difficult to keep an overview of the system and all information flows.

5.2   Risks to Users of the Node-RED Ecosystem

The additional, "hidden" information flows detected in the conformance analysis that are not captured by the specifications could expose sensitive information and allow infiltration of the system. The risk assessment presented in Sect. 4.2 shows the possible implications of using the analyzed nodes. A high severity rating is associated with slightly less than a third of the analyzed information flows, a medium and low severity with slightly more than a third each.

As a general observation, the results of the risk assessment indicate a substantial security risk for users of the Node-RED framework. Without the possibility to gauge the security implications of a specific node, chances are high that users build applications containing nodes with medium or high risk severity.

As shown in Table 1, roughly one third of all information flows pass messages between nodes, which is the primary intended use and is therefore associated with a low risk severity. Another large portion of information flows displays information in the terminal or dashboard or logs it. The corresponding groups

of information flow make up 517 of the analyzed information flows, corresponding to 55.1%. They are especially interesting because they do not influence the
behavior of the developed application, but instead support the development or
maintenance process – in other words: the developer's work. While logging is
important for failure analysis after an incident occurred and displaying information to the user during operation can be part of an application's functionality,
we estimate that the extent to which these actions are prevalent in the analyzed
node packages is higher than necessary. Especially so, when considering that
there are dedicated nodes for these use-cases, e.g., the *debug*-node to display
information in the Node-RED dashboard. Using a single node or small number of nodes made specifically for actions that could have security implications
would allow the realization of security mechanisms at a central point, for example, the sanitization of output values or logs. Instead, our analysis shows that
these functionalities are realized with custom implementations in the analyzed
nodes.

Other information flows interact with files, external servers, or hardware
devices. It is likely that these are information flows that are fundamental to the
implemented functionality of the corresponding nodes, and therefore a security
risk that has to be tolerated and mitigated by properly securing them.

6   Related Work

Security Conformance Analysis between Models and Code. Detecting
conformance issues between models of software systems and their implementation can help identify security issues at different abstraction levels and in different
steps of the software development lifecycle. For example, Peldszus et al. [27] and
Tuma et al. [34] identify non-conformance in the security design by automatically detecting mappings between models and implementation and detecting
deviations. Other approaches use similar techniques to detect architectural drift
or erosion, referring to discrepancies between implementation and design that
emerge over time. A systematic mapping study conducted by Li et al. [21] identified multiple approaches that address this issue. For example, Zhong et al. [41]
have proposed an approach based on software reflexion models introduced by
Murphy et al. [26] that checks UML diagrams for non-conformances at multiple
stages of the software development process. Other approaches explicitly formu-
late rules for mappings that need to hold and can automatically be checked, e.g.,
Uzun and Tekinerdogan [36] and Marchezan et al. [24]. While these approaches
also conduct non-conformance analyses between different system artifacts, they
assume a rich model representation beyond the specified inputs and outputs.

Code-Level Information Flow Security Analysis. Code-level security analysis omits the creation of a model of the analyzed software system and instead
works directly on the source code, as we do with the conducted information flow
analysis. A publication by Tabrizi and Pattabiraman [33] showed that a code-
level security analysis for IoT devices outperformed the same analysis based on
model-checking in terms of accuracy and execution time. Several approaches have

been proposed that aim to ease the often labor-intensive process of conducting information flow analysis by automating the identification of analysis specifications (such as sources and sinks), e.g., in C# (Livshits et al. [22]), Python (Chibotaru et al. [9]), and Android applications (Rasthofer et al. [28], Clapp et al. [10]). For JavaScript, Dutta et al. [13] have proposed a semi-automated approach that only considers the identification of sinks and is therefore not used in this paper. Staicu et al. [32] proposed an automated approach to detect both sources and sinks; however, their approach is dynamic and therefore not feasible for our work. While none of the above approaches were suitable in the context of this work, future research could include the adaption or extension of an existing approach to improve the creation process of the CodeQL query we used, especially if an approach such as our conformance analysis were to be used to implement automated compliance checks in Node-RED.

Node-RED and npm. The package manager npm and different security aspects of it have been investigated before and possible mitigations to increase its security have been proposed. Since Node-RED relies on npm, some of the more general findings pertain to it as well. For example, Zahan et al. [39] proposed multiple indicators for the detection of malicious packages, Decan et al. [12] and Alfadel et al. [4] investigated security vulnerabilities, and Zimmermann et al. [42] investigated security risks and their origins in npm packages. All these publications revealed wide-spread issues of vulnerable and exploitable packages in npm while also aiming to support developers in the identification of pressing security issues that need to be addressed. Ferreira et al. [14] identified, that a stricter access control scheme following the principle of least-privilege could be a mitigation to these issues and protect from malicious packages.

Some researchers also targeted Node-RED specifically. A suite of multiple tools designed to increase security and privacy for applications built with the Node-RED framework has been presented by Ioannidis et al. [19]. The authors provide techniques and tools to enable encrypted information flows between nodes, to perform code verification at runtime, to enforce access control policies in Node-RED applications, and to monitor Node-RED applications at runtime to detect security incidents. While these are valuable tools to enforce security in the ecosystem, their publications do not investigate the extent to which security issues could occur. Ancona et al. [5] proposed an approach for runtime monitoring of Node-RED applications. They use program traces to verify that API patterns comply with reference specifications in order to prevent unsafe program flows. Clerrisi et al. [11] follow the same idea but also capture static system information in their system models. Although these techniques do not specifically consider security, their dynamic approaches complement the static analysis approach we followed in our work, allowing a holistic security analysis if such approaches were to be combined. An approach proposed by Ahmadpanah et al. [2] goes beyond monitoring and instead enforces access control of modules and APIs based on pre-defined security policies via allow-lists. This resembles one of the possible mitigations we propose to the problem identified in this paper.

To the best of our knowledge, no investigation of the state of security of Node-RED nodes has been published before. This paper is the first to perform a comprehensive analysis of the source code that Node-RED applications are made from, concerning its information flow security.

7 Conclusion and Outlook on Possible Mitigations

Insecure applications running on IoT devices can have grave implications for users. This paper presents the results of a conformance analysis of nodes in the Node-RED library of nodes. By comparing the number of specified inputs and outputs against the number of endpoints detected via an information flow analysis with CodeQL, we identified a ratio of 55% divergent node packages within the complete library of 4798 node packages. These divergent node packages exhibit more possible information flow endpoints than are captured by their specifications, thus enabling "hidden" information flows. Such cases could potentially be exploited by attackers to obtain access to sensitive information that should be restricted from them. A risk assessment of a subset of the information flows showed, that 28% of them are associated with a high severity rating, imposing a substantial security risk to users of the Node-RED ecosystem.

Possible Mitigations. In a low-code environment such as Node-RED, the impact of security issues is increased because the user is likely not capable of addressing or even realizing such problems. We see a few main directions to mitigate the identified issue, revolving around improving the security of nodes, the information provided about nodes, and the information available to developers. These directions are discussed in the following paragraphs.

Improving the security of nodes could be either managed centrally by the framework itself, be left to the open-source developers, or realized in a mixture of these two. On the framework side, each contributed node could have to undergo a security analysis before being published. This analysis could, for example, resemble the information flow analysis we have conducted in this paper. If such a process is in place, it could also be extended with further security checks, such as the execution of a number of industry-standard static application security testing tools (SAST). The responsibility to perform this process could also be moved to the developers, who would have to run a standardized information flow analysis or other security checks and provide the results of it when submitting new or changed code to the framework. With such a mechanism in place, contributions could be rejected if they do not meet certain requirements, such as the realization of information flows only with whitelisted functionalities.

Another technical solution could be to adjust the framework to be more restrictive in regard to information flows. Nodes could be encapsulated more strictly and data only allowed to enter or exit the nodes via framework-specific channels. Such a solution would break the functionality of many nodes that are not adjusted to the new framework version, but it would greatly improve the security of developed applications. Compatibility issues could be mitigated by introducing the new version over an extended period of time in which existing nodes would have to be migrated, a standard practice for such updates.

Another direction to address the identified issue could be to enforce a security analysis process such as described above, but where the vetting process would not necessarily enforce any restrictions. Simply providing the results of the analysis to users would allow an informed decision on whether to use a specific node or refrain from it. This approach essentially matches the current idea of providing specifications for contributed nodes, with the difference that the non-conformances between implementation and specifications would be addressed.

More information should also be made available for developers of nodes. Currently, the only information about security provided by Node-RED concerns enforcing access control mechanisms to the development dashboard. No definition of inputs and outputs of nodes exists. There are no resources that discuss the security of node package contributions or what their specifications should capture. We believe it is likely that the lack of available information concerning security caused, in part, the issue this paper has identified in the ecosystem.

References

1. Ahmad, R., Alsmadi, I.: Machine learning approaches to IoT security: a systematic literature review. Internet Things **14**, 100365 (2021). https://doi.org/10.1016/j.iot.2021.100365
2. Ahmadpanah, M.M., Balliu, M., Hedin, D., Olsson, L.E., Sabelfeld, A.: Securing Node-RED Applications, pp. 1–21. Springer (2021). https://doi.org/10.1007/978-3-030-91631-2_1
3. Al-Garadi, M.A., Mohamed, A., Al-Ali, A.K., Du, X., Ali, I., Guizani, M.: A survey of machine and deep learning methods for internet of things (IoT) security. IEEE Commun. Surv. Tutor. **22**(3), 1646–1685 (2020). https://doi.org/10.1109/COMST.2020.2988293
4. Alfadel, M., Costa, D.E., Mkhallalati, M., Shihab, E., Adams, B.: On the threat of NPM vulnerable dependencies in node.js applications. CoRR **abs/2009.09019** (2020)
5. Ancona, D., Franceschini, L., Delzanno, G., Leotta, M., Ribaudo, M., Ricca, F.: Towards runtime monitoring of node.js and its application to the internet of things. Electron. Proc. Theoret. Comput. Sci. **264**, 27–42 (2018). https://doi.org/10.4204/eptcs.264.4
6. Anonymous authors of this paper: Replication package of this paper (2025). https://anonymous.4open.science/r/replication_package_ARES-CC51/
7. Bock, A.C., Frank, U.: Low-code platform. Bus. Inf. Syst. Eng. **63**, 733–740 (2021)
8. Chatterjee, A., Ahmed, B.S.: IoT anomaly detection methods and applications: a survey. Internet Things **19**, 100568 (2022). https://doi.org/10.1016/j.iot.2022.100568
9. Chibotaru, V., Bichsel, B., Raychev, V., Vechev, M.: Scalable taint specification inference with big code. In: Proceedings of the 40th ACM SIGPLAN Conference on Programming Language Design and Implementation, PLDI 2019, pp. 760–774. ACM (2019). https://doi.org/10.1145/3314221.3314648

10. Clapp, L., Anand, S., Aiken, A.: ModelGEN: mining explicit information flow specifications from concrete executions. In: Proceedings of the 2015 International Symposium on Software Testing and Analysis, ISSTA 2015, pp. 129–140. ACM (2015). https://doi.org/10.1145/2771783.2771810

11. Clerissi, D., Leotta, M., Reggio, G., Ricca, F.: Towards an approach for developing and testing node-red IoT systems. In: Proceedings of the 1st ACM SIGSOFT International Workshop on Ensemble-Based Software Engineering, EnSEmble 2018, pp. 1–8. ACM (2018). https://doi.org/10.1145/3281022.3281023

12. Decan, A., Mens, T., Constantinou, E.: On the impact of security vulnerabilities in the NPM package dependency network. In: Proceedings of the 15th International Conference on Mining Software Repositories, MSR 2018, pp. 181–191. ACM (2018). https://doi.org/10.1145/3196398.3196401

13. Dutta, S., Garbervetsky, D., Lahiri, S., Schäfer, M.: InspectJS: leveraging code similarity and user-feedback for effective taint specification inference for JavaScript. arXiv preprint arXiv:2111.09625 (2021)

14. Ferreira, G., Jia, L., Sunshine, J., Kästner, C.: Containing malicious package updates in NPM with a lightweight permission system. In: 2021 IEEE/ACM 43rd International Conference on Software Engineering (ICSE), pp. 1334–1346 (2021). https://doi.org/10.1109/ICSE43902.2021.00121

15. HaddadPajouh, H., Dehghantanha, A., M. Parizi, R., Aledhari, M., Karimipour, H.: A survey on internet of things security: Requirements, challenges, and solutions. Internet of Things **14**, 100129 (2021). https://doi.org/10.1016/j.iot.2019.100129

16. Halfond, W.G., Viegas, J., Orso, A., et al.: A classification of SQL injection attacks and countermeasures. In: ISSSE (2006)

17. Hassija, V., Chamola, V., Saxena, V., Jain, D., Goyal, P., Sikdar, B.: A survey on IoT security: application areas, security threats, and solution architectures. IEEE Access **7**, 82721–82743 (2019). https://doi.org/10.1109/ACCESS.2019.2924045

18. Huawei Technologies Co., L.: Global connectivity index. http://www.huawei.com/minisite/gci/en/index.html

19. Ioannidis, T., Bolgouras, V., Xenakis, C., Politis, I.: Securing the flow: security and privacy tools for flow-based programming. In: Proceedings of the 18th International Conference on Availability, Reliability and Security, ARES 2023. ACM (2023). https://doi.org/10.1145/3600160.3605089

20. Krohn, M., et al.: Information flow control for standard OS abstractions. In: Proceedings of Twenty-First ACM SIGOPS Symposium on Operating Systems Principles, SOSP 2007, pp. 321–334. ACM (2007). https://doi.org/10.1145/1294261.1294293

21. Li, R., Liang, P., Soliman, M., Avgeriou, P.: Understanding software architecture erosion: a systematic mapping study. J. Softw. Evol. Process **34**(3), e2423 (2022). https://doi.org/10.1002/smr.2423

22. Livshits, B., Nori, A.V., Rajamani, S.K., Banerjee, A.: Merlin: specification inference for explicit information flow problems. In: 30th ACM SIGPLAN Conference on Programming Language Design and Implementation, PLDI 2009, pp. 75–86. ACM (2009). https://doi.org/10.1145/1542476.1542485

23. Mahmoud, R., Yousuf, T., Aloul, F., Zualkernan, I.: Internet of things (IoT) security: current status, challenges and prospective measures. In: 2015 10th International Conference for Internet Technology and Secured Transactions (ICITST), pp. 336–341 (2015). https://doi.org/10.1109/ICITST.2015.7412116

24. Marchezan, L., Assunção, W.K.G., Herac, E., Keplinger, F., Egyed, A., Lauwerys, C.: Fulfilling industrial needs for consistency among engineering artifacts. In:

2023 IEEE/ACM 45th International Conference on Software Engineering: Software Engineering in Practice (ICSE-SEIP), pp. 246–257 (2023). https://doi.org/10.1109/ICSE-SEIP58684.2023.00028

25. binti Mohamad Noor, M., Hassan, W.H.: Current research on internet of things (IoT) security: a survey. Comput. Netw. **148**, 283–294 (2019). https://doi.org/10.1016/j.comnet.2018.11.025

26. Murphy, G., Notkin, D., Sullivan, K.: Software reflexion models: bridging the gap between design and implementation. IEEE Trans. Software Eng. **27**(4), 364–380 (2001). https://doi.org/10.1109/32.917525

27. Peldszus, S., Tuma, K., Strüber, D., Jürjens, J., Scandariato, R.: Secure dataflow compliance checks between models and code based on automated mappings. In: 2019 ACM/IEEE 22nd International Conference on Model Driven Engineering Languages and Systems (MODELS), pp. 23–33. IEEE (2019)

28. Rasthofer, S., Arzt, S., Bodden, E.: A machine-learning approach for classifying and categorizing android sources and sinks. In: NDSS, vol. 14 (2014)

29. Rokis, K., Kirikova, M.: Challenges of low-code/no-code software development: a literature review. In: Perspectives in Business Informatics Research, pp. 3–17. Springer (2022)

30. Schwartz, E.J., Avgerinos, T., Brumley, D.: All you ever wanted to know about dynamic taint analysis and forward symbolic execution (but might have been afraid to ask). In: 2010 IEEE Symposium on Security and Privacy, pp. 317–331 (2010). https://doi.org/10.1109/SP.2010.26

31. Smith, B., Williams, L., Austin, A.: Idea: using system level testing for revealing SQL injection-related error message information leaks. In: Engineering Secure Software and Systems, pp. 192–200. Springer (2010)

32. Staicu, C.A., Torp, M.T., Schäfer, M., Møller, A., Pradel, M.: Extracting taint specifications for JavaScript libraries. In: Proceedings of the ACM/IEEE 42nd International Conference on Software Engineering, ICSE 2020, pp. 198–209. ACM (2020). https://doi.org/10.1145/3377811.3380390

33. Tabrizi, F.M., Pattabiraman, K.: Design-level and code-level security analysis of IoT devices. ACM Trans. Embed. Comput. Syst. **18**(3), 1–25 (2019)

34. Tuma, K., Peldszus, S., Strüber, D., Scandariato, R., Jürjens, J.: Checking security compliance between models and code. Softw. Syst. Model., 1–24 (2022). https://doi.org/10.1007/s10270-022-00991-5

35. Udoh, I.S., Kotonya, G.: Developing IoT applications: challenges and frameworks. IET Cyber-Phys. Syst. Theory Appl. **3**(2), 65–72 (2018). https://doi.org/10.1049/iet-cps.2017.0068

36. Uzun, B., Tekinerdogan, B.: Architecture conformance analysis using model-based testing: a case study approach. Softw. Pract. Exp. **49**(3), 423–448 (2019). https://doi.org/10.1002/spe.2667

37. Williams, P., Dutta, I.K., Daoud, H., Bayoumi, M.: A survey on security in internet of things with a focus on the impact of emerging technologies. Internet Things **19**, 100564 (2022). https://doi.org/10.1016/j.iot.2022.100564

38. Xiao, L., Wan, X., Lu, X., Zhang, Y., Wu, D.: IoT security techniques based on machine learning: How do IoT devices use AI to enhance security? IEEE Signal Process. Mag. **35**(5), 41–49 (2018). https://doi.org/10.1109/MSP.2018.2825478

39. Zahan, N., Zimmermann, T., Godefroid, P., Murphy, B., Maddila, C., Williams, L.: What are weak links in the NPM supply chain? In: Proceedings of the 44th International Conference on Software Engineering: Software Engineering in Practice, ICSE-SEIP 2022, pp. 331–340. ACM (2022). https://doi.org/10.1145/3510457.3513044

40. Zhang, Z.K., Cho, M.C.Y., Wang, C.W., Hsu, C.W., Chen, C.K., Shieh, S.: IoT security: ongoing challenges and research opportunities. In: 2014 IEEE 7th International Conference on Service-Oriented Computing and Applications, pp. 230–234 (2014). https://doi.org/10.1109/SOCA.2014.58
41. Zhong, C., et al.: DOMICO: checking conformance between domain models and implementations. Softw. Pract. Exp. (2023). https://doi.org/10.1002/spe.3272
42. Zimmermann, M., Staicu, C.A., Tenny, C., Pradel, M.: Small world with high risks: a study of security threats in the NPM ecosystem. In: 28th USENIX Security Symposium, pp. 995–1010. USENIX Association (2019)

Scrambling Compiler: Automated and Unified Countermeasure for Profiled and Non-profiled Side Channel Attacks

Gabriele Magnani$^{(\boxtimes)}$ ⓘ, Isabella Piacentini, Giovanni Agosta ⓘ,
Alessandro Barenghi ⓘ, and Gerardo Pelosi ⓘ

Department of Electronics, Information and Bioengineering (DEIB),
Politecnico di Milano, Milan, Italy
{gabriele.magnani,isabella.piacentini,giovanni.agosta,
alessandro.barenghi,gerardo.pelosi}@polimi.it

Abstract. Side channel attacks extracting secrets carried by the power consumption variations or electromagnetic emissions in embedded devices are a consolidated threat to the security of edge computing systems. Such attacks either employ a synthetic model for the device behaviour to predict secret-dependent components of the measured power consumption (non-profiled attacks), or obtain such a model in a data-driven fashion (profiled attacks). Protections against both profiled and non-profiled attacks are characterized by a significant overhead, typically one or two orders of magnitude in computation time, and a comparatively significant engineering effort to deploy them. Furthermore, such protections are designed to hinder one of the two aforementioned attack strategies. In this work, we propose a compiler-based methodology to automate the application of a comparatively inexpensive countermeasure able to hinder both profiled and unprofiled attacks. We experimentally validate our approach employing the AES symmetric cipher as our case study, and a Cortex-M4 based microcontroller as the target device. Our solution increases the Measurements-to-Disclose security metric by at least 5000× in an attacker-optimal scenario, and proves to be immune to Bayesian template- and SVM-based profiled attacks.

Keywords: Embedded Systems Security · Side-Channel Attacks · Automated Countermeasure Instantiation

1 Introduction

The pervasive nature of embedded computers has led to a variety of devices, which are both interconnected and process data requiring security guarantees. One of the main threats to the cryptographic means employed to provide such security guarantees is represented by the so-called Side Channel Attacks (SCAs). SCAs allow to sidestep the computational hardness of the problems on which modern cryptographic primitives are built as they obtain information on values

M. Dalla Preda et al. (Eds.): ARES 2025, LNCS 15992, pp. 301–321, 2025.
https://doi.org/10.1007/978-3-032-00624-0_15

intended to be secret in the mathematical design of the primitive (e.g., symmetric keys, private signature keys). SCAs exploit the possibility to collect measures of physical properties, e.g., electromagnetic emissions, power consumption, or computation latency that are correlated to the secret data involved in the execution of the cryptographic primitives [26,27,33,35]. The information can be gathered either simply leveraging not-invasive observations of the system working as intended (passive SCAs), or observing the behaviour of the system under induced faults (active SCAs, also known as fault attacks). To extract information from the side channel measurements, the attacker devises a model of the power consumption of the device when an operation of the executed algorithm is performed. Such an operation is chosen in such a way that it takes as operand an (unknown) value depending from a small portion of the secret to be retrieved. The attacker then proceeds to determine the values of the model for all possible values of the secret and proceeds determining which of them best fits the measured behaviour of the device, in turn identifying the value of the portion of the secret she wants to retrieve. The model construction can be performed in a purely data-driven way (the case of *profiled* SCAs) or employing a synthetic model of the computing platform (*non-profiled* SCAs) [27]. For profiled SCAs, a large variety of statistical methods have been explored, from straightforward, but information theoretically optimal Bayes classifiers [14], to Support Vector Machines (SVMs) [25], and neural networks [17].

While a variety of SCA countermeasures are available to prevent non-profiled SCAs [2,27], there is experimental evidence that profiled SCAs can be performed even in the presence of such countermeasures [12]. *Scramble Suit* [7], on the other hand, is a dedicated countermeasure to profiled attacks designed for hardware accelerators implementing a specific cryptographic primitive. Essentially, it aims at differentiating the behaviour of each individual device, by inserting computation dependent on the secret values, the inputs and a device unique fingerprint. The differentiation is obtained duplicating the component computing the cryptographic primitive, and having the duplicate act on the same inputs as the original component, but employing a different, device dependent key. Such an approach prevents an attacker from separating the contribution of the differentiation element to the side channel behavior from the one related to the secret she's trying to extract.

However the Scramble Suit approach is vulnerable to non-profiled attacks. Indeed, a non-profiled attack can find out more than one fitting model to the device behaviour, and hence more than one admissible secret value, the attacker could simply try all the extracted secret values, at the cost of a relatively small amount of exhaustive search. *Computation Interleaving (CI)* was proposed in [30] as a unified countermeasure for both classes of attacks, once again targeting hardware implementations. CI relies on employing a single datapath to compute two, or more, instances of the cryptographic primitive to be protected, interleaving them temporally. In line of principle, temporal interleaving is replicable also in software implementations; however, the extremely high engineering cost of writing a tailored assembly-level algorithm, which is required to have the needed fine-grained control of the dataflow in a CPU pipeline, makes its transposition impractical without resorting to any automation mechanism.

Contribution. In this work, we propose a method to automate the application of the Computation Interleaving approach to software realizations of cryptographic primitives. Our approach relies on a modified compiler pipeline, which transforms an unprotected implementation of a cryptographic primitive into one protected with the computation interleaving countermeasure proposed by [30], without requiring human intervention. The proposed *CI hardening compiler* removes the demand for a per-platform engineering effort, enabling the widespread application of the approach on commodity off-the-shelf embedded platforms. Our compiler transformation takes care of tracking CPU register reuse and pipeline dataflow across the entire code being emitted, a difficulty which arises from transposing into a software realization the CI countermeasure, because dedicated hardware components are not available. Indeed, since the information leakage in side channels stems from the procedure employed to compute a value, and hence the hardware computing it, the implicit sharing of hardware resource that takes place in software implementations (e.g., register reuse) has long been known to be a source of vulnerabilities, which are challenging and time consuming to manage manually [5,13,34]. Our approach completely removes the need for specific expertise and additional engineering effort when it comes to secure a software implementation of a cipher and leverages the capabilities of a compiler infrastructure to obtain precise dataflow tracking and emit the protected assembly implementation, while fulfilling the requirements for the CI countermeasure. We validate our approach on a commercial-off-the-shelf Cortex-M4 microcontroller platform, performing profiled and non-profiled attacks and making our side channel measurements in a setting ideal for the attacker, i.e., on the ChipWhisperer [29] open evaluation platform for SCAs. We decided to take as our case study the Thumb-2 instruction set architecture (ISA) as it is supported by all ARM Cortex-M cores, which are optimized for low-cost and energy-efficient integrated circuits, and are embedded in billions of consumer devices.

Related Work. Side channel attacks and the related topics of detection of side channel vulnerabilities, countermeasure design, and their automated instantiation occupy a prominent place in the field of computer security [20]. As a recent systematic review reports [20], hardware and embedded systems security has steadily grown into the predominant topic in vulnerability analysis, during the course of the last decade. As such, a vast body of recent literature deals with the aforementioned problem, the coverage of which far exceeds the scope of this paper. We refer the reader to recent surveys for an overview of the various subtopics [22,26,35]. Providing automated instantiations of SCA countermeasures started with early attempts which employed a domain specific language or performed ad-hoc lexical analyses [6,9]. Employing dataflow analysis techniques from the domain of compiler engineering allowed the authors of [1] to automatically delineate the attack surface for power consumption based SCAs against software implementations of ciphers, and automatically apply masking countermeasures, tailoring them to avoid unneeded computational overheads. Similar approaches were also employed to prevent timing attacks [15,38]. Different approaches were also proposed, from automatic code polymorphism [10] to apply first-order boolean masking automatically [11]. Finally, the systematic code analysis and transformation capabilities of a compiler framework were also employed to introduce a new approach to counteracting SCAs that relies on modifying the runtime computation of a cryptographic primitive, while preserving the semantic equivalence of the corresponding machine code, an approach known as *code morphing* [2,3]. We advance the state of the art in the automated side channel attack countermeasure application by employing the code analysis and transformation capabilities of an industrial grade compiler, namely LLVM [23], to overcome the technical and performance limitations arising from a manual adaptation of the principles of the CI countermeasure to a software implementation of a cryptographic primitive. In particular, we leverage the compiler infrastructure to obtain systematic, instruction-level accurate scheduling, which prevents information leakage due to the sharing of the same microarchitectural components by the interleaved computations.

2   Background

In this section, we summarize the background on the Computation Interleaving countermeasure approach, and provide background notions on the structure of a compiler. Finally, we briefly describe the IT ARM instruction, available in the ARMv7 architecture, which we employ, in our chosen case study platform, to further enhance the efficiency of our approach.

2.1   Computation Interleaving Countermeasure

The Computation Interleaving (CI) countermeasure [30], employs the temporal interleaving of two (or more) computations of a block cipher as the means to introduce algorithmic noise to counteract both profiled and non-profiled side channel attacks. All the multiple computations of the same cipher are acting on the actual input of the primitive (in the following, a block cipher encryption for the sake of exposition clarity), while only one is employing the actual secret key. All other cipher instances employ different secret key values obtained combining a device fingerprint and the actual secret key so that the device keys are computationally indistinguishable from randomly drawn ones, and, knowing the actual secret key it is not possible to derive the device dependent keys. In [30] the authors propose either the use of a Physically Unclonable Function to derive the device dependent keys, or to encrypt the secret key under the device fingerprint as a key, assuming to have a dedicated encryption core to do so.

   In the following, we thus consider a CI protected symmetric block cipher $\text{ENC}(k, p)$, where k is the secret key and p the plaintext, and consider a single, device dependent, *fake* key k^f. The computation of $\text{ENC}(k, p)$ must be interleaved with the one of $\text{ENC}(k^f, p)$ in such a fashion that the three properties reported in [30] are guaranteed. To describe these properties, we will denote with $S_{i,k}$ the state of the block cipher before the i-th round computation, and therefore $S_{0,k}$ will represent the plaintext and $S_{n,k}$ as the ciphertext of an encryption procedure that applies consecutively n round computations. To realize the CI countermeasure the implementation must provide the following properties:

Property 1 (Execution Order Randomization). *The order of the operations on each pair of $S_{i,k}$ and S_{i,k^f} must be randomized.*

This property prevents the attacker from simply separating the true and fake computations by considering the time instant in which each one is being done by the device implementing the cryptosystem. Indeed, if the order in which the two cipher instances are computed is fixed, it is sufficient for an attacker to discard the computations over S_{i,k^f}, or employ the information deterministically provided by them for higher order side channel attacks [28].

Property 2 (No Same-Computation-State Overwriting). *A register should never store one after the other values from two subsequent states of the same computation, $S_{i,k}$ and $S_{i+1,k}$.*

Violating Property 2 would immediately imply that the side-channel behaviour of the implementation in the time instant when the value from $S_{i+1,k}$ overwrites the one from $S_{i,k}$ matches the one of an unprotected implementation. Indeed, such an overwriting action implies that the memory storing the values has a switching activity which is proportional to the Boolean difference, or xor the values being stored. Such a switching activity can be uniquely determined from a portion of the computation of the unprotected cipher acting on the correct secret key alone. Enforcing Property 2, instead, ensures that the value transitions in the memory elements have a side channel behavior which always depends on both the state of the cipher computing on the actual key, and the one of the cipher employing the fake key. This prevents an attacker from employing device model obtained via a data-driven strategy on a given device instance on a different one: their device keys will be different, in turn resulting in different side channel behaviours, in turn preventing a profiled attack from being effective Similarly, the dependence of the side channel behavior on both the correct and the fake key, and the dependence of the fake key on the entire correct key and device key prevents an attacker from modeling synthetically the behavior of the device to lead a non-profiled side channel attack, without requiring to guess both the user and device keys altogether, or trying to single out the contribution of the fake key (which is unfeasible if Property 1 holds).

Property 3 (No Consecutive-Computation-Operations). *The same computational operation should not be performed twice in a row on subsequent states of the same computation, $S_{i,k}$ and $S_{i+1,k}$ by the same combinatorial logic.*

Not implementing this property would enable a first-order non-profiled attack from the switching activity of the combinatorial logic, following the same line of reasoning of a violation of Property 2. Indeed, while modeling the transitions of a given arbitrary combinatorial cone is more challenging, the amount of information required to do so is the same as for memories, i.e., knowing the sequence of their inputs.

Ensuring that the three properties hold in a dedicated hardware design is relatively straightforward, as the designer has full control over the dataflow and may add dedicated memories to avoid unwanted overwriting actions. By contrast, ensuring that a CPU executing a software implementation of a cipher does not violate any of them requires precise and systematic control over the instruction scheduling and register allocation. In this work, we consider in-order, single issue CPUs, such as the ones in the overwhelming majority of microcontroller-oriented designs (e.g. ARM Cortex-M series), where it is possible to enforce such constraints from essentially an architectural point of view. Taking into account the effects of advanced microarchitectures, performing, e.g., dual issuing, requires to further specialize code emission per single microarchitecture. While this is feasible with a compiler based approach, including information on the microarchitectural leakage such as the ones from the analyses in [8] is beyond the scope of this work.

2.2 Preliminary Notions on Compiler Structure

We now provide a summary of the structure of a modern compiler pipeline, taking the LLVM compiler pipeline as an example and define the concepts from compiler theory which we will need in the following. The LLVM compiler infrastructure [23] works as a pipeline, where code, represented in the LLVM-IR format, is analysed and transformed through a sequence of separate steps called *passes*. The compiler is logically split onto three portions a *front-end*, a *middle-end* and a *back-end*. The front-end performs the parsing of the source code and produces an Intermediate Representation (IR) of it. The middle-end is composed of those passes that take as input and produce as output the LLVM-IR itself, thus remaining independent from both source and target languages. All the target machine-independent code optimization takes place there. Finally, the back-end performs machine-dependent optimization and produces the machine code. This modular and flexible infrastructure has made LLVM a trusted and popular choice for research and production compilers.

The LLVM-IR represents the source as a set of functions, each one of which has its code as a straight-line sequence of IR instructions, also known as *Basic Blocks* (BBs), delimited by branch IR instructions. Each instruction i is a tuple containing the instruction opcode (e.g., add) and its operands in the form of virtual registers. Virtual registers are meant to abstract from the actual number of available registers in the target architecture, and allow to represent the IR following the Static Single Assignment (SSA) principle [32]. An IR in SSA form is such that every instruction computing a new value sees the value stored into a new virtual register. It is praxis to say that an instruction *defines* its output virtual register, while *using* its inputs. We denote with $def(i)$ the set of virtual registers defined by the instruction i and with $use(i)$ the set of its used ones.

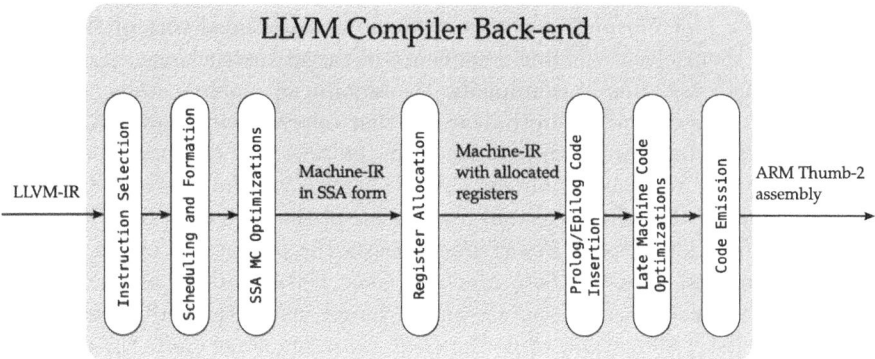

Fig. 1. High level overview of the LLVM compiler backend, highlighting the main sets of passes; the LLVM back-end

To perform automated analyses on the LLVM-IR of a program, it is commonplace to think of its instructions (or, if convenient its BBs), as logically arranged into a graph. Two graph representations are common: the *control flow graph* and the *data flow graph*. In the former, instructions represent nodes of the graph, while arcs connect two instructions if the source appears right before the destination in program order. Note that this implies that conditional branch instructions are sources for more than one arc. In the data flow graph representation, instructions are represented with nodes, while the arcs have as source node the one defining a variable and as destination nodes all the instructions which use the said variable. The data flow graph thus provides a representation of which nodes, i.e., instructions, depend on another one, as the latter will compute at runtime the values which they will use as inputs.

Our solution will use the Dominator Tree of LLVM, which is based on the notion *dominance*. An instruction i *dominates* another instruction j (and we denote it with $i \prec j$) when considering one of the two graph representations of the IR if all paths from the beginning of the function to j must pass through i. Furthermore, i *immediately dominates* j if it dominates it and no other instruction l dominates j, unless it also dominates i, that is $\forall l \in I, l \prec j \implies l \prec i$. The same notions of dominance and immediate dominance can be expressed for basic blocks rather than for individual instructions by simply coalescing together sequences of computational instructions uninterrupted by branches in the control flow graph. Being in need of controlling the scheduling of instructions and the register allocation, our modifications to the LLVM toolchain will mainly involve the LLVM backend, of which a logic view is represented in Fig. 1. The LLVM backend performs the *Instruction Selection* pass first, which replaces the LLVM-IR instructions with instructions from the target machine Instruction Set Architecture (ISA). It is commonplace to refer to the resulting IR as Machine-IR, to highlight the fact that its form depends on the target machine. The resulting Machine-IR is considered in its graph logical organizations described before, and the *Scheduling and Formation* passes, perform a topological sort of the nodes of the graph themselves, yielding a sequence of target instructions. In doing so, the Scheduling pass aims at minimizing the amount of pipeline stalls, wherever possible. Machine-dependent optimizations that operate with a program representation in SSA form are then performed by the *SSA MC Optimizations* stage. At this point, the representation *exits* the SSA form via the *Register Allocation* pass, which maps the infinite virtual register file of the SSA form onto the physical register file. The *Prolog/Epilog* stage inserts the prolog and epilog code for each function, and then the *Late Machine Code Optimizations* are performed, which are optimizations that operate on the target instructions after the resolution of the register allocation, while the *Code Emission* stage emits the assembly code.

```
ITETT  EQ
mov r0,  r4 # Then
mov r1,  r5 # Else
mov r2,  r6 # Then
mov r3,  r7 # Then
```

Listing 1.1: This list illustrates an example of IT (If-Then) instruction. In this case, <cond> is set to EQ (equal). The conditional flags are defined as ETT. This means that if the first instruction executes successfully, both the third and fourth instructions will also be executed. If the first instruction does not execute, only the second instruction will run

2.3   The ARM IT Instruction

Traditionally, the ARM architectures have always offered the possibility of computing *predicated instructions*, i.e., commit the result of an instruction if and only if a given flag, or set of flags is asserted in the program status word. Such a feature relied on a portion of the instruction encoding representing the encoding of the condition itself. Predicated instructions allow to essentially eliminate the cost of executing branch instructions in if-then-else conditional constructs. To retain this flexibility even in the compact encoding of the Thumb-2 encoded instruction sets (which are now used both in microcontroller grade and application grade ARM CPUs), the ARM Thumb-2 ISA includes an instruction known as the IT (If-Then) instruction. The IT instruction allows conditional execution of one to four instructions following it depending on a given condition code. IT instructions are also supported in the traditional ARM ISA as pseudo-instructions (and assembled into sequences of predicated instructions). The IT instruction works by specifying a condition (evaluating to a Boolean value) and a sequence of one to four markers stating if the following one to four instructions should be executed if the condition is true or false. This is encoded in assembly representing the IT instruction as IT[x[y[z]]] <cond> where <cond> serves as the condition for the initial instruction within the IT block, and x, y, and z represent the conditional flags for the subsequent instructions following the first one, with T

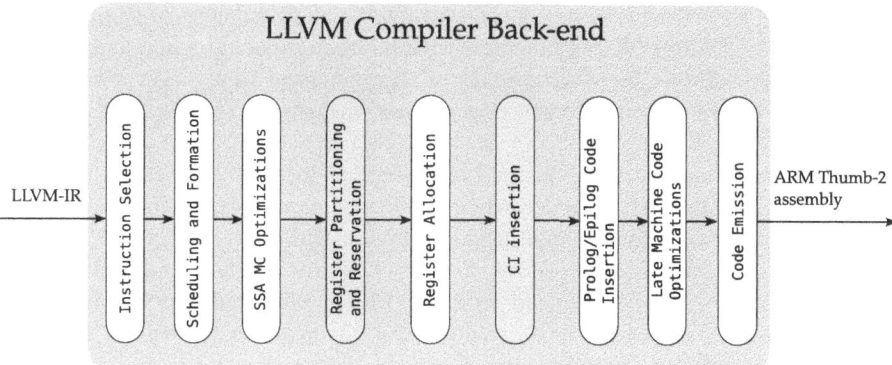

Fig. 2. LLVM pipeline modified to automate the insertion of the CI countermeasure: the additional passes are highlighted in teal.

(Then) and E (Else) being the available options. If an instruction is bound to a flag T, it will execute when <cond> evaluates to true. Conversely, an instruction with a flag E will execute if <cond> evaluates to false. Listing 1.1 is an example of an use of the IT instruction. In this instance, <cond> is set to EQ, i.e., the condition is true if result of the instruction preceding ITETT is equal to zero. The conditional flags are specified as ETT, which means that, if the first instruction executes, both the third and fourth instructions will also follow; otherwise, only the second instruction will be executed.

3   Scramble Hardening Compiler

In this section we detail how we designed a set of compiler passes which automatically realize the CI countermeasure in software, given an implementation of a cryptographic algorithm. A developer willing to employ our modified compiler pipeline only needs to provide the compiler with the name of the function implementing the cryptographic primitive to be protected and which parameter of the said function contains the secret key. This additional parameters are passed to the compiler as additional command line options. The function name is provided using the new command line option scrambleName. This option accepts a string input and is used to identify the function on which the transformation will be applied. It is not necessary to provide the mangled name of the function, as the scrambler will demangle the module's function name before making the comparison with scrambleName. Additionally, the index of the parameter containing the secret key is passed through the command line option scrambleSecretKey, which is specified as an enumerator in the argument list of the function. So in the case of the function aes_sbox_encrypt(uint8_t rk[RK_SIZE], uint8_t output[ABLOCK_SIZE], uint8_t input[BLOCK_SIZE]) the compiler requires two additional command line parameters *-scrambleName=aes_sbox_encrypt -scrambleSecretKey=0*. As the CI insertion passes need precise knowledge

about the register usage, as well as the arrangement in memory of the machine
instructions, it cannot be implemented within the middle-end where such information is unavailable. Instead, it must be implemented in a target-aware way,
within the LLVM back-end. To this end, we modified the LLVM compiler pipeline
as represented in Fig. 2.

While providing the three properties described in Sect. 2 is easiest tackling
them in their enumeration order when done in a hardware realization, doing
so through code transformations needs to first tackle the requirement of non-
memory element sharing imposed by Property 2, acting on the register allocation
strategies of the compiler. Considering the LLVM back-end pipeline depicted
in Fig. 2, we thus need to act before and after the *Register Allocation* pass. In
particular, we split our operations in a *Register partitioning and reservation* pass,
computed before the register allocation, and the *CI insertion* pass computed
after.

```
eor   r3, r3, r4        eor   r9, r3, r4
strb  r3, [sp, #12]     strb  r9, [sp, #12]

b     .LBB1_4           b     .LBB1_4
.LBB1_4:                .LBB1_4:
```

Listing 1.2: This listing demonstrates the impact of the CI insertion pass on
an instruction that uses and defines the same register. The original instruction
is shown on the left, with the use-def chain of r3 highlighted and underlined in
red. On the right, the instruction has been modified to use a new register, r9,
and this change has been propagated to all subsequent uses

3.1   Achieving Property 2 – Avoiding Register Overwrite with the Same Computation

Achieving Property 2 requires that no value from a state $S_{i+1,k}$ is stored in the
same register as the state from the same computation $S_{i,k}$. From a computation perspective, $S_{i,k}$ is represented by variables which are used by instructions
computing $S_{i+1,k}$ (i.e. defining variables which represent it). Therefore, for Property 2 to hold, it must hold that:

$$\forall i \in I, def(i) \cap use(i) = \emptyset \tag{1}$$

that is, an instruction should not use (read) and define (write) the same register.
This fact is usually not true, as instructions are allowed to employ the same
architectural register as both input and output. Listing 1.2 shows an example
of a basic block where instruction eor r3, r3, r4 uses and defines the same
register r3, as well as the transformed code that the CI insertion generates. It

can be noted that the definition of r3 is replaced with a different register r9, and the subsequent use of r3 in the next instruction is also replaced with a use of r9, preserving the original semantics. We note that, in case further uses of the replaced register, r3 are present in BBs which may follow it in program order, there is also a need to move back the value onto r3 before the branch leaving the current BB. To avoid violations of Property 2, we adopt a *random precharging* approach, i.e. we overwrite r3 right before inserting a move instruction which restores the value in r3 itself from r9.

```
ldr   r5, [sp, #320]        ittee     eq
                            ldr   r2, [sp, #596]
                            ldr   r5, [sp, #320]
                            ldr   r5, [sp, #320]
                            ldr   r2, [sp, #596]
```

Listing 1.3: This listing shows the effects of the CI insertion on an instruction that uses memory. On the left, we have the original instruction in red underlined. On the right, the instruction was duplicated (blue dashed underlined) and cloned in reverse order. Additionally, the CI insertion has allocated a new stack space for the instruction

Register Set Partitioning. To automatically enforce this transformation, the CI inserting compiler passes needs to control how the registers are allocated in each instruction. CI insertion divides the registers into three disjoint sets: the allocation (R_A), instruction-remapper (R_I), and mirror (R_M) sets. The allocation set R_A contains the minimum number of registers necessary to carry out the *Register Allocation* pass of LLVM. The instruction-remapper set R_I contains the register that will be used to remap a register if it is used and defined by the same instruction. The CI register partitioning pass attempts to build an isomorphism $f_I : R_A \xrightarrow{\sim} R_I$ between the allocation and remapper sets if possible, as this guarantees that the remapping process can always be performed. If that is not possible, the cardinality of the remapper set will be less than the allocation set, but there will be a chance that the remapping step will fail. For the mirror set it is always defined an isomorphism $f_M : R_A \cup R_I \xrightarrow{\sim} R_M$ between all the already allocated registers and itself. Thus, $|R_A| + |R_I| = |R_M|$ is always true, and $|R_A| \geq |R_I|$. If $|R_A| = |R_I|$, the CI insertion is guaranteed to be possible. Since the *Register Allocation* requires at least 3 registers, a total of 12 general purpose registers are needed to ensure the protection of an arbitrary cipher function. This is sufficient for a wide range of general purpose RISC ISAs. In particular, when implementing AES on an ARM architecture, which is endowed with 13 general-purpose registers, the CI insertion will store three registers in the allocation and instruction-remapper set, while six registers are reserved in the mirror set. For architectures with very small register files, there is a possibility that the scrambling process cannot be successfully completed, which will be analyzed in the following.

The R_A, R_I, and R_M sets are constructed on a per-function basis and are populated with randomly chosen registers, so for each CI-protected function, the registers in each set will be uncorrelated. CI register partitioning forces the *Register Allocation* pass to only use registers available in the R_A set generated for the specific function.

Register Remapping. After *Register Allocation*, CI insertion scans the machine instructions and detects those that violate the condition expressed in Eq. (1). For each such instruction i that defines and uses register r, the CI insertion employs the instruction remapper set R_I to find an available remapping register r'. It then performs a remapping of the definition performed by i from r to the new register r'. Then, all the uses of r must be remapped to uses of r' along the paths in the code until r is redefined by a different instruction. Therefore the remapping might need to be propagated through different basic blocks. If a basic block BB_j has only one parent, and the remapped basic block BB_i dominates it immediately, as explained in Sect. 2.2, the remapping can continue as if the instructions in BB_j belonged to BB_i (i.e., ignoring the branch), since no other definition of the same register can reach them. Otherwise, the CI insertion pass needs to insert a fragment of code that restores the remapped value from r' to the original register r. If the CI partitioning was able to create an isomorphism between the allocation and the instruction-remapper set, this process can be easily guaranteed to terminate. Indeed, every register in R_A has its own remapping register in R_I, and therefore the instruction that restores the original register r can be always performed, since the remapping register r' cannot have been overwritten except by another write to r in the original code, which however breaks the def-use chain, and therefore removes the need to restore the value of r. If this is not the case, the CI insertion keeps track of whether each register in R_I is currently in use, and attempts to use a free register when it is needed. If none can be found, then the modified LLVM compiler emits a warning as it is not possible to apply the CI insertion, given the resources at hand.

3.2 Adding the Fake Cipher Computation

A second step within the CI insertion is needed to address the insertion of the fake computation. This replica of the original cipher code must be interleaved with the original code. The availability of the mirror register set R_M ensures that the interleaving can be performed without affecting the semantics of the original (true) computation. Indeed, since $R_M \cap (R_A \cup R_I) = \emptyset$, the two computations are guaranteed not to interfere in terms of register usage.

Specifically, the CI insertion generates a new copy i^f of each instruction i in each basic block. Then, it performs a remapping of the registers used and defined by i^f with the isomorphism f_M. While the generated pair of instructions do no share any register, $(def(i) \cup use(i)) \cap (def(i^f) \cup use(i^f)) = \emptyset$, memory locations for the accesses of the fake cipher instruction i^f also need to be allocated in a separate space. Listing 1.3 shows how the CI insertion handles an instruction that accesses memory by allocating a mirror stack region. Since memory space is not as scarce as registers, allocating this mirror stack region is trivial, requiring only simple bookkeeping. In this, we assume, for the sake of simplicity, that the entire cipher is inlined in a single function (as it is common to be the case for symmetric ciphers). At this step, the code to generate the derived key is also included. For this purpose, a call is made to the unprotected cipher using the original key as plaintext and a random value computed at compile time as the key. The ciphertext will be used as the derived key

.LBB1_1:

```
movw    r7, #2056      @Only inserted
movt    r7, #20486     @when the random
ldr     r6, [r7]       @number needs
str     r6, [sp, #8]   @to be reloaded

ldr     r7, [sp, #8]
tst     r7, #1
lsr     r7, r7, #1
str     r7, [sp, #8]   @Optional
ittee   eq
...
```

Listing 1.4: This listing explains how the Scramble pass uses and reloads a random number. Red underlined instructions query the random number generator only if the stored number is depleted or at the beginning of a basic block with multiple parents. Blue dashed underlined instructions reload the random number and test if it is set. Orange wave underlined loads and stores the random number if the register is not cluttered

Randomizing the Ordering of True and Fake Instructions. The last property that the CI insertion compiler needs to enforce is that true and fake instructions are randomly interleaved during the execution – i.e., at each execution of each pair of instruction, it should be randomically decided whether the true or fake instruction is executed first. Indeed, a static order of execution would allow a side-channel attacker to separate statically the fake computation from the true one by simple timing.

To this end, an architecture-independent approach is to generate, for each instruction-fake instruction pair the assembly semantical equivalent of an if-then-else construct, where the then-block and else-block are constituted by the two possible schedules of the instruction pairs. The condition of the if-then-else construct is then obtained drawing a random bit, therefore guaranteeing that the order in which an instruction and the corresponding fake one are executed is chosen randomly. The aforementioned approach, which is architecture agnostic, however incurs in the overhead given by the insertion in the control flow of a non negligible amount of conditional branches. While this was shown to be acceptable in the context of the common overheads for side channel attack countermeasures [3], we chose to leverage the characteristics of the ARM Thumb-2 ISA to reduce the overhead to a minimum. To this end, we leverage the IT conditional block instructions. We recall that an IT instruction defines a block of one to four instructions that are executed conditionally, employing the same condition code that is read by the IT instruction itself. It is thus possible to employ an IT instruction driving the execution of the subsequent four computational instructions to our ends. To do so, Each instruction and its fake duplicate are emitted twice, the first time in a given order, while the second time in reverse order. The resulting four instructions sequence is then prefixed with an IT instruction. The condition of the IT block is set to execute the former pair of instructions if the condition is true, and the latter if the condition is false. Listing 1.3 shows how the CI insertion performs the cloning and wrapping, i.e., employing the ITTEE instruction which specialises IT with the correct conditions.

ITTEE employs the bits of the processor status word set by the previous instruction to drive the conditional execution. Therefore, to ensure the randomness of the selection, a random bit must be the result of the previous instruction. To enforce this, the CI insertion compiler employs a simple code fragment that requires a memory mapped true random number generator. We note that such a feature is common on microcontrollers [37], as a secure and fast TRNG is critical for key generation tasks which are typical of security oriented devices. Our approach considers a TRNG able to produce an architectural word (32 bit) of randomness per load operation. The snippet is inserted before the ITTEE block to read and test a single bit of the random filled register, which is filled loading from the address at which the true random number generator of the target ARM processor is mapped. CI insertion also loads a fresh random word after the current one is completely depleted or at the beginning of a basic block with multiple parents, where it is impossible to know a priori whether the current word is depleted or not. A stored random number is considered depleted if, from its loading, each of its bits was used to seed an IT block; this typically means reloading every 32 blocks. Since the TRNG is not guaranteed to provide fresh randomness at each clock cycle, but instead it requires a fixed amount of clock cycles to do so, all the basic blocks with an estimated cycle count less than the random number refresh time are padded with nop instructions to ensure getting a fresh random number each time. Listing 1.3 shows how CI insertion generates the appropriate code to handle the IT condition, including the (re)initialization of the random number. If a spare register is available (which is the case for the ARM register file), it can be used to reduce the number of load and store operations performed on the random number, by keeping it in a register.

These last passages fulfill the remaining required properties. In fact, even though this passage enforces randomization between the original instruction and a cloned one, the reloading of the random bit before each IT instruction is enough to ensure that no combinatorial Boolean function in the datapath is driven by two subsequent values of the same computation in two consecutive clock cycles.

3.3   Targeting Different Architectures

Although Scramble was tested and developed for ARM architecture, it can be easily adapted to new architectures. The Register Set Partitioning algorithm is already tuned to work with different numbers of registers and the only modification needed to support a new architecture is to tune the initial pool of registers for creating the R_I, R_M, and R_A sets. The register remapping algorithms are already architecture-independent. The most significant changes are required to generate the randomization of the order in architectures without IT instruction. In such architectures the IT instruction can be replaced with an if-then-else construct, as explained in Sect. 3.2. The only aspect that is entirely target-dependent is the generation of random numbers, which requires custom code to support different architectures.

4   Experimental Evaluation

In this section, we report the results of our experimental validation of the effectiveness of the proposed countermeasure in hindering both profiled and unprofiled attacks. Our benchmarking platform of choice is the ChipWhisperer 1200 Pro [29], a widely available hardware toolkit designed specifically to obtain high SNR measurements for side channel attacks, and provide a common ground for attack and countermeasure effectiveness comparisons. We employed a 32-bit STM32F4 ARM Cortex-M4 microcontroller. The same setup was employed to measure both the unprotected code, and the two instances of virtual devices having their power consumption profile altered with the scrambling countermeasure.

[[IMAGE DISCARDED DUE TO '/tikz/external/mode=list and make']] [[IMAGE DISCARDED DUE TO '/tikz/external/mode=list and make']]

[[IMAGE DISCARDED DUE TO '/tikz/external/mode=list and make']] [[IMAGE DISCARDED DUE TO '/tikz/external/mode=list and make']]

Fig. 3. Non-profiled CPA against an unprotected (left) and protected implementation (right): correlation coefficient as a function of the number of traces. Measurements to disclose for the unprotected implementation (99.9% confidence level): 15k, blue line; amount of traces where the GE is null for all 5 experiments: 20k, green line. For the protected implementation 5M traces do not allow the CPA to succeed; GE >0 in 20 experiments with 250k traces. (Color figure online)

Sampling occurred synchronously with the target device clock signal, providing one sample per clock cycle. This clock-locking approach eliminates artifacts caused by potential clock jitter and was facilitated by the ChipWhisperer acquisition feature, which synchronizes the target device clock with an external crystal oscillating at 7.37 MHz. This in turn implies that no portability issues in the models are coming from trace misalignments, clock jitter, or process variability across devices, leaving only our scrambling countermeasure as a defense against profiled attacks. As our case study, we chose a reference implementation of the AES-128 block cipher [36] employing a single S-Box to compute the SubBytes primitive. From a performance standpoint, we report that the Scramble hardened code runs the entire AES cipher in 64.9k clock cycles of the target platform, while the unprotected AES implementation takes 13.8k clock cycles. The resulting slowdown ($\approx 4.6\times$) compares quite favourably with common countermeasures tackling only unprofiled attacks such as masking, and is considered to be more than acceptable in practice. To put the figure in perspective, the state of the art, optimized masking schemes in [16] have the same AES run in 463k to 2.7M clock cycles on a 3.2 GHz Intel CPU.

Non-profiled Attack Security Validation. We validate the robustness of the proposed countermeasure in a threefold way: i) we perform a Correlation Power Analysis (CPA) attack, which is information theoretically optimal under the widely accepted assumption that the information leakage is proportional to the switching activity [18]; ii) a non-specific (i.e., model independent) t-test, as recommended by ISO/IEC 17825:2024 [21] and iii) the measured signal to noise (SNR) ratio w.r.t. the information which is expected to be leaked (i.e., Hamming distance between two intermediate values in a register). Figure 3 reports the results of both the CPA and the non-specific t-test. The results from the CPA, depicted in the two topmost figures show how Pearson's correlation coefficient for the correct key hypothesis (in blue), reaches a value close to the maximum possible (i.e., 1) after only 10 traces are employed for the attack in the unprotected device case (top left). We note that the Guessing Entropy (GE) score drops to its minimum consistently repeating the experiment 10 times. The protected design results (top right) show how employing $50k$ traces the correlation coefficient of the correct key hypothesis does not emerge w.r.t. the one of the wrong key hypotheses. This in turn implies an increase in the number of Measurements to Disclose (MtD) the secret value by at least even with $5000\times$, as no correct key retrieval is achieved even with all the $50k$ traces. The non-specific t-test results provide an analogous strong validation: indeed, the test on the unprotected implementation exceeds the threshold ±4.5 for 99.999% confidence in the protection by more than 40 times when employing only 500 traces (bottom right). The protected implementation retains t statistic values well within the threshold, even when $100\times$ the traces are employed for the test. Finally, we report that the peak SNR (measured with $50k$ traces) for the information leakage on the AES SubBytes operation is 3.3, while the one on the protected implementation it is lowered to $2.9 \cdot 10^{-3}$.

Table 1. Classification accuracy of TAs and SVM on an unprotected (**u**) and protected implementation (**p**). Templates with 2k traces; attacks performed against 10k traces per device

Attack type	Feature reduction	Accuracy**u**	Accuracy *p*
Template	**NICV**	91.2%	50.4%
	SOST	98.8%	51.3%
	PCA	96.8%	50.2%
SVM	**NICV**	89.4%	50.1%
	SOST	94.5%	50.3%
	PCA	92.5%	49.9%

Profiled Attack Security Validation. We evaluate the resistance against profiled attacks employing the information theoretically optimal Bayesian Templates Attack (TAs) and Support Vector Machines (SVMs), which were shown to be an efficient alternative to TAs, especially if paired with an appropriate feature reduction approach [24]. We note that the use of machine learning techniques (e.g. neural network classifiers and deep learning methods) yields an efficiency advantage over the aforementioned TAs in cases where experimental noise, clock jitter or other disturbances are hindering the measurements. To the end of providing the most favourable scenario to the attacker, we took measures to minimize noise and remove the other hindrances from our attack evaluation, so that the efficiency advantage is not needed for the evaluation. Feature reduction is practically mandatory in our scenario, as the number of samples per trace (corresponding to the dimensionality of the random variable of which we need to estimate a distribution) is in the tens of thousands range. Employing raw traces would indeed fall into a *curse-of-dimensionality* issue for the classifier [31]. We employ three different feature reduction approaches: sample selection with the maximum SOST [19] or Normalized InterClass Variance (NICV) [4] score, and Principal Component Analysis (PCA) [24]. For the NICV score, we choose to classify the traces according to the same intermediate value hypothesis yielding a successful unprofiled attack, to avoid the computation of an interclass variance across poorly classified traces. For the PCA-based feature reductions, we choose to keep the 25 most informative dimensions of the projected space, as they were measure to contain 95% of the information.

For all device instances, we build two device profiles, selecting the first round key bit as the target of our attack, employing 1k traces to build each profile. Subsequently, we classify 3k traces (none in common with the set used in the modeling phase) coming from different device instances. Table 1 reports the outcome of the classifications made model TA results.

Profiled attacks succeed on the unprotected implementation with extremely high accuracy (94.5% for SVMs and 98.8 for TAs) given an appropriate choice of the feature reduction strategy. Accuracy against the unprotected device instance, while they obtain an accuracy in the 49.9%–51.3% range for all protected implementations, regardless of the feature reduction technique, or profiled attack approach. This provides strong evidence of the non-effectiveness of TAs against our countermeasure, as the fluctuations around the accuracy of a random guess are within a range of plausibility for statistical artifacts. We note that, in our scenario where single-bit (i.e., two-class) template attacks are performed, the Guessing Entropy and the accuracy scores coincide. Indeed, computing the GE in our template attacks (with the possible key ranks being only 0 and 1) yields 0.51 as the average rank, further pointing to the ineffectiveness of template attacks against the protection, in our evaluation scenario.

5   Concluding Remarks

In this work, we proposed method to perform the fully automated application of a Scramble hardening countermeasure to a software implementation of a symmetric cipher, by means of a modified compiler pipeline. Our approach allows to obtain a significant improvement in the resistance against non profiled side channel attacks ($\geq 5000\times$ the MtD) and hinders successfully profiled attacks. The proposed countermeasure compares favourably in terms of computational efficiency, as it is more efficient than state-of-the-art masking schemes, while providing protection from both unprofiled and profiled attacks. Looking ahead, several promising directions remain to be explored. We intend to evaluate the applicability of Scramble beyond AES, testing it to other cryptographic ciphers to assess generality and robustness. Finally, we will investigate the resilience of our defenses against more advanced adversaries, including attacks based on deep neural networks, which are increasingly used to exploit subtle side-channel patterns. After this research we intend to release Scramble pass as open-source.

Acknowledgments. This work was supported in part by project SERICS (PE00000014) under the Italian NRRP MUR program funded by the EU - NGEU.

Disclosure of Interests. The authors have no competing interests to declare that are relevant to the content of this article.

References

1. Agosta, G., Barenghi, A., Pelosi, G.: A code morphing methodology to automate power analysis countermeasures. In: Groeneveld, P., Sciuto, D., Hassoun, S. (eds.) The 49th Annual Design Automation Conference 2012, DAC 2012, San Francisco, CA, USA, 3–7 June 2012, pp. 77–82. ACM (2012). https://doi.org/10.1145/2228360.2228376
2. Agosta, G., Barenghi, A., Pelosi, G.: Compiler-based techniques to secure cryptographic embedded software against side-channel attacks. IEEE Trans. Comput. Aided Des. Integr. Circuits Syst. **39**(8), 1550–1554 (2020). https://doi.org/10.1109/TCAD.2019.2912924

3. Agosta, G., Barenghi, A., Pelosi, G., Scandale, M.: The MEET approach: securing cryptographic embedded software against side channel attacks. IEEE Trans. Comput. Aided Des. Integr. Circuits Syst. **34**(8), 1320–1333 (2015). https://doi.org/10.1109/TCAD.2015.2430320

4. Archambeau, C., Peeters, E., Standaert, F.-X., Quisquater, J.-J.: Template attacks in principal subspaces. In: Goubin, L., Matsui, M. (eds.) CHES 2006. LNCS, vol. 4249, pp. 1–14. Springer, Heidelberg (2006). https://doi.org/10.1007/11894063_1

5. Balasch, J., Gierlichs, B., Grosso, V., Reparaz, O., Standaert, F.-X.: On the cost of lazy engineering for masked software implementations. In: Joye, M., Moradi, A. (eds.) CARDIS 2014. LNCS, vol. 8968, pp. 64–81. Springer, Cham (2015). https://doi.org/10.1007/978-3-319-16763-3_5

6. Barbosa, M., Moss, A., Page, D.: Constructive and destructive use of compilers in elliptic curve cryptography. J. Cryptol. **22**(2), 259–281 (2009). https://doi.org/10.1007/S00145-008-9023-0

7. Barenghi, A., Fornaciari, W., Pelosi, G., Zoni, D.: Scramble suit: a profile differentiation countermeasure to prevent template attacks. IEEE Trans. Comput. Aided Des. Integr. Circuits Syst. **39**(9), 1778–1791 (2020). https://doi.org/10.1109/TCAD.2019.2926389

8. Barenghi, A., Pelosi, G.: Side-channel security of superscalar CPUs: evaluating the impact of micro-architectural features. In: Proceedings of the 55th Annual Design Automation Conference, DAC 2018, San Francisco, CA, USA, 24–29 June 2018, pp. 120:1–120:6. ACM (2018). https://doi.org/10.1145/3195970.3196112

9. Bayrak, A.G., Regazzoni, F., Brisk, P., Standaert, F., Ienne, P.: A first step towards automatic application of power analysis countermeasures. In: Stok, L., Dutt, N.D., Hassoun, S. (eds.) Proceedings of the 48th Design Automation Conference, DAC 2011, San Diego, California, USA, 5–10 June 2011, pp. 230–235. ACM (2011). https://doi.org/10.1145/2024724.2024778

10. Belleville, N., Couroussé, D., Heydemann, K., Charles, H.P.: Automated software protection for the masses against side-channel attacks. ACM Trans. Archit. Code Optim. **15**(4) (2018). https://doi.org/10.1145/3281662, https://doi.org/10.1145/3281662

11. Belleville, N., Couroussé, D., Heydemann, K., Meunier, Q., El Ouahma, I.B.: Maskara: Compilation of a masking countermeasure with optimized polynomial interpolation. IEEE Trans. Comput. Aided Des. Integr. Circuits Syst. **39**(11), 3774–3786 (2020). https://doi.org/10.1109/TCAD.2020.3012237

12. Bronchain, O., Durvaux, F., Masure, L., Standaert, F.: Efficient profiled side-channel analysis of masked implementations. Extended. IEEE Trans. Inf. Forensics Secur. **17**, 574–584 (2022). https://doi.org/10.1109/TIFS.2022.3144871

13. Casalino, L., Belleville, N., Couroussé, D., Heydemann, K.: A tale of resilience: on the practical security of masked software implementations. IEEE Access **11**, 84651–84669 (2023). https://doi.org/10.1109/ACCESS.2023.3298436

14. Chari, S., Rao, J.R., Rohatgi, P.: Template attacks. In: Kaliski, B.S., Koç, K., Paar, C. (eds.) CHES 2002. LNCS, vol. 2523, pp. 13–28. Springer, Heidelberg (2003). https://doi.org/10.1007/3-540-36400-5_3

15. Cleemput, J.V., Coppens, B., Sutter, B.D.: Compiler mitigations for time attacks on modern x86 processors. ACM Trans. Archit. Code Optim. **8**(4), 23:1–23:20 (2012). https://doi.org/10.1145/2086696.2086702

16. Coron, J., Rondepierre, F., Zeitoun, R.: High order masking of look-up tables with common shares. IACR Trans. Cryptogr. Hardw. Embed. Syst. **2018**(1), 40–72 (2018). https://doi.org/10.13154/TCHES.V2018.I1.40-72

17. Das, D., Golder, A., Danial, J., Ghosh, S., Raychowdhury, A., Sen, S.: X-DeepSCA: cross-device deep learning side channel attack. In: Proceedings of the 56th Annual Design Automation Conference 2019, DAC 2019, Las Vegas, NV, USA, 02–06 June 2019, p. 134. ACM (2019). https://doi.org/10.1145/3316781.3317934

18. Durvaux, F., Standaert, F.-X., Veyrat-Charvillon, N.: How to certify the leakage of a chip? In: Nguyen, P.Q., Oswald, E. (eds.) EUROCRYPT 2014. LNCS, vol. 8441, pp. 459–476. Springer, Heidelberg (2014). https://doi.org/10.1007/978-3-642-55220-5_26

19. Gierlichs, B., Lemke-Rust, K., Paar, C.: Templates vs. stochastic methods. In: Goubin, L., Matsui, M. (eds.) CHES 2006. LNCS, vol. 4249, pp. 15–29. Springer, Heidelberg (2006). https://doi.org/10.1007/11894063_2

20. Heiding, F., Katsikeas, S., Lagerström, R.: Research communities in cyber security vulnerability assessments: a comprehensive literature review. Comput. Sci. Rev. **48** (2023). https://doi.org/10.1016/j.cosrev.2023.100551

21. ISO/IEC 17825:2024: Information technology - Security techniques - Testing methods for the mitigation of non-invasive attack classes against cryptographic modules (2024). www.iso.org

22. Javeed, A., Yilmaz, C., Savas, E.: Microarchitectural side-channel threats, weaknesses and mitigations: a systematic mapping study. IEEE Access **11**, 48945–48976 (2023). https://doi.org/10.1109/ACCESS.2023.3275757

23. Lattner, C., Adve, V.S.: LLVM: a compilation framework for lifelong program analysis and transformation. In: 2nd IEEE / ACM International Symposium on Code Generation and Optimization (CGO 2004), 20–24 March 2004, San Jose, CA, USA, pp. 75–88. IEEE Computer Society (2004). https://doi.org/10.1109/CGO.2004.1281665

24. Lerman, L., Bontempi, G., Markowitch, O.: Power analysis attack: an approach based on machine learning. Int. J. Appl. Cryptogr. **3**(2), 97–115 (2014). https://doi.org/10.1504/IJACT.2014.062722

25. Lerman, L., Bontempi, G., Markowitch, O.: A machine learning approach against a masked AES - reaching the limit of side-channel attacks with a learning model. J. Cryptogr. Eng. **5**(2), 123–139 (2015). https://doi.org/10.1007/S13389-014-0089-3

26. Lou, X., Zhang, T., Jiang, J., Zhang, Y.: A survey of microarchitectural side-channel vulnerabilities, attacks, and defenses in cryptography. ACM Comput. Surv. **54**(6), 122:1–122:37 (2022). https://doi.org/10.1145/3456629

27. Mangard, S., Oswald, E., Popp, T.: Power Analysis Attacks - Revealing the Secrets of Smart Cards. Springer (2007)

28. Messerges, T.S., Dabbish, E.A., Sloan, R.H.: Power analysis attacks of modular exponentiation in smartcards. In: Koç, Ç.K., Paar, C. (eds.) CHES 1999. LNCS, vol. 1717, pp. 144–157. Springer, Heidelberg (1999). https://doi.org/10.1007/3-540-48059-5_14

29. NewAE Technology Inc.: ChipWhisperer-Pro CW1200 (2024). https://rtfm.newae.com/Capture/ChipWhisperer-Pro/

30. Piacentini, I., Barenghi, A., Pelosi, G.: A non profiled and profiled side channel attack countermeasure through computation interleaving. In: 26th Euromicro Conference on Digital System Design, DSD 2023, Golem, Albania, 6–8 September 2023, pp. 718–725. IEEE (2023). https://doi.org/10.1109/DSD60849.2023.00103

31. Picek, S., Heuser, A., Jovic, A., Bhasin, S., Regazzoni, F.: The curse of class imbalance and conflicting metrics with machine learning for side-channel evaluations. IACR Trans. Cryptogr. Hardw. Embed. Syst. **2019**(1), 209–237 (2019). https://doi.org/10.13154/TCHES.V2019.I1.209-237

32. Rastello, F., Tichadou, F.B.: SSA-Based Compiler Design. Springer Nature (2022)
33. Ronen, E., Shamir, A., Weingarten, A., O'Flynn, C.: IoT goes nuclear: creating a ZigBee chain reaction. IEEE Secur. Priv. **16**(1), 54–62 (2018). https://doi.org/10.1109/MSP.2018.1331033
34. Seuschek, H., Santis, F.D., Guillen, O.M.: Side-channel leakage aware instruction scheduling. In: Brorsson, M., Lu, Z., Agosta, G., Barenghi, A., Pelosi, G. (eds.) Proceedings of the Fourth Workshop on Cryptography and Security in Computing Systems, CS2@HiPEAC 2017, Stockholm, Sweden, 24 January 2017, pp. 7–12. ACM (2017). https://doi.org/10.1145/3031836.3031838
35. Spreitzer, R., Moonsamy, V., Korak, T., Mangard, S.: Systematic classification of side-channel attacks: a case study for mobile devices. IEEE Commun. Surv. Tutorials **20**(1), 465–488 (2018). https://doi.org/10.1109/COMST.2017.2779824
36. National Institute of Standards and Technology: FIPS PUB 197 - Advanced Encryption Standard (AES) (2001). https://nvlpubs.nist.gov/nistpubs/fips/nist.fips.197.pdf
37. STMicroelectronics: STM32F407/417 32 bit Cortex-M Microcontroller Reference Manual (2025). https://www.st.com/en/microcontrollers-microprocessors/stm32f407-417/documentation.html
38. Wu, M., Guo, S., Schaumont, P., Wang, C.: Eliminating timing side-channel leaks using program repair. In: Tip, F., Bodden, E. (eds.) Proceedings of the 27th ACM SIGSOFT International Symposium on Software Testing and Analysis, ISSTA 2018, Amsterdam, The Netherlands, 16–21 July 2018, pp. 15–26. ACM (2018). https://doi.org/10.1145/3213846.3213851

Leaky Batteries: A Novel Set of Side-Channel Attacks on Electric Vehicles

Francesco Marchiori$^{(\boxtimes)}$⬤ and Mauro Conti⬤

University of Padova, Padua, Italy
francesco.marchiori@math.unipd.it , mauro.conti@unipd.it

Abstract. Advancements in battery technology have accelerated the adoption of Electric Vehicles (EVs) due to their environmental benefits. However, their growing sophistication introduces security and privacy challenges. Often seen as mere operational data, battery consumption patterns can unintentionally reveal critical information exploitable for malicious purposes. These risks go beyond privacy, impacting vehicle security and regulatory compliance. Despite these concerns, current research has largely overlooked the broader implications of battery consumption data exposure. As EVs integrate further into smart transportation networks, addressing these gaps is crucial to ensure their safety, reliability, and resilience.

In this work, we introduce a novel class of side-channel attacks that exploit EV battery data to extract sensitive user information. Leveraging only battery consumption patterns, we demonstrate a methodology to accurately identify the EV driver and their driving style, determine the number of occupants, and infer the vehicle's start and end locations when user habits are known. We utilize several machine learning models and feature extraction techniques to analyze EV power consumption patterns, validating our approach on simulated and real-world datasets collected from actual drivers. Our attacks achieve an average success rate of 95.4% across all attack objectives. Our findings highlight the privacy risks associated with EV battery data, emphasizing the need for stronger protections to safeguard user privacy and vehicle security.

Keywords: Electric Vehicles · Side-Channel Attacks · Privacy

1 Introduction

Electric Vehicles (EVs) have rapidly reshaped the automotive sector, providing notable environmental benefits and reducing reliance on fossil fuels. With global EV sales hitting 17.1 million units in 2024, a 55% increase from the previous year, electric mobility is expanding swiftly worldwide [23]. As EV adoption rises, these vehicles are increasingly integrated into smart transportation systems, impacting urban mobility, energy use, and data-centric vehicle ecosystems. This growing

M. Dalla Preda et al. (Eds.): ARES 2025, LNCS 15992, pp. 322–333, 2025.
https://doi.org/10.1007/978-3-032-00624-0_16

digitalization, however, raises significant data privacy and security concerns due to the large volumes of information generated and shared by modern EVs. To address these issues, regulations like the European GDPR and UNECE WP.29 cybersecurity directives (R155 and R156) have been introduced to enforce strong data protection and cybersecurity standards [1,28].

A crucial but underexplored area in EV security is the risk of sensitive data leakage from battery information. Previous studies have shown that lithium-ion batteries in smartphones can be vulnerable to side-channel attacks, exposing user behavior and even cryptographic keys [13,16]. Similar threats remain largely unstudied in EVs, leaving the implications uncertain. Battery data could be exploited for large-scale surveillance, targeted tracking, or stalking, presenting serious privacy issues. Existing research has demonstrated that charging data can be used to profile EV models, revealing unique recharging patterns [4,12], and has raised concerns about the potential tampering of charging infrastructure [9]. However, these works primarily focus on charging behavior and overlook battery consumption patterns during driving, which may reveal additional distinctive information. These gaps highlight the pressing need to study privacy risks related to battery data in EVs.

Contributions. This paper presents a novel set of side-channel attacks that extract sensitive user data and reveal confidential EV characteristics using only battery consumption information. By applying time-series feature extraction and training multiple Machine Learning (ML) classifiers, we expose critical privacy risks linked to battery consumption patterns. Our key contributions are:

- We propose a new category of side-channel attacks exploiting detailed EV battery consumption during driving, rather than focusing solely on charging behavior. This allows inference of sensitive attributes such as driver identity and style, vehicle model, number of occupants, auxiliary power use, and trip endpoints, especially when user habits are known. To our knowledge, this is the first comprehensive analysis targeting real-world consumption data instead of coarse telemetry or recharge patterns.
- We develop and compare multiple ML classifiers using time series feature extraction that leverages the causal relationships inherent in battery consumption data.
- We evaluate our approach on a dataset containing both simulated and real-world battery consumption traces from diverse conditions, achieving high accuracies: up to 0.972 for driving style, 0.999 for vehicle ID, 0.907 for occupancy, 0.967 for auxiliary power, 0.942 for driver ID, 0.955 for trip origin, and 0.935 for trip destination. Overall, our attacks average a 95.4% success rate across objectives.
- We propose a proof-of-concept countermeasure that significantly mitigates these attacks, lowering their success rate to around 45% in some scenarios while effectively neutralizing them in others.
- We make our methodology and code open-source at: https://github.com/Mhackiori/Leaky-Batteries.

2   Related Works

The battery is a core component of EVs, critically affecting their performance, efficiency, and lifespan. As dependence on lithium-ion technology increases, so do concerns regarding its security and privacy implications. A major issue is the infiltration of counterfeit batteries into the supply chain, which poses safety and performance risks and has led to the seizure of millions of dollars worth of products annually [10,15,24]. To mitigate these threats, regulatory authorities have enforced stringent standards covering battery design, usage, and disposal [3]. Beyond physical safety, data security is an emerging priority. EVs collect extensive sensitive data, such as battery health, GPS location, and user driving behavior, making them attractive cyberattack targets. Regulatory frameworks have responded accordingly: the EU Cybersecurity Act (EU) 2019/881 requires robust security measures across the product lifecycle [25], while UNECE WP.29 mandates cybersecurity standards and secure software updates for connected and autonomous vehicles [28]. These measures also address vulnerabilities in related infrastructure, including charging stations and cloud services. In parallel, side-channel attacks represent a growing threat. These attacks exploit indirect information leaks, such as power usage, electromagnetic emissions, or timing variations, to infer private data without breaching encryption. Prior studies on smartphones have shown that power consumption patterns during charging can expose sensitive information [6,13], and similar vulnerabilities exist in wireless charging systems [16]. In the EV domain, initial research indicates that monitoring charging current can enable vehicle profiling, raising privacy concerns [4]. Additional studies highlight the susceptibility of EV charging infrastructure to data leakage [12], suggesting that battery usage patterns may become a critical side channel in future attacks, warranting focused investigation.

3   System and Threat Model

We describe our system and threat model in Sects. 3.1 and 3.2. A comprehensive overview of the entire model is illustrated in Fig. 1.

3.1   System Model

EVs generate extensive data to maintain efficient operation, safety, and battery longevity. Central to this data ecosystem is the Battery Management System (BMS), which monitors and optimizes lithium-ion battery performance by continuously tracking parameters like voltage, current, temperature, State of Charge (SoC), and State of Health (SoH) [22]. This information is communicated internally via protocols such as the Controller Area Network (CAN) and may also be transmitted externally through telematics for remote diagnostics and fleet management. In addition to the BMS, EVs feature a network of sensors and computing units that track driving behavior, energy use, and vehicle location, supporting functions like range estimation, regenerative braking, and predictive

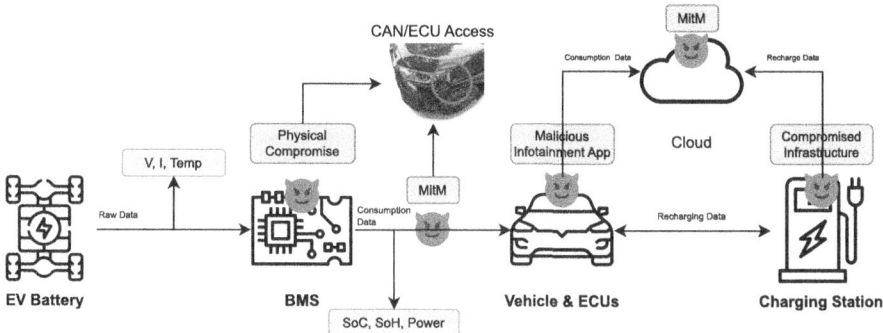

Fig. 1. Overview of the system model, the data flow, and the attack vectors. We refer to [27] for CAN/ECU access, and [4,9] for charging station compromise.

maintenance. Battery consumption data is tightly integrated with these systems, serving as a key input for performance evaluation and optimization [2,8,29]. Charging session details, including charge rate, energy delivered, and station location, are also recorded to promote battery health and facilitate better grid integration.

3.2   Threat Model

Attackers can exploit multiple vectors to access EV battery consumption data, using both physical and remote methods. They may compromise the BMS or onboard sensors through direct physical tampering [27] or cyberattacks targeting connected interfaces such as telematics units, infotainment systems, or diagnostic ports [20,21]. Notably, malicious Android apps on platforms like Android Auto can covertly collect vehicle data without explicit user permission [26]. Additionally, wireless communications between vehicles, cloud services, charging stations, or mobile apps are vulnerable to passive eavesdropping or active Man-in-the-Middle (MitM) attacks [9] Attackers might also manipulate public charging infrastructure to extract usage profiles [4] or use side-channel analysis via external sensors or power grid monitoring to infer battery consumption patterns. Once accessed, this data enables adversaries to reconstruct sensitive user behaviors, revealing driving habits, routines, and preferences [14]. Such profiling risks privacy violations and discrimination, for example, through usage-based insurance fraud or biased fleet management decisions [11]. More advanced threats include cyber-physical attacks that exploit energy consumption patterns to disrupt vehicle functions or impact grid stability.

4   Methodology

This section outlines the methodology and techniques of our proposed side-channel attacks. We begin by defining the specific objectives of our attacks in Sect. 4.1, detailing the private information we aim to infer. Next, Sect. 4.2 describes our data processing pipeline and feature extraction approach. Finally, in Sect. 4.3, we introduce the machine learning models employed in our attacks and discuss the methodology used for their optimization and tuning.

4.1   Attacks

Our side-channel attacks focus on inferring sensitive information from EV battery consumption data, targeting several key aspects. We analyze battery consumption patterns to determine *driving style*, distinguishing behaviors such as aggressive, neutral, and defensive driving, which reveal driver habits. *Vehicle identification* is achieved by exploiting unique energy consumption profiles to differentiate EV models. We also estimate the number of passengers through *occupancy detection*, as the battery load varies with passenger count. Additionally, we infer *auxiliary system usage*, such as air conditioning and infotainment power consumption, providing insight into user preferences and environmental conditions. Through consistent energy usage patterns, we perform *driver identification* to recognize individual drivers. Finally, assuming knowledge of user habits, we carry out *route inference*, estimating both the *origin* and *destination* of trips based on battery consumption patterns at the start and end of journeys. These objectives expose significant privacy risks tied to battery consumption data and underscore the need for enhanced protective measures against such inference attacks.

4.2   Feature Extraction

Our analysis relies on battery-related data collected at regular intervals. The specific features may vary depending on the dataset used. The key features consistently used across all our attacks and evaluations include the actual battery capacity (Wh), representing the battery's effective energy storage; the state of charge (SoC) as a percentage of remaining charge; total energy consumed (Wh) up to a given point; total energy regenerated (Wh) through regenerative braking; and average consumption (mWh) calculated over time. Additionally, we incorporate State of Health (SoH) to evaluate battery condition and aging, motor power to track energy usage by the motor, torque (Nm) as an indicator of motor output, and RPM (Revolutions Per Minute) to measure the motor's rotational speed. The raw battery consumption data is processed and fed into ML classifiers. For tasks like driving style and vehicle identification, the correlation between features is strong enough to enable accurate classification at the per-sample level, requiring minimal preprocessing. More complex inference tasks, however, necessitate additional feature engineering. To this end, we employ `tsfresh`, a Python library for automated time-series feature extraction [7]. This tool computes a wide range of statistical features, including Fourier transforms, autocorrelation, and trend metrics. Following feature extraction, the datasets are imputed to address missing values and then filtered to retain only the features most relevant to each attack objective. For occupancy and auxiliary power consumption inference, we analyze entire driving sessions, as cumulative energy usage provides important context. In the case of driver authentication, data is segmented into time windows of 10 samples to capture short-term behavioral signatures. For origin and destination inference, we use 5-sample time windows, focusing specifically on the initial and final portions of each driving event. This task-specific structuring ensures that the temporal resolution matches the nature of the classification objective, enabling efficient and effective analysis.

4.3   Models

We utilize ML models in this study due to their demonstrated ability to extract valuable insights from complex battery data, as shown in prior research [4,19]. To evaluate model performance for each classification task, we first apply a grid search to optimize hyperparameters, then split the tsfresh-processed dataset into training and testing sets using an 80%/20% ratio. The models assessed include Decision Tree (DT), K-Nearest Neighbors (KNN), Neural Network (MLP), and Random Forest (RF). Each model is tuned using grid search: for DT, we test both gini and entropy criteria and vary the maximum depth between 3 and 15. KNN is evaluated across values of k from 1 to 14 with both uniform and distance-based weighting. For the MLP, we explore hidden layer sizes of (50,) and (100,) with ReLU activation and the Adam optimizer. RF models are tested using the gini criterion with 100 or 200 estimators. We intentionally constrained the hyperparameter search space compared to prior battery-related ML work, as our initial tests showed that extensive tuning provided limited additional benefit [19]. Given the dataset and classification tasks, moderate optimization was sufficient to achieve strong performance.

5   Evaluation

We now evaluate the effectiveness of our proposed attacks and analyze their results. In Sect. 5.1, we provide an overview of the datasets used in our experiments, detailing their characteristics. In Sect. 5.2, we present the success rates of our attacks. In Sect. 5.3, we provide an analysis of feature importance for our classifiers, followed by a discussion of the attack's implications in Sect. 5.4.

5.1   Dataset

This work utilizes a dual EV dataset designed to improve battery range estimation through machine learning models trained on both simulated and real-world driving data. Due to our focus on battery-related inference using ML, this dataset aligns well with our objectives. It originates from a study that combines synthetic data generated using the Simulation of Urban MObility (SUMO) tool with real-world data collected from electric vehicles via onboard diagnostics (OBD-II) and environmental data obtained from external APIs [5]. The dataset supports a comprehensive analysis of energy consumption, offering insights that go beyond typical manufacturer specifications.

Simulated Dataset. The Dataset of Electric Vehicle Synthetic Trips (DEVST) contains 42,525 SUMO-generated EV trips across 21 routes, simulating varied conditions such as driving style, occupancy (1–5 passengers), auxiliary usage, wind, and traffic. Each simulation logs speed, SoC, energy use, slope, and range. It includes models like the BMW i3, VW ID.3/ID.4/e-Up, and a generic SUV. We use this dataset to perform side-channel attacks targeting driving style, vehicle type, occupancy, and auxiliary power use.

Real-World Dataset. The Dataset of Electric Vehicle Real Trips (DEVRT) includes 58 trips using a Nissan Leaf and Dacia Spring over four days in the Basque Country, Spain. Data was collected via OBD-II and APIs, capturing vehicle telemetry, weather, and traffic. We use this dataset to infer driver identity, trip origin, and destination. Due to class imbalance in origin/destination, we test both the original and an undersampled version for balanced evaluation.

5.2 Attacks Results

We present the experimental results demonstrating the effectiveness of our attacks. Accuracy directly reflects the success rate of each ML-based attack. While results are reported separately for each objective, multiple inferences can be performed concurrently using the same EV battery consumption data, provided the necessary features are present.

Simulated Dataset. As discussed in Sect. 4.2, driving style and vehicle identification do not require time-series analysis, allowing inference at the per-sample level on the simulated dataset. Results, shown in Fig. 2, indicate that our models achieve near-perfect accuracy for these tasks. Vehicle type inference performs especially well, reflecting the strong link between battery characteristics and car models. While past studies used similar features for legitimate battery authentication [19], our findings reveal their potential misuse in adversarial contexts.

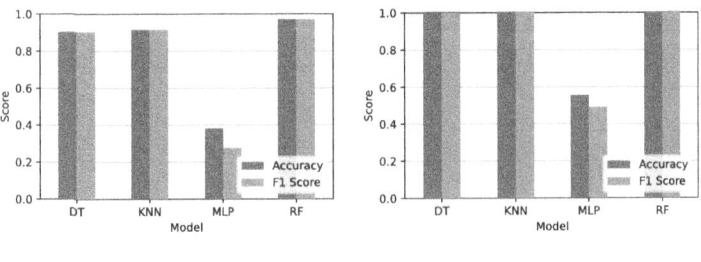

(a) Driving style inference.   (b) Car model inference.

Fig. 2. Results for attacks in the simulated dataset leveraging single sample feature correlation.

Figure 3 presents results for time-series attack objectives, occupancy and auxiliary power consumption, with high average accuracies of 0.907 and 0.967,

respectively, achieved by the RF model. While these reflect overall trip performance, some individual trips show even higher accuracy, as indicated by a
standard deviation of 0.092 for occupancy inference. However, since features are
extracted at the trip level, multiple data samples per trip would be needed to
confirm this variation.

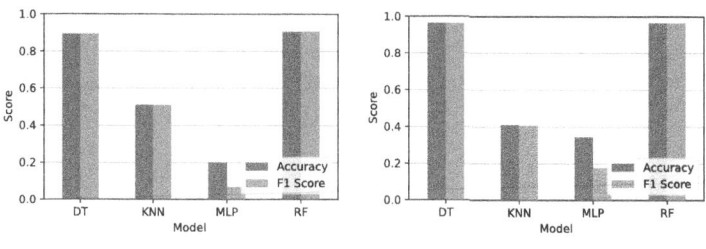

(a) Occupancy inference.   (b) Auxiliary consumption inference.

Fig. 3. Results for attacks in the simulated dataset leveraging single sample feature
correlation.

Real-World Dataset. In the real-world dataset, the RF model demonstrates the
highest performance among all tested models (with an accuracy of 0.942), which
is consistent with previous findings. However, the absence of labeled driving style
data in the real-world dataset limits our ability to explore potential correlations
between these results and those depicted in Fig. 2a, where driving style was
analyzed in the synthetic dataset. Table 1 shows the evaluation of origin and
destination city prediction attacks across 10 cities. The models achieve high
accuracy, demonstrating robustness to class imbalance since dataset balancing
has little effect on performance. This indicates that the attacks remain effective
in real-world scenarios where some locations are visited more often than others.

Table 1. Results for the trip inference attack.

(a) Origin identification.

Model	Balanced		Unbalanced	
	Acc.	F1	Acc.	F1
DT	0.909	0.908	0.967	0.966
KNN	0.182	0.180	0.279	0.275
MLP	0.045	0.009	0.197	0.158
RF	0.955	0.953	0.951	0.951

(b) Destination identification.

Model	Balanced		Unbalanced	
	Acc.	F1	Acc.	F1
DT	0.885	0.877	0.952	0.948
KNN	0.462	0.454	0.435	0.451
MLP	0.231	0.157	0.161	0.120
RF	0.923	0.927	0.935	0.936

5.3   Feature Analysis

To understand how battery consumption data influences our classification attacks, we apply eXplainable AI (XAI) techniques, specifically using SHapley Additive exPlanations (SHAP), a model-agnostic method for interpreting feature importance [18]. Given the large number of features generated by `tsfresh` from time-series data, we focus this analysis on the driving style inference attack, which relies directly on raw battery consumption data without preprocessing. Our findings show that average consumption is the most influential feature (importance value 0.261), followed by battery capacity (0.182), while state of charge (SoC) is the least important (0.039), likely because its time-dependent nature reduces its impact when features are treated independently by the classifier.

5.4   Discussion

In our evaluation, the RF model consistently outperformed other approaches across all attack objectives. Its strength stems from ensemble learning, which reduces overfitting by averaging predictions from multiple decision trees. This aligns with prior research demonstrating RF's effectiveness in battery data classification [19]. Conversely, the MLP showed lower accuracy, partly due to a limited grid search designed to reduce computational costs. Although some attack scenarios might allow for online processing, our main aim was to highlight that even simpler ML models with minimal overhead can effectively support these attacks.

6   Countermeasures

Our attacks successfully extract sensitive vehicle information from the dataset, exposing a notable security risk. However, since this data is crucial for normal vehicle operation, simply removing it is not an option. Applying traditional encryption or authentication on the CAN bus is challenging due to its limited bandwidth and legacy design [17], and many existing solutions require significant protocol upgrades like CAN-FD, which are often impractical. To address this, we propose a lightweight countermeasure based on time-based data aggregation that computes mean values over varying time windows. This approach disrupts the fine-grained time-series patterns exploited by our attacks, such as those detected by `tsfresh`, while preserving essential vehicle functions. Testing window sizes from 10 to 100 samples reveals a trade-off between privacy and utility: smaller windows maintain detailed behavior but leak more information, while larger windows enhance privacy at some cost to data usefulness. Our evaluation shows a significant drop in attack accuracy, down to 0.450 for driving style and 0.422 for car model inference with RF at the largest window size, demonstrating the countermeasure's effectiveness despite some outlier spikes (Fig. 4).

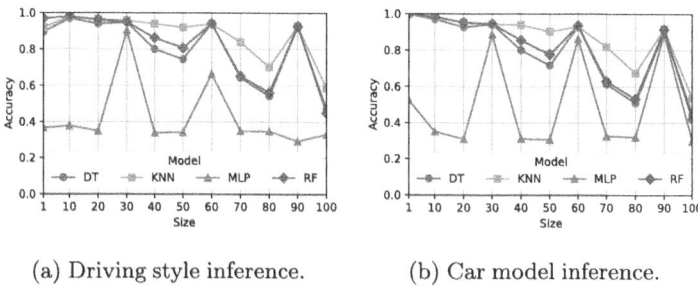

(a) Driving style inference.   (b) Car model inference.

Fig. 4. Countermeasure evaluation for different time window sizes.

7   Conclusions

With the increasing adoption of EVs, the volume of sensitive data they generate, particularly battery consumption patterns, raises notable security and privacy concerns. Although battery side-channel attacks have been studied in other domains, their implications for EVs remain largely unexplored. This paper addresses this gap by examining how battery data in EVs can be exploited to extract sensitive user information. We present novel side-channel attacks leveraging time-series feature extraction and machine learning classifiers to infer private details such as driver identity, trip attributes, and occupant count. Our evaluation on both simulated and real-world datasets demonstrates that battery consumption data can serve as a viable attack vector, achieving substantial classification accuracy.

Limitations and Future Work. Our approach assumes access to battery consumption data, and its effectiveness may be influenced by noise and variability in real-world conditions. Additionally, the datasets used, while diverse, do not capture the full spectrum of global EV types and driving scenarios. Future research will expand data diversity, improve model robustness, and explore countermeasures to mitigate privacy risks. Furthermore, investigating the interaction between battery data privacy and other connected vehicle data sources, such as charging stations, vehicle-to-vehicle communications, and in-vehicle sensors, will be crucial for a comprehensive understanding of EV security.

References

1. Regulation (EU) 2016/679 of the European parliament and of the council of 27 April 2016 on the protection of natural persons with regard to the processing of personal data and on the free movement of such data (general data protection regulation). Official J. Eur. Union (2016). https://eur-lex.europa.eu/eli/reg/2016/679/oj
2. Arandia, I., Cejudo, I., Irigoyen, E., Urbieta, I., Arregui, H., Loyo, E.: Analyzing the influence of driver, route and vehicle-related factors in electric vehicle energy

consumption, based on real life data. In: Proceedings of the 2022 3rd International Conference on Robotics Systems and Vehicle Technology, pp. 16–21 (2022)

3. Berger, K., Schöggl, J.P., Baumgartner, R.J.: Digital battery passports to enable circular and sustainable value chains: conceptualization and use cases. J. Clean. Prod. **353**, 131492 (2022)

4. Brighente, A., Conti, M., Donadel, D., Turrin, F.: EVScout2. 0: electric vehicle profiling through charging profile. ACM Trans. Cyber-Phys. Syst. **8**(2), 1–24 (2024)

5. Cejudo, I., Arandia, I., Urbieta, I., Irigoyen, E., Arregui, H., Loyo, E.: Electric vehicle battery consumption estimation model based on simulated environments. Int. J. Veh. Inf. Commun. Syst. **9**(3), 309–333 (2024)

6. Chawla, N., Singh, A., Kar, M., Mukhopadhyay, S.: Application inference using machine learning based side channel analysis. In: 2019 International Joint Conference on Neural Networks (IJCNN), pp. 1–8. IEEE (2019)

7. Christ, M., Braun, N., Neuffer, J., Kempa-Liehr, A.W.: Time series feature extraction on basis of scalable hypothesis tests (tsfresh-a Python package). Neurocomputing **307**, 72–77 (2018)

8. Chung, C.H., Jangra, S., Lai, Q., Lin, X.: Optimization of electric vehicle charging for battery maintenance and degradation management. IEEE Trans. Transp. Electrification **6**(3), 958–969 (2020)

9. Conti, M., Donadel, D., Poovendran, R., Turrin, F.: EVExchange: a relay attack on electric vehicle charging system. In: European Symposium on Research in Computer Security, pp. 488–508. Springer (2022)

10. U.S. Customs and Border Protection: CBP seizes record amount of counterfeit hoverboards (2016)

11. Efatinasab, E., Marchiori, F., Donadel, D., Brighente, A., Conti, M.: When authentication is not enough: on the security of behavioral-based driver authentication systems. arXiv preprint arXiv:2306.05923 (2023)

12. Gangwal, A., Jain, A., Conti, M.: On the feasibility of profiling electric vehicles through charging data. arXiv preprint arXiv:2210.05433 (2022)

13. Goller, G., Sigl, G.: Side channel attacks on smartphones and embedded devices using standard radio equipment. In: Mangard, S., Poschmann, A.Y. (eds.) COSADE 2014. LNCS, vol. 9064, pp. 255–270. Springer, Cham (2015). https://doi.org/10.1007/978-3-319-21476-4_17

14. Kang, L., Shen, H., Xu, S., Li, Y.: Electric vehicle trip information inference based on time-series residential electricity consumption. IEEE Internet Things J. **10**(17), 15666–15678 (2023)

15. Kong, L., Das, D., Pecht, M.G.: The distribution and detection issues of counterfeit lithium-ion batteries. Energies **15**(10), 3798 (2022)

16. La Cour, A.S., Afridi, K.K., Suh, G.E.: Wireless charging power side-channel attacks. In: Proceedings of the 2021 ACM SIGSAC Conference on Computer and Communications Security, pp. 651–665 (2021)

17. Lotto, A., Marchiori, F., Brighente, A., Conti, M.: A survey and comparative analysis of security properties of can authentication protocols. IEEE Commun. Surv. Tutorials (2024)

18. Lundberg, S.M., Lee, S.I.: A unified approach to interpreting model predictions. In: Guyon, I., et al. (eds.) Advances in Neural Information Processing Systems, vol. 30, pp. 4765–4774. Curran Associates, Inc. (2017). http://papers.nips.cc/paper/7062-a-unified-approach-to-interpreting-model-predictions.pdf

19. Marchiori, F., Conti, M.: Your battery is a blast! Safeguarding against counterfeit batteries with authentication. In: Proceedings of the 2023 ACM SIGSAC Conference on Computer and Communications Security, pp. 105–119 (2023)

20. Miller, C., Valasek, C.: A survey of remote automotive attack surfaces. Black Hat USA **2014**, 1–20 (2014)
21. Miller, C., Valasek, C.: Remote exploitation of an unaltered passenger vehicle. Black Hat USA **2015**(S 91), 1–91 (2015)
22. Mishra, S., Swain, S.C., Samantaray, R.K.: A review on battery management system and its application in electric vehicle. In: 2021 International Conference on Advances in Computing and Communications (ICACC), pp. 1–6. IEEE (2021)
23. Motion, R.: Over 17 million EVS sold in 2024 - record year (2025). https://rhomotion.com/news/over-17-million-evs-sold-in-2024-record-year/
24. O'Brien, M., Tatarka, G.: Lithium-ion batteries: an emerging focus of causation in consumer product fires. White Paper. Wilson Elser Moskowitz & Dicker LLP (2008)
25. European Parliament: Cybersecurity act (EU) 2019/881. European Union (2019). https://eur-lex.europa.eu/legal-content/EN/TXT/?uri=CELEX%3A32019R0881
26. Pese, M.D.: A first look at android automotive privacy. Technical report, SAE Technical Paper (2023)
27. Tindell, K.: Can injection: keyless car theft, April 2023. https://kentindell.github.io/2023/04/03/can-injection/
28. UNECE: Un regulation no. 155: Cybersecurity and cybersecurity management system (2021). https://unece.org/transport/documents/2021/03/standards/un-regulation-no-155-cyber-security-and-cyber-security
29. Yu, H., Tseng, F., McGee, R.: Driving pattern identification for EV range estimation. In: 2012 IEEE International Electric Vehicle Conference, pp. 1–7. IEEE (2012)

Machine Learning and Privacy

DP-TLDM: Differentially Private Tabular Latent Diffusion Model

Chaoyi Zhu[1] , Jiayi Tang[1] , Juan F. Pérez[3] , Marten van Dijk[4] ,
and Lydia Y. Chen[1,2(✉)]

[1] TU Delft, Delft, Netherlands
c.zhu-2@tudelft.nl, j.tang-14@student.tudelft.nl
[2] University of Neuchâtel, Neuchâtel, Switzerland
lydiaychen@ieee.org
[3] Universidad de los Andes, Bogotá, Colombia
jf.perez33@uniandes.edu.co
[4] Centrum Wiskunde & Informatica, Amsterdam, Netherlands
marten.van.dijk@cwi.nl

Abstract. Synthetic data from generative models emerges as the privacy-preserving data sharing solution. Such a synthetic data set shall resemble the original data without revealing identifiable private information. Till date, the prior focus on limited types of tabular synthesizers and small number of privacy attacks, particularly on Generative Adversarial Networks, and overlooks membership inference attacks and defense strategies, i.e., differential privacy. Motivated by the conundrum of keeping high data quality and low privacy risk of synthetic data tables, we propose DP-TLDM, Differentially Private Tabular Latent Diffusion Model, which is composed of an autoencoder network to encode the tabular data and a latent diffusion model to synthesize the latent tables. Following the emerging f-DP framework, we apply DP-SGD to train the auto-encoder in combination with batch clipping and use the separation value as the privacy metric to better capture the privacy gain from DP algorithms. Our empirical evaluation demonstrates that DP-TLDM is capable of achieving a meaningful theoretical privacy guarantee while also significantly enhancing the utility of synthetic data. Specifically, compared to other DP-protected tabular generative models, DP-TLDM improves the synthetic quality by an average of 35% in data resemblance, 15% in the utility for downstream tasks, and 50% in data discriminability, all while preserving a comparable level of privacy risk.

Keywords: synthetic tabular data · deep generative models · differential privacy

1 Introduction

High-quality synthetic data obtained from generative models are increasingly used to augment and substitute real data, boosting data utility for individuals

The link is: https://arxiv.org/abs/2403.07842

and enterprises [2,6,7]. As synthetic data resembles real data, it can be used to accelerate data-driven knowledge discovery and still abide by data protection regulations, e.g., GDPR [16], which restricts the collection and accessibility of real data. A key requirement for the adoption of these models in the industry is their ability to preserve the privacy of the real data [19,45]. Consider for instance medical institutes that own a subset of patients' data that cannot be shared freely and are subject to lengthy regulatory auditing. Alternatively, through a trusted party that first trains the generative model, a complete set of patients' synthetic data can be generated and distributed to all institutes that in turn design their own medical analysis based on these data. While the focus of generative models lies on producing synthetic data highly similar to and indiscernible from the real data, a rising concern is the real data privacy leakage caused by the synthetic data [5,14,26]. These studies highlight privacy vulnerabilities associated with synthetic data across specific domains, especially in image processing, and pertain to various generative models, including Bayesian networks, generative adversarial networks (GANs), and, more recently, diffusion processes. These privacy risks are materialized in attacks that are able to obtain training data, under various assumptions on the availability of model knowledge, i.e., white-box v.s. black-box attacks.

In the tabular data domain, Anonymeter [19] is the first framework that focuses on the privacy and utility trade-off of synthetic tables and introduces three privacy attacks relevant to tabular data: singling out attacks, linkability attacks, and attribute inference attacks. While it sheds light on quantifying the privacy-utility trade-off, [19] focuses on tabular GAN models, i.e., CTGANs [44], leaving the question of how this tradeoff behaves for different tabular generative models unaddressed. More importantly, the critically important category of Membership Inference Attacks (MIA) [9,21,32], which present stronger adversarial assumptions and infer whether specific data records are present in the training set, is overlooked. Last but not least, the impact of adopting privacy-enhancing strategies, such as differential privacy, on synthetic tabular data is largely unexplored by prior art.

Differential privacy (DP) [15] has received much attention as a solution to the problem of preserving individual privacy when releasing data. To incorporate DP in the training of deep neural models with stochastic gradient descent (SGD), DP-SGD [1] obfuscates gradient updates by adding calibrated statistical noise that is controlled by a privacy budget. There are two main DP analysis frameworks, (ϵ, δ)-DP [15], and emerging f-DP [13], where the former uses ϵ to define the privacy budget and the latter uses the separation value, which is the distance between the actual trade-off function of false positive and false negative and the ideal one, where no privacy leaks. A smaller privacy budget or separation value leads to adding more obfuscation noise to the gradients, degrading the performance of the underlying models. It is a long-standing challenge to apply meaningful ϵ or separation value while achieving satisfactory learning outcomes for image classification [1] and synthesizing [27]. The privacy enhancement of

DP on tabular generative models is yet to be explored, especially concerning different genres of generative models.

Based on the insights from our empirical study, we propose a novel differentially private latent tabular diffusion model, DP-TLDM, composed of an autoencoder and a diffusion model. Different from the existing TabDDPM, we first encode the tabular data into a continuous latent space, using the autoencoder network. This brings the advantage of a unified and compact representation of categorical variables, in contrast to the typical one-hot encoding. We then use the latent representation as input to the backbone diffusion model, which captures the data synthesis as a sequence of denoising processes [29]. To guard the proposed latent tabular diffusion against privacy attacks, we train the auto-encoder using DP-SGD. We follow the f-DP framework [13], which provides a precise parameterization of DP-SGD, specifically through the separation measure—a metric quantifying the maximum difference between false positive and false negatives when comparing a random guess and DP-protected algorithm. Thanks to the post-processing guarantees of DP, the backbone latent diffusion training is also protected by the DP. We extensively evaluate the proposed DP-TLDM against DP-CTGAN and DP-TabDDPM, where DP-SGD is used to train CTGAN and TabDDPM, showing a remarkable performance—reducing the privacy risk especially against MIA while maintaining a significant high data utility compared to the other two synthesizers. We make the following concrete contributions:

- We design DP-TLDM, a novel latent tabular diffusion model trained by DP-SGD that uses batch clipping on gradients and Gaussian noising mechanism. Our approach leverages the f-DP framework, where we propose a new theoretical privacy metric, termed *separation*, to enhance privacy guarantees.
- Our evaluation of DP-TLDM against DP-CTGAN and DP-TabDDPM shows that DP-TLDM can effectively reduce the privacy risks while maintaining high synthetic data quality across all privacy budget values. As a result DP-TLDM displays similar privacy risks levels than other synthesizers, but outperforms them by an average of 35% in data resemblance, 15% in the utility for downstream tasks, and a 50% in data discriminability.

2   Related Studies

In this section, we provide a general overview of the generative models and privacy on the tabular data.

Tabular Generative Models. Current state-of-the-art introduces several deep generative models for tabular data synthesis. TableGAN [34] implements an auxiliary classification model along with discriminator training to enhance column dependency in the synthetic data. CTGAN [44] improves data synthesis by introducing several preprocessing steps for categorical, continuous or mixed data types which encode data columns into suitable form for GAN training. The conditional vector designed by CTGAN [44] and later improved by Ctab-GAN [47] also helps the GAN training to reduce mode-collapse on minority categories. Drawback of these methods is also clear that there is loss of information during the transformation from table to latent vector. Therefore, GAN cannot learn the knowledge from the information that loses during this compression. TabDDPM [29] is based on denoising diffusion probabilistic models (DDPM) [22], it uses two different diffusion models to synthesize categorical and continuous columns. **Privacy attacks** Despite the impressive performance and application of deep generative models, recent works have also raised significant concerns regarding the potential privacy risks of these models. A vast body of related studies on **privacy attacks** can be categorized by various attack types, including (i) membership inference attacks (MIA) [5,9,21,36], inferring whether a certain data record is in the training set; (ii) attribute inference attacks [19,20], deducing sensitive attributes of the training data; (iii) replication attacks [5,25,37], reproducing the training data or hidden generative models; (iv) adversarial attacks [17,31,38], deceiving generative models through crafted input data at the inference stage. **Membership inference attacks** can be further categorized into white-box, no-box and black-box attacks based on the availability of model information. In white-box attacks, where attackers have access to the internals of generators, several works [5,26,48] have proposed loss-based techniques for conducting MIA on diffusion models. Black-box setting assumes the prior knowledge of attackers is limited only to generated samples [42,48].

Privacy enhancing methodologies have been studied to address potential privacy risks. DP-SGD and its variants have been widely adopted for privately training deep generative models. DPGAN [43] applies the DP-SGD algorithm directly to the discriminator component within GANs. In contrast, GS-WGAN [8] implements DP-SGD on the gradients transferred from the discriminator to the generator. The utility of DP-SGD is also extended beyond GANs and applied in normalizing flows for tabular data synthesis [30,40]. Moreover, in the context of emerging diffusion models, adaptions of DP-SGD are considered as well. One study [12] applied the classic DP-SGD algorithm with one modification involving sampling multiple time steps of a single data point when computing the loss. Building on this, another study [18] further presented the effectiveness of three other techniques, namely pre-training, augmentation multiplicity, and modified time step sampling. While DP-SGD is deemed a strong countermeasure for privacy leaks, it comes at the cost of sample quality and longer training times.

3 Empirical Analysis

In this section, we put our risk-utility quantification framework described in Appendix B.3 to the test on publicly available datasets that have been extensively employed in tabular data analysis and synthesis.

3.1 Datasets

We employ four datasets, two small (up to 20000 samples) and two larger. Since small datasets usually make models prone to overfitting, by comparing these datasets, we can understand how dataset size and overfitting affect the quality and privacy of synthetic data. Some characteristics of the datasets are listed in Table 4 in the appendix.

The **Loan dataset** [3] contains demographic information on 5000 customers. It holds 14 features divided into 4 different measurement categories, including binary, interval, ordinal, and nominal features. The **Housing dataset** [39] relates to houses in a given California district and provides summary statistics based on the 1990 Census data. It comprises 20,640 instances with 1 categorical and 9 numerical features and a total of 207 missing values. The **Adult dataset** [4] contains information on individuals' annual incomes and related variables. It consists of 48842 instances with 14 mixed datatype features in total, and a total of 6465 missing values. The **Cardiovascular Heart Disease dataset** [11] contains detailed information on the risk factors for cardiovascular disease, including 70000 instances with 13 mixed-type columns.

For all datasets, each synthesizer generated a synthetic dataset with the same size as the training dataset for evaluation. For the privacy evaluation, 1000 records are randomly sampled from each training set for every attack.

3.2   Privacy-Utility Trade-Off

Table 1 presents detailed results quantifying both utility and risk aspects of synthetic data for all four datasets employing the five generative models described in Appendix B.1. We present the three utility metrics discussed before (i.e., resemblance, discriminability, and utility), where a higher score indicates better performance, as well as the privacy risk for the four attacks considered (Singling out, Linkability, AIA, MIA), where a lower risk indicates better performance. Due to space reasons, we keep the detailed statistics of the five MIA attacks in the appendix. **Comparing the synthesizers**, TabDDPM generates synthetic data of the highest quality, outperforming other synthesizers. Across all four datasets, TabDDPM consistently secures top-three rankings in terms of resemblance, discriminability, and utility. CopulaGAN displays very good results in resemblance and discriminability but scores relatively low in utility. The Gaussian Copula sits at the other end of the spectrum, being outperformed by the other synthesizers across all datasets.

Despite the excellent performance of TabDDPM in generating high-quality synthetic data, it presents the highest risk, particularly in relation to Linkability and MIA. Its risk is especially high in terms of MIA attacks, where it displays a significantly higher risk than the other synthesizers.

On the contrary, the GAN family and Gaussian Copula, while not achieving superior synthetic data quality, showcase greater resilience to Linkability, AIA, and MIA attacks. This suggests that:

> Synthetic data with higher quality tend to closely resemble the original data, potentially resulting in heightened exposure of the genuine data and increased susceptibility to exploitation by attackers, especially shown in Tab-DDPM.

Table 1. Quantification of Risk-Utility for Five Generative Models Across Various Datasets. Here, "Resem." stands for Resemblance, "Distrim." refers to Discriminability, "S-out" denotes singling out attacks, and "Link" represents linkability attacks.

Dataset	Method	Quality Score ↑			Privacy Risk ↓			
		Resem.	Discri.	Utility	S-out	Link	AIA	MIA
Loan	CopulaGAN	92	95	70	52.81	2.31	6.98	2.86
	CTGAN	92	85	93	54.90	0.00	8.11	2.86
	ADS-GAN	93	95	73	17.23	0.00	0.00	22.86
	GC	86	82	78	28.68	0.00	0.00	5.72
	TabDDPM	98	100	97	26.31	2.23	16.68	45.72
Housing	CopulaGAN	94	90	62	8.14	0.00	1.54	20.00
	CTGAN	94	92	64	12.55	0.45	0.00	20.00
	ADS-GAN	93	87	74	1.73	1.43	0.98	48.58
	GC	91	84	32	4.16	0.00	0.00	5.72
	TabDDPM	96	98	93	1.30	0.16	0.00	88.58
Adult	CopulaGAN	93	97	81	10.25	0.05	5.08	17.14
	CTGAN	90	79	83	20.18	0.55	3.16	10.00
	ADS-GAN	88	59	83	19.74	0.00	0.00	20.00
	GC	80	50	56	32.80	0.38	2.86	8.58
	TabDDPM	96	98	98	22.72	0.46	0.00	94.28
Cardio	CopulaGAN	87	93	96	66.54	1.13	28.75	0.00
	CTGAN	84	68	97	62.04	1.11	24.07	11.42
	ADS-GAN	90	71	100	59.76	0.89	15.21	31.42
	GC	81	63	86	61.02	0.44	6.30	22.86
	TabDDPM	95	99	100	60.77	1.31	23.08	94.28

Across all types of attacks, AIA and MIA consistently display greater efficacy, as evidenced by their higher average risk observed across the four datasets. Notably, Linkability, AIA, and MIA attacks consistently manifest more detrimental effects on synthesizers that demonstrate superior utility, such as TabDDPM and ADS-GAN. Conversely, the Singling Out attack emerges as the predominant threat to synthesizers with lower utility, as exemplified by Gaussian Copula and Copula GAN.

This divergence underscores the intricate vulnerabilities of synthesizers to distinct attack methodologies. While Linkability, AIA, and MIA generally rely on the comprehensive attributes of synthetic data, the Singling Out Attack is based upon identifying outlier values within the synthetic dataset. This suggests that:

> Synthetic data of suboptimal quality may disclose more information about outliers to potential attackers as in Singling Out attacks. Conversely, high-quality synthetic data are prone to reveal more comprehensive and over-all information of the original data as shown in Linkability, AIA and MIA attacks.

Regarding MIA strategies, notable effectiveness is achieved by the Naive-Groundhog (NG), HistGroundhog (HG), and Closest Distance-Hamming (CD-H) strategies, which are able to reach success rates of 60% or higher in some cases. These results are detailed in Table 5 in Appendix D.1. Remarkably, Hist-Groundhog consistently outperforms other MIA strategies when applied to the TabDDPM synthesizer. In contrast, the NaiveGroundhog and Closest Distance-Hamming strategies demonstrate better efficacy when employed on other synthesizers.

In contrast, Closest Distance-L2 (CD-L) and Kernel Estimator (KE) strategies, exhibit a comparatively lower level of effectiveness. Given that half of the target records for MIA are from the training data, and both strategies consistently attain success rates close to 50%, the performance of these two strategies closely aligns with random guessing. This observation underscores the nuanced variations in the efficacy of MIA strategies for different synthesizer models. It indicates that:

> Sophisticated shadow modeling approaches (HistGroundhog) exhibit height-ened effectiveness when applied to high-quality synthetic data. In contrast, simpler shadow modeling methods (NaiveGroundhog) and distance-based strategies (Closest Distance-Hamming) may prove more effective when the synthetic data quality is suboptimal.

Across all data sets, the Linkability attack demonstrates higher average privacy risk, particularly when applied to smaller datasets such as Loan and Housing. As for other attacks, trends related to different dataset sizes are less evident.

In terms of synthetic data utility, larger datasets (Adult and Cardio) exhibit, on average, lower resemblance and discriminability scores compared to smaller ones (Loan and Housing). These findings prompt that larger datasets pose more challenges to the synthesizers, as increased dataset sizes may introduce greater diversity and complexity, thereby making data synthesis more difficult.

However, the utility scores are higher when dataset sizes increase. This phenomenon may be attributed to the fact that the utility metric is measured on the performance of downstream machine learning tasks, which are inherently influenced by the size of training data. In our experiments, the synthetic dataset size remains the same as the corresponding real dataset. Consequently, small real datasets result in small synthetic datasets, which may potentially engender suboptimal performance in machine learning tasks and lower utility scores.

This leads us to conclude that in our experiments:

The larger datasets are more challenging with regard to the data synthesis task and potentially less vulnerable to adversarial privacy attacks.

4   DP-TLDM

In this section, we introduce our latent tabular diffusion model (DP-TLDM), which effectively incorporates robust privacy protections by integrating Differential Privacy (DP) techniques. Illustrated in Fig. 1, our model consists of two components: the Autoencoder and the Latent Diffusion Model. Initially, the autoencoder performs the task of encoding both continuous and categorical features in the original tabular data into a unified latent space, meanwhile ensuring DP protection is applied throughout this transformation. Subsequently, the Latent Diffusion Model conducts a Gaussian diffusion process within the latent space.

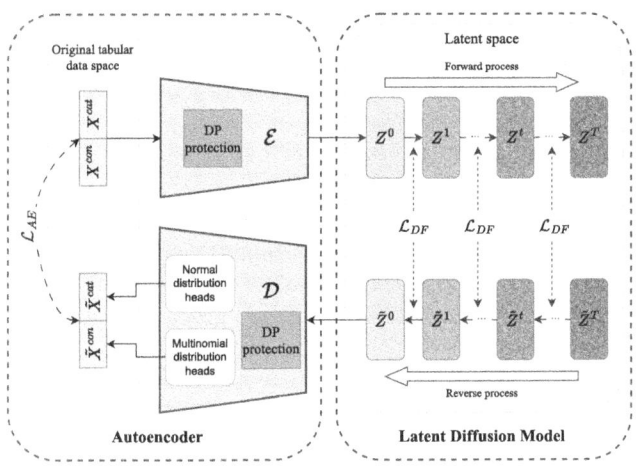

Fig. 1. The latent tabular diffusion model. Given the original tabular data with both continuous and categorical features, the autoencoder first encodes both features into a cohesive latent space, with the protection of Differential Privacy (DP). The Latent Diffusion Model then executes a Gaussian diffusion process within the latent space.

The essential background of diffusion models for tabular data is introduced in Sect. 4.1. Following this, in Sect. 4.2, we delineate the motivation behind the development of our latent tabular diffusion model, as well as details regarding the two components. Furthermore, the inclusion of DP-enhanced training and Differential Privacy measures are presented in Sects. 4.4 and 4.3, respectively.

4.1   Diffusion Primer

Diffusion models work with a forward process perturbing the data into Gaussian noise and a reverse process learning to recover the data from the pure noise.

Typically, given the original data x_0, and a total of T steps, the forward process $q(x_t|x_{t-1})$ at step t is modeled as a Markov chain that adds pure noise to the data. The whole forward process eventually ends at a simple distribution (e.g., standard Gaussian distribution) $p(x_T)$. The reverse process, starting at $p(x_T)$, is another Markov Chain with learned transitions $p_\theta(x_{t-1}|x_t)$, which are unknown and estimated by a neural network.

In the realm of modeling tabular data, the inherent heterogeneity among features necessitates tailored approaches for accurate modeling. TabDDPM [29] addresses this challenge by adopting different methods for noising and denoising continuous and categorical features, as shown in Fig. 2. TabDDPM employs Gaussian diffusion following [22], where the forward process gradually adds Gaussian noise to the input data, which eventually ends at $p_{con}(x_T) = \mathcal{N}(x_T; \mathbf{0}, \mathbf{I})$. Conversely, in the reverse process, a neural network is trained to predict the added noise, thereby facilitating the denoising of the data.

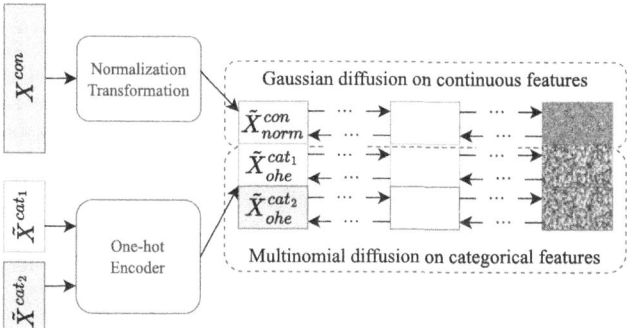

Fig. 2. The architecture of TabDDPM where different methods are adopted for continuous and discrete features separately. Continuous features are handled by the Gaussian diffusion process, whereas categorical features are one-hot encoded and diffused using the Multinomial diffusion process.

Meanwhile, categorical features are handled using Multinomial diffusion, as proposed by [23], with each categorical feature having a distinct Multinomial diffusion process. For a categorical feature with K classes, during the forward process, uniform noise over the K classes is applied to corrupt the one-hot encoded categorical feature, ending at the categorical distribution $p_{dis}(x_T) = \mathcal{C}(x_T; 1/K)$. Subsequently, the reverse process leverages a neural network to predict the probability vector to recover the noised data.

TabDDPM employs one multi-layer neural network for both the Gaussian diffusion and the Multinomial diffusions. The input to the network is the concatenated representation of both the normalized continuous features and one-hot encoded categorical features. The output has the same dimensionality as the input, with the first few coordinates being the predicted Gaussian noise and the rest being the predictions of probability vectors. The model is trained by minimizing a sum of the mean-squared error for the Gaussian diffusion and the KL divergences for each multinomial diffusion.

4.2 Tabular Latent Diffusion Model (TLDM)

While different diffusion processes for continuous and categorical features in TabDDPM underscore a strategy to accommodate the diverse nature of tabular data, there are two potential drawbacks. First, the utilization of one-hot encoded representations for categorical columns in tabular data introduces significant complexity. For instance, in the Adult dataset, the Educational Level column consists of 16 distinct categories, resulting in the transformation of a single column into a one-hot encoded feature vector with a dimensionality of 16. Second, the separation and discrepancy in the diffusion processes for continuous and categorical features could also lead to a potential loss of inter-feature relationships and dependencies. By treating continuous and categorical features with independent diffusion processes, the model may overlook the intricate correlations that could exist between features.

To address the mentioned limitations, we propose the latent tabular diffusion model following [35]. In our latent tabular diffusion model, both the continuous and categorical features are transferred to a unified continuous latent space by training an autoencoder. Subsequently, a unified diffusion model is deployed to noise and denoise the continuous latent features. The decoder component of the autoencoder is then employed to convert the denoised latent representation back to the original features.

Consequently, our model mitigates the sparsity and dimensional complexity associated with the one-hot encoding technique used in TabDDPM. With a unified continuous latent space, the diffusion model benefits from a more compact and streamlined input structure. Besides, jointly embedding both types of features into a latent representation also facilitates the preservation of inter-feature correlations within the original data.

Incorporating the autoencoder component provides an additional benefit in safeguarding the model through differential privacy (DP). In DP, a limited number of training epochs is set for a certain privacy budget. By decoupling the training procedures of the autoencoder and diffusion model components in our model, we are able to introduce DP mechanisms specifically to the training phase of the autoencoder. Thereby, only the autoencoder component will undergo a reduction in training epochs while the diffusion model can still be sufficiently trained. This deliberate separation of training procedures effectively balances privacy preservation and model efficacy for generating tabular data.

Autoencoder. The autoencoder component in our model comprises two parts: the encoder $\mathcal{E}$ and the decoder $\mathcal{D}$. Initially, given the original tabular data X, containing both continuous and categorical features, the encoder $\mathcal{E}$ jointly transforms the entire X into a continuous latent representation $Z = \mathcal{E}(X)$. Subsequently, the decoder $\mathcal{D}$ reconstructs the latent representation Z back into the original data space, yielding $\tilde{X} = \mathcal{D}(Z)$.

To handle the heterogeneity of features in tabular data, rather than treating continuous and categorical features with separate diffusion processes like Tab-DDPM, we add distinct heads in the output layer of the decoder to map each feature to a probability distribution.

For continuous features X^{con}, the Gaussian distribution is chosen and the head outputs the mean and variance of the distribution, representing the spread of different feature values. For categorical features X^{cat}, the distribution head is a multinomial distribution and each node outputs probabilities corresponding to different categories.

To train the autoencoder, we follow the common setting in Variational AutoEncoders [28], minimizing as loss function the negative Evidence Lower-Bound (ELBO), defined as

$$\mathcal{L}_{AE} = \mathbb{E}_{z \sim q_{\mathcal{E}}(z|x)}[-\log p_{\mathcal{D}}(x|z)] + D_{KL}(q_{\mathcal{E}}(z|x)||p(z)).$$

Here $q_{\mathcal{E}}(z|x)$ is the posterior distribution of the latent space given the input X after the encoder $\mathcal{E}$, and $p_{\mathcal{D}}(x|z)$ is the output distribution of the decoder $\mathcal{D}$ given the latent space Z. D_{KL} refers to the KL-divergence and $p(z)$ is a fixed prior distribution over the latent space Z. By setting $p(z)$ to a standard Gaussian distribution, the KL-divergence term serves as a regularizer that helps to avoid arbitrarily high-variance latent spaces.

Latent Diffusion Model. Once the input is mapped into the continuous latent space Z, a Gaussian diffusion process is the next component of the model. Within this process, for a latent variable z^0 generated by the encoder $\mathcal{E}$, the forward process in the diffusion model gradually adds Gaussian noise to the latent variable. Formally, with a total of T timesteps and a predefined variance schedule $\beta^1, \ldots, \beta^T$, the forward process at timestep t is

$$q(z^t|z^{t-1}) = \mathcal{N}(z^t; \sqrt{1 - \beta^t} z^{t-1}, \beta^t \mathbf{I}).$$

Notably, the sampling z^t at an arbitrary timestep t can be expressed in closed form as

$$q(z^t|z^0) - \mathcal{N}(z^t; \sqrt{\bar{\alpha}^t} z^0, (1 - \alpha^t)\mathbf{1}), \tag{1}$$

where $\alpha^t = 1 - \beta^t$ and $\bar{\alpha}^t = \prod_{s=1}^{t} \alpha^s$.

The progressive forward process eventually converges to a pure noise space, characterized by a standard Gaussian distribution $p(z^T) = \mathcal{N}(z^T; \mathbf{0}, \mathbf{I})$. Subsequently, the reverse process $p_\theta(z^{t-1}|z^t)$ is another Markov Chain with learned Gaussian transitions starting at $p(z^T)$.

To learn the reverse denoising transitions, we adopt the methodology proposed in [22]. The crux of this approach involves estimating the added noise. Thus, the training objective of the diffusion component is formulated as minimizing the loss

$$\mathcal{L}_{DF} = \mathbb{E}_{t, z^0, \epsilon} \left[\left\| \epsilon - \epsilon_\theta(z^t, t) \right\|^2 \right].$$

where ϵ is the true noise and ϵ_θ is the estimated noise given the sampling z^t and timestep t.

4.3 Differential Privacy Framework

To introduce a privacy protection in the latent space we employ the f-DP framework [13] since it is capable to provide better bounds on the privacy leakage under composition, which is key in the training of neural models, which is done iteratively by means of stochastic gradient descent. These better bounds result in a more faithful privacy-utility tradeoff analysis.

f-**DP Background.** In our paper, we adopt the f-DP framework to elevate privacy protection. This approach offers a clearer and more intuitive privacy explanation, encapsulating all necessary details to derive established DP metrics. Moreover, f-DP achieves a tighter privacy bound than traditional (ε, δ)-DP, allowing for a more precise privacy evaluation [13,41].

Differential Privacy (DP), as introduced by Dwork et al. [15], is a foundational framework for preserving the privacy of individuals' data within datasets. It quantifies the impact of an individual's data on the output of a randomized algorithm, ensuring minimal influence and thus protecting privacy.

In the (ε, δ)-DP framework, a randomized mechanism $\mathcal{M} : \mathbb{D} \to \mathbb{R}$, where $\mathbb{D}$ is the domain and $\mathbb{R}$ the range, achieves (ε, δ)-DP if for any two neighboring datasets D and D', differing by only a single record, it holds that

$$\Pr(\mathcal{M}(D) \in S) \le e^{\varepsilon} \Pr(\mathcal{M}(D') \in S) + \delta,$$

where S is a subset of possible outputs. The parameters ε and δ quantify the privacy level, with lower values indicating stronger privacy guarantees.

Transitioning from traditional (ε, δ)-DP analysis, the f-DP framework, proposed in [13], offers a refined perspective that relies on framing the adversary's challenge as a hypothesis testing problem. This framework introduces a trade-off function f that represents the trade-off between false negatives (FN) and false positives (FP) in distinguishing between datasets D and D'.

The FN and FP errors are defined as

$$\alpha_\phi = \mathbf{E}_{\mathcal{M}(D) \in S}[\phi(S)] \quad \text{and} \quad \beta_\phi = 1 - \mathbf{E}_{\mathcal{M}(D') \in S}[\phi(S)],$$

where $\phi \in [0, 1]$ denotes the rejection rule applied to the output of the DP mechanism $\mathcal{M}$. The trade-off function is given by

$$T(\mathcal{M}(D), \mathcal{M}(D'))(\alpha) = \inf_{\phi}\{\beta_\phi : \alpha_\phi \le \alpha\},$$

for a significance level $\alpha \in [0, 1]$, signifying the optimal trade-off between FN and FP errors. A mechanism $\mathcal{M}$ is said to be f-DP if $T(\mathcal{M}(D), \mathcal{M}(D')) \ge f$ for all neighboring datasets D and D'.

Thanks to its functional definition, the f-DP framework can provide much tighter composition bounds than other existing definitions of DP. f-DP encompasses (ϵ, δ)-DP as a special case, wherein a mechanism is (ϵ, δ)-DP if and only if it conforms to $f_{\epsilon,\delta}$-DP, with $f_{\epsilon,\delta}(\alpha) = \max\{0, 1 - \delta - e^{\epsilon}\alpha, (1 - \delta - \alpha)e^{-\epsilon}\}$.

DP-SGD. The Differentially Private Stochastic Gradient Descent algorithm (DP-SGD) [1] was designed for the differentially private training of neural networks. It achieves differential privacy by individually clipping (IC) the gradient of each individual sample within each mini-batch and adding Gaussian noise $\mathcal{N}(0, (C\sigma)^2\mathbf{I})$ as to the gradient

$$\tilde{g}_r \leftarrow \frac{1}{|B|}\left(\sum_{i\in B}[g_r(x_i)]_C + \mathcal{N}(0, (C\sigma)^2\mathbf{I})\right). \tag{2}$$

Here $[g_r(x_i)]_C = g_r(x_i)/\max(1, \|g_r(x_i)\|_2 /C)$ is clipped from $g_r(x_i)$, the original gradient of sample x_i at training round r, using the gradient norm bound C and a mini batch size B.

Separation Metric. To better illustrate the effectiveness of the f-DP guarantee, we introduce a novel metric called *separation*, which intuitively indicates the strength of DP in the hypothesis testing trade-off by measuring the distance between the ideal and actual trade-off functions.

Let N be the dataset size, $b = \mathbb{E}[|B|]$ the sample (mini batch) size, and σ the standard deviation of the Gaussian noise used in DP-SGD[1] as in (2). Thus, N/b equals the number of rounds in a single epoch and letting E denote the total number of epochs, the total number of rounds is $R = (N/b) \cdot E$.

Then DP-SGD is $C_{b/N}(G_{\sigma^{-1}})^{\otimes R}$-DP where $C_{b/N}$ is an operator representing the effect of subsampling in DP-SGD, $G_{\sigma^{-1}}$ is a Gaussian trade-off function characterizing the differential privacy (called Gaussian DP) due to adding Gaussian noise in DP-SGD, and the operator $\otimes R$ describes composition (of privacy leakage) over R rounds.

Following the asymptotic analysis in [13], DP-SGD converges to a μ-Gaussian DP defined as

$$G_{c \cdot h(\sigma)}\text{-DP} \quad \text{for} \quad c = \sqrt{bE/N},$$

where the function $h(\sigma)$ is calculated as

$$h(\sigma) = \sqrt{2\left(e^{\sigma^{-2}}\Phi\left(\frac{3}{2\sigma}\right) + 3\Phi\left(-\frac{1}{2\sigma}\right) - 2\right)}.$$

The ideal trade-off function is defined as $f(\alpha) = 1 - \alpha$, representing random guessing by the adversary; hence, it implies no privacy leakage. Since optimal trade-off functions are symmetric around the diagonal, separation between $1 - \alpha$ and $G_\mu(\alpha)$ can be measured as Euclidean distance between the point $(\frac{1}{2}, \frac{1}{2})$ on the curve $1 - \alpha$ and the point (a, a) on the curve $G_\mu(\alpha)$, i.e., where $G_\mu(a) = a$. Here, $G_\mu(a) = \Phi(\Phi^{-1}(1 - a) - \mu)$, with $\Phi(\cdot)$ being the cumulative distribution function of the standard normal distribution. Thus the separation is denoted as

$$sep = \sqrt{2}\left|a - \frac{1}{2}\right|, \quad \text{s.t. } G_\mu(a) = a. \tag{3}$$

For instance, taking the separation as 0.1, the μ calculated is 0.3563, and the distance between the trade-off function and the ideal curve is illustrated in Fig. 3.

---

[1] We consider probabilistic sampling as in the Opacus library [46] and use noise parameter $C \cdot \sigma$ and normalize with C rather than $2C$.

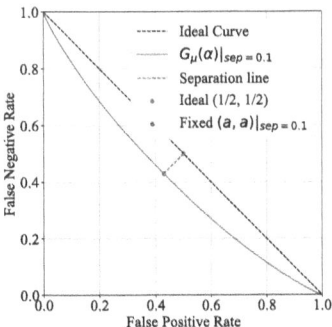

Fig. 3. The separation between the ideal curve and the trade-off function.

We notice that DP guarantee is influenced by three hyperparameters: σ, $\frac{N}{b}$, and E. Clearly, given a target utility, smaller values of E and larger values of $\frac{N}{b}$ enhance privacy protection. Based on these observations, we introduce the separation value as a novel term to evaluate privacy, which provides an intuitive explanation of the strength of DP.

4.4   Two-Stage DP-SGD Training

Instead of using the traditional individual clipping (IC) as in (2), as pointed out in [33], a better way is to utilize batch clipping (BC) for DP training, i.e.,

$$\tilde{g}_r \leftarrow \left[\frac{1}{|B|}\sum_{i \in B} g_r(x_i)\right]_C + \mathcal{N}(0, (C\sigma)^2 \mathbf{I}), \qquad (4)$$

In batch clipping, the average of the gradients within a batch is computed before applying clipping, as opposed to (2), which averages a sum of clipped individual gradients. This offers two key advantages. First, batch clipping allows for efficient computation of the sum of gradients across the entire mini-batch during both the forward and backward passes, thereby enhancing computational efficiency compared to individual clipping, which requires gradient computation for every single sample.

Second, batch clipping enables training Batch Normalization Layers in neural networks with a robust DP guarantee. As highlighted in [33], current implementations for IC that use batch normalization on the extensive training dataset lead to correlations among the updates across training rounds. Since these correlations are not considered, IC does not yield a solid DP guarantee from a theoretical perspective. However, batch normalization with BC over corresponding mini-batches can provide a solid DP argument within the $f-$DP framework.

Therefore, based on the mentioned advantages, we employ DP-SGD with batch clipping to enhance the differentially private training of our latent tabular diffusion model, as presented in Algorithm 1. The training procedure consists of two steps. First, given a privacy budget, we train the Autoencoder component utilizing batch clipping alongside the injection of DP noise. Second, the

---

Algorithm 1. DP enhanced two-stage training in DP-TLDM

1: **Input**: Tabular data $X = \{x_1, \ldots, x_N\}$, epochs E_1, E_2, batch sizes B_1, B_2, noise scale σ, norm bound C, timestep T
2: **Output**: Encoder $\mathcal{E}$, decoder $\mathcal{D}$, noise network ϵ_θ
3: **Initialize** $\mathcal{E}$, $\mathcal{D}$, ϵ_θ
4: **for** $e_1 = 1$ to E_1 **do**
5:     **for** $r_1 = 1$ to $\lceil N/B_1 \rceil$ **do**
6:         Compute $\bar{g}_{r_{1_\mathcal{E}}} \leftarrow \frac{1}{B_1} \nabla_\mathcal{E} \mathcal{L}_{AE}(\mathcal{E}, X_{r_1})$, $\bar{g}_{r_{1_\mathcal{D}}} \leftarrow \frac{1}{B_1} \nabla_\mathcal{D} \mathcal{L}_{AE}(\mathcal{D}, X_{r_1})$
7:         Clip and add noise for $\mathcal{E}$: $\tilde{g}_{r_{1_\mathcal{E}}} \leftarrow \frac{\bar{g}_{r_{1_\mathcal{E}}}}{\max(1, \|\bar{g}_{r_{1_\mathcal{E}}}\|_2/C)} + \mathcal{N}(0, (C\sigma)^2 \mathbf{I})$
8:         Clip and add noise for $\mathcal{D}$: $\tilde{g}_{r_{1_\mathcal{D}}} \leftarrow \frac{\bar{g}_{r_{1_\mathcal{D}}}}{\max(1, \|\bar{g}_{r_{1_\mathcal{D}}}\|_2/C)} + \mathcal{N}(0, (C\sigma)^2 \mathbf{I})$
9:     **end for**
10: **end for**
11: $Z^0 = \mathcal{E}(X)$
12: **for** $e_2 = 1$ to E_2 **do**
13:     **for** $r_2 = 1$ to $\lceil N/B_2 \rceil$ **do**
14:         Sample $Z_{r_2}^0 \sim q(Z^0)$, $t \sim \text{Uniform}(\{1, \ldots, T\})$, $\epsilon \sim \mathcal{N}(0, \mathbf{I})$
15:         Compute $g_{\epsilon_\theta} \leftarrow \nabla_{\epsilon_\theta} \mathcal{L}_{DF}(\epsilon, \epsilon_\theta, t, Z_{r_2}^0)$ and update ϵ_θ
16:     **end for**
17: **end for**

DP-trained encoder generates the latent features of the original data, and the Gaussian diffusion model is trained on this latent feature space.

5 Performance Evaluation

In this section, we evaluate the proposed DP-TLDM on the aforementioned four datasets, employing the same quality and privacy risk metrics used in Sect. 3. We aim to answer if DP-TLDM can take advantage of the privacy protection from the DP mechanism without degrading the synthetic data quality. We specifically compare DP-TLDM against two other baselines, DP-CTGAN and DP-TabDDPM, by applying the DP-SGD training algorithm on CTGAN and TabD-DPM, which represent the state-of-the-art GAN and diffusion-based generative models, respectively.

Evaluation Setup. Identical to Sect. 3, we use resemblance, discriminability and utility to measure synthetic data quality. We evaluate the privacy risk, ranging from 1–100, for four types of attacks, singling out, linkability, AIA and MIA. The privacy measure is the theoretical separation value in (3), representing the maximum difference of typeI-typeII error between the random guess and DP-SGD, illustrated in Fig. 3. Three separation values are evaluated, namely $[0.1, 0.15, 0.2]$, where lower values indicate a stronger privacy level. We conduct the DP-SGP training on each generator under a given σ value until the budget of separation depletes. For a fair comparison, we also apply batch clipping on all three synthesizers as outlined in (4).

Table 2. Impact of DP-SGD training on DP-CTGAN, DP-TabDDPM, and the proposed DP-TLDM. Here, "Resem." stands for Resemblance, "Distrim." refers to Discriminability, "S-out" denotes singling out attacks, and "Link" represents linkability attacks.

Dataset	Method	Quality Score ↑			Privacy Risk ↓			
		Resem.	Discri.	Utility	S-out	Link	AIA	MIA
Loan	TLDM	96	98	100	22.86	1.42	21.94	42.86
	DP-CTGAN	40	11	54	0	0.15	1.18	2.86
	DP-TabDDPM	40	9	55	0	0.13	2.43	10.48
	DP-TLDM	63	57	63	16.48	0.63	2.7	5.72
Housing	TLDM	98	98	85	2.53	0.12	0.98	97.14
	DP-CTGAN	37	9	21	0.34	0.01	0.05	8.58
	DP-TabDDPM	47	9	8	0.24	0.14	0.62	4.48
	DP-TLDM	86	81	30	1.22	0.09	0.81	10.48
Adult	TLDM	95	88	100	18.80	0.82	2.52	80.00
	DP-CTGAN	44	10	49	28.36	0.17	0.75	8.58
	DP-TabDDPM	49	9	48	0.3	0.27	2.7	5.72
	DP-TLDM	77	63	58	12.72	0.14	2.27	14.28
Cardio	TLDM	100	95	100	68.52	0.39	18.51	97.14
	DP-CTGAN	53	14	51	38.13	0.03	1.58	14.28
	DP-TabDDPM	43	9	71	0.99	0.15	1.06	0
	DP-TLDM	86	50	91	17.25	0.05	2.1	15.24

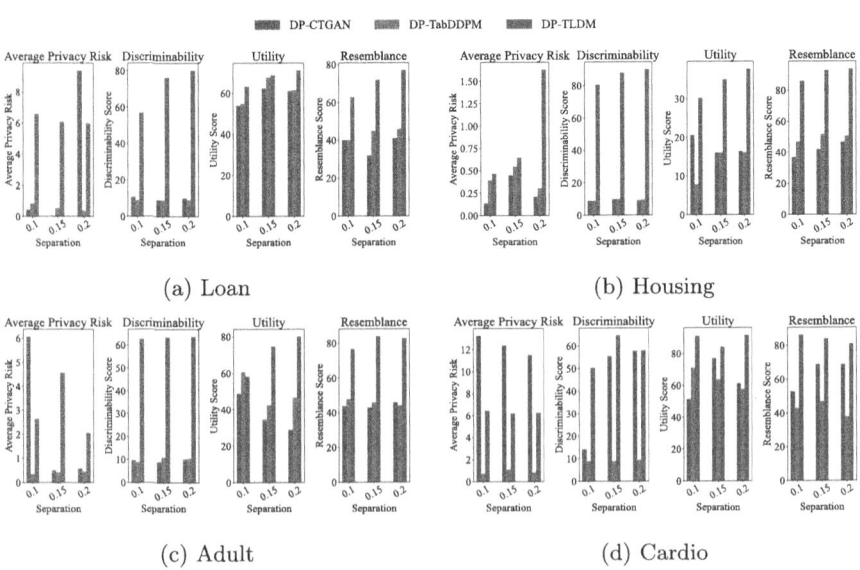

(a) Loan

(b) Housing

(c) Adult

(d) Cardio

Fig. 4. Comparison between three DP-enhanced synthesizers on various datasets.

5.1   Overview

We first present the overall performance for DP-CTGAN, DP-TabDDPM, and DP-TLDM in Table 2. The specific separation value is 0.1, which is the most meaningful DP protection level in our evaluation. We summarize the key observations as follows.

DP-TLDM Achieves the Optimal Balance Between Data Quality and Privacy Risk Mitigation. Across all DP-protected synthesizers, DP-TLDM consistently demonstrates the most favorable trade-off. It excels at achieving the highest resemblance, discriminability and utility scores, with comparable empirical risks. In sharp contrast, the two baseline methods fail to achieve any meaningful data quality scores with DP added, while DP-TLDM outperforms its counterparts by up to 3X across all four datasets.

DP Protection Yields a Notable Reduction in the Risk of MIA on DP-TabDDPM and DP-TLDM. Notably, among all attacks considered, the most pronounced enhancement is found in MIA, where the risk diminishes substantially from approximately 90 to around 10. Given that MIA exploits additional information about the training dataset and model, its potential implications for the privacy of synthetic data are particularly severe. However, DP mechanism employed here effectively mitigates these risks, successfully defending against MIA.

A Discernible Reduction in Privacy Risks and Data Quality Measures is Evident When Comparing DP and Non-DP Versions. Across all three DP-protected synthesizers, the privacy risks demonstrably decrease at the expense of data quality, compared with their non-DP versions. This phenomenon is observed across all four datasets and against all four attacks. Particularly noteworthy is the significant enhancement observed in the cardio dataset. Specifically, notable improvements are observed in the Singling Out attack (risk decreases from an average of 60 to approximately 20), AIA (from an average of 20 to 2), and MIA (from an average of 90 to 10).

DP-TLDM Exhibits the Highest Resilience to the DP Mechanism Considering Data Quality. Among all three data synthesizers, both DP-CTGAN and DP-TabDDPM experience substantial declines in data quality, particularly in discriminability, with scores dropping significantly from 92 (98) to 9 (9) in CTGAN (TabDDPM) on the housing dataset. In contrast, DP-TLDM manages to maintain a much higher data quality of synthetic data. We attribute the robust performance of DP-TLDM to its two-step training design. By implementing DP-SGD on the autoencoder networks and leveraging the diffusion backbone to offset the quality degradation in the autoencoder, DP-TLDM effectively preserves data utility despite the application of DP.

5.2   Impact of Privacy Budget

Here, we study the impact of varying separation values and summarize the results in Fig. 4. The notion of Average Privacy Risk refers to the average risk score of Singling Out, Linkability and AIA. A higher separation value offers limited privacy protection but also introduces a lower perturbation to the quality of synthetic data. Consequently, we present the following noteworthy observations.

DP-TLDM Consistently Exhibits the Best Synthetic Data Quality Across Varying Levels of Privacy Budget. Across all four datasets, a distinct hierarchy emerges among the three synthesizers, with DP-TLDM surpassing DP-TabDDPM and DP-CTGAN. This can be explained by the two benefits of our two-stage training scheme: firstly, Diffusion Models (DDPM) inherently exhibit great resilience to noisy input [10,24]. By integrating the autoencoder with DP, the algorithm outputs latent representations with added perturbations. The resilience of the diffusion model ensures the generation of high-quality synthetic data. Secondly, the isolated two-stage training approach, where the privacy budget is solely allocated to the autoencoder stage, ensures that the diffusion process can refine and generate synthetic data without further compromising privacy. This efficient use of the privacy budget allows for the production of synthetic data that is not only of high quality but also adheres strictly to the required privacy constraints. The diffusion stage, not requiring additional privacy budget, acts as a compensatory mechanism for any potential decrease in data utility due to the privacy-preserving perturbations introduced in the autoencoder stage.

Across Different Datasets and Separation Values, DP-TLDM and DP-CTGAN Generally Have Higher Privacy Risks. However, the significantly superior data quality produced by DP-TLDM does result in greater privacy leakage. Nonetheless, considering that the privacy risk is quantified on a scale from 0 to 100, all datasets demonstrate that our model maintains a privacy risk below 8. This indicates that *algo* successfully achieves an optimal balance between data quality and privacy protection.

Overall, these findings underscore that: The two-stage training scheme of DP-TLDM, which leverages the inherent robustness of diffusion models to noisy inputs, achieves the optimal privacy-utility tradeoff among three DP-generators at equivalent privacy levels.

6   Conclusion

Motivated by the increasing adoption of synthetic tables as a privacy-preserving data sharing solution, we design DP-TLDM, a latent tabular diffusion trained by DP-SGD, following the f-DP framework. Key components of DP-TLDM are i) an autoencoder network to transform tabular data into a compact and unified latent representation, and ii) a latent diffusion model to synthesize latent tables. Thanks to the two-component design, and by applying DP-SGD to train the autoencoder, DP-TLDM obtains a rigorous DP guarantee, measured by the separation value. Our evaluation results against tabular GAN and regular tabular diffusion models trained with DP-SGD show that DP-TLDM can effectively mitigate the empirical privacy risks of synthetic data while achieving 15–50% higher data quality than other synthesizers with a stringent theoretical privacy budget.

Acknowledgments. This research is part of the Priv-GSyn project, 200021E_229204 of Swiss National Science Foundation, and the DEPMAT project, P20-22/N21022, of the research programme Perspectief which is partly financed by the Dutch Research Council (NWO).

References

1. Abadi, M., et al.: Deep learning with differential privacy. In: Proceedings of the 2016 ACM SIGSAC Conference on Computer and Communications Security, pp. 308–318 (2016)
2. Ali, H., Murad, S., Shah, Z.: Spot the fake lungs: generating synthetic medical images using neural diffusion models. In: Irish Conference on Artificial Intelligence and Cognitive Science, pp. 32–39. Springer (2022)
3. Thera Bank: Bank Loan Modelling (2017). https://www.kaggle.com/datasets/itsmesunil/bank-loan-modelling
4. Becker, B., Kohavi, R.: Adult. UCI Machine Learning Repository (1996). https://doi.org/10.24432/C5XW20
5. Carlini, N., et al.: Extracting training data from diffusion models. In: 32nd USENIX Security Symposium (USENIX Security 23), pp. 5253–5270 (2023)
6. Chambon, P., et al.: RoentGen: vision-language foundation model for chest X-ray generation. arXiv preprint arXiv:2211.12737 (2022)
7. Chambon, P.J.M., Bluethgen, C., Langlotz, C., Chaudhari, A.: Adapting pre-trained vision-language foundational models to medical imaging domains. In: NeurIPS 2022 Foundation Models for Decision Making Workshop (2022)
8. Chen, D., Orekondy, T., Fritz, M.: GS-WGAN: a gradient-sanitized approach for learning differentially private generators. In: Advances in Neural Information Processing Systems, vol. 33, pp. 12673–12684 (2020)
9. Chen, W., Song, D., Li, B.: TrojDiff: Trojan attacks on diffusion models with diverse targets. In: IEEE/CVF Conference on Computer Vision and Pattern Recognition, CVPR, pp. 4035–4044 (2023)
10. Daras, G., Shah, K., Dagan, Y., Gollakota, A., Dimakis, A., Klivans, A.: Ambient diffusion: learning clean distributions from corrupted data. In: Advances in Neural Information Processing Systems, vol. 36 (2024)
11. Dempsy, K.: Cardiovascular Disease Dataset (2021). https://www.kaggle.com/datasets/thedevastator/exploring-risk-factors-for-cardiovascular-diseas
12. Dockhorn, T., Cao, T., Vahdat, A., Kreis, K.: Differentially Private Diffusion Models. CoRR abs/2210.09929 (2022)
13. Dong, J., Roth, A., Su, W.: Gaussian differential privacy. J. Roy. Stat. Soc. (2021)
14. Duan, J., Kong, F., Wang, S., Shi, X., Xu, K.: Are diffusion models vulnerable to membership inference attacks? In: International Conference on Machine Learning, ICML, vol. 202, pp. 8717–8730 (2023)
15. Dwork, C., McSherry, F., Nissim, K., Smith, A.: Calibrating noise to sensitivity in private data analysis. In: Halevi, S., Rabin, T. (eds.) TCC 2006. LNCS, vol. 3876, pp. 265–284. Springer, Heidelberg (2006). https://doi.org/10.1007/11681878_14
16. European Parliament and Council of the European Union: Regulation (EU) 2016/679 of the European parliament and of the council of 27 April 2016 on the protection of natural persons with regard to the processing of personal data and on the free movement of such data, and repealing directive 95/46/EC (general data protection regulation). Official Journal of the European Union, L119, 1-88 (2016). https://eur-lex.europa.eu/legal-content/EN/TXT/?uri=CELEX:32016R0679

17. Gao, H., Zhang, H., Dong, Y., Deng, Z.: Evaluating the robustness of text-to-image diffusion models against real-world attacks. CoRR abs/2306.13103 (2023)
18. Ghalebikesabi, S., et al.: Differentially private diffusion models generate useful synthetic images. CoRR abs/2302.13861 (2023)
19. Giomi, M., Boenisch, F., Wehmeyer, C., Tasnádi, B.: A unified framework for quantifying privacy risk in synthetic data. Proc. Priv. Enhancing Technol. **2**, 312–328 (2023)
20. Stadler, T., Oprisanu, B., Troncoso, C.: Synthetic data-a privacy mirage. arXiv preprint arXiv:2011.07018 (2020)
21. Hayes, J., Melis, L., Danezis, G., Cristofaro, E.D.: LOGAN: membership inference attacks against generative models. Proc. Priv. Enhancing Technol. **2019**(1), 133–152 (2019). https://doi.org/10.2478/POPETS-2019-0008
22. Ho, J., Jain, A., Abbeel, P.: Denoising diffusion probabilistic models. In: Advances in Neural Information Processing Systems 33: Annual Conference on Neural Information Processing Systems (2020)
23. Hoogeboom, E., Nielsen, D., Jaini, P., Forré, P., Welling, M.: Argmax flows and multinomial diffusion: learning categorical distributions. In: Advances in Neural Information Processing Systems, vol. 34, pp. 12454–12465 (2021)
24. Hsieh, Y.G., Kasiviswanathan, S., Kveton, B., Bloebaum, P.: Thompson sampling with diffusion generative prior. In: ICML 2023 (2023). https://www.amazon.science/publications/thompson-sampling-with-diffusion-generative-prior
25. Hu, H., Pang, J.: Model extraction and defenses on generative adversarial networks. arXiv preprint arXiv:2101.02069 (2021)
26. Hu, H., Pang, J.: Membership inference of diffusion models. CoRR abs/2301.09956 (2023)
27. Jordon, J., Yoon, J., Van Der Schaar, M.: PATE-GAN: generating synthetic data with differential privacy guarantees. In: International Conference on Learning Representations (2018)
28. Kingma, D.P., Welling, M.: Auto-encoding variational Bayes. arXiv preprint arXiv:1312.6114 (2013)
29. Kotelnikov, A., Baranchuk, D., Rubachev, I., Babenko, A.: TabDDPM: modelling tabular data with diffusion models. In: International Conference on Machine Learning, pp. 17564–17579. PMLR (2023)
30. Lee, J., Kim, M., Jeong, Y., Ro, Y.: Differentially private normalizing flows for synthetic tabular data generation. In: Thirty-Sixth AAAI Conference on Artificial Intelligence, AAAI, IAAI, EAAI, pp. 7345–7353 (2022)
31. Millière, R.: Adversarial attacks on image generation with made-up words. CoRR abs/2208.04135 (2022)
32. Mukherjee, S., Xu, Y., Trivedi, A., Patowary, N., Ferres, J.L.: privGAN: protecting GANs from membership inference attacks at low cost to utility. Proc. Priv. Enhancing Technol. **2021**(3), 142–163 (2021)
33. Nguyen, T.N., Nguyen, P.H., Nguyen, L.M., Van Dijk, M.: Batch clipping and adaptive layerwise clipping for differential private stochastic gradient descent. arXiv preprint arXiv:2307.11939 (2023)
34. Park, N., Mohammadi, M., Gorde, K., Jajodia, S., Park, H., Kim, Y.: Data synthesis based on generative adversarial networks. Proc. VLDB Endow. **11**(10), 1071–1083 (2018)
35. Rombach, R., Blattmann, A., Lorenz, D., Esser, P., Ommer, B.: High-resolution image synthesis with latent diffusion models. In: IEEE/CVF Conference on Computer Vision and Pattern Recognition, CVPR, pp. 10674–10685 (2022)

36. Shokri, R., Stronati, M., Song, C., Shmatikov, V.: Membership inference attacks against machine learning models. In: IEEE Symposium on Security and Privacy, SP, pp. 3–18 (2017)
37. Somepalli, G., Singla, V., Goldblum, M., Geiping, J., Goldstein, T.: Diffusion art or digital forgery? Investigating data replication in diffusion models. In: IEEE/CVF Conference on Computer Vision and Pattern Recognition, CVPR, pp. 6048–6058 (2023)
38. Szegedy, C., et al.: Intriguing properties of neural networks. In: 2nd International Conference on Learning Representations, ICLR (2014)
39. Torgo, L.: California Housing Prices (1990). https://www.kaggle.com/datasets/camnugent/california-housing-prices
40. Waites, C., Cummings, R.: Differentially private normalizing flows for privacy-preserving density estimation. In: AIES 2021: AAAI/ACM Conference on AI, pp. 1000–1009 (2021)
41. Wang, C., Su, B., Ye, J., Shokri, R., Su, W.: Unified enhancement of privacy bounds for mixture mechanisms via f-differential privacy. In: Advances in Neural Information Processing Systems, vol. 36 (2024)
42. Wu, Y., Yu, N., Li, Z., Backes, M., Zhang, Y.: Membership inference attacks against text-to-image generation models. CoRR abs/2210.00968 (2022)
43. Xie, L., Lin, K., Wang, S., Wang, F., Zhou, J.: Differentially private generative adversarial network. arXiv preprint arXiv:1802.06739 (2018)
44. Xu, L., Skoularidou, M., Cuesta-Infante, A., Veeramachaneni, K.: Modeling tabular data using conditional GAN. In: Advances in Neural Information Processing Systems, vol. 32 (2019)
45. Yoon, J., Drumright, L.N., Van Der Schaar, M.: Anonymization through data synthesis using generative adversarial networks (ADS-GAN). IEEE J. Biomed. Health Inform. **24**(8), 2378–2388 (2020)
46. Yousefpour, A., et al.: Opacus: user-friendly differential privacy library in PyTorch. CoRR (2021). https://arxiv.org/abs/2109.12298
47. Zhao, Z., Kunar, A., Birke, R., Chen, L.Y.: CTAB-GAN: effective table data synthesizing. In: Asian Conference on Machine Learning, pp. 97–112. PMLR (2021)
48. Zhu, D., Chen, D., Grossklags, J., Fritz, M.: Data forensics in diffusion models: a systematic analysis of membership privacy. CoRR abs/2302.07801 (2023)

Share Secrets for Privacy: Confidential Forecasting with Vertical Federated Learning

Aditya Shankar[1]([✉])[iD], Jérémie Decouchant[1][iD], Dimitra Gkorou[2],
Rihan Hai[1][iD], and Lydia Chen[1,3][iD]

[1] Delft University of Technology, Delft, The Netherlands
{a.shankar,j.decouchant,r.hai}@tudelft.nl
[2] ASML, Veldhoven, The Netherlands
dimitra.gkorou@asml.com
[3] Université de Neuchâtel, Neuchâtel, Switzerland
lydiaychen@ieee.org

Abstract. Vertical federated learning (VFL) is a promising area for time series forecasting in many applications, such as healthcare and manufacturing. Critical challenges to address include data privacy and overfitting on small and noisy datasets during both training and inference. Additionally, such forecasting models must scale well with the number of parties while ensuring strong convergence and low-tuning complexity. We address these challenges and propose "Secret-shared Time Series Forecasting with VFL" (STV), a novel framework with the following key features: i) a privacy-preserving algorithm for forecasting with SARIMAX and autoregressive trees on vertically-partitioned data; ii) decentralised forecasting using secret sharing and multi-party computation; and iii) novel N-party algorithms for matrix multiplication and inverse operations for exact parameter optimization, giving strong convergence with minimal tuning complexity. We evaluate on six representative datasets from public and industry-specific contexts. Results demonstrate that STV's forecasting accuracy is comparable to those of centralized approaches. Our exact optimization outperforms centralized methods, including state-of-the-art diffusion models and long-short-term memory, by 23.81% on forecasting accuracy. We also evaluate scalability by examining the communication costs of exact and iterative optimization to navigate the choice between the two. STV's code and supplementary material is available online: https://github.com/adis98/STV.

Keywords: Vertical Federated Learning · Time Series Forecasting · Multiparty Computation

1 Introduction

Vertically-partitioned or *feature*-partitioned time series data are prevalent in many areas, such as healthcare, manufacturing, and finance [30,40,46]. For example, consider the scenario in Fig. 1, where a mental health facility and a cardiac

M. Dalla Preda et al. (Eds.): ARES 2025, LNCS 15992, pp. 358–379, 2025.
https://doi.org/10.1007/978-3-032-00624-0_18

centre possess distinct features, such as stress levels and heart rate corresponding to a common patient. Each party can forecast patient risk levels using just their own feature sets, but it is likely that combining stress levels and heart rate could lead to better predictive precision due to the correlations between the two [10]. The straightforward way to use both sources is to first centralize the two feature sets at a server and then train a model. However, privacy restrictions, such as patient confidentiality agreements or laws (e.g. GDPR [33]), prevent data sharing between organizations. Such a scenario naturally extends to other domains, such as joint predictive maintenance in manufacturing [23,39], or stock predictions in finance [30].

Federated learning (FL) [19] is a promising research direction to address the privacy concern. Its training paradigm follows a *model-to-data* approach where data never leaves the premises of the source. Within FL, *Vertical federated learning* (VFL), considers cases where each participant owns different features pertaining to the same sample ID or timestamp [46], which corresponds to our problem scenario. However, time-series forecasting with VFL has received limited attention [40,45] and existing works overlook the following challenges.

First, VFL methods typically employ deep learning, which suffers when data is scarce due to overfitting. Data scarcity is a real issue—healthcare and manufacturing environments can be affected by slow collection and noisy measurements, leading to small datasets [22,26,47]. Second, VFL methods predominantly use a *split-learning* architecture, consisting of several bottom models at the clients and a single top model held by a server [7,17,42]. Final predictions are assumed to be generated by the top model at the server. However, since each party may have an interest in maintaining control or ownership over the final output, deciding which party should assume the server role can lead to conflicts. Moreover, centralizing predictions at a single party would be catastrophic in case of a data breach. Third, the models are generally trained iteratively—e.g., via gradient descent—needing extensive hyperparameter tuning. In contrast, analytical/exact methods can reach globally optimal solutions without any tuning, but may incur higher compute complexity. Therefore, we need a way to flexibly incorporate both approaches to handle diverse scenarios.

To address the challenges, we present a novel framework, *Secret-Shared Time Series Forecasting with Vertical Federated Learning* (STV), with the following contributions. **1. VFL forecasting framework**—built using *secret sharing* (SS) [36] and *multi-party computation* (MPC) [9,25] for cryptographic privacy guarantees. We propose STV_L for linear models such as $SARIMAX$ [14,20,32], and STV_T for autoregressive trees (ARTs) [29]. **2. Decentralized inference**— all outputs and intermediate data remain distributed across parties as shares when using MPC. Hence, responsibility of output generation is also distributed across all the involved parties, promoting trust through mutual dependence. **3. Adaptable optimization with Least Squares**—using a *two-step* approach that can flexibly be incorporated into both iterative and exact methods. This approach requires algorithms for N-*party* matrix multiplications and inverses on secret shares, a key novelty in our work.

Fig. 1. Problem scenario—forecasting risk levels needs corresponding input features from multiple parties, all of whom want to protect the confidentiality of their data.

Our evaluation compares the forecasting accuracy of STV_L and STV_T with centralized state-of-the-art forecasters based on diffusion models [2], Long Short Term Memory (LSTM), and SARIMAX with Maximum Likelihood Estimation (MLE) [14]. We also compare the communication costs of iterative and exact optimization of linear forecasters under different scaling scenarios, highlighting their trade-offs. We use a wide range of datasets: five public datasets (Air quality, flight passengers, SML 2010, PV Power, Rossman Sales) and one industrial semiconductor dataset for measuring chip overlays from alignment sensor data.

2   Background

In this section, we provide background knowledge on time series models and secure multiparty computation. We provide a summary of our notations and symbols in Table 1.

2.1   Time Series Forecasting

STV uses a popular linear forecaster, SARIMAX (Seasonal AutoRegressive Integrated Moving **A**verage with eXogenous variables) [20,32], that generalizes other autoregresive forecasters, such as ARMA, ARIMA, and ARIMAX [14,31]. It models the outputs as a linear function composed of autoregressive, moving averages, and exogenous variables along with their seasonal counterparts [32].

Autoregressive terms capture the influence of historical values on future predictions and moving average terms capture the influence of historical errors/residuals. Exogenous features serve as additional auxiliary features that aid in forecasting. The seasonal terms capture periodic patterns in the series. Mathematically, the output Y at time t can be modelled using a linear polynomial H, containing historical residuals $\epsilon(t-i)$, historical observations $Y(t-i)$, and exogenous features $X(t)$ as follows:

$$H : Y(t) = \alpha_1 Y(t-1) + \alpha_2 Y(t-2) + \beta_1 \varepsilon(t-1) + \gamma_1 X_1(t) + \gamma_2 X_2(t) + \varepsilon(t) \quad (1)$$

The coefficients (α, β, γ) are generally estimated using least-squares [16,27, 28,41] or Maximum Likelihood Estimation (MLE) [14]. However, implementing MLE with multiparty computation and secret sharing is limited to likelihood functions like the exponential or multivariate normal distributions [24,38], since computations with MPC are limited by a small number of supported mathematical operations. However, least-squares optimization is still possible by extending basic MPC protocols such as scalar addition and multiplication (see Sect. 2.2). First, we transform the datasets, (X, Y), into time-lagged design matrices (ϕ_X, ϕ_Y) representing Eq. (1):

$$
\underbrace{\begin{bmatrix} Y(3) \\ Y(4) \\ .. \\ Y(t) \end{bmatrix}}_{\phi_Y} = \underbrace{\begin{bmatrix} Y(2) & Y(1) & \varepsilon(2) & X_1(3)\, X_2(3) \\ Y(3) & Y(2) & \varepsilon(3) & X_1(2)\, X_2(2) \\ .. & .. & .. & .. \\ Y(t-1) & Y(t-2) & \varepsilon(t-1) & X_1(t)\, X_2(t) \end{bmatrix}}_{\phi_X} \times \underbrace{\begin{bmatrix} \alpha_1 \\ \alpha_2 \\ \beta_1 \\ \gamma_1 \\ \gamma_2 \end{bmatrix}}_{A} + \underbrace{\begin{bmatrix} \varepsilon(3) \\ \varepsilon(4) \\ .. \\ \varepsilon(t) \end{bmatrix}}_{\varepsilon}
\tag{2}
$$

Table 1. Summary of key mathematical notations

Variable	Description
X, Y	Exogenous features and output variable
H	Time series polynomial
(t)	Variable value at timestep t
ϵ	Residual features
α, β, γ	Autoregressive, moving average, exogenous coefficients
ϕ_X, ϕ_Y	Time-lagged design matrix of features and output
$C_1, C_{i \in [2:K]}$	Active party, passive parties
$\langle P \rangle$	Secret-shared state of a variable P. Union of $\langle P \rangle^i$
$\langle P \rangle^i$	C_i's share of a variable P
K	Number of parties or clients

With least-squares, A can be optimized using a *two-step* regression approach [16,27,28,41]. First, the residuals are estimated by modeling using only autoregressive (AR) and exogenous terms. Then, all the coefficients in A are jointly optimized by setting the residuals to the estimates.

Since the residuals, $\epsilon(.)$, in ϕ_X are unknown, they are initialized to zero to give $\hat{\phi}_X$, as shown below:

$$
\underbrace{\begin{bmatrix} Y(3) \\ Y(4) \\ .. \\ Y(t) \end{bmatrix}}_{\phi_Y} = \underbrace{\begin{bmatrix} Y(2) & Y(1) & 0\, X_1(3)\, X_2(3) \\ Y(3) & Y(2) & 0\, X_1(2)\, X_2(2) \\ .. & .. & .. & .. \\ Y(t-1) & Y(t-2) & 0\, X_1(t)\, X_2(t) \end{bmatrix}}_{\hat{\phi}_X} \times \underbrace{\begin{bmatrix} \hat{\alpha}_1 \\ \hat{\alpha}_2 \\ \hat{\beta}_1 \\ \hat{\gamma}_1 \\ \hat{\gamma}_2 \end{bmatrix}}_{\hat{A}} + \underbrace{\begin{bmatrix} \varepsilon(3) \\ \varepsilon(4) \\ .. \\ \varepsilon(t) \end{bmatrix}}_{\varepsilon}
\tag{3}
$$

With mean-squared-error (MSE), $\hat{A}$ is optimized using the *normal equation* (NE) [4] or gradient descent (GD):

Normal equation:

$$\hat{A} = ((\hat{\phi}_X)^T (\hat{\phi}_X))^{-1} ((\hat{\phi}_X)^T \phi_Y) \tag{4}$$

Gradient descent:

$$\hat{A} := \hat{A} - \frac{\alpha}{N} \times (\hat{\phi}_X)^T \times (\hat{\phi}_Y - \phi_Y) \text{ (for } e \text{ iterations)} \tag{5}$$

Here, $\hat{\phi}_Y = \hat{\phi}_X \times \hat{A}$ are the predictions at a particular step, α is the learning rate and N is the number of samples.

Following this initial estimate, the residuals, ε, are then obtained as follows:

$$\varepsilon = \phi_Y - \hat{\phi}_X \times \hat{A} \tag{6}$$

These residual estimates are then re-substituted in Eq. (2) to refine $\hat{A}$ via a second optimization step. Although we describe the two-step optimization procedure in the context of linear forecasters, the idea of autoregression can also be extended to tree-based models like XGBoost [6]. *Autoregressive trees* (ARTs) [29] build on this premise and use historical outputs/observations as decision nodes in a gradient-boosted regression tree. Therefore, extending XGBoost-based VFL methods [8,11,44] to ARTs only requires transforming the datasets into lagged design matrices using a polynomial like Eq. (1). This architecture enables modelling forecasts in a non-linear fashion.

2.2   MPC

Multi-Party Computation methods use the principle of *secret sharing* [36] for privacy by scattering a value into random shares among parties. These methods offer strong privacy guarantees, i.e., **information-theoretic security** [11]. Assume there are K parties, $C_{i \in [1,K]}$. If party C_i wants to secure its private value, V, it does so by generating $K - 1$ random shares, denoted $\langle V \rangle^{i'}$; $\forall i' \in [1, K]$; $i' \neq i$. These are sent to the corresponding party $C_{i'}$. C_i's own share is computed as $\langle V \rangle^i = V - \sum_{i' \neq i}^{K} \langle V \rangle^{i'}$. The whole ensemble of K shares representing the shared state of V, is denoted as $\langle V \rangle$.

Parties cannot infer others' data from their shares alone, as shares are completely random. However, the value can be recovered by combining all shares. We can extend this idea to machine learning by distributing feature *vectors* and outputs as shares to preserve their privacy. All parties then jointly utilize decentralized training protocols on the secretly shared data to obtain a local model. Inference/forecasting is then done by distributing features into secret shares and then computing the prediction as a distributed share across all parties. Training and forecasting on secretly shared features requires primitives for performing mathematical operations on distributed shares, which we explain as follows.

Addition and Subtraction: If X and Y exist as secret shares, $\langle X \rangle$ and $\langle Y \rangle$, each party performs a local addition or subtraction, i.e., $\langle Z \rangle^k = \langle X \rangle^k +(-) \langle Y \rangle^k$. To obtain $Z = X + (-)Y$, the shares are aggregated: $Z = \sum_k^K \langle Z \rangle^k$.

Knowing the value of $\langle Z \rangle^k$ makes it impossible to infer the private values X or Y, as each participant only owns a share of the whole secret. Moreover, the individual values of the shares, $\langle X \rangle^k$ and $\langle Y \rangle^k$, are also masked by adding them.

Multiplication (using Beaver's triples) [3,44]: Consider $Z = X * Y$, where $*$ denotes element-wise multiplication, and X and Y, are secretly shared. The coordinator first generates three numbers a, b, c such that $c = a * b$. These are then secretly shared, i.e., C_k, receives $\langle a \rangle^k$, $\langle b \rangle^k$, and $\langle c \rangle^k$. C_k computes $\langle e \rangle^k = \langle X \rangle^k - \langle a \rangle^k$ and $\langle f \rangle^k = \langle Y \rangle^k - \langle b \rangle^k$, and sends it to C_1. C_1 then aggregates these shares to recover e and f and broadcasts them to all parties. C_1 then computes $\langle Z \rangle^1 = e * f + f * \langle a \rangle^1 + e * \langle b \rangle^1 + \langle c \rangle^1$, and the others calculate $\langle Z \rangle^k = f * \langle a \rangle^k + e * \langle b \rangle^k + \langle c \rangle^k$. It is easy to see that aggregation of the individual shares gives the product Z. Despite knowing e and f, X and Y are hidden since the parties do not know a, b, and c. Moreover, the values of X and Y are also hidden from the coordinator, who is only responsible for the generation of a, b, and c, and does not hold any features or outputs. Similar to addition, the individual shares, $\langle Z \rangle^k$, do not reveal anything about the local share values, i.e., $\langle X \rangle^k$, $\langle Y \rangle^k$, $\langle a \rangle^k$, $\langle b \rangle^k$, and $\langle c \rangle^k$. Additional primitives for division and argmax can also be computed using MPC, as detailed in Fang et al. [11] and Xie et al. [44].

3   Related Work

As shown in Table 2, we compare VFL methods on their applicability to time series forecasting, potential for achieving inference privacy, adaptability to alternative optimization choices, and generalizability to N-parties.

Time-Series Forecasting. Earlier, we mentioned that industries require easy-to-understand and low-complexity models to avoid overfitting on small datasets. Hence we focus on linear/logistic regression (LR) [15,17,37], and tree-based models [8,44]. Yan et al. [45] modifies the split learning architecture using Gated Recurrent Units (GRUs) with a shared upper model for predictions. However, it

Table 2. Comparison of related works in VFL.

Method	Time Series	Serverless inference	Dual optimization	N-party (≥ 2)
Yan et al. [45]	✔	✘	✘	✔
Han et al.[15]	✘	✔	✔	✘
Xie et al.[44]	✘	✔	✘	✔
Shi et al.[37]	✘	✔	✘	✔
STV (this work)	✔	✔	✔	✔

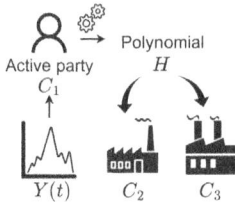
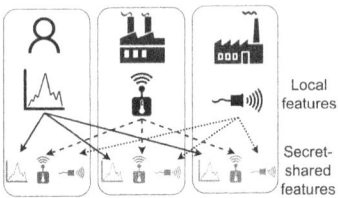

(a) Polynomial generation through pre-processing

(b) Secretly sharing features

Fig. 2. Time-series pre-processing and secret sharing of features in STV.

depends on a single server to produce forecasts, which is a bottleneck and can lead to trust issues among the involved parties.

Decentralized Inference. We consider schemes adopting SS as potential candidates for our inference requirements, as they are straightforward to integrate into a decentralized approach like ours [15,37,44]. Shi et al. [37] and Han et al. [15] train linear models while Xie et al. [44] implement XGBoost. Homomorphic encryption methods, such as Hardy et al. [17], require the predictions to be decrypted at the server, violating the requirement.

Optimization. When it comes to optimization techniques, all selected works, except for Han et al. [15], employ solely iterative approaches. Notably, Han et al. [15] offer iterative and matrix-based methods for exact optimization using Eq. (4). However, they only provide 2-party protocols for matrix multiplications and inverses, which we extend to the N-party case.

4   STV Framework

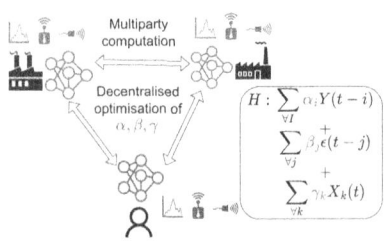
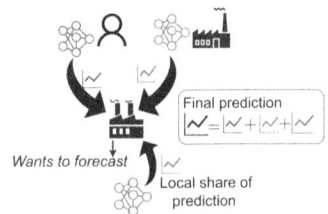

(a) MPC optimization of time-series polynomial H with secret-shared features

(b) Decentralized inference through flexible selection of share-aggregator

Fig. 3. Training and inference in STV.

Algorithm 1. General protocol STV

Data: X_k on party C_k $\forall k \in [1, K]$, and Y on C_1
Accepted Parameters: Task: *Training/Inference*, Model *type*, number of trees T,
Optimization method O, learning rate α, iterations, e, Trained distributed *Model*,
Requesting party C_j
Output:Trained model distributed across K parties or predicted forecast at party C_j

1: **if** *Training* and active party C_1 **then**
2:     $params = ProcessSeries(Y)$
3:     $H = GenPoly$ *(params, type)*
4:     Broadcast H to C_i $\forall i \in [1, K]$
5: **end if**
6: Share local features $\langle X_k \rangle$ and (or) outputs $\langle Y \rangle$
7: $\langle \phi_X \rangle, \langle \phi_Y \rangle = TransformData$ $(H)\{$ (2)$\}$
8: **if** *type* $==$ *Tree* and *Training* **then**
9:     **return** $Model = STV_T$ $(\langle \phi_X \rangle, \langle Y \rangle, T)$
10: **else if** *type* $==$ *Linear* and *Training* **then**
11:     **return** $Model = STV_L$ $(\langle \phi_X \rangle, \langle \phi_Y \rangle, O, \alpha, e)$
12: **end if**
13: **if** *Inference* **then**
14:     $\langle Result \rangle = Model.Predict(\langle \phi_X \rangle)$
15:     **if** requesting party C_j **then**
16:         $Result = \sum_{k=1}^{K} \langle Result \rangle^k$ {Aggregate predictions}
17:     **end if**
18: **end if**

Here we introduce the adversarial model and problem statement, followed by STV's design and implementation for trees (STV$_T$), and SARIMAX (STV$_L$). Both models employ secret sharing and MPC to protect the privacy of features.

Adversarial Models. We assume that all parties are *honest-but-curious/semi-honest* [17,46], i.e., they adhere to protocol but try to infer others' private data using their own local data and whatever is communicated to them. Also, it is assumed that parties do not collude. This is a standard assumption in VFL as all parties are incentivised to collaborate due to their mutual dependence on one another for training and inference [17,46]. In addition, we also assume that communication between parties is encrypted to prevent snooping.

Problem Statement. We assume a setup with K parties, C_1 to C_K, grouped into two types: *active* and *passive*. Without loss of generality, we denote the active party as C_1, which holds the ground truth outputs of the training data for the time series, $Y(t)$, for a timestep t. It also possesses exogenous features, $X_1(t)$. The passive parties only have exogenous features, $X_i, \forall i \in [2, K]$. The common samples between parties are assumed to be already identified using privacy-preserving entity alignment approaches [17,35]. Our goal is to forecast future values using exogenous and autoregressive features without sharing them with others in plaintext. We further assume that there is a *coordinator*, a trusted third party that oversees the training process and is responsible for generat-

---

Algorithm 2. STV_T

Data: Secretly shared transformed matrices $\langle \phi_X \rangle$, $\langle \phi_Y \rangle$
Parameter: number of trees T
Output: Distributed autoregressive XGBoost tree

1: Initialize predictions $\langle \hat{\phi}_Y \rangle^k = 0$ on all parties C_k
2: Initialize $Trees_k = [\,]$ on all parties C_k
3: **for** $t \in [1, T]$ **do**
4:    $tree_{t_k} = \mathbf{\textit{SecureFit}}(\langle \phi_X \rangle^k, \langle \phi_Y \rangle^k, \langle \hat{\phi}_Y \rangle^k)$
5:    $\langle \hat{\phi}_{Y_t} \rangle^k = tree_{t_k}.Predict(\langle \phi_X \rangle^k)$
6:    **if** active party C_1 **then**
7:        $\hat{\phi}_{Y_t} = \sum_{i=1}^{K} \langle \hat{\phi}_{Y_t} \rangle^k$ {Aggregate predictions}
8:        $\hat{\phi}_Y = \hat{\phi}_Y + \hat{\phi}_{Y_t}$ {Add to final predictions}
9:    **end if**
10:    $Trees_k.append(tree_{t_k})$ on every party C_k
11: **end for**
12: **return** $Trees_k$ on party C_k

---

ing randomness, such as Beaver's triples for element-wise multiplication with MPC [3,11]. However, this coordinator cannot access private data and intermediate results, so it does not pose a privacy threat, as mentioned in Xie et al. [44].

4.1   Protocol Overview

An overview of STV is provided in Algorithm 1. The framework consists of preliminary steps for pre-processing the series and secretly sharing features (Fig. 2), followed by distributed **training** and **inference** (Fig. 3).

Training. The active party initiates by pre-processing the output and determines parameters like the auto-correlations and partial auto-correlations of the series (line 2) to identify the time lags of the autoregressive and moving average terms in Eq. (1). As shown in Fig. 2a, these are then used to generate a polynomial for SARIMAX or ARTs (line 3). As illustrated in Fig. 2b, the features and outputs are then secretly shared and transformed into lagged design matrices (line 7), like in Eq. (2). All parties then follow decentralized training protocols, Algorithm 2 or Algorithm 3 to train a distributed model. Training is illustrated in Fig. 3a.

Privacy-Preserving Inference. During inference (Fig. 3b), the final prediction exists as a distributed share (line 14), which is aggregated on the requesting party (line 16). Since the result is computed as a distributed share, the outputs are not tied to a particular party.

4.2 STV_T: Autoregressive Tree (ART)

STV_T focuses on the autoregressive tree and transforms the original datasets, X and Y, into time-lagged design matrices. Following the training framework in

Algorithm 3. STV_L

Data: Secretly shared transformed matrices $\langle \phi_X \rangle$, $\langle \phi_Y \rangle$
Accepted Parameters: O, α, e
Output: Shared optimized coefficients $\langle A \rangle$

```
1:  for step ∈ [1, 2] do
2:      if step = 1 then
3:          Initialize residuals to zero in ⟨φ_X⟩^k for all C_k
4:      end if
5:      if O = "iterative" then
6:          Randomly initialize ⟨A⟩^k for all C_k
7:          for e iterations do
8:              Get ⟨φ̂_Y⟩ = ⟨φ_X⟩ × ⟨A⟩ using Alg. 4
9:              ⟨dl/dA⟩ = (⟨φ_X⟩)^T × (⟨φ̂_Y⟩ - ⟨φ_Y⟩) (Alg. 4)
10:             Perform update: ⟨A⟩ := ⟨A⟩ - (α/N)⟨dl/dA⟩
11:         end for
12:     else if O = "exact" then
13:         ⟨Z⟩ = (⟨φ_X⟩)^T × ⟨φ_X⟩ using Alg. 4
14:         ⟨W⟩ = ⟨Z^{-1}⟩ using Alg. 5
15:         ⟨V⟩ = (⟨φ_X⟩)^T × ⟨φ_Y⟩ using Alg. 4
16:         ⟨A⟩ = ⟨W⟩ × ⟨V⟩
17:     end if
18:     if step = 1 then
19:         Predict: ⟨φ̂_Y⟩ = ⟨φ_X⟩ × ⟨A⟩ using Alg. 4
20:         Estimate residuals ⟨ε⟩ = ⟨φ_Y⟩ - ⟨φ̂_Y⟩
21:         Set ⟨φ_X⟩^k using residuals from ⟨ε⟩^k for all C_k
22:     end if
23: end for
24: return ⟨A⟩^k on all parties C_k
```

Xie et al. [44], we train a distributed autoregressive XGBoost model using the secretly-shared design matrices. The details are provided in Algorithm 2. Training proceeds iteratively, finally resulting in the generation of T trees on each party. At each step, every party learns a new tree and makes a local prediction (lines 4–5). The active participant aggregates the distributed shares of the prediction to compute the first and second order gradients needed for generating the next distributed tree. These gradients are then secretly shared with the other parties for them update their local tree ensembles. Details on the tree-building function, **SecureFit**, are provided in Appendix C. During training, individual predictions are aggregated on the active party since gradients are computed by C_1 (see Appendix C). For inference, aggregation can be performed on any party since gradients are not calculated.

Algorithm 4. Secure Matrix Multiplication

Data: Secretly shared matrices $\langle U \rangle$ and $\langle V \rangle$ across K parties, $C_1, C_2, .., C_K$
Output: $\langle W \rangle$, i.e., product $W = U \times V$ as shares across K parties

1: **for** each row index i **do**
2:    **for** each column index j **do**
3:        $\langle T \rangle = \langle U[i, :] \rangle * \langle V[:, j] \rangle$ {Element-wise product} $\langle W_{i,j} \rangle^k = sum\{\langle T \rangle^k\}$
4:    **end for**
5: **end for**
6: **return** $\langle W \rangle^k$ on party C_k

Algorithm 5. Secure Matrix Inverse

Data: Secretly shared matrix $\langle U \rangle$ across K parties, $C_1, C_2, .., C_K$
Output: $\langle V \rangle$, i.e., inverse, $V = U^{-1}$, as a distributed share

1: **if** active party (P_1) **then**
2:    Generate random non-singular perturbation matrix P and secretly share as $\langle P \rangle$
3: **end if**
4: Get $\langle Q \rangle = \langle U \rangle \times \langle P \rangle$ using Alg. 4
5: Aggregate $Q = \sum_{k=1}^{K} \langle Q \rangle^k$ on passive party $C_j; j > 1$
6: **if** Passive party C_j **then**
7:    Compute $R = Q^{-1} = (UP)^{-1} = P^{-1}U^{-1}$
8:    Generate shares $\langle R \rangle$
9: **end if**
10: Compute $\langle T \rangle = \langle U^{-1} \rangle = \langle P \rangle \times \langle R \rangle$ using Alg. 4
11: **return** $\langle T \rangle^k$ on party C_k

4.3   STV$_L$: **SARIMAX**

With STV$_L$, the objective is optimizing the coefficients, A, in Eq. 2. This can be done either analytically (exactly) or iteratively using the two-step regression process explained in Sect. 2.1. Details are provided in Algorithm 3.

Algorithm 3 requires matrix operations like *multiplication* (lines 8–9; 13–19) and *inverse* (line 14) on secretly shared data. This is a requirement for both iterative and exact methods, as seen in Eq. 4 and Eq. 5. The N-party (≥ 2) algorithms for performing these operations are detailed below.

N-Party Matrix Multiplication. To perform matrix multiplication with secretly shared data (Algorithm 4), we view the computation of every output element $W_{i,j}$ as a scalar product of row and column vectors (line 3). This is implemented using the N-party element-wise product of the row and column vectors with Beaver's triples followed by an addition, as shown in Sect. 2.2.

N-Party Matrix Inverse. As shown in Algorithm 5, we compute the inverse of a secretly-shared matrix, U, using a non-singular perturbation matrix, P, generated by the active party (line 2). Subsequently, the aggregation of product UP on a passive party does not leak U as P is unknown (line 5). $(UP)^{-1}$ can then be computed locally and secretly shared, followed by a matrix multiplication with P, i.e., $P \times (UP)^{-1} = U^{-1}$, giving the result as a secret share (lines 7–10).

Similar to the tree-based models, forecasting is done by secretly sharing features and computing the output as a distributed share (see Fig. 3b). The true value of the forecast can be obtained by summing the shares across all parties, avoiding the need for having a server act as a middleman for producing forecasts.

5   Performance Evaluation

We evaluate the forecasting accuracy of STV against centralized approaches. We also compare the scalability of iterative and exact optimization for linear forecasters using the total communication cost.

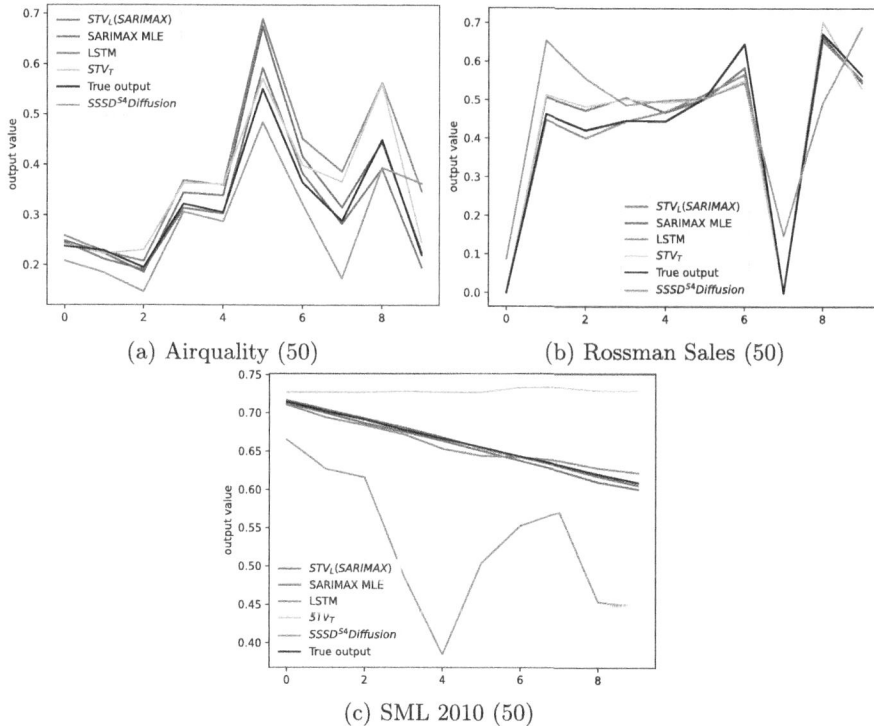

(a) Airquality (50)   (b) Rossman Sales (50)

(c) SML 2010 (50)

Fig. 4. Forecasts (y-axis) of different methods, total window size 50 (40 steps horizon and forecasts 10 steps ahead). The x-axis shows the forecasted timesteps.

5.1   Forecasting Accuracy

We compare the performance of STV_L (exact optimization) and STV_T with other centralized methods: Long-Short-Term Memory (LSTM), SARIMAX with

Table 3. Average n-MSE and (standard deviation) results for different datasets and methods. Relative improvement of the best VFL method with the best centralized one is also shown (rel. imp). Lowest MSE values are highlighted in bold. SML 2010, Air quality, and Rossman Sales have prequential window sizes 50, 100, 200, and 400. PV Power uses 25, 50, 100, and 200. Airline passengers uses 60, 80, 100, 120, and 140. Finally, the industrial data uses 25, 50, and 100.

Dataset	STV_L (SARIMAX, VFL)	STV_T (ART, VFL)	$SARIMAX$ (MLE, Centralized)	$LSTM$ (Centralized)	$SSSD^{S4}$ (Centralized)	Rel. imp. (%)
Airquality	**0.00069** (0.00008)	0.00100 (0.00056)	0.00088 (0.00031)	0.00114 (0.00076)	0.00150 (0.00073)	21.59
Airline passengers	0.00304 (0.00086)	0.00808 (0.00379)	**0.00222** (0.00148)	0.04130 (0.04086)	0.00392 (0.00226)	-36.94
PV Power	**0.00138** (0.00136)	0.00249 (0.00254)	0.00159 (0.00095)	0.14333 (0.23033)	0.00167 (0.00058)	15.22
SML 2010	**0.00787** (0.00711)	0.01875 (0.01458)	0.01033 (0.01061)	0.01716 (0.01086)	0.01085 (0.00871)	23.81
Rossman Sales	**0.00074** (0.00012)	0.00243 (0.00153)	0.00077 (0.00006)	0.00639 (0.00280)	0.00331 (0.00151)	3.89
Industrial data	**0.00602** (0.00049)	0.04118 (0.04051)	0.00969 (0.00449)	0.00617 (0.00203)	0.01875 (0.00313)	2.43

MLE[1], and diffusion models for forecasting ($SSSD^{S}4$) [2]. The LSTM has two layers with 64 units, followed by two dense layers of sizes 32 and 1. We train the model for 500 epochs with a batch size of 32 and a learning rate of 0.001. The diffusion configuration has the following settings[2] $T = 200, \beta_0 = 0.0001, \beta_T = 0.02$. The model uses two residual layers, four residual and skip channels, with three diffusion embedding layers of dimensions 8×16. Training is done for 4000 iterations with a learning rate of 0.002.

Five public forecasting datasets are used: Airline passengers [21], Air quality data [43], PV Power [18], SML 2010 [34], and Rossman Sales [1]. An industry-specific dataset to estimate a performance parameter for chip overlays from inline sensor values in semiconductor manufacturing is also included [12,13]. Evaluation and pre-processing steps are given in Appendix A and Appendix B. A variant of prequential window testing [5] is used since industrial time series data can significantly change after intervals due to machine changes/repairs. The dataset is partitioned into multiple windows of a given size, each further divided into an 80–20 train-test split. After forecasting the test split, the model is retrained on the next window (cf. Appendix B). All features and outputs are scaled between 0 and 1 for a consistent comparison. We thus present the predictions' normalized mean-squared errors (n-MSE). Ground truths on the test set are measured and averaged across multiple windows. We average the n-MSE scores across different window sizes to generalize performance scores across varying forecasting ranges, as shown in Table 3.

---

[1] https://www.statsmodels.org/devel/generated/statsmodels.tsa.statespace.sarimax. SARIMAX.html.

[2] Using https://github.com/AI4HealthUOL/SSSD.git.

Table 4. Network overhead (B) with varying parties, feature counts and samples.

		NE	GD iterations		
			10	100	1000
Parties	2	2.54×10^8	2.33×10^7	2.33×10^8	2.33×10^9
	4	5.85×10^8	4.65×10^7	4.65×10^8	4.65×10^9
	8	1.48×10^9	9.31×10^7	9.31×10^8	9.31×10^9
Features	10	9.77×10^6	8.34×10^6	8.34×10^7	8.34×10^8
	100	1.92×10^9	1.23×10^8	1.23×10^9	1.23×10^{10}
Samples	10	1.16×10^6	2.76×10^5	2.76×10^6	2.76×10^7
	100	4.53×10^8	1.24×10^7	1.24×10^8	1.24×10^9
	1000	1.48×10^9	1.23×10^8	1.23×10^9	1.23×10^{10}

Table 3 demonstrates that our approach STV_L outperforms other centralized methods in terms of performance. We use exact optimization since iterative gradient descent eventually converges to the same value in the long run. Due to its guaranteed convergence, exact optimization improves against centralized methods by up to 23.81%. Though it does worse than SARIMAX MLE on the passenger data, it is still among the top two methods. Regression plots from a prequential window of size 50 from three datasets are shown in Fig. 4. Generally, all methods can capture patterns in the time series, like in Fig. 4a and Fig. 4b. Occasionally, deep models such as $SSSD^{S4}$ overfit, showing the drawback of NNs on small windows (see Fig. 4c).

5.2 Scalability

We measure the total communication costs of exact optimization using the normal equation (NE) and iterative batch gradient descent (GD) to analyze the scalability of the two methods under increasing parties, features, and samples. We vary the parties between 2, 4, and 8, features between 10 and 100, and samples between 10, 100, and 1000. Since communication costs depend only on the dataset dimensions and the number of parties, we generate random data matrices for all valid combinations of features and samples on each party, i.e., #features ≤ #samples. We then optimize the coefficients using either the exact approach (Algorithm 3, lines (13–19)), or batch gradient descent (lines (6–10)), for a different number of iterations (10, 100, 1000). For party-scaling, we average the total communication costs across various feature and sample combinations for a given number of parties. Similarly, we measure feature and sample scaling by averaging the total costs across different (sample, party) and (feature, party) combinations. Results are shown in Table 4.

We observe that when the number of parties/samples/features is small, exact optimization's cost is comparable to an iterative version with more iterations. For example, when the number of parties is 2, we see that the cost of NE is close to GD with 100 iterations. However, when we increase to 8 parties, the cost of NE exceeds GD with 100 iterations. Similarly, we see that NE has a lower cost than GD with 100 iterations for smaller magnitudes of features and samples. This is no longer the case when increasing the features and samples. However, the cost of GD increases proportionally with the iterations, eventually surpassing NE, as seen with 1000 iterations. In practice, hyperparameters like the learning rate and batch size affect the convergence rate, which may be hard to tune in a distributed setup. So, choosing between iterative or exact optimization depends on several factors, requiring adaptability in frameworks.

6   Conclusion

We present a generalizable, novel decentralized and privacy-preserving forecasting framework. For instance, healthcare centers can share patient data to assess risks, but confidentiality agreements limit data sharing. Our results show that the approach competes well with centralized methods. Scalability analyses reveal the trade-offs between iterative and exact optimization, emphasizing the need for adaptability. Future directions include enabling deep models, such as LSTMs and diffusion, in VFL and exploring hybrid approaches that combine horizontal and vertical FL for improved forecasting. Additionally, moving beyond semi-honest to adversarial participants is a potential area of exploration.

Acknowledgments. This research is part of the Priv-GSyn project, 200021E_229204 of Swiss National Science Foundation and the DEPMAT project, P20-22 / N21022, of the research programme Perspectief which is partly financed by the Dutch Research Council (NWO).

Disclosure of Interests. The authors have no competing interests to declare that are relevant to the content of this article.

A   Datasets and Pre-Processing

We make use of the following public datasets in our work: Air Quality [43], SML 2010 [34], PV Power [18], Airline Passengers [21], and Rossman Sales [1]. We do not provide the details on the industrial dataset due to confidentiality agreements. Here we provide a brief description of each dataset and the pre-processing steps applied to the dataset itself. These steps are unconnected with the series pre-processing steps which are part of the STV framework. For all datasets, we scale all features and output values between the range 0 to 1 using a MinMax scaler to ensure that all datasets have the same range of values for comparing the MSE losses.

A.1   Air Quality

The dataset contains approximately 9300 samples of multivariate time-series data, with 15 attributes. Five of these are true output values on five gases: Carbon Monoxide (CO), Non Metanic Hydrocarbons (NMHC)), Benzene (C6H6)), Total Nitrogen Oxides (NOx), and Nitrogen Dioxide (NO2). Exogenous features such as the temperature, ozone levels, and humidity are provided, along with strongly correlated sensor data for each of the five gases. The dataset contains missing values and duplicates, and contains hourly data for each of the five gases.

We preprocess the data by discarding all rows with any missing information and remove duplicate rows. We predict the ground truth values of CO using the other sensor values and information such as temperature and humidity as the exogenous regressors.

A.2   SML 2010

The SML 2010 dataset contains information from a monitor system in a domotic house. It contains approximately 4100 samples with 24 attributes in total, corresponding to 40 days of monitoring data. The attributes contain values such as the indoor and outdoor temperature, lighting levels, Carbon Dioxide levels, relative humidity, rain, windspeed, etc. We predict the indoor habitation temperature using the others as exogenous features.

A.3   Airline Passengers

Airline Passengers is a small dataset of 145 samples containing the number of international airline passengers (in thousands) on a monthly basis. The exogenous features are also just two: the year and the month. We predict the number of passengers using the year and month as exogenous regressors.

A.4   PV Power

The PV Power dataset contains around 3100 samples of solar power generation data from each of two power plants over a 34-day period. Attributes include features such as the DC power, AC power, yield, ambient temperature, irradiation levels, and the data and time.

We drop identifiers, empty, and duplicate data. We also drop the DC power attribute, and total yield as these features are very strongly correlated with the AC output. As outputs, we predict the AC power generation using the remaining features as exogenous regressors.

A.5   Rossman Sales

The Rossman Sales dataset contains sales data for 1115 store outlets. The attributes consists of features such as holidays, store type, competitor distance, number of customers, and promotional details among others. We predict the sales of the store with ID 1, using the other features as exogenous regressors.

B   Experimental Evaluation

As mentioned in the main text, we use a variation of prequential window testing
[5], whereby the entire data is broken into windows of a defined length, each one
internally split in an 80–20 train-test ratio. This is illustrated in Fig. 5.

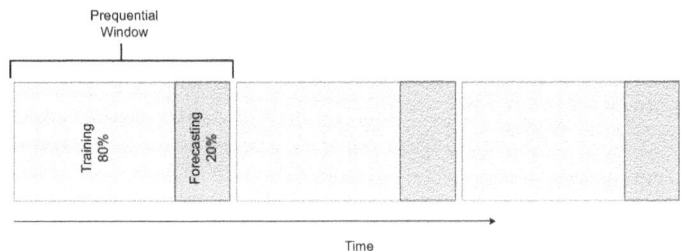

Fig. 5. Prequential window evaluation with re-training in every window.

For each window, we train on the portion allotted for training and forecast
the remaining. Within a given training window, we first generate the polynomial
by processing the time series as in Algorithm 1 from the main text. Identifying
the parameters for generating the polynomial can be automated using implementations such as auto arima[3].

For each window size, such as 50, 100, 200, 400, we average the MSE loss
between the forecasts and the true values across all windows. The average MSE
per-window size is given in Table 5, which is an expanded version of Table 1 from
the main text.

---

[3] https://alkaline-ml.com/pmdarima/modules/generated/pmdarima.arima.auto_
arima.html.

Table 5. Average normalized MSE values for different public datasets, with different prequential window sizes

Dataset	Window size	STV_L	SARIMAX MLE	LSTM	STV_T	$SSSD^{S4}$
Air quality	50	0.00071	0.00110	0.00244	0.00198	0.00270
	100	0.00059	0.00048	0.00055	0.00075	0.00086
	200	0.00066	0.00124	0.00069	0.00067	0.00100
	400	0.00080	0.00068	0.00087	0.00061	0.00144
	Avg.	**0.00069**	0.00088	0.00114	0.00100	0.00150
SML 2010	50	0.00645	0.00621	0.00343	0.00755	0.01373
	100	0.01958	0.02819	0.02778	0.04305	0.02384
	200	0.00500	0.00662	0.02781	0.01709	0.00336
	400	0.00045	0.00030	0.00960	0.00729	0.00249
	Avg.	**0.00787**	0.01033	0.01716	0.01875	0.01085
Rossman Sales	50	0.00070	0.00079	0.00464	0.00183	0.00589
	100	0.00064	0.00071	0.00340	0.00496	0.00281
	200	0.00068	0.00086	0.00674	0.00088	0.00233
	400	0.00095	0.00072	0.01079	0.00206	0.00220
	Avg.	**0.00074**	0.00077	0.00639	0.00243	0.00331
PV Power	25	0.00133	0.00093	0.00950	0.00660	0.00131
	50	0.00360	0.00307	0.01037	0.00258	0.00143
	100	0.00004	0.00063	0.01115	0.00010	0.00267
	200	0.00054	0.00175	0.54227	0.00068	0.00128
	Avg.	**0.00138**	0.00159	0.14333	0.00249	0.00167
Airline Passengers	60	0.00261	0.00113	0.11651	0.00673	0.00110
	80	0.00450	0.00444	0.00339	0.00628	0.00403
	100	0.00308	0.00066	0.01982	0.00270	0.00798
	120	0.00316	0.00136	0.05164	0.01134	0.00356
	140	0.00185	0.00351	0.01512	0.01332	0.00293
	Avg.	0.00304	**0.00222**	0.04130	0.00808	0.00392

C SMPC-Based XGBoost with VFL

XGBoost [6] is a tree-based gradient-boosting algorithm, that iteratively generates an ensemble of trees by greedily learning a new tree at every step to improve on the earlier one. Each tree has weights assigned to its leaf nodes. When making a prediction for a sample, the weights corresponding to the leaf to which the sample was assigned to are summed to give the final prediction score.

To generate a tree at every iteration, it uses first and second order gradients of the latest predictions, i.e., from the previous tree, in order to set the optimal weights for the new one.

For each sample with index i, the first and second order gradients are denoted as g_i and h_i, respectively. The sum of the gradients of all instances on a particular node is used to set the new weights for it. For example, for node j and corresponding instance set I_j, the accumulated values of g and h are computed as follows: $G_j = \sum_{i \in I_j} g_i$, and $H_j = \sum_{i \in I_j} h_i$. Based on this, for a tree with T nodes, the weights and objective are calculated as follows:

$$w_j = -G_j/(H_j + \lambda) \tag{7}$$

$$obj = -0.5 \times \sum_{j=1}^{T} ((G_j)^2/(H_j + \lambda)) + \gamma T \tag{8}$$

, where γ, λ are regularizers. While Eq. (7) sets the new weights, Eq. (8) is used to identify how to split nodes at each iteration.

With this in mind, using the secret sharing primitives it is possible to compute these functions to extend XGBoost to VFL, which we show in Algorithm 6.

When XGBoost is trained for VFL using secret sharing, each client obtains a local tree with their own weights as shown in Fig. 6. In the figure, the weights for clients 1 and 2 are distributed such that their local weights are shares of the weights of the centralized version, i.e., $wi = wi1 + wi2 \; \forall i \in [1, 4]$

The indicator vector s on line 1 of Algorithm 6, is a binary vector that is used to point out the location of instances on nodes. We explain this with the help of the example in Fig. 7. To calculate the updated weight of the node with instances that have an age greater than 30 (bottom left), we need to find the sum of $\sum_{i \in I_j} g_i$, where $I_j = \{2, 4\}$ Eq. (7). The indicator vector in this case would be $s = [0, 1, 0, 1]$, meaning that nodes 2 and 4 are part of node j. If we have a vector of the gradients, $g = [g1, g2, g3, g4]$, we can compute $g_2 + g_4$ as $s \odot g$, i.e., the inner product. Under VFL, both the gradients g, and the indicator vector s, exist as secret shares across clients, i.e., $s = \sum_k^K \langle s_k \rangle^k$, and $g = \sum_k^K \langle g_k \rangle^k$. Therefore, we can compute the product using MPC primitives for matrix multiplication.

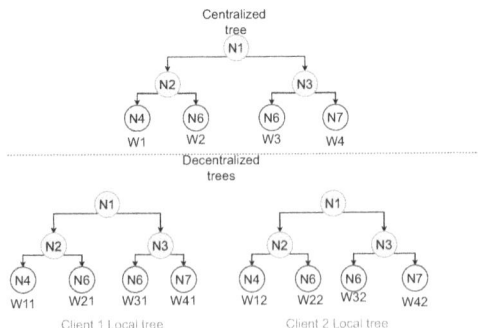

Fig. 6. Centralized vs Secretly shared XGBoost trees.

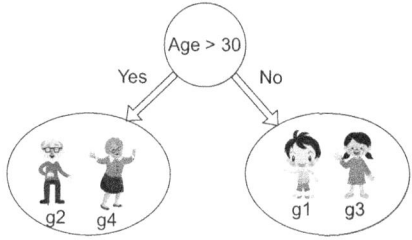

Fig. 7. Mapped instances to a node in XGBoost.

Algorithm 6. Fit XGBoost [44]

Data: Secretly shared matrices: $\langle X \rangle$, $\langle Y \rangle$, $\langle \hat{Y} \rangle$ across K clients, $C_1, C_2, .., C_K$
Output: Learned   tree   for   the   current   iteration,   one   on   each
client.

1: Initialize indicator vector $s \leftarrow 1$ on all C_k
2: **if** active client C_1 **then**
3:     Compute derivatives g, h
4:     Generate shares $\langle g \rangle$, $\langle h \rangle$, $\langle s \rangle$
5: **end if**
6: $Tree_k = \textbf{\textit{SecureBuild}}(\langle g \rangle^k, \langle h \rangle^k, \langle s \rangle^k)$ on each C_k
7: **return** $Tree_k$ on C_k

The process of split-finding and setting weights is done using the **_Secure-Build_** function, which makes use of secret sharing primitives to compute the functions in Eq. (8) and Eq. (7). We defer readers to the implementation in Xie et al. [44] for additional details on this.

References

1. Rossman store sales (2015). https://www.kaggle.com/c/rossmann-store-sales
2. Alcaraz, J.M.L., Strodthoff, N · Diffusion based time series imputation and forecasting with structured state space models. arXiv preprint arXiv:2208.09399 (2022)
3. Beaver, D.: Efficient multiparty protocols using circuit randomization. In: Advances in Cryptology—CRYPTO'91: Proceedings 11, pp. 420–432. Springer (1992)
4. Blais, J., et al.: Least squares for practitioners. Math. Probl. Eng. **2010** (2010)
5. Cerqueira, V., Torgo, L., Mozetič, I.: Evaluating time series forecasting models: an empirical study on performance estimation methods. Mach. Learn. **109**, 1997–2028 (2020)
6. Chen, T., et al.: XGBoost: extreme gradient boosting. R package version 0.4-2 **1**(4), 1–4 (2015)
7. Chen, T., Jin, X., Sun, Y., Yin, W.: VAFL: a method of vertical asynchronous federated learning. arXiv preprint arXiv:2007.06081 (2020)
8. Cheng, K., et al.: Secureboost: a lossless federated learning framework. IEEE Intell. Syst. **36**(6), 87–98 (2021)
9. Cramer, R., Damgård, I.B., et al.: Secure Multiparty Computation. Cambridge University Press (2015)

10. De Hert, M., Detraux, J., Vancampfort, D.: The intriguing relationship between coronary heart disease and mental disorders. Dialogues Clin. Neurosci. **20**(1), 31–40 (2018)
11. Fang, W., et al.: Large-scale secure XGB for vertical federated learning. In: Proceedings of the 30th ACM International Conference on Information & Knowledge Management, pp. 443–452 (2021)
12. Gkorou, D., Larranaga, M., Ypma, A., Hasibi, F., van Wijk, R.J.: Get a human-in-the-loop: feature engineering via interactive visualizations (2020)
13. Gkorou, D., et al.: Towards big data visualization for monitoring and diagnostics of high volume semiconductor manufacturing. In: Proceedings of the Computing Frontiers Conference. CF'17, New York, NY, USA, pp. 338–342. Association for Computing Machinery (2017). https://doi.org/10.1145/3075564.3078883
14. Hamilton, J.D.: Time Series Analysis. Princeton University Press (2020)
15. Han, S., Ng, W.K., Wan, L., Lee, V.C.: Privacy-preserving gradient-descent methods. IEEE Trans. Knowl. Data Eng. **22**(6), 884–899 (2009)
16. Hannan, E.J., Kavalieris, L.: A method for autoregressive-moving average estimation. Biometrika **71**(2), 273–280 (1984)
17. Hardy, S., et al.: Private federated learning on vertically partitioned data via entity resolution and additively homomorphic encryption. arXiv preprint arXiv:1711.10677 (2017)
18. Kannal, A.: Solar power generation (2020). https://www.kaggle.com/datasets/anikannal/solar-power-generation-data
19. Konečný, J., McMahan, B., Ramage, D.: Federated optimization: distributed optimization beyond the datacenter. arXiv preprint arXiv:1511.03575 (2015)
20. Korstanje, J.: The SARIMAX Model, pp. 125–131. Apress, Berkeley (2021). https://doi.org/10.1007/978-1-4842-7150-6_8
21. Kothari, C.: Airline Passengers (2018). https://www.kaggle.com/datasets/chirag19/air-passengers
22. Li, L., Damarla, S.K., Wang, Y., Huang, B.: A gaussian mixture model based virtual sample generation approach for small datasets in industrial processes. Inf. Sci. **581**, 262–277 (2021)
23. Lin, C.Y., Hsieh, Y.M., Cheng, F.T., Huang, H.C., Adnan, M.: Time series prediction algorithm for intelligent predictive maintenance. IEEE Robot. Autom. Lett. **4**(3), 2807–2814 (2019)
24. Lin, X., Karr, A.F.: Privacy-preserving maximum likelihood estimation for distributed data. J. Priv. Confident. **1**(2) (2010)
25. Lindell, Y.: Secure multiparty computation for privacy preserving data mining. In: Encyclopedia of Data Warehousing and Mining, pp. 1005–1009. IGI global (2005)
26. Litjens, G., et al.: A survey on deep learning in medical image analysis. Med. Image Anal. **42**, 60–88 (2017)
27. Liu, C., Hoi, S.C., Zhao, P., Sun, J.: Online Arima algorithms for time series prediction. In: Proceedings of the AAAI Conference on Artificial Intelligence, vol. 30 (2016)
28. Lütkepohl, H.: General-to-specific or specific-to-general modelling? An opinion on current econometric terminology. J. Econ. **136**(1), 319–324 (2007)
29. Meek, C., Chickering, D.M., Heckerman, D.: Autoregressive tree models for time-series analysis. In: Proceedings of the 2002 SIAM International Conference on Data Mining, pp. 229–244. SIAM (2002)

30. Menegatti, D., Ciccarelli, E., Viscione, M., Giuseppi, A.: Vertically-advised federated learning for multi-strategic stock predictions through stochastic attention-based lstm. In: 2023 31st Mediterranean Conference on Control and Automation (MED), pp. 521–528 (2023). https://doi.org/10.1109/MED59994.2023.10185757

31. Montgomery, D.C., Jennings, C.L., Kulahci, M.: Introduction to Time Series Analysis and Forecasting. Wiley (2015)

32. Perktold, J.: Sarimax (2023). https://www.statsmodels.org/dev/generated/statsmodels.tsa.statespace.sarimax.SARIMAX.html

33. Regulation, P.: Regulation (eu) 2016/679 of the european parliament and of the council. Regulation (EU) **679**, 2016 (2016)

34. Romeu-Guallart, P., Zamora-Martinez, F.: SML2010. UCI Machine Learning Repository (2014). https://doi.org/10.24432/C5RS3S

35. Scannapieco, M., Figotin, I., Bertino, E., Elmagarmid, A.K.: Privacy preserving schema and data matching. In: Proceedings of the 2007 ACM SIGMOD International Conference on Management of Data, pp. 653–664 (2007)

36. Shamir, A.: How to share a secret communications of the ACM 22 (1979)

37. Shi, H., Jiang, Y., Yu, H., Xu, Y., Cui, L.: MVFLS: multi-participant vertical federated learning based on secret sharing. Federate Learn. 1–9 (2022)

38. Snoke, J., Brick, T.R., Slavkovic, A., Hunter, M.D.: Providing accurate models across private partitioned data: secure maximum likelihood estimation (2017)

39. Susto, G.A., Beghi, A.: Dealing with time-series data in predictive maintenance problems. In: 2016 IEEE 21st International Conference on Emerging Technologies and Factory Automation (ETFA), pp. 1–4. IEEE (2016)

40. Tang, F., Liang, S., Ling, G., Shan, J.: IHVFL: a privacy-enhanced intention-hiding vertical federated learning framework for medical data. Cybersecurity 6 (2023)

41. Tarsitano, A., Amerise, I.L.: Short-term load forecasting using a two-stage SARIMAX model. Energy **133**, 108–114 (2017)

42. Vepakomma, P., Gupta, O., Swedish, T., Raskar, R.: Split learning for health: distributed deep learning without sharing raw patient data. arXiv preprint arXiv:1812.00564 (2018)

43. Vito, S.: Air Quality. UCI Machine Learning Repository (2016). https://doi.org/10.24432/C59K5F

44. Xie, L., Liu, J., Lu, S., Chang, T.H., Shi, Q.: An efficient learning framework for federated XGBoost using secret sharing and distributed optimization. ACM Trans. Intell. Syst. Technol. (TIST) **13**(5), 1–28 (2022)

45. Yan, Y., Yang, G., Gao, Y., Zang, C., Chen, J., Wang, Q.: Multi-participant vertical federated learning based time series prediction. In: Proceedings of the 8th International Conference on Computing and Artificial Intelligence, pp. 165–171 (2022)

46. Yang, Q., Liu, Y., Chen, T., Tong, Y.: Federated machine learning: concept and applications. ACM Trans. Intell. Syst. Technol. (TIST) **10**(2), 1–19 (2019)

47. Zhu, Q.X., Zhang, H.T., Tian, Y., Zhang, N., Xu, Y., He, Y.L.: Co-training based virtual sample generation for solving the small sample size problem in process industry. ISA Trans. **134**, 290–301 (2023)

GIDM: Gradient Inversion of Federated Diffusion Models

Jiyue Huang[1(✉)], Chi Hong[1], Stefanie Roos[2], and Lydia Y. Chen[1,3]

[1] TU Delft, Delft, Netherlands
{j.huang-4,c.hong}@tudelft.nl
[2] RPTU Kaiserslautern, Kaiserslautern, Germany
stefanie.roos@cs.rptu.de
[3] University of Neuchâtel, Neuchâtel, Switzerland
yiyu.chen@unine.ch

Abstract. Diffusion models are becoming the most prevalent generative models, producing exceptional high-quality image data through a stochastic process of diffusion steps based on Gaussian noises. Recent studies explore the federated training of diffusion models, enabling the collaborative training of a model without clients sharing raw data. We demonstrate that even without direct sharing of the data, the shared gradients of federated diffusion models already leak sensitive information about the raw data. We design the first gradient inversion attack GIDM for diffusion, which can reconstruct the training data from the shared model updates. GIDM is a two-phase fusion attack that is both efficient and effective. In its first phase, GIDM leverages the trained diffusion model itself as prior knowledge to constrain the inversion search (latent) space, followed by a second phase of pixel-wise fine-tuning. Different from existing inversion attacks on the classification models, inverting diffusion models present new challenges, most notably that the noise term and randomly sampled diffusion step are not known to the attacker but are required for the reconstruction. To tackle this challenge, we propose a joint triple-optimization algorithm to approximate the raw data, sampling step, and noise term simultaneously. GIDM is shown to be able to reconstruct images almost identical to the original ones and clearly outperforms baselines, i.e., GIDM without the second phase and state-of-the-art attacks on classifiers adapted to diffusion. The code of our method is available at https://github.com/GillHuang-Xtler/Diffusion_inversion.

Keywords: Gradient inversion · Diffusion models · Reconstruction attack

1 Introduction

The emergence of likelihood-based diffusion models empowers probabilistic models to generate high-quality data, such as image and video data [11,20,24]. Diffusion models are trained by finding the reverse Markov transitions that maximize

M. Dalla Preda et al. (Eds.): ARES 2025, LNCS 15992, pp. 380–401, 2025.
https://doi.org/10.1007/978-3-032-00624-0_19

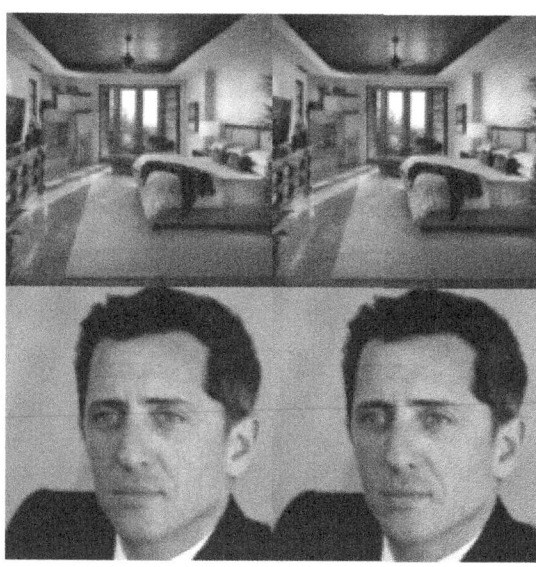

Fig. 1. Original training image (left) v.s. Recovered images (right) by our proposed GIDM on diffusion models: reconstructing almost identical to the original image of 128×128 size.

the likelihood of the training data. In practice, the training is done by gradually adding noise to and denoising the images over multiple steps.

However, training high-quality diffusion models usually requires a large amount of data. Practically, such data may be owned by different parties. Following data privacy regularization such as HIPAA [2] and GDPR [28], data owners are not allowed to share such data if it contains personally identifiable information, which includes in particular sensitive data such as medical records. As a consequence, prior works argue that diffusion models need to be trained in a distributed manner without sharing raw data, e.g., in a federated learning manner [17,22]. Indeed, the design of the Denoising Diffusion Probabilistic Model (DDPM) [11], the most common architecture for training diffusion models, enables distribution trivially: in each round, the algorithm independently samples a random Gaussian noise ϵ for data sample(s) x_0 at each sampling step t. Thus, there exist multiple designs for federated diffusion, which—while differing in the details of their implementation—all share the following approach: at each global round of training, multiple distributed data owners (clients) train the diffusion sub-models based on their local data. Then, the central server, which connects to every client, aggregates their gradients before returning the aggregated gradient to the clients for further training until convergence is reached.

Such a federated diffusion method successfully avoids direct data sharing and enables the server to obtain the intermediate training gradients and the diffusion model in the end. In this paper, we consider the privacy leakage caused by the shared gradients. While there have been privacy attacks on diffusion models, they do not consider gradients. For example, relying on inferring information from the trained model, e.g., error comparison of the forward process posterior estimation [5,22], adversaries are able to launch membership inference attacks [5, 13,32] or attribute inference attacks.

Although studies on federated training classifiers demonstrate that the server is able to invert the client's raw data from their gradients [8,34,40,41], we argue that existing attacks cannot be easily transferred to diffusion models. The key idea of previous attacks is to reconstruct images from dummy data by using the gradients to constrain the search space. In the context of classification, label information needs to be present or reconstructed as part of the attack. In contrast, diffusion does not have labels; rather it requires the sampling step t during the training process and the noise prediction ϵ in each step, so that a novel approach is needed.

In this paper, we systematically study the data reconstruction risk when training federated diffusion models. We first define the common factors of federated training methods for diffusion models, according to related studies. Afterwards, we design our attack, which relies on diffusion-specific information that other scenarios lack. Specifically, at the end of the training process, the server owns a trained diffusion model, which we can use to constrain the search space for the reconstructed images. Using generative models has been explored in prior studies on inversion attacks on classification [7,15] but these studies rely on external models.

Concretely, to reconstruct images that resemble the training data, we thus design a fusion optimization, GIDM, that includes two phases. The generating phase maps the dummy data into a narrow latent space to optimize in-distribution images by utilizing the diffusion model as prior knowledge. Then the fine-tuning phase further optimizes the similarity between the dummy and real gradients to update the dummy data generated during the first phase of the attack.

Approximating the gradient of diffusion models also requires the knowledge of ϵ and t, which may only be known to the clients, a key challenge of inversion attacks on diffusion models. To solve this, the two phases of GIDM include a novel triple-optimization for dummy data, ϵ, and t. Specifically, the triple-optimization includes three independent optimizers for the dummy data, the noise, and the sampling step to refine the joint training. By coordinating the three optimizers with updating intervals, we are able to recover images without knowing the exact values of ϵ and t.

Our proposed GIDM is able to recover images almost identical to the original data up to size 128×128, as shown in Fig. 1. Our evaluation further shows that the fine-tuning phase is indeed required and GIDM cannot reliable reconstruct images without using the triple-optimization. For comparison, we adapt two attacks for image classifiers, DLG [41] and InvG [8], to the scenario of diffusion. Note that as these attacks do not consider ϵ and t, we weaken the adversarial model for them by providing the concrete parameter values. Despite these attacks having more information, which would not be available in a real-world setting, GIDM outperforms them in terms of four key image similarity metrics.

We summarize our main contributions as follows. We present the first gradient inversion attack GIDM on diffusion models, leveraging three key novel ideas: the use of the trained diffusion model to constrain the search space; a two-phase attack consisting of a phase based on the existing diffusion model, and a fine-tuning phase; a triple-optimization method that jointly reconstructs the data, the sampling step, and the noise parameter. Our evaluation shows that GIDM can successfully reconstruct images of a large size and highlights the impact of the different attack components through ablation studies.

2 Related Work

Diffusion Models and Privacy. Diffusion models employ a two-step process: First, they deconstruct the training data structure step by step in a forward manner. Second, they master the reconstruction of the structure from noise in a reverse process. The Denoising Diffusion Probabilistic Model (DDPM) [11] introduces a stable and efficient implementation of diffusion for high-quality image synthesis. DDPM relies on a forward process without learnable parameters while employing simplified Gaussian noise in the reverse phase. Further variants of diffusion models such as DDIM [24], Stable Diffusion [20], and Imagen [21] improve the sampling efficiency or involve deep language understanding for text-to-image generation. However, well-trained diffusion models have been shown to be vulnerable to privacy attacks, i.e., information leakage on the training data. Recent studies on privacy concerns of diffusion models mainly focus on membership inference attacks [5,13,32] or training data memorizing attacks [4, 23]; both of which are executed on the trained model. None of the studies has addressed the data reconstruction from the gradients of diffusion models.

Privacy Defenses of Federated Learning. In order to enhance system privacy against privacy leakage attacks and not significantly reduce model accuracy [3,10,26,35], current defenses are primarily conducted individually by clients, falling into two categories: gradient perturbation and input perturbation. Gradient perturbation [1,3,6,10,14,25,27,35], preferred for its efficiency and maintaining global model accuracy, involves transmitting perturbed gradients. In contrast, input perturbation, such as mixing images before local training, is less common [38]. Prominent gradient perturbation defenses include differential private stochastic gradient descent [6], which adds noise and clips gradients to limit sensitivity [1]. Gradient sparsification accelerates training by setting small gradient entries to zero [3], differing from dropout by removing small entries rather than randomly selecting them [10,14,25]. Soteria proposes a fully-connected defense layer to perturb data representation, crucial for preventing inversion attacks while preserving Federated Learning performance [26]. Overall, defense efficacy depends on parameters like noise level, clipping bound, sparsity, and pruning rate, which need to be carefully chosen to balance model quality and privacy.

Gradient Inversion. As the first practical gradient inversion attack for classifiers, Deep Leakage from Gradients (DLG) reconstructs data and label simultaneously by directly approximating gradients from the dummy data input [41].

DLG tends to reconstruct images of low quality and cannot deal with large training batches. To strengthen DLG, one line of work improves DLG by developing different optimizers [8,34], distance metrics [8], or integrating direct features [40], e.g., they first infer labels before reconstructing. The other line of work focuses on leveraging external knowledge for inversion. Such knowledge includes prior data distributions for more accurate embeddings [9], adding batch normalization regularizers to manage larger batches [36], applying pre-trained generator models to ensure high-quality reconstructed data [7,15,18] and utilizing auxiliary datasets [31]. GGDM iteratively refines the noise via a pre-trained unconditional DDPM as a guidance, but also targeting invert classifiers. These advanced attacks [7,15,16,36] successfully integrate additional information to improve the attack effectiveness. However, such knowledge can also be further integrated to our proposed GIDM. Thus, our direct comparison baselines are DLG and InvG.

Apart from classification models, inversion can be applied to Generative Adversarial Networks (GANs), where the attacks aim to invert a generated image back into the latent space of a pre-trained GAN model [33], i.e., reconstructing the latent code instead of the training images. Currently, there exist no inversion attack studied for inverting diffusion models.

3   Methodology

In this section, we first introduce preliminaries on federated diffusion models, highlighting the common components of existing frameworks. Then, we propose our inversion attack GIDM, which leverages the trained diffusion model as prior knowledge for constrained optimization, consisting of two phases. The generative phase improves the quality of a dummy image to achieve fast convergence, followed by a fine-tuning phase to increase the pixel-wise similarity. For both phases, we argue that the prior art of gradient inversion attacks does not apply to diffusion models due to the inability to handle more unknown factors, namely the noise ϵ and sampling step t, according to the DDPM training strategy. Thus, we design a triple-optimization algorithm to infer the original image, ϵ, and t simultaneously.

3.1   Federated Diffusion Model Preliminaries

We consider a federated image generation task following the standard DDPM diffusion models [11], which aims to optimize the weighted variational bound:

$$L(\theta) = \mathbb{E}_{t,\mathbf{x}_0,\epsilon} \left[\left\| \epsilon - \epsilon_\theta \left(\sqrt{\bar{\alpha}_t}\mathbf{x}_0 + \sqrt{1 - \bar{\alpha}_t}\epsilon, t \right) \right\|^2 \right], \tag{1}$$

where $\mathbf{x}_0 \in \mathbb{R}^m$ are training samples of dimension m = width × height × color, $L(\cdot)$ is the point-wise loss function, θ denotes the diffusion model network parameters and $\bar{\alpha}_t$ is a hyper-parameter controlling the forward noising process. Note that the sampling step t is chosen uniformly between 1 and T and we follow the definition [11] that ϵ_θ is a function approximator intended to predict the Gaussian noise ϵ added to the image $\mathbf{x}_t$ of step t.

Algorithm 1. Federated Diffusion Model Training

Input: The number of clients K, number of global training round R, local datasets $X_k, k \in [1, K]$, diffusion steps T, global learning rate η.
Initialize model θ
for $r = 1, 2, ..., R$ **do**
 for $k = 1, 2, ..., K$ **do**
  $t \sim \text{Uniform}(\{1, ..., T\})$
  $\epsilon \sim \mathcal{N}(\mathbf{0}, \mathbf{I})$
  $\mathbf{x}_0 \sim X_k$
  $g_k = \nabla_{\theta_k} \left\| \epsilon_k - \epsilon_{\theta_k} \left(\sqrt{\bar{\alpha}_t} \mathbf{x}_0 + \sqrt{1 - \bar{\alpha}_t} \epsilon_k, t \right) \right\|^2$
 $g = 1/K \sum_{k=1}^{K} g_k$
 Update $\theta = \theta - \eta g$

Return the trained θ^* (θ from the last round)
Result: the trained θ^*

There are K clients serving as data owners who are responsible for diffusion model training. The kth federated learning client owns the local real dataset $X_k, k \in \{1, 2, ..., K\}$, which is not shared with others. Each client reports the gradient:

$$\nabla_\theta \left\| \epsilon_k - \epsilon_{\theta_k} \left(\sqrt{\bar{\alpha}_t} \mathbf{x}_0 + \sqrt{1 - \bar{\alpha}_t} \epsilon_k, t \right) \right\|^2 ,$$

for the locally sampled data $\mathbf{x}_0$. We use R global training rounds. The single server $\mathcal{S}$, which does not own any data itself, aggregates, usually by computing their average, and distributes the aggregated model in each global training round.

In contrast to other federated learning models, e.g., classification tasks, diffusion models require sampling the parameters ϵ and t. We assume that they are sampled by the clients who own the data during the training process. Consequentially, the server does not know which parameters were chosen by each client. In the evaluation, we compare this setting to a less privacy-preserving variant where the server chooses ϵ and t and distributes them to the clients in Sect. 4.4 and Sect. 4.5. Both settings can be implemented as equivalent optimization problems to centralized diffusion models. The general training process is given in Algorithm 1.

3.2   Threat Model

Our threat model considers the federated server $\mathcal{S}$ as the adversary to reconstruct the input training data X_k of the target client C_k. The threat model is as follows.
Objective. The adversarial server aims to recover the input data X_k trained by client C_k based on the gradient:

$$g_k = \nabla_\theta \left\| \epsilon_k - \epsilon_{\theta_k} \left(\sqrt{\bar{\alpha}_t} \mathbf{x}_0 + \sqrt{1 - \bar{\alpha}_t} \epsilon_k, t \right) \right\|^2 ,$$

during a specific global training round r. As the inversion can be executed at one given global round, we drop the index r for simplicity. The attack is successful if the recovered image $\hat{X}$ is almost identical to X_k.

Capability. We assume that the honest-but-curious server does not have access to the real data of data owners. Moreover, the servers' computational resources are limited, so it cannot, e.g., break cryptographic primitives.

Knowledge. To recover input data at a specific round, we assume $\mathcal{S}$ naturally owns the global model and can access the model parameters and the submitted gradient of all clients. However, the initialization of ϵ and the sampling step of t are unknown to the adversary unless stated otherwise.

3.3 Two-Phase Inversion with Diffusion Prior

To assess the privacy leakage of federated diffusion, we propose the first gradient inversion attack GIDM: an honest-but-curious server reconstructs a victim client's data using the gradients submitted by the client. We model the inversion process as an optimization problem that iteratively modifies the dummy data by minimizing the distance between known and approximated gradients, as proposed by the inversion attacks for federated classifier training [41]. Following Algorithm 1, when client k computes the gradient for the training data $\mathbf{x}_0$, the gradient is:

$$g_k = \nabla_{\theta_k} \left\| \epsilon_k - \epsilon_{\theta_k} \left(\sqrt{\bar{\alpha}_t} x_0 + \sqrt{1 - \bar{\alpha}_t} \epsilon_k, t \right) \right\|^2.$$

Note that since a gradient inversion attack can be launched at any specific global training round for any client, we drop the round and client indexes r and k in the following. Assuming that θ is second-order differentiable, we suppose that the dummy data $\hat{\mathbf{x}}_0$ is an approximation of $\mathbf{x}_0$ if $\hat{g} \sim g$, where $\hat{g}$ is the dummy gradient calculated based on $\hat{\mathbf{x}}_0$. Thus, our gradient inversion objective turns to:

$$\min_{\hat{x}_0} Dist(\nabla_\theta \left\| \epsilon - \epsilon_\theta \left(\sqrt{\bar{\alpha}_t} \hat{x}_0 + \sqrt{1 - \bar{\alpha}_t} \epsilon, t \right) \right\|^2, g), \tag{2}$$

where $Dist(\cdot)$ is a distance metric for two gradients.

Without constraining the search space, the difficulty of inversion increases exponentially with the image size [41]. We leverage the final trained diffusion model, which the server naturally possesses as it is the result of the training process, to constrain the search space. In contrast to prior work, no external pretrained model is required. Concretely, we propose a constrained fusion model consisting of two phases: the generative phase and the fine-tuning phase. First, the generative phase leverages prior knowledge of the trained final diffusion model, $\mathcal{D}_{\theta^*} : \mathbb{R}^m \to \mathbb{R}^m$, where θ^* is the diffusion model parameter. Then, the fine-tuning phase improves the dummy image from the generative phase by efficiently minimizing the pixel-wise similarity. The overall workflow is summarized in Fig. 2, where the first generative phase outputs the optimized latent code as the input to the fine-tuning phase. The fine-tuning phase then output the final recovered images.

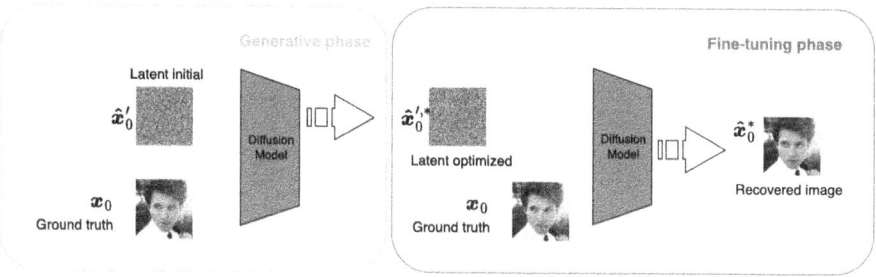

Fig. 2. The workflow of two phases of GIDM: Generative phase to optimize the latent code, while the fine-tuning phase continues to improve the pixel-wise similarity between the recovered images and the original ones to achieve both efficiency and effectiveness.

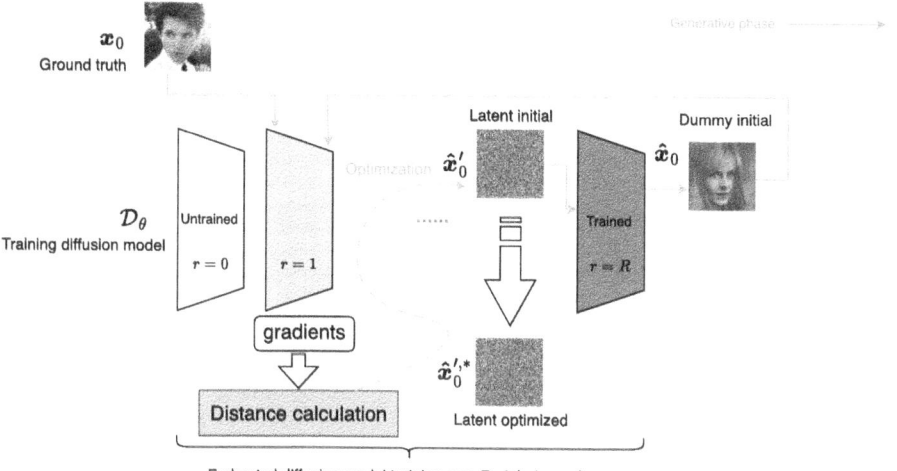

Fig. 3. We utilize one 128×128 image from *CelebA* as an example to show every intermediate result above. The generative phase executes 5000 iterations in this example, finally outputting the high-quality latent code which is able to sample resembled images from the trained diffusion models.

Generative Phase. We aim to generate images that resemble the training dataset as the starting point for dummy data optimization by gradient approximation. Our approach is to map the original search space into a narrow latent space with constraints (based on prior knowledge). The details of the generative phase is presented in Fig. 3. Let the latent code $\hat{\mathbf{x}}_0'$ [29] be of the same dimension as the dummy data $\hat{\mathbf{x}}_0$ from Eq. 2 and $\hat{\mathbf{x}}_0 = \mathcal{D}_\theta(\hat{\mathbf{x}}_0', t)$. We execute multiple iterations to optimize $\hat{\mathbf{x}}_0'$, as described below, so that the gradient computed on $\hat{\mathbf{x}}_0$ has a small distance to the real gradient. Thus, instead of directly updating the dummy data, we perform a latent space search over $\hat{\mathbf{x}}_0'$, which is the input of $\mathcal{D}_\theta$, outputting $\hat{\mathbf{x}}_0$. That is:

$$\hat{\mathbf{x}}_0^{\prime,*} = \mathcal{D}_\theta \left(\underset{\hat{\mathbf{x}}_0'}{\arg\min} \, Dist(\delta, g), t \right),$$

with:

$$\delta = \nabla_\theta \left\| \boldsymbol{\epsilon} - \boldsymbol{\epsilon}_\theta \left(\sqrt{\bar{\alpha}_t} \mathcal{D}_\theta(\hat{\mathbf{x}}_0', t) + \sqrt{1 - \bar{\alpha}_t} \boldsymbol{\epsilon}, t \right) \right\|^2.$$

Fine-Tuning Phase. The generative phase is able to generate high-quality data, yet, indirectly optimizing $\hat{\mathbf{x}}_0$ does not guarantee pixel-wise similarity. Moreover, each iteration of optimizing the latent code $\hat{\mathbf{x}}_0'$ requires T sampling steps of the trained diffusion model, e.g., $T = 1000$ in DDPM, which is computationally expensive. Therefore, our fine-tuning phase executes direct optimizing of $\hat{\mathbf{x}}_0$ following Eq. 2 based on the output of the generative phase $\hat{\mathbf{x}}_0^{\prime,*}$ to increase the pixel-wise similarity. The details of the finet-tuning phase is presented in Fig. 4.

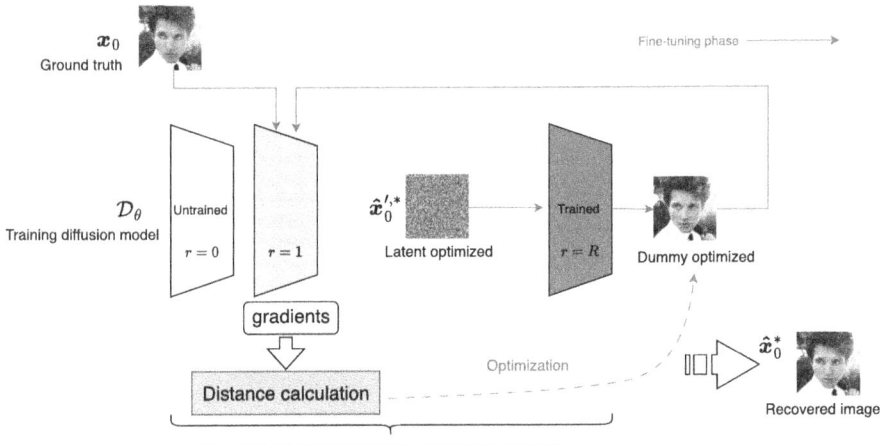

Fig. 4. We utilize one 128×128 image from *CelebA* as an example to show every intermediate result above. The fine-tuning phase consists of 1500 iterations. The latent optimized $\hat{\mathbf{x}}_0^{\prime,*}$ is the output of the generative phase.

The output of the generative phase, i.e., the intermediate dummy data, generated by the optimized latent code $\hat{\mathbf{x}}_0^{\prime,*}$, is then optimized by the fine-tuning phase. From Fig. 4, we see that the generative phase is already able to reconstruct a high-quality image that overall resembles the original picture while the pixel-wise similarity with the original data is low. As in the comparison example, The output of the generative phase differs from the original data in hair, face, and background. By integrating the generative phase and the fine-tuning phase, we recover high-quality data efficiently and effectively with high pixel-wise similarity.

Within both phases, calculating the gradients requires the knowledge of private $\boldsymbol{\epsilon}$ and t. We first conduct an exploratory experiment to determine whether inversion methods for classifiers adapted for diffusion models enable successful attacks. The result, presented in Sect. 4.4, demonstrates that adapted existing attacks are unable to recover training samples when applied to diffusion models due to the large search space of the diffusion optimization procedure. This motivates the novel design for gradient approximation on diffusion models.

3.4 Triple-Optimization

To enable inversion without knowing $\{\epsilon, t\}$, we optimize three different parameters simultaneously while taking their design principles and differences into consideration. Concretely, we design a triple-optimization method to refine the coordination of the three independent optimizations, namely, of $\mathbf{x}_0$, ϵ, and t by determining the approximations $\hat{\mathbf{x}}_0$, $\hat{\epsilon}$, and $\hat{t}$, respectively. Note that all three optimizations are based on backpropagating with the goal approximating the gradient.

Optimizing $\hat{\epsilon}$. In DDPM, we compute the distribution of the noisy sample after t iterations of the forward process in closed-form by:

$$q\left(\mathbf{x}_t \mid \mathbf{x}_0\right) = \mathcal{N}\left(\mathbf{x}_t; \sqrt{\bar{\alpha}_t}\mathbf{x}_0, (1 - \bar{\alpha}_t)\mathbf{I}\right).$$

The number of iterations in the forward process is set to a large T, and the variance levels $\beta_t \in (0, 1)$ increase linearly (ranging from 10^{-4} to 0.02), which means that $\bar{\alpha}_t = \prod_{i=1}^{t}(1 - \beta_t)$ approximates 0 for large t. Thus, the latent distribution is a Gaussian distribution ϵ sampled locally by the client, i.e., we should have $\epsilon \sim \mathcal{N}(\mathbf{0}, \mathbf{I})$. To follow such a Gaussian distribution, i.e., reduce the probability of sampling unlikely values, when implementing stochastic gradient descent requires a small learning rate η_ϵ to update $\hat{\epsilon}$. Also, following Eq. 1, training diffusion models is to predict the noise added during the forward process and the training performs well without changing the noise term during every iteration of inversion. Thus, we utilize an interval updating strategy for $\hat{\epsilon}$. The updating is achieved by:

$$\hat{\epsilon}^{i+1} = \hat{\epsilon}^i - \eta_\epsilon \frac{\partial Dist(\hat{g}, g)}{\partial \hat{\epsilon}^i}.$$

Optimizing $\hat{t}$. In contrast to ϵ and $\mathbf{x}_0$, which are floating tensors, t is an discrete integer in $\{1, \ldots, T\}$. To find the optimal t by stochastic gradient descent, we initialize a $1 \times T$ auxiliary vector following the uniform distribution: $\hat{t} \sim \text{Uniform}(\mathbf{0}, \mathbf{J})$ where $\mathbf{J}$ is a vector of ones. In each iteration of optimization for approximating the dummy gradient to the real gradient, $\hat{t}$ is updated by the learning rate η_t. The inferred $\hat{t}$ is chosen as the index of the maximum element in the vector after softmax transition: $\hat{t} = \arg\max(softmax(\hat{t}))$. $\hat{t}$ is updated at each inversion iteration:

$$\hat{t}^{i+1} = \hat{t}^i - \eta_t \frac{\partial Dist(\hat{g}, g)}{\partial \hat{t}^i}.$$

Optimizing $\hat{\mathbf{x}}_0$. Replacing ϵ and t in Eq. 2 with $\hat{\epsilon}$ and $\hat{t}$, we perform the optimization of $\hat{\mathbf{x}}_0$ starting with a random initialized image $\hat{\mathbf{x}}_0 \sim \text{Uniform}(\mathbf{0}, 2^p \mathbf{I})$, given that the source data is a p-bit binary encoded value. With each iteration, we update $\hat{\mathbf{x}}_0$ by back-propagating the distance between $\hat{g}$ and g. We set the learning rate of the dummy data as η_x. $\hat{\mathbf{x}}_0$ is updated at each inversion iteration:

$$\hat{\mathbf{x}}_0^{i+1} = \hat{\mathbf{x}}_0^i - \eta_x \frac{\partial Dist(\hat{g}, g)}{\partial \hat{\mathbf{x}}_0^i}.$$

The optimizers are coordinated based on an optimization interval S. After every S iterations of updating $\hat{\mathbf{x}}_0$ and $\hat{t}$, we perform S iterations of $\hat{\epsilon}$, $\hat{\mathbf{x}}_0$ and $\hat{t}$ simultaneously.

In summary, the triple-optimization gradient inversion coordinates three independent optimization processes to perform data reconstruction for the practical federated diffusion models without knowledge of the private noise and step sampled by each client.

4   Experimental Evaluation

We design a set of experiments to study the impact and effectiveness of gradient inversion attacks on diffusion models, as well as the ablation studies. The experimental setups, baselines, evaluation metrics, employment details, and results are presented in this section.

4.1   Setups

Datasets. Unless stated otherwise, our experiments use two datasets : *Celeb-A* [19] and *LSUN-Bedroom* [37], both with images resized to 128×128 since the original images from these datasets are of varying sizes. Both datasets are trained using the standard DDPM model [11] as by Algorithm 1 with 50 rounds. The optimization interval of GIDM for $\hat{\epsilon}$ optimizer is set to be $S = 50$. For all three optimizations of our triple-optimization, we use Adam as the optimizer. We choose $Dist(\cdot)$ to be the L2-Norm [41] distance, as the distance calculated by cosine similarity is large in our model, which may cause exploding gradients during training.

Hardware. For hardware, we conducted our experiments using an Alienware Aurora R13 running Ubuntu 20.04. This system boasts 64 GB of memory, a GeForce RTX 3090 GPU, and a 16-core Intel i9 CPU. With each of its 8 P-cores supporting two threads, the machine houses a total of 24 logical CPU cores.

Hyperparameters. The project of this paper is based on Pytorch 2.3.0. In our gradient inversion attackers, we apply Adam as the optimizer for both ϵ, t and the dummy image. The learning rate used in this paper is 0.01 without any scheduler for learning rate decay. The diffusion model for our experiments is the commonly used DDPM, which uses UNet to implement the sampling of each step. For our topic, the server can reconstruct the data from each client. Thus, we experiment on one random client for this work, following the settings of the baseline works [34,41].

4.2   Baselines with Adaptation

Since we are the first to study the gradient inversion attack on diffusion models, there is no direct baseline to compare to. State-of-the-art inversion attacks are designed for classifiers. Thus, we compare GIDM with adapted versions of the attacks that are compatible with diffusion models: DLG-dm [41] and InvG-dm [8] with Adam optimizer. Please note that without knowing $\{\epsilon, t\}$, DLG-dm and InvG-dm are **not** able to invert images similar to the original. As a consequence, we provide $\{\epsilon, t\}$ for these methods, giving them additional information that GIDM does not have. Specifically, for the same training input of images, the initialization works the same for DLG-dm and InvG-dm as for DLG and InvG. The backpropagation for calculating the gradients of diffusion models requires the additional inputs of ϵ and t, which does not apply to the baseline DLG and InvG. Thus, for DLG-dm and InvG-dm on diffusion models, we randomly sample ϵ following a Gaussian distribution of the same size of the dummy image and t from $[1, T]$ following a uniform distribution. They are kept constant over all inversion iterations. When it comes to the distance metric, we keep L2-Norm for DLG-dm and cosine similarity for InvG-dm, as for DLG and InvG.

4.3   Metrics

In evaluating the gradient inversion attack, which aims to reconstruct data that closely matches the original client data, we employ four metrics to gauge the resemblance between the reconstructed and real data: Mean Squared Error (MSE), Structural Similarity Index (SSIM) [30], Peak Signal-to-Noise Ratio (PSNR) [12], and Learned Perceptual Image Patch Similarity (LPIPS) score [39]. Statistically, *MSE* calculates the average squared difference on a pixel level between the reconstructed and original images:

$$\text{MSE}\,(q_1, q_2) = \frac{1}{MN} \sum_{i=0}^{M-1} \sum_{j=0}^{N-1} \left(q_1(i,j) - q_2(i,j)\right)^2,$$

where $q_1(i,j)$ and $q_2(i,j)$ indicate the original and recovered images, respectively. *PSNR* relates this *MSE* to the maximum pixel values, concretely, considering the ratio of the maximal value to *MSE* in a logarithmic manner:

$$\text{PSNR} = 10 \log_{10} \frac{R^2}{\text{MSE}},$$

where R is the maximum possible pixel value of the image. When the pixels are represented using 8 bits per sample, this is 255. For more modern visual assessments, *SSIM* mimics the human visual system to measure the structural variance of images based on luminance, contrast, and structure:

$$SSIM = \frac{2\mu_{x_r}\mu_{x_x} + c_1 2\sigma_{x_x x_x} + c_2}{\mu_{x_r}^2 + \mu_{x_z}^2 + c_1 \sigma_{x_r}^2 + \sigma_{x_y}^2 + c_2},$$

where μ_{x_r} and μ_{x_g} represent the means of the ground truth and the generated image, respectively. Accordingly, $\sigma_{\hat{x}_r}$ and σ_{x_g} are the standard deviations of $\hat{x}_r$ and x_g. Moreover, σ denotes the covariance between both images, while c_1 and c_2 are constants set to avoid instability.

LPIPS determines the perceptual similarity between the original and reconstructed images by learning the inverse mapping from the generated image back to the original. For MSE and LPIPS, lower values indicate greater similarity, whereas for SSIM and PSNR, higher values signify closer resemblance.

4.4   Final Reconstructed Images

The performance of our GIDM is assessed by the similarity between the final recovered image and the original image used during training. To demonstrate our inversion effectiveness, we report the final MSE, LPIPS, PSNR, SSIM results in Fig. 5. We also visualize examples of the final reconstructed images in Fig. 6 for *CelebA* and *LSUN-bedroom*. For GIDM, we assume $\{\epsilon, t\}$ is sampled by the client and randomly initialized: $\hat{\epsilon} \sim \mathcal{N}(\mathbf{0}, \mathbf{I})$ and $\hat{t} \sim \text{Uniform}(\{1, ..., T\})$. Recall that for the baselines, $\{\epsilon, t\}$ is assumed to be known. "Generative" refers to only the output of the generative phase before the fine-tuning phase, with $\{\epsilon, t\}$ known.

From Fig. 5, it is evident that GIDM outperforms baseline methods consistently for all four evaluation metrics, demonstrating superior reconstructing results. Yet, our generative phase does not always recover better images than DLG-dm and InvG-dm, which can be explained by the difference in goals in terms of similarity. The four evaluation metrics compute the quality of similarity based on pixels. In contrast, "Generative" optimizes the latent space to conduct indirect inversion. Thus, the high-quality output (semantically similar and clear) from the diffusion model may result in lower pixel-wise similarity than baselines, which appear comparably blurred in Fig. 6. Adding the fine-tuning phase resolves the issue and achieves better performance in terms of the metrics despite using less information.

Figure 6 visualizes and compares the recovered images on both datasets. GIDM successfully reconstructs high-quality images from the gradients that are nearly indistinguishable from the ground truth perceptually. As a comparison, DLG-dm and InvG-dm, which are designed for classifiers, fail to recover images resembling the ground truth. Specifically, they are only able to create images of similar color palettes as the original data without recreating the original object, let alone high-quality details. This meets our expectations since they conduct pixel-wise optimization. These methods suffer from exponentially increased difficulty when the image size is large.

When it comes to the difference between "Generative" and GIDM, we observe that our generative phase can already recover good approximations of the original image. Generally, the main color, object outline, and positions after the generative phase are almost identical to the ground truth, though there are still minor differences in the details of the images. For example, the face and hair shape, the background texture, or sometimes the makeup color is different from the ground truth for the *CelebA* human-facial dataset. The fine-tuning phase

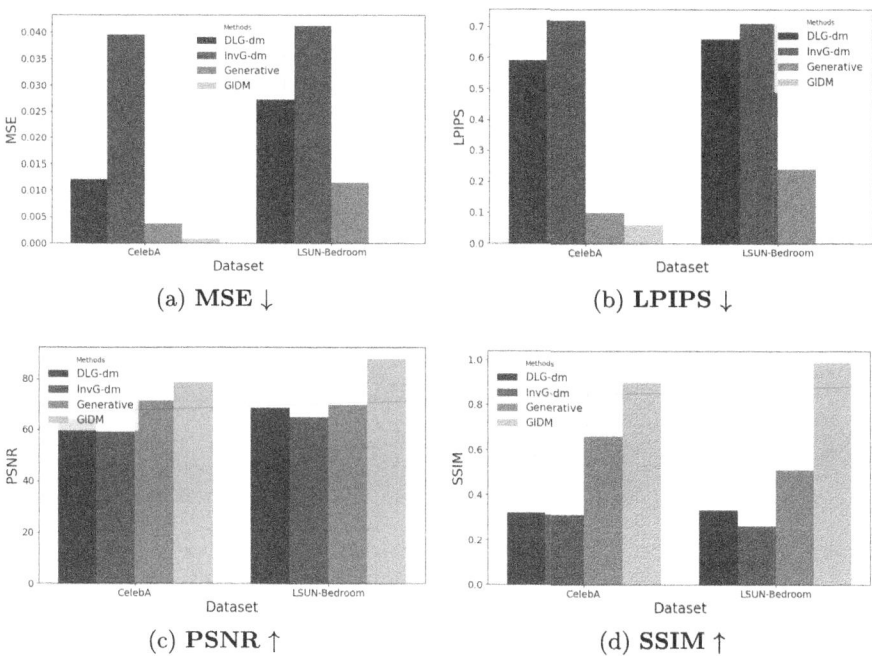

Fig. 5. Inversion results of diffusion models on *CelebA* and *LSUN-Bedroom*. We compare our GIDM (unknown $\{\epsilon, t\}$) with DLG-dm, InvG-dm, and our generative phase result (all three known $\{\epsilon, t\}$). ↓ stands for the lower the better, ↑ for the higher the better.

adjusts the generated images by direct gradient approximation, which results in successful reconstruction.

To summarize, gradient inversion of diffusion models is possible. Using the trained diffusion model to constrain the search space is highly effective. Still a fine-tuning phase is required to indeed recover high-quality images. With this phase, GIDM clearly outperforms the adapted baselines, despite using less knowledge.

4.5   Intermediate Inversion Outputs of GIDM

We now analyze the quality of the reconstructed images during the optimization process. We use example images from the *CelebA* dataset, both for known and unknown $\{\epsilon, t\}$.

Figure 7 shows the intermediary results for our example image. It highlights that both phases are necessary for the inversion process. For both known and unknown $\{\epsilon, t\}$, we observe gradual improvements, with the color palette and the profile details getting more similar to the original image in each step.

For the generative phase, the initialized random Gaussian noise can directly output a distinguishable image of a human face. However, this image shows an

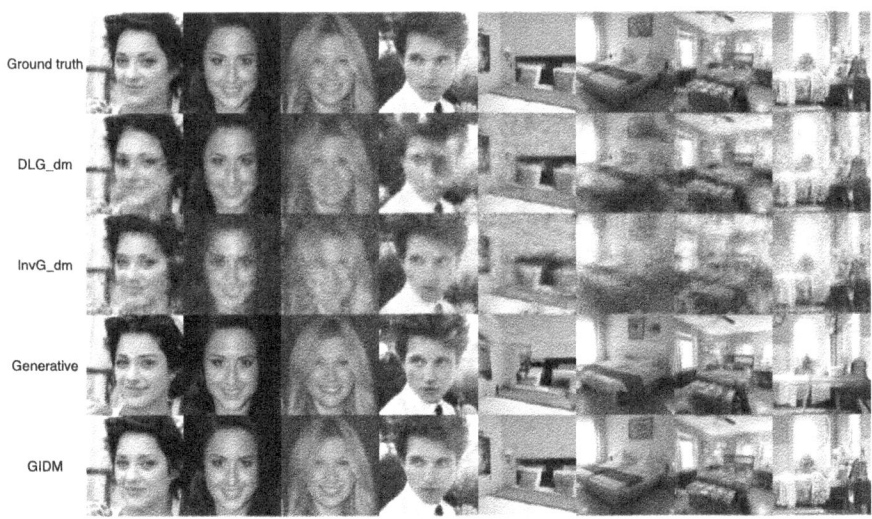

Fig. 6. Visualization of recovered images comparing with baselines on *CelebA* and *LSUN-Bedroom* datasets. "Generative" in the figure is the output of our generative phase before the fine-tuning phase. For GIDM, we assume that the server does not know $\{\epsilon, t\}$, while the baselines assume known $\{\epsilon, t\}$.

arbitrary human face, with no strong similarity to the original image. Thus, we have constrained the search space to images of human faces, which now enables finding one particular human face. We hence see that leveraging the trained diffusion model as a prior is highly effective in narrowing down the set of potential results.

After calculating the dummy gradient based on the previous image, our back-propagation adjusts the Gaussian noise so that it gradually generates an image of a similar color palette and object profiles. One interesting finding is that GIDM can reconstruct similar colors at an early stage of the training. In contrast, object outlines, such as the hair, converge slowly and gradually. Upon reaching the 3000-th iteration of the generative phase, the recovered image has been gradually started resembling the original image but does not mirror all the details of the original. Note that increasing the number of iterations to 10,000 does still not result in a fully recovered image, further motivating the need for the fine-tuning phase.

The fine-tuning phase starts with the output of the generative phase and we train 1500 iterations. Following the red arrows, the hair outline, and background start to approximate the original data. The fine-tuning phase does not utilize the diffusion model for optimizing alternative space. Thus, the reconstruction is efficient by not unnecessarily executing diffusion model sampling at each optimization iteration as in the generative phase.

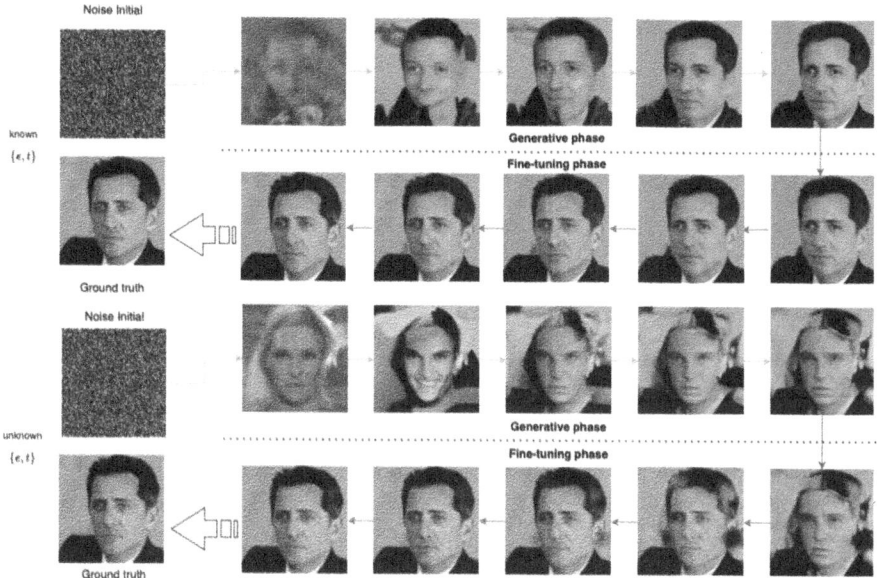

Fig. 7. Step-by-step gradient inversion intermediate results visualization for known and unknown $\{\epsilon, t\}$. The generative phase is marked by yellow arrows while the fine-tuning phase is red arrows. We initialize the latent code using 128×128 Gaussian noise. The generative phase is trained for $r_g = 5000$ and the fine-tuning phase for $r_f = 1500$ iterations. The same number n_i of images is shown for both phases, with the iterations between images being r_g/n_i and r_f/n_i for the generative and fine-tuning phases, respectively. (Color figure online)

4.6 The Impact of Knowing t or ϵ on GIDM

Our results in Sect. 4.4 consider ϵ and t initialized together by the client, which is unknown to the server. Here we provide an ablation study on the impact of knowing one factor and keeps the other one unknown respectively. We start by discussing the impact of known and unknown t. Hence, we assume that ϵ is known in this section. We use an image from *CelebA* as an example and show the process of optimization in Fig. 8. From the steps, it can be observed that when t is known to the server, the optimization process is smooth. This demonstrates that generating the changing t as the input of $\mathcal{D}(\hat{x}_0, t)$ influences the approximation during the optimization process of t. However, even without knowing t, the 128×128 images can be recovered in the end due to the less randomness than ϵ.

As a comparison, we also evaluate the impact of known or unknown ϵ for the reconstruction. Here, it is also assumed that t is known to the server (adversary). The results are shown in Fig. 9. Similarly, in the end, our GIDM is shown to be able to reconstruct images that resembles the original (ground truth in the figure). However, the intermediate output shows different way approaching the end. In general, the middle steps looks more natural perceptually with ϵ known by the

Fig. 8. Step-by-step gradient inversion intermediate results visualization, comparing known or unknown t. We initialize the latent code by 128×128 Gaussian noise. We present some of the representative intermediate outputs through the whole process. The total number of inversion iterations is 4000.

server. We could observe smooth changes towards the final results. Additionally, each output demonstrates high quality in terms of both the color blocks and facial profiles (figures above). As a comparison, unknown ϵ causes some deformed images, represented by both color and profiles (figures below). When it comes to the difference between Fig. 9 and Fig. 8, we find that t influences more on the image content (e.g., natural undistorted face) while ϵ controls more on the image clarity (blurness and random dots).

Fig. 9. Step-by-step gradient inversion intermediate results visualization, comparing known or unknown ϵ. We initialize the latent code by 128×128 Gaussian noise. We present some of the representative intermediate outputs through the whole process. The total number of inversion iterations is 4000.

4.7 Effectiveness of Triple-Optimization

In this part, we conduct an ablation study to showcase the significance of our joint triple-optimization. We apply the two-phase fusion model to compare the final recovered image without optimizing $\hat{t}$ or $\hat{\epsilon}$. An example reconstruction can be seen in Fig. 10.

In Fig. 10, we can first observe that it is indeed necessary to optimize the three factors jointly. Without such a joint optimization, the reconstructed images do not resemble the original image closely. The difference in importance between the two terms is notable. Concretely, when $\hat{t}$ is not optimized, the resulting image is very close to random pixels. In contrast, when $\hat{t}$ is optimized but $\hat{\epsilon}$ not, the reconstructed images is clearly that of a human face, though the details are not reconstructed.

Although $\hat{t}$ is only a single value that has a limited range, e.g., integer values between 0 and 999 for the classical DDPM, it decides the specific position on the Markov chain to train on. It guides the training process, similar to the label of classification tasks, which has a huge impact on the gradients. Thus, without having $\hat{t}$ resemble the parameter used during training, we have a very noisy image.

Without optimizing the noise term $\hat{\epsilon}$, which is a float tensor with more randomness, the image quality remains low but the attack is able to recover most color palettes and some outline information. We argue that there might be two reasons. First, $\hat{\epsilon}$ is introduced as a prediction target for training, which is less sensitive to incorrect sampling than $\hat{t}$, which directly instructs the noising process through the position of the chain. Second, the noise term is designed to follow a Gaussian distribution, avoiding unlikely values during inversion avoids extreme differences. In summary, our triple-optimization is indeed required.

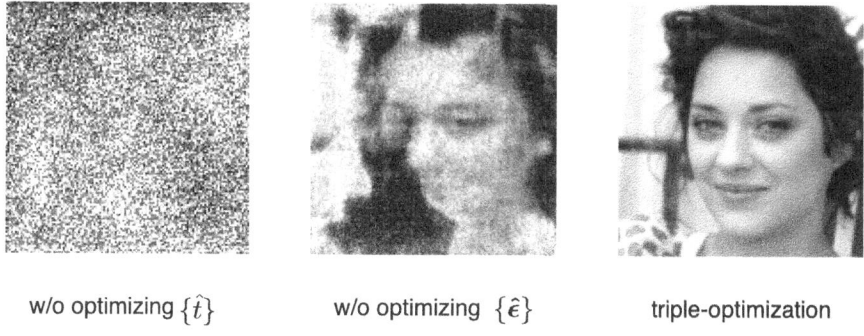

w/o optimizing $\{\hat{t}\}$ w/o optimizing $\{\hat{\epsilon}\}$ triple-optimization

Fig. 10. The reconstruction results of without optimizing $\hat{t}$ (random sampled), without optimizing $\hat{\epsilon}$ (random sampled) and triple-optimization on an example of *CelebA*.

5   Conclusion

In this paper, we are the first to study gradient inversion attacks on diffusion models. Leveraging the trained diffusion models as prior knowledge to constrain the search space, we propose an attack GIDM consisting of two phases. In the first phase, we use the trained diffusion model to approximate the image before fine-tuning the image to closer resemble the origin on a pixel-by-pixel basis in the second phase. The key challenge in designing GIDM is that the noise and sampling step are not known to the attacker, which we solved by the use of a joint optimization algorithm. Our reconstruction results are impressive, almost perfectly recreating images up to 128×128 in size.

In the future, we aim to develop a defense mechanism against the inversion attack, e.g., by using differential privacy [6]. It is unclear how differential privacy can be integrated in such a manner that the quality of the trained diffusion model is not severely impacted.

Acknowledgement. This research was partly funded by the SNSF/DFG project Priv-GSyn at 200021E_229204/550302673.

References

1. Abadi, M., et al.: Deep learning with differential privacy. In: Proceedings of the 2016 ACM SIGSAC Conference on Computer and Communications Security, Vienna, Austria, 24–28 October 2016, pp. 308–318. ACM (2016)
2. Act, A.: Health insurance portability and accountability act of 1996. Public Law **104**, 191 (1996)
3. Aji, A.F., Heafield, K.: Sparse communication for distributed gradient descent. In: Proceedings of the 2017 Conference on Empirical Methods in Natural Language Processing, EMNLP 2017, Copenhagen, Denmark, 9–11 September 2017, pp. 440–445. Association for Computational Linguistics (2017)
4. Carlini, N., et al.: Extracting training data from diffusion models. In: Calandrino, J.A., Troncoso, C. (eds.) 32nd USENIX Security Symposium, USENIX Security 2023, Anaheim, CA, USA, 9–11 August 2023, pp. 5253–5270. USENIX Association (2023)
5. Duan, J., Kong, F., Wang, S., Shi, X., Xu, K.: Are diffusion models vulnerable to membership inference attacks? In: International Conference on Machine Learning, ICML 2023, 23–29 July 2023, Honolulu, Hawaii, USA, vol. 202. Proceedings of Machine Learning Research, pp. 8717–8730. PMLR (2023)
6. Dwork, C.: The differential privacy frontier (extended abstract). In: Reingold, O. (ed.) TCC 2009. LNCS, vol. 5444, pp. 496–502. Springer, Heidelberg (2009). https://doi.org/10.1007/978-3-642-00457-5_29
7. Fang, H., Chen, B., Wang, X., Wang, Z., Xia, S.-T.: GIFD: a generative gradient inversion method with feature domain optimization. In: IEEE/CVF International Conference on Computer Vision, ICCV 2023, Paris, France, 1–6 October 2023, pp. 4944–4953. IEEE (2023)
8. Geiping, J., Bauermeister, H., Dröge, H., Moeller, M.: Inverting gradients - how easy is it to break privacy in federated learning? In: Advances in Neural Information Processing Systems 33: Annual Conference on Neural Information Processing Systems 2020, NeurIPS 2020, 6–12 December 2020, Virtual (2020)
9. Guan, Z., Zhou, Y., Gu, X., Li, B.: GIE: gradient inversion with embeddings. In: IEEE International Conference on Multimedia and Expo, ICME 2024, Niagara Falls, ON, Canada, 15–19 July 2024, pp. 1–6. IEEE (2024)
10. Hinton, G.E., Srivastava, N., Krizhevsky, A., Sutskever, I., Salakhutdinov, R.: Improving neural networks by preventing co-adaptation of feature detectors. CoRR, abs/1207.0580 (2012)

11. Ho, J., Jain, A., Abbeel, P.: Denoising diffusion probabilistic models. In: Advances in Neural Information Processing Systems 33: Annual Conference on Neural Information Processing Systems 2020, NeurIPS 2020, 6–12 December 2020, Virtual (2020)

12. Horé, A., Ziou, D.: Image quality metrics: PSNR vs. SSIM. In: 20th International Conference on Pattern Recognition, ICPR 2010, Istanbul, Turkey, 23–26 August 2010, pp. 2366–2369. IEEE Computer Society (2010)

13. Hu, H., Pang, J.: Loss and likelihood based membership inference of diffusion models. In: Athanasopoulos, E., Mennink, B. (eds.) Information Security - 26th International Conference, ISC 2023, Groningen, The Netherlands, 15–17 November 2023, Proceedings. LNCS, vol. 14411, pp. 121–141. Springer (2023)

14. Huang, Y., Gupta, S., Song, Z., Li, K., Arora, S.: Evaluating gradient inversion attacks and defenses in federated learning. In: Advances in Neural Information Processing Systems 34: Annual Conference on Neural Information Processing Systems 2021, NeurIPS 2021, 6–14 December 2021, Virtual, pp. 7232–7241 (2021)

15. Jeon, J., Kim, J., Lee, K., Oh, S., Ok, J.: Gradient inversion with generative image prior. In: Ranzato, M., Beygelzimer, A., Dauphin, Y.N., Liang, P., Vaughan, J.W. (eds.) Advances in Neural Information Processing Systems 34: Annual Conference on Neural Information Processing Systems 2021, NeurIPS 2021, 6–14 December 2021, Virtual, pp. 29898–29908 (2021)

16. Jin, X., Chen, P.-Y., Hsu, C.-Y., Chia-Mu, Yu., Chen, T.: CAFE: catastrophic data leakage in vertical federated learning. In: Advances in Neural Information Processing Systems, vol. 34, pp. 994–1006 (2021)

17. Li, D., Xie, W., Wang, Z., Yibing, L., Li, Y., Fang, L.: FedDiff: diffusion model driven federated learning for multi-modal and multi-clients. IEEE Trans. Circuits Syst. Video Technol. **34**(10), 10353–10367 (2024)

18. Li, Z., Zhang, J., Liu, L., Liu, J.: Auditing privacy defenses in federated learning via generative gradient leakage. In: IEEE/CVF Conference on Computer Vision and Pattern Recognition, CVPR 2022, New Orleans, LA, USA, 18–24 June 2022, pp. 10122–10132. IEEE (2022)

19. Liu, Z., Luo, P., Wang, X., Tang, X.: Deep learning face attributes in the wild. In: 2015 IEEE International Conference on Computer Vision, ICCV 2015, Santiago, Chile, 7–13 December 2015, pp. 3730–3738. IEEE Computer Society (2015)

20. Rombach, R., Blattmann, A., Lorenz, D., Esser, P., Ommer, B.: High-resolution image synthesis with latent diffusion models. In: IEEE/CVF Conference on Computer Vision and Pattern Recognition, CVPR 2022, New Orleans, LA, USA, 18–24 June 2022, pp. 10674–10685. IEEE (2022)

21. Saharia, C., et al.: Photorealistic text-to-image diffusion models with deep language understanding. In: Advances in Neural Information Processing Systems 35: Annual Conference on Neural Information Processing Systems 2022, NeurIPS 2022, New Orleans, LA, USA, 28 November–9 December 2022 (2022)

22. Shankar, A., Brouwer, H., Hai, R., Chen, L.Y.: SiloFuse: cross-silo synthetic data generation with latent tabular diffusion models. CoRR, abs/2404.03299 (2024)

23. Somepalli, G., Singla, V., Goldblum, M., Geiping, J., Goldstein, T.: Diffusion art or digital forgery? Investigating data replication in diffusion models. In: IEEE/CVF Conference on Computer Vision and Pattern Recognition, CVPR 2023, Vancouver, BC, Canada, 17–24 June 2023, pp. 6048–6058. IEEE (2023)

24. Song, J., Meng, C., Ermon, S.: Denoising diffusion implicit models. In: 9th International Conference on Learning Representations, ICLR 2021, Virtual Event, Austria, 3–7 May 2021. OpenReview.net (2021)

25. Srivastava, N., Hinton, G.E., Krizhevsky, A., Sutskever, I., Salakhutdinov, R.: Dropout: a simple way to prevent neural networks from overfitting. J. Mach. Learn. Res. **15**(1), 1929–1958 (2014)

26. Sun, J., Li, A., Wang, B., Yang, H., Li, H., Chen, Y.: Soteria: provable defense against privacy leakage in federated learning from representation perspective. In: IEEE Conference on Computer Vision and Pattern Recognition, CVPR 2021, Virtual, 19–25 June 2021, pp. 9311–9319. Computer Vision Foundation/IEEE (2021)

27. Sun, X., Ren, X., Ma, S., Wang, H.: meProp: sparsified back propagation for accelerated deep learning with reduced overfitting. In: Proceedings of the 34th International Conference on Machine Learning, ICML 2017, Sydney, NSW, Australia, 6–11 August 2017, Proceedings of Machine Learning Research, vol. 70, pp. 3299–3308. PMLR (2017)

28. Voigt, P., Von dem Bussche, A.: The EU General Data Protection Regulation (GDPR). A Practical Guide, 1st edn. Springer, Cham (2017). 10(3152676):10–5555

29. Wang, Z., Wang, J., Liu, Z., Qiu, Q.: Binary latent diffusion. In: IEEE/CVF Conference on Computer Vision and Pattern Recognition, CVPR 2023, Vancouver, BC, Canada, 17–24 June 2023, pp. 22576–22585. IEEE (2023)

30. Wang, Z., Bovik, A.C., Sheikh, H.R., Simoncelli, E.P.: Image quality assessment: from error visibility to structural similarity. IEEE Trans. Image Process. **13**(4), 600–612 (2004)

31. Wu, R., Chen, X., Guo, C., Weinberger, K.Q.: Learning to invert: simple adaptive attacks for gradient inversion in federated learning. In: Evans, R.J., Shpitser, I. (eds.) Uncertainty in Artificial Intelligence, UAI 2023, 31 July–4 August 2023, Pittsburgh, PA, USA. Proceedings of Machine Learning Research, vol. 216, pp. 2293–2303. PMLR (2023)

32. Wu, Y., Yu, N., Li, Z., Backes, M., Zhang, Y.: Membership inference attacks against text-to-image generation models. CoRR, abs/2210.00968 (2022)

33. Xia, W., Zhang, Y., Yang, Y., Xue, J.-H., Zhou, B., Yang, M.-H.: GAN inversion: a survey. IEEE Trans. Pattern Anal. Mach. Intell. **45**(3), 3121–3138 (2023)

34. Xu, J., Hong, C., Huang, J., Chen, L.Y., Decouchant, J.: AGIC: approximate gradient inversion attack on federated learning. In: 41st International Symposium on Reliable Distributed Systems, SRDS 2022, Vienna, Austria, 19–22 September 2022, pp. 12–22. IEEE (2022)

35. Ye, X., et al.: Accelerating CNN training by pruning activation gradients. In: Vedaldi, A., Bischof, H., Brox, T., Frahm, J.-M. (eds.) ECCV 2020. LNCS, vol. 12370, pp. 322–338. Springer, Cham (2020). https://doi.org/10.1007/978-3-030-58595-2_20

36. Yin, H., Mallya, A., Vahdat, A., Álvarez, J.M., Kautz, J., Molchanov, P.: See through gradients: image batch recovery via Gradinversion. In: IEEE Conference on Computer Vision and Pattern Recognition, CVPR 2021, Virtual, 19–25 June 2021, pp. 16337–16346. Computer Vision Foundation/IEEE (2021)

37. Yu, F., Zhang, Y., Song, S., Seff, A., Xiao, J.: LSUN: construction of a large-scale image dataset using deep learning with humans in the loop. CoRR, abs/1506.03365 (2015)

38. Zhang, H., Cissé, M., Dauphin, Y.N., Lopez-Paz, D.: mixup: beyond empirical risk minimization. In: 6th International Conference on Learning Representations, ICLR 2018, Vancouver, BC, Canada, 30 April–3 May 2018, Conference Track Proceedings. OpenReview.net (2018)

39. Zhang, R., Isola, P., Efros, A.A., Shechtman, E., Wang, O.: The unreasonable effectiveness of deep features as a perceptual metric. In: 2018 IEEE Conference on

Computer Vision and Pattern Recognition, CVPR 2018, Salt Lake City, UT, USA, 18–22 June 2018, pp. 586–595. Computer Vision Foundation/IEEE Computer Society (2018)

40. Zhao, B., Mopuri, K.R., Bilen, H.: iDLG: improved deep leakage from gradients. CoRR, abs/2001.02610 (2020)

41. Zhu, L., Liu, Z., Han, S.: Deep leakage from gradients. In: Advances in Neural Information Processing Systems 32: Annual Conference on Neural Information Processing Systems 2019, NeurIPS 2019, 8–14 December 2019, Vancouver, BC, Canada, pp. 14747–14756 (2019)

Privacy-Preserving Encoding and Scaling of Tabular Data in Horizontal Federated Learning Systems

Tim Piotrowski[1]([envelope]) [iD], Zoltán Nochta[1] [iD], Manuel Karl[2] [iD], and Martin Johns[2] [iD]

[1] Karlsruhe University of Applied Sciences, Karlsruhe, Germany
{tim.piotrowski,zoltan.nochta}@h-ka.de,
[2] TU Braunschweig, Braunschweig, Germany
{m.karl,m.johns}@tu-braunschweig.de

Abstract. Federated Machine Learning (FML) enables multiple entities to collaboratively train a shared ML model while keeping their local datasets private. By combining data and knowledge across participants, FML can produce better models than those trained on isolated datasets. The preprocessing of training data, such as scaling numerical features and encoding categorical variables, is essential to ensure data uniformity and thus improve model quality. In horizontal FML systems, participants have data with the same features, but own different samples. Achieving a uniform preprocessing among participants usually requires revealing statistics about training data or even the exchange of sensitive categorical values, which undermines privacy. To avoid it, privacy-preserving preprocessing methods are necessary. This work addresses the secure scaling of numerical features and the consistent encoding of categorical data in FML systems. We propose a privacy-preserving approach for Z-Score normalization that allows participants to scale numerical features collaboratively without revealing local statistics. We evaluate eight methods for a uniform encoding of categorical values across the system and assess their impact on model quality, dimensionality, scalability, and privacy. Our experimental evaluation on five datasets demonstrates that system-wide consistent preprocessing improves model performance compared to isolated approaches. However, we observe a trade-off between privacy preservation and efficiency. Based on our findings, we provide practical recommendations for selecting suitable encoding strategies depending on the use case, aiming to balance privacy, data consistency, and model performance in FML settings.

Keywords: Federated Learning · Preprocessing · Tabular Data · Encoding · Scaling · Secure Multiparty Computation · Security

M. Dalla Preda et al. (Eds.): ARES 2025, LNCS 15992, pp. 402–424, 2025.
https://doi.org/10.1007/978-3-032-00624-0_20

1   Introduction

In the recent decade, Machine Learning (ML) has become increasingly capable of tackling complex problems such as credit card fraud, or detect cancer based on images. ML models are typically created and managed by a single entity that stores and utilizes large volumes of data, including images, text files, and structured tabular data, for model training and testing purposes. However, storing and processing the data of multiple data owners raise security and privacy concerns and can also violate legal regulations. In sectors, such as finance or healthcare, sensitive data must not leave the respective institution.

Horizontal FML enables multiple independent data owners to collaboratively train ML models to solve a common business problem. In FML, participants train models locally on their datasets and share only the calculated model weights (or gradients) across multiple rounds to build a common global model. During the training, no training or test data is exchanged between participants.

In centralized FML systems, a server collects the locally calculated weights from connected participants and computes the resulting global model [12]. In decentralized FML settings, participants train the model without involving a central entity or server [16,26]. In both setups, all participants receive the same (initially untrained) ML model, use the same optimization algorithm, and agree on specific training parameters, including learning rates, target accuracy, and the maximum number of iteration rounds. In addition, they must prepare their training datasets before the training can begin.

Pre-processing is particularly crucial when using structured (tabular) data stored in relational databases for model training. It consists of multiple tasks, such as feature selection, data cleaning and data transformation, which encompasses encoding categorical feature values and scaling numerical features. Previous work on tabular data in FML has focused mainly on feature selection, with limited consideration of data transformation steps. Consequently, existing FML research implicitly assumes that data transformation is carried out independently by each participant or performed by a central server. Both assumptions lead to problems: The isolated preprocessing of local training data at each site can lead to inconsistent feature representations in the overall system. These inconsistencies can degrade the quality of the jointly trained model. Conversely, centralized preprocessing ensures high model quality, but requires the transfer of sensitive data to the server. For example, system-wide consistent encoding of categorical features requires the transfer of all distinct values of all categorical features in plain text, e.g., patient names, medical records, which is infeasible when dealing with sensitive information. Many studies bypass these challenges entirely by preprocessing the entire dataset before splitting it into simulated federated datasets, neglecting the complexities and constraints of real-world FML settings.

So far, limited attention has been paid to the challenges posed by data transformation in FML. The specific information required to be transmitted to a central server for consistent encoding and scaling across all datasets in FML has not yet been thoroughly examined.

Our paper addresses these gaps, examines the limitations of local preprocessing in FML, determines the required information exchange between participants to perform uniform preprocessing, and introduces a federated approach to run data transformation tasks that enable consistency while preserving data confidentiality. We propose and evaluate specific protocols and cryptographic techniques that prevent the exchange of sensitive data during encoding and scaling. Our main contributions are as follows:

1. The presentation of a federated data transformation schema consisting of federated scaling and federated encoding applicable in horizontal FML environments.
2. A privacy-preserving protocol for Z-Score normalization, allowing numerical feature scaling within federations without exposing local statistical data, thus maintaining the confidentiality of participant information while ensuring effective preprocessing.
3. Introduction of eight protocols, that partly leverage cryptographic methods, to uniformly encode categorical features in FML systems without sharing confidential or sensitive data.
4. A comprehensive evaluation of the approaches through experiments, focusing on model quality, federated scalability, the impact of input dimensionality, and the extent of shared information, followed by a discussion and selection of appropriate algorithms for different use cases.

2   Background

2.1   Federated Machine Learning

In a FML system, n independent entities jointly train the ML model to address a common challenge without revealing training data D_i [12]. Conventionally, each participant P_i exchanges only locally computed model updates, such as gradients $\nabla \mathcal{L}_i$ or model weights θ_i^t with a central server. The server creates and refines the aggregated model using Federated Stochastic Gradient Descent (FedSGD) or Federated Averaging (FedAVG) respectively:

$$\theta^{(t+1)} = \theta^{(t)} - \eta \sum_{i=1}^{n} \frac{|D_i|}{\sum_j |D_j|} \nabla \mathcal{L}_i \quad (1) \qquad \theta^{(t+1)} = \sum_{i=1}^{n} \frac{|D_i|}{\sum_j |D_j|} \theta_i^{(t+1)} \quad (2)$$

In FedSGD (Eq. 1), the server updates the global model by computing a weighted average of the gradients received from all clients, where each client computes $\nabla \mathcal{L}_i$ using a small batch of its local dataset D_i. The weight $\frac{|D_i|}{\sum_j |D_j|}$, ensures that clients with larger datasets contribute more to the global update, whereby $\sum_j |D_j|$ represents the total size of the data of all participants and η is the learning rate. In FedAVG (Eq. 2), the server aggregates θ_i^t of all clients, after each client has trained on its entire dataset for multiple rounds. After aggregation, the new global model $\theta^{(t+1)}$ is sent back to all clients for the next round of training. This iterative process continues until the model converges or a stopping criterion is met.

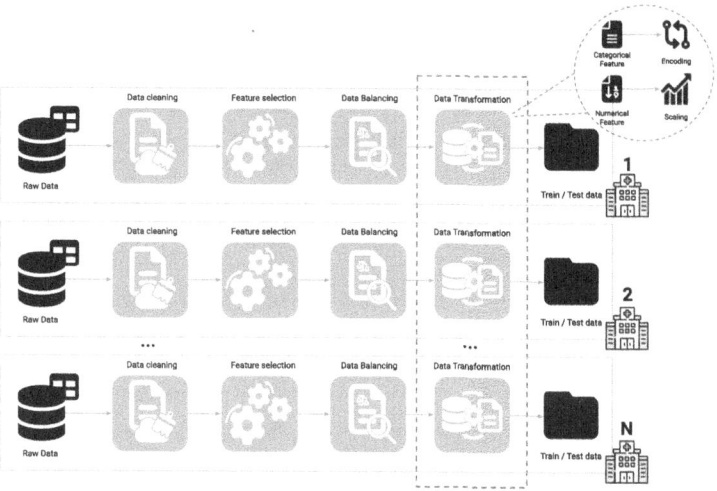

Fig. 1. Example of a federated preprocessing pipeline applying uniform data transformations across all clients.

2.2 Preprocessing of Tabular Data

Preprocessing of training and testing data is crucial for ensuring high data quality and enhancing the learning capability of machine learning models. Figure 1 illustrates a potential preprocessing pipeline for tabular data in federated learning, comprising feature selection, data cleaning, balancing, and transformation. As research on preprocessing in federated tabular settings is still limited, this pipeline represents our conceptual framework to guide future exploration.

The goal of feature selection is to identify and select the most relevant features from the dataset, eliminate irrelevant, redundant, or highly correlated features, and reduce dimensionality if necessary.

Data cleaning aims to remove duplicates and outliers from the dataset and to handle missing values. Duplicates add little value to ML model training, while outliers can negatively affect the model's performance. Missing values often arise in datasets, such as time-series data, due to failures during data collection. If not addressed, these gaps prevent the model from interpreting the affected data points. Common handling methods include imputing likely values manually, replacing missing values by the feature's mean, or removing incomplete data points.

The data balancing phase applies sampling (over-sampling or under-sampling) of data to ensure a more equal distribution of classes to improve model performance and prevent bias due to dominant classes.

In this work, we focus on the data transformation phase as highlighted in Fig. 1. This phase encompasses encoding of categorical features and scaling of numerical features to ensure consistency and to enhance the resulting model's performance.

Scaling is a transformation that maps data from its original space $\mathbb{R}^n$ into a standardized subspace of $\mathbb{R}^n$ to ensure numerical stability and improve model performance. Mathematically, it applies a function $f : \mathbb{R}^n \rightarrow \mathbb{R}^n$, where each feature x_i is transformed into $\tilde{x}_i = f(x_i)$ to adjust its range, variance, or distribution while preserving relative structures within the dataset. This transformation facilitates better optimization, by preventing features with larger magnitudes from dominating the learning process.

Encoding methods, such as one-hot encoding and label encoding, map categorical variables to numerical representations, facilitating their processing by ML models. Both methods begin by extracting the unique categorical values of a feature, forming a set $S = \{s_1, s_2, \ldots, s_n\}$, commonly referred to as "bag of words." A dictionary function $f : S \rightarrow \mathbb{N}_0$ assigns each value a unique non-negative integer, based on alphabetical order or metrics like term frequency-inverse document frequency [5]. In label encoding, each $s_i \in S$ is replaced by its label $f(s_i)$, which is especially suitable for ordinal features with natural ordering, such as European dress sizes.

If a categorical feature cannot be sorted or relationships between the values are of importance, one-hot encoding should be preferred. For one-hot encoding, a categorical value s_i is represented as a binary vector $v_i \in \{0, 1\}^{|S|}$, where the j-th entry is a 1 if $f(s_i) = j$ and a 0 otherwise.

This ensures that each categorical value is mapped to a unique basis vector in $\mathbb{R}^{|S|}$, preserving categorical distinctions without imposing an artificial ordinal structure. For example, when using this method to encode the feature "illness" with a dictionary $d_{illness} = \{arthritis = 0, diabetes = 1, pneumonia = 2\}$, the resultant vector for a patient with arthritis would be represented as $v = [1\ 0\ 0]$.

3 Threat Model and Privacy Requirements

We consider FML systems involving a small number (n < 20) of independent participants, such as hospitals, that collaborate to address shared challenges while considering organizational and legal constraints. The FML system uses a central server provided by one of the participants or by a third-party orchestrator. We assume that the participants have already completed the data cleaning and balancing tasks locally and reached a consensus on feature selection as well. Now, they want to encode and scale relevant features in a federated manner. To properly encode categorical features, participants must transmit plaintext data, e.g., about patients' medical conditions, to the server. Hospitals are understandably unwilling to share such data, as it could expose details about the prevalence of specific diseases within their patient populations. Such disclosures would compromise privacy and violate trust. Scaling of numerical data, on the other hand, requires the exchange of local statistical properties, like *std* or *mean* of each feature. Features, such as the Charlson Comorbidity Index (CCI) may contain highly sensitive information. The CCI is a weighted metric designed to predict the one-year mortality risk for patients with specific comorbidities. Access to statistical properties of the CCI could allow FML participants to gain insights into others' datasets. For instance, observing higher *mean* or *std* values than those in their own data could indicate an elevated mortality risk among patients at a specific institution or reveal trends in patients' health.

With regard to trustworthiness, we assume that every participant and the server are Honest-but-Curious (HBC) entities. An HBC participant basically follows the protocol, but attempts to extract as much information as possible from legitimately received messages. In our scenario, it includes categorical feature values in clear text and numerical statistics of local data sets.

Concerning privacy, we aim to minimize the amount of data that have to be exchanged in the FML system with emphasis on these requirements:

1. The server cannot access or learn any specific value of the categorical data.
2. The server cannot access the local statistics about numerical data of individual participants.
3. Each participant gains only knowledge about the categorical values that are also present in its own data set.
4. No participant has access or can learn statistics about numerical data of other participants.

4 Related Work

We are not aware of previous research that explicitly addresses the privacy problem of encoding and scaling in FML systems. However, there are publications that discuss security aspects of feature selection in the field of FML analysis. FML analytics has emerged to enable secure federated data insights without disclosing data [24].

Akavia et al. [2] proposed the first Secure Multiparty Computation (SMPC) based protocol for private feature selection. It combines multiple SMPC methods and leverages Gini impurity for efficient feature scoring. Li et al. [17] propose a privacy-preserving feature selection method using Homomorphic Encryption (HE). It builds sparse ridge regression models on horizontally partitioned data, outsourcing computation to two non-colluding servers and integrating Recursive Feature Elimination for feature pruning.

Eleks et al. [9] enable data consumers to analyze data without exposure and propose strategies for handling missing or unclean data, such as reformatting, feature generation, or adding attributes. Hsu and Huang [14] propose an FML framework using HE to secure training data and model aggregation. An initiator selects participants by sending encrypted queries and suggests pre-processing based on a shared schema. While providing strong data protection, HE incurs high computational costs and scales poorly with complex models.

Privacy vulnerabilities in training have been widely studied. FedSGD-based systems, in particular, are susceptible to data reconstruction under HBC assumptions [11,19,28]. In contrast research on FedAVG when participants have large data silos is limited, especially for tabular data, as most studies focus on image or speech data. Fowl et al. [10] demonstrate the feasibility of inferring local data even in a FedAVG environment. Vero et al. [23] propose the first attack on tabular data in FML settings. The paper even highlights our privacy implications of sharing data during preprocessing, as the server leverages information about categorical values and numerical statistics to reconstruct the data of participants. Wu et al. [27] also explored tabular data, using label property inference with a Generative Adversarial Network to extract information about target class distributions.

While general privacy-enhancing techniques such as SMPC, HE and Differential Privacy (DP) are widely applied to model aggregation [1,4,18] to tackle these attacks. Recent research includes Das et al. [7], which propose a communication-efficient protocol that combines DP and SMPC for collaborative deep learning in vertical and horizontal FML, significantly reducing overhead while maintaining strong privacy guarantees, and highlighting the feasibility of scalable privacy-preserving training. Further Eichner et al. [8] introduce a federated system architecture combining Trusted Execution Environments, Differential Privacy, and SMPC to secure both client and server-side computations, enabling verifiable privacy guarantees at scale.

However, application of these techniques to preprocessing remains limited. Our work addresses this gap by researching privacy-preserving protocols for encoding and scaling in horizontal FML.

5   Local and Server-Based Data Transformation

This section presents an analysis of local versus server-based data transformation in FML, highlighting the trade-offs and the information exchanges required for the server-based approach. We will examine the strengths and limitations of both methods, before assessing their performance in terms of model quality.

5.1   Local Scaling and Encoding in FML

A numerical feature f can be scaled using methods, such as Min-Max or Z-Score Normalization, reducing values to a standardized range:

$$\tilde{x}_i = \frac{x_i - f_{\min}}{f_{\max} - f_{\min}} \qquad (3) \qquad\qquad z_i = \frac{x_i - \mu_f}{\sigma_f} \qquad (4)$$

Min-Max normalization (Eq. 3) uses the feature's minimum and maximum values $f_{\min}$ and $f_{\max}$ to transform a value x_i. Z-Score normalization (Eq. 4) requires the mean μ_f and the standard deviation σ_f of f for standardization. Due to deviations of the parameters μ_f and σ_f as well as of f_{max} and f_{min} in the local data sets of participants, performing the normalization independently at each site would result in inconsistent scaling of numerical features, making it challenging for the model to recognize similarities in the input data during training.

Categorical feature encoding involves each participant generating a local mapping of unique values in their dataset to numerical identifiers, creating a dictionary for all distinct categorical values. These values are then transformed into

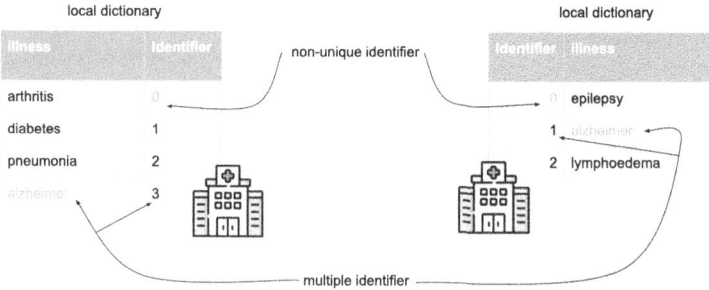

Fig. 2. The dictionary problems visualized on illnesses held by two FML hospitals (Icon source: https://www.flaticon.com/de/kostenlose-icons/krankenhaus)

numerical representations, through label encoding or one-hot encoding. However, isolated local encoding in FML can lead to two types of *dictionary problems*, as illustrated in Fig. 2. When participants independently perform the encoding, the same identifiers are used for different categorical values, thus creating non-unique identifiers. In the example, both participants use a 0 to identify two different illnesses, "arthritis" and "epilepsy", resulting in a collision. Furthermore, identical values are represented by multiple different identifiers. For example, both participants possess the feature value "alzheimer" but encode it as 3 and 1, respectively. Consequently, a system-wide unique identification of the strings is not guaranteed.

5.2   Server-Based Encoding and Scaling in FML

In FML, the central server typically oversees the orchestration of the protocol and the model aggregation, making it a suitable entity to facilitate uniform encoding and scaling of features. However, achieving consistency requires participants to share specific information with the server. For example, for Min-Max normalization, each participant provides its local minimum and maximum values of the numerical features. The server then determines the global minimum and maximum across all datasets and shares these values with the clients.

The uniform encoding of categorical data on the other hand relies on establishing a shared dictionary. In a centralized FML environment, the server aggregates the clear text local dictionaries into a global dictionary, eliminating the dictionary problems. This global dictionary is then shared with the participants. Alternatively, an open-source dictionary can be used to encode categorical features containing words of a language, such as diseases. For example, hospitals collaborating to train a model might have a feature listing treated illnesses. Using a global dictionary of worldwide known diseases for encoding would produce an excessively large one-hot encoding, containing more illnesses than encountered in the local datasets. This leads to sparse representations that reduce model performance and computational efficiency. Moreover, this approach fails when

Table 1. Comparison of Local vs. Server-Based preprocessing using the F1-Score in an FML environment with four participants

	Method			
Dataset	Local Preproc.	Uniform Encoding	Uniform Scaling	Server-Based
Adult	0.60	0.66	0.65	**0.69**
German	0.30	0.77	0.56	**0.79**
Health Heritage	0.63	0.67	0.64	**0.69**
Lawschool	0.69	0.69	0.70	**0.71**
CC Fraud	0.80	0.84	0.81	**0.90**

categorical features include custom terms, as often seen in computer science, due to the lack of predefined dictionaries for such data.

5.3 Performance Assessment

In the following, we investigate the impact of unified federated scaling and encoding on model quality compared to isolated local preprocessing. In our experiments we used the datasets Adult Census [3], German Credit Card [13], Health Heritage[1], Lawschool Admission [25], and the Simulated Credit Card Transactions[2]. These datasets include numerical and categorical features, representing a two-class prediction problem.

We partitioned each dataset into four subsets, each assigned to a different participant in the simulated federation. The data is non-independently and identically distributed (non-IID) among participants to simulate real-world scenarios, with varying categorical values, dataset sizes, and label distributions across participants, thus maximizing divergence. However, this distribution approach is inherently constrained, particularly for datasets with limited variability in their categorical features.

We conducted four experiments by varying the encoding and scaling methods during data preprocessing. In the first, the participants performed isolated local preprocessing and exchanged only input sizes to apply the padding needed to construct the encoding vectors. In the second, the server created a global dictionary for uniform encoding, and the clients scaled their own data locally. The third experiment combined server-based uniform scaling with client-side data encoding. In the fourth, the server orchestrated both uniform encoding and scaling tasks. After each preprocessing, we performed federated model training using FedAVG. Hereby, a small neural network tailored to each dataset, optimizing its architecture to fit the specific features and patterns was used. The results shown in Table 1 demonstrate that uniform scaling and encoding using a server, significantly improve the model's quality. A notable example is the German Credit Card dataset, which showed a 49% increase in the F1-score. The

---

[1] https://www.kaggle.com/c/hhp.

[2] https://www.kaggle.com/datasets/kartik2112/fraud-detection.

Lawschool dataset, on the other hand, showed minimal benefit from federated preprocessing, likely due to its limited categorical values. Therefore, most unique values are already present locally, thus participants' dictionaries closely align or match with the global dictionary. The best results can be achieved, combining both uniform encoding and scaling.

In addition, the experiments showed that the datasets mostly benefit from uniform encoding, while uniform scaling seems to have a lower impact on these datasets. We attribute this to the influence of categorical values on the model's decision-making.

6 Privacy-Preserving Z-Score Normalization

Z-score normalization (see Eq. 4) is a well-known and widely used data preprocessing technique to scale numerical features in ML training datasets. In FML systems, it especially helps avoid model quality deterioration caused by undetected outliers in participants' private datasets.

As the required μ_f and σ_f differ on each local dataset, we propose a protocol that achieves uniform Z-Score in FML systems. However, in FML system, revealing local statistics raises privacy concerns. To address this, we extend our approach with a privacy preserving method so that no local statistics need to be exchanged. The n participants have to collaboratively compute the global mean μ_{gf} and the global standard deviation σ_{gf} for each numerical feature f that requires normalization:

$$\mu_{gf} = \frac{\sum_{i=1}^{n}(\mu_{if} * |D_i|)}{\sum_{i=1}^{n}|D_i|} \qquad \sigma_{gf} = \sqrt{\frac{\sum_{i=1}^{n}\sigma_{if}^2}{\sum_{i=1}^{n}|D_i|}} \tag{5}$$

First, μ_{gf} is computed as the weighted average of local means μ_{if}, where weights are the dataset sizes $|D_i|$. Next, each participant calculates its local variance σ_{if}^2 using μ_{gf}. Afterwards, σ_{gf} is derived by aggregating these σ_{if}^2 values, devided by the total dataset size, and taking the square root.

Knowing both values, each participant can carry out the Z-score normalization of a feature f locally. However, to carry out the required calculations, each participant P_i would normally disclose $|D_i|$ as well as μ_{if} and σ_{if}^2 of each numerical feature. To protect participants' sensitive data, we adopt and apply the Secure Average Computation (SAC) algorithm introduced by Wink and Nochta [26]. Originally designed for decentralized FML, we adapt SAC to the centralized setting with the server acting as a passive message relay.

To compute $\sum_{i=1}^{n}(\mu_{if} * |D_i|)$ for a feature f, each participant P_j generates n positive random numbers, $r_{1j}, r_{2j}, ..., r_{nj}$, one for each participant in the federation and multiplies its local μ_n by $|D_i|$. Afterwards, each participant P_j calculates n weighted parts of its own μ_n accordingly:

$$\mu_{i,j} = \mu_j * \frac{r_{ij}}{\sum_{i=1}^{n}r_{ij}} \tag{6}$$

where P_i is the intended receiver, P_j is the sender, and μ_j is the local mean of f that P_j wants to keep secret. These parts are exchanged between the participants, with each participant keeping its self-calculated $\mu_{i,j}$ value for $i = j$. By summing their own value where $i = j$ with the received values, each participant computes the partial sum $s_i = \sum_{i=1}^{i=n} \mu_{i,j}$, which is then exchanged with the others. Finally, the sum $s = \sum_{i=1}^{i=n} s_i$ is computed by each participant, representing $\sum_{i=1}^{n} (\mu_{if} * |D_i|)$.

By using this algorithm, all three required sums $\sum_{i=1}^{n} (\mu_{if} * |D_i|)$, $\sum_{i=1}^{n} |D_i|$ and $\sum_{i=1}^{n} \sigma_{if}^2$ can be calculated without disclosing any local values.

7   Privacy-Preserving Feature Encoding Methods

In the following, we present eight approaches to encode categorical data that aim to minimize or even eliminate the need for exchanging sensitive data. We categorize them as Round-Robin Identifier Allocation Protocols, Secure Multiparty Computation Protocols, and Alternative Encoding Protocols.

7.1   Round-Robin Identifier Allocation Protocols

All three protocols in this group utilize a round-robin (RR) approach—proposed in this work—for assigning globally unique identifiers to categorical values across the FML system. As shown in Fig. 3, this approach organizes all FML participants into a logical ring, enabling message exchange in a coordinated RR fashion. The process starts at participant P_1, who creates a dictionary d_f for a given categorical feature f. P_1 then transmits the highest identifier value assigned in the dictionary $max_1(d_f)$ to the next participant P_2 in the ring. P_2 generates its own dictionary by incrementing the just received value to create the lowest identifier $min_2(d_f) = max_1(d_f) + 1$. This procedure continues sequentially through all participants until the last participant, P_n, sends $max_n(d_f)$ to P_1, which then broadcasts $max_n(d_f)$ as the highest identifier value of f to all other participants. This guarantees that all participants are aware of the maximum encoding length, enabling, for example, a consistent one-hot encoding of f at all FML nodes. To ensure scalability and efficiency, each participant's message includes the highest identifiers from all their categorical features, rather than covering just one feature at a time.

Unique Identifier One-Hot Encoding (UHE) requires the participants to generate a unique one-hot encoding for all categorical features locally, after the RR protocol established unique identifiers and the global maximum $max_n(d_f)$ for each categorical feature. These encodings have a length corresponding to the $max_n(d_f)$ for a given feature f, replacing the original features.

This process enhances upon isolated local one-hot encoding by ensuring FML-wide unique identifiers for categorical values, while minimizing information disclosure in contrast to server-based encoding. This approach does not address the

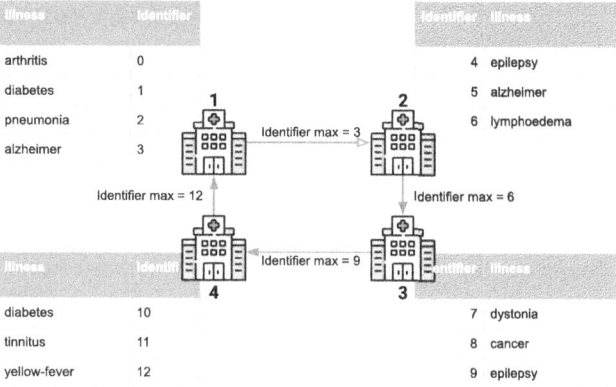

Fig. 3. Our Round-Robin protocol to assign unique identifiers to categorical features.

challenge of multiple identifiers for the same categorical value. Instead, we investigate whether simply establishing unique identifiers is sufficient for the model to learn and generalize across different encodings of the same underlying value.

Private Set Intersection (PSI) is a cryptographic protocol that allows users, to determine the intersection of their datasets (i.e., common elements) without revealing the rest of their data [6]. We apply PSI to resolve cases where multiple identifiers have been assigned to the same categorical value in participants' dictionaries. This collaborative process ensures a consistent encoding of identical values of a feature f while maintaining privacy.

Our protocol follows these steps: After assigning unique identifiers using the RR protocol, all n participants perform PSI with all other $n-1$ participants to identify their categorical value intersections $\bigcap_n = concat(\bigcap_1, \bigcap_2, ..., \bigcap_{n_1})$, then standardize encoding by adopting the lowest identifier value among intersections. For example, if participant P_x assigns *alzheimer = 3* and P_y sets *alzheimer = 0*, P_x updates to *0*, ensuring consistent representation of this disease across the federation.

We focus on the asymmetric PSI methods Asymmetrical Labeled PSI (APSI) and Practical Over-Threshold Multi-Party PSI (OT-MP-PSI), chosen for their adaptability to varying dictionary sizes, code availability, scientific recognition, and suitability for centralized and decentralized FML settings.

Asymmetrical Labeled Private Set Intersection (APSI) introduced by Cong et al. [6], uses a one-to-one communication pattern, where one participant acts as a client and the other as a server. Note that only the client learns the intersection of the two sets during a single protocol execution.

In our FML setting each participant runs the APSI protocol twice with every other participant: once as a client and once as a server, ensuring that all parties learn all potential intersections. To deploy APSI in FML participant must offer separate service instances for each other participant, because requests cannot be processed simultaneously due to the encryption. For a federation with n participants, this design requires $n \times (n-1)$ protocol executions to compute pairwise intersections across all participants.

Given the central FML server's role in managing communication in the federation, our protocol ensures that all APSI interactions are routed through the server. Since PSI requests are encrypted, the server cannot access the exchanged information, preserving participant privacy. One key advantage of APSI is its ability to exchange labels during the intersection computation. Thus, participants automatically receive the corresponding labels from intersecting values, eliminating the need for sending additional label requests.

Practical Over-Threshold Multi-Party PSI (OT-MP-PSI) by Mahdavi et al. [20] enables n entities to compute the intersection of their datasets, revealing an element only if it appears in at least $t \leq n$ datasets. It employs Shamir's Secret Sharing, encoding each element into a polynomial with a secret fixed at 0. An intersection is detected if any t shares reconstruct to 0.

Chosen participants are assigned as a keyholder (generating polynomials) or a reconstructor (verifying intersections). The keyholder engage in polynomial share generation with the participants, which then put these shares into padded bins. The reconstructor iterates over these bins, reconstructing secrets from different participants' shares. If a reconstructed value is 0, the intersection is reported.

To adapt this approach in our use case, we set $t = 2$, detecting all pairwise intersections. As the method is designed for numerical sets, we convert each categorical value x into an integer by first encoding it as bytes and then casting to integer: $x_t = int(bytes(x))$. At the start, the central server assigns the first and last participants in the RR ring structure as keyholder and reconstructor, respectively.

The reconstructor learns only the bin positions of intersections, not their contents. Upon detection, it informs participants of intersecting positions. For instance, P_1 learns that its element at position $(2, 3)$ in the padded bins intersects with P_2's element at position $(1, 4)$. Using these positions, participants exchange their identifiers, but not their values.

To minimize data transfer between participants, only participants with lower indices in the RR ring provide identifiers, as they assigned lower identifiers. Specifically, P_1 never requests identifiers, while P_n queries $P_1, \ldots, P_{n-1}$ as needed.

7.2   Secure Multiparty Computation Protocols

The following methods were designed to achieve encoding within the federation with minimal effort and without relying on complex encryption techniques. Both approaches leverage the SAC protocol previously employed in Sect. 6, enabling participants to collaboratively compute specific metrics without disclosing local values.

Bytes-Norm (BN) employs the encoding scheme for categorical features introduced in Sect. 7.1, where each categorical value x of a feature f is cast to an integer via its byte representation, formally $x_t = int(bytes(x))$. We treat the resulting numerical values x_t as standard numerical features, enabling the application of privacy-preserving Z-Score normalization using the μ_g and σ_g of the transformed feature f_t. The Z-Score normalization eliminates the extreme dimension differences of the x_t values. Unlike one-hot encoding, this approach treats categorical values as continuous numerical data, yielding a distinct encoding scheme. However, similar to label encoding, it does not preserve semantic relationships between categorical values when no natural order is present.

Mod-Norm (MN) extends the typecasting approach $x_t = int(bytes(x))$ by incorporating a binning approach based on a modulo operation, enabling the mapping of categorical values into a smaller numerical range. Each participant first transforms every categorical value x of the categorical feature f_i to x_t. Participants then compute the number of unique values $unq_i = |unq(f_i)|$ locally and securely aggregate the global sum $s_i = \sum_{j=1}^{n} unq_{ij}$ with the other n participants using SAC. The result s_i serves as an upper bound estimate of the distinct categorical values (duplicates or rather intersections are not considered between participants). Finally, each x_t is then encoded as $H_i = x_t \bmod (2s_i)$, with the factor 2 included to reduce the likelihood of collisions.

7.3   Alternative Encoding Strategies

This section explores encoding strategies from related work, proposed as alternatives to generic methods like one-hot or label encoding. Originating from natural language processing tasks or standard (i.e., non-federated) training settings, we evaluate their feasibility to encode tabular data in a FML setting.

FastText (FT) is a pre-trained word embedding model designed to map words into high-dimensional vector spaces [15]. Formally, given a bag of words S and a predefined embedding dimension d, FT assigns each entry $r \in S$ a dense vector representation $\phi(x)$. These embeddings are typically trained on extensive corpora to capture semantic relationships effectively. For example, synonyms or related terms like "illness" and "alzheimer" are positioned close to each other in the feature space, reflecting their contextual similarities. While this property is valuable for text representation, our work focuses on a different application: We utilize FT mainly to encode categorical features within a dataset.

A key advantage of FT is its ability to generate embeddings for out-of-vocabulary words using subword information. This property ensures that any categorical value $x \notin S$ can still be mapped to a unique vector $\phi(x)$ by leveraging character-level n-grams.

In a FML setting, this guarantees that all participants can independently compute identical vector representations for the same categorical feature value without exchanging raw data. Specifically, given a categorical feature f with a dictionary of unique values D_f, we apply FT to obtain a fixed-length vector representation for each entry $\forall x \in D_f, v_x = \phi(x), v_x \in \mathbb{R}^{300}$ where we utilize the pre-trained English word embedding model of FT with a vector dimension of $d = 300$. This enables a consistent and privacy-preserving encoding mechanism for categorical features across all federated learning participants.

Target Encoding (TE) replaces categorical values with the mean of their corresponding target variable, with the target class typically set to 1 in binary classification problems [21]. A categorical value x of a feature f is transformed such that:

$$x_t = \frac{frequency(x) * p(f = x|c = 1) + \alpha * \mu_c}{frequency(x) + \alpha} \tag{7}$$

where frequency(x) represents the frequency of x in the feature, $p(f = x \mid c = 1)$ is the probability of x occurring given the target class $c = 1$, μ_c is the mean of the target label c, and α is a smoothing parameter to mitigate overfitting or poor encoding for small datasets. TE is prone to overfitting and target leakage, where information from the target variable unintentionally influences predictions, causing overly optimistic results and misleading model performance assessments.

For federated TE, we propose two strategies: local TE without communication, ensuring privacy but risking inconsistent encodings, and sharing probability values to unify encodings, compromising privacy, as probabilities and clear text values are revealed. To prioritize privacy, we adopt the first approach, allowing participants to encode values independently without data exchange.

Rolling Hash (RH) proposed by Nagy et al. [22] serves as a benchmark to compare our proposed approaches against an established technique for federated encoding. While originally applied to NLP tasks, this method is one the only work we are aware of that addresses federated encoding, making it a valuable point of reference. Adapting the protocol for categorical features, each categorical value is lowercased and hashed using $H = \sum_{i=1}^{|s|} s_i * P^i \mod M$ where $|s|$ is the string length, s_i is the position of the i-th character in the alphabet ($a = 1, b = 2, \ldots, z = 26$), $P = 31$ is a prime exceeding the alphabet size, and $M = 5000$ defines the vector length. The resulting H determines the position in the M-length vector set to 1 for a word's occurrence. Repeating this for each categorical value produces a 5000-length one-hot vector encoding. Following the original work, which represents an entire text features in a single 5000-length vector, we similarly encode all categorical features in a shared 5000-length vector. This reduces sparsity compared to the standard one-hot encoding per feature, leveraging the assumption that this dimensionality suffices for multiple categorical variables, as it does for text data.

8   Experimental Evaluation

To identify the most suitable secure encoding protocol, we evaluate them based on four dimensions: impact on model quality, scalability in federated settings

Table 2. Dataset specifications, including amount of categorical and numerical features as well as categorical features encoded under different approach

Dataset	Features	Categorical	Numerical	One-Hot	FT	RH	Data Points
Adult	13	8	5	105	2404	5013	45222
German	20	13	7	63	3908	5020	1000
Health Heritage	17	6	11	110	1811	5011	218415
Lawschool	7	5	2	39	1502	5006	96584
CC Fraud	7	4	4	1206	904	5004	137775

(message exchange and runtime), changes in input vector dimensionality, and information leakage to participants or the central server.

For this evaluation, we utilize the same datasets described in Sect. 5.3. In Table 2 we collected an overview of the datasets, incl. the number of numerical and categorical features, size of the full dataset, and input dimensions using different encodings. The number of features describes the state after the datasets were feature engineered, i.e., by adding or removing different features.

The proposed protocols were implemented using Protocol Buffers for message formatting and ZeroMQ for message transmission between clients and the server. Preprocessing and federated training were simulated on a single machine with four NVIDIA TITAN Xp GPUs (12 GB VRAM), four Intel(R) Xeon(R) CPU E5-2660 v4 @ 2.00GHz, and 64 GB RAM. Unless stated otherwise, the simulated federation included one server and four participants. This baseline was chosen because the SAC protocol requires at least three participants and aligns with the available resources, allowing each participant to use a dedicated GPU and CPU.

8.1   Impact on Model Quality

We first assess each method's impact on model quality by applying the selected encoding for preprocessing, followed by federated training. We track test F1-scores across epochs and stop training once performance stabilizes. The F1-scores across the federation were calculated by summing the local confusion matrices derived from each participant's test data. However, in real federations, such matrices should never be exchanged, as they could reveal sensitive information, including participant labels and data quantities. This approach was used solely for evaluation in the context of this work.

Both PSI methods produce the same results, therefore we collectively evaluated them as "PSI". We integrated the authors' PSI implementations into our preprocessing service using a C-to-Python wrapper. As shown in Table 3, PSI outperformed all other methods by preserving both the input data and the underlying model. It delivers results identical to unsecured server-based encoding with a global dictionary while also ensuring data privacy.

Table 3. F1-Scores of federated model training with four participants using different approaches for encoding, including isolated local preprocessing, in a non-IID setting. The best results are highlighted in bold for each dataset

Dataset	Server-Based Benchmark	Privacy Preserving Methods PSI	Local	UHE	BN	MN	FT	RH	TE
Adult	0.69	**0.69**	0.60	0.50	0.0	0.30	0.62	0.65	**0.69**
German	0.79	**0.79**	0.30	0.55	0.0	0.53	0.75	0.31	0.55
Health Heritage	0.69	0.69	0.63	0.63	0.54	0.59	0.67	**0.70**	0.65
Lawschool	0.71	**0.71**	0.69	0.46	0.53	0.56	0.66	0.69	0.67
CC Fraud	0.90	**0.90**	0.80	0.64	0.0	0.83	0.89	0.88	0.84

The Bytes algorithm performed worst, consistently underperforming local preprocessing and yielding F1-Scores of 0 for three datasets. MN and UHE showed moderate but unstable performance, often degrading model quality. UHE only outperformed local preprocessing once, highlighting that establishing unique identifiers alone is insufficient.

FT, RH, and TE emerged as the best-performing alternatives to PSI. Although TE matched federated preprocessing in one instance, it struggled on the German dataset. Similarly, RH beats local preprocessing by only 1% on the German dataset. FT demonstrated stable performance across all five datasets, outperforming local preprocessing on those with numerous categorical values. Apart from FT and PSI, the other approaches resulted in significant loss of model quality. We attribute this to the fact that they introduce a lot of sparsity or use numerical representation for features that can't be sorted.

8.2   Scaling Analysis

We assess federated scalability by evaluating message complexity among n participants using O-notation. For OT-MP-PSI we estimate the worst-case scenario, where participants in the ring must request intersections from all preceding participants. PSI achieves the highest model quality but incurs the highest communication overhead. APSI, in particular, exhibits rapid growth in communication demands as n increases, while BN, MN, and UHE scale moderately. FT, RH, and TE are the most efficient, requiring no inter-participant communication.

Empirical runtime evaluations on the Adult dataset confirm these trends. We measure the time from the server's preprocessing request to completion (Table 4). Since experiments were conducted locally, network-related delays in real-world federations were not considered. Execution times were measured as n increased from 4 to 10. BN, MN, and Local Encoding exhibit the fastest runtimes (< 100 ms), with Local Preprocessing unaffected by federation size. RH, TE, and UHE take longer, with TE being four times faster than RH.

Among research-based methods, FT is the slowest (20 s) due to embedding model loading. PSI-based methods have the highest latency. APSI is more effi-

Table 4. Runtimes (in msec) of encoding approaches using the Adult dataset

Participants	Local	MPSI	APSI	UHE	BN	MN	FT	RH	TE
4	≈41	63673	28280	264	89	52	≈20799	≈853	≈183
6	≈41	105210	64819	377	96	52	≈20799	≈853	≈183
8	≈41	119530	140913	520	99	62	≈20799	≈853	≈183
10	≈41	148776	227524	636	111	67	≈20799	≈853	≈183

cient than OT-MP-PSI for small federations (4âĂŞ6 participants) but less so beyond eight. These results indicate a clear trade-off between model quality and preprocessing time.

8.3 Input Dimension

We evaluate the input dimension by measuring the size of the original data point vector $|V|$ after encoding the categorical features $|C|$ and adding the numerical features $|N|$. For instance, in one-hot encoding, the original features are removed from the vector, and the encoding is added to the data point. The same applies to FT and RH, where a new encoding replaces the original features.

TE, MN, and BN achieve the smallest input dimensions by converting categorical features into numerical values. Unique Identifier One-Hot and PSI methods result in input dimensions comparable to traditional one-hot encoding, offering more efficient dimensions compared to isolated local encoding by avoiding padding. FT and RH substantially increase input dimensions, leading to higher hardware costs. FT scales linearly with the embedding size (300 in these experiments) and the number of categorical values, whereas RH generates fixed-size sparse vectors of 5000 in our setup.

8.4 Privacy Analysis

All introduced algorithms meet the established privacy requirements, defined in Sect. 3. While neither the server nor participants gain knowledge of others' local datasets, this does not eliminate the need for exchanging or disclosing certain information. PSI-based approaches reveal intersections $\bigcap_f$ of a feature f between participants, thereby they only gain information about values present in their local datasets. Therefore, all parties have to consent to share potential intersections.

Additionally, BN and the protocols utilizing the RR, disclose an approximation of the sum of all unique values $\approx |unq(f)|$ in feature f. However, no intersections between participants are considered, and meaningful inferences are complex to draw for categorical features without limiting the value range. Furthermore, the second participant in the ring during RR can infer the size of the first participant's dictionary. Adding padding or noise can obscure this but increases one-hot encoding dimensionality, thus introducing sparsity.

Table 5. Comparison of the privacy-preserving categorical feature encodings

Method	Federated Scaling	Input Dimension	Δ F1-Score	Shared Infos
Local	$O(1)$	$|N|$ + One-Hot	15.4%	$|V|$
APSI	$O(4n - 2n - 1)$	$|N|$ + One-Hot	0%	$\approx |unq(f)| + \bigcap_f$
OT-MP-PSI	$O(8n - 7 + \sum_{i=1}^{n} n - i)$	$|N|$ + One-Hot	0%	$\approx |unq(f)| + \bigcap_f$
UHE	$O(2n - 1)$	$|N|$ + One-Hot	18.2%	$\approx |unq(f)|$
BN	$O(2n - 2)$	$|V|$	52.6%	Z-Score statistics
MN	$O(4n - 4)$	$|V|$	19.4%	$\approx |unq(f)|$
FT	$O(1)$	$|N|$ + Embed	3.8%	None
RH	$O(1)$	$|V|$ + Bucket	11.0%	None
TE	$O(1)$	$|V|$	7.6%	None

Z-Score normalization does not disclose local values. However, it reveals aggregated metrics, such as the sums of weighted local means, the total number of data points in the federation, and the sum of variances. Furthermore, both the server and participants gain access to μ_g and σ_g for each normalized feature. The same applies to MN, which uses the Z-Score to normalize the casted categorical values. Nonetheless, the exposure of these values offers limited actionable information, as the large numerical range of encoded strings makes it challenging to derive meaningful insights.

The FT, RH, and TE protocols meet all of our established privacy goals and exceed them in several areas. By eliminating the need to share data among participants, they prevent disclosing sensitive information and introduce no additional communication overhead. As a result, these protocols provide a higher level of privacy than all other approaches evaluated, achieving a standard comparable to the robust data confidentiality of locally isolated label encoding.

8.5   Discussion

Categorical feature preprocessing in FML must balance privacy, scalability, and model quality. Among the evaluated methods, PSI and FT offer the best trade-offs, while others compromise model quality, provide limited privacy benefits, or perform similarly to local preprocessing. Table 5 summarizes these results.

PSI ensures consistent encoding and model quality preservation, especially on datasets like the German dataset where other methods underperform. However, it poses privacy risks by revealing intersections and leaking metadata via the RR protocol. PSI also incurs high runtimes and scalability costs, though it integrates easily without hardware changes or model adjustments. We recommend PSI when model quality is critical, scalability is manageable, and a certain trust between participants and the server can be ensured. It is also preferable when FT's hardware demands are impractical. Between OT-MP-PSI and APSI, the latter is better for federations with up to 10 participants due to its decentralized design, which improves resilience by enabling seamless continuation despite node failures or late additions.

FT offers a privacy-first approach by encoding data locally without participant communication, ensuring scalability with constant computational costs. However, it demands substantial resources, including a 7 GB pre-trained model, high memory usage, and increased neural network input sizes due to word embedding size. Additionally, it degrades model quality by about 3.8%. FT is ideal when privacy and scalability are priorities, particularly in untrusted environments where HBC assumptions don't hold and extra hardware is available.

Limitations: Privacy-related limitations of secure Z-Score normalization in FML arise from the exposure of global statistics, such as μ_g and σ_g. While these values might be accessible, inferring exact local contributions becomes increasingly difficult as the number of participants grows, reducing the risk of individual data leakage. However, global statistics remain essential to ensure consistent preprocessing across all participants.

As an alternative to SAC, we considered DP and HE for Secure Z-Score normalization, but their limitations make them unsuitable for this problem. DP protects individual values by introducing noise and could be viable in two-party settings where SMC is infeasible. However, it reduces precision while still requiring the exchange of global scaling parameters for consistent preprocessing. HE, on the other hand, imposes significant computational overhead, particularly in multi-party settings. Operations like standard deviation require square roots, which HE does not natively support and must approximate using complex polynomial functions, further increasing computational costs. Since both methods ultimately necessitate sharing global statistics, they offer no advantage over SMC, which we selected for its efficiency and practicality.

Additionally, we only cover Z-Score in its paper due to its resistance to outliers. If an Outlier Detection is integrated into a federated preprocessing pipeline, other alternatives, such as Min-Max scaling or Robust Scaling should be adapted and investigated in FML as well. Incorporating these techniques while preserving privacy poses challenges, requiring methods, such as Garbled Circuits, which demand further refinement. A comprehensive evaluation and implementation of various scaling methods within a FL setting warrant a dedicated research study.

In conclusion, none of the investigated approaches fully preserved model quality while ensuring complete privacy. Striking a balance between privacy and performance often necessitates some degree of data exchange, highlighting the ongoing challenge and the need for further novel methodologies to achieve both objectives effectively.

9   Conclusion

This paper examined the impact of encoding and scaling in horizontal FML, showing that inconsistent local preprocessing significantly degrades model performance. Primary contributors to poor model quality are the so-called "dictionary problems", resulting in duplicate or mismatched identifiers for the same feature values. However, achieving uniform scaling and encoding requires sharing sensitive clear text categorical values and statistical properties, posing privacy risks. To address these concerns, we proposed a privacy-preserving Z-Score normalization method using Secure Multiparty Computation, ensuring that only aggregated global statistics are shared. For categorical encoding, we introduced eight privacy-preserving methods, each offering different trade-offs between privacy, scaling, input dimensionality and model quality. Experiments on five datasets demonstrated that a Round-Robin protocol combined with PSI matched the performance of unsecured uniform preprocessing but incurred high computational costs and requires trust between participants. The most private methods Rolling Hash and fastText avoid direct data exchange, though only fastText maintained competitive model quality. However, it also increased model complexity and hardware demands due to its use of word embeddings. Since our scaling and encoding methods are ML framework-agnostic, they are compatible with TensorFlow, PyTorch, and Scikit-learn. Leveraging our gRPC and ZMQ setup, the preprocessing prototype can be integrated into Flower pipelines prior to training, enabling secure and scalable preprocessing in practice. We recommend PSI when high model quality is essential, provided trust among participants and scalable resources are available. When privacy and scaling are the primary concerns, FT offers a secure alternative, though with efficiency trade-offs and local hardware requirements. To support future research and adoption, our source code and implementation details will be publicly released upon publication.

Acknowledgments. This work was co-funded by the European Union in the Interreg Upper Rhine program (project aura.ai).

References

1. Adnan, M., Kalra, S., Cresswell, J.C., Taylor, G.W., Tizhoosh, H.R.: Federated learning and differential privacy for medical image analysis. Sci. Rep. **12**(1), 1953 (2022)
2. Akavia, A., Galili, B., Shaul, H., Weiss, M., Yakhini, Z.: Privacy preserving feature selection for sparse linear regression. Cryptology ePrint Archive (2023)
3. Becker, B., Kohavi, R.: Adult. UCI Machine Learning Repository (1996). https://doi.org/10.24432/C5XW20
4. Byrd, D., Polychroniadou, A.: Differentially private secure multi-party computation for federated learning in financial applications (2020). https://doi.org/10.48550/ARXIV.2010.05867
5. Ceri, S., Bozzon, A., Brambilla, M., Valle, E.D., Fraternali, P.: Web Information Retrieval. Data-Centric Systems and Applications. Springer, Berlin, Heidelberg (2013). https://doi.org/10.1007/978-3-642-39314-3
6. Cong, K., et al.: Labeled psi from homomorphic encryption with reduced computation and communication. Cryptology ePrint Archive, Paper 2021/1116 (2021). https://eprint.iacr.org/2021/1116

7. Das, S., Ray Chowdhury, S., Chandran, N., Gupta, D., Lokam, S., Sharma, R.: Communication efficient secure and private multi-party deep learning. Proc. Priv. Enhancing Technol. **2025**, 169–183 (2025)
8. Eichner, H., et al.: Confidential federated computations. arXiv preprint arXiv:2404.10764 (2024)
9. Eleks, M., Rebstadt, J., Kortum, H., Thomas, O.: Privacy aware processing (2023)
10. Fowl, L., Geiping, J., Czaja, W., Goldblum, M., Goldstein, T.: Robbing the fed: Directly obtaining private data in federated learning with modified models. arXiv preprint arXiv:2110.13057 (2021)
11. Geiping, J., Bauermeister, H., Dröge, H., Moeller, M.: Inverting gradients - how easy is it to break privacy in federated learning? CoRR abs/2003.14053 (2020). https://arxiv.org/abs/2003.14053
12. Hard, A., et al.: Federated learning for mobile keyboard prediction. CoRR abs/1811.03604 (2018)
13. Hofmann, H.: Statlog (German Credit Data). UCI Machine Learning Repository (1994). https://doi.org/10.24432/C5NC77
14. Hsu, R.H., Huang, T.Y.: Private data preprocessing for privacy-preserving federated learning. In: 2022 IEEE 5th International Conference on Knowledge Innovation and Invention (ICKII), pp. 173–178. IEEE (2022)
15. Joulin, A., Grave, E., Bojanowski, P., Mikolov, T.: Bag of tricks for efficient text classification. arXiv preprint arXiv:1607.01759 (2016)
16. Kalra, S., Wen, J., Cresswell, J.C., Volkovs, M., Tizhoosh, H.R.: ProxyFL: decentralized federated learning through proxy model sharing. CoRR abs/2111.11343 (2021). https://arxiv.org/abs/2111.11343
17. Li, X., Dowsley, R., Cock, M.D.: Privacy-preserving feature selection with secure multiparty computation (2021). https://arxiv.org/abs/2102.03517
18. Liu, Z., Chen, S., Ye, J., Fan, J., Li, H., Li, X.: DHSA: efficient doubly homomorphic secure aggregation for cross-silo federated learning (2022)
19. Lyu, L., Chen, C.: A novel attribute reconstruction attack in federated learning (2021). https://doi.org/10.48550/ARXIV.2108.06910
20. Mahdavi, R.A., et al.: Practical over-threshold multi-party private set intersection. In: Proceedings of the 36th Annual Computer Security Applications Conference, pp. 772–783. ACSAC '20, Association for Computing Machinery (2020). https://doi.org/10.1145/3427228.3427267
21. Micci-Barreca, D.: A preprocessing scheme for high-cardinality categorical attributes in classification and prediction problems. ACM SIGKDD Explor. Newsl **3**(1), 27–32 (2001)
22. Nagy, B., et al.: Kiss: privacy-preserving federated learning and its application to natural language processing. Knowl.-Based Syst. **268**, 110475 (2023). https://www.sciencedirect.com/science/article/pii/S0950705123002253
23. Vero, M., Balunović, M., Dimitrov, D.I., Vechev, M.: TabLeak: tabular data leakage in federated learning (2023)
24. Wang, Z., Ji, H., Zhu, Y., Wang, D., Han, Z.: A survey on federated analytics: taxonomy, enabling techniques, applications and open issues (2025). https://arxiv.org/abs/2404.12666
25. Wightman, F.L.: LSAC national longitudinal bar passage study (2017)
26. Wink, T., Nochta, Z.: An approach for peer-to-peer federated learning. In: Proceedings of 51st Annual IEEE/IFIP International Conference on Dependable Systems and Networks Workshops (DSN-W) (2021)

27. Wu, H., Zhao, Z., Chen, L.Y., Moorsel, A.V.: Federated learning for tabular data: exploring potential risk to privacy. In: 2022 IEEE 33rd International Symposium on Software Reliability Engineering (ISSRE), pp. 193–204. IEEE Computer Society, Los Alamitos, CA, USA (2022). https://doi.ieeecomputersociety.org/10.1109/ISSRE55969.2022.00028
28. Zhu, J., Blaschko, M.B.: R-GAP: recursive gradient attack on privacy. In: International Conference on Learning Representations (2021). https://openreview.net/forum?id=RSU17UoKfJF

BTDT: Membership Inference Attacks Against Large Language Models

Shadi Farokhghate$^{(\boxtimes)}$, Ali Abbasi Tadi, and Dima Alhadidi

University of Windsor, 401 Sunset Ave, Windsor, ON N9B 3P4, Canada
{farokhg,abbasit,dima.alhadidi}@uwindsor.ca

Abstract. Given a machine learning model and a record, Membership Inference Attacks (MIAs) determine whether this record was used as part of the model training dataset. This can raise privacy issues. MIAs pose a significant threat to the privacy of machine learning models, particularly when the training dataset contains confidential information. MIAs often take advantage of a model's tendency to overfit its training data, resulting in lower loss values for the training data than for non-training data. Recently, a new MIA against language models was designed based on a decision rule that compares the difference between the loss value of the target sample under the target model and the average loss of its neighboring samples against a threshold. They generate neighborhoods with simple word replacements that preserve the semantics and fit the context of the original word using Masked Language Models (MLMs). In this work, we propose Back Translation and Dynamic Thresholding (BTDT), a novel MIA. BTDT generates more realistic and diverse neighbor samples using back translation and introduces a dynamic thresholding mechanism, resulting in more adaptive and accurate membership inference. The results indicate that by employing dynamic thresholding, the attack's false positive and false negative rates can be effectively managed, thereby enhancing its robustness and efficiency.

Keywords: Membership Inference Attacks (MIAs) · Large Language Models (LLMs) · Back Translation

1 Introduction

Membership Inference Attacks (MIAs) [1] are a type of privacy attack in which an adversary aims to determine whether a specific data point was part of the training dataset, potentially leaking confidential information such as medical records or personal identifiers. By analyzing the behaviour of the model, the adversary can identify patterns that differentiate between data points included in the training set and those that are not. This ability poses significant privacy risks, mainly when training data contains sensitive information. MIAs have emerged as one of the most widely used approaches to assess data leakage and empirically examine the privacy vulnerabilities of machine learning models. Building

M. Dalla Preda et al. (Eds.): ARES 2025, LNCS 15992, pp. 425–436, 2025.
https://doi.org/10.1007/978-3-032-00624-0_21

on the identified privacy risks in machine learning models, this work focuses on evaluating the potential for information leakage in Large Language Models (LLMs) through MIAs. Given their extensive training on vast datasets, LLMs are particularly susceptible to exposing sensitive data from their training set.

Shokri et al. [1] introduced an approach based on shadow models for MIAs, which requires significant resources and knowledge of the target model's architecture, making them impractical for LLMs. Likelihood Ratio Attacks (LiRAs) [3,4,6,8,9] address some limitations by using auxiliary data for calibration, but such datasets are often unavailable in privacy-sensitive contexts. A new MIA through neighborhood comparison proposed by Mattern et al. [2] avoids auxiliary datasets by generating neighbors using Masked Language Models (MLMs), although these neighbors often lack semantic diversity. We aim to create a more realistic and diverse set of neighbors that better capture the characteristics of data points by utilizing back translation. Back translation, a technique commonly used in Natural Language Processing (NLP) for data augmentation, involves translating a text sample to another language and then translating it back to the original language. This process preserves the semantic content of the sample while introducing natural variations. This approach ensures that the generated neighbors remain contextually relevant. These neighbors closely resemble the target point, but are not part of the training set. The paraphrased text produced through back translation retains the contextual coherence of the original text. Unlike random replacements or synonym substitutions, neighbors generated using back translation are more likely to fit naturally within the original context, providing more realistic variations that better reflect the nuances of the training data. We determined membership by comparing the model's loss value for the target data point with those of its neighbors. The target data point is likely not in the training set if the loss values are similar. If the loss value of the target data point is significantly lower, it indicates overfitting and suggests that the target sample is from the training data. For this comparison and inferring membership, recent work uses a static threshold. In this work, we propose a novel mechanism, the Neighborhood Loss Coefficient (NLC) and dynamic thresholding, to enhance the accuracy of MIAs. NLC introduces a dynamic adjustment to the decision boundary. NLC enables us to infer the membership of a target data point using dynamic thresholding, providing a more adaptive and precise method for attack decision making. It offers flexibility and enhances attack robustness in complex, high-variance datasets while reducing false positives and false negatives by dynamically adapting to the target sample's neighborhood. In particular, our contributions are as follows.

- **New Back Translation and Dynamic Thresholding (BTDT) MIA**. We propose a new MIA attack BTDT against LLMs that depends on the following techniques:
  - **Novel Neighborhood Generation Strategy for MIAs Against LLMs.** We introduce a new method for generating neighborhood samples for MIAs against LLMs. This approach utilizes back translation to

generate neighboring samples and provides a new perspective on how to create realistic and contextually coherent neighbors.

- **Introduction of Neighborhood Loss Coefficient and Dynamic Thresholding.** We introduce a novel mechanism, the Neighborhood Loss Coefficient (NLC) and dynamic thresholding, to enhance the robustness of the MIA. This method dynamically adapts the threshold, offering more robust performance compared to fixed-threshold approaches.
- **Experimental Results.** We evaluate the performance BTDT, using AUC score, recall, precision, and F1 score. Our results demonstrate that BTDT performs better in inferring membership compared to existing methods [2,13, 14].

2   Related Work

MIAs have emerged as a critical concern in machine learning, especially regarding the privacy of training data. Shokri *et al.* [1] pioneered this domain, introducing the concept of MIAs. They demonstrated that adversaries could infer whether specific data points were part of the training set by training shadow models that mimic the behaviour of the target model. This foundational work laid the groundwork for subsequent research, highlighting the privacy risks of machine learning models. A membership inference attack using the shadow training technique [1] involves creating numerous shadow models, often hundreds [4]. These shadow models are designed to have the same or similar architecture as the target model. However, relying on shadow training limits its applicability to LLMs. Gaining full details of the training algorithms used by these state-of-the-art models is often challenging, as they are considered intellectual property and are not publicly disclosed.

MIAs often take advantage of a model's tendency to overfit its training data, resulting in lower loss values for the training data than for non-training data [5,10]. One common and straightforward MIA is the LOSS attack [5], which classifies a sample as part of the training set if its loss value falls below a specific threshold. Although these attacks often show high accuracy, a significant issue is that the high accuracy is mainly due to the attack's ability to correctly identify non-training samples rather than training samples, which does not pose a significant privacy threat [4]. The problem arises because specific samples, such as repetitive or straightforward short sentences, naturally receive higher probabilities from the model [7,11]. This inherent characteristic of the samples affects the model's score more than the model's tendency to overfit its training data. To solve this, researchers introduced difficulty calibration mechanisms [6,12]. These mechanisms assess the intrinsic complexity of a data sample and use this complexity to adjust model scores before comparing them to a threshold. Practically, difficulty calibration is mostly implemented through Likelihood Ratio Attacks (LiRAs) [3,4]. LiRAs evaluate the difficulty of a target point by feeding it to reference models, which offer a view of the likelihood that target point is within

428 S. Farokhghate et al.

the given domain [6,8,9]. LiRAs assume that an adversary is aware of the target model's training data distribution and has access to a sufficient number of samples to train reference models. However, this assumption is overly optimistic and often unrealistic, particularly in privacy-sensitive fields where data leakage is a concern (e.g., the medical domain). In such cases, high-quality public data within the same domain is typically unavailable, rendering reference-based attacks ineffective.

Recently, Mattern *et al.* [2] designed a membership inference attack against language models that does not rely on additional data. This attack is via neighborhood comparison, where the membership decision is based on comparing the loss difference of a sample with the average loss of its synthetic neighbors. This method leverages the model's tendency to produce lower loss values for training samples compared to synthetic neighbors generated through perturbations. In this study, Mattern *et al.* [2] generated neighborhoods with simple word replacements that preserve semantics and fit the context of the original word using MLMs. Furthermore, the MIN-K% PROB [13] method introduces an approach that examines the probability distribution of words in a text, identifying outlier probabilities to infer membership status without knowing the pretraining corpus. Based on this, the Min-K%++ [14] method offers a theoretically motivated enhancement by identifying training samples as local maxima in the modeled distribution along each input dimension. These methods are also reference-free and do not rely on additional data.

Building on the limitations of previously discussed methods, we propose a novel MIA leveraging neighborhood comparison. Our approach, BTDT, utilizes back translation to generate diverse and realistic neighbors and incorporates dynamic thresholds in the decision rule, enabling more precise membership inference for each sample.

3 BTDT

In this section, we present a detailed explanation of our attack (BTDT), beginning with the general idea and then outlining the proposed process for MIA.

3.1 General Idea

Let M refer to a model trained on a dataset D_{train}. We aim to evaluate the privacy risks of M for the members of the training data set D_{train}. We consider grey-box access to the target model, where the adversary can only provide inputs to the model and receive the model output(s). We assume that the attacker knows the loss values of the model for the inputs. Given a sample s we want to determine whether $s \in D_{train}$ or $s \notin D_{train}$.

In a LOSS attack, the adversary uses the model's loss values to infer membership status. The assumption is that the model exhibits lower loss values for data points it has seen during training than those it has not. The adversary computes the model's loss for a given sample s and compares it against a predetermined threshold λ. If the loss value for the data sample identified by $\mathcal{L}(M, s)$ is less than this threshold, the adversary classifies the data point as a member of the training set; otherwise, it is classified as a non-member. Recent attacks use a similar framework, but include difficulty calibration to consider the intrinsic complexity of the sample s within the target distribution, adjusting its loss value accordingly. They use a function $d : S \rightarrow \mathbb{R}$ that assigns difficulty scores to data samples and then they compute $\mathcal{L}(M, s) - d(s)$. If this value is less than the threshold $(\mathcal{L}(M, s) - d(s) < \lambda)$, the adversary classifies the data point as a member of the training set; otherwise, it is classified as a non-member.

LiRAs involve the use of a reference model f_ϕ to assign a difficulty score to each data point, as shown in Eq. 1. This score is derived from the loss value $\mathcal{L}(f_\phi, s)$ of the reference model when evaluated on the data point s, making the suitability of this score dependent on the quality of the reference model and the availability of data from the training distribution.

$$d(s) = \mathcal{L}(f_\phi, s) \tag{1}$$

Mattern *et al.* [2] designed a new difficulty calibration function that does not need any reference model and data from the training distribution. For a given sample s, they produce a set of n neighbors using MLMs. Then, they calculate the difference between the target model's loss value for the target data point s and its neighbors and classify the target sample as a member if

$$\mathcal{L}(M, s) - \sum_{i=1}^{n} \frac{\mathcal{L}(M, s_i')}{n} < \lambda. \tag{2}$$

where s_i' denotes a neighboring data point of s.

3.2   Proposed Architecture

BTDT introduces back translation as a novel technique for the generation of neighborhoods in MIAs. Back translation involves translating a text sample to another language and then translating it back to the original language. This process generates semantically equivalent but syntactically diverse samples that can be used as neighbors for the original data point. Furthermore, we add a new condition to the decision rule. We know that the target model has a lower loss value for its training dataset than for other samples, including neighborhood samples. Considering this in the decision rule, we classify the target sample as a member if

$$\mathcal{L}(M, s) - \sum_{i=1}^{n} \frac{\mathcal{L}(M, s_i')}{n} < \lambda \quad \text{and} \quad \mathcal{L}(M, s) < \sum_{i=1}^{n} \frac{\mathcal{L}(M, s_i')}{n} \tag{3}$$

This means that we should choose a negative threshold for comparison, so the second condition will be automatically considered. To enhance the accuracy of MIAs, we introduce a new factor called the Neighborhood Loss Coefficient (NLC), which allows us to use a dynamic threshold for each sample instead of a static one. NLC is a parameter applied to the average loss of neighboring samples. Unlike a static threshold, NLC allows the decision boundary to be dynamically adjusted based on the characteristics of the loss values of the neighbors, ensuring that the attack is sensitive to varying loss distributions. Specifically, the decision function compares the loss of the target sample with the scaled average loss of its neighbors, as expressed by:

$$\mathcal{L}(M, s) - \sum_{i=1}^{n} \frac{\mathcal{L}(M, s_i')}{n} < -NLC. \sum_{i=1}^{n} \frac{\mathcal{L}(M, s_i')}{n} \qquad (4)$$

The introduction of the Neighborhood Loss Coefficient and using a dynamic threshold add a layer of flexibility to the decision function, allowing it to be more adaptive to different scenarios. Figure 1 outlines the overall flow of our proposed method.

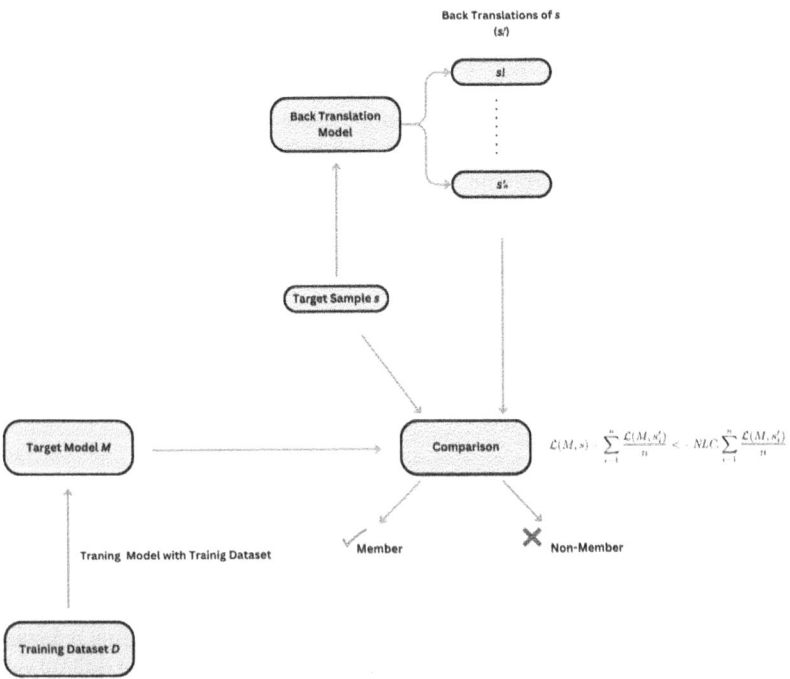

Fig. 1. BTDT Framework. Given a target sample s, we use back translation to generate neighbors. Then, the target model's loss values for these neighbors are compared to the loss value of the original sample under the target model. As the neighbors are close in context to the target sample, their loss values are expected to be similar unless the target sample is part of the model's training set. In that case, the loss difference will be below the threshold.

4   Evaluation

In this section, we conduct a comprehensive evaluation of the performance of BTDT against LLMs. The code for this study is available at this anonymous GitHub repository [16].

4.1   Experimental Setup

Datasets. We conducted our experiments using subsets of the AG News and DBpedia datasets, accessed via the Hugging Face datasets library [15]. The subset of the AG News dataset used in our experiments contains 15,200 samples, split into two equal, non-overlapping subsets of 7,600 samples each. One subset is used to train the target model, providing positive examples for the membership classification task, while the other subset, which is not utilized for training, serves as the source of negative examples. Also, the sunset of the DBpedia dataset consists of 2,000 samples, with 1,000 used for training and the remaining 1,000 as non-members for further evaluation.

Target Model. As our target model, we acquire and fine-tune the pre-trained 117M parameter version of GPT-2 using the Huggingface transformers library and PyTorch.

4.2   Experimental Results

In this section, we present the results of our experiments, including a comparison with existing methods [2, 13, 14].

Benchmarking. For comparative analysis, we selected the approaches introduced by Mattern *et al.* [2], Zhang *et al.* [14], and Shi *et al.* [13] as our baselines. As seen in the following tables, BTDT consistently outperforms existing approaches in terms of AUC, precision, recall, and F1 score. Table 1 shows the comparison of BTDT with the baseline methods on the AG News dataset. For the MIN-K% PROB and Min-K%++ methods, we evaluated the performance by setting K to 10%. In these methods, K denotes the percentage of tokens with the lowest probabilities used to compute the average log-likelihood. Our method outperforms the others across all metrics. This is due to a combination of back translation for generating semantically diverse neighbors and dynamic thresholding with the Neighborhood Loss Coefficient (NLC), which together allow for more accurate membership inference.

Table 2 illustrates the True Positive Rate (TPR) at fixed False Positive Rates (FPR) on the AG News dataset. Our method achieves higher TPRs. The dynamic thresholding mechanism, aided by NLC, provides more flexibility in adjusting the decision boundary, improving recall without increasing false positives compared to the static thresholds used by the baseline methods.

Table 1. Comparison of Performance Metrics - AG News Dataset

Method	AUC%	Precision%	Recall%	F1 Score%
Shi *et al.* [13] (MIN-K% PROB)	53.36	43.46	54.20	57.57
Zhang *et al.* [14] (Min-K%++)	52.75	50.76	52.87	53.67
Mattern *et al.* [2] (neighbor Attack)	80.32	83.84	78.32	79.60
BTDT	**98.35**	**96.71**	**100**	**98.38**

Table 2. True Positive Rate (TPR) at 2%, 5% and 10% False Positive Rate (FPR) - AG News Dataset

Method	2%	5%	10%
Shi *et al.* [13] (MIN-K% PROB)	2.23	5.59	11.19
Zhang *et al.* [14] (Min-K%++)	2.22	5.55	11.11
Mattern *et al.* [2] (neighbor Attack)	9.05	23.76	47.53
BTDT	**60.80**	**100**	**100**

Table 3 compares the performance of BTDT with the baseline methods on the DBpedia dataset. For the MIN-K% PROB and Min-K%++ methods, we evaluated the performance by setting K to 10%. BTDT consistently surpasses the others in terms of AUC, precision, recall, and F1 score.

Table 3. Comparison of Performance Metrics - DBpedia Dataset

Method	AUC%	Precision%	Recall%	F1 Score%
Shi *et al.* [13] (MIN-K% PROB)	65.30	30.80	99.35	74.20
Zhang *et al.* [14] (Min-K%++)	89.80	79.80	99.75	90.72
Mattern *et al.* [2] (neighbor Attack)	87.95	91.40	85.50	87.51
BTDT	**99.90**	**99.80**	**100**	**99.90**

In Table 4, our approach demonstrates higher TPR values at various FPR thresholds on the DBpedia dataset. The flexibility provided by dynamic thresholding with NLC enables our method to handle diverse datasets more effectively.

Impact of NLC. One of the primary contributions of this study is the introduction of NLC and dynamic thresholding. We evaluated the performance of the attack via generating neighbors using back translation and inferring membership using dynamic thresholding based on Eq. 4. To evaluate the impact of the NLC on the performance of BTDT, we conducted a series of experiments using different values for NLC. Table 5 and Table 6 illustrate the impact of different NLCs on the attack's performance across various metrics on the AG News dataset.

Table 4. True Positive Rate (TPR) at 2%, 5% and 10% False Positive Rate (FPR) -
DBpedia Dataset

Method	2%	5%	10%
Shi *et al.* [13] (MIN-K% PROB)	2.88	7.21	14.42
Zhang *et al.* [14] (Min-K%++)	9.88	24.70	49.40
Mattern *et al.* [2] (neighbor Attack)	19.65	49.12	84.73
BTDT	**100**	**100**	**100**

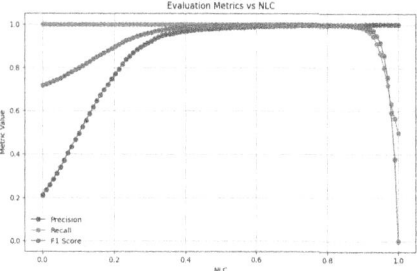

Fig. 2. Evaluation metrics on 100 different NLCs on AG News Dataset.

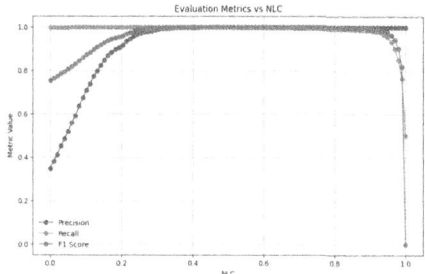

Fig. 3. Evaluation metrics on 100 different NLCs on DBpedia Dataset.

Table 5. Results Using different Neighborhood Loss Coefficients (NLCs) - AG News
Dataset

NLC	AUC%	Precision%	Recall%	F1 Score%
0.4	98.35	96.71	100	98.38
0.5	99.07	98.14	100	99.08
0.6	99.41	98.82	100	99.41
0.7	99.63	99.27	99.98	99.63

Also, Table 7 and Table 8 shows how varying the NLC value affects the performance of the attack on the DBpedia dataset. One of the primary impacts of the

NLC is on the precision and recall of the attack. When we increase the NLC, we effectively make the decision threshold stricter. This means that only target samples with a loss significantly lower than their neighbors will be identified as members. As a result, the precision of our attack improves—we're less likely to falsely label non-members as members. However, this comes at the cost of recall. Some true members may have loss values closer to their neighbors and, therefore, might not be flagged by the attack. Conversely, lowering the NLC makes the decision threshold more lenient. This boosts recall, as the attack becomes more aggressive in labeling samples as members. However, this increase in recall might reduce precision, leading to more false positives, where non-members are incorrectly identified as members. Figure 2 and Fig. 3 illustrate evaluation metrics on 100 different NLCs ranging from 0 to 1 on the performance of the attack on the datasets.

Table 6. True Positive Rate (TPR) at 2%, 5% and 10% False Positive Rate (FPR) Using different Neighborhood Loss Coefficients (NLCs) - AG News Dataset

NLC	2%	5%	10%
0.4	60.80	100	100
0.5	100	100	100
0.6	100	100	100
0.7	99.98	99.98	99.98

Table 7. Results Using different Neighborhood Loss Coefficients (NLCs) - DBpedia Dataset

NLC	AUC%	Precision%	Recall%	F1 Score%
0.4	99.90	99.80	100	99.90
0.5	99.94	99.90	100	99.95
0.6	99.90	100	99.80	99.89
0.7	99.75	100	99.50	99.74

Table 8. True Positive Rate (TPR) at 2%, 5% and 10% False Positive Rate (FPR) Using different Neighborhood Loss Coefficients (NLCs) - DBpedia Dataset

NLC	2%	5%	10%
0.4	100	100	100
0.5	100	100	100
0.6	99.80	99.81	99.82
0.7	99.51	99.52	99.55

5   Conclusion

MIAs pose a critical challenge, especially for LLMs trained on vast datasets that may contain sensitive information. BTDT introduces an innovative approach to MIAs by using back translation to generate diverse and contextually relevant neighborhood samples, coupled with a novel dynamic thresholding mechanism; Neighborhood Loss Coefficient (NLC). Through experiments, we have demonstrated that our method significantly enhances attack's performance. By moving away from static thresholds and incorporating an adaptive decision-making process, BTDT is more robust and adaptable to different datasets. Future research could broaden the scope of our attack to other domains, such as image and audio data, to examine its applicability beyond text.

Acknowledgments. This research is supported by the Natural Sciences and Engineering Research Council of Canada (NSERC) Discovery Grant (RGPIN-2019-05689).

References

1. Shokri, R., et al.: Membership inference attacks against machine learning models. In: 2017 IEEE Symposium on Security and Privacy (SP), pp. 3–18 (2017)
2. Mattern, J. et al.: Membership inference attacks against language models via neighborhood comparison. arXiv preprint (2023). arXiv:2305.18462
3. Ye, J. et al.: Enhanced membership inference attacks against machine learning models. In: Proceedings of the 2022 ACM SIGSAC Conference on Computer and Communications Security, pp. 3093–3106 (2022)
4. Carlini, N., et al.: Membership inference attacks from first principles. In: 2022 IEEE Symposium on Security and Privacy (SP), pp. 1897–1914 (2022)
5. Yeom, S. et al.: Privacy risk in machine learning: Analyzing the connection to overfitting. In: IEEE 31st Computer Security Foundations Symposium (CSF), pp. 268–282 (2018)
6. Watson, L. et al.: On the importance of difficulty calibration in membership inference attacks. arXiv preprint arXiv:2111.08440. (2021)
7. Fan, A. et al.: Hierarchical neural story generation. arXiv preprint arXiv:1805.04833 (2018)
8. Mireshghallah, F. et al.: Quantifying privacy risks of masked language models using membership inference attacks. arXiv preprint arXiv:2203.03929 (2022)
9. Mireshghallah, F., et al.: Memorization in nlp fine-tuning methods. arXiv preprint arXiv:2205.12506 (2022)
10. Sablayrolles, A. et al.: White-box vs black-box: Bayes optimal strategies for membership inference. In: International Conference on Machine Learning, pp. 5558–5567 (2019)
11. Holtzman, A. et al.: The curious case of neural text degeneration. arXiv preprint arXiv:1904.09751. (2019)
12. Long, Y., et al.: Understanding membership inferences on well-generalized learning models. arXiv preprint arXiv:1802.04889. (2018)
13. Shi, W., et al.: Detecting pretraining data from large language models. arXiv preprint arXiv:2310.16789. (2023)

14. Zhang, J., et al.: Min-k%++: Improved baseline for detecting pre-training data from large language models. arXiv preprint arXiv:2404.02936. (2024)
15. Lhoest, Q., et al.: Datasets: a community library for natural language processing. arXiv preprint arXiv:2111.08782 (2021)
16. https://anonymous.4open.science/r/MIA-800B/README.md

Author Index

The manufacturer's authorised representative in the EU is Springer
Nature Customer Service Centre GmbH, Europaplatz 3, 69115 Heidelberg,
Germany. If you have any concerns regarding our products, please
contact ProductSafety@springernature.com

Printed and bound by CPI Group (UK) Ltd, Croydon, CR0 4YY
28/04/2026
02098521-0015